THE 1999 CHRISTIAN WRITERS' MARKET GUIDE

SALLY E. STUART

CHRISTIAN WRITERS'

MARKET GUIDE

1999

Harold Shaw Publishers
Wheaton, Illinois

CONTENTS

III. PERIODICALS

INTRODUCTION

As I prepare this fourteenth annual edition of the market guide, I am again surprised at the number of changes. Most of the publishers who did not have e-mail last year now have it, and a higher percentage also have Websites—indicating an even greater movement into the electronic age. For the first time the listings will indicate if they accept submissions by e-mail, and whether the material should be sent as an attached file or copied into the message.

This year the individual listings will also tell if their guidelines are available by e-mail or on their Website. Some will also send you to the Website for their book catalog—or at least for a listing of current books. All of this is changing how we do our market research, making it much easier and less time-consuming to learn a great deal more about the publishers and publications we want to write for. Keep in mind that you can easily access all those publishers with e-mail or Websites through my Website at http://www.stuart market.com.

The change, tightening up, and fluctuation in the market has continued over the last year. Yet this 1999 edition still has 85 new periodicals and 44 new book publishers. The number of periodical publishers is just slightly higher than last year, but the book publisher's list is up about 20. I encourage you to seek out some possible new markets from this list. At the same time I want to share what for me is a new philosophy in approaching the market. In the past it has been assumed that we would all be most interested in the paying markets, often ignoring the nonpaying. In fact, some of you have asked that I delete the nonpaying markets, or at least put them in a separate section. As the market has begun the shrink, and many publishers are closing their doors to freelance submissions, I have started hearing a different message from those publishers. They are now looking primarily for writers who have paid their dues and are already well-published. That means that in the long run we need to be more concerned with regular publication and establishing our reputations in specific areas of writing than we are about being paid. I am now encouraging writers to seek out all the best publications for their topic or type of writing—whether paying markets or not—and get published as often as they can. In this changing market, those unpaid submissions may make the difference in your success in the future.

One of the behind-the-scenes changes I made this year was sending each publisher a copy of their current listing. It was a lot of work for me, but resulted in more publishers responding to update their listing. I also sent out the largest number of questionnaires ever, nearly 2,500.

You will also find a number of new topics this year, in both the book and periodical sections. Those are identified in the contents and topical listings with an asterisk. Be sure to also spend some time in the resources section which has been greatly expanded and contains some outstanding Websites. Not only are there correspondence courses and writing courses on tape, you will find a number of how-to-write Websites that will lead you through a virtual hands-on writing course. Another section will link you to a good number of writing-related organizations that may be of help to you, as well as all kinds of Websites that will be invaluable in your research projects. And yet another offers invaluable resources to help you deal with any legal questions or concerns. The answers to most of the questions I am asked over the year are now readily available in this resource section.

For those interested in subsidy publishing, the list of possible distributors for those books has also been expanded. See that list following the list of subsidy publishers at the end of the regular book publisher's section. The list of online magazines has also grown, with more publications producing both a print and an online edition. Note that some of the online editions are the same as the print edition, but some are entirely different.

I'm excited about this year's listing of agents, which has grown considerably—for the first time since I started the list. Each year I have dropped a few and added a few, but never managed to make the list grow significantly. The list has gone from 28 agents last year to 74 this year. Be sure to note that some of these are secular agents who are willing to handle religious books. The introduction to that literary agent section now also includes some resources for investigating a possible agent before contacting or signing a contract with him or her. Since I cannot personally vouch for the integrity of each agent listed, you will need to check out each one thoroughly.

Some of you have been asking for more information on those offering editorial services, so you will know if they are qualified to critique your manuscripts. This year I have started to add credentials to their listings. Not all the listings will reflect that this year, but should in the next year or two.

It is a good idea each year to study the market analysis sections of this book for more insight into what's happening in the industry. As with any new reference book, I suggest you spend some quality time becoming familiar with its contents and structure. Discover the supplementary lists available throughout the book. Read through the glossary and spend a few minutes learning terms you are not familiar with. Review the lists of writer's groups and conferences and mark those you might be interested in pursuing during the coming months. The denominational listing will help you start making the important connection between periodicals and book publishers associated with different denominations, and the list I started last year will help you put the "families" of publishers together that are not denominational. With so many publishers being bought out or merging, it will help keep you up-to-date with the new members of these often growing families.

Be sure to carefully study the "How to Use This Book" section. It will save you a lot of time and frustration in trying to understand the meaning of all the notations in the primary listings, and it's full of helpful hints. Remember to send for sample copies (or catalog) and guidelines for any of these publishers or periodicals you are not familiar with. Then study those carefully before submitting anything to that publisher.

Editors tell me repeatedly that they are looking for writers who understand them, their periodical or publishing house, and most of all, their unique approach to the marketplace. One of the biggest complaints I've gotten from publishers over the years is that the material they receive routinely is not appropriate for their needs. I got fewer of those complaints this year. I hope that is an indication that you are all doing a better job of marketing. With a little time and effort, you can fulfill all their expectations, distinguish yourself as a professional, and sell what you write.

Again, I wish you well as you embark on this exciting road to publication, whether for the first time or as a long-time veteran. And as I remind you every year, each of you has been given a specific mission in the field of writing. You and I often feel inadequate to the task, but I learned a long time ago that the writing assignments God has given me cannot be written quite as well by anyone else.

Sally E. Stuart
1647 SW Pheasant Dr.
Aloha, OR 97006
(503)642-9844 (Please call after 9 A.M. Pacific time.)
Fax (503)848-3658
E-mail: stuartcwmg@aol.com.
Website: http://www.stuartmarket.com

P.S. For information on how to receive the market guide automatically every year and freeze the price at $21.99 for future editions, or for information on getting the guide at a discounted group rate or getting books on consignment for your next seminar or conference, contact me at the address or numbers above.

HOW TO USE THIS BOOK

The purpose of this market guide is to make your marketing job easier and more targeted. However, it will serve you well only if you put some time and effort into studying its contents and using it as a springboard for discovering and becoming an expert on those publishers best suited to your writing topics and style.

Below you will find information on its general set-up and instructions for its use. In order to help you become more of an expert on marketing, I am including an explanation of each entry in the alphabetical listings for both the book section and the periodical section. Be sure to study these before trying to use this book.

1. Spend some time initially getting acquainted with the contents and set-up of this resource book. You cannot make the best use of it until you know exactly what it has to offer.

2. Study the Contents pages, where you will find listings of all the periodical and book topics. When selecting a topic, be sure to check related topics as well. Some cross-referencing will often be helpful. For example, if you have a novel that deals with doctor-assisted suicide, you might find the list for adult novels and the list for controversial issues and see which publishers are on both lists. Those would be good potential markets. In the topical sections you will find a letter "R" following publishers that accept reprints (pieces that have been printed in other publications, but for which you retain the rights).

3. The Primary/Alphabetical Listings for book and periodical publishers contain those publishers who answered the questionnaire and those who did not. The listings preceded by an asterisk (*) are those publishers who didn't respond and whose information I was unable to update from other sources. Those with a number symbol (#) were updated from their printed guidelines or other current sources. Since the information in those two groups was not verified by the publisher, you are encouraged to send for sample copies or catalogs and writer's guidelines before submitting to them or get that information by e-mail or on their Websites.

4. In each **book publisher listing** you will find the following information (as available) in this format:

a) Name of publisher

b) Address, phone and fax numbers, e-mail address, Website

c) Denomination or affiliation

d) Name of editor—This may include the senior editor's name, followed by the name of another editor to whom submissions should be sent. In a few cases, several editors are named with the type of books each is responsible for. Address to appropriate editor.

e) Sometimes a statement of purpose

f) Sometimes a list of imprint names

g) Number of inspirational/religious titles published per year

h) Number of submissions received annually

i) Percentage of books from first-time authors

j) Those publishers who do not accept books through agents. If it says nothing about agents, you may assume they do accept books through agents.

k) The percentage of books from freelance authors they subsidy publish (if any). This does not refer to percentage paid by author. If percentage of subsidy is over 50%, the publisher will be listed in a separate section under Subsidy Publishers.

l) Whether they reprint out-of-print books from other publishers

m) Preferred manuscript length in words or pages

n) Average amount of royalty, if provided. If royalty is a percentage of wholesale or net, it is based on price paid by bookstores or distributors. If it is on retail price, it is based on cover price of the book.

o) Average amount paid for advances—Whether a publisher pays an advance or not is noted in the listing; if they did not answer the question, there is no mention of it.

p) Whether they make any outright purchases and amount paid. In this kind of sale, an author is paid a flat fee and receives no royalties

q) Average first printing (number of books usually printed for a first-time author)

r) Average length of time between acceptance of a manuscript and publication of the work

s) Whether they consider simultaneous submissions. This means you can send a query or complete manuscript simultaneously to more than one publisher, as long as you advise everyone involved that you are doing so.

t) Length of time it should take them to respond to a query/proposal or to a complete manuscript (when two lengths of time are given, the first generally refers to a query and the latter to a complete manuscript). Give them a one-month grace period beyond that and then send a polite follow-up letter if you haven't heard from them.

u) Whether a publisher "Accepts," "Prefers," or "Requires" the submission of an ACCEPTED manuscript on disk. Most publishers now do accept or require that books be sent on a computer disk (usually along with a hard copy), but since each publisher's needs are different, that information will be supplied to you by the individual publisher when the time comes. For the first time this year, this section also indicates if they will accept submissions by e-mail.

v) Availability and cost for writer's guidelines and book catalogs—If the listing says "Guidelines," it means they are available for a #10 (business-sized) SASE with a first-class stamp. The cost of the catalog (if any), the size of envelope, and amount of postage are given, if specified (affix stamps to envelope; don't send loose). Tip: If postage required is more than $1.24, I suggest you put $1.24 in postage on the envelope and clearly mark it "Special Standard Mail." (That is enough for up to 1 pound.) (Please note that if the postage rates increase this year, this amount may change. Check with your local post office.) If the listing says "free catalog," it means you need only request it; they do not ask for payment or SASE. Note: If sending for both guidelines and catalog, it is not necessary to send two envelopes; guidelines will be sent with catalog. If guidelines are available by e-mail or Website, that will be indicated.

w) Nonfiction Section—Preference for query letter, book proposal, or complete manuscript, and if they accept phone, fax, or e-queries (if it does not say they accept them, assume they do not; this reference applies to fiction as well as nonfiction). If they want a query letter, send just a letter describing your project. If they want a query letter/proposal, you can add a chapter-by-chapter synopsis and the number of sample chapters indicated. If not specified, send one to three chapters. This is often followed by a quote from them about their needs or what they don't want to see.

x) Fiction Section—Same information as nonfiction section

y) Special Needs—If they have specific topics they need that are not included in the subject listings, they are indicated here.

z) Ethnic Books—Usually specifies which ethnic groups they target or any particular needs

aa) Also Does—Indicates which publishers also publish booklets, pamphlets or tracts.

bb) Tips—Specific tips provided by the editor/publisher

Note: At the end of some listings you will find an indication that the publisher receives mailings of book proposals from The Writer's Edge (see Editorial Services/Illinois for an explanation of that service).

5. In each **periodical listing** you will find the following information (as available) in this format:

a) Name of periodical

b) Address, phone, fax, e-mail address, Website

c) Denomination or affiliation

d) Name of editor and editor to submit to (if different)

e) Theme of publication—This will help you understand their particular slant.

f) Format of publication, frequency of publication, number of pages and size of circulation—tells whether magazine, newsletter, journal, tabloid, newspaper, or take-home paper. Frequency of publication indicates quantity of material needed. Number of pages usually indicates how much material they can use. Circulation indicates the amount of exposure your material will receive and often indicates how well they might pay or the probability that they will stay in business.

g) Subscription rate—Amount given is for a one-year subscription in the country of origin. I suggest you subscribe to at least one of your primary markets every year to become better acquainted with its specific focus.

h) Date established—included only if 1994 or later

i) Openness to freelance; percentage freelance written. If they buy only a small percentage, it often means they are open but receive little that is appropriate. The percentage freelance written indicates how great your chances are of selling to them. When you have a choice, choose those with the higher percentage, but only if you have done your homework and know they are an appropriate market for your material.

j) Preference for query or complete manuscript tells if they want a cover letter with complete manuscripts and whether they will accept phone, fax, or e-mail queries. (If it does not mention cover letters or phone, fax, or e-mail queries, assume they do not accept them.)

k) Payment schedule, payment on acceptance (they pay when the piece is accepted) or publication (they pay when it is published), and rights purchased (See glossary for definitions of different rights.)

l) If a publication does not pay, or pays in copies or subscription, that is indicated in bold, capital letters.

m) If a publication is not copyrighted, that is indicated. That means you should ask for your copyright notice to appear on your piece when they publish it, so your rights will be protected.

n) Preferred word lengths and average number of manuscripts purchased per year (in parentheses)

o) Response time—The time they usually take to respond to your query or manuscript submission (add at least two weeks for delays for mailing)

p) Seasonal material (also refers to holiday)—If sending holiday or seasonal material, it should reach them at least the specified length of time in advance.

q) Acceptance of simultaneous submissions and reprints—If they accept simultaneous submissions, it means they will look at submissions (usually timely topic or holiday material) sent simultaneously to several publishers. Best to send to non-overlapping markets (such as denominational), and be sure to always indicate that it is a simultaneous submission. Reprints are pieces you have sold previously, but to which you hold the rights (which means you sold only first or one-time rights to the original publisher and the rights reverted to you as soon as they were published).

r) If they accept, prefer or require submissions on disk or by e-mail. Most of them seem to want a disk after the piece is accepted, but want a query or hard copy first. If it does not say they prefer or require disks, you should wait and see if they ask for them. If they accept an e-mail submission, it will indicate whether they want it as an attached file or copied into the message. If it says they accept e-mail submissions, but doesn't indicate a preference, it means they will take it either way.

s) Average amount of kill fee, if they pay one (see glossary for definition).

t) Whether or not they use sidebars (see glossary for definition), and whether they use them regularly or sometimes.

u) Their preferred Bible version is indicated. The most popular version is the NIV (New International Version). If no version is indicated, they usually have no preference. See glossary for Bible Versions list.

v) Availability and cost for writer's guidelines, theme list, and sample copies—If the listing says "Guidelines," it means they are available for a #10 SASE (business-sized) with a first-class stamp. The cost for a sample copy, the size of envelope, and number of stamps required are given, if specified (affix stamps to envelope; don't send loose). Tip: If postage required is more than $1.24, I suggest you put $1.24 in postage on the envelope and clearly mark it "Special Standard Mail." (That is enough for up to one pound). If the listing says "Free sample copy," it means you need only to request them; they do not ask for payment or SASE. Note: If sending for both guidelines and sample copy, it is not necessary to send two envelopes; guidelines will be sent with sample copy. If a listing doesn't mention guidelines or a catalog, they probably don't have them. For the first time this year, this section will also indicate if the guidelines/theme list are also available by e-mail or on their Website.

w) "Not in topical listings" means the publisher has not supplied a list of topics they are interested in. Send for their guidelines to determine topics used.

x) Poetry—Name of poetry editor (if different). Average number of poems bought each year. Types of poetry; number of lines. Payment rate. Maximum number of poems you may submit at one time.

y) Fillers—Name of fillers editor (if different). Types of fillers accepted; word length. Payment rate.

z) Columns/Departments—Name of column editor. Names of columns in the periodical (information in parentheses gives focus of column); word length requirements; payment. Be sure to see sample before sending ms or query. Most columns require a query.

aa) Special Issues or Needs—Indicates topics of special issues they have planned for the year, or unique topics not included in regular subject listings

bb) Ethnic—Any involvement they have in the ethnic market

cc) Contest—Information on contests they sponsor or how to obtain that information

dd) Tips—Tips from the editor on how to break into this market or how to be successful as an author

ee) At the end of some listings you will find a notation as to where that particular periodical placed in the Top 50 Plus Christian Periodical list in 1998, and/or their place in previous years. This list is compiled annually to indicate the most writer-friendly publications. To receive a complete listing, plus a prepared analysis sheet and writer's guidelines for the top 50 of those markets, send $25 (includes postage) to: Sally Stuart, 1647 SW Pheasant Dr., Aloha OR 97006, or call (503)642-9844 for more information.

Some listings also include EPA winners. These awards are made annually by the Evangelical Press Association (a trade organization for Christian periodicals).

6. It is important that you adhere closely to the guidelines set out in these listings. If a publisher asks for a query only, do not send a complete manuscript. Following these guidelines will mark you as a professional.

7. If your manuscript is completed, select the proper topical listing and target audience, and make up a list of possible publishers. Check first to see which ones will accept a complete manuscript (if you want to send it to those that require a query, you will have to write a query letter or book proposal to send first). Please do not assume that your manuscript will be appropriate for all those on the list. Read the primary listing for each and if you are not familiar with a publisher, read their writer's guidelines and study one or more sample copies or book catalog. (The primary listings contain information on how to get these.) Be sure the slant of your manuscript fits the slant of the publisher.

8. If you have an idea for an article, short story, or book but you have not written it yet, a reading of the appropriate topical listing will help you decide on a possible slant or approach. Select some publishers to whom you might send a query about your idea. If your idea is for an article, do not overlook

the possibility of writing on the same topic for a number of different periodicals listed under that topic, either with the same target audience or another from the list that indicates an interest. For example, you could write on money management for a general adult magazine, a teen magazine, a women's publication, or one for pastors. Each would require a different slant, but you would get a lot more mileage from that idea.

9. If you do not have an idea, simply start reading through the topical listings or the primary listings. They are sure to trigger any number of book or magazine ideas you could go to work on.

10. If you run into words or terms you are not familiar with, check the glossary at the back of the book for definitions.

11. If you need someone to look at your material to evaluate it or to give it a thorough editing, look up the section on Editorial Services and find someone to send it to for such help. That often will make the difference between success or failure in publishing.

12. If you are a published author with other books to your credit, you may be interested in finding an agent. Unpublished authors generally don't need or won't be able to find an agent. However, some agents will consider unpublished authors (their listing will indicate that), but you must have a completed manuscript before you approach an agent (see agent list). Christian agents are at a premium, so realize it will be hard to find an agent unless you have had some success in book writing.

13. Check the Group list to find a group to join in your area. Go to the Conference list to find a conference you might attend this year. Attending a conference every year or two is almost essential to your success as a writer.

14. **ALWAYS SEND AN SASE WITH EVERY QUERY OR MANUSCRIPT.**

15. **DO NOT RELY SOLELY ON THE INFORMATION PROVIDED IN THIS MARKET GUIDE.** It is just that—a guide—and is not intended to be complete in itself. It is important to your success as a freelance writer that you learn how to use writer's guidelines and study book catalogs or sample copies before submitting to any publisher. Be a professional!

ADDITIONAL RESOURCES TO HELP WITH YOUR WRITING AND MARKETING

1. New!!**Sally Stuart's Guide to Getting Published**— At last, the author of the Christian Writers' Market Guide has compiled all the information you need to understand and function in the world of Christian publishing. Takes you through all the steps needed to be successful as a freelance writer. Serves as both a text and a reference book. This book will be published about August 1999. Call, write, or e-mail Sally Stuart for information.

2. **1999 Top 50+ Christian Periodical Publishers Packet**—Includes a list of the Top 50+ "writer-friendly" periodicals, pre-prepared analysis sheets, and publisher's guidelines for each of the top 50, and a master form for analyzing your own favorite markets. Saves more than $40 in postage and 25-30 hours of work. $25, postpaid. New packet every year.

3. **The 1999 Christian Writers' Market Guide on computer disk**— ASCII Text on $3\frac{1}{2}''$ HD disk, for quick marketing reference. This is in text form as it appears in the book, not in a database. $30 postpaid.

4. **A Market Plan for More Sales**—A step-by-step plan to help you be successful in marketing. Includes 5 reproducible forms. $5 postpaid.

5. **The Complete Guide to Christian Writing and Speaking**—A how-to handbook for beginning and advanced writers and speakers written by the 19 members of the editorial staff of *The Christian Communicator.* $13, postpaid.

6. New!! **The Complete Guide to Writing for Publication**—$18 postpaid. Written by top experts in the field. Contains chapters on various genres of fiction, marketing tips, and chapters on writing for children, plus everything you wanted to know about writing for publication.

7. New!! **The Complete Guide to Writing & Selling the Christian Novel**—This guide not only gives you the how-to for writing excellent fiction, it give insight into how to successfully sell it, and specifically how to make it Christian without being preachy. $18 postpaid.

8. **Permissions Packet**—A compilation of over 16 pages of information directly from publishers on how and when to ask permission to quote from other people's material or from Bible paraphrases. Information not available elsewhere in printed form. $6 postpaid. Note: Sometime this year, this packet may be available in book form, in which case you will be sent the book instead of the packet.

9. New!! **Electronic Research Sites and How to Use Them**—This manual is a must-have for any writer wanting to pursue electronic research. It not only lists all the best research sites on the Web, it includes a copy of the home page for each one so you know exactly what each site has to offer. $13 postpaid.

10. **The Christian Writer's Book**—This book focuses on the writing and selling of Christian books. Many valuable sections, including what an editor does, a guided tour of the book contract, an extensive bibliography of writer's resources, and a style guide for authors and editors. $19 postpaid.

11. **Copyright Law, What You Don't Know Can Cost You**—Answers all the questions about rights and copyright law that affect you as a writer. Simple Q & A format followed by the actual wording of the law. Includes reproducible copyright forms & instructions. $18 postpaid.

12. **Write on Target, A Five-Phase Program for Nonfiction Writers, by Dennis Hensley & Holly Miller**—The craft of writing, the nuts and bolts, finding your niche, selling your manuscript, and mapping your future success as a writer. $15 postpaid.

13. **100 Plus Motivational Moments for Writers and Speakers**—A devotional book specifically for writers and speakers written by successful writers and speakers. $13 postpaid.

14. **You Can Do It! A Guide to Christian Self-Publishing** (revised edition) by Athena Dean. Dean shares insider self-publishing secrets for the Christian market. Takes you step-by-step through the project, including actual budgets and current cost estimates. $13 postpaid.

15. **1999 Internet Directory of Christian Publishers**—A handy listing of over 500 Christian publishers who have Websites or e-mail addresses. Note: Since this list is growing daily and is too long to maintain in a booklet format, it now comes on $8\frac{1}{2}$ x11 sheets, 3-hole punched to put in a loose-leaf notebook. $7 postpaid.

16. The following resources are all 8-page, 8½ x 11 booklets on areas of specific interest, as indicated:

a) **Keeping Track of Your Periodical Manuscripts**—These pages can be duplicated to keep track of every step involved in sending out your periodical manuscripts to publishers. $5 postpaid.

b) **Keeping Track of Your Book Manuscripts**—A similar booklet summarizing the steps in tracking a book manuscript from idea to publication. $5 postpaid.

c) **How to Submit a Book Proposal to a Publisher**—Contains all you need to know to present a professional-looking book proposal to a publishing house (includes a sample book proposal). $5 postpaid.

d) **How to Submit an Article or Story to a Publisher**—Shows how to write a query, prepare a professional-looking manuscript, and more. $5 postpaid.

e) **How to Write That Sure-Sell Magazine Article**—Contains a 3-step writing plan for articles, a list of article types, 12 evaluation questions, sample manuscript page, and more. $5 postpaid.

f) **How to Write a Picture Book**—An inside look at how to write, format, and lay out a children's picture book, with tips for those all-important finishing touches. $5 postpaid.

g) **How to Write Daily Devotionals That Inspire**—Includes the basic format and patterns for daily devotionals, marketing tips, 12 evaluation questions, and polishing. $5 postpaid.

h) **How to Write Personal Experience Articles**—Includes how to write a query letter/sample, components of personal experience article, interviewing tips, and more. $5 postpaid.

17. The following resources are all 8½ x 5½ booklets, 12-20 pages, on areas of specific interest, as indicated:

a) **The Art of Researching the Professional Way**—$5 postpaid.

b) **Interviewing the Professional Way**—$5 postpaid.

c) **The Professional Way to Write Dialogue**—$5 postpaid.

d) **The Professional Way to Create Characters**—$5 postpaid.

e) **Writing Junior Books the Professional Way (for ages 8-12)**—$5 postpaid.

f) **Writing for Young Adults the Professional Way**—$5 postpaid.

Note: Any of the above $5 booklets may be purchased at 2 for $9, 4 for $17, 6 for $25, 8 for $33, 10 for $40, or all 14 for $54.

To order any of the above resources, send a list of what you want with your check or money order to: Sally E. Stuart, 1647 SW Pheasant Dr., Aloha OR 97006, (503)642-9844. Fax: (503)848-3658.

18. **The Writer's Edge**—A service that links book writers and Christian publishers. The writer fills out a book information form and sends that along with 3 sample chapters, a synopsis, and a check for $45. The writer receives a brief critique of the manuscript or, if the manuscript is accepted by The Writer's Edge, a synopsis of the manuscript will appear in a newsletter that goes to more than 40 Christian publishers who use The Writer's Edge as a

screening tool for unsolicited manuscripts. Writer's Edge now also considers previously pubvlished books. *For further information, send an SASE to The Writer's Edge, PO Box 1266, Wheaton, IL 60189, or obtain an application by e-mail at writersedge@usa.net or from their Website: http://members.tri pod.com/~writersedge/.* The Writer's Edge cannot be reached by phone.

RESOURCES FOR WRITERS

Below you will find a variety of resources that will help you as you carry out your training or work as a freelance writer. In addition to the resources here, also check out the separate listings for groups, conferences, editorial services, contests (see periodical topics). You are encouraged to spend some time checking out these resources, as they represent a wealth of knowledge and contacts that will help you be more successful in this business of writing and publishing.

CORRESPONDENCE COURSES

+**AMERICAN SCHOOL OF CHRISTIAN WRITING.** This division of American Christian Writers offers a 3-year, 36-lesson correspondence course that covers the entire field of Christian writing. Students may purchase full course or selected portions. Several payment plans available. For lesson list and enrollment forms contact: American Christian Writers, PO Box 110390, Nashville TN 37222. (800)21-WRITE. Website: http://www.ecpa.org/acw.

AT-HOME WRITING WORKSHOPS. Director: Marlene Bagnull, Write His Answer Ministries, 316 Blanchard Rd., Drexel Hill PA 19026. E-mail: mbagnull@ aol.com. Offers 3 courses of study with 6-10 study units in each. (1) Putting Your Best Foot Forward (lays foundation for your writing ministry), 6 units, $170; (2) Nonfiction (articles, tracts, curriculum, devotionals, how-tos, etc., plus planning a nonfiction book and book proposal), 10 units, $272; (3) Fiction, 10 units, $255. Units may also be purchased individually for $30-34.

+**BETHESDA POETRY CLASSES.** Advanced study, includes: poetry terms, ideas, resource list, study outlines, and more. Contact with SASE: Margaret L. Been, S. 63 W 35530 Piper Rd., Eagle WI 53119.

+**THE CHRISTIAN COMMUNICATOR MANUSCRIPT CRITIQUE SERVICE E-MAIL HANDS-ON COURSE.** For information contact: Susan Titus Osborn, 3133 Puente St., Fullerton CA 92835-1952. (714) 990-1532. E-mail: Susanosb@aol.com. Web site: http://www.christiancommunicator. com. Offers basic writing course available by e-mail. Includes 6 lessons online, handouts, and critiqued assignments. Cost for entire course: $120, by the lesson: $25. Completion of entire course entitles you to one unit of Continuing Education Credit (CEU) from Pacific Christian College of Hope International University for an additional $30.

CHRISTIAN WRITERS GUILD. Director: Norman B. Rohrer, 65287 Fern Ln., Hume CA 93628. (209)335-2333. Offers a 3-year home study course: Discover Your Possibilities in Writing. Includes an introduction to writing, article writing, short inspirational pieces, and fiction, plus a number of additional benefits. Send for your free Starter Kit. Cost for 3-year course is $495. Offers several payment plans and a $75 discount for full payment up front. Special offer through the Christian Writers' Market Guide: Instead of paying $150 down payment, you may pay $25 down, plus $15/month for the next 27 months as you study. Ask about the CWMG special when you request your starter kit.

CHRISTIAN WRITERS INSTITUTE CORRESPONDENCE COURSES. This 54-year-old institution, founded by veteran publisher Robert Walker, is now a division of American Christian Writers. Offers six, 1-year courses with an assigned instructor/mentor. Writing assignments are given with a goal of having a publishable manuscript by the end of each course. Two payment plans available. Contact: Christian Writers Institute, PO Box 110390, Nashville TN 37222. (800)21-WRITE.

+GLORY PRESS/DICK BOHRER, PO Box 624, West Linn OR 97068. (503)638-7711. E-mail: glorypress@juno.com. Offers a writing course based on his 228-page text, How to Write What YOU Think. Cost of book $25. Then you pay him $1 per page as you write the assignments in the text. To enroll, send $25 with a short Christian testimony. Also offers courses entitled, How To Write Features Like a Pro, or 21 Ways to Write Stories for Christian Kids.

+THE LITTFIN PRATT AGENCY/VALINDA LITTFIN/LONNI COLLINS PRATT, 518 W. Nepessing, Ste. 201, Lapeer MI 48446. (810)664-1267. Fax (810)664-4610. E-mail: lcollpr@tir.com. Offers mentoring programs for serious new or intermediate writers (must have access to e-mail). Choose Beginning Career Mentoring (12-14 wks) or Intermediate Career Mentoring (6-8 wks). Send for application information and details.

ONLINELEARNING.NET/UCLA EXTENSION. Offers an extensive selection of writing courses, called The Writers' Program. Call (800)784-8436, ext. 350. Website: http://www.onlinelearning.net/wjp.

POETRY WRITING SESSIONS. Mary Harwell Sayler, PO Box 730, DeLand FL 32721-0730. Encourages Christian poets to write poems, then revise with purpose and style. Seven study units address poetry content, theme, language, rhyme, rhythm, traditional patterns, and free verse forms. Complete course, including instructor's evaluation of assignments is $200. Or order Session One with notebook for $40 (subsequent units $30 each). Instructional tapes and critique service also available.

+RIGHTEOUS WRITING. Intensive writing course covering research, library strategy, note taking, cultivating a topic, outlining, polishing, avoiding pitfalls, approaching editors, copyrighting, marketing, and more. Contact: Dr. Kenneth Gentry, 1749 Kingston Rd., Placentia CA 92870. E-mail: KennethGentry@compuserve.com.

+WRITER'S DIGEST WORKSHOPS. Writers Digest School, 1507 Dana Ave., Cincinnati OH 45207. (800)759-0963. This is a secular course, but you may request a Christian instructor.

+THE WRITING ACADEMY SEMINAR. Sponsors year-round correspondence writing program and annual seminar in various locations. Contact: Nancy Remmert, (314)524-3718. E-mail: nremm10335@aol.com. Website: http://www.wams.org.

WRITING SERVICES INSTITUTE (WSI)/MARSHA L. DRAKE, 6341 Beatrice St., Vancouver BC V5P 3R5, Canada. Phone/fax (604)321-3555. E-mail:

103270.1722@compuserve.com. Website: http://www.vsb-adult-ed.com. Offers correspondence course: Write for Fun and Profit. Write for details and information on correspondence course.

WRITING CLASSES ON CASSETTE TAPES

+**THE CHRISTIAN COMMUNICATOR MANUSCRIPT CRITIQUE SERVICE CASSETTE HANDS-ON COURSE.** For information contact: Susan Titus Osborn, 3133 Puente St., Fullerton CA 92835-1952. (714) 990-1532. E-mail: Susanosb@aol.com. Web site: http://www.christiancommunicator. com. Offers basic writing course available by cassette. Includes 6 lessons on 12 cassettes, handouts, and critiqued assignments. Cost for entire course: $150, by the lesson: $30. Completion of entire course entitles you to one unit of Continuing Education Credit (CEU) from Pacific Christian College of Hope International University for an additional $30.

CHRISTIAN WRITERS LEARNING CENTER. Over 1,000 cassette tapes to choose from. Cost is $5-6 each, depending on quantity. Send SASE for list of topics to: American Christian Writers, Reg Forder, PO Box 110390, Nashville TN 37222. (800)21-WRITE.

CREATIVE CHRISTIAN MINISTRIES. Tapes on a variety of topics. $4.95 ea.; or order five tapes and select one, of your choice, absolutely free. Also has other resources to help you become an effective, productive writer. Send SASE for free Writer's Catalog: Creative Christian Ministries, PO Box 12624, Roanoke VA 24027. (540)342-7511. E-mail: ccmbbr@juno.com.

WRITE HIS ANSWER MINISTRIES. Director: Marlene Bagnull, 316 Blanchard Rd., Drexel Hill PA 19026. E-mail: mbagnull@aol.com. Website: http://nancpub.com/cwf. Tapes on 20+ topics, $5 ea. Topics include: Taking the Pain Out of Marketing; Writing Manuscripts That Sell and Touch Lives; Turning Personal Experience into Print; and Self-Publishing. Tapes of Marlene's day-long Christian Writers Seminar (emphasis on writing for periodicals) or Book Writers Symposium (four 90-minute sessions) are $18.95 and include handouts.

WRITING INSTRUCTION & HELPS

+**THE ARROW.** Http://www.wport.com/cawilcox/start2.htm. Good help with leads and endings and self-editing.

+**THE ART OF WRITING.** Http://www.webcom.com/wordings/artofwrite/ artofwriting.html. A section called Hodgepodge includes interesting tips and information on writing, plus several other helpful links.

+**CARTOONING.** Http://www.cartoon.org. Website for the International Museum of Cartoon Art. Includes information on how to become a cartoonist. Click on "Advice".

+**CHILDREN'S WRITING.** Http://www.users.interport.net/hdu/chchange.htm. Includes recent changes at children's book publishers and articles of interest to children's writers.

+**CHILDREN'S WRITING RESOURCE CENTER.** A Website sponsored by Children's Book Insider (a newsletter for children's writers). Http://

www.write4kids.com. Offers market news, tutorials, FAQ, files to download, surveys, and links to other resources for children's writers. CBI offers other resources, including a complete children's writing course for under $20.

+**CRISCADIAN'S ACTIVE VOICE.** Http://members.aol.com/criscadian/index. html. Includes sections on self-editing, writing press releases, preparing manuscripts, and an interesting section called " A Body of Verbs " that give all kinds of descriptive verbs.

+**EEI PRESS.** Offers reference books for writers, professional editors, and proofreaders. Visit their Website: http://www.eeicom.com/press, or for a catalog, send to 66 Canal Center Plaza, Ste. 200, Alexandria VA 22314-5507, or call (800)683-8380.

+**FREELANCE WRITING.** Http://www.suite101.com/topics/page.cfm/1639. Practical helps for freelancers, such as how to write a query letter.

+**ONLINE WORKSHOPS FOR WRITERS.** Http://www.mlode.com/verlakay/index34.html. Provides transcripts of online chats on a variety of writing topics.

+**RENSSELEAR WRITING CENTER ONLINE HANDOUTS.** Http://www.rpi. edu/dept/llc/writecenter/web/text/proseman.html. Includes 12, one-page handouts on Basic Prose Styles, and 18 handouts on Basic Punctuation and Mechanics.

+**STYLE AND PROOFREADING HELPS.** Http://www.proofread.com.

+**TRACKING WRITING SUBMISSIONS.** Http://www.utahlinx.com/users/kcummings. This is freeware.

+**WRITERS CLUB UNIVERSITY COURSE CATALOG.** Http://www.writers club.com/scripts/wcu/coursecatalog.cfm.

GROUPS/ORGANIZATIONS OF INTEREST

+**AMERICAN BOOKSELLERS ASSOCIATION,** Http://www.ambook.org/bookweb.

AMERICAN CHRISTIAN WRITERS, PO Box 110390, Nashville TN 37222. (800)21-WRITE. Reg Forder, director. Ministry with a goal to provide full service to Christian writers and speakers. Publishes two writers periodicals, operates two correspondence schools, hosts three dozen conferences each year, offers a critique service and book publishing division, and has a mail-order learning center that offers thousands of books, cassette tapes, and software programs for writers.

AMERICAN SOCIETY OF JOURNALISTS AND AUTHORS, 1501 Broadway, Ste. 302, New York NY 10036. (212)997-0947. E-mail: asja@compuserve. com. Website: www.asja.org.

THE AMY FOUNDATION sponsors two annual contests for prizes up to $10,000. One for publication in the secular media (The Amy Awards)and the other for publication in the religious media (Awakening the Giant Writing Awards). For details on both contests, and a copy of last year's winning entries, contact: The Amy Foundation, PO Box 16091, Lansing MI 48901-6091. (517)323-6233. Website: http://www.amyfound.org.

*ASSOCIATED CHURCH PRESS, PO Box 30215, Phoenix AZ 85046-0215. (602)569-6371. New executive director.

+THE ASSOCIATION OF AUTHOR'S REPRESENTATIVES, INC. Http:// www.bookwire.com/AAR. Includes a list of agents who don't charge fees (except for office expenses).

+ASSOCIATION OF CHRISTIAN WEB AUTHORS, http://acwa.hypermart. net.

+R.R. BOWKER, 121 Chanlon Rd., New Providence NJ 07974, (908)464-6800. Website: www.bowker.com/standards/home/isbn. This company issues International Standard Book Numbers (ISBN), Standard Account Numbers (SAN), and Advanced Book Information forms. Forms can be printed off their Website.

+THE CHILDREN'S BOOK COUNCIL, http://www.cbcbooks.org. Go to the Authors/Illustrators Page for marketing information and beginner instruction for writers and illustrators of children's books, plus lots of good links.

CHRISTIAN BOOKSELLERS ASSN., PO Box 200, Colorado Springs CO 80901-0200. (800)252-1950. E-mail: webmaster@cba-intl.org. Website: http://www.cbaonline.org. Bill Anderson, president.

+EDITORIAL FREELANCERS ASSN., http://www.the-efa.org.

EVANGELICAL CHRISTIAN PUBLISHERS ASSN., 1969 E. Broadway Rd. Ste. 2, Tempe AZ 85282. (602)966-3998. Fax (602)966-1944. E-mail: Jmeegan@ecpa.org. Website: http://www.ecpa.org. Doug Ross, pres./CEO. Trade organization of more than 200 Christian book publishers around the world. Offers a submission service on the Internet, called First Edition, where your book proposal can be reviewed by the Christian publishers who are members of this association. Cost is $79. Visit their Website for addition information.

EVANGELICAL PRESS ASSN., 314 Dover Rd., Charlottesville VA 22901. (804)973-5941. Fax (804)973-2710. E-mail: 74473.272@compuserve. com. Ronald E. Wilson, director. Trade association for Christian periodicals and associate members (open to writers).

+FAITH, HOPE & LOVE is the inspirational chapter of Romance Writers of America. Dues for the chapter are $15/yr, but you must also be a member of RWA to join (dues $65/yr). Chapter offers these services: online list service for members, a Website, 20-pg bimonthly newsletter, annual contest, connects critique partners by mail or e-mail, and latest romance market information. To join, contact RWA National Office, 3707 FM 1960 West, Ste. 550, Houston TX 77068. (281)440-6885. Fax (281)440-7510. Website: http://www.rwanational.com. Or go to FHL Website: http://www.webpak. net/robinlee/FHL/info.html. Over 120 members.

INTERNATIONAL CHRISTIAN WRITERS GROUP, Stanley C. Baldwin, director, 12900 SE Nixon, Milwaukie OR 97222 (include SASE for reply). E-mail: SCBaldwin@juno.com. A point of contact for writers around the world. Prayer Fellowship: Joyce Tomanek, e-mail: neh8_10_@stc.net. Networking: Susan Peel, e-mail: suepeel@your-office.com.

+LITERATURE PRAYER FELLOWSHIP, contact: Ethel Herr, 731 Lakefair Dr., Sunnyvale CA 94089. (408)734-4707. E-mail: ethel@mylawfirm.com.

Sends out a quarterly prayer letter that lists prayer concerns of members broken down to facilitate daily prayer. Send letter or e-mail to join group (no cost) and ask for deadline for next letter.

NATIONAL RELIGIOUS BROADCASTERS., 7839 Ashton Ave., Manassas VA 20109. (703)330-7000. Request information on the Directory of Religious Media.

+NATIONAL WRITERS UNION, 113 University Pl. 6th Fl., New York NY 10003-4527. (212)254-0279. Website: www.nwu.org/nwu. Trade union for freelance writers in all genres publishing in U.S. markets.

+PUBLISHERS WEEKLY is the international news magazine and trade journal for the secular book publishing and bookselling industry. Website: www.publishersweekly.com.

*RELIGION NEWS SERVICE, 1101 Connecticut Ave. NW, Ste 350, Washington DC 20036. (202)463-8777. Fax (202)463-0033. Dale Hanson Bourke, publisher.

+SMALL PUBLISHERS ASSN. OF NORTH AMERICA, Box 1306, Buena Vista CO 81211. (719)395-4790. Fax (719)395-8374. Website: www. SPANnet.org. A nonprofit professional trade association for independent presses, self-publishers and authors. See Website for membership benefits.

+THE SOCIETY OF CHILDREN'S BOOK WRITERS AND ILLUSTRATORS, http://www.scbwi.org. This is the professional organization for children's book writers.

+WRITERS GUILD OF AMERICA EAST, 555 W 57th St., New York NY 10019. (212)767-7800. Website: www.wga.org.

+WRITERS GUILD OF AMERICA WEST, 7000 W 3rd St., Los Angeles CA 90048. (213)951-4000. Website: www.wga.org.

+WRITERS INFORMATION NETWORK, PO Box 11337, Bainbridge Island WA 98110. (206)842-9103. Newsletter, seminars, editorial services.

+WRITERS' UNION OF CANADA, 24 Ryerson Ave., Toronto ON M5T 2P3 Canada. (416)703-8982. Website: www.swifty.com/twuc

ON LEGAL CONCERNS

COPYRIGHT ATTORNEY/SALLIE G. RANDOLPH, 160 E. Niagra St., Tonawanda NY 14150. (716)693-5669. E-mail: SallieRandolph @compu serve.com. Reviews and/or negotiates book contracts.

+COPYRIGHT LAW - LIBRARY OF CONGRESS COPYRIGHT OFFICE, 101 Independence Ave. SE, Washington DC 20559-6000. (202)707-3000. Website: http://lcweb.loc.gov/copyright. You may call or write for forms, or get them from the Website. Also check out this copyright information site: http://www.benedict.com.

+FAIR BUSINESS PRACTICES BRANCH, INDUSTRY CANADA, 50 Victoria St., 17th Floor, Hull QB K1A 0C9 Canada. (819)953-7735 or (800)348-5358. Attn.: George Bennett. Contact about illegal or unethical behavior by an agent or publisher in Canada. You also might notify or contact The Canadian Author's Assn. at (705)653-0323.

+THE FEDERAL TRADE COMMISSION, BUREAU OF CONSUMER PRO-TECTION, 6th & Pennsylvania Ave. NW, Washington DC 20580. (202)326-2676. Fax (202)326-2050. Website: http://www.ftc.com. Lydia Parnes, Deputy Director. Contact about illegal or unethical behavior by an agent or publisher in the U.S..

LEGAL CONCERNS FOR WRITERS AND PUBLISHERS, http://home.earth link.net/ivanlove/helpful.html. Contains a long list of articles on various aspects of copyright, book contracts, and other legal topics written by a lawyer in easy-to-understand terms.

+LITNET: LEGAL & LITIGATION SUPPORT SERVICES DIRECTORY, http://www.litnet.com. The most comprehensive Web directory of legal and litigation support service providers.

+UNITED STATES POSTAL INSPECTION SERVICE, 475 L'Enfant Plaza West SW, Washington DC 20260-2166. Manager, Fraud and Prohibited mailings. Contact about incidents of potential mail fraud.

Note: If you are the victim of fraud or have questions/concerns about an agent or publisher, contact the Better Business Bureau in their town, as well as their local attorney general or their state attorney general's office of consumer protection.

CONNECTING WITH OTHER WRITERS

CHRISTIAN WRITER'S WORKSHOP. This is an interactive Christian writer's group that meets once a week on the Internet for discussion and has a weekly newsletter that comes by e-mail. To find the club at 9:00 ET on Thursday nights, go to Key Word: Writers—Writer's Club—Chat rooms. Select the Writer's Workshop chat room. They will tell you how to sign up for the newsletter. Contact person is Bill Yates, e-mail: WTYates@aol.com.

+CHURCH WRITERS GROUP. Leader: George McBride. Offers critiques of your manuscripts online. Anyone interested in joining can e-mail George at: gmcbride@shianet.org.

FICTION WRITERS CONNECTION. Website: http://www.fictionwriters.com. Helpful instruction for fiction and nonfiction writers. Also hosts chat nights. E-mail: Bcamenson@fictionwriters.com, for details.

INTERNATIONAL@WRITERS CLUB. Provides writers worldwide with a host of services and opportunities with a base for networking, job opportunities, and invaluable writing resources. Membership is $35/year. For more information, visit their Website at: http://members.tripod.com/awriters/iwc.htm.

INTERNET FOR CHRISTIANS. A book by Quentin J. Schultze, Gospel Films, Inc., $12.95. Available at your local Christian bookstore. Author also offers a free newsletter, Internet for Christians. To subscribe send the message "SUBSCRIBE and your e-mail address" to: ifc-request@gospel com.net. Website: http://www.gospelcom.net/ifc (includes hyperlinks to all listed sites).

KINGDOM WRITERS. Leader: Marilyn Phemister. An e-mail critique group and fellowship for Christian writers. You may submit work for critique, and critique the works of others in return. To sign up, write to: owner-kingwrit@netside.com. Leave subject blank (AOL members type *). In body of message type: subscribe kingwrit Your Name. Website: http://www.angelfire.com/ks/kingwrit/index.html. Membership (60 & growing) open.

+**OHZONE: WHERE CHRISTIAN AUTHORS MEET.** Http://www.christpages. net/ohzone/index.html. Features Christian poetry and fiction submitted by Christian authors.

+**THE SPIRITUAL MIND.** This is a Web and discussion list for Christian artists, writers, musicians, and creative-thinking people. It is intended as a resource to inspire and educate, spark new relationships and connections, to pool resources and share experience, knowledge, and know-how, practical and spiritual. To subscribe, send an e-mail to: major-domo@ncis.ml.org, with "subscribe spirit-mind" in the message box.

THE WISE STEWARD'S CLUB. Website: http://home.sprynet.com/sprynet/ WiseStewards/writers.htm. Leader: Melissa Morgan.

+**A WORD A DAY.** Http://www.wordsmith.org/awad/index.html. This is the Website for the mailing list by the same day. At the Website you can sign up to get a new word and its definition sent each day.

+**WRITING UPDATE FROM WRITER'S DIGEST.** This is a periodic, free, e-mail newsletter from the editors at Writer's Digest that includes up-to-date writing-related news and tips. To subscribe, contact: newsletter-request@writersdigest.com, with "Subscribe Newsletter" in the message box, or sign up at their Website: http://www.writersdigest.com.

WEBSITES OF INTEREST TO WRITERS

GENERAL:

ACW PRESS: RESOURCES FOR THE CHRISTIAN WRITER. Http://www.acw press.com/links.htm. Links to lots of great resources.

+**AMERICAN JOURNALISM REVIEW'S NEWS LINK.** Http://www.newslink. org. Links more than 60 Websites including The Freedom Forum, Pulitzer Prizes, American Society of Magazine Editors, American Society of Newspaper Editors, Newsletter Publishers Assn., and the Committee to Project Journalists.

+**BARTLETTS FAMILIAR QUOTATIONS.** Http://www.columbia.edu/acis/ bartleby/bartlett. Just enter the word or words and it gives you the quotations.

+**BOOK WIRE.** Http://www.bookwire.com. The most complete listing of book resources on the Web.

+**CANADIAN MAGAZINE PUPLISHERS ASSN.** Http://www.cmpa.ca.

CHRISTIAN BOOK DISTRIBUTORS (CBD). Http://www.christianbook.com. Check out what's selling in the marketplace. Books can be found by publisher, author or subject.

+**CHRISTIAN WRITERS' MARKET GUIDE.** Http://www.stuartmarket.com. Sally Stuart's Website with information on the latest guide, links to the

Websites or e-mail of all the Christian publishers or publications that have them. Lots more in the works.

+**EPA NEW SERVICE.** C/o Doug Trouten, Minnesota Christian Chronicle, 7317 Cahill Rd., Minneapolis MN 55439. (612)941-1605.

+**DICTIONARIES.** Http://northshores.com/sylvania/ref/diction.htm. A WEB OF ON-LINE DICTIONARIES, Http://www.facstaff.bucknell.edu/rbeard/diction,html. Linked to more than 600 dictionaries in 150 different languages.

+**HOW TO PROMOTE YOUR WEBSITE.** Http://www.wilsonweb.com.

+**INDUSTRY NEWS SITE.** Http://www.mediacentral.com.

+**INFORMATION PLEASE.** Http://www.InfoPlease.com. This 50-year-old print resource is now available on the Internet.

+**INKSPOT, THE WRITER'S RESOURCE.** Http://www.inkspot.com. A comprehensive writing resource full of market information, tips on improving your writing, articles, interviews with professional authors and editors, networking opportunities, and a guide to the best resources for writers on the Web.

+**INTERNET RESEARCH RESOURCES:** Http://www.dailyplanit.com/resources.htm. Designed to put a library reference room at your fingertips; links to a broad range of resources.

+**JOURNALISM QUOTES.** Http://www.schindler.org/quote.

+**MARANATHA CHRISTIAN JOURNAL.** 12240 Perris Blvd. #112, Moreno Valley CA 92557. (909)247-0958. E-mail: editor@mcjonline.com. Http://www.mcjonline.com. A wealth of news and views for today's online Christian.

+**ON-LINE LITERARY RESEARCH TOOLS.** Http://www.english.upenn.edu/jlynch/lit.

+**PHOTOSOURCEBANK.** PhotoSource Intl., Ron Engh, director, Pine Lake Farm, 1910 - 35th Rd., Osceola WI 54020. (715)248-3800. Fax (715)248-7394. E-mail: web@photosource.com. Http://www.photosource.com. For an informational message, call: (715)248-1512. Good source of stock photos, and an opportunity for you to post a description of the photos you have for sale on this Website.

+**POOR RICHARD'S WEBSITE.** Http://www.poorrrichard.com. Information on setting up your own Website, including almost 800 links to related sites, and examples of free and low-cost Website utilities.

+**RESEARCH & RESOURCES FOR WRITERS.** Http://www.fontayne.com/linkresource.html. Links to lots of great sites, such as Bartlett's Familiar Quotations, other quotation resources, grammar/style notes, a rhyming dictionary, speech writing resources, etc.

+**SEARCH ENGINES.** Http://www.711.net. This site connects you to 12 search engines. Also check out: http://google.stanford.edu.

+**TOURBUS.** Http://www.TOURBUS.com. A newsletter about what's happening on the Internet, including information on current Internet hoaxes.

+**THE WORD DETECTIVE ON THE WEB.** Http://www.users.interport.net/words1. An online version of the popular newspaper column that answers reader's questions about words and language.

+**WRITER'S DIGEST WEBSITE.** Http://www.writersdigest.com. Lots of writer's helps, including copies of writer's guidelines you can print right off the site. Website for guidelines: http://www.writersdigest.com/guidelines/index.htm.

+**WRITERS GUIDELINES DATABASE.** Http://mav.net/guidelines/religious. shtml. Another site where you can print out guidelines.

+**WRITERSNET: INTERNET RESOURCES FOR WRITERS.** Http://www.writers.net/index.html. A place to search for published writers, literary agents, editors, or publishers by name or specialty. Also offers writing assignments.

+**YAHOO'S LIST OF CHRISIAN PUBLICATIONS ON THE WEB.** Go to the search engine Yahoo—Society and Culture: Religion: Christian.

SPECIALTY TOPICS:

BIBLE PROPHECY. Http://www.armageddonbooks.com. Links to every Bible Prophecy site on the Web.

+**A CHILDREN'S BOOK EDITOR'S SITE.** Http://www.users.interport.net/ hdu. Includes articles written by a children's book editor, links to children's literature sites, and direct links to a number of children's book editor Websites.

CHRISTIAN COMICS INTERNATIONAL. Http://members.aol.com/ChriCom/ or, http://members.aol.com/ChriCat/. Nate Butler can be reached by e-mail at: ChrisCom@aol.com. Also a bimonthly newsletter for writers of Christian Comics is available: New Creation, Kevin Yong, PO Box 254, Dept. C, Temple City CA 91780, or e-mail: Densign888@aol.com. The first issue is free on request. Another contact person for writers interested in scripting a comic or other aspects of comic ministry is: Len Cowan, 519 - 164th Pl. SE, Bothell WA 98012, e-mail: clcowan@xc.org.

CHRISTIAN MUSIC SITES. Christian Music Online at http://www.cmo.com; and Steve Green Ministries at http://www.stevegreenministries.org.

+**CLOTHING OF PAST ERAS.** Covers everything from ancient Greece to the Middle Ages to the 1950's. Http://members.aol.com/nebula5/tcpinfo2. html#history.

+**ETHICAL STANDARDS FOR JOURNALISM.** Http://www.webethics.com. Includes a set of ethical standards for both online and print journalism and links to other sites on this topic.

HOMESCHOOLING. Http://www.learnathome.com/. For writers in home schooling market.

+**INSPIRATIONAL ROMANCE.** Http://members.aol.com/inspirlvg. Includes links to publishers of inspirational romances.

PARENT SOUP. Http://www.parentsoup.com. For writers of parenting articles.

+**SELLING TO HOLLYWOOD.** Http://www.sellingtohollywood.com. Information for scriptwriters and announcement of a scriptwriters conference.

PROMOTION & SELF-PROMOTION

+**ADVOCATE MEDIA GROUP.** 908 Ventures Way, Chesapeake VA 23320. (800)439-5055. Fax (757)547-5544. Contact: Shelly Simone. AMG is an all-inclusive media marketing company that promotes authors, musicians, and other product producers through their nationally syndicated TV & radio show, Interviews & Reviews, as well as their nationally circulated Interviews & Reviews magazine and their Website at http://www.advocate-media.com. Specializes in generating TV and radio exposure in the Christian marketplace.

+**BOOK MARKETING UPDATE** is a newsletter for book writers that guarantees to get you national publicity and more book sales (at least $25,000 worth), or your money back. Contact: Bradley Communications Corp., 135 E. Plumstead Ave., PO Box 1206, Lansdowne PA 19050-8206. (800)784-4359x432. Fax (610)284-3704.

+**BOOKWIRE.** This is an author tour database for Internet browsers. Lets general public and industry professionals know about authors touring in their area. For more information or to list your tour, contact Roger Williams at roger.williams@bookwire.com, or call him at (212)982-7008. Website: http://www.bookwire.com.

+**CLASS PROMOTIONAL SERVICES.** Http://www.classervices.com. See Website for information on speaker-training seminars, media publicity services, and a speaker's bureau.

+**COFFEEHOUSE BOOKSTORE** is a cyberstore for self-published Christian writers, artists and musicians. For $20/mo (plus a small origination/set-up fee) CoffeeHouse will design and host your site, advertise to the Christian community through magazines, conferences and other media, register and update regularly with major Web search engines and maintain your site with appropriate links. There are no commissions or fees to pay on product sales. You sell your products and keep all profits. For more information, call (800)336-5691 or go to http://www.coffeehouse.com.

+**CREATIVE RESOURCES, INC.** PO Box 1665, Sandpoint ID 83864. (208)263-8055. Fax (208)263-9055. Interview scheduling line: (800)858-9388. E-mail: CMResources@aol.com. Contact: Don S. Otis. One of the largest Christian publicity firms in the country. Provides services for direct mail, communications and media relations.

+**THE MIDWEST BOOK REVIEW.** 278 Orchard Dr., Oregon WI 53575. James Cox, editor-in-chief. Send copy of your book to be reviewed for library resource newsletters, etc.

+**THE WRITE CONNECTION/MARY HAMPTON**, 1535 NE 86th Ave., Portland OR 97220. (503)251-8678. Offers help in promoting your published book. Will help you develop a marketing plan to help get the best exposure for you and your book. Send an SASE for details.

SERVICES FOR WRITERS

+**AMERICA'S LARGEST NEWSPAPERS.** 14 Hickory Ave., Takoma Park MD 20912. A computerized list of the 120 largest daily newspapers with the names of over 700 key editors. Available on disk or hard copy.

CHRISTIAN INFORMATION MINISTRY/RESEARCH SERVICE. Provides fee-based custom research and information retrieval for authors, churches, individuals, publishers, ministries, speakers; primarily topics pertaining to Bible, theology and Christian living. Basic research fee is $35/hr, plus expenses, such as photocopying and shipping. Cecil R. Price, Th.M., PO Box 141055, Dallas TX 75214. (214)827-0057. E-mail: cecil_r_price@ acd.org. Also ask about The Booklet Book, a database of booklets available on religious topics.

+**COFFEEHOUSE BOOKSTORE** is a cyberstore for self-published Christian writers, artists and musicians. For $20/mo (plus a small origination/set-up fee) CoffeeHouse will design and host your site, advertise to the Christian community through magazines, conferences and other media, register and update regularly with major Web search engines and maintain your site with appropriate links. There are no commissions or fees to pay on product sales. You sell your products and keep all profits. For more information, call (800)336-5691 or go to http://www.coffeehouse.com.

CORRESPONDENCE COURSE FOR MANUSCRIPT EDITING. The University of Wisconsin offers a correspondence course in manuscript editing for those wanting to do editing on a professional level or for writers wanting to improve their personal editing skills. Reasonable cost. Contact: U of Wisconsin Learning Innovations, Rm 104, 432 N. Lake St., Madison WI 53706. Ask about Manuscript Editing A52.

+**CORNERSTONE INDEXING/SHIRLEY WARKENTIN**, 1862 Tenaya Ave., Clovis CA 93611. (559)322-2145. E-mail: indexer@juno.com. Website: http://home.earthlink.net/warkentin4. Writes subject and scripture indexes for nonfiction books from a Christian perspective, conforming to publisher specifications.

+**FORTUNECITY.** Offers 20 megabytes of space for your Website, plus all kinds of additional resources to help you get started and to make your site successful. For details visit: http://www.adz.net/fc345.html.

*****INTERACTIVE DATA MANAGEMENT.** David Gibby, 1786 NW Jay St., Roseburg OR 97470, (541)957-1786. Can help you develop a web page; design business logos or brochures; develop interactive CD magazines and books; put all your articles, artwork, or other data on a CD; plus much more. Call or write for information.

JUNO OFFERS FREE E-MAIL SERVICE. This service is free (if you qualify) and an easy solution for those who want an e-mail address and the ability to correspond with others by e-mail, but don't need or want additional access to the Internet. There is no obligation for requesting the software or trying it out. E-mail your request to: signup@juno.com, or call (800)654-5866. This service is advertiser supported, and membership is limited to the US for now (although you can communicate with e-mail users in other countries). You may sign up at their Website: http://www. juno.com.

+**LOGOS RESEARCH SYSTEMS,** 715 SE Fidalgo Ave., Oak Harbor WA 98277-4049. (360)679-6575. Fax (360)675-8169. E-mail: info@logos.com. Website: http://www.logos.com. Offers electronic publishing solutions for academic and reference book publishers; converts books to CD Roms.

WRITERS' PUBLICATIONS/SPECIALIZED

*THE CHRISTIAN MUSIC DIRECTORY. Easy-to-use guide to the Christian music, film, and video business. James Lloyd Group, PO Box 448, Jacksonville OR 97530. (541)899-8888. Fax (541)488-0418. (Call for current price). Also has The Christian Artist Survival Guide, How to Produce, Manufacture, Distribute & Promote an Independent Christian Record., $33.45, incl. postage.

TAX TIPS FOR WRITERS. A book that deals with tax law and tax return preparation from a writer's standpoint. Cost is $12.95, plus $1.55 postage. Tower Enterprises, 2130 Sunset Dr., #47, Vista CA 92083. (760)941-9293. Fax (760)941-5718. E-mail: lizklung@earthlink.net. Also offers a writer's newsletter called Writer's News, and a book called "GRANDMA, I WANT TO WRITE A BOOK", on developing your child's creative writing ability.

TOTALLY HONEST TAX TIP FOR WRITERS by Sandy Cathcart, a licensed tax preparer. Helps you decide if and when you need to start considering your writing as a business, and takes you through all the steps involved. Includes several helpful forms. Cost is $10, including postage. Order from Needle Rock Publishing, 341 Flance Rock Rd., Prospect OR 97536.

+**WRITING FOR PROFIT.** A 1999 updated edition of this classic writing how-to by Dr. Dennis Hensley is now available to review and download for $10 from a Website at: http://www.blueroses.com/writingforprofit. Also available on disk for $12 from: Denehen, Inc., 6824 Kanata Ct., Fort Wayne IN 46815.

WRITERS' SOFTWARE

AMERICAN CHRISTIAN WRITERS SOFTWARE FOR WRITERS, PO Box 110390, Nashville TN 37222. (800)21-WRITE. Reg Forder, director. Send a #10 SASE/1 stamp for an 8-page catalog of software (mostly shareware) of special interest to writers.

*BESTSELLER: A SUBMISSION TRACKING SOFTWARE FOR WRITERS. For a demo copy send $12 US or $17.50 CAN; for complete program, send $73.95 US or $99.45 CAN (prices include postage) to: Salt Spring Island Software, 137 McPhillips Ave., Salt Spring Island BC, V8K 2T6 Canada. For more information call (604)537-4339.

TOPICAL/SUBJECT LISTINGS OF BOOK PUBLISHERS

One of the most difficult aspects of marketing is trying to determine which publishers might be interested in the book you want to write. This topical listing was designed to help you do just that.

First, look up your topic of interest in the following lists. If you don't find the specific topic, check the list of topics in the table of contents and find any related topics. Once you have discovered which publishers are interested in a particular topic, the next step is to secure writer's guidelines and book catalogs from those publishers. Don't assume, just because a particular publisher is listed under your topic, that it would automatically be interested in your book. It is your job to determine whether your approach to the subject will fit within the unique scope of that publisher's catalog. It is also helpful to visit a Christian bookstore to actually see some of the books produced by each publisher you are interested in pursuing.

Note, too, that the primary listings for each publisher indicate what the publisher prefers to see in the way of a query, book proposal, or complete manuscript.

R—Indicates which publishers reprint out-of-print books from other publishers.

APOLOGETICS

ACU Press
Ambassador House
Baker Books—R
Bethany House
Black Forest—R
Brentwood—R
Bridge/Logos
Broadman & Holman
Catholic Univ./America—R
Christian Publications
Christian Univ Press—R
College Press—R
Comments Publishing—R
Cornerstone Press
Cross Cultural
Crossway Books
Eerdmans Publishing—R
Essence Publishing—R
FOG Publishing
Franciscan Univ Press—R
Gospel Publishing House—R
Hendrickson—R
Holy Cross—R
Huntington House—R
InterVarsity Press
Kregel—R

Lightwave Publishing
Longwood—R
Magnus Press—R
Master Books—R
Master Design
Messianic Jewish—R
Morehouse—R
Multnomah
Our Sunday Visitor—R
Oxford University
Presbyterian & Reformed
Promise Publishing
Read 'N Run—R
Regnery—R
Revell
Review & Herald
Rose Publishing
St. Bede's—R
Son-Rise
Still Waters Revival—R
Sword of the Lord—R
TEACH Services—R
Tekna Books
Trinity Foundation—R
Tyler Press—R
Univ Press of America—R
Vital Issues Press—R
Zondervan

ARCHAEOLOGY

Baker Books—R
Black Forest—R
Brentwood—R
Christopher Publishing
College Press—R
Doubleday
Eerdmans Publishing—R
Essence Publishing—R
Facts on File
Hendrickson—R
Huntington House—R
Journey Books—R
Kregel—R
Monument Press
New Leaf Press—R
Oxford University
Promise Publishing
Ragged Edge—R
Read 'N Run—R
Review & Herald
Schocken Books—R
Trinity Press Intl.—R
Tyler Press—R
Univ/Ottawa Press
Univ Press of America—R
West Coast Paradise—R

Westminster John Knox
Yale Univ Press—R
Zondervan

AUTOBIOGRAPHY

Bantam Books
Bethany House
Black Forest—R
Blue Dolphin
Brentwood—R
Bridge/Logos
Christopher Publishing
Daybreak Books—R
Doubleday
Eerdmans Publishing—R
Essence Publishing—R
Fairway Press—R
FOG Publishing
Friends United Press—R
Guernica Editions—R
Hearth Publishing—R
Longwood—R
Lowenbrown Publishing
McDougal Publishing
Messianic Jewish—R
Openbook—R
Paragon House—R
Promise Publishing
Read 'N Run—R
Regnery—R
Review & Herald
St. Bede's—R
Schocken Books—R
Son-Rise
Southern Baptist Press—R
Still Waters Revival—R
Sword of the Lord—R
Tekna Books
Tyler Press—R
VESTA—R
Vital Issues Press—R
West Coast Paradise—R
Westminster John Knox
Zondervan

BIBLE/BIBLICAL STUDIES

Abingdon Press—R
Accent Publications
ACU Press
Ambassador House
Baker Books—R
Bantam Books
Bethany House
Black Forest—R
Brentwood—R
Bridge/Logos

Broadman & Holman
Brown-ROA
Chalice Press
Chariot Victor
Christian Ed Pub.
Christian Publications
Christopher Publishing
College Press—R
Contemporary Drama Service
Cornell Univ Press—R
Creation House
Cross Cultural
Crossway Books
CSS Publishing
Daybreak Books—R
Doubleday
Eerdmans Publishing—R
Essence Publishing—R
Fairway Press—R
FOG Publishing
Franciscan Univ Press—R
Goetz Publishing, B.J.
Gospel Publishing House—R
HarperSanFrancisco
Hendrickson—R
Hensley Publishing —R
Holy Cross—R
Huntington House—R
Intl. Awakening Press—R
InterVarsity Press
Judson Press—R
Kindred Productions
Kregel—R
Libros Liguori
Lightwave Publishing
Logion Press
Loizeaux (commentary)
Longwood—R
Lowenbrown Publishing
Magnus Press—R
Master Design
McDougal Publishing
Mercer University Press
Messianic Jewish—R
Morehouse—R
Mt. Olive College Press
New City Press—R
New Hope—R
Northstone—R
Omega House—R
Our Sunday Visitor—R
Oxford University
Paragon House—R
Pauline Books
Paulist Press
Presbyterian & Reformed
Promise Publishing
Ragged Edge—R

Rainbow/Legacy Press—R
Read 'N Run—R
Resource Publications
Revell
Review & Herald
Royal Productions—R
St. Anthony Messenger—R
St. Bede's—R
Schocken Books—R
Shaw Publishers, Harold—R
Sheed & Ward—R
Shining Star
Smyth & Helwys
Son-Rise
Sonstar Publishing—R
Southern Baptist Press—R
Starburst Publishers
Sword of the Lord—R
Tekna Books
Thomas More—R
Toccoa Falls
Treasure Learning—R
Trinity Foundation—R
Trinity Press Intl.—R
Tyler Press—R
United Church Pub.
Univ Press of America—R
VESTA—R
Vital Issues Press—R
Wadsworth—R
Wesleyan Publishing House
Westminster John Knox
Wood Lake Books—R
Yale Univ Press—R
Zondervan

BIOGRAPHY

Alexander Books
Ambassador House
Bantam Books
Barbour Publishing—R
Bethany House
Black Forest—R
Blue Dolphin
Brentwood—R
Bridge/Logos
Catholic Univ/America—R
Christian Publications
Christopher Publishing
Cornell Univ. Press—R
Counterpoint
Daybreak Books—R
Dimension Books—R
Doubleday
Eerdmans Publishing—R
Eerdmans/Young Readers
Erica House

Essence Publishing—R
Facts on File
Fairway Press—R
Hay House
Hearth Publishing—R
ICS Publications—R
Intl. Awakening Press—R
Journey Books—R
Kaleidoscope Press—R
Kregel—R
Lifetime Book—R
Light and Life—R
Longwood—R
Lowenbrown Publishing
McDougal Publishing
Messianic Jewish—R
Middle Atlantic—R
Morehouse—R
Morrow and Co., Wm
Mosaic Press
Mt. Olive College Press
New Hope—R
One World
Openbook—R
Oxford University
Pacific Press
Paragon House—R
Promise Publishing
G.P. Putnam's Sons
Read 'N Run—R
Regnery—R
Review & Herald
Royal Productions—R
St. Bede's—R
Schocken Books—R
Shaw Publishers, Harold—R
Son-Rise
Southern Baptist Press—R
Still Waters Revival—R
Summit Pub. Group—R
Sword of the Lord—R
TEACH Services—R
Tekna Books
Toccoa Falls
Tyler Press—R
United Church Pub.
VESTA—R
Vital Issues Press—R
West Coast Paradise—R
Westminster John Knox
Windflower—R
Yale Univ Press—R
YWAM Publishing—R
Zondervan

BOOKLETS

Barbour Publishing—R

Barclay Press—R
Christian Publications
Comments Publishing—R
Cross Way Pub.
Dry Bones Press—R
Essence Publishing—R
Forward Movement
Franciscan Univ Press—R
Good Book—R
Good News Publishers
Gospel Publishing House—R
Hearth Publishing—R
Huntington House—R
Intl. Awakening Press—R
InterVarsity Press
Kindred Productions
Libros Liguori
Lightwave Publishing
Liguori Publications
Longwood—R
Lowenbrown Publishing
Lydia Press
Messianic Jewish—R
Middle Atlantic—R
Moody Press (series only)
Omega House—R
Our Sunday Visitor—R
Paradise Research—R
Pilgrim Press—R
Review & Herald
St. Anthony Messenger Press
Sonstar Publishing—R
Sword of the Lord—R
TEACH Services—R
Trinity Foundation—R
Tyler Press—R
West Coast Paradise—R
Wine Press Publishing

CANADIAN/FOREIGN

Cerdic Publications
Essence Publishing
Guernica Editions
Hunt and Thorpe
Inheritance Publications
Kindred Productions
Openbook
Still Waters
Summit Publishing
United Church Pub. Hs
Univ. of Ottawa Press
VESTA
West Coast Paradise
Windflower
Wood Lake Books—R

CELEBRITY PROFILES

Black Forest—R
Blue Dolphin
Bridge/Logos
Christopher Publishing
Cross Cultural
Daybreak Books—R
Doubleday
Essence Publishing—R
Judson Press—R
Lifetime Books—R
New Leaf Press—R
Promise Publishing
G.P. Putnam's Sons
Read 'N Run—R
Royal Productions—R
Shaw Publishers, Harold—R
Sword of the Lord—R
Zondervan

CHILDREN'S EASY-READERS*

Abingdon Press—R
Black Forest—R
Concordia
Eerdmans/Young Readers
Essence Publishing—R
Henry Holt
Lightwave Publishing
PACE Publications—R
Pacific Press
Read 'N Run—R
Review & Herald

CHILDREN'S PICTURE BOOKS

Abingdon Press—R
Art Can Drama—R
Boyds Mills Press
Bridge/Logos
Chariot Victor
Concordia
CSS Publishing
Eerdmans/Young Readers
Essence Publishing—R
Fairway Press—R
Focus Publishing
Gold 'n' Honey Books
Henry Holt
Hunt & Thorpe
Kaleidoscope Press—R
Lightwave Publishing
Living the Good News
Lowenbrown Publishing
Loyola Press
McDougal Publishing

Messianic Jewish—R
Morehouse—R
Morris, Joshua
National Baptist—R
Pauline Books
Paulist Press
Read 'N Run—R
Regina Press
Royal Productions—R
Son-Rise
Sword of the Lord—R
Vital Issues Press—R
Zondervan

CHRISTIAN EDUCATION

Abingdon Press—R
Accent Publications
ACU Press
Baker Books—R
Bantam Books
Black Forest—R
Brentwood—R
Bristol House—R
Broadman & Holman
Brown-ROA
Chalice Press
Chariot Victor
Christian Ed Pub.
Christopher Publishing
College Press—R
Concordia
Contemporary Drama Service
Crossway Books
CSS Publishing
Educational Ministries
Eerdmans Publishing—R
Essence Publishing—R
Fairway Press—R
Goetz Publishing, B.J.
Gospel Publishing House—R
GROUP Publishing—R
Group's FaithWeaver
Hensley Publishing —R
Holy Cross—R
Hunt & Thorpe
Kregel—R
Liguori Publications
Lightwave Publishing
Liturgical Press
Logion Press
Longwood—R
Lowenbrown Publishing
Master Books—R
Meriwether—R
Moody Press
Morehouse—R
National Baptist—R

New Canaan
New Hope—R
New Leaf Press—R
Omega House—R
Openbook—R
Perigee Books
Presbyterian & Reformed
Preservation Press
Ragged Edge—R
Rainbow/Legacy Press—R
Rainbow/Rainbow Books—R
Read 'N Run—R
Religious Education
Resource Publications
Rose Publishing
Royal Productions—R
St. Bede's—R
Smyth & Helwys
Sonstar Publishing—R
Southern Baptist Press—R
Standard
Still Waters Revival—R
Sword of the Lord—R
TEACH Services—R
Trinity Foundation—R
Tyler Press—R
United Church Press
United Church Pub.
Vital Issues Press—R
West Coast Paradise—R
Westminster John Knox
Windflower—R
Wood Lake Books—R
Zondervan

CHRISTIAN HOME SCHOOLING

Art Can Drama—R
Baker Books—R
Bantam Books
Barbour Publishing—R
Bay Public., Mel
Black Forest—R
Brentwood—R
Bridge/Logos
Brown-ROA
Christian Publications
Concordia
Crossway Books
Eerdmans Publishing—R
Essence Publishing—R
Fairway Press—R
Focus Publishing
Hunt & Thorpe
Huntington House—R
Kaleidoscope Press—R
Longwood—R

Morehouse—R
New Canaan
Omega House—R
Promise Publishing
Rainbow/Legacy Press—R
Rainbow/Rainbow Books—R
Rainbow's End
Read 'N Run—R
Royal Productions—R
Saint Mary's Press—R
Shaw Publishers, Harold—R
Son-Rise
Sonstar Publishing—R
Standard
Starburst Publishers
Still Waters Revival—R
Sword of the Lord—R
TEACH Services—R
Tyler Press—R
Vital Issues Press—R
YWAM Publishing—R
Zondervan

CHRISTIAN LIVING

Abingdon Press—R
ACTA Publications
Albury Publishing—R
Ambassador House
Baker Books—R
Bantam Books
Barbour Publishing—R
Barclay Press—R
Beacon Hill Press
Bethany House
Black Forest—R
Brentwood—R
Bridge/Logos
Bristol House—R
Broadman & Holman
Chalice Press
Chariot Victor
Chosen Books
Christian Publications
Christopher Publishing
College Press—R
Concordia
Creation House
Cross Cultural
Crossway Books
CSS Publishing
Daybreak Books—R
Destiny Image
Dimensions for Living—R
Doubleday
Eerdmans Publishing—R
Element Books—R
Essence Publishing—R

Fairway Press—R
FOG Publishing
Forward Movement
Franciscan Univ Press—R
Friends United Press—R
Gesher—R
Gospel Publishing House—R
HarperSanFrancisco
Haworth Press—R
Hearth Publishing—R
Hendrickson—R
Hensley Publishing —R
Holy Cross—R
Honor Books
Horizon House—R
Howard Publishing
Huntington House—R
Impact Christian Books—R
InterVarsity Press
Judson Press—R
Kregel—R
Libros Liguori
Life Cycle Books—R
Light and Life—R
Liguori Publications
Liturgical Press
Living Books for All
Longwood—R
Lowenbrown Publishing
Magnus Press—R
McDougal Publishing
Moody Press
Morehouse—R
Multnomah
New City Press—R
New Leaf Press—R
Omega House—R
Openbook—R
Our Sunday Visitor—R
Paraclete Press—R
Perigee Books
Presbyterian & Reformed
Promise Publishing
Ragged Edge—R
Rainbow/Legacy Press—R
Read 'N Run—R
Resurrection Press—R
Revell
Review & Herald
Royal Productions—R
St. Bede's—R
Shaw Publishers, Harold—R
Sheed & Ward—R
Shining Star
Small Helm Press—R
Smyth & Helwys
Son-Rise
Sonstar Publishing—R

Standard
Starburst Publishers
Still Waters Revival—R
TEACH Services—R
Tekna Books
Thomas More—R
Tyler Press—R
United Church Press
United Church Pub.
Vital Issues Press—R
Wellness
West Coast Paradise—R
Western Front—R
Westminster John Knox
Zondervan

CHRISTIAN SCHOOL BOOKS

Art Can Drama—R
Baker Books—R
Black Forest—R
Christian Publications
Fairway Press—R
Hunt & Thorpe
Huntington House—R
Kaleidoscope Press—R
Lowenbrown Publishing
Morehouse—R
New Canaan
Read 'N Run—R
Royal Productions—R
St. Bede's—R
Son-Rise
Southern Baptist Press—R
Sword of the Lord—R
Tyler Press—R
West Coast Paradise—R

CHURCH LIFE

ACTA Publications
ACU Press
Alban Institute
Albury Publishing—R
Art Can Drama—R
Baker Books—R
Bethany House
Black Forest—R
Brentwood—R
Bridge/Logos
Bristol House—R
Broadman & Holman
Cerdic Publications
Chalice Press
Christian Publications
Christopher Publishing
Crossway Books
CSS Publishing

Destiny Image
Eerdmans Publishing—R
Essence Publishing—R
Fairway Press—R
Forward Movement
Friends United Press—R
Gesher—R
Gospel Publishing House—R
GROUP Publishing—R
HarperSanFrancisco
Hendrickson—R
Holy Cross—R
Impact Christian Books—R
InterVarsity Press
Judson Press—R
Kregel—R
Libros Liguori
Light and Life—R
Liguori Publications
Longwood—R
McDougal Publishing
Moody Press
Morehouse—R
Multnomah
New Leaf Press—R
Openbook—R
Our Sunday Visitor—R
Presbyterian & Reformed
Ragged Edge—R
Rainbow/Legacy Press—R
Read 'N Run—R
Review & Herald
St. Anthony Messenger—R
St. Bede's—R
Sheed & Ward—R
Smyth & Helwys
Sonstar Publishing—R
Sword of the Lord—R
Tekna Books
Tyler Press—R
United Church Press
United Church Pub.
Vital Issues Press—R
Wood Lake Books—R
Zondervan

CHURCH RENEWAL

ACTA Publications
Alban Institute
Baker Books—R
Barclay Press—R
Bethany House
Black Forest—R
Brentwood—R
Bridge/Logos
Bristol House—R
Broadman & Holman

Cerdic Publications
Chosen Books
Christian Publications
Church Growth Inst.
Cross Cultural
Crossway Books
CSS Publishing
Destiny Image
Dimension Books—R
Doubleday
Eerdmans Publishing—R
Essence Publishing—R
Evangel Publishing—R
Fairway Press—R
Franciscan Univ Press—R
Gospel Publishing House—R
HarperSanFrancisco
Hendrickson—R
Holy Cross—R
Impact Christian Books—R
Intl. Awakening Press—R
InterVarsity Press
Judson Press—R
Libros Liguori
Light and Life—R
Longwood—R
Lowenbrown Publishing
Master Design
McDougal Publishing
Middle Atlantic—R
Moody Press
Morehouse—R
Multnomah
Omega House—R
Our Sunday Visitor—R
Pastor's Choice
Presbyterian & Reformed
Ragged Edge—R
Read 'N Run—R
Royal Productions—R
Resurrection Press—R
Review & Herald
Royal Productions—R
St. Bede's—R
Schocken Books—R
Sheed & Ward—R
Smyth & Helwys
Southern Baptist Press—R
Tekna Books
Thomas More—R
Tyler Press—R
United Church Press
United Church Pub.
Vital Issues Press—R
Westminster John Knox
Wood Lake Books—R
Zondervan

CHURCH TRADITIONS*

Black Forest—R
CSS Publishing
Eerdmans Publishing—R
Essence Publishing—R
Forward Movement
HarperSanFrancisco
Holy Cross—R
Longwood—R
Loyola Press
Our Sunday Visitor—R
Paragon House—R
Read 'N Run—R
St. Anthony Messenger—R
St. Bede's—R
Tekna Books
Thomas More—R
United Church Pub.
Univ Press of America—R
Wood Lake Books—R

CONTROVERSIAL ISSUES

Accent Books
Ambassador House
Baker Books—R
Bantam Books
Black Forest—R
Blue Dolphin
Brentwood—R
Bridge/Logos
Chalice Press
Christian Publications
Comments Publishing—R
Cross Cultural
Daybreak Books—R
Destiny Image
Doubleday
Dry Bones Press—R
Element Books—R
Erica House
Essence Publishing—R
FOG Publishing
HarperSanFrancisco
Haworth Press—R
Hay House
Hendrickson—R
Huntington House—R
Innisfree Press
InterVarsity Press
Kregel—R
Lifetime Books—R
Light and Life—R
Lowenbrown Publishing
Magnus Press—R
Monument Press
Morehouse—R

Multnomah
Pilgrim Press—R
Presbyterian & Reformed
Read 'N Run—R
Regnery—R
Schocken Books—R
Sonstar Publishing—R
Starburst Publishers
Still Waters Revival—R
Sword of the Lord—R
Tekna Books
Trinity Foundation—R
Tyler Press—R
United Church Pub.
Univ/Ottawa Press
Vital Issues Press—R
West Coast Paradise—R
White Stone Circle
Zondervan

COOKBOOKS

Bantam Books
Barbour Publishing—R
Black Forest—R
Brentwood—R
Christopher Publishing
Daybreak Books—R
Doubleday
Fairway Press—R
Hearth Publishing—R
Huntington House—R
Longwood—R
Morrow & Company, Wm.
Mt. Olive College Press
Omega House—R
One World
Pacific Press
Perigee Books
Rainbow/Legacy Press—R
Read 'N Run—R
Review & Herald
Royal Productions—R
Schocken Books—R
Son-Rise
Southern Baptist Press—R
Starburst Publishers
Summit Pub. Group—R
Tekna Books
Tyler Press—R

COUNSELING AIDS

Accent Publications
Baker Books—R
Bethany House
Black Forest—R
Brentwood—R

Bridge/Logos
Brown-ROA
Christopher Publishing
Crossroad Publishing—R
Dimension Books—R
Eerdmans Publishing—R
Erica House
Essence Publishing—R
Fairway Press—R
Gospel Publishing House—R
Haworth Press—R
InterVarsity Press
Judson Press—R
Kaleidoscope Press—R
Kregel—R
Life Cycle Books—R
Liguori Publications
Longwood—R
McDougal Publishing
Morehouse—R
Neibauer Press—R
New Leaf Press—R
Pastor's Choice
Presbyterian & Reformed
Rainbow's End
Read 'N Run—R
Resource Publications
Resurrection Press—R
Royal Productions—R
Shaw Publishers, Harold—R
Son-Rise
Southern Baptist Press—R
Tekna Books
Tyler Press—R
United Church Pub.
West Coast Paradise—R
Westminster John Knox
White Stone Circle
Zondervan

CREATION SCIENCE

Albury Publishing—R
Black Forest—R
Bridge/Logos
Christopher Publishing
Crossway Books
Essence Publishing—R
Hendrickson—R
Huntington House—R
InterVarsity Press
Kaleidoscope Press—R
Lightwave Publishing
Longwood—R
Pacific Press
Presbyterian & Reformed
Promise Publishing
Rainbow's End

Read 'N Run—R
Review & Herald
Rose Publishing
Sword of the Lord—R
TEACH Services—R
Tekna Books
Zondervan

CULTS/OCCULT

Albury Publishing—R
Ambassador House
Baker Books—R
Bantam Books
Bethany House
Black Forest—R
Bridge/Logos
Comments Publishing—R
CSS Publishing
Essence Publishing—R
Hendrickson—R
Huntington House—R
Impact Christian Books—R
InterVarsity Press
Longwood—R
Monument Press
Moody Press
New Leaf Press—R
Open Court—R
Paragon House—R
Presbyterian & Reformed
Promise Publishing
Read 'N Run—R
Rose Publishing
Schocken Books—R
Son-Rise
Starburst Publishers
Tekna Books
Tyler Press—R
Vital Issues Press—R
Wood Lake Books—R
Zondervan

CURRENT/SOCIAL ISSUES

Accent Books
Ambassador House
Baker Books—R
Bantam Books
Barclay Press—R
Baylor University Press
Beacon Hill Press
Bethany House
Black Forest—R
Blue Dolphin
Brentwood—R
Bridge/Logos
Bristol House—R

Chalice Press
Christian Media—R
Christian Publications
Christopher Publishing
Cornell Univ. Press—R
Cross Cultural
Crossroad Publishing—R
Crossway Books
Destiny Image
Eerdmans Publishing—R
Element Books—R
Erica House
Essence Publishing—R
Fairway Press—R
FOG Publishing
Haworth Press—R
Hay House
Hendrickson—R
Horizon House—R
Howard Publishing
Huntington House—R
InterVarsity Press
Judson Press—R
Kregel—R
Libros Liguori
Life Cycle Books—R
Lifetime Books—R
Liguori Publications
Living the Good News
Longwood—R
Lowenbrown Publishing
Moody Press
Morehouse—R
Multnomah
New Hope—R
Openbook—R
Oxford University
Paragon House—R
Paulist Press
PREP Publishing—R
Presbyterian & Reformed
Promise Publishing
Ragged Edge—R
Read 'N Run—R
Regnery—R
Resurrection Press—R
Review & Herald
Shaw Publishers, Harold—R
Small Helm Press—R
Smyth & Helwys
Son-Rise
Sonstar Publishing—R
Starburst Publishers
Still Waters Revival—R
Summit Pub. Group—R
Sword of the Lord—R
Tekna Books
Tyler Press—R

United Church Pub.
Univ/Ottawa Press
VESTA—R
Vital Issues Press—R
Western Front—R
Westminster John Knox
Wood Lake Books—R
Zondervan

CURRICULUM

Art Can Drama—R (drama,
  arts)
Black Forest—R
Christian Ed Pub.
CSS Publishing
Educational Ministries
Facts on File
Gospel Publishing House—R
Group's FaithWeaver
Hensley Publishing —R
Master Books—R
Morehouse—R
Openbook—R
Rainbow/Legacy Press—R
Rainbow/Rainbow Books—R
Read 'N Run—R
Rose Publishing
Royal Productions—R
Smyth & Helwys
Standard
Tekna Books
Treasure Learning—R
Tyler Press—R
United Church Press
Wellness
Wesleyan Publishing House
Wonder Time (mag.)
Wood Lake Books—R

DEATH/DYING

Abingdon Press—R
ACTA Publications
Albury Publishing—R
Black Forest—R
Blue Dolphin
Bridge/Logos
Broadman & Holman
Christopher Publishing
Conari Press—R
Crossroad Publishing—R
CSS Publishing
Daybreak Books—R
Doubleday
Eerdmans Publishing—R
Erica House
Essence Publishing—R

Fairway Press—R
Forward Movement
Gilgal Publications
HarperSanFrancisco
Haworth Press—R
Hay House
Hendrickson—R
InterVarsity Press
Kregel—R
Life Cycle Books—R
Liguori Publications
Liturgy Training
Longwood—R
Morehouse—R
Paraclete Press—R
Paragon House—R
Perigee Books
Promise Publishing
Rainbow/Legacy Press—R
Read 'N Run—R
Resurrection Press—R
Review & Herald
St. Bede's—R
Schocken Books—R
Sheed & Ward—R
Smyth & Helwys
Sonstar Publishing—R
Tekna Books
Thomas More—R
United Church Press
Univ/Ottawa Press
White Stone Circle
Wood Lake Books—R
Zondervan

DEVOTIONAL BOOKS

ACU Press
Albury Publishing—R
Barbour Publishing—R
Barclay Press—R
Black Forest—R
Brentwood—R
Bridge/Logos
Broadman & Holman
Chariot Victor
Christian Publications
Christopher Publishing
Church Street Press
Concordia
Contemporary Drama Service
Crossroad Publishing—R
Crossway Books
CSS Publishing
Daybreak Books—R
Destiny Image
Dimensions for Living—R
Doubleday

Dry Bones Press—R
Eerdmans Publishing—R
Essence Publishing—R
Fairway Press—R
FOG Publishing
Franciscan Univ Press—R
Friends United Press—R
Gesher—R
Gilgal Publications
Gospel Publishing House—R
HarperSanFrancisco
Hendrickson—R
Hensley Publishing —R
Honor Books
Howard Publishing
Impact Christian Books—R
J. Countryman
Judson Press—R
Libros Liguori
Light and Life—R
Lightwave Publishing
Liguori Publications
Longwood—R
Loyola Press
Master Design
McDougal Publishing
Morehouse—R
New Leaf Press—R
Openbook—R
Pacific Press
Paraclete Press—R
Pauline Books
Promise Publishing
Rainbow/Legacy Press—R
Rainbow's End
Read 'N Run—R
Resurrection Press—R
Revell
Review & Herald
St. Anthony Messenger—R
St. Bede's—R
Saint Mary's Press—R
Schocken Books—R
Shaw Publishers, Harold—R
Sheed & Ward—R
Sheer Joy! Press
Smyth & Helwys
Son-Rise
Sonstar Publishing—R
Standard (for kids)
Starburst Publishers
TEACH Services—R
Tekna Books
Thomas More—R
Toccoa Falls
Tyler Press—R
United Church Press
United Church Pub.

West Coast Paradise—R
Westminster John Knox
White Stone Circle
Wood Lake Books—R
World Bible
Zondervan

DISCIPLESHIP

Accent Publications
ACU Press
Albury Publishing—R
Baker Books—R
Barbour Publishing—R
Barclay Press—R
Beacon Hill Press
Bethany House
Black Forest—R
Brentwood—R
Bridge/Logos
Bristol House—R
Broadman & Holman
Chalice Press
Chariot Victor
Chosen Books
Christian Publications
Church Growth Inst.
College Press—R
Creation House
Crossway Books
CSS Publishing
Eerdmans Publishing—R
Essence Publishing—R
Fairway Press—R
Gesher—R
Gospel Publishing House—R
HarperSanFrancisco
Hendrickson—R
Hensley Publishing—R
Horizon House—R
Howard Publishing
InterVarsity Press
J. Countryman
Judson Press—R
Kregel—R
Libros Liguori
Light and Life—R
Lightwave Publishing
Longwood—R
Lowenbrown Publishing
Master Design
McDougal Publishing
Messianic Jewish—R
Middle Atlantic—R
Moody Press
Morehouse—R
Multnomah
Neibauer Press—R

New Hope—R
New Leaf Press—R
Omega House—R
Paragon House—R
Presbyterian & Reformed
Promise Publishing
Rainbow/Legacy Press—R
Review & Herald
St. Bede's—R
Schocken Books—R
Sheed & Ward—R
Smyth & Helwys
Southern Baptist Press—R
Standard
Sword of the Lord—R
Tekna Books
Thomas More—R
Toccoa Falls
Treasure Learning—R
Tyler Press—R
Vital Issues Press—R
Westminster John Knox
Wood Lake Books—R
YWAM Publishing—R
Zondervan

DIVORCE

ACTA Publications
Albury Publishing—R
Baker Books—R
Bantam Books
Bethany House
Black Forest—R
Brentwood—R
Bridge/Logos
Broadman & Holman
Erica House
Essence Publishing—R
Forward Movement
Gilgal
Haworth Press—R
Hay House
Huntington House—R
InterVarsity Press
Longwood—R
Lowenbrown Publishing
Morehouse—R
Perigee Books
PREP Publishing—R
Presbyterian & Reformed
Promise Publishing
Read 'N Run—R
Regnery—R
Resurrection Press—R
Schocken Books—R
Sheer Joy! Press
Sonstar Publishing—R

Southern Baptist Press—R
Tekna Books
Tyler Press—R
Vital Issues Press—R
West Coast Paradise—R
Wood Lake Books—R
Zondervan

DOCTRINAL

ACU Press
Alba House—R
Albury Publishing—R
Ambassador House
Baker Books—R
Beacon Hill Press
Bethany House
Black Forest—R
Brentwood—R
Broadman & Holman
Catholic Univ./America—R
Christian Publications
Christian Univ Press—R
CSS Publishing
Doubleday
Eerdmans Publishing—R
Essence Publishing—R
Fairway Press—R
Friends United Press—R
Gospel Publishing House—R
Hearth Publishing—R
Hendrickson—R
Impact Christian Books—R
Intl. Awakening Press—R
Kregel—R
Libros Liguori
Light and Life—R
Liturgical Press
Loizeaux
Longwood—R
Magnus Press—R
Master Design
McDougal Publishing
Moody Press
Our Sunday Visitor—R
Paragon House—R
Paulist Press
Pilgrim Press—R
Presbyterian & Reformed
Promise Publishing
Review & Herald
Royal Productions—R
St. Anthony Messenger—R
St. Bede's—R
Shaw Publishers, Harold—R
Sheed & Ward—R
Southern Baptist Press—R
Still Waters Revival—R

Sword of the Lord—R
Tekna Books
Trinity Foundation—R
Tyler Press—R
Univ Press of America—R
West Coast Paradise—R
Westminster John Knox
Zondervan

DRAMA

Art Can Drama—R
Baker Books—R
Baker's Plays
Black Forest—R
Brentwood—R
Christian Media—R
Church Street Press
Concordia
Contemporary Drama Service
CSS Publishing
Eldridge Pub.
Fairway Press—R
Guernica Editions—R
Lillenas
Lowenbrown Publishing
Meriwether—R
New Hope—R (missions)
Read 'N Run—R
Sheer Joy! Press
Southern Baptist Press—R
Standard
Tyler Press—R
United Church Pub.
West Coast Paradise—R
Western Front—R
Windflower—R
Zondervan

ECONOMICS

Black Forest—R
Brentwood—R
Bridge/Logos
Christopher Publishing
Cross Cultural
Dimension Books—R
Eerdmans Publishing—R
Essence Publishing—R
FOG Publishing
Forward Movement
Haworth Press—R
Huntington House—R
Lowenbrown Publishing
Moody Press
New World Library
Oxford University
Paragon House—R

Paulist Press
Pilgrim Press—R
Read 'N Run—R
Regnery—R
Schocken Books—R
Summit Pub. Group—R
Trinity Foundation—R
Tyler Press—R
Univ/Ottawa Press
Vital Issues Press—R

ENVIRONMENTAL ISSUES

Baker Books—R
Bantam Books
Black Forest—R
Blue Dolphin
Boyds Mills Press
Chalice Press
Christian Univ Press—R
Christopher Publishing
Counterpoint
Cross Cultural
CSS Publishing
Daybreak Books—R
Doubleday
Eerdmans Publishing—R
Element Books—R
Essence Publishing—R
Facts on File
Forward Movement
Haworth Press—R
Hay House
Hearth Publishing—R
Holy Cross—R
Huntington House—R
Judson Press—R
Liturgy Training
Lowenbrown Publishing
Monument Press
Morehouse—R
Oxford University
Paulist Press
Promise Publishing
Read 'N Run—R
Resurrection Press—R
Royal Productions—R
Schocken Books—R
Sonstar Publishing—R
Southern Baptist Press—R
Summit Pub. Group—R
Tekna Books
Tyler Press—R
United Church Press
United Church Pub.
Univ/Ottawa Press
Vital Issues Press—R
West Coast Paradise—R

White Stone Circle
Zondervan

ETHICS

Abingdon Press—R
ACU Press
Ambassador House
Baker Books—R
Bantam Books
Baylor University Press
Bethany House
Black Forest—R
Brentwood—R
Catholic Univ./America—R
Chalice Press
Christian Publications
Christian Univ Press—R
Christopher Publishing
Cornell Univ. Press—R
Creation House
Crossroad Publishing—R
Crossway Books
CSS Publishing
Daybreak Books—R
Doubleday
Dry Bones Press—R
Eerdmans Publishing—R
Erica House
Essence Publishing—R
Forward Movement
Gospel Publishing House—R
Haworth Press—R
Hay House
Hearth Publishing—R
Holy Cross—R
Howard Publishing
Huntington House—R
InterVarsity Press
Judson Press—R
Kregel—R
Life Cycle Books—R
Lifetime Books—R
Logion Press
Longwood—R
Lowenbrown Publishing
McDougal Publishing
Mercer University Press
Morehouse—R
Multnomah
New Leaf Press—R
New World Library
Open Court—R
Oxford University
Paragon House—R
Paulist Press
Perigee Books
Pilgrim Press—R

Presbyterian & Reformed
Promise Publishing
Read 'N Run—R
Regnery—R
Resource Publications
Royal Productions—R
St. Anthony Messenger—R
St. Bede's—R
Schocken Books—R
Sheed & Ward—R
Smyth & Helwys
Still Waters Revival—R
Summit Pub. Group—R
Tekna Books
Trinity Foundation—R
Trinity Press Intl.—R
Tyler Press—R
United Church Press
United Church Pub.
Univ/Ottawa Press
Univ Press of America—R
Vital Issues Press—R
Wadsworth—R
Westminster John Knox
White Stone Circle
Yale Univ Press—R
Zondervan

ETHNIC/CULTURAL

Abingdon Press—R
ACU Press
Baker Books—R
Bantam Books
Barclay Press—R
Beacon Hill Press
Black Forest—R
Boyds Mills Press
Broadman & Holman
Chalice Press
Christian Univ Press—R
Christopher Publishing
College Press—R
Cross Cultural
Daybreak Books—R
Doubleday
Eerdmans Publishing—R
Facts on File
Franciscan Univ Press—R
Friends United Press—R
Gospel Publishing House—R
Haworth Press—R
Hay House
Hearth Publishing—R
Hensley Publishing
Holy Cross —R
Huntington House—R
InterVarsity Press

Judson Press—R
Kaleidoscope Press—R
Kregel—R
Libros Liguori
Liguori Publications
Living Books for All
Longwood—R
Lowenbrown Publishing
Lydia Press
Messianic Jewish—R (Jewish only)
Middle Atlantic—R
Monument Press
Morehouse—R
Mosaic Press
National Baptist—R
One World
Palisades
Paragon House—R
Pelican Publishing—R
Pilgrim Press—R
Read 'N Run—R
Review & Herald
St. Anthony Messenger—R
Schocken Books—R
Shaw Publishers, Harold—R
Standard (few)
Tekna Books
United Church Press
United Church Pub.
Univ/Ottawa Press
VESTA—R
World Bible
Zondervan

EVANGELISM/ WITNESSING

Accent Publications
ACU Press
Albury Publishing—R
Ambassador House
Baker Books—R
Bethany House
Brentwood—R
Bridge/Logos
Bristol House—R
Broadman & Holman
Chariot Victor
Chosen Books
Christian Publications
Christopher Publishing
Church Growth Inst.
Concordia
Crossway Books
CSS Publishing
Doubleday
Eerdmans Publishing—R
Erica House

Essence Publishing—R
Fairway Press—R
Forward Movement
Friends United Press—R
Gospel Publishing House—R
HarperSanFrancisco
Hendrickson—R
Horizon House—R
Huntington House—R
Impact Christian Books—R
InterVarsity Press
Judson Press—R
Kregel—R
Langmarc
Light and Life—R
Longwood—R
Lowenbrown Publishing
McDougal Publishing
Messianic Jewish—R
Middle Atlantic—R
Moody Press
Morehouse—R
Multnomah
Neibauer Press—R
New Hope—R
New Leaf Press—R
Omega House—R
Openbook—R
Paragon House—R
Presbyterian & Reformed
Ragged Edge—R
Rainbow/Legacy Press—R
Read 'N Run—R
Resurrection Press—R
Review & Herald
Rose Publishing
Royal Productions—R
St. Bede's—R
Shaw Publishers, Harold—R
Sheer Joy! Press
Son-Rise
Sonstar Publishing—R
Southern Baptist Press—R
Still Waters Revival—R
Sword of the Lord—R
Tekna Books
Toccoa Falls
Tyler Press—R
United Church Press
Vital Issues Press—R
West Coast Paradise—R
Westminster John Knox
Zondervan

EXEGESIS*

Eerdmans Publishing—R
Essence Publishing—R

HarperSanFrancisco
Hendrickson—R
Holy Cross—R
Longwood—R
Master Design
Monument Press
Review & Herald
St. Bede's—R
Sonstar Publishing—R
Tekna Books
Wood Lake Books—R

EXPOSÉS

Ambassador House
Brentwood—R
Christian Publications
Huntington House—R
Lifetime Books—R
Open Court—R
Promise Publishing
Read 'N Run—R
Schocken Books—R
Southern Baptist Press—R
Sword of the Lord—R
Trinity Foundation—R
Tyler Press—R
Vital Issues Press—R

FAMILY LIFE

ACTA Publications
ACU Press
Albury Publishing—R
Baker Books—R
Bantam Books
Barclay Press—R
Beacon Hill Press
Bethany House
Black Forest—R
Blue Dolphin
Brentwood—R
Bridge/Logos
Broadman & Holman
Chalice Press
Chariot Victor
Christian Publications
Christopher Publishing
College Press—R
Concordia
Crossroad Publishing—R
Crossway Books
CSS Publishing
Daybreak Books—R
Destiny Image
Dimensions for Living—R
Eerdmans Publishing—R
Erica House

Essence Publishing—R
Fairway Press—R
Focus Publishing
Gospel Publishing House—R
GROUP Publishing—R
Haworth Press—R
Hay House
Hensley Publishing—R
Holiday House
Honor Books
Howard Publishing
Huntington House—R
InterVarsity Press
J. Countryman
Judson Press—R
Kindred Productions
Langmarc
Libros Liguori
Life Cycle Books—R
Light and Life—R
Lightwave Publishing
Liguori Publications
Longwood—R
Lowenbrown Publishing
Loyola Press
McDougal Publishing
Moody Press
Morehouse—R
Multnomah
New City Press—R
New Hope—R
New Leaf Press—R
Openbook—R
Our Sunday Visitor—R
Paragon House—R
Pauline Books
Pelican Publishing—R
Perigee Books
Peter Pauper Press
Presbyterian & Reformed
Promise Publishing
Ragged Edge—R
Rainbow/Legacy Press—R
Rainbow's End
Read 'N Run—R
Recovery Communications
Resurrection Press—R
Revell
Schocken Books—R
Shaw Publishers, Harold—R
Son-Rise
Southern Baptist Press—R
Sower's Press
Starburst Publishers
Still Waters Revival—R
Sword of the Lord—R
TEACH Services—R
Tekna Books

Treasure Learning—R
Tyler Press—R
Vital Issues Press—R
Wellness
Westminster John Knox
Windflower—R
Wood Lake Books—R
Zondervan

FICTION: ADULT/ RELIGIOUS

Alexander Books
Ambassador House
Baker Books—R
Bantam Books
Barbour Publishing—R
Bethany House
Black Forest—R
Blue Dolphin
Books in Motion
Cerdic Publications
Chariot Victor
Christopher Publishing
Comments Publishing—R
Cornerstone Press
Counterpoint
Creation House
Crossway Books
CSS Publishing
Daybreak Books—R
Dry Bones Press—R
Eerdmans Publishing—R
Erica House
Essence Publishing—R
Focus Publishing
Friends United Press—R
Genesis Publishing
Guernica Editions—R
Hay House
HeartQuest
Heartsong Presents
Hearth Publishing—R
Horizon House—R
Huntington House—R
J. Countryman
Kregel—R
Lowenbrown Publishing
Marlton Publishers
McDougal Publishing
Messianic Jewish—R
Morrow & Company, Wm.
Mosaic Press
MountainView—R
Mt. Olive College Press
MountainView Publishing
Multnomah
Pacific Press

Palisades
Pelican Publishing—R
PREP Publishing—R
G.P. Putnam's Sons
Read 'N Run—R
Recovery Communications
Revell
Review & Herald
Shaw Publishers, Harold—R
Sheer Joy! Press
Sonstar Publishing—R
Starburst Publishers
West Coast Paradise—R
Western Front—R
Windflower—R
Wine Press—R
Wood Lake Books—R
Zondervan

FICTION: ADVENTURE

Ambassador House
Bantam Books
Barbour Publishing—R
Bethany House
Black Forest—R
Books in Motion
Boyds Mills Press
Brentwood—R
Christian Ed Pub.
Christopher Publishing
Concordia
Crossway Books
Dry Bones Press—R
Erica House
Essence Publishing—R
Fairway Press—R
Forward Movement
GROUP Publishing—R (juv/
   teen)
Hearth Publishing—R
HeartQuest
Henry Holt
Huntington House—R
Kaleidoscope Press—R (juv)
Lowenbrown Publishing
Morehouse—R
Morris, Joshua
Morrow & Co., Wm. (juv)
MountainView—R
Palisades
PREP Publishing—R
G.P. Putnam's Sons
Read 'N Run—R
Revell
Review & Herald
Shaw Publishers, Harold—R
Sonstar Publishing—R

Southern Baptist Press—R
Starburst Publishers
Sword of the Lord—R
Toccoa Falls
West Coast Paradise—R
Windflower—R
Wine Press—R

FICTION: ALLEGORY

Ambassador House
Black Forest—R
Chariot Victor
Creation House
CSS Publishing
Eerdmans Publishing—R
Erica House
Essence Publishing—R
Fairway Press—R
GROUP Publishing—R
Huntington House—R
Lowenbrown Publishing
McDougal Publishing
Morris, Joshua
Morehouse—R
MountainView—R
Palisades
Read 'N Run—R
Revell
Sonstar Publishing—R
Sword of the Lord—R
Wine Press—R
Zondervan

FICTION: BIBLICAL

Ambassador House
Black Forest—R
Brentwood—R
Christopher Publishing
College Press—R
Concordia
Creation House
CSS Publishing
Eerdmans/Young Readers
Fairway Press—R
Friends United Press—R
GROUP Publishing—R
HeartQuest
Kregel—R
Lowenbrown Publishing
McDougal Publishing
Messianic Jewish—R
Middle Atlantic—R (juv)
Morehouse—R
Morris, Joshua
MountainView—R
Mt. Olive College Press

New Hope—R (juv)
Palisades
Pacific Press
PREP Publishing—R
Ragged Edge—R (juv)
Read 'N Run—R
Revell
Review & Herald
Sheer Joy! Press
Southern Baptist Press—R
Sword of the Lord—R
Toccoa Falls
Western Front—R
Windflower—R
Wine Press—R
Zondervan

FICTION: CONTEMPORARY

Baker Books—R
Bantam Books
Barbour Publishing—R
Bethany House
Black Forest—R
Books in Motion
Boyds Mills Press
Brentwood—R
Christian Ed Pub.
Christopher Publishing
Concordia
Cornerstone Press
Counterpoint
Creation House
Crossway Books
Dry Bones Press—R
Eerdmans Publishing—R
Erica House
Essence Publishing—R
Fairway Press—R
Guernica Editions—R
HarperSanFrancisco
HeartQuest
Heartsong Presents
Henry Holt
Journey Books—R
Kindred Productions
Lowenbrown Publishing
Marlton Publishers
Middle Atlantic—R (juv)
Morehouse—R
Morris, Joshua
Mosaic Press
MountainView—R
Mt. Olive College Press
Multnomah
National Baptist—R
One World
Palisades

Pleasant Co.
Read 'N Run—R
Revell
Shaw Publishers, Harold—R
Sonstar Publishing—R
Southern Baptist Press—R
Starburst Publishers
Toccoa Falls
West Coast Paradise—R
Western Front—R
Windflower—R
Wine Press—R
Zondervan

FICTION: ETHNIC

Baker Books—R
Black Forest—R
Blue Dolphin
Boyds Mills Press
CSS Publishing
Eerdmans Publishing—R
Essence Publishing—R
Guernica Editions—R
Henry Holt
Kaleidoscope Press—R (juv)
Lowenbrown Publishing
Messianic Jewish—R
Mosaic Press
MountainView—R
Palisades
Pelican Publishing—R
Shaw Publishers, Harold—R
Wine Press—R

FICTION: FANTASY

Bantam Books
Books in Motion
Boyds Mills Press
Dry Bones Press—R
Eerdmans Publishing—R
Fairway Press—R
Forward Movement
Henry Holt
Marlton Publishers
MountainView—R
Palisades
Read 'N Run—R
Shaw Publishers, Harold—R
Wine Press—R
Zondervan

FICTION: FRONTIER

Bantam Books
Bethany House
Black Forest—R

Books in Motion
Boyds Mills Press
Brentwood—R
Christopher Publishing
Fairway Press—R
Hearth Publishing—R
Kaleidoscope Press—R (juv)
MountainView—R
Multnomah
Palisades
Read 'N Run—R
Revell
Sonstar Publishing—R
Southern Baptist Press—R
Windflower—R
Wine Press—R

FICTION: FRONTIER/ ROMANCE

Bantam Books
Barbour Publishing—R
Bethany House
Brentwood—R
Chariot Victor
Christopher Publishing
Fairway Press—R
HeartQuest
Heartsong Presents
Hearth Publishing—R
MountainView—R
Multnomah
Palisades
Proclaim Publishing
Read 'N Run—R
Revell
Sonstar Publishing—R
Southern Baptist Press—R
Wine Press—R
Zondervan

FICTION: HISTORICAL

Bantam Books
Bethany House
Black Forest—R
Books in Motion
Boyds Mills Press
Brentwood—R
Christopher Publishing
Cornerstone Press
Counterpoint
Crossroad Publishing—R
Crossway Books
Dry Bones Press—R
Eden Publishing
Eerdmans Publishing—R
Eerdmans/Young Readers

Erica House
Essence Publishing—R
Fairway Press—R
Friends United Press—R
HarperSanFrancisco
Hearth Publishing—R
HeartQuest
Henry Holt
Holiday House
Horizon House—R
J. Countryman
Journey Books—R
Kregel—R
Lowenbrown Publishing
Misty Hill Press
Morehouse—R
Morris, Joshua
Morrow & Company, Wm.
Mosaic Press
MountainView—R
Multnomah
One World
Palisades
Pleasant Co.
Ragged Edge—R (juv)
Read 'N Run—R
Revell
Son-Rise
Sonstar Publishing—R
Southern Baptist Press—R
West Coast Paradise—R
Western Front—R
Windflower—R
Wine Press—R
YWAM Publishing—R
Zondervan

FICTION: HISTORICAL/ ROMANCE

Bantam Books
Barbour Publishing—R
Bethany House
Brentwood—R
Chariot Victor
Christopher Publishing
Creation House
Crossway Books
Erica House
Fairway Press—R
HeartQuest
Heartsong Presents
Hearth Publishing—R
Horizon House—R
Kregel—R
MountainView—R
Multnomah
Palisades

Read 'N Run—R
Revell
Sonstar Publishing—R
Southern Baptist Press—R
Wine Press—R
Zondervan

FICTION: HUMOR

Ambassador House
Bantam Books
Black Forest—R
Christopher Publishing
Counterpoint
CSS Publishing
Essence Publishing—R
Fairway Press—R
Hearth Publishing—R
Holiday House
Henry Holt
Journey Books—R
Kaleidoscope Press—R (juv)
Lowenbrown Publishing
Morehouse—R
Morris, Joshua
Mosaic Press
MountainView—R
Palisades
Read 'N Run—R
Revell
Shaw Publishers, Harold—R
Sheer Joy! Press
Sonstar Publishing—R
Sword of the Lord—R
West Coast Paradise—R
Wine Press—R

FICTION: JUVENILE
(Ages 8-12)

Barbour Publishing—R
Bethany House
Black Forest—R
Boyds Mills Press
Chariot Victor
Concordia
Cornerstone Press
CSS Publishing
Eerdmans/Young Readers
Erica House
Essence Publishing—R
Fairway Press—R
Focus Publishing
Forward Movement
Friends United Press—R
Gold 'n' Honey
GROUP Publishing—R
Hearth Publishing—R

Holiday House
Henry Holt
Horizon House—R
Huntington House—R
Journey Books—R
Kaleidoscope Press—R
Kindred Productions
Lightwave Publishing
Living the Good News
McDougal Publishing
Messianic Jewish—R
Misty Hill Press
Morehouse—R
Morris, Joshua
MountainView—R
PACE Publications—R
Pacific Press
Pauline Books
Pelican Publishing—R
Read 'N Run—R
Sheer Joy! Press
Sonstar Publishing—R
Sword of the Lord—R
Toccoa Falls
Tyler Press—R
Wine Press—R
YWAM Publishing—R
Zondervan

FICTION: LITERARY

Baker Books—R
Black Forest—R
Counterpoint
Dry Bones Press—R
Eerdmans Publishing—R
Eerdmans/Young Readers
Erica House
FOG Publishing
Guernica Editions—R
J. Countryman
Morrow & Company, Wm.
Mosaic Press
Mt. Olive College Press
Multnomah
Palisades
Read 'N Run—R
Shaw Publishers, Harold—R
West Coast Paradise—R
Wine Press—R

FICTION: MYSTERY

Baker Books—R
Bantam Books
Bethany House
Black Forest—R
Books in Motion

Boyds Mills Press
Christian Ed Pub.
Concordia
Dry Bones Press—R
Eerdmans Publishing—R
Erica House
Essence Publishing—R
Henry Holt
Journey Books—R
Lowenbrown Publishing
Morehouse—R
Morrow & Company, Wm.
Mosaic Press
MountainView—R
Mt. Olive College Press
Multnomah
Palisades
Prescott Press—R
Rainbow Books
Read 'N Run—R
Revell
Shaw Publishers, Harold—R
Sonstar Publishing—R
Sword of the Lord—R
Toccoa Falls
Wine Press—R
Western Front—R
Zondervan

FICTION: MYSTERY/
ROMANCE

Bantam Books
Barbour Publishing—R
Bethany House
Black Forest—R
Brentwood—R
Chariot Victor
Erica House
Fairway Press—R
HeartQuest
Heartsong Presents
Love Inspired
MountainView—R
Palisades
Read 'N Run—R
Revell
Sonstar Publishing—R
Southern Baptist Press—R
Sword of the Lord—R
Wine Press—R
Zondervan

FICTION: PLAYS

Baker's Plays
Bantam Books
Brentwood—R

Creatively Yours
CSS Publishing
Eldridge Pub. (& musicals)
Essence Publishing—R
Fairway Press—R
Lillenas
Lowenbrown Publishing
Meriwether—R
Mosaic Press
Mt. Olive College Press
National Baptist—R
Read 'N Run—R
Resource Publications
Sheer Joy! Press
Southern Baptist Press—R

FICTION: ROMANCE

Bantam Books
Barbour Publishing—R
Bethany House
Chariot Victor
Erica House
Fairway Press—R
Heartsong Presents
Hearth Publishing—R
HeartQuest
Love Inspired
Lowenbrown Publishing
Marlton Publishers
Morrow & Company, Wm.
MountainView—R
Multnomah
Palisades
PREP Publishing—R
Read 'N Run—R
Revell
Sheer Joy! Press
Sonstar Publishing—R
Sword of the Lord—R
Wine Press—R

FICTION: SCIENCE FICTION

Bantam Books
Black Forest—R
Books in Motion
Boyds Mills Press
Dry Bones Press—R
Forward Movement
GROUP Publishing—R
Huntington House—R
Morrow & Company, Wm.
MountainView—R
Read 'N Run—R
Skysong Press
Wine Press—R

FICTION: SHORT STORY COLLECTION

Black Forest—R
Boyds Mills Press
Christopher Publishing
Concordia
Counterpoint
Essence Publishing—R
Fairway Press—R
GROUP Publishing—R
Hearth Publishing—R
J. Countryman
Kaleidoscope Press—R (juv)
Lowenbrown Publishing
Morehouse—R
Mosaic Press
MountainView—R
Mt. Olive College Press
National Baptist—R
Read 'N Run—R
Sonstar Publishing—R
West Coast Paradise—R

FICTION: TEEN/YOUNG ADULT

Bethany House
Black Forest—R
Boyds Mills Press
Comments Publishing—R
Eerdmans/Young Readers
Essence Publishing—R
Fairway Press—R
Focus Publishing
Friends United Press—R
GROUP Publishing—R
Hearth Publishing—R
Henry Holt
Horizon House—R
Huntington House—R
Journey Books—R
Living the Good News
Lowenbrown Publishing
McDougal Publishing
Messianic Jewish—R
MountainView—R
PACE Publications—R
Palisades
Ragged Edge—R
Read 'N Run—R
Review & Herald
Saint Mary's Press—R
Sheer Joy! Press
Sword of the Lord—R
Toccoa Falls
Windflower—R
Wine Press—R

YWAM Publishing—R
Zondervan

GAMES/CRAFTS

Bay Public., Mel
Brown-ROA
Concordia
Contemporary Drama Service
Educational Ministries
Essence Publishing—R
Gospel Publishing House—R
GROUP Publishing—R
Hunt & Thorpe
Judson Press—R
Kaleidoscope Press—R
Lightwave Publishing (games)
Lowenbrown Publishing
Meriwether—R
Messianic Jewish—R
Morehouse—R
Our Sunday Visitor—R
Perigee Books
Pleasant Co.
Rainbow/Rainbow Books—R
Read 'N Run—R
Review & Herald
Schocken Books—R
Shining Star
Standard
Starburst Publishers
Tekna Books
Tyler Press—R
Wood Lake Books—R
Zondervan

GIFT BOOKS

Albury Publishing—R
Baker Books—R
Barbour Publishing—R
Berrie, Russ
Black Forest—R
Bridge/Logos
Calligraphy Collection
Chariot Victor
Christian Publications
Church Street Press
Conari Press—R
Concordia
Contemporary Drama Service
Counterpoint
Creation House
Daybreak Books—R
Dimensions for Living—R
Eerdmans Publishing—R (art)
Element Books—R
Erica House

Essence Publishing—R
Hay House
Hearth Publishing—R
Hensley Publishing—R
Honor Books
Howard Publishing
Hunt & Thorpe
Huntington House—R
Image Craft
J. Countryman
Judson Press—R
Kaleidoscope Press—R
Living the Good News
Longwood—R
Lowenbrown Publishing
Manhattan Greeting Card
Morehouse—R.
Mt. Olive College Press
Multnomah
New Leaf Press—R
Our Sunday Visitor—R
Painted Hearts & Friends
Palisades (romantic)
Peter Pauper Press
Preservation Press
Promise Publishing
Read 'N Run—R
Resurrection Press—R
Schocken Books—R
Shaw Publishers, Harold
Starburst Publishers
Summit Pub. Group—R
Sunrise Publications
West Coast Paradise—R
Western Front—R
Westminster John Knox
Wine Press—R
Zondervan

GROUP STUDY BOOKS

Alban Institute
Baker Books—R
Brentwood—R
Bridge/Logos
Chariot Victor
CSS Publishing
Essence Publishing—R
Fairway Press—R
FOG Publishing
HarperSanFrancisco
Hendrickson—R
Hensley Publishing—R
Innisfree Press
Judson Press—R
Langmarc
Longwood—R
Morehouse—R

New Hope—R
New Leaf Press—R
Paradise Research—R
Presbyterian & Reformed
Ragged Edge—R
Rainbow's End
Read 'N Run—R
Resource Publications
St. Anthony Messenger—R
Sheed & Ward—R
Smyth & Helwys
Sonstar Publishing—R
Southern Baptist Press—R
Standard
Tekna Books
Tyler Press—R
Wood Lake Books—R
Zondervan

HEALING

Alba House—R
Albury Publishing—R
Baker Books—R
Bantam Books
Bethany House
Black Forest—R
Blue Dolphin
Brentwood—R
Bridge/Logos
Chosen Books
Christian Publications
Christopher Publishing
Conari Press—R
Crossroad Publishing—R
CSS Publishing
Daybreak Books—R
Destiny Image
Doubleday
Eerdmans Publishing—R
Elder Books—R
Element Books—R
Erica House
Essence Publishing—R
Fairway Press—R
Gilgal
Gospel Publishing House—R
HarperSanFrancisco
Haworth Press—R
Hay House
Hensley Publishing—R
Impact Christian Books—R
InterVarsity Press
Libros Liguori
Lifetime Books—R
Lowenbrown Publishing
McDougal Publishing
Middle Atlantic—R

Morehouse—R
Northstone—R
Omega House—R
Paradise Research—R
Paragon House—R
Perigee Books
Promise Publishing
Read 'N Run—R
Recovery Communications
Resource Publications
Resurrection Press—R
Saint Mary's Press—R
Schocken Books—R
Son-Rise
Southern Baptist Press—R
Starburst Publishers
Tekna Books
Tyler Press—R
United Church Press
United Church Pub.
Univ/Ottawa Press
White Stone Circle
Wood Lake Books—R
Zondervan

HEALTH

Accent Books
Albury Publishing—R
Baker Books—R
Bantam Books
Bethany House
Black Forest—R
Blue Dolphin
Brentwood—R
Bridge/Logos
Broadman & Holman
Christopher Publishing
Crossroad Publishing—R
Daybreak Books—R
Doubleday
Dry Bones Press—R
Eerdmans Publishing—R
Elder Books—R
Element Books—R
Essence Publishing—R
Facts on File
Fairway Press—R
HarperSanFrancisco
Haworth Press—R
Hay House
Hensley Publishing—R
Huntington House—R
Journey Books—R
Kaleidoscope Press—R
Life Cycle Books—R
Lifetime Books—R
Longwood—R

McDougal Publishing
Morehouse—R
Mosaic Press
New World Library
Northstone—R
Pacific Press
Paradise Research—R
Perigee Books
Promise Publishing
Read 'N Run—R
Recovery Communications
Regnery—R
Review & Herald
Schocken Books—R
Shaw Publishers, Harold—R
Son-Rise
Southern Baptist Press—R
Starburst Publishers
Summit Pub. Group—R
TEACH Services—R
Tekna Books
Tyler Press—R
Univ/Ottawa Press
VESTA—R
Vital Issues Press—R
Wellness
West Coast Paradise—R
White Stone Circle
Zondervan

HISTORICAL

Albury Publishing—R
Ambassador House
Bantam Books
Barbour Publishing—R
Baylor University Press
Bethany House
Black Forest—R
Brentwood—R
Catholic Univ./America—R
Christian Publications
Christian Univ Press—R
Christopher Publishing
Cistercian Publications
Cornell Univ. Press—R
Counterpoint
Cross Cultural
Crossroad Publishing—R
Custom Communications
Daybreak Books—R
Dimension Books—R
Doubleday
Eerdmans Publishing—R
Element Books—R
Erica House
Essence Publishing—R
Facts on File

Friends United Press—R
Gesher—R
Good Book—R
Hearth Publishing—R
Holiday House
Holy Cross—R
Huntington House—R
Impact Christian Books—R
Intl. Awakening Press—R
Journey Books—R
Judson Press—R
Kregel—R
Light and Life—R
Magnus Press—R
Mercer University Press
Middle Atlantic—R
Monument Press
Morehouse—R
Morrow & Company, Wm.
Mosaic Press
Our Sunday Visitor—R
Oxford University
Paradise Research—R
Paragon House—R
Promise Publishing
Ragged Edge—R
Read 'N Run—R
Regnery—R
Schocken Books—R
Son-Rise
Sonstar Publishing—R
Southern Baptist Press—R
Still Waters Revival—R
Summit Pub. Group—R
Tekna Books
Trinity Foundation—R
Tyler Press—R
United Church Pub.
Univ/Ottawa Press
Univ Press of America—R
VESTA—R
Vital Issues Press—R
West Coast Paradise—R
White Stone Circle
Windflower—R

HOMILETICS*

Abingdon Press—R
Alba House—R
Black Forest—R
Chalice Press
CSS Publishing
Eerdmans Publishing—R
Hendrickson—R
Holy Cross—R
Judson Press—R
Longwood—R

Master Design
Our Sunday Visitor—R
Review & Herald
St. Anthony Messenger—R
St. Bede's—R
Tekna Books
Thomas More—R
Univ Press of America—R

HOW-TO

Accent Books
Accent Publications
ACTA Publications
Albury Publishing—R
Alexander Books
Baker Books—R
Bantam Books
Bethany House
Black Forest—R
Blue Dolphin
Brentwood—R
Bridge/Logos
Broadman & Holman
Brown-ROA
Christian Publications
Christopher Publishing
Church Growth Inst.
Church Street Press
Elder Books—R
Element Books—R
Erica House
Essence Publishing—R
Facts on File
Fairway Press—R
Gesher—R
Gilgal
GROUP Publishing—R
Hay House
Hearth Publishing—R
Hensley Publishing—R
Howard Publishing
Huntington House—R
InterVarsity Press
Judson Press—R
Kaleidoscope Press—R
Lifetime Books—R
Living the Good News
Longwood—R
Lowenbrown Publishing
McDougal Publishing
Meriwether—R
Morehouse—R
Morrow & Company, Wm.
Mt. Olive College Press
Multnomah
New City Press—R
New Leaf Press—R

Pauline Books
Perigee Books
PREP Publishing—R
Presbyterian & Reformed
Promise Publishing
Ragged Edge—R
Read 'N Run—R
Resource Publications
Resurrection Press—R
Revell
Review & Herald
St. Anthony Messenger—R
Schocken Books—R
Shaw Publishers, Harold—R
Sheed & Ward—R
Sheer Joy! Press
Sonstar Publishing—R
Southern Baptist Press—R
Sower's Press
Standard
Starburst Publishers
Still Waters Revival—R
Sword of the Lord—R
Tekna Books
Tyler Press—R
Vital Issues Press—R
Westminster John Knox
Wood Lake Books—R
Zondervan

MEN'S BOOKS

ACTA Publications
Albury Publishing—R
Baker Books—R
Bantam Books
Barbour Publishing—R
Beacon Hill Press
Bethany House
Black Forest—R
Blue Dolphin
Bridge/Logos
Broadman & Holman
Chalice Press
Christian Publications
Concordia
Crossway Books
CSS Publishing
Daybreak Books—R
Destiny Image
Dimensions for Living—R
Doubleday
Essence Publishing—R
Focus on the Family
Forward Movement
Gospel Publishing House—R
Hay House
Hendrickson—R

Hensley Publishing—R
Honor Books
Huntington House—R
Judson Press—R
Kregel—R
Liguori Publications
Longwood—R
Lowenbrown Publishing
McDougal Publishing
Moody Press
Morehouse—R
Multnomah
New Leaf Press—R
Perigee Books
Pilgrim Press—R
Presbyterian & Reformed
Promise Publishing
Read 'N Run—R
Resource Publications
Resurrection Press—R
St. Anthony Messenger—R
Schocken Books—R
Son-Rise
Sonstar Publishing—R
Starburst Publishers
Sword of the Lord—R
Tekna Books
Thomas More—R
Tyler Press—R
United Church Press
Vital Issues Press—R
White Stone Circle
Zondervan

MIRACLES

Albury Publishing—R
Baker Books—R
Black Forest—R
Brentwood—R
Bridge/Logos
Chosen Books
Christian Publications
CSS Publishing
Erica House
Essence Publishing—R
Fairway Press—R
FOG Publishing
Friends United Press—R
Gospel Publishing House—R
HarperSanFrancisco
Hay House
Honor Books
Impact Christian Books—R
Lowenbrown Publishing
Loyola Press
McDougal Publishing
Omega House—R

Our Sunday Visitor—R
Pacific Press
Paragon House—R
Promise Publishing
Read 'N Run—R
Review & Herald
Royal Productions—R
St. Bede's—R
Schocken Books—R
Shaw Publishers, Harold—R
Southern Baptist Press—R
Starburst Publishers
Tyler Press—R
United Church Press
Zondervan

MISSIONARY

ACU Press
Albury Publishing—R
Bethany House
Black Forest—R
Brentwood—R
Bridge/Logos
Christian Publications
Christian Univ Press—R
Christopher Publishing
CSS Publishing
Eerdmans Publishing—R
Essence Publishing—R
Fairway Press—R
Friends United Press—R
Gospel Publishing House—R
Horizon House—R
Journey Books—R
Judson Press—R
Living Books for All
Longwood—R
Lowenbrown Publishing
Master Design
McDougal Publishing
Messianic Jewish—R
Middle Atlantic—R
New Hope—R
Omega House—R
PACE Publications—R
Promise Publishing
Read 'N Run—R
Review & Herald
St. Bede's—R
Sonstar Publishing—R
Southern Baptist Press—R
Sword of the Lord—R
TEACH Services—R
Tekna Books
Treasure Learning—R
Tyler Press—R
Vital Issues Press—R

West Coast Paradise—R
Westminster John Knox
YWAM Publishing—R

MONEY MANAGEMENT

Alban Institute
Baker Books—R
Bantam Books
Bethany House
Black Forest—R
Blue Dolphin
Brentwood—R
Bridge/Logos
Broadman & Holman
Cerdic Publications
Christopher Publishing
Essence Publishing—R
Facts on File
Fairway Press—R
Gesher—R
Hay House
Hensley Publishing—R
Howard Publishing
Lifetime Books—R
Longwood—R
Lowenbrown Publishing
New Leaf Press—R
Perigee Books
Read 'N Run—R
Regnery—R
Review & Herald
Schocken Books—R
Southern Baptist Press—R
Starburst Publishers
Summit Pub. Group—R
Tyler Press—R
Zondervan

MUSIC-RELATED BOOKS

ACU Press
Albury Publishing—R
American Cath. Press—R
Bay Public., Mel
Christian Media—R
Christopher Publishing
Church Street Press
Contemporary Drama Service
Cornell Univ. Press—R
Cornerstone Press
Destiny Image
Dimension Books—R
Essence Publishing—R
Hay House
Judson Press—R
Lifetime Books—R
Lillenas

Liturgy Training
Longwood—R
Lowenbrown Publishing
Middle Atlantic—R
Morehouse—R
Ragged Edge—R
Read 'N Run—R
Standard
Tyler Press—R
United Church Pub.
West Coast Paradise—R
Windflower—R
Zondervan

PAMPHLETS

Barclay Press—R
Cross Way Pub.
Dry Bones Press—R
Essence Publishing—R
Forward Movement
Franciscan Univ Press—R
Good Book—R
Huntington House—R
Intl. Awakening Press—R
Kindred Productions
Libros Liguori
Life Cycle Books
Liguori Publications
Lowenbrown Publishing
Lydia Press
Messianic Jewish—R
Middle Atlantic—R
Neibauer Press—R
Omega House—R
Our Sunday Visitor—R
Paradise Research—R
Partnership Book
Review & Herald
Rose Publishing
St. Anthony Messenger
Sword of the Lord—R
TEACH Services—R
West Coast Paradise—R

PARENTING

ACTA Publications
ACU Press
Albury Publishing—R
Baker Books—R
Bantam Books
Barbour Publishing—R
Beacon Hill Press
Bethany House
Black Forest—R
Brentwood—R
Bridge/Logos

Broadman & Holman
Chalice Press
Chariot Victor
Christian Publications
Christopher Publishing
Conari Press—R
Concordia
Crossroad Publishing—R
Crossway Books
CSS Publishing
Daybreak Books—R
Dimensions for Living—R
Doubleday
Eerdmans Publishing—R
Erica House
Essence Publishing—R
Facts on File
Fairway Press—R
Focus on the Family
Focus Publishing
Forward Movement
HarperSanFrancisco
Hay House
Hensley Publishing—R
Horizon House—R
Howard Publishing
Huntington House—R
InterVarsity Press
Judson Press—R
Kaleidoscope Press—R
Kregel—R
Liguori Publications
Lightwave Publishing
Living the Good News
Longwood—R
Loyola Press
McDougal Publishing
Morehouse—R
Multnomah
New Leaf Press—R
Northstone—R
Openbook—R
Our Sunday Visitor—R
Paragon House—R
Pauline Books
Perigee Books
Presbyterian & Reformed
Ragged Edge—R
Read 'N Run—R
Resurrection Press—R
Revell
Review & Herald
Schocken Books—R
Shaw Publishers, Harold—R
Sheed & Ward—R
Standard
Starburst Publishers
Still Waters Revival—R

Sword of the Lord—R
Tekna Books
Thomas More—R
Tyler Press—R
United Church Press
Vital Issues Press—R
Westminster John Knox
Zondervan

PASTORS' HELPS

Abingdon Press—R
Accent Publications
ACTA Publications
Alban Institute
Albury Publishing—R
Baker Books—R
Beacon Hill Press
Bethany House
Brentwood—R
Bristol House—R
Broadman & Holman
Brown-ROA
Christian Publications
Christopher Publishing
College Press—R
CSS Publishing
Eerdmans Publishing—R
Essence Publishing—R
Fairway Press—R
Gesher—R
Gospel Publishing House—R
GROUP Publishing—R
Haworth Press—R
Hendrickson—R
InterVarsity Press
Judson Press—R
Kregel—R
Langmarc
Liguori Publications
Loizeaux
Longwood—R
Master Design
Morehouse—R
Neibauer Press—R
New Leaf Press—R
Our Sunday Visitor—R
Pastor's Choice
Paulist Press
Pelican Publishing—R
Presbyterian & Reformed
Read 'N Run—R
Resurrection Press—R
Southern Baptist Press—R
Standard
Sword of the Lord—R
Tekna Books
Tyler Press—R

United Church Press
Vital Issues Press—R
Wellness
Wesleyan Publishing House
Westminster John Knox
Wood Lake Books—R
Zondervan

PERSONAL EXPERIENCE

Bantam Books
Black Forest—R
Brentwood—R
Chicken Soup Books
Cross Cultural
Daybreak Books—R
Dry Bones Press—R
Eerdmans Publishing—R
Erica House
Essence Publishing—R
Fairway Press—R
Friends United Press—R
Gesher—R
Gilgal
Hay House
Hensley Publishing—R
Honor Books
Huntington House—R
Innisfree Press
Libros Liguori
Longwood—R
Lowenbrown Publishing
McDougal Publishing
Omega House—R
Openbook—R
Perigee Books
Promise Publishing
Rainbow's End
Read 'N Run—R
St. Bede's—R
Schocken Books—R
Shaw Publishers, Harold—R
Son-Rise
Southern Baptist Press—R
Starburst Publishers
Tekna Books
Thomas More—R
Tyler Press—R
United Church Press
VESTA—R
Vital Issues Press—R
Windflower—R
Zondervan

PERSONAL GROWTH*

Broadman & Holman
Chariot Victor

Concordia
CSS Publishing
Destiny Image
Eerdmans Publishing—R
Erica House
Essence Publishing—R
Forward Movement
Gesher—R
HarperSanFrancisco
Hay House
Hendrickson—R
Hensley Publishing—R
Holy Cross—R
Innisfree Press
InterVarsity Press
J. Countryman
Judson Press—R
Longwood—R
Magnus Press—R
Multnomah
New World Library
Northstone—R
Paragon House—R
Perigee Books
Read 'N Run—R
Review & Herald
St. Bede's—R
Shaw Publishers, Harold—R
Sonstar Publishing—R
Starburst Publishers
Tekna Books
Thomas More—R
United Church Pub.
White Stone Circle

PERSONAL RENEWAL

Ambassador House
Baker Books—R
Barclay Press—R
Bethany House
Black Forest—R
Blue Dolphin
Bridge/Logos
Chosen Books
Christian Publications
Christopher Publishing
Creation House
Cross Cultural
CSS Publishing
Daybreak Books—R
Destiny Image
Eerdmans Publishing—R
Erica House
Essence Publishing—R
Friends United Press—R
Gesher—R
Haworth Press—R

Hay House
Impact Christian Books—R
Intl. Awakening Press—R
J. Countryman
Judson Press—R
Libros Liguori
Longwood—R
McDougal Publishing
Middle Atlantic—R
Multnomah
Omega House—R
Perigee Books
Promise Publishing
Read 'N Run—R
St. Bede's—R
Schocken Books—R
Shaw Publishers, Harold—R
Starburst Publishers
Tekna Books
Thomas More—R
Tyler Press—R
United Church Pub.
Zondervan

PHILOSOPHY

ACU Press
Bantam Books
Black Forest—R
Brentwood—R
Catholic Univ./America—R
Christopher Publishing
Cornell Univ. Press—R
Cornerstone Press
Counterpoint
Cross Cultural
Crossroad Publishing—R
CSS Publishing
Daybreak Books—R
Doubleday
Dry Bones Press—R
Eerdmans Publishing—R
Element Books—R
Erica House
Essence Publishing—R
Fairway Press—R
Friends United Press—R
Genesis Publishing
Gesher—R
Hay House
Huntington House—R
Mercer University Press
Mosaic Press
Mt. Olive College Press
Open Court—R
Oxford University
Paragon House—R
Paulist Press

Promise Publishing
Read 'N Run—R
Regnery—R
Schocken Books—R
Still Waters Revival—R
Tekna Books
Trinity Foundation—R
Univ/Ottawa Press
Univ Press of America—R
VESTA—R
Vital Issues Press—R
Wadsworth—R
Yale Univ Press—R
Zondervan

POETRY

Black Forest—R
Boyds Mills Press
Brentwood—R
Christopher Publishing
Cornerstone Press
Creatively Yours
Cross Way Pub.
CSS Publishing
Dry Bones Press—R
Essence Publishing—R
Fairway Press—R
Focus Publishing
Guernica Editions—R
Image Books—R
Lowenbrown Publishing
Middle Atlantic—R
Morrow & Company, Wm.
Mosaic Press
Mt. Olive College Press
Poets Cove Press
Rainbow's End
Read 'N Run—R
St. Bede's—R
Southern Baptist Press—R
Tyler Press—R
VESTA—R
Vital Issues Press—R
West Coast Paradise—R
Westminster John Knox
White Stone Circle
Windflower—R

POLITICAL THEORY

Ambassador House
Bantam Books
Baylor University Press
Black Forest—R
Brentwood—R
Catholic Univ./America—R
Christopher Publishing

Daybreak Books—R
Doubleday
Essence Publishing—R
Huntington House—R
Judson Press—R
Lowenbrown Publishing
Monument Press
Mosaic Press
Open Court—R
Paragon House—R
Pilgrim Press—R
Promise Publishing
Read 'N Run—R
Regnery—R
Schocken Books—R
Still Waters Revival—R
Summit Pub. Group—R
Trinity Foundation—R
Tyler Press—R
United Church Pub.
Univ/Ottawa Press
Univ Press of America—R
Vital Issues Press—R
White Stone Circle
Zondervan

PRAYER

ACTA Publications
ACU Press
Alba House—R
Albury Publishing—R
Baker Books—R
Bantam Books
Barbour Publishing—R
Barclay Press—R
Beacon Hill Press
Bethany House
Black Forest—R
Brentwood—R
Bridge/Logos
Bristol House—R
Broadman & Holman
Brown-ROA
Catholic Book Publishing
Chariot Victor
Chosen Books
Christian Publications
Concordia
Creation House
Crossroad Publishing—R
CSS Publishing
Daybreak Books—R
Destiny Image
Doubleday
Dry Bones Press—R
Eerdmans Publishing—R
Essence Publishing—R

Fairway Press—R
FOG Publishing
Forward Movement
Friends United Press—R
Gesher—R
Gospel Publishing House—R
HarperSanFrancisco
Hay House
Hendrickson—R
Hensley Publishing—R
Holy Cross—R
Howard Publishing
ICS Publications—R
Impact Christian Books—R
InterVarsity Press
J. Countryman
Judson Press—R
Kregel—R
Libros Liguori
Light and Life—R
Lightwave Publishing
Liguori Publications
Liturgy Training
Living the Good News
Longwood—R
Lowenbrown Publishing
Loyola Press
Master Design
McDougal Publishing
Middle Atlantic—R
Moody Press
Morehouse—R
Multnomah
New Hope—R
New Leaf Press—R
Northstone—R
Omega House—R
Our Sunday Visitor—R
Paraclete Press—R
Pauline Books
Presbyterian & Reformed
Preservation Press
Promise Publishing
Rainbow/Legacy Press—R
Read 'N Run—R
Regina Press
Resource Publications
Resurrection Press—R
Revell
Review & Herald
Rose Publishing
Royal Productions—R
St. Anthony Messenger—R
St. Bede's—R
Saint Mary's Press—R
Schocken Books—R
Shaw Publishers, Harold—R

Sheed & Ward—R
Smyth & Helwys
Sonstar Publishing—R
Southern Baptist Press—R
Standard
Starburst Publishers
Still Waters Revival—R
Sword of the Lord—R
TEACH Services—R
Tekna Books
Toccoa Falls
Tyler Press—R
United Church Press
United Church Pub.
Vital Issues Press—R
Westminster John Knox
White Stone Circle
Wood Lake Books—R
World Bible
Zondervan

PROPHECY

Albury Publishing—R
Ambassador House
Black Forest—R
Blue Dolphin
Brentwood—R
Bridge/Logos
Creation House
CSS Publishing
Destiny Image
Element Books—R
Essence Publishing—R
Fairway Press—R
FOG Publishing
Gospel Publishing House—R
HarperSanFrancisco
Kregel—R
Longwood—R
McDougal Publishing
Messianic Jewish—R
Multnomah
New Leaf Press—R
Omega House—R
Read 'N Run—R
Review & Herald
Rose Publishing
Schocken Books—R
Small Helm Press
Southern Baptist Press—R
Starburst Publishers
Still Waters Revival—R
Sword of the Lord—R
Tyler Press—R
Vital Issues Press—R
Western Front—R

Zondervan

PSYCHOLOGY

Alba House—R
Baker Books—R
Bantam Books
Barclay Press—R
Bethany House
Black Forest—R
Blue Dolphin
Brentwood—R
Catholic Univ./America—R
Christopher Publishing
Conari Press—R
Cross Cultural
Crossroad Publishing—R
Daybreak Books—R
Dimension Books—R
Doubleday
Dry Bones Press—R
Eerdmans Publishing—R
Elder Books—R
Element Books—R
Erica House
Essence Publishing—R
Fairway Press—R
Gesher—R
HarperSanFrancisco
Haworth Press—R
Hay House
Huntington House—R
Innisfree Press
InterVarsity Press
Judson Press—R
Liguori Publications
Longwood—R
Lowenbrown Publishing
Morehouse—R
Mosaic Press
Open Court—R
Oxford University
Paragon House—R
Perigee Books
PREP Publishing—R
Rainbow Books
Read 'N Run—R
Recovery Communications
Religious Education
Resurrection Press—R
Revell
Review & Herald
Schocken Books—R
Shaw Publishers, Harold—R
Southern Baptist Press—R
Starburst Publishers
Thomas More—R

Tyler Press—R
Univ/Ottawa Press
Univ Press of America—R
Vital Issues Press—R
Yale Univ Press—R
Zondervan

RECOVERY BOOKS

Baker Books—R
Black Forest—R
Christopher Publishing
Crossroad Publishing—R
CSS Publishing
Daybreak Books—R
Elder Books—R
Erica House
Essence Publishing—R
Forward Movement
Gilgal Publications
Haworth Press—R
Huntington House—R
Judson Press—R
Libros Liguori
Liguori Publications
Longwood—R
Lowenbrown Publishing
Morehouse—R
New World Library
Openbook—R
Our Sunday Visitor—R
Perigee Books
PREP Publishing—R
Rainbow's End
Read 'N Run—R
Recovery Communications
Resource Publications
Rose Publishing
Schocken Books—R
Starburst Publishers
Tekna Books
Tyler Press—R
White Stone Circle
Zondervan

REFERENCE BOOKS

Abingdon Press—R
Baker Books—R
Bantam Books
Baylor University Press
Bethany House
Brentwood—R
Christian Univ Press—R
Crossroad Publishing—R
CSS Publishing
Doubleday

Dry Bones Press—R
Eerdmans Publishing—R
Element Books—R
Fairway Press—R
Hendrickson—R
Impact Christian Books—R
Intl. Awakening Press—R
Judson Press—R
Kaleidoscope Press—R
Kregel—R
Lifetime Books—R
Lightwave Publishing
Loizeaux
Longwood—R
Lowenbrown Publishing
Master Design
Middle Atlantic—R
Morehouse—R
Oxford University
Paragon House—R
Perigee Books
Presbyterian & Reformed
Ragged Edge—R
Read 'N Run—R
Religious Education
Review & Herald
Scarecrow Press
Schocken Books—R
Sonstar Publishing—R
Southern Baptist Press—R
Still Waters Revival—R
Sword of the Lord—R
Tekna Books
Tyler Press—R
Univ/Ottawa Press
VESTA—R
Westminster John Knox
World Bible
Zondervan

RELIGION

Abingdon Press—R
ACU Press
Alexander Books
Ambassador House
Baker Books—R
Bantam Books
Bethany House
Black Forest—R
Blue Dolphin
Brentwood—R
Catholic Univ./America—R
Cerdic Publications
Chariot Victor
Christian Publications
Christopher Publishing

Cornell Univ. Press—R
Counterpoint
Cross Cultural
Crossroad Publishing—R
Crossway Books
CSS Publishing
Daybreak Books—R
Dimension Books—R
Doubleday
Dry Bones Press—R
Eerdmans Publishing—R
Eerdmans/Young Readers
Element Books—R
Erica House
Essence Publishing—R
Facts on File
Fairway Press—R
Focus Publishing
FOG Publishing
Forward Movement
Franciscan Univ Press—R
Friends United Press—R
Genesis Publishing
HarperSanFrancisco
Hay House
Hendrickson—R
Holy Cross—R
Honor Books
Huntington House—R
Impact Christian Books—R
Judson Press—R
Kregel—R
Light and Life—R
Liguori Publications
Liturgy Training
Living the Good News
Lowenbrown Publishing
Mercer University Press
Middle Atlantic—R
Morehouse—R
More Press, Thomas
Morrow & Co, Wm.
Mosaic Press
Mt. Olive College Press
New Hope—R
New World Library
Northstone—R
One World
Open Court—R
Oxford University
Our Sunday Visitor—R
Paragon House—R
Paulist Press
Pilgrim Press—R
Presbyterian & Reformed
Preservation Press
G.P. Putnam's Sons

Ragged Edge—R
Read 'N Run—R
Regnery—R
Religious Education
Resurrection Press—R
Rose Publishing
St. Bede's—R
Saint Mary's Press—R
Scarecrow Press
Schocken Books—R
Sheed & Ward—R
Sheer Joy! Press
Smyth & Helwys
Southern Baptist Press—R
Still Waters Revival—R
Summit Pub. Group—R
Sword of the Lord—R
Tekna Books
Thomas More—R
Trinity Press Intl.—R
Tyler Press—R
United Church Press
United Church Pub.
Univ/Ottawa Press
Univ Press of America—R
VESTA—R
Vital Issues Press—R
Wadsworth Publishing
Westminster John Knox
Wood Lake Books—R
Yale Univ Press—R
Zondervan

RETIREMENT

ACTA Publications
Baker Books—R
Bethany House
Black Forest—R
Broadman & Holman
Chalice Press
Christian Publications
College Press—R
Elder Books—R
Essence Publishing—R
Fairway Press—R
Judson Press—R
Liguori Publications
Longwood—R
Northstone—R
Read 'N Run—R
Regnery—R
Schocken Books—R
Southern Baptist Press—R
Starburst Publishers
Tekna Books
Tyler Press—R
United Church Pub.

Westminster John Knox
Zondervan

SCHOLARLY

Baker Books—R
Baylor University Press
Black Forest—R
Catholic Univ./America—R
Crossroad Publishing—R
Crossway Books
Dry Bones Press—R
Eerdmans Publishing—R
Essence Publishing—R
Haworth Press—R
Hendrickson—R
Holy Cross—R
Huntington House—R
Impact Christian Books—R
Intl. Awakening Press—R
Logion Press
Master Design
Messianic Jewish—R
Monument Press
Morehouse—R
Our Sunday Visitor—R
Oxford University
Paragon House—R
Paulist Press
Pilgrim Press—R
Presbyterian & Reformed
Ragged Edge—R
Read 'N Run—R
Religious Education
Royal Productions—R
Scarecrow Press
Shaw Publishers, Harold—R
Smyth & Helwys
Tekna Books
Toccoa Falls
Trinity Foundation—R
Trinity Press Intl.—R
Tyler Press—R
Univ/Ottawa Press
Univ Press of America—R
VESTA—R
Vital Issues Press—R
Zondervan

SCIENCE

Bantam Books
Black Forest—R
Christopher Publishing
Cornell Univ. Press—R
Counterpoint
Crossroad Publishing—R
Dry Bones Press—R

Eerdmans Publishing—R
Facts on File
Huntington House—R
Journey Books—R
Kaleidoscope Press—R
Master Books—R
Northstone—R
Open Court—R
Oxford University
Paragon House—R
Promise Publishing
Read 'N Run—R
Royal Productions—R
Regnery—R
Schocken Books—R
Summit Pub. Group—R
Tekna Books
Trinity Foundation—R
Tyler Press—R
Univ/Ottawa Press
Vital Issues Press—R
Zondervan

SELF-HELP

Accent Books
Albury Publishing—R
Alexander Books
Black Forest—R
Blue Dolphin
Christian Publications
Christopher Publishing
Crossroad Publishing—R
Daybreak Books—R
Dimensions for Living—R
Doubleday
Erica House
Essence Publishing—R
Facts on File
Fairway Press—R
Gesher—R
Good Book—R
HarperSanFrancisco
Hay House
Hensley Publishing—R
Howard Publishing
Huntington House—R
Innisfree Press
Judson Press—R
Libros Liguori
Liguori Publications
Living the Good News
Longwood—R
Lowenbrown Publishing
Morehouse—R
Mt. Olive College Press
One World
Openbook—R

Pacific Press
Paradise Research—R
Perigee Books
Peter Pauper Press
Preservation Press
G.P. Putnam's Sons
Ragged Edge—R
Rainbow's End
Read 'N Run—R
Resurrection Press—R
Revell
Schocken Books—R
Shaw Publishers, Harold—R
Sheed & Ward—R
Sonstar Publishing—R
Starburst Publishers
Summit Pub. Group—R
Tekna Books
Thomas More—R
United Church Pub.
West Coast Paradise—R
Zondervan

SENIOR ADULT CONCERNS

ACTA Publications
Baker Books—R
Bethany House
Black Forest—R
Broadman & Holman
Chalice Press
Christian Publications
Christopher Publishing
Essence Publishing—R
Facts on File
Fairway Press—R
Gospel Publishing House—R
Haworth Press—R
Horizon House—R
Howard Publishing
Huntington House—R
Judson Press—R
Langmarc
Liguori Publications
Lowenbrown Publishing
Morehouse—R
New Leaf Press—R
Perigee Books
Promise Publishing
Read 'N Run—R
Schocken Books—R
Shaw Publishers, Harold
Southern Baptist Press—R
Tekna Books
Tyler Press—R
United Church Pub.
Westminster John Knox
Zondervan

SERMONS

Albury Publishing—R
Brentwood—R
Bridge/Logos
Church Growth Inst.
CSS Publishing
Destiny Image
Doubleday
Eerdmans Publishing—R
Fairway Press—R
GROUP Publishing—R
Hendrickson—R
Judson Press—R
Kregel—R
Liguori Publications
Liturgical Press
Longwood—R
Master Design
Pastor's Choice
Proclaim Publishing
Read 'N Run—R
St. Bede's—R
Southern Baptist Press—R
Still Waters Revival—R
Sword of the Lord—R
Tekna Books
Tyler Press—R
United Church Press
United Church Pub.
Vital Issues Press—R
Wood Lake Books—R

SINGLES ISSUES

Abingdon Press—R
Albury Publishing—R
Baker Books—R
Barbour Publishing—R
Bethany House
Brentwood—R
Broadman & Holman
Christian Publications
Erica House
Essence Publishing—R
Gospel Publishing House—R
Horizon House—R
Huntington House—R
InterVarsity Press
Judson Press—R
Langmarc
Liguori Publications
Longwood—R
Lowenbrown Publishing
Morehouse—R
New Leaf Press—R
Perigee Books
Rainbow/Legacy Press—R

Read 'N Run—R
Schocken Books—R
Tekna Books
Tyler Press—R
Vital Issues Press—R
Zondervan

SOCIAL JUSTICE ISSUES

Alban Institute
Ambassador House
Baker Books—R
Bantam Books
Barclay Press—R
Bethany House
Black Forest—R
Brentwood—R
Catholic Univ./America—R
Chalice Press
Cross Cultural
CSS Publishing
Daybreak Books—R
Eerdmans Publishing—R
Essence Publishing—R
Haworth Press—R
Huntington House—R
Innisfree Press
Judson Press—R
Libros Liguori
Life Cycle Books—R
Lifetime Books—R
Liguori Publications
Liturgy Training
Lowenbrown Publishing
Morehouse—R
Northstone—R
Openbook—R
Oxford University
Paulist Press
Pilgrim Press—R
Ragged Edge—R
Read 'N Run—R
Regnery—R
Resurrection Press—R
Schocken Books—R
Shaw Publishers, Harold—R
Sheed & Ward—R
Still Waters Revival—R
Tekna Books
Tyler Press—R
United Church Press
United Church Pub.
Univ/Ottawa Press
Univ Press of America—R
Vital Issues Press—R
Westminster John Knox
White Stone Circle
Wood Lake Books—R

Zondervan

SOCIOLOGY

Baker Books—R
Bethany House
Black Forest—R
Brentwood—R
Christopher Publishing
Daybreak Books—R
Essence Publishing—R
Haworth Press—R
Hay House
Huntington House—R
InterVarsity Press
Judson Press—R
Longwood—R
Lowenbrown Publishing
Mosaic Press
Oxford University
Paragon House—R
Paulist Press
Read 'N Run—R
Schocken Books—R
Still Waters Revival—R
Tekna Books
Univ/Ottawa Press
Univ Press of America—R
Vital Issues Press—R

SPIRITUALITY

Abingdon Press—R
ACTA Publications
ACU Press
Alba House—R
Alban Institute
Baker Books—R
Bantam Books
Barclay Press—R
Bethany House
Black Forest—R
Blue Dolphin
Brentwood—R
Bridge/Logos
Broadman & Holman
Catholic Univ./America—R
Chalice Press
Chosen Books
Christian Publications
Christopher Publishing
Cistercian Publications
Conari Press—R
Crossroad Publishing—R
Crossway Books
CSS Publishing
Daybreak Books—R
Dimension Books—R

Doubleday
Dry Bones Press—R
Eerdmans Publishing—R
Elder Books—R
Element Books—R
Erica House
Essence Publishing—R
Fairway Press—R
Forward Movement
Franciscan Univ Press—R
Friends United Press—R
Gesher—R
HarperSanFrancisco
Hay House
Hendrickson—R
Hensley Publishing—R
Holy Cross—R
Honor Books
Huntington House—R
Impact Christian Books—R
Innisfree Press
InterVarsity Press
Judson Press—R
Kregel—R
Libros Liguori
Light and Life—R
Liguori Publications
Living the Good News
Longwood—R
Lowenbrown Publishing
Loyola Press
Magnus Press—R
McDougal Publishing
More Press, Thomas
Morehouse—R
Multnomah
New World Library
Northstone—R
Omega House—R
Our Sunday Visitor—R
Oxford University
Paraclete Press—R
Paragon House—R
Pauline Books
Peter Pauper Press
Pilgrim Press—R
PREP Publishing—R
Promise Publishing
Ragged Edge—R
Rainbow/Legacy Press—R
Read 'N Run—R
Regnery—R
Resurrection Press—R
St. Anthony Messenger—R
St. Bede's—R
Saint Mary's Press—R
Schocken Books—R
Shaw Publishers, Harold—R

Sheed & Ward—R
Smyth & Helwys
Sonstar Publishing—R
Southern Baptist Press—R
Starburst Publishers
Sword of the Lord—R
Tekna Books
Thomas More—R
Toccoa Falls
Tyler Press—R
United Church Press
United Church Pub.
Univ/Ottawa Press
Vital Issues Press—R
West Coast Paradise—R
Westminster John Knox
White Stone Circle
Zondervan

SPIRITUAL WARFARE

Albury Publishing—R
Black Forest—R
Bridge/Logos
Chosen Books
Christian Publications
Creation House
CSS Publishing
Destiny Image
Essence Publishing—R
Gesher—R
Gospel Publishing House—R
Hendrickson—R
Hensley Publishing—R
Huntington House—R
Impact Christian Books—R
InterVarsity Press
Longwood—R
Lowenbrown Publishing
Lydia Press
Marlton Publishers
Master Design
Multnomah
Omega House—R
Read 'N Run—R
St. Bede's—R
Schocken Books—R
Shaw Publishers, Harold—R
Starburst Publishers
Sword of the Lord—R
Zondervan

SPORTS/RECREATION

ACTA Publications
Bantam Books
Boyds Mills Press
Christopher Publishing

Essence Publishing—R
Facts on File
Lifetime Books—R
Mosaic Press
New Leaf Press—R
Openbook—R
Read 'N Run—R
Royal Productions—R
Schocken Books—R
Sonstar Publishing—R
Starburst Publishers
Summit Pub. Group—R
Tekna Books
Tyler Press—R
Zondervan

STEWARDSHIP

Albury Publishing—R
Baker Books—R
Black Forest—R
Chalice Press
Christian Publications
Creation House
CSS Publishing
Eerdmans Publishing—R
Essence Publishing—R
Forward Movement
Gesher—R
Gospel Publishing House—R
Hensley Publishing—R
Huntington House—R
Judson Press—R
Kregel—R
Lightwave Publishing
Longwood—R
Lowenbrown Publishing
McDougal Publishing
Messianic Jewish—R
Morehouse—R
Multnomah
Neibauer Press
Presbyterian & Reformed
Rainbow/Legacy Press—R
Read 'N Run—R
Review & Herald
Schocken Books—R
Shaw Publishers, Harold—R
TEACH Services—R
Tekna Books
Tyler Press—R
United Church Pub.
Vital Issues Press—R
Wood Lake Books—R
Zondervan

THEOLOGICAL

Abingdon Press—R
ACU Press
Alba House—R
Baker Books—R
Bethany House
Black Forest—R
Blue Dolphin
Brentwood—R
Bridge/Logos
Broadman & Holman
Catholic Univ./America—R
Chalice Press
Christian Publications
Christian Univ Press—R
Christopher Publishing
Cistercian Publications
Crossroad Publishing—R
Crossway Books
CSS Publishing
Dimension Books—R
Doubleday
Dry Bones Press—R
Eerdmans Publishing—R
Erica House
Essence Publishing—R
Fairway Press—R
FOG Publishing
Friends United Press—R
HarperSanFrancisco
Hay House
Hendrickson—R
Holy Cross—R
Huntington House—R
Impact Christian Books—R
Intl. Awakening Press—R
InterVarsity Press
Judson Press—R
Kregel—R
Light and Life—R
Liguori Publications
Liturgical Press
Liturgy Training
Loizeaux
Magnus Press—R
Master Design
Mercer University Press
Messianic Jewish—R
Morehouse—R
Multnomah
New City Press—R
New Leaf Press—R
Open Court—R
Our Sunday Visitor—R
Oxford University
Paragon House—R
Paulist Press

Pilgrim Press—R
Presbyterian & Reformed
Promise Publishing
Ragged Edge—R
Read 'N Run—R
Religious Education
Resurrection Press—R
Review & Herald
St. Anthony Messenger—R
St. Bede's—R
Schocken Books—R
Shaw Publishers, Harold—R
   (lay)
Sheed & Ward—R
Smyth & Helwys
Southern Baptist Press—R
Still Waters Revival—R
Sword of the Lord—R
Tekna Books
Trinity Foundation—R
Trinity Press Intl.—R
Tyler Press—R
United Church Press
Univ/Ottawa Press
Univ Press of America—R
Vital Issues Press—R
Westminster John Knox
White Stone Circle
Wood Lake Books—R
Zondervan

TIME MANAGEMENT*

Black Forest—R
Broadman & Holman
Concordia
Erica House
Essence Publishing—R
Gesher—R
HarperSanFrancisco
Hensley Publishing—R
Read 'N Run—R
Shaw Publishers, Harold—R
Starburst Publishers
Tekna Books

TRACTS

American Tract Society
Dry Bones Press—R
Essence Publishing—R
Franciscan Univ Press—R
Good News Publishers
Intl. Awakening Press—R
Liguori Publications
Lowenbrown Publishing
Messianic Jewish—R
Middle Atlantic—R

Neibauer Press—R
Partnership Book
Review & Herald
Trinity Foundation—R

TRAVEL

Accent Books
Black Forest—R
Boyds Mills Press
Brentwood—R
Christopher Publishing
Doubleday
Eerdmans Publishing—R
Essence Publishing—R
Image Books—R
Journey Books—R
Longwood—R
Morehouse—R
Mt. Olive College Press
Rainbow Books
Read 'N Run—R
Schocken Books—R
Tekna Books
United Church Pub.
West Coast Paradise—R

WOMEN'S ISSUES

Alban Institute
Albury Publishing—R
Baker Books—R
Bantam Books
Baylor University Press
Beacon Hill Press
Bethany House
Black Forest—R
Blue Dolphin
Bridge/Logos
Broadman & Holman
Chalice Press
Chariot Victor
Christian Publications
Christopher Publishing
Conari Press—R
Concordia
Cornell Univ. Press—R
Creation House
Cross Cultural
Crossway Books
Daybreak Books—R
Destiny Image
Doubleday
Eerdmans Publishing—R
Elder Books—R
Element Books—R
Essence Publishing—R
Facts on File

Fairway Press—R
Focus Publishing
Forward Movement
Gospel Publishing House—R
Guernica Editions—R
HarperSanFrancisco
Haworth Press—R
Hay House
Hendrickson—R
Hearth Publishing—R
Hensley Publishing—R
Holy Cross—R
Honor Books
Horizon House—R
Howard Publishing
Huntington House—R
Innisfree Press
InterVarsity Press
J. Countryman
Judson Press—R
Kregel—R
Life Cycle Books—R
Liguori Publications
Longwood—R
Lowenbrown Publishing
Monument Press
Moody Press
Morehouse—R
Mosaic Press
Multnomah
New Hope—R
New Leaf Press—R
New World Library
Northstone—R
Openbook—R
Pacific Press
Pelican Publishing—R
Perigee Books
Pilgrim Press—R
PREP Publishing—R
Promise Publishing
Rainbow/Legacy Press—R
Rainbow Books
Read 'N Run—R
Resurrection Press—R
Revell
Review & Herald
St. Anthony Messenger—R
Schocken Books—R
Shaw Publishers, Harold—R
Sheed & Ward—R
Son-Rise
Sonstar Publishing—R
Southern Baptist Press—R
Starburst Publishers
Still Waters Revival—R
Summit Pub. Group—R
Tekna Books

Thomas More—R
Tyler Press—R
United Church Press
Univ/Ottawa Press
Vital Issues Press—R
Westminster John Knox
White Stone Circle
Wood Lake Books—R
Zondervan

WORLD ISSUES

Ambassador House
Baker Books—R
Bantam Books
Barclay Press—R
Bethany House
Black Forest—R
Blue Dolphin
William Carey Library
Chalice Press
Christopher Publishing
Cross Cultural
Daybreak Books—R
Destiny Image
Essence Publishing—R
Hendrickson—R
Huntington House—R
InterVarsity Press
Liguori Publications
Longwood—R
Lowenbrown Publishing
Monument Press
Morehouse—R
New Leaf Press—R
Orbis Books
Paragon House—R
Pilgrim Press—R
Read 'N Run—R
Regnery—R
Schocken Books—R
Shaw Publishers, Harold—R
Sonstar Publishing—R
Still Waters Revival—R
Tekna Books
Tyler Press—R
United Church Pub.
VESTA—R
Vital Issues Press—R
Wood Lake Books—R
Zondervan

WORSHIP RESOURCES

Abingdon Press—R
Art Can Drama—R
Baker Books—R
Barclay Press—R

Bethany House
Catholic Book Publishing
Chalice Press
Christian Publications
Church Street Press
Educational Ministries
Eerdmans Publishing—R
Essence Publishing—R
Fairway Press—R
Hendrickson—R
InterVarsity Press
Judson Press—R
Kregel—R
Liturgical Press
Liturgy Training
Longwood—R
Lowenbrown Publishing
McDougal Publishing
Meriwether—R
Morehouse—R
Rainbow/Legacy Press—R
Read 'N Run—R
Royal Productions—R
St. Anthony Messenger—R
Sheed & Ward—R
Smyth & Helwys
Standard
Tekna Books
Thomas More—R
Tyler Press—R
United Church Press
United Church Pub.
Vital Issues Press—R
Westminster John Knox
Wood Lake Books—R
Zondervan

WRITING HOW-TO

Black Forest—R
Bridge/Logos
Essence Publishing—R
Fairway Press—R
Lowenbrown Publishing
Perigee Books
Promise Publishing
Schocken Books—R
Shaw Publishers, Harold—R
Sheed & Ward—R
Sonstar Publishing—R

Tekna Books

YOUTH BOOKS
(Nonfiction)

Note: Listing denotes books for 8- to 12-year-olds, junior highs or senior highs. If all three, it will say "all."

Albury Publishing—R (all)
Art Can Drama—R (all)
Baker Books—R (all)
Bethany House (all)
Black Forest—R (all)
Broadman & Holman (all)
Christian Ed Pub. (8-12)
Christian Publications (Jr/Sr High)
Concordia (Jr/Sr High)
Contemporary Drama Service
Creation House (Sr High)
CSS Publishing (all)
Eerdmans/Young Readers (all)
Erica House (all)
Essence Publishing—R
Facts on File (all)
Fairway Press—R (all)
Friends United Press—R (Jr High)
Gospel Publishing House—R
Horizon House—R (Jr/Sr High)
Huntington House—R (8-12)
Journey Books—R (all)
Judson Press—R
Kaleidoscope Press—R (8-12)
Langmarc (Jr/Sr High)
Libros Liguori (all)
Lightwave Publishing (8-12)
Liguori Publications (all)
Living the Good News
Lowenbrown Publishing (Jr/Sr High)
Morehouse—R (all)
Morris, Joshua (all)
New Canaan (all)
New Hope—R (8-12)
PACE Publications—R (8-12)
Pauline Books—R (all)

Ragged Edge—R (8-12)
Rainbow/Legacy Press—R (8-12)
Read 'N Run (all)
Royal Productions—R (8-12)
Resurrection Press—R
Review & Herald (all)
St. Anthony Messenger—R (all)
Shining Star (8-12)
Son-Rise (all)
Sonstar Publishing—R (Jr/Sr High)
So. Baptist Press—R (all)
Still Waters Revival—R (all)
Sword of the Lord—R (all)
TEACH Services—R (8-12/Jr High)
Tekna Books (all)
Tyler Press—R (all)
Vital Issues Press—R
Windflower—R (all)
World Bible (all)
YWAM Publishing—R (all)
Zondervan (all)

YOUTH PROGRAMS

Baker Books—R
Church Growth Inst.
Concordia
Contemporary Drama Service
CSS Publishing
Educational Ministries
Fairway Press—R
GROUP Publishing—R
Group's FaithWeaver
Hensley Publishing—R
Judson Press—R
Langmarc
Liguori Publications
Morehouse—R
Read 'N Run—R
Resurrection Press—R
St. Anthony Messenger—R
Sheer Joy! Press
Standard
Vital Issues Press—R
Wood Lake Books—R
Zondervan

ALPHABETICAL LISTINGS OF BOOK PUBLISHERS

(*) An asterisk before a listing indicates no or unconfirmed information update.

(#) A number symbol before a listing indicates it was updated from their guidelines or other current sources.

(+) A plus sign before a listing indicates it is a new listing this year and was not included last year.

If you do not find the publisher you are looking for, look in the General Index. See the introduction of that index for the codes used to identify the current status of each unlisted publisher.

+ABINGDON PRESS, 201 8th Ave. S, Nashville TN 37203. (615)749-6000. E-mail: (first initial and last name)@umpublishing.org. Website: http://www.abingdon.org. United Methodist Publishing House. Editors: Harriett Jane Olson (books), Cynthia Gadsden (professional books), Ulrike Guthrie (academic books), Peg Augustine (children's books). Books and church supplies directed primarily to a religious market. Publishes 120 titles/yr. Receives 1,000 submissions annually. 5% of books from first-time authors. Reprints books. Prefers 144 pgs. Royalty 7½% on retail; no advance. Average first printing 3,000. Publication within 2 yrs. No simultaneous submissions. Requires disk. Responds in 6-8 wks. Guidelines; free catalog.

> **Nonfiction:** Proposal/2 chapters; no phone query.
>
> **Ethnic Books:** African-American, Hispanic, Native-American, Korean.
>
> **Tips:** "Looking for general-interest books: mainline, social issues, marriage/family, self-help, exceptional people."

*ACCENT BOOKS & VIDEOS, PO Box 700, Bloomington IL 61702. (309)378-8296. Fax (309)378-4420. E-mail: acntlug@aol.com. Website: http://www.blvd.com/blvd. Cheever Publishing. Betty Garee, ed. Information for the mobility impaired. Publishes 1-2 titles/yr (mostly how-to books). Receives 15-20 submissions annually. 85% of books from first-time authors. No mss through agents. Prefers 64 pgs (max). Outright purchases. Average first printing 300. Publication within 6 mos. Considers simultaneous submissions. Responds in 2 wks. Accepts disk. Guidelines; catalog $3.50.

> **Nonfiction:** Query only first; phone/fax/e-query OK.
>
> **Also Does:** Booklets.

#ACCENT PUBLICATIONS, PO Box 36640, Colorado Springs CO 80936-3664. (719)536-0100x3337. Imprint of Cook Communications Ministries. Cheryl Crews, acq ed. Evangelical church resource products. Publishes 6-

8 titles/yr. Receives 500 submissions annually. 90% of books from first-time authors. No mss through agents. Royalty on retail or outright purchase; no advance. Publication within 1 yr. Considers simultaneous submissions. Responds in 3 mos. Guidelines; catalog for 9x12 SAE/3 stamps.

Nonfiction: Query letter only; no phone query. "Looking for church resource products that promote the work of the local church in any ministry aspect; also series ideas for Bible studies/group study books."

Tips: "Be fresh, creative, and in tune with the needs and ministries of the local church's Christian education programs."

ACTA PUBLICATIONS, 4848 N. Clark St., Chicago IL 60640-4711. (773)271-1030. Fax (773-271-7399. E-mail: acta@one.org. Catholic. Gregory F. Augustine Pierce and Thomas R. Artz, co-pubs. Resources for the "end-user" of the Christian faith. Imprints: Buckley Publications; National Center for the Laity. Publishes 10 titles/yr. Receives 65 submissions annually. 50% of books from first-time authors. Prefers 150-200 pgs. Royalty 10-12 1/2% of net; no advance. Average first printing 3,000. Publication within 1 yr. Disk accepted. Responds in 2 mos. Guidelines; catalog for 9x12 SAE/2 stamps.

Nonfiction: Query or proposal/1 chapter; no phone/e-query.

Tips: "Most open to books that are useful to a large number of average Christians. Read our catalog and one of our books first."

*ACU PRESS, 1648 Campus Ct., Abilene TX 79601. (915)674-2720. Fax (915)674-6471. E-mail: LEMMONST@acuprs.acu.edu. Church of Christ/Abilene Christian University. Thom Lemmons, ed. Guidance in the religious life for members and leaders of the denomination. Publishes 10 titles/yr. Receives 100 submissions annually. 10% of books from first-time authors. Royalty 10%. Average first printing 5,000. Publication within 3 mos. Considers simultaneous submissions. Responds in 1 mo. Catalog.

Nonfiction: Proposal/3 chapters.

ALBA HOUSE, 2187 Victory Blvd., Staten Island NY 10314-6603. (718)761-0047. Fax (718)761-0057. Website: http://www.albahouse.org. Catholic/Society of St. Paul. Father Victor Viberti, S.S.P., acq ed. Publishes 24 titles/yr. Receives 450 submissions annually. 20% of books from first-time authors. No mss through agents. Reprints books. Royalty 7-10% on retail; no advance. Publication within 9 mos. Prefers disk. Responds in 1-2 mos. Free guidelines/catalog.

Nonfiction: Query.

#THE ALBAN INSTITUTE, INC., 7315 Wisconsin Ave. Ste. 1250 W, Bethesda MD 20814-3211. (301)718-4407. Fax (301)718-1958. Episcopal Church. Linda Marie Delloff, dir. Publishes 10 titles/yr. Receives 100 submissions annually. No mss through agents. Prefers 100 pgs. Royalty 7-10% of net; outright purchases for $50-100 for 450-2,000 wd articles on congregational life; advance $100. Publication within 1 yr. Responds in 4 mos. Guidelines; catalog for 9x12 SAE/3 stamps.

Nonfiction: Proposal only first. Books for clergy and laity.

Tips: "Books on congregational issues: problems and opportunities in congregational life; the clergy role and career; the ministry of the laity in church and world." Intelligent/liberal audience.

#ALBURY PUBLISHING, 2448 E. 81st St., Ste. 4700, Tulsa OK 74137. (800)811-3921 or (918)496-2200. Fax (918)496-7702. Website: http:// www.alburypublishing.com. Elizabeth Sherman, ed. mng Charismatic Christian lifestyle and doctrinal issues. Publishes 12 titles/yr. Receives 96 submissions annually. 2% of books from first-time authors. Reprints books. Prefers 192 pgs. Royalty; advance. Average first printing 10,000. Publication within 10 mos. No simultaneous submissions. Responds in 3 mos. Guidelines; catalog for 9x12 SAE/2 stamps.

> **Nonfiction:** Query only; e-mail query OK. "Want well-written and compelling content, whether the topic has to do with personal or corporate Christian experience."

ALEXANDER BOOKS, 65 Macedonia Rd., Alexander NC 28701. (828)252-9515. Fax (828)255-8719. E-mail: susan@abooks.com. Website: http:// www.abooks.com. Susan Parker, ed. Imprint: Farthest Star. Publishes 8-10 titles/yr. Receives 300 submissions annually. 10% of books from first-time authors. Royalty 12-15% on net; few advances. Publication within 1 yr. Considers simultaneous submissions. Responds in 1-3 mos. Guidelines; catalog for #10 SAE/2 stamps.

> **Nonfiction:** Query or proposal/3 chapters. "Subjects include religion."
>
> **Fiction:** Query or proposal/3 chapters. Adult.
>
> **Tips:** "Know your market and send a professionally prepared manuscript."

AMERICAN CATHOLIC PRESS, 16565 State St., South Holland IL 60473-2025. (708)331-5485. Catholic worship resources. Father Michael Gilligan, ed dir. Publishes 4 titles/yr. Reprints books. Pays $25-100 for outright purchases only. Average first printing 3,000. Publication within 1 yr. Considers simultaneous submissions. Responds in 2 mos. Catalog for SASE.

> **Nonfiction:** Query first.
>
> **Tips:** "We publish only materials on the Roman Catholic liturgy. Especially interested in new music for church services."

ART CAN DRAMA RESOURCES, Promise Productions, Inc., PO Box 927, Glen Rose TX 76043. (800)687-2661. Fax (817)897-3388. E-mail: drama@ thepromise.org. Website: http://www.thepromise.org. Ted Oliver, ed. Supplies Christian schools, churches, and home schools with drama study materials. Publishes 2-3 titles/yr. Receives 50-100 submissions annually. 10% of books from first-time authors. Reprints books. Prefers 150-250 pgs. Royalty 5-10% on retail; $250-500 advance. Average first printing 500-1,000. Publication within 3-6 mos. No simultaneous submissions. Responds in 1-3 mos. Requires disk. Free guidelines/catalog.

> **Nonfiction:** Proposal/1chapter. Fax query OK.
>
> **Special Needs:** Stage or radio playscripts. Youth plays (contemporary comedies); children's plays (short sketches), creation dramatics (how-to).
>
> **Tips:** "Most open to books on the arts in a Christian context; playscripts which have been produced, won awards, and explore the Christian experience."

AUGSBURG BOOKS, 100 S. 5th St., Suite 700 (55402), Box 1209, Minneapolis MN 55440-1209. (612)330-3300. Fax (612)330-3215. No longer accepting freelance submissions.
**Note: This publisher is serviced by The Writer's Edge.

BAKER BOOKS, Box 6287, Grand Rapids MI 49516-6287. (616)676-9185. Fax (616)676-9573. Website: http://www.bakerbooks.com. Evangelical. Allan Fisher, dir. of publications; submit to Rebecca Cooper, asst. Publishes 120 titles/yr. Receives 2,000 submissions annually. 10% of books from first-time authors. Reprints books. Prefers 150-300 pgs. Royalty 14% of net; some advances. Average first printing 5,000. Publication within 1 yr. Considers simultaneous submissions. Responds in 3 mos. No disk. Guidelines (on Website); catalog for 9x12 SAE/6 stamps.
   Nonfiction: Proposal/3 chapters; no e-query. "Request our brochure on how to prepare a proposal."
   Fiction: Query. "We are interested in mysteries and contemporary women's fiction from a Christian world view without being preachy. Our fiction is more literary than popular. Request summary of contemporary women's fiction."
   Ethnic Books: Would be interested in publishing specifically for the African-American market; also multicultural fiction.
   Tips: "Please prepare a complete, well-organized proposal. Request our guidelines for guidance."
   **Note: This publisher serviced by The Writer's Edge.

BAKER'S PLAYS, 100 Chauncy St., Boston MA 02111-1783. (617)482-1280. Fax (617)482-7613. E-mail: info@bakersplays.com. Website: http://www.bakersplays.com. Raymond Pape, assoc ed. Publishes 20-25 plays/yr. Receives 600 submissions annually. 40% of plays from first-time authors. Production royalty varies; no advance. Average first printing 1,000. Considers simultaneous submissions. Accepts disk. Responds in 2-6 mos. Free guidelines; no catalog.
   Plays: Complete ms.
   Tips: "We currently publish full-length or one-act plays, theater texts and musicals, with a separate division which publishes plays for religious institutions. The ideal time to submit work is from September to April."

#BALLANTINE BOOKS, 201 E. 50th St., New York NY 10022. (212)572-4910. Fax (212)572-4912. A Division of Random House. Joanne Wyckoff, religion ed. General publisher that does a few religious books. No guidelines or catalog. Not in topical listings.
   Nonfiction & Fiction: Proposal/100 pages of manuscript.

#BANTAM BOOKS, 1540 Broadway, New York NY 10036. (212)354-6500. General trade publisher with a religious/inspirational list. Thomas Cahill, dir. Accepts mss only through agents. Prefers at least 80,000-100,000 wds. Royalty 4-15%; advance. Publication within 8 mos. Considers simultaneous submissions from agents. Responds in 1 mo. Catalog for SASE.
   Nonfiction: Proposal/2-3 chapters. "Want all types of religious/inspirational books." No humor, no triumph over tragedy unless subject is well known or a celebrity.

Fiction: Proposal/2-3 chapters. "Books must cross over into the trade market."

Tips: "We want books that appeal to a large, general audience and fresh ideas. Be sure to investigate the competition and include an author bio. The author's relevant experience and authority is very important to us."

BARBOUR PUBLISHING, INC., 1810 Barbour Dr., PO Box 719, Uhrichsville OH 44683. (614)922-6045. Fax (614)922-5948. Website: http://www.barbourbooks.com. Susan Johnson, sr ed. Distributes Christian books at bargain prices. Imprints: Barbour Books (nonfiction), Promise Press (original nonfiction and gift books—see separate listing); and Heartsong Presents (fiction—see separate listing); Inspirational Library. Publishes 75 titles/yr. Receives 450 submissions annually. 40% of books from first-time authors. No mss through agents. Reprints books. Prefers 50,000-60,000 wds or 300 pgs. Outright purchases $750-2,500; advance is half of outright purchase. Average first printing 15,000-20,000. Publication within 1 yr. Considers simultaneous submissions. Responds in 9-12 wks. No disk; prefers e-mail (with prior arrangement). Guidelines; catalog $2.

Nonfiction: Query; no phone/fax/e-query.

Fiction: Proposal/2 chapters to Rebecca Germany, fiction ed. "We are interested in a mystery/romance series." See separate listing for Heartsong Presents.

Also Does: Booklets.

Tips: "We seek solid, evangelical books with the greatest mass appeal. A good gift book for mothers will go much farther with Barbour than will a commentary on Jude. Do your homework before sending us a manuscript; send material that will work well within our publishing philosophy."

BARCLAY PRESS, 110 S. Elliott Rd., Newberg OR 97132-2144. (503)538-7345. Fax (503)538-7033. E-mail: info@barclaypress.com. Website: http://www.barclay press.com. Friends/Quaker. Dan McCracken, general manager. Books dealing with Christian spirituality and contemporary issues that Christians should address. Publishes 1-5 titles/yr. Receives 40-50 submissions annually. 1% of books from first-time authors. No mss through agents. Reprints books. Prefers 100-200 pgs. Royalty 10% on net; no advance. Average first printing 1,500. Publication within 18 mos. Considers simultaneous submissions. Responds in 6 wks. Prefers disk. No guidelines; free book list.

Nonfiction: Query only; fax/e-query OK. "Looking for books on spirituality and current social issues."

Also Does: Booklets and pamphlets.

**Note: This publisher serviced by The Writer's Edge.

MEL BAY PUBLICATIONS, INC., #4 Industrial Dr., Pacific MO 63069-0066. (314)257-3970. Fax (314)257-5062. E-mail: email@melbay.com. Website: http://www. melbay.com. William A. Bay, pres/ed-in-chief. Imprints: Cathedral Music Press; Creative Keyboard Publications; Editions Classicae; Building Essence Series; You Can Teach Yourself. Also distributes secular and sacred organ and choral music from Kevin Mayhew Ltd. of England. Publishes 25 inspirational/religious titles/yr. Royalty 10% on retail; no advance. Publication within 6-9 mos. Responds in 1-6 wks. Free guidelines/catalog.

Nonfiction: Concept statement and brief resume; complete ms or proposal/3-4 chapters or 3-4 musical compositions (photocopy only); cassette recording of sample pieces; no fax/e-query. Does not print contemporary pop vocal music, nor music for large ensembles.

Tips:"We specialize in instrument method books, song books, and historically or thematically related solo instrument anthologies. Prior to submission, please examine our catalogs to gather a sense of the type of material we publish and confirm that your proposal hasn't already been done. Free Guitar/Bass catalog available on request; the 400-page Complete Catalog costs $5 prepaid if ordered separately, but is free with any order on request."

BAYLOR UNIVERSITY PRESS, PO Box 97363, Waco TX 76798-7363. (254)710-3164. Fax (254)710-3440. E-mail: steven-heyduck@baylor.edu. Website: http://www.baylor.edu/~BUPress. Baptist. Janet L. Burton, ed. Imprint: Markham Press Fund. Academic press producing scholarly books on religion and social sciences; separation of church and state. Publishes 4 titles/yr. Receives 120 submissions annually. Royalty 10% of net; no advance. Average first printing 1,000. Publication within 1 yr. Responds in 2 mos. Free catalog.

Nonfiction: Query/outline; no phone query, e-mail query OK.

#BEACON HILL PRESS OF KANSAS CITY, PO Box 419527, Kansas City MO 64141. (816)931-1900. Fax (816)753-4071. E-mail: bjp@bhillkc.com. Website: http://www.nphdirect.com. Nazarene Publishing House/Church of the Nazarene. Kelly Gallagher, acq ed. A Christ-centered publisher that provides authentically Christian resources that are faithful to God's Word and relevant to life. Imprint: Beacon Hill Books. Publishes 30 titles/yr. Receives 1,000 submissions annually. 10% of books from first-time authors. No mss through agents. Prefers 30,000-60,000 wds or 250 pgs. Royalty 12-18% of net; advance; some outright purchases. Average first printing 5,000. Publication within 1 yr. Considers simultaneous submissions. Responds in 3 mos. Free guidelines/catalog.

Nonfiction: Query or Proposal/2-3 chapters; no phone/fax query. "Looking for applied Christianity, spiritual formation, and leadership resources."

Ethnic Books: Spanish division—Casa Nazarena De Publicaciones. Publishes in several languages.

BETHANY HOUSE PUBLISHERS, 11300 Hampshire Ave. S, Minneapolis MN 55438 (moving in March 1999). (612)829-2500. Fax (612)829-2768. A ministry of Bethany Fellowship, Inc. Cindy M. Alewine, ms review ed; Steve Laube, acq ed (stevelaube@bethanyhouse.com); David Horton, acq ed; Barbara Lilland, sr ed, adult fiction; Kevin Johnson, sr ed, adult nonfiction; Rochelle Gloege, sr ed, children and youth. To publish information that communicates biblical truth and assists people in both spiritual and practical areas of life. Imprint: Portraits (Barbara Lilland, ed). Publishes 120-150 titles/yr. Receives 3,000 submissions annually. 2% of books from first-time authors. Negotiable royalty on net and advance. Publication within 1 yr. Considers simultaneous submissions. Responds in 3 mos. Guidelines for fiction/nonfiction/juvenile; catalog for 9x12 SAE/5 stamps.

Nonfiction: Cover letter, synopsis, 3 chapters; no phone/fax query. "Seeking well-planned and developed books in the following categories: personal growth, devotional, contemporary issues, marriage and family, reference, applied theology and inspirational."

Fiction: Cover letter/synopsis/3 chapters. "PORTRAITS is our new contemporary fiction line. We also publish adult historical fiction, teen/young adult fiction, children's fiction series (7-12 yrs; no picture books). Send SASE for guidelines."

Tips: "Seeking high quality fiction and nonfiction that will inspire and challenge our audience—the man and woman in the pew. "

**Note: This publisher serviced by The Writer's Edge.

BETHEL PUBLISHING. Sold to Evangel Press.

+BIRCH LANE PRESS, 120 Enterprise Ave., Secaucus NJ 07094. (201)866-0490. No response to questionnaire.

BLUE DOLPHIN PUBLISHING, INC., PO Box 8, Nevada City CA 95959. (916)265-6925. Fax (916)265-0787. E-mail: Bdolphin@netshel.net. Website: http://www.bluedolphinpublishing.com. Paul M. Clemens, pub. Imprint: Pelican Pond. Books that help people grow in their social and spiritual awareness. Publishes 12-15 titles/yr. Receives 4,000 submissions annually. 90% of books from first-time authors. Prefers about 60,000 wds or 200 pgs. Royalty 10-15% of net; no advance. Average first printing 3,000-5,000. Publication within 10 mos. Considers simultaneous submissions. No disk until contract. Responds in 1-3 mos. Guidelines (also on Website); catalog for 6x9 SAE/2 stamps.

Nonfiction: Proposal/1 chapter; e-query OK. "Looking for books on interspecies and relationships."

Fiction: Query/2-pg synopsis.

Tips: "We look for topics that would appeal to the general market, are interesting, different and that will aid in the growth and development of humanity."

+BOOKS IN MOTION, 9212 E. Montgomery #501, Spokane WA 99206. (509)922-1646. Secular fiction publisher that does some religious books. Gary Challender, pres. Publishes unabridged audio books. Publishes 70-80 titles/yr. 25% of books from first-time authors. Royalty 10% of retail or net. Publication within 3 mos. Considers simultaneous submissions. Response time varies. Free guidelines/catalog.

Fiction: Query/synopsis/1st chapter.

Tips: "Our audience is 20% women and 40% men (mostly truck drivers). "

+BOYDS MILLS PRESS, 815 Church St., Honesdale PA 18431-1895. (717)253-1164. Highlights for Children. Beth Troop, ms coord. Publishes a wide range of literary children's titles, for preschool through young adult; some religious. Publishes 50 titles/yr. Receives 10,000 submissions annually. 20% of books from first-time authors. Reprints books. Royalty 8-15% on retail; advance varies. Considers simultaneous submissions. Responds in 3 mos. Free guidelines/catalog.

Nonfiction: Proposal/1 chapter and sample art."No self-help books."

Fiction: Synopsis/3 chapters for novel; complete ms for picture book. "We are always interested in multicultural settings."

BRIDGE/LOGOS, 1300 Airport Rd. #E, North Brunswick NJ 08902-1700. (732)435-8700. Fax (732)435-8701. E-mail: editor@bridgelogos.com. Website: Ronnie Belanger, ed-in-chief. Purpose is to clearly define God's changeless Word to a changing world. Imprints: Logos, Bridge. Publishes 25 titles/yr. Receives 370 submissions annually. 20% of books from first-time authors. **SUBSIDY PUBLISHES 12%.** Prefers 180 pgs. Royalty 6-25% of net; some advances, $1,000-10,000. Average first printing 5,000. Publication within 6 mos. Considers simultaneous submissions. Responds in 6 wks. No disk. Guidelines; catalog for 9x12 SAE/4 stamps.

Nonfiction: Query only; phone query OK. "Most open to evangelism, spiritual growth, self-help and education."

Tips: "Have a great message, a well-written manuscript, and a willingness, as well as ways, to market your book."

BRISTOL HOUSE, LTD., PO Box 4020, Anderson IN 46013-0020. (765)644-0856. Fax (765)622-1045. Sara Anderson, sr. ed. Imprint: Bristol Books. Publishes 4 titles/yr. Receives 35-55 submissions annually. Few books from first-time authors. Reprints books. **SOME SUBSIDY.** Prefers 160-240 pgs. Royalty 14% of net; no advance. Average first printing 1,000. Publication within 6-9 mos. Responds in 4 mos. Requires disk, no e-mail. Catalog for 9x12 SAE/2 stamps.

Nonfiction: Proposal/2 chapters; fax/e-query OK. "Looking for books on renewal. Most of our books are Methodist/Wesleyan in emphasis."

BROADMAN & HOLMAN PUBLISHERS, 127 9th Ave. N, Nashville TN 37234. (615)251-3638. Fax (615)251-3752. Website: http://www.broadman holman.com. Southern Baptist. Richard P. Rosenbaum, Jr., ed. Publishes 60 titles/yr. Receives 2,500 submissions annually. 10% of books from first-time authors. Prefers 60,000-80,000 wds. Variable royalty on net; advance. Average first printing 5,000. Publication within 12-18 mos. Considers simultaneous submissions. Responds in 8 wks. Requires disk. Guidelines; no catalog.

Nonfiction: Query only; no phone/fax query.

Ethnic: Spanish translations.

Tips: "Follow guidelines when submitting. Be informed about the market in general and specifically related to the book you want to write."

**Note: This publisher serviced by The Writer's Edge.

BROWN-ROA, 1665 Embassy West Dr., Ste. 200, Dubuque IA 52002-2259. (800)922-7696. Fax (319)557-3720. E-mail: mkrawczuk@harcourtbrace. com. Website: http://www.brownroa.com. Catholic. Marge Krawczuk, mng ed. Publishes 50-100 titles/yr. Receives 100-300 submissions annually. Variable royalty or outright purchase; rarely pays advance. Average first printing 1,000-3,000. Publication within 1 yr. Considers simultaneous submissions. Responds in 2 mos. Free catalog.

> **Nonfiction:** Complete ms. "Looking primarily for school and parish text books and easy-to-use help books."

WILLIAM CAREY LIBRARY, 1705 N. Sierra Bonita Ave., Pasadena CA 91104. (626)798-4067. Fax (626)794-0477. Eugene Klingman, gen mgr. Publishes 10-15 titles/yr. Not in topical listings.

> **Nonfiction:** Query only. "As a specialized publisher, we do only books and studies of church growth and world missions. "

CATHOLIC BOOK PUBLISHING CORP., 77 West End Rd., Totowa NJ 07512. (973)890-2400. Fax (973)890-2410. Catholic. Anthony Buono, mng ed. Inspirational books for Catholic Christians. Publishes 15-20 titles/yr. Receives 75 submissions annually. 30% of books from first-time authors. No mss through agents. Variable royalty or outright purchases; no advance. Average first printing 3,000. Publication within 12-15 mos. No simultaneous submissions. Responds in 2-3 mos. Catalog for 9x12 SAE/5 stamps.

> **Nonfiction:** Query letter only; no phone/fax query.

> **Tips:** "We publish mainly Liturgical books, Bibles, Missals, and prayer books. Most of the books are composed in-house or by direct commission with particular guidelines. We strongly prefer query letters in place of full manuscripts."

THE CATHOLIC UNIVERSITY OF AMERICA PRESS, 620 Michigan Ave. NE, Washington DC 20064. (202)319-5052. Fax (202)319-4985. E-mail: cuapress@ cua.edu. Website: http://www.cua.edu/www/pubs/cupr. Catholic. Dr. David J. McGonagle, dir. Publishes 6 titles/yr. Receives 100 submissions annually. 75% of books from first-time authors. No mss through agents. Reprints books. Prefers 400 pgs. Variable royalty on net; no advance. Average first printing 750. Publication within 6 mos. Considers simultaneous submissions. Responds in 2 wks. Prefers e-mail submission. Guidelines; catalog for 9x12 SASE.

> **Nonfiction:** Query first; phone/fax/e-query OK. "Looking for history, literature, philosophy, political theory and theology."

> **Tips:** "We publish only works of original scholarship of interest to practicing scholars and academic libraries; works that are aimed at college and university classrooms. We do not publish for the popular religious audience."

CERDIC PUBLICATIONS, PJR-RIC, 11, rue Jean Sturm, 67520 Nordheim, France. Phone (03)88.87.71.07. Fax (03)88.87.71.25. Marie Zimmerman, dir. Publishes 3-5 titles/yr. 50+% of books from first-time authors. Prefers 230 pgs. The first print run in the field of law in religion does not make money; no payment. Average first printing 2,200. Publication within 3 mos (varies). Considers simultaneous submissions. Responds in 4 wks. No guidelines; free catalog.

> **Nonfiction:** Complete ms; phone/fax query OK. "Looking for books on law and religion. All topics checked in topical listings must relate to the law."

> **Tips:** "We publish original studies in law of religion (any) with preference for young, beginning authors; in French only."

CHALICE PRESS, Box 179, St. Louis MO 63166-0179. (314)231-8500. Fax (314)231-8524. E-mail: chalice@cbp21.com. Website: http://www.chalice press.com. Christian Church (Disciples of Christ). Dr. David P. Polk, ed-in-chief; Dr. Jon L. Berquist, academic ed. Books for a thinking, caring church; in Bible , theology, ethics, homiletics, pastoral care, and congregational studies. Publishes 40-50 titles/yr. Receives 400+ submissions annually. 5% of books from first-time authors. No mss through agents. Prefers 144-160 pgs for general books, 160-300 pgs for academic books. Royalty 12-14% of net; advances negotiable. Average first printing 2,500-3,000. Publication within 1 yr. Disk required on acceptance. Responds in 1-3 mos. Guidelines on Website; catalog for 9x12 SAE/2 stamps.

> **Nonfiction:** Proposal/2 chapters; fax/e-query OK. "Looking for books that treat current issues perceptively, especially from a moderate-to-liberal perspective."
>
> **Ethnic Books:** African-American and Hispanic.

CHARIOT VICTOR PUBLISHING, 4050 Lee Vance View, Colorado Springs CO 80918. (719)536-0100. Fax (719)536-3269. E-mail: chariotpub@aol.com. Website: http://www.chariotvictor.com. Cook Communications Ministries. Melissa Borger, ed asst. Leading the way with spiritual growth products. Publishes 45-50 titles/yr. Receives 1,200 submissions annually. 15% of books from first-time authors. Royalty .05-20% on net; advance $8,750; outright purchases for $500-5,000. Average first printing 15,000. Publication within 1 yr. Considers simultaneous submissions. Responds in 3 mos. Guidelines; catalog for 9x12 SAE/2 stamps.

> **Nonfiction:** Query, then proposal/3 chapters; no phone/fax/e-query.
>
> **Fiction:** Query/proposal/3-5 chapters. Promises line (historical or contemporary). Query, then proposal/2 chapters. 80,000 words. Releasing one each season. For adults.
>
> **Note:** This publisher serviced by The Writer's Edge.

CHOSEN BOOKS, Division of Baker Book House, 3985 Bradwater St., Fairfax VA 22031-3702. (703)764-8250. Fax (703)764-3995. E-mail: JECampbell@aol.com. Website: http://www.bakerbooks.com. Charismatic. Jane Campbell, ed. Books that recognize the gifts and ministry of the Holy Spirit and help the reader live a more empowered and effective life for Christ. Publishes 8 titles/yr. Receives 300 submissions annually. 10% of books from first-time authors. Prefers 60,000 wds or 200 pgs. Royalty on net; modest advance. Average first printing 5,000-7,500. Publication within 18 mos. Considers simultaneous submissions. Prefers disk. Responds in 2-3 mos. Guidelines (also on Website); no catalog.

> **Nonfiction:** Query or proposal/2 chapters (summary, outline, author resume); e-query OK (no e-proposal). "Looking for books that help the reader live a more empowered and effective life for Jesus Christ."
>
> **Tips:** "State your theme clearly in your cover letter, along with your qualifications for writing on that subject, and be sure to enclose an SASE."
>
> **Note:** This publisher serviced by The Writer's Edge.

CHRISTIAN ED. PUBLISHERS, Box 26639, San Diego CA 92196. (619)578-4700. Fax (619)578-2431(for queries only). E-mail: Lackelson@aol.com.

Website: http://www.ChristianEdPublishers.com. Dr. Lon Ackelson, acq ed. An evangelical publisher of Bible Club materials for ages two through high school; church special-event programs, and Bible-teaching craft kits. Publishes 80 titles/yr. Receives 150 submissions annually. 10% of books from first-time authors. No mss through agents. Outright purchases for .03/wd; no advance. Publication within 1 yr. Considers simultaneous submissions. Responds in 1-2 mos. Guidelines (also by e-mail); catalog for 9x12 SAE/4 stamps.

Nonfiction: Query; phone/fax/e-query OK. Bible studies, curriculum and take-home papers.

Fiction: Query first. Juvenile fiction for take-home papers. "Each story is about 1,000 wds. Write for an application."

Tips: "All writing done on assignment. Request our guidelines, then complete a writer application before submitting. Need Bible-teaching ideas for preschool through sixth grade. Also publishes Bible stories for primary take-home papers, 300 wds."

CHRISTIAN LITERATURE CRUSADE, 701 Pennsylvania Ave., Fort Washington PA 19034. (215)542-1242. Fax (215)542-2580. E-mail: 76043.3053@ compuserve. com or CLCBooks@juno.com. Willard Stone, publications coordinator. Accepting no freelance submissions at this time.

*CHRISTIAN MEDIA, Box 448, Jacksonville OR 97530. (541)899-8888. Fax on request. James Lloyd, ed/pub. Publishes 5 titles/yr. Receives 12 submissions annually. Most books from first-time authors. Would consider reprints. Prefers 200 pgs. Royalty on net; no advance. Considers simultaneous submissions. Responds in 3 wks. Catalog for 9x12 SAE/2 stamps.

Nonfiction: Query; phone query OK. Works dealing with the internal workings of the media industry; publishing, broadcasting, records, etc.

Tips: "Produces manuals, instructional or otherwise. Exposés; also books of prophetic interpretation, end times, eschatology, interpolations of political events, etc."

CHRISTIAN PUBLICATIONS, 3825 Hartzdale Dr., Camp Hill PA 17011. (717)761-7044. Fax (717)761-7273. E-mail: editors@cpi-horizon.com. Website: http://www.cpi-horizon.com. Christian and Missionary Alliance. David E. Fessenden, mng ed. Publishes books which emphasize Christ as Savior, Sanctifier, Healer, and Coming King. Imprint: Horizon Books. Publishes 40 titles/yr. Receives 1,200-1,500 submissions annually. 20% of books from first-time authors. Prefers 150-300 pgs. Royalty 5-10% of retail or net; outright purchases $100-400 (booklets); variable advance. Average first printing 3,000-5,000. Publication within 12 mos. Considers simultaneous submissions on full proposals. Prefers disk. Responds in 1-2 mos. Guidelines (also by e-mail); catalog for 9x12 SAE/5 stamps.

Nonfiction: Query/proposal/2 chapters (include 1st); one-page fax/e-query OK. "Looking for books on applying the power of the Spirit to practical, daily life."

Also Does: Booklets, 10-32 pages.

Tips: "Have a compelling idea that you are passionate about, combined with a thorough grounding in Scripture."

**Note: This publisher serviced by The Writer's Edge.

CHRISTIAN UNIVERSITIES PRESS, 7831 Woodmont #345, Bethesda MD 20814. (301)654-7414. Fax (301)654-7336. E-mail: AUSTINISP1@aol. com. Website: http://www.interscholars.com. An imprint of International Scholar's Publications. Dr. Robert West, ed-in-chief. The best obtainable projects in evangelical/Christian research. Publishes 100+ titles/yr. Receives 250+ submissions annually. 60% of books from first-time authors. No mss through agents. Reprints books. Prefers up to 264 pgs. Royalty 8-12% of net; no advance. Average first printing 500+. Publication within 8 mos. Considers simultaneous submissions. Responds in 1 mo. No disk. Guidelines; free catalog.

> **Nonfiction:** Proposal/2 chapters; fax/e-query OK. "Looking for history and theology."
>
> **Ethnic Books:** Hispanic (Latin America) or (West) African.
>
> **Tips:** "Most open to scholarly monograph/dissertation, non-fiction research; New Testament."

THE CHRISTOPHER PUBLISHING HOUSE, 24 Rockland St., Hanover MA 02339. (781)826-7474. Fax (781)826-5556. E-mail: info@atigroupinc. com. Nancy A. Lucas, mng ed. Produces fine quality books for the public's reading enjoyment. Publishes 6-8 titles/yr. Receives 200+ submissions annually. 90% of books from first-time authors. **SUBSIDY PUBLISHES 8-10%.** Prefers 100+ pgs. Prefers 120 pgs. Royalty 5-30% of net; no advance. Average first printing 2,000. Publication within 12-14 mos. Considers simultaneous submissions. Responds in 6-8 wks. Accepts disk or e-mail. Guidelines; catalog for #10 SAE/2 stamps.

> **Nonfiction:** Complete ms. Most topics; no juvenile material.
>
> **Fiction:** Complete ms. Adult only. About 100 pgs.

+CHRISTOPHER SCOTT PUBLISHING, LTD., 25 Fullerton St., Boothbay Harbor MA 04538. (207)633-9739. Fax (207)633-7865.Website: http://www.cspublishing.com. Chris H. Scott, mng ed. Hard cover books only. Imprint: S and S Press.

> **Nonfiction:** Complete ms/cover letter & synopsis.
>
> **Fiction:** Children's books.

CHURCH & SYNAGOGUE LIBRARY ASSN., PO Box 19357, Portland OR 97280-0357. (503)244-6919. Fax (503)977-3734. E-mail: csla@world accessnet. com. Website: http://www.worldaccessnet.com/~csla. Karen Bota, ed. An interfaith group set up to help librarians set up and organize/reorganize their religious libraries. Publishes 6 titles/yr. No mss through agents. No royalty. Average first printing 750. Catalog.

CHURCH GROWTH INSTITUTE, PO Box 7000, Forest VA 24551. (804)525-0022. Fax (804)525-0608. E-mail: cgimail@churchgrowth.org. Ephesians Four Ministries. Cindy G. Spear, ed. Publishes 4-6 titles/yr. Receives 52 submissions annually. 7% of books from first-time authors. No mss through agents. Prefers 64-160 pgs. Royalty 5% on retail or outright purchase; no advance. Average first printing 500. Publication within 1 yr.

Considers simultaneous submissions. Responds in 3 mos. Requires disk. Guidelines; catalog for 9x12 SAE/5 stamps.

Nonfiction: Proposal/1 chapter; no phone/fax/e-query. "We prefer our writers to be experienced in what they write about, to be experts in the field."

Special Needs: Topics that help churches grow spiritually and numerically; leadership training; attendance and stewardship programs; new or unique ministries (how-to).

Tips: "Most open to a practical manual or complete resource packet for the pastor or other church leaders. Write with a conservative Christian slant; be very practical. "

*CHURCH STREET PRESS, 127 Ninth Ave. N., Nashville TN 37234. (800)436-3689. Genevox Music Group. Does music, academic, how-to, drama, and coffee-table books.

*CISTERCIAN PUBLICATIONS, INC., Wallwood Hall, WMU Station, Kalamazoo MI 49008. (616)387-8920. Fax (616)387-8921. St. Joseph's Abbey/Catholic/Order of Cistercians of the Strict Observance. Dr. E. Rozanne Elder, ed dir. Publishes 8-14 titles/yr. Receives 30 submissions annually. 50% of books from first-time authors. No mss through agents. Prefers 204-286 pgs. Variable payment. Average first printing 1,500. Publication within 2-10 yrs. Free style sheet/catalog.

Nonfiction: Proposal/1 chapter. History, spirituality and theology.

Tips: "We publish only on the Christian Monastic Tradition."

COLLEGE PRESS PUBLISHING CO., INC., 223 W. Third St. (64801), Box 1132, Joplin MO 64802. (417)623-6280. Fax (417)623-8250. E-mail: collegepress@collegepress.com. Website: http://www.collegepress.com. Christian Church/Church of Christ. John M. Hunter, ed. Imprint: Forerunner Books. Christian materials that will help fulfill the Great Commission and promote unity on the basis of biblical truth and intent. Publishes 30 titles/yr. Receives 400+ submissions annually. 1-5% of books from first-time authors. Reprints books. Prefers 250-300 pgs (paperback) or 300-600 pgs (hardback). Royalty 5-15% of net; no advance. Average first printing 2,000. Publication within 6 mos. Considers simultaneous submissions. No e-mail submissions. Responds in 2-3 mos. Guidelines; catalog for 9x12 SAE/5 stamps.

Nonfiction: Query only, then proposal/2-3 chapters; no phone/fax/e-query. "Looking for Bible commentaries, books on blended families, home schooling and integrity."

Ethnic Books: Reprints their own books in Spanish.

Tips: "Most open to conservative, biblical exposition with an 'Armenian' view and/or 'amillennial' slant."

CONARI PRESS, 2550 9th St., Ste. 101, Berkeley CA 94710-2551. (510)649-7175. Fax (510)649-7190. E-mail: conaripub@aol.com, or conari@ix.netcom.com. Website: http://www.readersndex.com/conari. Mary Jane Ryan, exec ed; Claudia Schaab, mng ed. Focus is on the human experience. Publishes 30 titles/yr. Receives 1,000 submissions annually. 50% of books from first-time authors. Reprints bks. Royalty 12-16% of net; variable advance. Average first printing 20,000. Publication within 1-3 yrs. Considers simultaneous submissions. Responds in 3 mos. Guidelines; catalog for 6x9 SAE/3 stamps.

Nonfiction: Proposal/3 chapters; no phone/fax query.

+CONCILIAR PRESS, PO Box 76, Ben Lomand CA 95005. (831)336-5118. Fax (831)336-8882. E-mail:marketing@conciliarpress.com. Website: http://www.conciliarpress.com. Antiochian Orthodox Christian Archdiocese of N.A. Dr. Thomas Zell, ed. Publishes 2-5 titles/yr. Receives 50 submissions annually. 20% of books from first-time authors. **SUBSIDY PUBLISHES 10%.** Royalty; no advance. Average first printing 5,000. Prefers e-mail submission. Guidelines; catalog for 9x12 SAE/5 stamps. Not in topical listings.

Nonfiction: Query only; phone/fax/e-query OK.

Fiction: Query only. "We do publish children's materials."

CONCORDIA PUBLISHING HOUSE, 3558 S. Jefferson Ave., St. Louis MO 63118-3968. (314)268-1000. Fax (314)268-1329. Website: http://www.cph.org. Lutheran Church/Missouri Synod. Rachel Hoyer: adult nonfiction, drama, youth; Dawn Weinstock: adult, family, children's devotionals; Jane Wilke: children's, teaching resources; Brandy Simmons: guidelines for adults, children's drama. Publishes 120 titles/yr. Receives 3,000 submissions annually. 10% of books from first-time authors. Royalty 2-14% on retail; some outright purchases; some advances $500-2000. Average first printing 8,000-10,000 (up to 30,000 on Arch Books). Publication within 2 yrs. Considers simultaneous submissions. Responds in 4 mos. Prefers disk. Guidelines.

Nonfiction: Proposal/2 chapters; no phone/fax query. No poetry, personal experience or biography.

Fiction: Proposal/2 chapters. No adult fiction. Children's categories: beginning reader, chapter, juvenile, youth. Must have strong Christian message.

Christian Drama: Individual scripts and collections; seasonal and topical. Outright purchases; some royalty.

Tips: "Most open to family, inspirational/devotional, children's picture books, and teaching resources. Any proposal should be Christ-centered, Bible-based, and life-directed."

**Note: This publisher serviced by The Writer's Edge.

CONTEMPORARY DRAMA SERVICE—See Meriwether Publishing, Ltd.

COOK COMMUNICATIONS MINISTRIES—See Chariot Victor Books.

DAVID C. COOK PUBLISHING CO.—See Chariot Victor Books.

#CORNELL UNIVERSITY PRESS, Sage House, 510 E. State St., Ithaca NY 14850. (607)277-2338. Nondenominational. Frances Benson, ed-in-chief; Kay Scheuer, mng ed. Publishes 6-8 titles/yr. Receives 20 submissions annually. 50% of books from first-time authors. Reprints books. Prefers 100,000 wds. Royalty to 15%; advance to $5,000. Average first printing 1,250. Publication within 1 yr. May consider simultaneous submission. Responds in 3 mos. Free guidelines/catalog.

Nonfiction: Query first. "Looking for historical (especially medieval and early modern) and philosophical books."

CORNERSTONE PRESS CHICAGO, 939 W. Wilson Ave., Ste. 202C, Chicago IL 60640. (773)561-2450. Fax (773)989-2076. E-mail: cspress@jpusa.chi.il. us. Website: http://www.geocities.com/Paris/Metro/9478/index.html.Tom Montgomery, ed. Publishes 4 titles/yr. Receives 60 submissions annually. Prefers 200-250 pgs. Royalty 12%; no advance. Average first printing 2,000-3,000. Publication within 1 yr. Considers simultaneous submissions. Catalog for SASE.

> **Nonfiction:** Proposal/3 chapters.
> **Fiction:** Proposal/3 chapters. Children, teen, adults.
> **Tips:** "We focus on nonfiction, especially social issues, music and the arts, C.S. Lewis and Inklings-related works, and generally engaging popular culture without being reactionary—pointing out underlying worldviews and assumptions, showing their disparity with Christianity without demonizing them. No Chicken-Soup or feel-good type books, Sunday school or home school curricula."

+COUNTERPOINT, 1627 I St. NW Ste. 850, Washington DC 20006. (202)887-0363. Fax (202)887-0562. Perseus Book Group. Jack Shoemaker, ed-in-chief. Publishes serious literary work; secular but does some religious books. Publishes 20-25 titles/yr. Receives 800 submissions annually. 2% of books from first-time authors. Reprints books. Royalty 7½-15% on retail. Publication within 18 mos. Considers simultaneous submissions. Responds in 2 mos.

> **Nonfiction:** Agented submissions only.
> **Fiction:** Agented submissions only.

+J. COUNTRYMAN, (800)251-4000. Fax (615)902-3200. Jack Countryman, pub/exec VP; Terri Gibbs, mng ed. Gift-book imprint; presenting strong, Bible-based messages in beautifully designed books. Publishes 15-20 titles/yr. Receives 100+ submissions annually. Might consider a reprint. Prefers 128 pgs. Royalty; advance. Average first printing 40,000. Publication within 1 yr. Considers simultaneous submissions. Responds in 2-3 wks. No guidelines; free catalog.

> **Nonfiction:** Query; no phone/fax/e-query."We will look at other material, but will not guarantee its return."
> **Fiction:** Query. Adult."We are looking for short pieces of fiction."

#CREATION HOUSE, 600 Rinehart Rd., Lake Mary FL 32746-4872. (407)333-3132. Fax (407)333-7100. E-mail: creationhouse@strang. com. Website: http://www.creationhouse.com. Strang Communications. Alyse Lounsberry, ed dir; Ginger Schmaus, acq ed. To provide the charismatic market with books on Spirit-led living. Publishes 25-30 titles/yr. Receives 700 submissions annually. 2% of books from first-time authors. Prefers 40,000 wds or 200 pgs. Royalty 4-18% on retail; advance $1,500-5,000. Average first printing 5,000. Publication within 9 mos. Considers simultaneous submissions. Responds in 2-3 mos. No disk. Free guidelines; no catalog.

> **Nonfiction:** Proposal/3 chapters; fax query OK. "Looking for books of Spirit-filled interest, devotional life, practical Christian living, and Bible study/foundational." Note: Accepting no freelance at this time.
> ****Note:** This publisher serviced by The Writer's Edge.

*CREATIVELY YOURS**, 2906 W. 64th Pl., Tulsa OK 74132. Phone/fax (918)446-2424. Creatively Yours Puppetry. Jill Morris, pub. Publishes individual scripts and books of plays, poems, and related material; general religious. Send complete ms. Responds in 2 mos or less. Pays $25 for plays; $5 for poems (4-20 lines/action), and $10 for choral readings. Buys all rts. Guidelines/brochure for SASE.

> **Tips:** "Try the material on children—if they don't like it, don't send it to us. Use humor whenever possible. The plays we publish can be used with puppets or children, so don't overload on characters, props, or setting—keep it simple."

> **Note:** Since this publisher wants individual plays or poems, it is listed in the topical section for periodicals.

CROSS CULTURAL PUBLICATIONS, INC., PO Box 506, Notre Dame IN 46556. (800)561-6526 or (219)272-0889. Fax (219)273-5973. E-mail: crosscult@ aol.com. Website: http://www.crossculturalpub.com. Cyriac K. Pullapilly, gen ed. Promotes intercultural and interfaith understanding. Imprint: CrossRoads Books. Publishes 5-8 titles/yr. Receives 2,000-3,000 submissions annually. 75% of books from first-time authors. Prefers 200-250 pgs. Royalty 5-10% of net; no advance. Average first printing 1,000-1,500. Publication within 5-12 mos. Considers simultaneous submissions. Requires disk. Responds in 2-3 mos. Free catalog.

> **Nonfiction:** Query first; no phone/fax/e-query.

> **Ethnic Books:** Seeks to serve the cross cultural, intercultural, and multicultural aspects of religious traditions.

> **Tips:** "Most open to solidly researched, well-written books on serious issues. Do a thorough job of writing/editing, etc."

THE CROSSROAD PUBLISHING CO., 370 Lexington Ave., New York NY 10017. (212)532-3650. Fax (212)532-4922. Michael Leach, pub. Books on religion, spirituality, and personal growth that speak to the diversity of backgrounds and beliefs; books that inform, enlighten, and heal. Publishes 50 titles/yr. Receives 1,000 submissions annually. 10% of books from first-time authors. Rarely subsidy publishes (5%). Reprints books. Prefers 50,000-60,000 wds or 160 pgs. Royalty 6-15% of net; advance $1,000 (more for established authors). Average first printing 5,000. Publication within 6-8 mos. Considers simultaneous submissions. Responds in 3 mos. Accepts disk. Free catalog.

> **Nonfiction:** Proposal/2 chapters or complete ms; fax query OK.

> **Fiction:** Proposal/2 chapters or complete ms. Prefers historical fiction that focuses on important figures or periods in the history of Christianity.

CROSSWAY BOOKS, 1300 Crescent St., Wheaton IL 60187. (630)682-4300. Fax (630)682-4785. A division of Good News Publishers. Marvin Padgett, VP editorial; submit to Jill Carter, ed asst. Publishes books that combine the Truth of God's Word with a passion to live it out; with unique and compelling Christian content. Publishes 70 titles/yr. Receives 2,500 submissions annually. 2% of books from first-time authors. Prefers 25,000 wds & up. Royalty 14-21% on net; advance varies. Average first printing 5,000-10,000. Publication within 18 mos. Considers simultaneous submissions. Requires disk (compatible with Macintosh and Microsoft Word). Responds in 6-8 wks. Guidelines; catalog for 9x12 SAE/7 stamps.

Nonfiction: Query only, then proposal/2 chapters; fax query OK.

Fiction: Proposal/2 chapters (no complete mss). Adult.

Also Does: Tracts. See Good News Publishers.

Tips: "Most open to books that are consistent with what the Bible teaches and stand within the stream of historic Christian truth; books that give a clear sense that the author is a genuine Christian seeking to live a consistent Christian life. Be clear and concise in your synopsis."

**Note: This publisher serviced by The Writer's Edge.

C.S.S. PUBLISHING CO., PO Box 4503, 517 S. Main St., Lima OH 45802-4503. (419)227-1818. Fax (419)228-9184. E-mail: Tom@csspub.com. Website: http://www.csspub.com. Terry Rhoads, ed; Tom Lentz, acq. ed. A clearing house for the promotion and exchange of creative ideas used in ministry. Publishes 200 titles/yr. Receives 1,200-1,500 submissions annually. 50% of books from first-time authors. **SUBSIDY PUBLISHES 40%** through Fairway Press. Prefers 100-125 pgs. Royalty 3-7% or outright purchases for $25-400. Average first printing 1,000. Publication within 6-10 mos. Considers simultaneous submissions. Responds in 3-4 mos. Accepts disk. Free guidelines/catalog.

Nonfiction: Complete ms; fax/e-query OK. "Looking for church programs and practical resources."

Fiction: Complete ms. For all ages. Inspirational; plays (Advent/Christmas); short-story collections. Children's books, 6-12 years, series or single books.

Tips: "Suggest what you can do to help promote the book."

*CUSTOM COMMUNICATIONS SERVICES, INC./SHEPHERD PRESS/CUSTOMBOOK, 77 Main St., Tappan NJ 10983. (914)365-0414. Norman Shaifer, pres. Publishes 50-75 titles/yr. 50% of books from first-time authors. No mss through agents. Royalty on net; some outright purchases for specific assignments. Publication within 6 mos. Responds in 1 month. Guidelines.

Nonfiction: Query/proposal/chapters. "Histories of individual congregations, denominations, or districts."

Tips: "Find stories of larger congregations (750 or more households) who have played a role in the historic growth and development of the community or region."

#DAYBREAK BOOKS/RODALE, 733 Third Ave., 15th Floor, New York NY 10017-3204. (212)573-0250. Fax (212)682-0665. E-mail: karchar@aol.com. Website: http://www.rodalepress.com. Karen Kelly, ed dir. Publishes books that empower and enlighten. Publishes 9-12 inspirational titles/yr. Receives 100+ submissions annually. 50% of books from first-time authors. Some reprints. Prefers 35,000-50,000 pgs. Royalty 6-15% on retail; advance $10,000 & up. Average first printing 12,000. Publication within 12-18 mos. Considers simultaneous submissions. Responds in 4-9 wks. Requires disk. Free guidelines/catalog.

Nonfiction: Proposal 1-2 chapters; fax/e-query OK. "Looking for books of personal stories, work, and ethics." Prefers agented submissions.

Fiction: Query first. For adults. "We want non-genre fiction of a spiritual, not religious, nature."

Tips: "An expert writing in their area, or a professional with some credentials in the area they are writing about, has the best chance of succeeding."

DESTINY IMAGE PUBLISHERS, INC., 167 Walnut Bottom Rd., PO Box 310, Shippenburg PA 17257. (717)532-3040. Fax (717)532-9291. E-mail: dlm@reapernet.com. Website: http://www.reapernet.com. Charismatic/Pentecostal. Don Milam, ed; submit to Don Nori, Jr. Publishes books that speak to the purposes of God in this generation. Imprints: Revival Press, Treasure House and Destiny Image. Publishes 40-45 titles/yr. Receives 1,000 submissions annually. 60% of books from first-time authors. Prefers 176 pgs. Royalty 8-20% on net; no advance. Average first printing 5,000-10,000. Publication within 5 mos. Considers simultaneous submissions. Prefers disk or e-mail. Responds in 2 wks. No guidelines; free catalog.

Nonfiction: Query only; phone/fax/e-query OK.

Special Needs: Revival/renewal books.

Also Does: Video/audio tapes; provides Internet services.

*DIMENSION BOOKS, INC., Box 811, Denville NJ 07835. (201)627-4334. Catholic. Thomas P. Coffey, ed. Publishes 12 titles/yr. Receives 800 submissions annually. 2% of books from first-time authors. Reprints books. Prefers 200 pgs. Royalty 10-15% on retail; advance. Average first printing 6,000-20,000. Publication within 6 mos. Considers simultaneous submissions. Responds in 2-5 wks. Catalog for #10 SAE/1 stamp.

Nonfiction: Query. Christian spirituality, music, biography and psychology.

+DIMENSIONS FOR LIVING, 201 8th Ave. S, Nashville TN 37203. (615)749-6000. E-mail: jcrowe@umpublishing.org. Website: http://www.abingdon.org. United Methodist Publishing House. Joseph A. Crowe, ed. Books for the general Christian reader. Publishes 120 titles/yr. Receives 1,000 submissions annually. 5% of books from first-time authors. Reprints books. Prefers 144 pgs. Royalty 7½% on retail; some outright purchases; no advance. Average first printing 3,000. Publication within 2 yrs. No simultaneous submissions. Requires disk. Responds in 6-8 wks. Guidelines; free catalog.

Nonfiction: Proposal/2 chapters; no phone query.

Ethnic Books: African-American, Hispanic, Native-American, Korean.

Special Needs: Inspiration/devotion, self-help, home/family, special occasion gift books.

#DISCOVERY PUBLISHING HOUSE, Box 3566, Grand Rapids MI 49501. (616) 942-0218. Fax (616) 957-5741. E-mail: cholquist@rbc.org. Website: http://www.rbc.org. Radio Bible Class. Robert DeVries, pub.; submit to Carol Holquist, assoc pub. Guidelines. Not in topical listings.

**Note: This publisher serviced by The Writer's Edge.

DOUBLEDAY/RELIGION, 1540 Broadway, New York NY 10036. (212)354-6500. Fax (212)782-8911. Website: http://www. bdd.com. Random House, Inc. Eric Major, VP of Religion; submit to Mark Fretz or Trace Murphy, sr eds. Imprints: Image, Galilee, Doubleday Hardcover, Anchor Bible Commentaries. Publishes 36-40 titles/yr. Receives 1,000 submissions annually. 10% of books from first-time authors. Royalty 6-15% on retail; advance. Average first printing varies. Publication within 1 yr. Considers simultaneous submissions. Responds in 1-3 mos. No disk. No guidelines; free catalog.

Nonfiction: Proposal/3 chapters; no phone query.

Fiction: Proposal/3 chapters. For adults.

Ethnic Books: African American.

Tips: "Most open to a book that has a big and well-defined audience. Have a clear proposal, lucid thesis and specified audience."

DRY BONES PRESS, PO Box 640345, San Francisco CA 94164. (415)292-7371. Fax (415)292-7314. E-mail: jrankin@drybones.com. Website: http://www. drybones.com/. Jim Rankin, ed/pub. Nursing and specialty books. Publishes 2-3 titles/yr. Receives 10 submissions annually. 90% of books from first-time authors. Open to subsidy publishing. Reprints books. Prefers 50-200 pgs (unless poetry, special topic or tract). Royalty 6-10% on retail or as per arrangement; no advance. Average first printing 1,000. Publication within 18-24 mos. Considers simultaneous submissions. Requires disk. Responds in 1-2 mos. No guidelines; catalog for 6x9 SAE/3 stamps.

Nonfiction: Proposal/table of contents & chapters 1-3; fax/e-query OK. "Looking for books written by patients about their experience of illness."

Fiction: Proposal/1-3 chapters. Adults.

Also Does: Pamphlets, booklets, tracts.

Tips: "Most open to liturgical books, e.g. psalter; poetry, if not overly trite or sentimental; patient experiences, if well-told and suitable to examination along with professional literature."

*EDITORIAL CARIBE, 9300 S. Dadeland Blvd. Ste. 203, Miami FL 33156. (800)322-7423. Subsidiary of Thomas Nelson. Targets the needs and wants of the Hispanic community.

*EDITORIAL PORTAVOZ, PO Box 2607, Grand Rapids MI 49333. (616)451-4775. (800)733-2607. Fax (616)451-9330. Website: http://www.portavoz. com. Spanish Division of Kregel Publishing.

+EERDMANS BOOKS FOR YOUNG READERS, 255 Jefferson SE, Grand Rapids MI 49503. (616)459-4591. Fax (616)459-6540. E-mail: jzylstra@ eerdmans.com. Wm. B. Eerdmans Publishing. Judy Zylstra, ed-in-chief. Books that nurture children's faith in God and help children and young people understand and explore life in God's world. Publishes 10-12 titles/yr. Receives 1,500-2,000 submissions annually. 5% of books from first-time authors. Age-appropriate length. Royalty 5- $6\frac{1}{4}$% of retail; advance to previously published authors. Average first printing 10,000 (picture books) and 5,000-6,000 (chapter books/novels). Publication within 18 mos. Considers simultaneous submissions. Responds in 2-4 mos. Guidelines; catalog for 9x12 SAE/4 stamps.

Nonfiction: Proposal/3 chapters for book-length; complete ms for picture books. For children and teens.

Fiction: Proposal/3 chapters for book-length; complete ms for picture books. For children and teens.

Tips: "Please do not send illustrations with picture book manuscripts unless you are a professional illustrator. When submitting artwork, send color copies, not originals. "

WM B. EERDMANS PUBLISHING CO., 255 Jefferson Ave. SE, Grand Rapids MI 49503. (616)459-4591. Fax (616)459-6540. Protestant/Academic/Theological. Jon Pott, ed-in-chief. Publishes 200 titles/yr. Receives 2,000 submissions annually. 5% of books from first-time authors. Reprints books. Royalty. Average first printing 4,000. Publication within 1 yr. Considers simultaneous submissions. Responds in 3-4 wks Guidelines (also by e-mail: akayayan@eerdmans.com, send name and address); free catalog.

Nonfiction: Proposal/2 chapters; fax query OK. "Looking for religious approaches to contemporary issues; spiritual growth; scholarly works; biography for middle readers through young adults; children's picture books expressing positive family values."

Fiction: Query letter only. Children/teen/adult. "We are looking for adult novels with high literary merit. For our children's program we look for manuscripts that help a child explore life in God's world, and to foster a child's exploration of her or his faith."

Ethnic Books: Spanish imprint is Nueva Creacion.

Tips: "Most open to material with general appeal, but well researched, cutting-edge material that bridges the gap between evangelical and mainline worlds."

**Note: This publisher serviced by The Writer's Edge.

ELDER BOOKS, PO Box 490, Forest Knolls CA 94933. (415)488-9002. Carmel Sheridan, dir. Publishes 6-10 titles/yr. Receives 250 submissions annually. 50% of books from first-time authors. Reprints books. Prefers 130 pgs. Royalty 7% of retail; no advance. Average first printing 3,000. Publication within 9 months. Responds in 3 mos.

Nonfiction: Proposal/2 chapters. "Most open to parenting, health, women's or seniors' issues."

ELDRIDGE PUBLISHING CO., INC., PO Box 1595, Venice FL 34284. (800)95-CHURCH. Fax (800)453-5179. E-mail: info@95church.com. Website: http://www.95church.com. Independent Christian drama publisher. Dottie Dunham, religion ed. To provide superior religious drama to enhance preaching and teaching, whatever your Christian faith. Publishes 35 plays/yr. Receives 350-400 plays annually. 75% of plays from first-time authors. One-act to full-length plays. Outright purchases of $100-1,000; no advance. Publication within 1 yr. Considers simultaneous submissions. Responds in 1-3 mos. Requires disk or e-mail submission. Free guidelines (also by e-mail or Website)/catalog.

Plays: Complete ms; e-query OK. For children, teens and adults.

Special Needs: Always looking for high quality Christmas and Easter plays but open to other holiday and "anytime" Christian plays too. Can be biblical or current day, for performance by all ages, children through adult.

Tips: "Have play produced at your church and others prior to submission, to get out the bugs. At least try a stage reading. T-shirts, posters and sound effects tapes accompany our dramas."

ELEMENT BOOKS, 160 N. Washington St., Boston MA 02114. (617)915-9400. Fax (617)248-9494. E-mail: element@cove.com. Website: http://www.east west.com/Element. Roberta Scimone, acq ed. Books for broad religious market. Publishes 100 titles/yr. Receives hundreds of submissions annually. 15% of books from first-time authors. Reprints books. Prefers 125-250 pgs. Variable royalty & advance. Average first printing 3,000-5,000. Publication within 18 mos. Considers simultaneous submissions. Responds in 6-8 wks. Free guidelines (also by e-mail) & catalog.

Nonfiction: Query only; no phone query; e-query OK.

Tips: "Try to reach a broad-based market—no books on very scholarly or limited-interest subjects."

+ERICA HOUSE, PO Box 1109, Frederick MD 21702. (301)631-9073. Fax (301)631-1922. E-mail: eribooks@ericahouse.com. Website: http://www. ericahouse.com. Willem Meiners, ed; submit to Mae Argilan. Casting a bright light in the darkness. Publishes 5-10 titles/yr. Receives 250 submissions annually. 75% of books from first-time authors. Various payment arrangements. Publication within 1 yr. Considers simultaneous submissions. No disk or e-mail. Responds in up to 6 mos. Guidelines (also by e-mail/Website)/catalog on Website.

Nonfiction: Query only; e-query preferred."Always looking for works about/for people who overcome steep challenges in life."

Fiction: Query only. For all ages.

Tips: "We encourage new talent to contact us."

FACTS ON FILE, 11 Penn Plaza, New York NY 10001. (212)967-8800. Website: http://factsonfile.com. Infobase Holdings. Laurie Likoff, ed. School and library reference and trade books tied to curriculum and areas of cross-cultural studies, including religion. Publishes 3-5 titles/yr. Receives 10-20 submissions annually. 2% of books from first-time authors. Prefers 224-480 pgs. Royalty 8-15% on retail; outright purchases of $2,000-10,000; advance $5,000. Some work for hire. Average first printing 5,000. Publication within 9-12 mos. Considers simultaneous submissions. Responds in 4-6 wks. Requires disk. Free guidelines/catalog.

Nonfiction: Query or proposal/2 chapters; fax/e-query OK.

FOCUS PUBLISHING, 1375 Washington Ave. S., Bemidji MN 56601. (218)759-9817. Fax (218)751-2183. E-mail: focus@paulbunyan.net. Website: http://www.paulbunyan.net/focus. Jan Haley, V.P. Does Christian books geared toward children and homeschooling families. Publishes 4-6 titles/yr. Receives 350 submissions annually. 90% of books from first-time authors. Reprints books. Royalty 7-10% on retail; no advance. Publication within 1 yr. Responds in 2 mos. Free catalog.

Nonfiction: Proposal. Adult Bible study books. Also hopes to build their children's dept.

Fiction: Query with synopsis. "Need Christian fiction for children, men, and young adults."

Tips: "Include your target market with proposals, and send SASE."

Note: Full through the year 2000.

*FOCUS ON THE FAMILY PUBLISHERS, 8605 Explorer Dr., Colorado Springs CO 80920-1051. (719)531-3496. Fax (719)531-3484. Website: http://www.family.org. Larry Weeden, mng ed. Dedicated to the preservation of marriage and the family. Publishes 15-20 titles/yr. Receives 2,000 submissions annually. Prefers 200 pgs. Average first printing 25,000. Publication within 1 yr. Considers simultaneous submissions. Responds in 6-8 wks. Free guidelines.

Nonfiction: Submit ONLY a 1-pg query letter.

Tips: "Need highly practical books—tell how to do something and don't make it too complicated. Also looking for writers who are verbal and can do a good, lively interview."

**Note: This publisher serviced by The Writer's Edge.

FOG (FRIENDS OF GOD) PUBLISHING HOUSE, PO Box 2703, Houston TX 77252-2703. (713)759-0207. Submit to The Editor. To be a servant of God, so that all will boast in the Lord and know His grace. Publishes 5+ titles/yr. Receives 200 submissions annually. 20% of books from first-time authors. Negotiated royalty; no advance. Average first printing 5,000. Publication within 8 mos. Considers simultaneous submissions. Requires disk on request. Responds in 2 mos. Guidelines; no catalog.

Nonfiction: Complete ms only; no phone query.

Fiction: Complete ms only. "Must be classic/timeless stories stressing values gained through learned experience."

Special Needs: Will consider computer games, especially if created for MACINTOSH.

Tips: "Must be extremely well researched and well written. We toss anything remotely unprofessional." Does not return manuscripts.

Note: They are creating a Website and plan to do electronic publishing.

FORTRESS PRESS, 100 S. 5th St., Suite 700 (55402), Box 1209, Minneapolis MN 55440-1209. (612)330-3300. Fax (612)330-3215. No longer accepting freelance submissions.

FORWARD MOVEMENT PUBLICATIONS, 412 Sycamore St., Cincinnati OH 45202. (513)721-6659. Fax (513)721-0729. E-mail: forwardmovement @msn.com. Website: http://www.forwardmovement.org. Episcopal. Edward S. Gleason, ed/dir. Publishes 12 titles/yr. Receives 50 submissions annually. 50% of books from first-time authors. No mss through agents. Rarely reprints books. Prefers 150 pgs. One-time honorarium; no advance. Average first printing 5,000. Publication within 9 mos. Reluctantly considers simultaneous submissions. Prefers disk. Responds in 1-2 mos. Guidelines; catalog for 6 stamps (no envelope).

Nonfiction: Query for book, complete ms if short; fax/e-query OK.

Fiction: Query. For children and teens."We are just beginning to publish fiction for middle-school readers."

Ethnic Books: Hispanic pamphlets.

Also Does: Booklets, 4-32 pgs; and pamphlets 4-8 pgs.

Tips: "We sell primarily to a mainline Protestant audience."

FRANCISCAN UNIVERSITY PRESS, 1235 University Blvd., Steubenville OH 43952. (740)283-6357 or (800)783-6357. Fax (614)283-6427. E-mail: fuspress@franuniv.edu. Website: http://www.franuniv.edu. Catholic/Franciscan University of Steubenville. James Fox, exec. dir. To provide literature to inform and inspire readers on their pilgrimage of faith. Publishes 7 titles/yr. Receives 50 submissions annually. 5% of books from first-time authors. No mss through agents. Reprints books. Prefers 300 pgs. Royalty 5-15% on retail; no advance. Average first printing 3,000. Publication within 1 yr. Considers simultaneous submissions. Prefers disk. Responds 3 mos. Free guidelines/catalog.

Nonfiction: Proposal/3 chapters. "Looking for Catholic apologetic/catechetical books in a popular vein."

Ethnic Books: "Spanish translations of our best-selling devotional works."

Also Does: Pamphlets, booklets, tracts.

Tips: "Most of our books are solicited from university professors and associates."

FRIENDS UNITED PRESS, 101 Quaker Hill Dr., Richmond IN 47374. (765)962-7573. Fax (765)966-1293. E-mail: friendspress@xc.org. Website: http://www.fum.org. Friends United Meeting (Quaker). Barbara Bennett Mays, ed. To gather persons into a fellowship where Jesus Christ is known as Lord and Teacher. Publishes 4-6 titles/yr. Receives 50-75 submissions annually. 80% of books from first-time authors. No mss through agents. Rarely does subsidy, 5%. Reprints books. Prefers 200 pgs. Royalty 7.5% of net; no advance. Average first printing 1,000-1,500. Publication within 1 yr. Considers simultaneous submissions. Responds in 4-6 mos. Prefers disk or e-mail submissions. Guidelines (also on Website); free catalog.

Nonfiction: Proposal/2 chapters; fax/e-query OK.

Fiction: Proposal/2 chapters. For all ages. Very limited. "Quaker faith must be a significant part of the story or the characters."

Ethnic Books: Howard Thurman Books (African American).

Tips: "Most open to Quaker authors. Looking for Quaker-related spirituality, or current faith issues/practice addressed from a Quaker experience or practice."

GILGAL PUBLICATIONS, Box 3399, Sunriver OR 97707. (541)593-8418. Fax (541)593-5604. Judy Osgood, exec. ed. Focuses on collections of meditations on specific themes. Publishes 1 title/yr. Receives 100+ submissions annually. 25-30% of submissions from first-time authors. No mss through agents. Pays $25/meditation on acceptance, plus 2 copies of the book. Average first printing 3,000. Publication time varies. Responds in 1-2 mos. No disk. Guidelines (required).

Nonfiction: Complete ms (after reading guidelines); fax query OK. "Our books are all anthologies on coping with stress and resolving grief. Not interested in other book mss. Currently interested in meditations on bereavement of various kinds."

Tips: "Our readers are hungry for shared experiences."

*B.J. GOETZ PUBLISHING CO., 3055 W. John Beers Rd., Stevensville MI 49127. (616)429-6442. Fax (616)429-5353. B.J. Goetz, pub. Specializes in materials to enhance Christian education programs; experiential/environmental concepts. Publishes 1 title/yr. Receives 12 submissions annually. 100% of books from first-time authors. Variable payment for outright purchase. Average first printing 1,000. Responds in 1-3 mos. Catalog.

Nonfiction: Proposal or complete ms. "We need an interdenominational approach in Christian education programs or Bible studies for children 5-12."

GOLD 'N' HONEY BOOKS/MULTNOMAH. Children's books imprint for Multnomah Publishers.

GOOD BOOK PUBLISHING COMPANY, PO Box 837, Kihei HI 96753-0837. Phone/fax (808)874-4876. E-mail: dickb@dickb.com. Website: http://www. dickb.com. Christian/Protestant/Bible Fellowship. Ken Burns, pres. Researches and publishes books on the biblical/Christian roots of Alcoholics Anonymous. Publishes 1 title/yr. Receives 8 submissions annually. 80% of books from first-time authors. No mss through agents. Reprints books. Prefers 250 pgs. Royalty 10%; no advance. Average first printing 3,000. Publication within 2 mos. Considers simultaneous submission. Responds in 1 wk. No disk. No guidelines; free catalog.

Nonfiction: Proposal; no phone/fax/e-query. Books on the spiritual history and success of A.A.; 12-step spiritual roots.

Also Does: Pamphlets and booklets.

GOOD NEWS PUBLISHERS, 1300 Crescent St., Wheaton IL 60187. (630)682-4300x308. Fax (630)682-4785. E-mail: gdennis@goodnews-crossway.org. Geoffrey Dennis, mngr. Tracts only; publishing the gospel message in an attractive and relevant format. Publishes 30 tracts/yr. Receives 500 submissions annually. 2% of tracts from first-time authors. Prefers 650-800 wds. Pays about $150 or a quantity of tracts. Average first printing 250,000. Publication within 8 mos. Considers simultaneous submissions. Responds in 6 wks. Guidelines; free tract catalog.

Tracts: Complete ms.

Also Does: Booklets.

GOSPEL LIGHT PUBLICATIONS—See Regal Books.

GOSPEL PUBLISHING HOUSE, 1445 Boonville Ave., Springfield MO 65802. (417)862-2781. Glen Ellard, sr. book ed. Supports the pastors and churches of the Assemblies of God. Publishes 3-5 nondepartmental and 7-9 departmental titles/yr. Receives 260 submissions annually. 33-50% of books from first-time authors. Reprints books. Prefers 50,000 wds or 160 pgs. Royalty on net; no advance. Average first printing 5,000. Publication within 12-18 mos. Considers simultaneous submissions. Responds in 4 wks. Requires disk. Guidelines.

Nonfiction: Query only; no phone query.

Special Needs: Books on Pentecostal and pastoral leadership; Holy Spirit; deaf culture ministries.

Ethnic Books: Hispanic.

Also Does: Booklets.

Tips: "Any books related to departmental ministries would require the interest and support of the corresponding department (such as Christian education or youth)."

GROUP PUBLISHING, INC., Box 481, Loveland CO 80539. (970)669-3836. Fax (970)679-4370. E-mail: kloesche@grouppublishing.com. Website: http://www.grouppublishing.com. Non-denominational. Kerri Loesche, ed asst. Imprints: Group Books and Vital Ministry. Encourages Christian growth in children, youth and adults. Publishes 50 titles/yr. Receives 300-400 submissions annually. 5% of books from first-time authors. No mss through agents. Reprints books. Prefers 200 pgs. Outright purchases; no advance. Average first printing 6,500. Publication within 12-18 mos. Considers simultaneous submissions. Responds in 3 mos. Prefers disk. Guidelines (also by e-mail); catalog for 9x12 SAE/2 stamps.

> **Nonfiction:** Query only; fax/e-query OK. "Most open to practical ministry tools for pastors, youth workers, C.E. directors, and teachers with an emphasis on active learning. Read *Why Nobody Learns Much of Anything at Church: And How to Fix It* and *The Dirt on Learning* by Thom & Joani Schultz."

+GROUP'S FAITHWEAVER BIBLE CURRICULUM, Box 481, Loveland CO 80539. (970)669-3836. Fax (970)669-4370. E-mail: kloesche@group publishing.com. Website: http://www.grouppublishing.com. Kerri Loesche, ed asst. Publishes 24 titles/yr. Receives 200 submissions annually. 40% of books from first-time authors. No mss through agents. Outright purchase. Publication within 12-18 mos. Responds in 3 mos. Accepts disk. Trial assignment guidelines (also by e-mail)/catalog for 9x12 SAE/2 stamps.

> **Nonfiction:** Query requesting a trial assignment for children or youth; phone/fax query OK. Produces curriculum for preschoolers, 1st-2nd, 3rd-4th, 5th-6th graders; junior highs and senior highs. Submissions received are only kept on file for 30 days.

GUERNICA EDITIONS, PO Box 117, Stn. P, Toronto ON M5S 2S6 Canada. (616)658-9888. Fax (616)657-8885. E-mail: 102026:1331@compuserve. com. Website: http://www.compuserve.com/homepage/Guernica. Toward creating an essential library. Antonio D'Alfonso, ed. Publishes 1 religious title/yr. Receives 50 submissions annually. 10% of books from first-time authors. No mss through agents. Reprints books. Prefers 128 pgs. Royalty 7-10% of net; advance $1,000. Average first printing 1,000. Publication within 18-24 mos. Responds in 1 mo. Requires disk; no e-mail. No guidelines (read one of our books to see what we like); for catalog send money order for stamps (if from US).

> **Nonfiction:** Query first; no phone query. "Looking for books on world issues."
>
> **Fiction:** Query first. Interested in ethnic and translations.
>
> **Ethnic Books:** Concentration on other cultures. "We are involved in translations and ethnic issues."

Tips: "Know what we publish. We're in a transitional period, so try us."

HARPERSANFRANCISCO, 353 Sacramento St. #500, San Francisco CA 94111-1213. (415)477-4400. Fax (415)477-4444. E-mail: hcsanfrancisco@ harpercollins. com. Website: http://www.harpercollins.com. Religious division of HarperCollins. David Hennessy, sr ed asst. Dedicated to publishing books of highest quality that illuminate diverse religious traditions and spiritual journeys and offer paths toward personal growth and holistic well-being. Publishes 36-46 titles/yr. Receives 200-300 submissions annually. 10% of books from first-time authors. Prefers 160-256 ms pgs. Royalty 10-15% on cloth, 7.5% on paperback, on retail; advance $20,000-50,000. Average first printing 7,500-10,000. Publication within 8-12 mos. Considers simultaneous submissions. Responds in 3-4 mos. Requires disk. No guidelines/catalog.

   Nonfiction: Query only; fax query OK.

   Tips: "Agented proposals get a good deal more attention in-house. "

   **Note: This publisher serviced by The Writer's Edge.

HARRISON HOUSE PUBLISHERS, Box 35035, Tulsa OK 74153. (918)494-5944. Evangelical/Charismatic. This company is booked up for the next 3-4 years.

HARVEST HOUSE PUBLISHERS, 1075 Arrowsmith, Eugene OR 97402. (541)343-0123. Evangelical. Books and products that affirm biblical principles and help people grow spiritually strong. Publishes 100 titles/yr. No longer accepting unsolicited submissions, proposals, queries, etc.

   **Note: This publisher serviced by The Writer's Edge and ECPA First Edition Website.

#THE HAWORTH PASTORAL PRESS, An imprint of The Haworth Press, 10 Alice St., Binghamton NY 13904-1580. (607)722-5857. Fax (607)722-6362. Website: http://www.haworthpressinc.com. Bill Palmer, mng ed. Publishes 10 titles/yr. Receives 100 submissions annually. 50% of books from first-time authors. Reprints books. Prefers up to 250 pgs. Royalty 7½-15% of net; advance $500-1,000. Average first printing 1,500. Publication within 1 yr. Requires disk. Responds in 2 mos. Guidelines; free catalog.

   Nonfiction: Proposal/3 chapters; no phone/fax query. "Looking for books on psychology/social work, etc., with a pastoral perspective."

+HAY HOUSE, PO Box 5100, Carlsbad CA 92018-5100. (760)431-7695. Fax (760)431-6948. E-mail: HayHouseSD@aol.com. Website: http://www. hayhouse.com. Jill Kramer, ed dir. Books to help heal the planet. Publishes 4 titles/yr. Receives 200 submissions annually. 60% of books from first-time authors. Prefers 70,000 wds or 250 pgs. Royalty; advance. Average first printing 5,000. Publication within 10 mos. Considers simultaneous submissions. Requires disk. Responds in 1 mo. Guidelines; free catalog.

   Nonfiction: Proposal/3 chapters; fax/e-mail query OK. "Looking for self-help/spiritual with a unique angle."

   Fiction: Query only. Rarely publishes fiction."Only accept spiritual, adult fiction, if by a well-known author."

   Also Does: Some gift books and flip books.

Tips: "We are looking for books with a unique slant, ecumenical, but not overly religious. "

#HEALTH COMMUNICATIONS, 3201 S. 15th St., Deerfield Beach FL 33442. (954)360-0909. Fax (954)472-7288. Website: http://www.hci-online.com. Christiane Belleris, ed dir. Nonfiction that emphasizes self-improvement, personal motivation, psychological health and overall wellness; recovery/ addiction, self-help/psychology, health/wellness, soul/spirituality, inspiration, women's issues, relationships and family. Publishes 40 titles/yr. 20% of books from first-time authors. Prefers 250 pgs. Royalty 15% of net. Publication within 9 mos. Considers simultaneous submissions. Responds in 1-3 mos. Must get and follow guidelines for submission. Guidelines; catalog for 9x12 SASE. Not in topical listings.

Nonfiction: Query/outline & 2 chapters; no phone query.

+HEART ARBOR BOOKS, 5061 Forest Rd., Mentor Road OH44060. Karla Whitsitt, pub. No response to questionnaire; send SASE for guidelines.

HEARTH PUBLISHING, 212 N. Ash, Hillsboro KS 67063. (316)947-3966. Fax (316)947-3392. Stan Thiessen, ed/dir. Wholesome literature of a classic nature, not necessarily religious. Publishes 4-6 titles/yr. Receives 600 submissions annually. 80+% of books from first-time authors. No mss through agents. Reprints books. Prefers 96-224 pgs (poetry 96 pgs). Negotiable royalty and advance. Average first printing 1,500-20,000. Publication within 8+ mos. Considers simultaneous submissions. Responds in 1-3 mos. Requires disk. Guidelines; no catalog.

Nonfiction: Proposal/3-4 chapters; no phone/fax query. "Any topic, including genealogy and cookbooks."

Fiction: Proposal/3-4 chapters. "Looking for juvenile and young adult (7-12) series or single books, classic adventure, fun to read; should fit secular markets as well as religious. Call about ongoing anthologies."

Also Does: Booklets and chapbooks.

Tips: "Most open to books espousing Christian ethics but not necessarily religious. Good, wholesome adventure of any kind. Specialty cookbooks."

+HEART QUEST/TYNDALE HOUSE PUBLISHERS, PO Box 80, Wheaton IL 60189-0080. (630)668-8300. Fax (630)668-6885. Website: http://www.tyndale. com. Catherine Palmer, consulting ed; Rebekah Nesbitt, acq ed. Romance imprint. To encourage and challenge readers in their faith journey and/or Christian walk. Responds in 3 mos. Guidelines.

Fiction: One-page query/synopsis/3chapters."Must incorporate three plot lines—action, emotional, and faith (see guidelines for details). None set in Civil War period." Also considering novellas for anthologies (Victorian and Prairie).

Tips: "We want only historical romances (set in 1600-1945), contemporary romances, novellas and series (no stand-alone romances)."

HEARTSONG PRESENTS, Imprint of Barbour Publishing, Inc., PO Box 719, 1810 Barbour Dr., Uhrichsville, OH 44683. (614)922-6045. Fax (614)922-5948. E-mail: rgermany@barbourbooks.com. Website: http://www. barbourbooks.com. Rebecca Germany, ed; Tracie Peterson, acq ed. Produces affordable, wholesome entertainment through a book club that also helps to enhance and spread the Gospel. Publishes 52 titles/yr. Receives 700+ submissions annually. 25-35% of books from first-time authors. Prefers 50,000-55,000 wds. Outright purchases $2,000-2,500; rare advance. Average first printing 20,000. Publication within 6-9 months. Considers simultaneous submissions. Responds in 6-9 wks. Requires disk. Guidelines; no catalog.

> **Fiction:** Proposal/3-4 chapters; fax/e-query OK. "We publish 2 contemporary and 2 historical romances every 4 weeks. We cover all topics and settings. Specific guidelines available."

> **Tips:** "Most open to romance with a strong conservative-Christian theme. Read our books and study our style before submitting."

HENDRICKSON PUBLISHERS, 140 Summit St., PO Box 3473, Peabody MA 01961. (508)532-2248. Fax (508)532-8248. E-mail: DPenwell@hendrick son. com. Dan Penwell, mngr of trade products. To provide biblically oriented books for reference, learning and personal growth. Publishes 30-40 titles/yr. Receives 100-150 submissions annually. 25% of books from first-time authors. Reprints books. Prefers 200-500 pgs. Royalty 10-14% of net; some advances. Average first printing 3,000. Publication within 9-12 mos. Considers simultaneous submissions. Responds in 1-2 mos. Prefers e-mail submissions. Follow *Chicago Manual of Style*. Guidelines(also by e-mail); catalog for 9x12 SAE/6 stamps.

> **Nonfiction:** Query/summary or sample chapters; fax/e-query OK. Also publishes academic books through their Academic Book Division.

> **Special Needs:** Books that help the reader's confrontation and interaction with Scripture, leading to a positive change in thought and action; books that give a hunger to studying, understanding and applying Scripture; books that encourage and facilitate personal growth in such areas as personal devotions and a skillful use of the Bible.

> **Tips:** "A well-organized, thought-provoking, clear, and accurate proposal has the best chance of being read and accepted."

> ****Note:** This publisher serviced by The Writer's Edge.

HENSLEY PUBLISHING, 6116 E. 32nd St., Tulsa OK 74135. (918)664-8520. Fax (918)664-8562. E-mail: neal@hensleypublishing.com. Website: http://www.hensleypublishing.com.Terri Kalfas, ed dir. To edify and challenge the readers to a higher level of spiritual maturity in their Christian walk. Publishes 5-10 titles/yr. Receives 800 submissions annually. 50% of books from first-time authors. Reprints books. Prefers up to 250 pgs. Royalty 5% on net; some outright purchases of $250 & up; no advance. Average first printing 5,000. Publication within 18 mos. Considers simultaneous submissions. Disk required in MAC format; no e-mail. Responds in 2 mos. Guidelines (also on Website); catalog for 9x12 SAE/2 stamps.

> **Nonfiction:** Query or proposal/3 consecutive chapters, or complete ms; no phone/fax/e-query. "Looking for short, inspirational-study, adaptable to our new format, for use by small or large groups or individuals."

> **Ethnic Books:** Will have a limited number of titles available this year.

Tips: "Most open to a Bible study that can be used by anyone; no denominational influences."

+HENRY HOLT & COMPANY BOOKS FOR YOUNG READERS, 115 W. 18th St., New York NY 10011. (212)886-9200. Henry Holt & Co., Inc. Submit to BYR Submissions. Cutting-edge fiction and nonfiction for the very young through young adults; some religious. Publishes 70-80 titles/yr. 5% of books from first-time authors. Royalty on retail; advance $3,000 & up. Publication within 18 mos. Responds in 5 mos. Guidelines; catalog for 9x12 SAE/5 stamps.

    Nonfiction: Query. Juvenile illustrated books.

    Fiction: Query. Picture books, chapter books, novels.

HOLY CROSS ORTHODOX PRESS, 50 Goddard Ave., Brookline MA 02445. (617)731-3500. Fax (617)850-1460. Greek Orthodox. Anton C. Vrame, mng ed. Academic and general works of interest to Orthodox Christians in church history, worship, spirituality and life. Publishes 8-10 titles/yr. Receives 15-20 submissions annually. 50% of books from first-time authors. No mss through agents. Reprints bks. Prefers 200-300 pgs. Royalty 8-12% on retail; no advance. Average first printing 750-1,000. Publication within 12-18 mos. Considers simultaneous submissions. Requires disk (MAC). Responds in 3-4 mos. Free catalog.

    Nonfiction: Complete ms. Also open to saints and iconography. "Most open to a book on historic Orthodox Christianity with a sound theological basis."

    Ethnic Books: Greek (orthodox).

HONOR BOOKS, PO Box 55388, Tulsa OK 74155. (918)496-9007. Fax (918)496-3588. Website: http://www.HonorBooks.com. Inspirational/devotional. Catherine Dodd, acq sec. To inspire, encourage, and motivate readers to draw nearer to God, to experience His love and grace. Publishes 60+ titles/yr. Receives 2,200 submissions annually. 2% of books from first-time authors. Royalty on net, outright purchase or work-for-hire assignments; negotiable advance. Publication within 2 yrs. Considers simultaneous submissions. Responds in 1-6 mos. Guidelines.

    Nonfiction: Proposal/2 chapters. Send photocopies.

    Special Needs: Seasonal gift books; third-person stories reflecting God's wisdom applied to everyday life, in a devotional format.

    Tips: "Our books are for busy, achievement-oriented people who are looking for balance between reaching their goals and knowing that God loves them unconditionally. Our books should challenge spiritual growth, victorious living, and an intimate knowledge of God. Write about what you are for, not what you are against. We look for scripts that are biblically correct and which edify the reader."

HOWARD PUBLISHING CO., INC., 3117 N. 7th St., West Monroe LA 71291. (318)396-3122 Fax (318)397-1882. E-mail: dennyb@howardpublishing. com. Website: http://www.howardpublishing.com. John Howard, pres.; submit to Denny Boultinghouse. Christian publisher. Publishes 23-28 titles/yr. Receives 250 submissions annually. 20% of books from first-time authors. Prefers 200-250 pgs. Negotiable royalty & advance. Average first printing 10,000. Publication within 1 yr. Considers simultaneous submissions. Responds in 4-6 wks. No disk. Free guidelines/catalog.

Nonfiction: Proposal/3 chapters; no phone query.

Tips: "Our authors must first be Christ-centered in their lives and writing, then qualified to write on the subject of choice. Public name recognition is a plus. Authors who are also public speakers usually have a ready-made audience."

HUNT AND THORPE, Deershot Lodge, Park Lane, Ropley, Hants, UK S024 OBE. (01962) 735320. John Hunt, ed. Children's books for the international Christian market. Publishes 25 titles/yr. Receives 100 submissions annually. 1% of books from first-time authors. Prefers 1,000 wds or 10 pgs for color books. Royalty 5-10% on net; advance $500. Average first printing 20,000. Publication within 2 yrs. No simultaneous submissions. Responds in 1 mo. No disk. Free catalog.

Nonfiction: Proposal/1 chapter; no phone query.

Fiction: For young teens to age 20. No children's fiction.

+HUNTINGTON HOUSE, PO Box 53788, Lafayette LA 70505. (318)237-7049. Fax (318)237-7060. Mark Anthony, ed. Focus is on educating readers on current events and the culture war. Publishes 25-30 titles/yr. Receives 1,500 submissions annually. 25% of books from first-time authors. Reprints books. Prefers 50,000-60,000 wds or 208-224 pgs. Royalty 10% on net; negotiable advance. Average first printing 5,000-10,000. Publication within 1 yr. Considers simultaneous submissions. Responds in 4 mos. Guidelines; free catalog.

Nonfiction: Proposal. "Looking for political, social, current events, One World Government exposes, and anti-New Age. "

Fiction: Query. For all ages.

Also Does: Pamphlets and booklets.

Tips: "Authors must be available to perform interviews at our expense. "

#ICS PUBLICATIONS, 2131 Lincoln Rd NE, Washington DC 20002. (202)832-8489. Fax (202)832-8967. Website: http://www.ocd.or.at/ics. Catholic/Institute of Carmelite Studies. Steven Payne, OCD, ed. dir. For those interested in the Carmelite tradition with focus on prayer and spirituality. Publishes 8 titles/yr. Receives 30 submissions annually. 10% of books from first-time authors. Reprints books. Prefers 200 pgs. Royalty 2-6% on retail; some outright purchases; advance $500. Average first printing 3,000-7,000. Publication within 2 yrs. Considers simultaneous submissions. Responds in 2 mos. Guidelines; catalog for 7x10 SAE/2 stamps.

Nonfiction: Query or outline/1 chapter; phone query OK. "Most open to translation of Carmelite classics; popular introductions to Carmelite themes which show a solid grasp of the tradition."

IN CELEBRATION, a division of Instructional Fair/TS Denison, 2400 Turner NW, Grand Rapids MI 49544. (616)363-1290. Fax (616)363-2156. E-mail: akieda@tribune.com. Alyson Kieda, prod mgr. Producer of specialty products, including cards and books. 90% freelance. Query or outright submission. Pays varying amounts on acceptance for all rts. Rarely pays royalties. Responds in 4-8 wks. Does a few inspirational or religious cards (doesn't need cards, but will look at ideas). Open to ideas for new card lines or specialty products. Send 1-2 ideas. Open to ideas for audio tapes, banners, clip-art books, coloring books, computer software, craft/activity books, post cards, posters, puzzles, stickers, note pads, award certificates, parent/teacher resources, children's books for church/home. Guidelines; free catalog.

Tips: "Open to new book ideas. Looking for authors/artists to produce books to match our ideas."

+INFINITY PUBLISHING CO., 17400 South Blvd., Gulfport MS 39503. (228)863-5916. Nora Collins, pub. Publishes poetry anthologies. August 31 each year is the deadline for poems for their annual winter book project.

Special Needs: Send 1 or 2 original poems of 24 lines or less on any topic. Poems will not be returned. Any that miss the deadline will automatically be considered for the next year's book project.

*INHERITANCE PUBLICATIONS, Box 154, Neerlandia AB T0G 1R0 Canada. (403)674-3949. No response to questionnaire.

INNISFREE PRESS, 136 Roumfort Rd., Philadelphia PA 19119-1632. (215)247-4085. Fax (215)247-2343. E-mail: InnisfreeP@aol.com. Website: http://www.innisfreepress.com. Marcia Broucek, ed-in-chief. Specializes in books that go beyond traditional boundaries to investigate all aspects of spirituality. Publishes 8 titles/yr. Receives 500 submissions annually. 60% of books from first-time authors. Prefers 40,000-50,000 wds. Royalty 10% of net; advance $500. Average first printing 5,000. Publication within 1 yr. Considers simultaneous submissions. Responds in 6 wks. Requires disk. Free guidelines (also on Website)/catalog.

Nonfiction: Proposal/2 chapters; no phone/fax/e-query. "Looking for books with a spiritual perspective on everyday living in the workplace, in relationships, in personal growth."

Tips: "Looking for books that demonstrate original thinking, not a rehash of what is already available in other forms." Books with personal experience and women's perspective are of special interest.

INTERNATIONAL AWAKENING PRESS, 139 N. Washington, PO Box 232, Wheaton IL 60189. Phone/fax (630)653-8616. E-mail: international awakening@juno.com. Intl. Awakening Ministries, Inc. Richard Owen Roberts, pres. Scholarly books on religious awakenings or revivals. Publishes 4 titles/yr. Receives 12 submissions annually. Reprints books. Royalty 10% on retail; no advance. Average first printing 3,000. Publication within 6 mos. Responds in 3 mos. Requires disk. No guidelines; free catalog.

Nonfiction: Query only; no phone/fax query. "Looking for books on revival."

Also Does: Booklets, pamphlets, tracts.

INTERVARSITY PRESS, Box 1400, Downers Grove IL 60515. (630)887-2500. Fax (630)887-2520. E-mail: mail@ivpress.com. Website: http://www. ivpress.com. InterVarsity Christian Fellowship. Andrew T. LePeau, ed dir; submit to Rodney Clapp or Cindy Bunch Hotaling. To communicate the

Lordship of Christ in all of life through a serious-minded approach to Scripture, the church and the world. Imprint: LifeGuide Bible Studies. Publishes 80 titles/yr. Receives 450 submissions annually. 35% of books from first-time authors. Prefers 50,000 wds or 200 pgs. Negotiable royalty on retail; negotiable advance. Average first printing 5,500. Publication within 10 mos. Considers simultaneous submissions. Requires disk; no e-mail. Responds in 8-10 wks. Guidelines; catalog for 9x12 SAE/5 stamps.

Nonfiction: All unsolicited mss (from people they have had no previous contact with) are referred to The Writer's Edge (see their listing under Editorial Services—IL); fax/e-query OK. "Looking for academic and reference books."

Ethnic Books: Black, Hispanic, Asian.

Also Does: Booklets.

Tips: "We look for a thoughtful approach. We shy away from black and white treatments. Writers who are nuanced, subtle, discerning and perceptive will get farther at IVP."

**Note: This publisher serviced by The Writer's Edge.

JOSSEY-BASS INC., PUBLISHERS/RELIGION IN PRACTICE, 350 Sansome St., San Francisco CA 94104. (415)433-1740. Fax (415)433-0499. Website: http://www.josseybass.com. Simon & Shuster, Inc. Sarah Polster, ed. 25% of books from first-time authors. Royalty 10-15%. Publication within 1 yr. Considers simultaneous submissions. Responds in 1-2 mos. No e-mail submissions.

Nonfiction: Query or proposal."Our editorial mission is (1) to enrich people's understanding of the life and possibilities of congregations and other religious organizations, and (2) to aid in the education and development of those who serve in them, both as religious leaders and as committed, active laity. We also explore the role of religious institutions in their communities and in society as a whole."

JOURNEY BOOKS/BOB JONES UNIVERSITY PRESS, 1700 Wade Hampton Blvd., Greenville SC 29614. (864)370-1800x4350. Fax (864)298-0268 x4324. E-mail: grepp@bju.edu. Website: http://www.bjup.com. Bob Jones University Press. Gloria Repp, acq ed. Imprints: Light Line and Pennant Books. Goal is to publish books for children that excel in both literary and moral content. Publishes 8-10 titles/yr. Receives 500 submissions annually. 30% of books from first-time authors. Reprints books. Prefers up to 10,000 wds (depends on age group). Royalty on net; outright purchases of $1,000 (for first-time authors); advance $1,000. Average first printing 5,000. Publication within 12-18 months. Considers simultaneous submissions. Accepts disks. Responds in 4-6 wks. Guidelines (also by e-mail); catalog for 9x12 SAE/2 stamps.

Nonfiction: No phone/fax/e-query. Biography only; 10,000-30,000 wds.

Fiction: Proposal/5 chapters or complete ms. For children and teens; 8,000-40,000 wds; young adult 40,000-60,000 wds."Looking for humor or mystery; problem realism; historical fiction."

Also Does: Story cassettes and book sets.

Tips: "Most open to realistic or historical fiction for upper elementary through teens; biography with a good moral tine; or easy readers with satisfying content. Follow guidelines."

JUDSON PRESS, Box 851, Valley Forge PA 19482-0851. (610)768-2109. Fax (610)768-2441. Website: http://www.judsonpress.com. American Baptist Churches USA. Randy Frame, acq ed. Publishes 30 titles/yr. Receives 500 submissions annually. 50% of books from first-time authors. Reprints books. Prefers 160-180 pgs. Royalty 5-10% on retail; some work-for-hire agreements; advance $300. Average first printing 3,000. Publication within 9-18 mos. Considers simultaneous submissions. Responds in 2-3 mos. Prefers disk. Free guidelines/catalog.

Nonfiction: Proposal/2 chapters; phone query OK.

Ethnic Books: African-American and Asian-American.

Tips: "Authors should avoid books based primarily on their own experiences and personal reflections. Writing style must be engaging and the writer should be well qualified to address the topic. We want books that are unusually well-written."

**Note: This publisher serviced by The Writer's Edge.

*KALEIDOSCOPE PRESS, 2507 94th Ave. E., Edgewood WA 98371. Phone/fax (253)848-1116. Penny Lent, ed/pub. Providing tools for growth and enrichment that are unavailable. Publishes 7 titles/yr. Receives 175 submissions annually. 90% of books from first-time authors. No mss through agents. Reprints books. Variable length. Royalty 10% on retail; no advance. Average first printing 2,000. Publication within 1 yr. Considers simultaneous submissions. Responds in 2 mos. Requires disk. Guidelines; catalog for #10 SAE/1 stamp.

Nonfiction: Query letter only; no phone/fax query. "Actively seeking submissions of inspiration, short poetry, anecdotes, humor, short poetry, quips and quotes, and bizarre rejections from/about writers for a book in progress."

Fiction: For children only; also picture books. Query only. "Show us in your query how the piece is unique or needed in the marketplace."

Tips: "Most open to nonfiction that fills a need. Do and show your market research. Grab our interest."

KINDRED PRODUCTIONS, 169 Riverton Ave., Winnipeg MB R2L 2E5 Canada. (204)669-6575. Fax (204)654-1865. E-mail: kindred@cdnmbconf.ca. Website: http://www.mbconf.org/mbc/kp/kindred.htm. Mennonite Brethren. Marilyn Hudson, mgr. To resource the churches within the denomination (Anabaptist perspective) for Christ-like living and ministry. Publishes 3-4 titles/yr. Receives 60 submissions annually. 90% of books from first-time authors. **SUBSIDY PUBLISHES 5%.** Prefers 200-250 pgs. Royalty 10-15% on retail; no advance. Average first printing 1,000-2,000. Publication within 9-12 mos. Considers simultaneous submissions. Responds within 4-5 mos. Requires disk or e-mail. Free guidelines (also by e-mail)/catalog.

Nonfiction: Proposal/2 chapters; fax/e-query OK. Also does pamphlets and booklets. "Looking for inspirational books, story-based, with cross-over potential."

Tips: "Most open to inspirational books; maintain the human element in your writing. Stories, thoughts, and people need to be real. Also Bible studies from an evangelical point of view."

KREGEL PUBLICATIONS, PO Box 2607, Grand Rapids MI 49501. (616)451-4775. Fax (616)451-9330. E-mail: Editorial@kregel.com. Website: http://www. kregel.com. Evangelical/Conservative. Dennis R. Hillman, pub. To provide tools for ministry and Christian growth from a conservative, evangelical perspective. Publishes 60 titles/yr. Receives 250+ submissions annually. 20% of books from first-time authors. Reprints books. Royalty 8-16% of net; some outright purchases; $1,000-2,000 advance. Average first printing 5,000. Publication within 16 mos. Considers simultaneous submissions. Requires disk. Responds in 1-2 mos. Guidelines; catalog for 9x12 SAE/3 stamps.

> **Nonfiction:** Query only; fax/e-query OK.
>
> **Fiction:** Query only. Looking for biblical/historical fiction with strong Christian themes and characters.
>
> **Ethnic Books:** Spanish division: Editorial Portavoz.
>
> **Tips:** "Most open to biblically based books of practical Christian teaching or books of interest to the vocational Christian worker. Take the time to study our line of books and tell us how your book meets our needs."
>
> ****Note:** This publisher serviced by The Writer's Edge.

LANGMARC PUBLISHING, PO Box 33817, San Antonio TX 78265. (210)822-2521. Fax (210)822-5014. E-mail: langmarc@flash.net. Lutheran. Lois Qualben, pub. Focuses on spiritual growth of readers. Publishes 4 titles/yr. Receives 200 submissions annually. 50% of books from first-time authors. No mss through agents. Prefers 150-300 pgs. Royalty 8-10% on retail; no advance. Average first printing 1,500. Publication usually within 1 yr. Considers simultaneous submissions. Responds in 2-4 mos. Requires disk. Catalog for SASE.

> **Nonfiction:** Proposal/3 chapters; phone query OK. "Most open to inspirational, congregational leadership, or materials for teens."
>
> **Fiction:** Does some.

LIBROS LIGUORI, 1 Liguori Dr., Liguori MO 63125. (314)464-2500. Fax (314)464-8449. E-mail: LibrosLiguori@compuserve.com. Website: http://www. Liguori.org. Spanish division of Liguori Publications. Vincent Hamon-Enriquez, ed. To spread the gospel in the Hispanic community by means of low-cost publications. Publishes 15 titles/yr. Receives 6-8 submissions annually. 5% of books from first-time authors. Prefers up to 30,000 wds. Royalty 4-12% of net or outright purchases of $400 (book and booklet authors get royalties; pamphlet authors get $400 on acceptance); advance. Average first printing 3,500-5,000. Publication within 18 mos. No simultaneous submissions. Requires disk. Responds in 4-8 wks. Free guidelines/catalog.

> **Nonfiction:** Query first; fax/e-query OK. "Looking for issues families face today—substance abuse, unwanted pregnancies, etc.; family relations; religion's role in immigrant's experiences."

Ethnic Books: Focuses on Spanish-language products.

Also Does: Pamphlets and booklets; PC software, and clip art.

Tips: "Needs books on the Hispanic experience in the U.S. Keep it concise; avoid academic/theological jargon; and stick to the tenets of the Catholic faith—avoid abstract arguments."

LIFE CYCLE BOOKS, Box 420, Lewiston NY 14092. (416) 690-8532. Fax (416)690-5860. E-mail: pbroughton@lcbooks.com. Website: http://www.lifecyclebooks.com. Paul Broughton, gen mgr. Publishes 1-3 pro-life titles/yr. Receives 50 submissions annually. 50% of books from first-time authors. Reprints books. Royalty 8% of net; outright purchase of brochure material, $250+; advance $100-300. **SUBSIDY PUBLISHES 10%.** Publication within 10 mos. Responds in 6 wks. Free catalog.

Nonfiction: Query or complete ms. "Our emphasis is on pro-life and pro-family titles."

Tips: "We are most involved in publishing leaflets of about 1,500 wds, and welcome submissions of mss of this length."

#LIFETIME BOOKS, 2131 Hollywood Blvd., Hollywood FL 33020. (954)925-5242. Fax (954)925-5244. E-mail: lifetime@shadow.net. Website: http://www. lifetimebooks.com. Callie Rucker, sr ed. General publisher that publishes 2-4 religious titles/yr. Receives 100 submissions annually. 95% of books from first-time authors. Reprints books. Prefers 60,000 wds or 200-300 pgs. Royalty 6-15% on retail; advance of $500-10,000. Average first printing 10,000. Publication within 1 yr. Considers simultaneous submissions. Responds in 1-2 mos. Free guidelines/catalog.

Nonfiction: Proposal/1 chapter; fax query OK. Include a clear marketing and promotional strategy.

Tips: "Spirituality, optimism, and a positive attitude have international appeal. Steer clear of doom and gloom; less sadness and more gladness benefits all." Also publishes some New Age books.

*LIGHT AND LIFE COMMUNICATIONS, PO Box 535002, Indianapolis IN 46253-5002. Free Methodist. Submit to The Editor. Denominational publisher; publishes books that minister. Publishes 30 titles/yr. Receives 60 submissions annually. 33% of books from first-time authors. Reprints books. Royalty & advance negotiable. Publication within 6-12 mos. Reluctantly accepts simultaneous submissions. Responds in 6 wks. (or after next acquisitions committee meeting). Requires disk. Guidelines.

Nonfiction: Proposal/3 chapters.

Tips: "Most open to books that have obvious marketability; and books that speak more to the heart than to the head."

LIGHTWAVE PUBLISHING, INC., Box 160, Maple Ridge BC V2X 7G1 Canada. (604)462-7890. Fax (604)462-8208. E-mail: christie@lightwave publishing.com. Website: http://www.lightwavepublishing.com. Interdenominational. Christie Bowler, ed. To help children understand the basics of the Christian faith, and to help parents pass these values on to their children. Publishes 24 titles/yr. Receives 110 submissions annually. No mss through agents. Outright purchases or work for hire (pays an hourly or per-project rate, amount depends on project size; wages up front, on delivery of manuscript). Publication within 4-8 mos. Considers simultaneous submissions. Responds in 1 mo (if requested). Guidelines (also on Website); catalog on Website.

Nonfiction: Query only to inquire about work-for-hire and send resume; fax/e-query OK.

Fiction: Query only. "We do very little fiction, and only as related to teaching children about prayer, stewardship, general Bible knowledge, or creation science. Picture books."

Special Needs: Books related to children and parenting issues from a variety of angles.

Also Does: Some booklets.

Tips: "We usually come up with book ideas, then hire a writer/researcher, with expertise in that particular field, to write it."

**Note: This publisher serviced by The Writer's Edge.

LIGUORI PUBLICATIONS, 1 Liguori Dr., Liguori MO 63057. (314)464-2500. Fax (314)464-8449. E-mail: 73451.1652@compuserve.com, or 104626. 1563@compuserve.com., or jbauer@liguori.org. Website: http://www. Liguori.org. Catholic/Redemptorists. Anthony Chiffolo, acq ed. Publishes 50 titles/yr. Prefers 100-300 pgs for books; 40-100 pgs for booklets; pamphlets 16-18 pgs. Royalty 10-11% on retail; outright purchase of pamphlets for $400; advance varies. Average first printing 3,500-5,000 on books & booklets, 10,000 on pamphlets. Publication within 2 yrs. Accepts disks. Responds in 9-13 wks. Guidelines.

Nonfiction: Proposal/2 chapters (complete ms for pamphlets). "Looking for books on teen issues."

Fiction: Complete ms. "Generally we don't do fiction, but will consider children's picture books, allegory or biblical books for children."

Ethnic Books: Publishes books in Spanish. See separate listing for Libros Liguori.

Also Does: Booklets, pamphlets and tracts; computer games and screen savers. Electronic publishing division does 4 books/yr.

Tips: "Manuscripts accepted by us must have a strong, practical application."

LILLENAS PUBLISHING CO., Program Builder Series and Other Drama Resources, Box 419527, Kansas City MO 64141-6527. (816)931-1900. Fax (816)753-4071. E-mail: drama@lillenas.com. Website: http://www. lillenas.com/drama. Paul M. Miller, ed; submit to Kim Messer, asst. Publishes 15 drama resource books and 3 program builders/yr. Royalty 10% for drama resources; outright purchase of program builder material; no advance. No simultaneous submissions. Responds in 3 mos. Guidelines; catalog.

Drama Resources: Query or complete ms; phone/fax/e-query OK. Accepts readings, one-act and full-length plays, puppet scripts, program and service features, monologues, and sketch collections.

Tips: "We have added a new line of full-length plays for use in schools and dinner theater that are wholesome but not specifically religious."

LION PUBLISHING, 4050 Lee Vance View, Colorado Springs CO 80918-7102. (719)536-3271. Cook Communications. Accepts no freelance submissions.

THE LITURGICAL PRESS, PO Box 7500, St. John's Abbey, Collegeville MN 56321. (320)363-2213. Fax (800)445-5899. E-mail: mtwomey@osb.org. Website: http://www.litpress.org/edit.html. St. John's Abbey (a Benedictine group). Imprints: Liturgical Press Books, Michael Glazier Books and Pueblo Books. Mark Twomey, mng ed. Academic manuscripts to Linda Maloney (lmmaloney@osb.org). Publishes 70 titles/yr. Prefers 100-300 pgs. Royalty 10% of net; some outright purchases; no advance. Responds in 3 mos. Guidelines; free catalog.

> **Nonfiction:** Query/proposal. Adult only.
>
> **Tips:** "We publish liturgical, scriptural, and pastoral resources."

*LITURGY TRAINING PUBLICATIONS, Office of Divine Worship, 1800 N. Hermitage Ave., Chicago IL 60622-1101. (773)486-8970. Fax (773)486-7094. E-mail: editors@LTP.org. Catholic/Archdiocese of Chicago. Victoria Tufano, sr acq ed. Resources for liturgy in Christian life. Publishes 25 titles/yr. Receives 150 submissions annually. 50% of books from first-time authors. Variable royalty. Average first printing 2,000-5,000. Publication within 1 yr. Considers simultaneous submissions. Responds in 2-10 wks. Requires disk. Catalog.

> **Nonfiction:** Proposal/1 chapter; phone/fax/e-query OK.

+LIVING BOOKS FOR ALL, PO Box 98425 (TST), Kowloon, Hong Kong. 852-2723-1525. Fax 852-2366-6519. E-mail: clchk@hkstar.com. Website: Http://www.hkstar.com/~clchk/lbaguide.html. Christian Literature Crusade (CLC) Hong Kong. Mrs. M. Allison, ed. Prefers books of interest to Asians or Western readers interested in Asia. mos. Incomplete topical listings. Guidelines on Website.

> **Nonfiction:** Proposal with 2-3 chapters (up to 30 pages); no e-mail submissions.
>
> **Ethnic Books:** For Asian market.
>
> **Tips:** "Write in direct, personal, inclusive style; then simplify. No dissertations." Prefers American spelling to English spelling.

#LIVING THE GOOD NEWS, 600 Grant St., Ste. 400, Denver CO 80203. Fax (303)832-4971. Division of the Morehouse Group. Liz Riggleman, ed. admin. Publishes 15 titles/yr. Royalty. Publication within 1 yr. Considers simultaneous submissions. Responds in 2 mos. Guidelines; catalog for 9x12 SAE/4 stamps.

> **Nonfiction:** Query or proposal/1 chapter. "Seeking books on practical, personal, spiritual growth for all ages."
>
> **Fiction:** Query with synopsis. For children and teens; also picture books.
>
> **Special Needs:** Grandparenting and storytelling; youth resources.
>
> **Tips:** "Readers are mainly from liturgical and mainline church backgrounds. Seeking creative ways to connect with self, others, God and the earth."

LOGION PRESS, 1445 Boonville Ave., Springfield MO 65802. (417)862-2781. Assemblies of God. Dr. Stanley Horton, ed. Academic Line of Gospel Publishing House; primarily college textbooks. Publishes 2 titles/yr. Receives 5 submissions annually. 20% of books from first-time authors. No mss through agents. Prefers up to 185,000 words. Royalty on retail; no advance. Average first printing 3,500. Publication within 1 yr. No simultaneous submissions. Responds in 3 mos. Requires disk. Free guidelines/catalog.

Nonfiction: Proposal/1-2 chapters.

Tips: "Books must not contradict our statement of Fundamental Truths that all our ministers must sign annually."

LOIZEAUX, PO Box 277, Neptune NJ 07754-0277. (732)918-2626. Fax (732)922-9487. Website: http://www.biblecompanion.org. Evangelical. Marjorie Carlson, mng ed. Publishes 10-15 titles/yr. Receives 50 submissions annually. 2% of books from first-time authors. No mss through agents. Negotiable royalty on net; no advance. Average first printing 4,000. Publication within 24 mos. No simultaneous submissions. No e-mail submissions. Responds in 2-3 wks. Guidelines; free catalog.

Nonfiction: Query only; no phone/fax query. Looking for Bible commentaries.

LOVE INSPIRED/STEEPLE HILL, 300 E. 42nd St., New York NY 10017. (212)682-6080. Fax (212)682-4539. Website: http://www.romance.net. Harlequin Enterprises. Christian romance imprint. Tara Gavin, ed dir; Tracy Farrell, sr ed; Melissa Jeglinski, ed; Patience Smith, asst ed; Anne Canedeo, freelance ed. Publishes 36 titles/yr. 10% of books from first-time authors. Rarely reprints books. Prefers 75,000-80,000 wds or 300-320 pgs. Royalty on net; advance. Publication within 12-24 mos. Responds in 4-6 wks. No disk. Guidelines.

Fiction: Query letter or 3 chapters and up to 5-page synopsis. Contemporary romance. "Portray Christian characters learning an important lesson about the powers of truth and faith. Include humor, drama, and the many challenges of life and faith. Want strong romance."

+LOWENBROWN PUBLISHING, 3489 Newberry Trail, Decatur GA 30034. (770)322-2196. Lowenbrown Communications. Dr. Pamela M Brown, ed. Focuses on ethnic issues and sound spiritual instructions. Publishes 6-12 religious titles/yr. Receives 165 submissions annually. 60% of books from first-time authors. **SUBSIDY PUBLISHES 30%.** Negotiable royalty & advance. Considers simultaneous submissions. Responds in 2-3 mos. Guidelines; no catalog.

Nonfiction: Query only; phone query OK.

Fiction: Query only. For teens and adults.

Special Needs: Ethnic products. Also board games, gifts, novelty items, and ceramic products.

Ethnic Books: Black, Hispanic, Asian.

Also Does: Pamphlets, booklets, tracts.

Tips: "Follow through."

LOYOLA PRESS, 3441 N. Ashland Ave., Chicago IL 60657-1397. (773)281-1818. Fax (773)281-4129. E-mail: schroeder@loyolapress.com. Catholic. LaVonne Neff, ed dir. Serving faith formation in the Jesuit tradition. Publishes 20+ titles/yr. Receives 500 submissions annually. 10% of books from first-time authors. Rarely reprints books. Prefers 60,000-80,000 wds or 200-400 pgs. Variable royalty on net; advance. Average first printing 5,000-7,500. Publication within 2-18 mos. Considers simultaneous submissions. Responds in 3 mos. Accepts disk or e-mail. Guidelines (also by e-mail); free catalog.

Nonfiction: Proposal/2 chapters; fax query OK. "Most open to professionally written mss; spirituality for laypersons in the Catholic tradition."

LYDIA PRESS, Box 62069, Colorado Springs CO 80962-2069. (719)481-8149. Nondenominational. Alaine Pakkala, pres; submit to Carolyn Reynolds. Specializes in discipleship and encouragement materials to rebuild shattered lives. Publishes 10-15 titles/yr. 60% of books from first-time authors. **SUBSIDY PUBLISHES 2%.** Reprints books. Prefers 200 pgs. Royalty 25-50% on net; no advance. Average first printing 2,000. Publication within 10 mos. Considers simultaneous submissions. Responds in 1 mo. Guidelines; catalog for 9x12 SAE/5 stamps.

Nonfiction: Query; phone query OK. Books on spiritual warfare.

Ethnic Books: Encouragement and discipleship for Black youth; also Hispanic.

Also Does: CD-Rom discipleship materials for teens; pamphlets and booklets.

MAGNUS PRESS, PO Box 2666, Carlsbad CA 92018. (760)806-3743. Fax (760)806-3689. Warren Angel, ed dir. To publish biblical studies which are written for the average person and which minister life to Christ's Church. Publishes 6 titles/yr. Receives 60 submissions annually. 50% of books from first-time authors. Reprints books. Prefers 125-375 pgs. Graduated royalty on retail; no advance. Average first printing 5,000. Publication within 10 mos. Considers simultaneous submissions. No disk. Responds in 1 mo. Guidelines; free catalog.

Nonfiction: Query or proposal/2-3 chapters; fax query OK. "Looking for biblical studies, any subject, including apologetics and controversial issues. Inspirational books which teach the Bible while nurturing growth in Christ."

Tips: "Our writers need solid knowledge of the Bible, and a mature spirituality which reflects a profound relationship with Jesus Christ."

+MARLTON PUBLISHERS, INC., PO Box 223, Severn MD 21144. (800)859-0173. Fax (410)519-1439. Bruce Rory Thomas, ed. To spread the Gospel truth through Christian fiction. Publishes 3 titles/yr. Receives 10 submissions annually. 75% of books from first-time authors. Prefers 50,000-60,000 wds. Outright purchase $500-5,000. Average first printing 5,000. Publication within 6 mos. All books solicited.

Nonfiction: Query only; no phone/fax query. On spiritual warfare; uses little nonfiction.

Fiction: Query only. "We want adult Christian fiction only. Must deal with contemporary conflicts faced by people who have become Christians as adults. "

Tips: "We prefer character novels of inner conflict, with the story having action, drama and romance (when possible). "

MASTER BOOKS, PO Box 726, Green Forest AR 72638-0726. (870)438-5288. Fax (870)438-5120. E-mail: mbnlp@cswnet.com. New Leaf Press. Jim Fletcher, ed. Publishes 8-10 titles/yr. Receives 100 submissions annually.

10% of books from first-time authors. No mss through agents. **SUBSIDY PUBLISHES 5-15%.** Reprints books. Royalty 10-15% of net; no advance. Average first printing 5,000. Publication within 6 mos. Considers simultaneous submissions. Responds in 7-10 days. Free catalog.

> **Nonfiction:** Query. "Looking for biblical creationism; biblical science; creation/evolution debate material."
> **Special Needs:** Children's books and homeschool science books.
> **Also Does:** Videos.

+MCDOUGAL PUBLISHING, 727 N. Mulberry St., Hagerstown MD 21742. (301)797-6637. Fax (301)733-2767. Website: http://www.mcdougal.org. Charismatic, non-denominational. Harold McDougal, pres; Barbara Lanzdorf, ed. Publishes 30 titles/yr. Receives 60 submissions annually. 70% of books from first-time authors. No mss through agents. **SUBSIDY PUBLISHES 30%.** Prefers 112-250 pgs. Royalty 10%; no advance. Average first printing 3,000-5,000. Publication within 6 mos. Considers simultaneous submissions. Responds in 3 mos. Free guidelines/catalog.

> **Nonfiction:** Complete ms; phone/fax/e-query OK.
> **Fiction:** Complete ms. For all ages, including picture books.
> **Tips:** "Most open to worship and revival. "

MERCER UNIVERSITY PRESS, 6316 Peake Rd., Macon GA 31210. (912)752-2880. Fax (912)752-2264. E-mail: mupressorders@mercer.edu. Website: http://www.mupress.org. Marc Jolley, mng ed.

> **Nonfiction:** Query. "We are looking for books on history, philosophy, theology and religion, including history of religion, philosophy of religion, Bible studies and ethics."

MERIWETHER PUBLISHING LTD., 885 Elkton Dr., Colorado Springs CO 80918. (719)594-4422. Fax (719)594-9916. E-mail: Merpcos@aol.com. Arthur L. Zapel, ed; submit to Rhonda Wray. Publishes 2-3 titles/yr.; 25-30 plays/yr. Primarily a publisher of plays for Christian and secular; must be acceptable for use in a wide variety of Christian denominations. Imprint: Contemporary Drama Service. Publishes 3 bk/25 plays/yr. Receives 800 submissions annually (mostly plays). 50% of books from first-time authors. Reprints books. Prefers 200 pgs. Royalty 10% on net or retail; no advance. Average first printing of books 2,500, plays 500. Publication within 1 yr. Considers simultaneous submissions. Prefers disk. Responds in 2-8 wks. Guidelines; catalog $1/9x12 SAE/3 stamps.

> **Nonfiction:** Query letter only; fax query OK. "Looking for creative worship books, i.e., drama, using the arts in worship, how-to books with ideas for Christian education."
> **Fiction:** Plays only. Always looking for Christmas and Easter plays. Send complete ms.
> **Tips:** "Our books are on drama or any creative, artistic area that can be a part of worship."

MESSIANIC JEWISH PUBLISHERS, 6204 Park Heights Ave., Baltimore MD 21215. (410)358-6471. Fax (410)764-1376. E-mail: messjewcom@aol.com. Website: http://www.MessianicJewish.net. Lederer/Messianic Jewish Communications. Alan J. Tannenbaum, ed. Books that witness to the unsaved Jewish person or teach the Christian about the Jewish roots of

Christianity. Imprint: Remnant Books (for subsidy books only). Publishes 6-12 titles/yr. Receives 50 submissions annually. 50% of books from first-time authors. No mss through agents. **SUBSIDY PUBLISHES 10%.** Reprints books. Prefers 52,000-88,000 wds. Royalty 7-15% on net; no advance. Average first printing 3,000 (subsidy), 5,000 (royalty). Publication within 6-12 mos. No simultaneous submissions. Requires disk or e-mail submissions (in MS Word). Responds in 3-6 mos. Requires disk. No guidelines; free catalog.

    Nonfiction: Proposal/2-3 chapters; no phone/fax/e-query. Jewish evangelism or Jewish roots of Christian faith.

    Fiction: Proposal/2-3 chapters. All ages. "Need Jewish themes."

    Ethnic Books: Jewish.

    Also Does: Booklets, pamphlets and tracts. Children's curriculum.

*MIDDLE ATLANTIC REGIONAL PRESS, 100 Bryant St. NW, Washington DC 20001. (202)265-7609. Middle Atlantic Regional Gospel Ministries. Myron Noble, pres. Helps publish works of unpublished African American authors. Publishes 1-3 titles/yr. Receives 8-12 submissions annually. 75% of books from first-time authors. **SUBSIDY PUBLISHES 20%.** Reprints books. Prefers 80-125 pgs. Royalty 10-15% of net; no advance. Average first printing 5,000. Publication within 6-18 mos. Considers simultaneous submissions. Responds in 3-6 mos. No disk. Guidelines; free catalog.

    Nonfiction: Proposal/3 chapters or complete ms; phone query OK.

    Fiction: Query.

    Ethnic Books: African-American.

    Also Does: Pamphlets, booklets, tracts.

MISTY HILL PRESS, 5024 Turner Rd., Sebastopol CA 95472. (707)823-7437. Small press that does some religious titles. Sally C. Karste, ed. Publishes 1 title/yr. Negotiable royalty. Responds in 1 week. Guidelines; catalog for 9x12 SAE/2 stamps.

    Fiction: Query first. Historical fiction for children.

    Note: Not accepting manuscripts at this time.

MONUMENT PRESS, PO Box 140361, Irving TX 75014-0361. (972)681-9190. Fax (972)686-5332. Website: http://www.publishers-associates.com/monument. Member of the consortium Publishers Associates (8 publishers). Belinda Buxjom, sr ed; submit to Mary Markal. Publishes only scholarly books. Other imprints: Ide House and Tangelwuld. Publishes 20 titles/yr. Receives 1,200 submissions annually. 100% of books from first-time authors. No mss through agents. Any length. Royalty 2-8% on retail; no advance. Average first printing 3,000. Publication within 4 mos. No simultaneous submissions. Prefers disk. Responds in 4 mos (goes to all houses in the consortium). Guidelines; catalog for 4 stamps.

    Nonfiction: Query only; no phone/fax query.

    Ethnic: Publishes for all ethnic groups.

    Tips: "Most open to liberation theology. Scholarly works only. "

#MOODY PRESS, 820 N. LaSalle Blvd., Chicago IL 60610. (312)329-2101. Fax (312)329-2144. Website: http://www.moodypress.org. Imprint: Northfield Publishing. Moody Bible Institute. Submit to The Editor. To provide books that evangelize, edify the believer, and educate concerning the

Christian life. Publishes 65-70 titles/yr. Receives 3,500 submissions annually. 1% of books from first-time authors. Reprints books. Royalty on net; advance $500-50,000. Average first printing 10,000. Publication within 6 mos. Considers simultaneous submissions (reluctantly). Responds in 2 mos. Guidelines; catalog for 9x12 SAE.

Nonfiction: Proposal/3 chapters; no phone/fax query.

Also Does: Booklets in series only.

Tips: "Most open to books where the writer is a recognized expert and already has a platform to promote the book. Not currently accepting fiction."

**Note: This publisher serviced by The Writer's Edge.

THOMAS MORE/An RCL Company, 200 E. Bethany Dr., Allen TX 75002. (972)390-6923. Fax (972)390-6620. E-mail: dhampton@rcl-enterprises. com. Website: http://www.rclweb.com. Catholic/Resources for Christian Living. Debra Hampton, mng ed. Dedicated to providing the highest quality books, video and interactive media that contribute to the dialogue on religion, ethics, social policy, lifestyle and spirituality shaping our future. Publishes 25 titles/yr. Receives 100 submissions annually. 30% of books from first-time authors. Reprints books. Prefers 200 pgs. Royalty 7-15% on retail; advance $5,000. Average first printing 10,000. Publication within 6 mos. Considers simultaneous submissions. Requires disk (Macintosh). Responds in 6-9 wks. No guidelines; free catalog.

Nonfiction: Proposal/1 chapter or complete ms. "Looking for books on family, psychology/spiritual growth, scripture (meditation, prayer), spirituality (men's, women's, general), religion (saints), and resources for religion teachers. "

Tips: "Looking for books on theology, commentary, reflection, spirituality and reference—for the serious, but non-scholarly reader (written in popular style)."

MOREHOUSE PUBLISHING CO., 4775 Linglestown Rd., Harrisburg PA 17112. (717)541-8130. Fax (717)541-8136. Website: http://www. more housegroup.com. Episcopal/ecumenical. Deborah K. Farrington, ed dir; artists submit illustration packages to Valerie Gittings, mng ed. Laura Hudson, children's ed (lhudson@morehousegroup.com). Academic, devotional, reference, and Bible study materials for Christians of all denominations. Publishes 35 titles/yr; 4-5 picture books/yr. Receives 500 submissions annually. 40% of books from first-time authors. Reprints books. Prefers 80-150 pgs. Royalty on net; modest advance. Average first printing 2,500-3,500. Publication within 8 mos. Considers simultaneous submissions. Responds in 6-9 wks. Guidelines; for free catalog call (800)877-0012 .

Nonfiction: Proposal/1 chapter; no phone/fax query. "Looking for books on marriage, parenting skills, single parenting, relations, marriage counseling helps for clergy, stewardship, Bible studies, dealing with grief/loss, and current social issues."

Fiction: Complete ms/resume. For children/teens. Picture books for 3-8 year olds. "Books on Christian themes, such as prayer, God, Jesus, creation and care of God's earth, the church, Bible stories, seasonal titles, hymns, saints, and Christian concepts such as grace, forgiveness, healing, etc., from a mainline Christian perspective."

Tips: "Stories should contain rich theological concepts in terms children can understand. Seeking manuscripts that are unique, that either approach a topic from a fresh angle, or explore a subject not covered in currently available children's material. Books should appeal to children and adults alike, be theologically sound, as well as fun and entertaining for all."

*JOSHUA MORRIS PUBLISHING, Readers Digest Rd., Pleasantville NY 10570. Anglican/Evangelical. Beverly Larson, ed. To create unique novelty-type books that bring the stories and truth of the Bible to life for young children. Imprint: Reader's Digest Young Families. Publishes 60 titles/yr. Receives 200 submissions annually. 5% of books from first-time authors. Makes outright purchases. Average first printing 25,000. Publication within 9 mos. Considers simultaneous submissions. Responds in 2-3 mos. No guidelines/catalog.

Nonfiction: Proposal/1 chapter.

Fiction: Proposal/1 chapter. Children's picture books.

Special Needs: Produces board games and all kinds of novelty books for children.

Tips: "We are looking for writers who are excellent at rhyming and can write for preschoolers particularly. We commission authors to write books that we have come up with. Authors should send samples of their best work, rather than sending a specific proposal."

#WILLIAM MORROW AND CO., 1350 Avenue of the Americas, New York NY 10019. (212)261-6500. Fax (212)261-6595. Website: http://www.williamm orrow.com. The Hearst Corp. Debbie Mercer-Sullivan, mng ed. General trade publisher that does a few religious titles. Publishes 5 religious titles/yr. Receives 1,000 submissions annually. 30% of books from first-time authors. Only accepts mss through agents. Prefers 50,000-100,000 wds. Standard royalty on retail; advance varies. Publication within 2 yrs. Considers simultaneous submissions. Responds in 3 mos.

Nonfiction & Fiction: Query only; mss and proposals accepted only through an agent.

Note: Morrow Junior Books accepts no unsolicited manuscripts.

+MOSAIC PRESS, 85 River Rock Dr., Buffalo NY 14207. Phone/fax (800)387-8992. E-mail: cp507@freenet.toronto.on.ca. Secular publisher that does some religious books. Submit to Book Editor. Publishes 20 titles/yr. Royalty 10% of retail. Considers simultaneous submissions. Free guidelines.

Nonfiction: Proposal/sample chapters.

Fiction: Synopsis.

Special Needs: Poetry books. Submit sample poems.

+MOUNTAINVIEW PUBLISHING COMPANY, 1022 NE O'Leary St., Oak Harbor WA 98277. (360)675-2183. E-mail: junebug@whidbey.net. Website: http://www.whidbey.com/mountainview. Susan Johnson, ed/pub. New online Christian publisher specializing in romance novels. Imprint: Glory Books. Launching spring 1999. Will consider reprint.. Prefers 80,000-100,000 wds. Royalty 20-30% of retail; no advance. Books printed on an as-

ordered basis. Publication within 6 mos. Considers simultaneous submissions. Responds in 2 mos. Guidelines (also by e-mail, Website); no catalog.
Fiction: Mailed proposal/4-5 chapters or e-query/short synopsis. Historical romances, 80,000-100,000 wds; contemporary romances, 65,000-80,000 wds. "Seeking high-quality manuscripts that evoke emotion in the reader, cutting edge books that challenge reader's minds, as well as the tried and true old fashioned romance that readers love so much."
Tips: "Christian romances should contain a faith element. Challenge the reader to think, to look at things through different eyes. Avoid head-hopping and clichés; avoid heavy-handed preaching."

MOUNT OLIVE COLLEGE PRESS, 634 Henderson St., Mount Olive NC 28365. (919)658-2502. Dr. Pepper Worthington, ed. Publishes 5 titles/yr. Receives 1,000 submissions annually. 70% of books from first-time authors. Prefers 220 pgs. Negotiated royalty. Average first printing 500. Publication within 1-3 yrs. No simultaneous submissions. Responds in 6-12 mos. No disk. Free guidelines/catalog.
Nonfiction: Proposal/3 chapters; no phone query. Religion. For poetry submit 6 sample poems.
Fiction: Proposal/3 chapters. Religious.

MULTNOMAH PUBLISHERS (formerly Questar Publishers), Box 1720, 204 W. Adams St., Sisters OR 97759. (541)549-1144. Fax (541)549-2044. E-mail: chuber@multnomahpubl.com. Website: Up in January 1999. Rod Morris, gen fiction; Dan Benson, Christian Living books; Alice Gray, gift bks. Imprint information listed below. Publishes 120 titles/yr. Receives 2,400 submissions annually. 5% of books from first-time authors. Length depends on project. Negotiable royalty and advance. Average first printing 12,500. Publication within 12-24 mos. Considers simultaneous submissions. Responds in 3-6 mos. Requires disk. Guidelines (also by e-mail); catalog for 9x12 SAE/7 stamps.
Multnomah Books: Christian living and popular theology books. Submit to: Editorial Dept.
Gold 'n' Honey: Children's books. Cover letter and complete ms. Submit to: Don Goodman, children's ed.
Multnomah Fiction: Message-driven, clean, moral, uplifting fiction. Cover letter, synopsis and 3 chapters. Submit to Rod Morris.
Palisades and Alabaster: Contemporary (pure) romance (Palisades) and women's fiction (Alabaster). Length for Palisades is 75,000-90,000 wds. For Alabaster, looking for longer (90,000-105,000 wds), more developed stories within a variety of genres: stand alone, comedy, cozy mystery and suspense, all with a thread of romance. Cover letter, synopsis and 3 chapters. Each line publishes 6 new titles/yr. Submit to Julie Schwarzburg (Palisades) or Karen Ball (Alabaster). No phone/fax query; e-query OK. Accepts disk or e-mail.
Multnomah Gift Books: Looking for proposals on substantive topics with beautiful, lyrical writing. Cover letter, synopsis and 2-3 chapters. Submit to Editorial Dept.
**Note: This publisher serviced by The Writer's Edge.

*NATIONAL BAPTIST PUBLISHING BOARD, 6717 Centennial Blvd., Nashville TN 37209. (615)350-8000. Fax (615)350-9018. E-mail: nbpb@nbpb. org. Website: http://www.nbpb.org. National Missionary Baptist Convention of America. Rev. Willie N. Paul, dir of publications. To provide quality Christian education resources to be used by African-American churches. Receives 200 submissions annually. 30% of books from first-time authors. Reprints books. Prefers 130 pgs. Outright purchases; advance. Average first printing 20,000. Publication within 1 yr.

Nonfiction: Complete ms; phone query OK.

Fiction: Complete ms. "We need biblically based fiction for children."

Ethnic Books: African-American publisher.

Tips: "Most open to religious books that can be used for Christian education."

NAVPRESS/PIÑON PRESS, Box 35001, Colorado Springs CO 80935. (719)548-9222. Website: http://www.navpress.org or http://www.gospel com.net/navs/NP. "We are no longer accepting any unsolicited submissions, proposals, queries, etc."

**Note: This publisher serviced by The Writer's Edge.

NAZARENE PUBLISHING HOUSE—See Beacon Hill Press of Kansas City.

NEIBAUER PRESS, 20 Industrial Dr., Warminster PA 18974. (215)322-6200. Fax (215)322-2495. E-mail: Nathan@Neibauer.com. Evangelical/Protestant clergy and church leaders. Nathan Neibauer, ed. Publishes 8 titles/yr. Receives 100 submissions annually. 5% of books from first-time authors. No mss through agents. Reprints books. Prefers 200 pgs. Royalty on net; some outright purchases; no advance. Average first printing 2,500. Publication within 6 mos. Considers simultaneous submissions. Responds in 2 wks. Prefers e-mail submissions. No guidelines/catalog.

Nonfiction: E-query OK.

Also Does: Pamphlets and tracts.

Tips: "Publishes only religious books on stewardship and church enrollment, stewardship and tithing, and church enrollment tracts."

THOMAS NELSON PUBLISHERS, 501 Nelson Pl., Nashville TN 37214. Accepts no freelance submissions.

**Note: This publisher serviced by The Writer's Edge.

TOMMY NELSON, a division of Thomas Nelson, Inc., 404 BNA Dr., Ste. 508, Nashville TN 37217. (615)889-9000. Accepting no freelance submissions for now.

**Note: This publisher serviced by The Writer's Edge.

NEW CANAAN PUBLISHING CO., INC., PO Box 752, New Canaan CT 06840. Phone/fax (203)966-3408. E-mail: newcan@sprynet.com. Website: http://newcanaanpublishing.com. Kathy Mittelstadt, ed. Children's books with strong educational and moral content; for grades 1-9. Publishes 1-2 titles/yr. Receives 100 submissions annually. 50% of books from first-time authors. Prefers 20,000-40,000 wds or 140 pgs. Royalty 8-12 % on net; no advance. Average first printing 500-5,000. Publication within 6-8 mos. No simultaneous submissions. Responds in 10-12 wks. Requires disk; no e-mail submissions. Guidelines (also on Website); free catalog.

Nonfiction: Query letter; proposal/2-3 chapters; e-query OK.

Fiction: Complete ms. For children and teens, 6-14 yrs. "We want children's books with strong educational and moral content; 10,000-20,000 wds." No picture books.

Special Needs: Middle-school-level educational books.

*NEW CITY PRESS, 202 Cardinal Rd., Hyde Park NY 12538. (914)229-0335. Fax (914)229-0351. E-mail: PATNCP@aol.com. Catholic. Pat Markey, ed. Focus is on Christian living and unity. Publishes 12 titles/yr. Receives 60 submissions annually. 5% of books from first-time authors. Reprints books. Prefers 56,000 wds. Royalty 10% on net; no advance. Average first printing 5,000. Publication with 16 mos. Considers simultaneous submissions. Responds in 3 mos. Requires disk. Free catalog.

Nonfiction: Query only; fax/e-query OK. "Looking for how-to and family topics."

NEW HOPE, Box 12065, Birmingham AL 35202-2065. (205)991-8100. Fax (205)991-4015. E-mail: new_hope@wmu.org. Website: http://www.new hopepubl.com. Imprint of Woman's Missionary Union; Auxiliary to Southern Baptist Convention. Coy Batson, dir. Publishes 12-15 titles/yr. Receives 80-100 submissions annually. 10-15% of books from first-time authors. Reprints books occasionally. Prefers 150-250 pgs. Royalty on retail or outright purchases; no advance. Average first printing 5,000-10,000. Publication within 18 mos. Considers simultaneous submissions. Responds in 3 mos. Requires disk. Guidelines; catalog for 9x12 SAE/4 stamps.

Nonfiction: Complete ms or proposal/3-4 chapters; no phone/fax/e-query. "All that we publish must have a missions/ministry emphasis, preferably for women or children."

Fiction: Complete ms or proposal/3-4 chapters. For women or children only. Subject matter must include a ministry/missions emphasis. Children's picture books or storybooks, especially with a multicultural focus.

Tips: "Most open to books which focus on spiritual growth that turns faith outward into action; books that equip women and children to share Christ with others; books that lead to involvement in missions; books that teach appreciation for other cultures and people groups. Follow guidelines."

NEW LEAF PRESS, PO Box 726, Green Forest AR 72638-0726. (870)438-5288. Fax (870)438-5120. Pentecostal/Charismatic. Jim Fletcher, ed. Imprint: Master Books. Publishes 15-20 titles/yr. Receives 500 submissions annually. 15% of books from first-time authors. Reprints books. Prefers 100-400 pgs. Royalty 10% on net; no advance. Average first printing 10,000. Publication within 10 mos. Considers simultaneous submissions. Responds in 3 mos. Guidelines; catalog for 9x12 SAE/5 stamps.

Nonfiction: Complete ms; phone/fax query OK. "Looking for devotional, gift books and Christian living."

Tips: "Tell us why this book is marketable and why it will be a blessing and fulfill the needs of others."

+NEW WORLD LIBRARY, 14 Pamaron Way, Novato CA 94949. Submit to Submissions Editor. Dedicated to awakening individual and global potential;

inspirational and practical books. Royalty. Considers simultaneous submissions.

Nonfiction: Query/outline & sample chapters.

Special Needs: Audio cassettes.

NORTHSTONE PUBLISHING, INC., 9025 Jim Bailey Rd., Kelowna BC V1Y 9G8 Canada. (250)766-2778. Fax (250)766-2736. E-mail: info@woodlake. com. Website: http://www.joinhands.com. Wood Lake Books, Inc. Michael Schwartzentruber, ed. To provide high quality products promoting positive social and spiritual values. Publishes 8-12 titles/yr. Receives 900 submissions annually. 30% of books from first-time authors. Prefers 192-256 pgs. Royalty 8-12% on retail; some advances $1,000. Average first printing 4,000. Publication within 9 mos. Considers simultaneous submissions. Responds in 3 mos. Prefers disk or e-mail. Guidelines; catalog $2.

Nonfiction: Proposal/2 chapters; phone/fax/e-query OK.

Tips: "Although we publish from a Christian perspective, we seek to attract a general audience. Our target audience is interested in spirituality and values, but may not even attend church (nor do we assume that they should)."

ONE WORLD, 201 E. 50th St., New York NY 10022. (212)572-2620. Fax (212)940-7539. Website: http://www.randomhouse.com/BB. Imprint of Ballantine Books. Cheryl Woodruff, assoc pub; submit to Gary Brozek, assoc ed. Books that are written by and focus on African Americans, Native Americans, Asian Americans and Latino Americans; but from an American multicultural perspective. Publishes 8-10 titles/yr. Receives 1,200 submissions annually. 25% of books from first-time authors. Reprints books. Royalty 8-12% on retail; variable advance. Publication within 2 yrs. Considers simultaneous submissions. No disk or e-mail. Responds in 4 mos. Guidelines/catalog for #10 SASE.

Nonfiction: Query or proposal with 100 pgs; no e-query. "Religious/ inspirational books for Americans of color."

Fiction: Query or proposal/3 chapters. "Looking for contemporary or historical."

Ethnic Books: All are ethnic books.

+OPENBOOK PUBLISHERS, Box 1368, GPO, Adelaide, Australia 5001. (618)8223 5468. Fax (618)8223 4552. E-mail: cpfeiffer@openbook.com. au. Lutheran. John Pfitzner, ed; submit to Christopher Pfeiffer. Australian resources for Christians of all denominations. Publishes 20 titles/yr. Receives 100+ submissions annually. 60% of books from first-time authors. Reprints books. Prefers 160 pgs. Royalty 10-15% on net; no advance. Average first printing 1,000-2,000. Publication within 6 mos. Considers simultaneous submissions. Prefers e-mail submissions. Responds in 1 mo. No guidelines/catalog.

Nonfiction: Complete ms; phone/fax/e-query OK.

Tips: "Most open to resources for use in congregations and homes."

*OPEN COURT PUBLISHING CO., 332 S. Michigan Ave., Ste. 2000, Chicago IL 60604-9968. David Ramsey Steele, ed dir. Publishes 4 religious titles/yr. Receives 600 submissions annually. 20% of books from first-time authors. Reprints books. Prefers 350-400 pgs. Royalty 5-12% of net; advance

$1,000-2,000. Average first printing 500 (cloth), 1,500 (paperback). Publication within 1-3 yrs. Considers simultaneous submissions. Responds in 6 mos. Free catalog.

Nonfiction: Proposal/2 chapters. "We're looking for works of high intellectual quality for a scholarly or general readership on comparative religion, philosophy of religion, and religious issues."

*ORBIS BOOKS, PO Box 308, Maryknoll NY 10545-0308. (914)941-7590. Fax (914)945-0670. E-mail: orbisbooks@aol.com. Catholic Foreign Mission Society. Robert Ellsberg, ed. Publishes 50-55 titles/yr. Receives 2,200 submissions annually. 2% of books from first-time authors. Accepts few mss through agents. Prefers 250-350 pgs. Royalty 10-15% of net; advance $500-3,000. Publication within 15 mos. Responds in 2 mos. Free guidelines/catalog.

Nonfiction: Proposal/1 chapter. "Global justice and peace; religious development in Asia, Africa, and Latin America; Christianity and world religions."

+ORIGINAL WORD PUBLISHERS, PO Box 799, Roswell GA 30077. (800)235-9673 or (404)552-8879. Website: http://www.originalword.com. Dr. Charles Goodwin, ed. A trans-denominational, nonprofit teaching ministry devoted to biblical studies.

OUR SUNDAY VISITOR, INC., 200 Noll Plaza, Huntington IN 46750-4303. (219)356-8400. Fax (219)359-9117. E-mail: Jlindsey@osv.com. Website: http://www.osv.com. Catholic. Greg Erlandson, ed-in-chief; submit to Jacquelyn Lindsey. To assist Catholics to be more aware and secure in their faith and capable of relating their faith to others. Publishes 30 titles/yr. Receives 100+ submissions annually. 10% of books from first-time authors. Reprints books. Royalty 10-13% on net; advance $2,000. Average first printing 5,000. Publication within 1 yr. Considers simultaneous submissions. Responds in 6 wks. Requires disk. Free guidelines/catalog.

Nonfiction: Proposal/2 chapters; phone/fax/e-query OK. "Most open to devotional books (not 1st person), church histories, heritage and saints, the parish, prayer and family."
Also Does: Pamphlets and booklets.
Tips: "All books published must relate to the Catholic Church. Give as much background information as possible on why the topic was chosen. Follow our guidelines."

OXFORD UNIVERSITY PRESS, 198 Madison Ave., New York NY 10016-4314. (212)679-7300. Website: http://www.oup-usa.org. Academic press. Cynthia Read, exec ed. Service to academic community. Publishes 60+ titles/yr. Receives hundreds of submissions annually. 20% of books from first-time authors. Prefers 250 pgs. Royalty & advance negotiable. Average first printing 900. Publication within 1 yr. Considers simultaneous submissions. Responds in 3 mos. Free catalog.

Nonfiction: Proposal/2 chapters. "Most open to academic books."

+PACE PUBLICATIONS, PO Box 1982, Independence MO 64055. (816)350-8431. Fax (816)350-7462. E-mail: pace1982@aol.com. Julia Hansen, ed dir. Focus is on Christian children's books for ages 8-14 years; fundamental, Bible-believing and obedient Christian living in a pagan society; being witnesses for Christ by life and word. Publishes 6-12 titles/yr. Receives 20 submissions annually. 50% of books from first-time authors. Reprints books. Prefers 150 pgs. Royalty 10% of net; no advance. Average first printing 5,000. Publication within 1 yr. Considers simultaneous submissions. Responds in 1-2 mos. Guidelines.

Nonfiction: Proposal/3 chapters; e-query OK. Easy-readers, missionary stories; books for 8-12 year old.

Fiction: Proposal/3 chapters. For children and teens. "Juvenile fiction must NOT have Christians dancing, drinking, or involved in romantic situations. No New Age ideas. Respect for authority a must."

PACIFIC PRESS PUBLISHING ASSN., Box 5353, Nampa ID 83653-5353. (208)465-2511. Fax (208)465-2531. E-mail: editor.book@pacificpress. com. Website: http://www.pacificpress.com. Seventh-day Adventist. Jerry Thomas, book ed; submit to Kenneth Wade, acq ed. Books of interest and importance to Seventh-day Adventists and other Christians of all ages. Publishes 30 titles/yr. Receives 900 submissions annually. 20% of books from first-time authors. Prefers 40,000-70,000 wds or 128-256 pgs. Royalty 12-15% of net; advance $1,500. Average first printing 6,000. Publication within 10 mos. Considers simultaneous submissions. Responds in 3 mos. Requires disk/accepts by e-mail. Guidelines (also on Website).

Nonfiction: Query only; e-query OK.

Fiction: Proposal/3 chapters. Adults and children (7-12 years old), series or single books. "Must be true-to-life, focus on some important truth, and have a strong spiritual message. No talking animals."

Ethnic Books: Occasionally publishes for ethnic market.

Tips: "Our Website has the most up-to-date information, including samples of recent publications. Do not send full manuscript unless we request it after reviewing your proposal."

PALISADES/MULTNOMAH. Pure romance novels. See Multnomah Publishers.

PARACLETE PRESS, PO Box 1568, Orleans MA 02653. (508)255-4685. Fax (508)255-5705. E-mail: mail@paraclete-press.com. Website: http://www. paralete-press.com. Ecumenical. Lillian Miao, sr ed. Publishes 10 titles/yr. Receives 160 submissions annually. Few books from first-time authors. Reprints few books. Prefers 200 pgs. Royalty 10-12% on retail or net; no advance. Average first printing 3,000-5,000. Publication within 6-12 mos. Responds in 3-4 wks. Requires disk or e-mail. Guidelines (also by e-mail); catalog for 9x12 SAE/3 stamps.

Nonfiction: Proposal/1 chapter; phone/fax/e-query OK. "Looking for books on deeper spirituality that appeal to all denominations."

Tips: Vision statement: "In all times, in different branches of the Christian family, there are people who have written, sung, or spoken things that encouraged us to give our lives to God and to listen to His voice. We gather and share these treasures."

PARADISE RESEARCH PUBLICATIONS, INC., PO Box 837, Kihei HI 96753-0837. Phone/fax (808)874-4876. E-mail: dickb@dickb.com. Website: http://www. dickb.com. Ken Burns, ed. Imprint: Tincture of Time Press.

Publishes 5 titles/yr. Receives 8 submissions annually. 80% of books from first-time authors. No mss through agents. Reprints books. Prefers 250 pgs. Royalty 10% on retail; no advance. Average first printing 5,000. Publication within 2 mos. Considers simultaneous submission. Responds in 1 wk. No disk. No guidelines; free catalog.

Nonfiction: Query only; no phone/fax/e-query. Books on the biblical/Christian history of early Alcoholics Anonymous.

Also Does: Pamphlets and booklets.

+PARAGON HOUSE, 2700 University Ave. W., Ste. 200, St. Paul MN 55114-1016. (651)644-3087. Fax (651)644-0997. E-mail: paragon@paragon house.com. Website: http://www.paragonhouse.com. Intercultural Foundation. Thomas Walsh, religion ed. Serious nonfiction and texts with an emphasis on religion and philosophy. Imprints: New Era Books, Athena, Omega. Publishes 4-7 titles/yr. Receives 500 submissions annually. 5-10% of books from first-time authors. Reprints books. Prefers 256+ pgs. Royalty 5-12% of net; advance $1,000. Average first printing 2,000-3,000. Publication within 1 yr. Considers few simultaneous submissions. Requires disk. Guidelines; catalog available online.

Nonfiction: Query; proposal/2-3 chapters, or complete ms; fax/e-mail query OK. "Looking for scholarly overviews of religious teachers and movements; text books in philosophy; and reference books."

+PARTNERSHIP PRESS. A partnership of authors, pastors and theologians in 22 Holiness and Wesleyan denominations. Publishes 1 title/yr.

Nonfiction: Spiritual formation.

PAULINE BOOKS & MEDIA, 50 St. Paul's Ave., Boston MA 02130. (617)522-8911. Fax (617)541-9805. Website: http://www. pauline.org. Catholic. Sr. Mary Mark Wickenheiser, F.S.P., acq ed. To help clarify Catholic belief and practice for the average reader. Publishes 25-35 titles/yr. Receives 1,300 submissions annually. 75% of books from first-time authors. No ms through agents. Royalty 8-12% of net; advance $200. Average first printing 3,000. Publication within 2-3 yrs. Responds in 3 mos. No disk. Guidelines; catalog for 9x12 SAE/4 stamps.

Nonfiction: Query only, fax query OK. "Looking for books on faith and moral values, spiritual growth and development, and Christian formation for families."

Fiction: Query or proposal/chapters. Children's picture books, 150-500 wds; easy-to-read, 750-1,500 wds; and middle reader, 15,000-25,000 wds. No adult fiction.

Tips: "Open to religion teacher's resources and adult catechetics. No biographical or autobiographical material."

#PAULIST PRESS, 997 Macarthur Blvd., Mahwah NJ 07430. (201)825-7300. Fax (201)825-8345. Catholic. Donald Brophy, mng ed; Karen Scialabba, children's book ed. Imprints: Newman Press; Stimulus Books. Publishes 90-100 titles/yr. Receives 500 submissions annually. 5-8% of books from first-time authors. Prefers 100-400 pgs. Royalty 10% on retail; advance $500. Average first printing 3,500. Publication within 10 mos. Responds in 2 mos. Guidelines.

Nonfiction: Proposal/2 chapters. "Looking for theology (Catholic and ecumenical Christian), popular spirituality, liturgy, and religious education texts." Children's books for 5-7 years or 8-10 years; complete ms.

Tips: "Most open to progressive, world-affirming, theologically sophisticated, growth-oriented, well-written books. Have strong convictions but don't be pious. Stay well-read. Pay attention to contemporary social needs."

PELICAN PUBLISHING CO., INC., PO Box 3110, Gretna LA 70054-3110. (504)368-1175. Website: http://www.pelicanpub.com/. Nina Kooij, ed. Imprints: Firebird Press. Publishes 2 titles/yr. Receives 500 submissions annually. 50% of books from first-time authors. Reprints books. Prefers 200+ pgs. Royalty; some advances. Publication within 9-18 mos. Responds in 1 mo. Disk on request. Guidelines (also on Website); catalog for 9x12 SAE/7 stamps.

Nonfiction: Proposal/2 chapters; no phone query.

Tips: "On inspirational titles we need a high-profile author who already has an established speaking circuit so books can be sold at these appearances."

+PERIGEE BOOKS, 375 Hudson St., New York NY 10014. (212)366-2000. Website: http://www.penguinputnam.com. Penguin Putnam, Inc. Dolores McMullan, ed. Publishes 10 titles/yr. Receives 200 submissions annually. 20% of books from first-time authors. Prefers 60,000-80,000 wds. Royalty; advance. Average first printing varies. Publication within 12-18 mos. Considers simultaneous submissions. Prefers disk. Responds in 1-2 mos. No guidelines or catalog

Nonfiction: Query only; no phone query.

+PETER PAUPER PRESS, 202 Mamaroneck Ave., White Plains NY 10601. (914)681-0144. Fax (914)681-0389. E-mail: pauperp@aol.com. Sol Skolnick, creative dir. Does small-format illustrated gift books. Imprint: Inspire Books (evangelical imprint being launched 3/99). Publishes 24 titles/yr. No mss through agents. Prefers 800-2,000 wds. Outright purchase $250-1,000. Average first printing 10,000. Publication within 8-12 mos. Considers simultaneous submissions. Requires disk. Responds in 1 mo. Guidelines; no catalog.

Nonfiction: Query only; no phone/fax/e-query.

Tips: "We want original aphorisms, 67-75 to a book. Title should be focused on a holiday or special occasion, such as mother, sister, graduation, new baby, wedding, etc. "

PILGRIM PRESS, 700 Prospect Ave. E., Cleveland OH 44115-1100. (216)736-3715. Fax (216)736-3703. E-mail: stavet@ucc.org. Website: http://www.pilgrimpress.com. United Church of Christ. Timothy G. Staveteig, ed. Scholarly and trade books on social issues and the moral life. Publishes 35 titles/yr. Receives 500 submissions annually. 50% of books from first-time authors. Reprints books. Prefers 65,000 wds. Royalty 8% of net; negotiable advance. Publication within 1 yr. Might consider simultaneous submissions. Disk required. Responds in 12 wks. Free guidelines/catalog.

Nonfiction: Query only; phone/fax/e-query OK.

Ethnic Books: Black, Hispanic and Asian. Always interested in books on pluralism and multiculturalism.

Also Does: Booklets; journal/calendar for women.

Tips: "Looking for a timely topic with a fresh thesis."

+PLEASANT COMPANY PUBLICATIONS, 8400 Fairway Pl., Middleton WI 53562. Material of interest to girls 8-12. Submit to Submissions Editor. Imprints: American Girls Collection (historical fiction); American Girls Library (contemporary nonfiction); also adding a contemporary fiction imprint. Prefers 100-200 pgs. Royalty; negotiable advance. Responds in 3-4 mos. Guidelines.

Nonfiction: Complete ms. "We need advice and activity books and nonfiction specifically targeted to girls. "

Fiction: Complete ms. "All fiction for historical imprint must feature an American girl, age 8-12, from an historical period. We are also open to contemporary fiction for new imprint; stories must capture the spirit of contemporary American girls (ages 10-12)."

Tips: "If your idea would work for both boys and girls, it probably isn't for us."

PREP PUBLISHING, 1110½ Hay St., Fayetteville NC 28305. (910)483-6611. Fax (910)483-2439. E-mail: PREPPub@aol.com. Website: http://www. prep-pub.com. PREP, Inc. Anne McKinney, mng ed. Books to enrich people's lives and help them find joy in human experience. Publishes 10 titles/yr. Receives 1,500+ submissions annually. 85% of books from first-time authors. Reprints books. Prefers 250 pgs. Royalty 6-10% on retail; advance. Average first printing 3,000-5,000. Publication within 18 mos. Considers simultaneous submissions. Prefers e-mail submissions. Responds in 1 mo. Guidelines (also on Website) & catalog for #10 SAE/1 stamp.

Nonfiction: Query only; no phone query.

Fiction: Query only. All ages.

Tips: "Rewrite, rewrite, rewrite with your reader clearly in focus. "

PRESBYTERIAN AND REFORMED (P & R) PUBLISHING CO., PO Box 817, Phillipsburg NJ 08865. (908)454-0505. Fax (908)859-2390. Not a denominational house. Thom E. Notaro, ed. All books must be consistent with the Westminster Confession of Faith. Imprints: Craig Press; Evangelical Press. Publishes 8-10 titles/yr. Receives 200 submissions annually. 20% of books from first-time authors. Prefers 140-240 pgs. Royalty 5-14% of net; no advance. Average first printing 3,000. Publication within 8-10 mos. Considers simultaneous submissions. Disk required. Responds in 1-3 mos. Free guidelines/catalog.

Nonfiction: Proposal/3 chapters; fax query OK.

Tips: "Clear, engaging, and insightful applications of reformed theology to life. Offer us fully developed proposals and polished sample chapters."

*PRESERVATION PRESS, PO Box 612, 25 Russell Mill Rd., Swedesboro NJ 08085. (609)467-8902. Fax (609)467-3183. Website: http://www.preserva tionpress. com. Norma J. Del Viscio, pres. Seeks to release titles that speak to the restoration of the orthodox faith. Est. 1994. Publishes 16 titles/yr. Receives 80 submissions annually. 33% of books from first-time authors.

No mss through agents. Royalty 15% of net; no advance. Publication within 1 yr. Considers simultaneous submissions. Responds in 1-3 mos. Free guidelines/catalog.

Nonfiction: Query or proposal/2-3 chapters; phone query OK.

+PROMISE PRESS/BARBOUR PUBLISHING, INC., 1810 Barbour Dr., PO Box 719, Uhrichsville OH 44683. (614)922-6045. Fax (614)922-5948. E-mail: booksbarbour@ tusco.net. Website: http://www.barbourbooks.com. Susan Johnson, sr ed. Imprint of Barbour Publishing. Focuses on original nonfiction and gift titles by contemporary authors. Est. 1998.

+PROVIDENCE PRESS, PO Box 328, St. Eugene ON K0B 1P0 Canada. E-mail: provpress@hawk.igs.net. Independent, nondenominational. Sponsors an annual poetry and prose contest.

#G.P. PUTNAM'S SONS, 345 Hudson St., New York NY 10014. (212)951-8405. Fax (212)951-8694. Website: http://www.putnam.com. Imprint of Penguin Putnam. David Briggs, mng ed.; submit to Mayo Rao, ed asst, OR Children's Editorial Dept. 5% of books from first-time authors. Accepts mss through agents only. Variable royalty on retail; variable advance. Considers simultaneous submissions. Responds in 6 mos. Guidelines; request catalog through book order dept..

Nonfiction: Query only. "We publish some religious/inspirational books and books for ages 2-18."

Fiction: Adult or for ages 2-18. Primarily picture books or middle-grade novels.

Tips: "We prefer agented submissions."

QUESTAR PUBLISHERS—See Multnomah Publishers.

RAGGED EDGE, PO Box 152, Shippenburg PA 17257. (717)532-237.White Mane Publishing Co., Inc. Harold E. Collier, acq ed. Christian, social science and self-help books; to make a difference in people's lives. Publishes 10-15 titles/yr. Receives 50-75 submissions annually. 50% of books from first-time authors. **SUBSIDY PUBLISHES 20%.** Reprints books. Prefers 200 pgs. Variable royalty on net; advance. Average first printing 3,000. Publication within 1 yr. Considers simultaneous submissions. Responds in 60 days. Free guidelines/ catalog.

Nonfiction: Query only; fax query OK.

Fiction: Query only. For children (8-12) or teens (12-17).

Tips: "Most open to a Protestant book in the middle of the spectrum."

RAINBOW BOOKS, PO Box 430, Highland City FL 33846-0430. (888)613-2665. Fax (941)648-4420. E-mail: RBIbooks@aol.com. Betsy A. Lampe, sr ed. To provide solutions to real problems on an ethical level. Publishes 5 titles/yr. Receives 600 submissions annually. 90% of books from first-time authors. Minimum 15,000 wds. Royalty 6-10% on retail; variable advance. Average first printing 5,000. Publication within 10 mos. Considers simultaneous submissions. Disk on request. Responds in 8-10 wks. Guidelines; free copy.

Nonfiction: Query only; no phone/fax/e-query. Looking for self-help/ how-to books from authors with credentials on their subject matter. Wants something refreshing from the religious left; nothing from the religious right.

Fiction: Query only. For adults. No graphic violence or sex; good taste must prevail.

Tips: "We want to see books that deal with real world problems and provide solutions on a very ethical level. Write a good query and synopsis first."

RAINBOW PUBLISHERS/LEGACY PRESS, PO Box 261129, San Diego CA 92196. (619)271-7600. E-mail: celmed@aol.com. Christy Allen, ed. Publishes nondenominational, nonfiction for children and adults in the evangelical Christian market. Publishes 10 titles/yr. Receives 250 submissions annually. 50% of books from first-time authors. Reprints books. Prefers 150 pgs & up. Royalty 8% and up on net; advance $500. Average first printing 5,000. Publication within 2 yrs. Considers simultaneous submissions. Responds in 3 mos. Prefers disk. Guidelines; catalog for 9x12 SAE/2 stamps.

Nonfiction: Proposal/3-5 chapters; e-query OK. "Looking for nonfiction for girls ages 2-12 and women ages 30-60."

Tips: "We are interested in expanding our line for girls called The Criss-Cross Collection. We are also interested in books for adults, particularly women ages 30-60. All books must offer solid Bible teaching."

RAINBOW PUBLISHERS/RAINBOW BOOKS, Box 261129, San Diego CA 92196. (619)271-7600. Fax (612)578-4795. E-mail: celmed@aol.com. Christy Allen, ed. Publishes Bible-teaching, reproducible books for children's teachers. Publishes 20 titles/yr. Receives 250 submissions annually. 50% of books from first-time authors. Reprints books. Prefers 96 pgs. Outright purchases $640. Average first printing 2,500. Publication within 2 yrs. Considers simultaneous submissions. Responds in 3 mos. Accepts disk, no e-mail. Guidelines; catalog for 9x12 SAE/2 stamps.

Nonfiction: Proposal/3-5 chapters; e-query OK. "Looking for fun and easy ways to teach Bible concepts to kids, ages 2-12."

Special Needs: Creative puzzles and unique games.

Tips: "Request a catalog or visit your Christian bookstore to see what we have already published. You can either send a unique proposal or propose an addition to one of our existing series."

RAINBOW'S END CO., 354 Golden Grove Rd., Baden PA 15005. Phone/fax (412)266-4997. E-mail: Btucker833@aol.com. Website: http://rainbows-end-publish.com. Wayne P. Brumagin, ed; Bettie Tucker, dir of publications. To reach out in Christ and impact lives. Publishes 2-4 titles/yr. Receives 100 submissions annually. 100% of books from first-time authors. Prefers 150-200 pgs. Royalty 12-14% on retail; advance $250. Average first printing 1,000-3,000. Publication within 12-15 mos. Considers simultaneous submissions. Responds in 4-12 wks. Prefers disk. Guidelines; catalog for 9x12 SAE.

Nonfiction: Complete ms; e-query OK. "Looking for recovery books, self-help and how-to."

READ 'N RUN BOOKS, PO Box 294, Rhododendron OR 97049. (503)622-4798. Crumb Elbow Publishing. Michael P. Jones, pub. Books of lasting interest. Publishes 2 titles/yr. Receives 150 submissions annually. 90% of books from first-time authors. Reprints books. Royalty on net or copies; no advance; **SOME COOPERATIVE PUBLISHING**. Average first printing 1,000+. Publication within 3 mos. Considers simultaneous submissions. Responds in 3 mos. Guidelines; catalog $3.25.

> **Nonfiction:** Complete ms; no phone query. "Looking for historical (particularly Old West); the Pacific Northwest; missionary work among American Indians; fur trade and environmental."
>
> **Fiction:** Complete ms or proposal/3 chapters. Any type; any age. "Historical fiction would be great, especially if it involves the Old West or the Pacific NW. Realism is important."
>
> **Special Needs:** Also does postcards, note card, posters.
>
> **Ethnic Books:** Open to.
>
> **Tips:** "Nature and history are two areas we are seriously looking at, but also interested in poetry and short-story collections."

REGAL BOOKS, 2300 Knoll Dr., Ventura CA 93003. Does not accept unsolicited manuscripts.

*THE REGINA PRESS, 10 Hub Dr., Melville NY 11747-3503. (516)694-8600. Fax (516)694-2205. Catholic/Christian. George Malhame, juvenile ed. Publishes 5-10 titles/yr. Royalty on net; some outright purchases; some advances. Sometimes sends free catalog.

> **Fiction:** Query/proposal. Children's picture books for ages 3-8; coloring books.

#REGNERY PUBLISHING, 1 Massachusetts Ave. NW, Washington DC 20001-1401. (202)546-5005. Fax (202)546-8759. Eagle Publishing. Harry Crocker, exec ed; submit to Submissions Editor. Trade publisher that does scholarly Catholic books and evangelical Protestant books. Imprint: Gateway Editions. Publishes 2-4 religious titles/yr. Receives 30-50 submissions annually. Few books from first-time authors. Reprints books. Prefers 250-500 pgs. Royalty 8-15% on retail; advances to $50,000. Average first printing 5,000. Publication within 1 yr. Considers simultaneous submissions. Responds in 6 mos. Free catalog.

> **Nonfiction:** Proposal/1-3 chapters; no fax query. Looking for history, popular biography and popular history.
>
> **Tips:** "Religious books should relate to politics, history, current affairs, biography, and public policy. Most open to a book that deals with a topical issue from a conservative point of view—something that points out a need for spiritual renewal; or a how-to book on finding spiritual renewal."

RELIGIOUS EDUCATION PRESS, 5316 Meadow Brook Rd., Birmingham AL 35242-3315. (205)991-1000. Fax (205)991-9669. E-mail: ewlwsux@ix. netcom.com. Website: http://www.bham.net/releduc. Unaffiliated. James Michael Lee, ed. Mission is specifically directed toward helping fulfill, in an interfaith and ecumenical way, the Great Commission. Publishes 5-6 titles/yr. Receives 500 submissions annually. 40% of books from first-time authors. Prefers 200-500 pgs. Royalty 5% on net; advance. Average first printing 2,000. Publication within 9 mos. Responds in 1 mo. Requires disk. Guidelines; free catalog.

Nonfiction: Query only; phone/fax/e-query OK. Also publishes books on religious psychology and pastoral care.

Tips: "We publish serious, scholarly books written on a professional level in the field of religious education and closely related subject areas. Our books are intentionally multifaith, written for an ecumenical audience."

*RENLOW PUBLISHING, 4327 Pennswood Dr., Middletown OH 45042-2931. A general publisher that does a few inspirational or religious titles. D.E. Margerum, ed/pub. Send proposal/sample chapters. Not in topical listings.

#RESOURCE PUBLICATIONS, INC., Ste. 290, 160 E. Virginia St., San Jose CA 95112-5876. (408)286-8505. Fax (408)287-8748. E-mail: editor@rpinet.com, or roders@rpinet.com. Website: http://www.rpinet.com/ml/ml.html. Nick Wagner, ed dir. Publishes 20 titles/yr. Receives 450 submissions annually. 30% of books from first-time authors. Prefers 50,000 wds. Royalty 8% of net: rare advance. Average first printing 3,000. Publication within 1 yr. Responds in 10 wks. Prefers disk. Guidelines; catalog for 9x12 SAE/10 stamps.

Nonfiction: Proposal/1 chapter; phone/fax/e-query OK.

Fiction: Query. Adult/teen/children. Only read-aloud stories for storytellers. "Must be useful in ministerial, counseling, or educational settings."

Also Does: Computer programs; aids to ministry or education.

Tips: "Know our market. We cater to ministers in Catholic and mainstream Protestant settings. We are not an evangelical house or general interest publisher."

#RESURRECTION PRESS LTD, PO Box 248, Williston Park NY 11596. (516)742-5686. Fax (516)746-6872. Http://www.catholicity.cm/market/rpress. Catholic. Imprint: Spirit Life Series. Emilie Cerar, pub. Publishes 10-12 titles/yr. Receives 200 submissions annually. 25% of books from first-time authors. No mss through agents. Reprints books. Prefers 200 pgs. Royalty 5-10% on retail; advance $250-2,000. Average first printing 3,000. Publication within 1 yr. Considers simultaneous submissions. Responds in 1-2 mos. Free guidelines & catalog.

Nonfiction: Proposal/2 chapters; fax query OK. "Most open to pastoral resources, self-help, and spirituality for the active Christian."

FLEMING H. REVELL CO., Box 6287, Grand Rapids MI 49516. (616)676-9185. Fax (616)676-9573. E-mail: lholland@bakerbooks.com. Website: http://www. bakerbooks.com. Subsidiary of Baker Book House. Imprints: Revell, Chosen, Spire. Linda Holland, ed dir; submit to Sheila Ingram. Publishes 60 titles/yr. Receives 1,000 submissions annually. 10% of books from first-time authors. Prefers 60,000 wds. Royalty 10-14% on net; advance. Average first printing 5,000. Publication within 1 yr. Considers simultaneous submissions. Responds in 3 mos. Requires disk. Free guidelines (also on Website)/catalog.

Nonfiction: Proposal/2 chapters; no phone/fax/e-query.

Fiction: Proposal/2 chapters. Adult.

Tips: "Research the market for what's needed; maintain excellence; address a felt need; use good clarity and focus on topic."

**Note: This publisher serviced by The Writer's Edge.

REVIEW AND HERALD PUBLISHING ASSN., 55 W. Oak Ridge Dr., Hagerstown MD 21740-7390. (301)393-3000. Fax (301)393-4055. Seventh-Day Adventist. Jeannette Johnson, acq ed. Proclaims and upholds to the world the character of a loving Creator God and nurtures a growing relationship with God by providing products that teach and enrich people spiritually, mentally, physically, and socially. Publishes 50-60 titles/yr. Receives 400 submissions annually. 35-50% of books from first-time authors. Prefers 128-160 pgs. or 45,000 wds. Royalty 7-16% of net; advance $500. Average first printing 4,000. Publication within 12-18 mos. Considers simultaneous submissions. Requires disk. Responds in 1 mo. Requires disk. Guidelines; free catalog.

>   **Nonfiction:** Query, proposal/3 chapters or complete ms; phone/fax/e-query OK. "Looking for Christian living and spiritual growth books."
>
>   **Fiction:** Proposal/3 chapters or complete ms. All ages.
>
>   **Also Does:** Pamphlets, booklets, tracts.
>
>   **Tips:** "Looking for books that are practical, how-to, crisp and relevant."

ROSE PUBLISHING, 4455 Torrance Blvd. #259, Torrance CA 90503. (310)370-7152. Fax (310)370-7492. E-mail: rosepubl@aol.com (make subject Carol). Website: http://members.aol.com/rosepublis. Nondenominational. Carol Witte, mng ed. Publishes only large Sunday school charts and teaching materials. Publishes 5 titles/yr. 5% of books from first-time authors. Outright purchases. Publication within 6-12 mos. Free catalog.

>   **Special Needs:** Query with sketch of proposed chart (non-returnable); fax query OK; e-query OK if less than 100 wds (copied into message). Large teaching charts for Sunday schools; church history time lines; charts for children and youth. Also books on the Trinity, creation vs. evolution, Christian history, how we got the Bible, Ten Commandments, and the Lord's Prayer.
>
>   **Tips:** "Now accepting more freelance submissions. Material for children, youth, Bible study charts and study guides, pamphlets, maps, timelines."

*ROYAL PRODUCTIONS, 7127 Little River Turnpike, Ste. 205, Annandale VA 22003. (703)750-3078. Fax (703)916-7773. E-mail: TWMgroup@ipo.net. Nondenominational Christian and educational publisher. Fidelis Iyebote, mng ed. Publishes 8 titles/yr. 50% of books from first-time authors. Reprints books. Prefers 200 pgs. Royalty on net; no advance. Average first printing 5,000. Publication within 6 mos. Responds in 3 mos. Guidelines/catalog.

>   **Nonfiction:** Query only. Looking for Christian school books, celebrity profiles, environmental issues, ethics and sports, biographies/autobiographies of Christian music, entertainment or sports stars.
>
>   **Fiction:** Children's picture books.

Special Needs: Considering ideas for production of educational audio and video films, instructional and study aid material for math, biology, chemistry, physics, French and Spanish, and Christian education.

ST. ANTHONY MESSENGER PRESS, 1615 Republic St., Cincinnati OH 45210. (513)241-5615. (800)488-0488. Fax (513)241-0399 or 241-1197. E-mail: StAnthony@AmericanCatholic.org. Website: http://www.American Catholic.org. Catholic. Lisa Biedenbach, mng ed. Seeks to publish affordable resources for living a Catholic-Christian lifestyle. Imprint: Franciscan Communications and Ikonographics (videos). Publishes 18-20 titles/yr. Receives 240 submissions annually. 5% of books from first-time authors. No mss through agent. Reprints books. Prefers 25,000-50,000 wds or 100-200 pgs. Royalty 10-12% of net; advance $1,000. Average first printing 5,000. Publication within 12-18 mos. Responds in 2 mos. Accepts disk. Guidelines; catalog for 9x12 SAE/4 stamps.

Nonfiction: Query only/500-wd summary; fax/e-query OK. "Looking for resources for prayer and liturgy, and Catholic identity."

Special Needs: Family-based catechetical programs; children's books that teach Catholic-Christian values and doctrine; Catholic identity and how to pass on faith to children.

Ethnic Books: Hispanic, occasionally.

Also Does: Pamphlets and booklets.

Tips: "Know our audience. Books should be written in popular (not academic) style, use anecdotes or stories liberally to illumine your points or thesis, and reflect the best of modern Catholic teaching."

SAINT BEDE'S PUBLICATIONS, Box 545, Petersham MA 01366-0545. (978)724-3407 or (800)507-1000. Fax (978)724-3574 or (800)919-5600. E-mail: Meddy@hhcc.com. Website: http://www.stbedes.org. Catholic. Submit to St. Scolastica Priory. Evangelization focus. Publishes 8-12 titles/yr. Receives 200 submissions annually. 30% of books from first-time authors. Reprints books. **SUBSIDY PUBLISHES 1%.** Prefers 150-200 pgs. Royalty 5-8% on net or retail; no advance. Average first printing 500-2,000. Publication within 2 yrs. Accepts simultaneous submissions. Responds in 2 mos. Accepts disk. Guidelines; free catalog.

Nonfiction: Query only; phone/fax/e-query OK.

Tips: "Just state what you've got simply without gimmicks or attention-getting ploys that usually turn off editors before they've even read your proposal. If your work is worthy of publication, it will stand on its own."

SAINT MARY'S PRESS, 702 Terrace Heights, Winona MN 55987-1320. (507)457-7900. (800)533-8095. Fax (507)457-7990. E-mail: snagel@smp.org. Website: http://www.smp.org. Catholic. Steve Nagel, ed-in-chief. Fiction for teens, ages 11-17. Publishes 20-25 titles/yr. Reprints books. Prefers up to 40,000 wds. Royalty; advance. Average first printing 5,000. Publication within 2 mos. Accepts simultaneous submissions. Guidelines (also by e-mail); free catalog.

Fiction: Query/outline & chapters; e-query OK.

Tips: "Books that give insight into the struggle of teens to become healthy, hopeful adults and also shed light on Catholic experience, history or cultures."

SCARECROW PRESS, 4720 Boston Way., Lanham MD 20706. (301)459-3366. Fax (301)459-2118. Website: http://www.scarecrowpress.com. University Press of America. Shirley Lambert, ed dir; submit to Katie Regen, asst ed. Publishes 5-15 titles/yr. Receives 50 submissions annually. 35% of books from first-time authors. Prefers 250-350 pgs. Royalty 10-15% of net; no advance. Average first printing 525. Publication within 8-12 mos. Considers simultaneous submissions. Responds in 2-4 mos. Requires disk. Free guidelines/catalog.

Nonfiction: Proposal/2-3 chapters; phone/fax/e-query OK. "Looking for reference, religion and scholarly books."

SCHOCKEN BOOKS, INC., 201 E. 50th St., New York NY 10022. (212)572-2559. Fax (212)572-6030. Website: http://www.Randomhouse.com. Imprint of Random House. Arthur Samuelson, ed dir. Publishes trade nonfiction in a variety of areas that have potential for substantial backlist life. Publishes 4 religion titles/yr. Receives 1,000 submissions annually. 5% of books from first-time authors. Reprints books. Royalty; advance. Average first printing 10,000. Publication within 1 yr. Considers simultaneous submissions. Responds in 4-6 wks. No disk. No guidelines; free catalog.

Nonfiction: Send proposal or complete ms. "Looking for general non-fiction."

SCRIPTURE PRESS—See Chariot Victor Books.

HAROLD SHAW PUBLISHERS, Box 567, Wheaton IL 60189. (630)665-6700. Fax (630)665-6793. E-mail: shawpub@compuserve.com. Website: www.shawpub.com. Submit to Editorial Assistant. Publishes a diverse range of books to meet the diverse needs of readers. Imprints: Wheaton Literary Series, North Wind. Publishes 40-45 titles/yr. Receives 800 submissions annually. 10-20% of books from first-time authors. Reprints books. Royalty on retail; outright purchases $375-2,000 (for Bible study guides and compilations); advance. Average first printing 5,000. Publication within 9-18 mos. Prefers no simultaneous submissions. Prefers disk. Responds in 6-8 wks. Guidelines on Website; catalog for 9x12 SAE/5 stamps.

Nonfiction: Proposal/2-3 chapters; no phone/fax/e-query. "Looking for stellar books on felt need just developing in the marketplace."

Fiction: Proposal/4 chapters. Prefers high-quality, literary fiction; no phone/fax/e-query.

Tips: "Authors must have an audience and a purpose in mind before they begin. Most manuscripts are the author's thoughts on some topic few people care about."

**Note: This publisher serviced by The Writer's Edge.

SHEED & WARD, 7373 S. Lovers Lane Rd., Franklin WI 53132. (800)558-0580. E-mail: jereditor@aol.com. Website: http://www.theobooks.org. National Catholic Reporter Publishing Co. Jeremy Langford, ed-in-chief (773-404-7449). Publishes 30 titles/yr. Receives 200 submissions annually. 10% of books from first-time authors. No mss through agents. **SUBSIDY PUBLISHES 2%.** Reprints books. Prefers 100-200 pgs. Royalty 6/8/10% on retail; some work-for-hire; flexible advance. Average first printing 2,000. Publication within 6 mos. Responds in 3 mos. Requires disk. Guidelines; catalog for 7x11 SAE/2 stamps.

Nonfiction: Complete ms; phone/fax/e-query OK. "Looking for parish ministry (euthanasia, health care, spirituality, leadership, sacraments, small group or priestless parish facilitating books)."

Tips: "Be in touch with needs of progressive/changing parishes."

*SHINING STAR PUBLICATIONS, 1204 Buchanan St., Carthage IL 62321. Fax (217)357-6095. Division of Frank Schaffer Publications. Mary Tucker, ed. Publishes 20 titles/yr. Receives 30-40 submissions annually. 25% of books from first-time authors. No mss through agents. Prefers 48-96 pgs. Outright purchases $20/pg.; no advance. Average first printing 3,000. Publication within 12 mos. No simultaneous submissions. Prefers disk. Responds in 2 mos. Guidelines; free catalog.

Nonfiction: Query first; phone/fax query OK. "We need reproducible workbooks to teach Scriptures and Christian values; Bible activities; Bible story crafts; skits and songs with a Christian emphasis."

Tips: "We publish only Bible activity books with reproducible pages for teachers and parents to use in home or church teaching situations; no picture books or children's novels."

SKYSONG PRESS, 35 Peter St. S., Orillia ON L3V 5A8 Canada. E-mail: skysong@bconnex.net. Website: http://www.bconnex.net/~skysong. Steve Stanton, ed. Guidelines on Website.

Fiction: Christian science-fiction only. "New authors should not submit novel manuscripts. Send us something for Dreams & Visions (see periodical section) first."

SMALL HELM PRESS, 622 Baker St., Petaluma CA 94952-2525. (707)763-5757. E-mail: smllhelm@sonic.net. Website: http://www.sonic.net/~smll helm. Alice Pearl Evans, pub. Interprets direction in contemporary life. Publishes 1 title/yr. Receives few submissions. Reprints books. Prefers 96-224 printed pgs. Outright purchase, negotiable. Average first printing 1,000-2,000. Publication within 9 mos. Considers simultaneous submissions. Responds in 2-4 wks. Catalog for 9x12 SAE/3 stamps.

Nonfiction: Query, proposal or complete ms; prefers phone query.

Tips: "Most open to nonfiction of interest to general public and based on cultural or philosophical issues with a Christian worldview. Write with conviction and credibility."

SMYTH & HELWYS PUBLISHING, INC., 6316 Peake Rd., Macon GA 31210-3960. (912)752-2217. Fax (912)752-2264. E-mail: shelwys@mindspring. com. Website: http://www.helwys.com. Theresa Peterlein, VP Marketing. Quality resources for the church and individual Christians that are nurtured by faith and informed by scholarship. Publishes 35 titles/yr. Receives 600 submissions annually. 25% of books from first-time authors. Prefers 144 pgs. Royalty 7%. Considers simultaneous submissions. Responds in 3 mos. Free guidelines/catalog.

Nonfiction: Query only; fax/e-query OK. "Most open to books appropriate for mainline church community."

Tips: "Most open to books with a strong secondary or special market beyond the trade."

+SONSTAR PUBLISHING, PO Box 214, Houghton Lake MI 48629. (517)422-3647. Fax (517)42-2730. E-mail: info@sonstar.com. Jack Metzler, ed. Books that tackle difficult problems, especially from first-time authors. Imprints: Sonstar, Trail's End, Blue Goose. Publishes 1-5 titles/yr. Receives 15-20 submissions annually. 95% of books from first-time authors. Reprints books. Prefers 70,000 wds. Royalty 8-15% of net; no advance. Average first printing 3,00-5,000. Publication within 12-18 mos. Considers simultaneous submissions. No disk or e-mail submissions. Responds in 2 mos. No guidelines or catalog.

    Nonfiction: Proposal/2-3 chapters; fax/e-query OK. "Looking for books on child and spouse abuse; children of divorce."

    Fiction: Query or complete ms. For all ages.

    Also Does: Booklets.

SOWER'S PRESS, PO Box 666306, Marietta GA 30066. (770)977-3784. Jamey Wood, ed. Books to further establish the ministries of speakers and teachers. Publishes 2-3 titles/yr. Responds in 1 mo.

    Nonfiction: Proposal/chapters. Marriage and family books.

STANDARD PUBLISHING, 8121 Hamilton Ave., Cincinnati OH 45231. (513)931-4050. Fax (513)931-0950. E-mail: standardpub@attmail.com. Standex Intl. Corp. Diane Stortz, dir of new product development. An evangelical Christian publisher of curriculum, classroom resources, teen resources, children's books, and drama. Publishes 150 titles/yr. Receives 1,500 submissions annually. 25% of books from first-time authors. Royalty & work for hire; advance. Average first printing 10,000 (depends on product). Publication within 12-18 mos. Considers simultaneous submissions. Responds in 2 mos. Prefers disk. Guidelines; catalog $2.

    Nonfiction: Send complete proposal, including sample chapters, to Christian Education Team, Children's Editor, Teen Editor, Drama Team, or Adult Editor.

    **Note: This publisher serviced by The Writer's Edge.

STARBURST PUBLISHERS, PO Box 4123, Lancaster PA 17604. (717)293-0939. Fax (717)293-1945. E-mail: starburst@starburstpublishers.com. Website: http://www.starburstpublisher.com. Evangelical. David A. Robie, ed. Publishes books that will reach the Christian and general market. Publishes 15 titles/yr. Receives 1,000 submissions annually. 50% of books from first-time authors. Prefers 200-300 pgs. Royalty 6-15% of net; some advances. Average first printing 5,000-10,000. Publication within 12-18 mos. Considers simultaneous submissions. No disks. Responds in 2-4 wks. Guidelines (also on Website); catalog for 9x12 SAE/4 stamps.

    Nonfiction: Proposal/3 chapters; e-mail query OK, no phone query.

    Fiction: Proposal/3 chapters. Adult. "We are looking for good, wholesome fiction. Inspirational self-help."

    Tips: "Most open to nonfiction that can be sold in both Christian and general markets. Be fresh!"

STILL WATERS REVIVAL BOOKS, 4710–37A Ave., Edmonton AB T6L 3T5 Canada. (403)450-3730. E-mail: swrb@swrb.com. Website: http://

www.swrb.com. Reformed Church. Reg Barrow, pres. Publishes 100 titles/yr. Receives few submissions. Very few books from first-time authors. Reprints books. Prefers 128-160 pgs. Negotiated royalty or outright purchase. Considers simultaneous submissions. Catalog for 9x12 SAE/2 stamps.

Nonfiction: Proposal/2 chapters. "Reformed (especially Covenanter) books of scholarly value, for the use of educated laymen." No non-Reformed or premillennial.

Tips: "Most open to books based on the system of doctrine found in the Westminster confession of faith, as it applies to our contemporary setting."

+**THE SUMMIT PUBLISHING GROUP**, 2000 Lamar Blvd. Ste. 600, Arlington TX 76006. (817)588-3013. Jill Bertolet, pub. Secular publisher of contemporary nonfiction books, including some religious. Publishes 35 titles/yr. 40% of books from first-time authors. Reprints books. Royalty 5-20% of net; advance $2,000 & up. Publication within 6 mos. Considers simultaneous submissions. Responds in 1-3 mos. Guidelines; catalog for 9x12 SAE/5 stamps.

Nonfiction: Proposal/2 chapters.

Tips: "Books need national distribution appeal. Author's media experience, contacts and exposure are a strong plus. "

*****SUMMIT PUBLISHING, LTD.**, Denvigh House, Denvigh Rd., Milton Keynes MK1 1YP, England. Charismatic. Noel Halsey, pres. Send query with a summary, table of contents, and excerpts from the manuscript.

SWORD OF THE LORD PUBLISHERS, PO Box 1099, Murfreesboro TN 37133-1099. (615)893-6700. Fax (615)895-7447. E-mail: editorial@ swordofthelord.com. Website: http://www.swordofthelord.com. Independent Baptist. Dr. Shelton Smith, ed. Publishes 24 titles/yr. Receives 60-75 submissions annually. 20% of books from first-time authors. No mss through agents. Reprints books. Royalty 5-10% on net or retail; no advance. Average first printing 7,500. Publication within 6-12 mos. Considers simultaneous submissions. Disk OK. Responds in 6-9 mos. Prefers KJV. Free guidelines/catalog.

Nonfiction: Complete ms; no phone/fax/e-query.

Fiction: Complete ms. For all ages, including picture books.

Also Does: Booklets, pamphlets.

Tips: "Check spelling and grammar. Have professionally edited."

TABOR PUBLISHING. Replaced by Thomas More.

+**TEKNA BOOKS**, PO Box 461, Chanhassen MN 55317. Phone/fax (612)401-9695. E-mail: submissions@teknbooks.com. Website: http://www.tekna books.com. Ecumenical. Submit to Acquisitions Editor. Seeks to pass the torch of faith to future generations. Publishes 2-5 titles/yr. Receives 30 submissions annually. **SUBSIDY PUBLISHES SOME BOOKS.** No length preference. Royalty 4-12% of retail; no advance. Average first printing 1,000. Publication within 10 mos. Considers simultaneous submissions. Prefers e-mail submissions (in rich text format). Responds in 1-2 mos. Guidelines (also by e-mail or on Website); catalog on Website. For guidelines, e-mail: guide@teknabooks.com.

Nonfiction: Proposal/chapters or complete ms; e-query OK.

Tips: "We realize that it is almost impossible for new authors with fresh insight to have a voice in a publishing industry with already-established agendas. While we certainly work with published authors, we are exceptionally receptive to new authors."

+TIME FOR LAUGHTER/WATERBROOK PRESS, 7814 Potomac Dr., Colorado Springs CO 80920. (719)590-4999. Fax (719)590-8977. Autonomous subsidiary of Bantam Doubleday Dell Publishing Group. New romance line. 62,000 wds.

TOCCOA FALLS COLLEGE PRESS, Toccoa Falls College, PO Box 800067, Toccoa Falls GA 30598. (706)886-6831. Fax (706)886-0210. Marcille P. Jordan, ed. Publishes quality Christian material for the church and academic community. Publishes 4 titles/yr. Receives 7 submissions annually. 75% of books from first-time authors. Very limited subsidy. Prefers 150-250 pgs. Royalty 10% of retail; no advance. Average first printing 1,500-3,000. Publication within 3 mos. Considers simultaneous submissions. Responds ASAP. Guidelines.

Nonfiction: Query, proposal or complete ms; phone/fax query OK.

Fiction: Query, proposal, or complete ms. For children or teens.

Tips: "We are looking for material that is biblical, practical and well written."

TOUCH PUBLICATIONS, PO Box 19888, Houston TX 77224-9888. (281)497-7901. Fax (281)497-0904. E-mail: eliz@touchusa.org. Website: http://www.touchusa.org. Touch Outreach Ministries. Elizabeth Bruns, ed; Scott Boren, dir of new products. To awaken the church in North America to dynamic life and outreach so more brought to Christ through cell churches. Publishes 8 titles/yr. Receives 25 submissions annually. 40% of books from first-time authors. Reprints books. Prefers 75-200 pgs. Royalty 10-15% of net; no advance. Average first printing 2,000. Not in topical listings.

Nonfiction: Query only. "Must relate to cell church life."

Tips: "Our market is extremely focused. We publish books, resources and discipleship tools for churches, using a cell group strategy."

TREASURE LEARNING SYSTEMS (formerly Treasure Publishing), 1133 Riverside Ave., Fort Collins CO 80524. (970)484-8483. Fax (970)495-6700. E-mail: mark@treasurelearning.com. Website: http://www.treasurelearning.com. Mark Steiner, sr. ed. To assist the church in fulfilling the Great Commission. Publishes 10 titles/yr. Receives 100 submissions annually. 80% of books from first-time authors. Reprints books. Prefers 1,200 wds or 32 pgs. Royalty 5-10% of net; outright purchases of $1,000-5,000; advance. Publication within 1 yr. Considers simultaneous submissions. Responds in 4 wks. Accepts disk, no e-mail. Guidelines; catalog for SAE/2 stamps.

Nonfiction: Proposal/2 chapters. Children's picture books or topical and exegetical Bible study resources for adults.

Tips: "We need Bible-based material and curriculum writers for children, teens and adults."

THE TRINITY FOUNDATION, PO Box 68, Unicoi TN 37692. (423)743-0199. Fax (423)743-2005. E-mail: JROB1517@aol.com. Website: http://www.

trinityfoundation.org. John W. Robbins, pres. To promote the logical system of truth found in the Bible. Publishes 6 titles/yr. Receives 3 submissions annually. No books from first-time authors. No mss through agents. Reprints books. Prefers 200 pgs. Outright purchase; free books; no advance. Average first printing 3,000. Publication within 9 mos. No simultaneous submissions. Requires disk. Responds in 2 mos. No guidelines: catalog for #10 SAE/1 stamp.

Nonfiction: Query letter only. Most open to Calvinist/Clarkian books.

Also Does: Booklets and tracts.

Tips: "Most open to well-written, Calvinist, biblical books. Read Gordon Clark first."

TRINITY PRESS INTERNATIONAL, PO Box 1321, Harrisburg PA 17105. (717)541-813o. Fax (717)541-8136. E-mail: hrast@morehousegroup. com. Website: http://www.morehousegroup.com. Dr. Harold W. Rast, dir. A nondenominational, academic religious publisher. Publishes 35 titles/ yr. Receives 150-200 submissions annually. 3% of books from first-time authors. Reprints books. Royalty 10% on net; advance $500 & up. Average first printing 2,000. Publication within 8-12 mos. Responds in 3-6 mos. Guidelines; free catalog.

Nonfiction: Complete ms or proposal/3 chapters. "Religious material only in the area of Bible studies, theology, ethics, etc." No dissertations or essays.

Tips: "Most open to a book that is academic, to be used in undergraduate biblical studies, theology or religious studies program."

TYNDALE HOUSE PUBLISHERS, 351 Executive Dr., Box 80, Wheaton IL 60189-0080. (630)668-8300. Fax (630)668-3245. Website: http://www.tyndale. com. Submit to The Editor. Imprints: Heart Quest (see separate listing). Publishes 100 titles/yr. 5-10% of books from first-time authors. Reprints books. Royalty; outright purchase of some children's books. Average first printing 5,000-10,000. Publication within 12-18 mos. No unsolicited mss. Guidelines; catalog for 9x12 SAE/9 stamps.

Nonfiction: Query only; no phone/fax query.

Fiction: Query only. "All must have a distinct Christian message."

**Note: This publisher serviced by The Writer's Edge.

UNITED CHURCH PRESS, 700 Prospect Ave. E., Cleveland OH 44115-1100. (216)736-3704. Fax (216)736-3703. E-mail: sadlerk@ucc.org. Website: http:// www.ucpress.com. United Church of Christ/Board for Homeland Missions. Kim M. Sadler, ed. Publishes 15-25 titles/yr. Receives 150+ submissions annually. 50% of books from first-time authors. Royalty 8% of net; work for hire, one-time fee; advance negotiable. Average first printing 3,000. Publication within 9-12 mos. Considers simultaneous submissions. Responds in 6-8 wks. Requires disk. Free guidelines/catalog.

Nonfiction: Proposal/2 chapters or complete ms; e-query OK.

Special Needs: Children's sermons, worship resources, youth materials, religious materials for ethnic groups.

Ethnic Books: African-American, Native-American, Asian-American, Pacific Islanders, and Hispanic.

Tips: "Most open to well-written mss that are United Church of Christ specific and/or religious topics that cross denominations. Use inclusive language and follow the *Chicago Manual of Style*."

UNITED CHURCH PUBLISHING HOUSE, 3250 Bloor St. W., 4th floor, Toronto ON M8X 2Y4 Canada. (416)231-5931. Fax (416)232-6004. E-mail: bookpub@uccan.org. Website: http://www.uccan.ucph.org. The United Church of Canada. Submit to Acquisitions Editor. Publishes socially important books that raise awareness of timely issues. Publishes 10 titles/yr. Receives 75 submissions annually. 60% of books from first-time authors. No mss through agents. Prefers 150-200 pgs. Royalty 10% of net; advance $100. Average first printing 1,500. Publication within 6 mos. considers simultaneous submissions. Responds in 4-8 wks. Accepts disk or e-mail submissions. Guidelines; free catalog.

Nonfiction: Proposal/1-2 chapters; phone/e-query OK. Publishes Canadian authors only. "Books on Jubilee."

Tips: "We publish books in the areas of Christian education; resources for church, worship, music; social issues; United Church History and leaders; and women and religion. Liberal viewpoints and theology."

UNITED METHODIST PUBLISHING HOUSE. See Abingdon Press and Dimensions for Living.

UNIVERSITY OF OTTAWA PRESS, 542 King Edward Ave., Ottawa ON K1N 6N5 Canada. (613)562-5246. Fax (613)562-5247. E-mail: press@uottawa. ca. Website: http://www.uopress.uottawa.ca/en/welcome.html. Dr. V. Bennett, ed-in-chief. Promotes scholarly, academic publications. Publishes 2-4 titles/yr. Receives 300 submissions annually. No mss through agents. Prefers 250-300 pgs. Royalty 8-10% on net; no advance. Average first printing 800. Publication within 10-12 mos. Accepts simultaneous submissions. Responds in 2 wks. Accepts disk. Free guidelines/catalog.

Nonfiction: Query/proposal/at least 2 chapters; fax/e-query OK. Scholarly books only (peer reviewed). Social scientific study of religion.

UNIVERSITY PRESS OF AMERICA, 4720 Boston Way, Lanham MD 20706. (301)731-9540. Fax (301)459-2118. E-mail: pcooper@univpress.com. Website: http://www.univpress.com. Rowman & Littlefield Publishing Group/academic. Peter Cooper, acq ed. Publishes scholarly works in the social sciences and humanities; established by academics for academics. Publishes 50 religious titles/yr. Receives 100 submissions annually. 75% of books from first-time authors. Reprints books. Prefers 200 pgs. Royalty 12% of net; no advance. Average first printing 500. Publication within 6 mos. Considers simultaneous submissions. Responds in 1-2 mos. Requires disk. Guidelines; free catalog.

Nonfiction: Complete ms/resume; phone/fax/e-query OK. "Looking for scholarly manuscripts."

Ethnic Books: African studies; Black studies.

Tips: "We publish academic and scholarly books only. Authors are typically affiliated with a college, university or seminary."

UPPER ROOM BOOKS, 1908 Grand Ave., Box 189, Nashville TN 37202-0189. (615)340-7256. Fax (615)340-7006. Website: http://www.upperroom.org. No freelance.

VICTOR BOOKS—See Chariot Victor Books.

VICTORY HOUSE, INC., Box 700238, Tulsa OK 74170. (918)747-5009. Fax (918)747-1970. E-mail: vhigw@aol.com. Lloyd B. Hildebrand, mng ed. To edify the body of Christ. Publishes 4-5 titles/yr. Not accepting unsolicited mss at this time. No mss through agents. No guidelines; catalog for #10 SAE/1 stamp.

VITAL ISSUES PRESS, Box 53788, Lafayette LA 70505-3788. (318)237-7049. Fax (318)237-7060. Imprint of Huntington House Publishers. Mark Anthony, ed-in-chief. Focus is on educating readers on current events. Publishes 25-30 titles/yr. Receives 1,500 submissions annually. 25% of books from first-time authors. Reprints books. Prefers 50,000-60,000 wds or 208-224 pgs. Royalty 10% on net; negotiable advance. Average first printing 5,000-10,000. Publication within 1 yr. Considers simultaneous submissions. Responds in 4 mos. Free guidelines/catalog.

> **Nonfiction:** Query/outline.

WADSWORTH PUBLISHING COMPANY, 10 Davis Dr., Belmont CA 94002. (415)595-2350. Fax (415)637-7544. E-mail: peter_adams@wadsworth. com. Website: http://www.thomson.com/wadsworth.html. Division of International Thomson Publishing, Inc.; secular publisher that does some religious books. Mr. Robin Zwettler, ed dir. Publishes 5-10 higher education religious textbooks/yr. Receives 200 submissions annually. 35% of books from first-time authors. No mss through agents. Reprints books. Royalty 5-15% on net; few advances. Average first printing 5,000. Publication within 1 yr. Considers simultaneous submissions. Responds in 1 mo. Free guidelines/catalog (by subject area).

> **Nonfiction:** Query or proposal/chapters; fax/e-query OK. "Looking for college textbooks, especially on world religions; anthologies."

WATERBROOK PRESS, 5446 N. Academy Dr. Ste. 200, Colorado Springs CO 80918. (719)590-4999. Fax (719)590-8977. Autonomous subsidiary of Bantam Doubleday Dell Publishing Group. Not currently open to freelance submissions.

> ****Note:** This publisher serviced by The Writer's Edge.

WESLEYAN PUBLISHING HOUSE, Box 50434, Indianapolis IN 46250. (317)570-5100. Fax (317)570-5370. E-mail: publisher@wesleyan.org. Website: http://www.wesleyan.org. The Wesleyan Church. Nathan Birky, pub. Denominational publisher. Does full royalty publishing, printing, and helps authors with self-publishing. Royalty. Requires disk. Guidelines. Incomplete topical listings.

> **Nonfiction:** Proposal/1 chapter.

> **Tips:** "We provide Christian curriculum and ministry resources, Bible study materials and books of general interest to Wesleyans. While membership in the Wesleyan Church is not required of our writers, we carefully examine manuscripts for such things as doctrinal compatibility and biblical interpretation."

WESTERN FRONT, LTD., 2275 San Ysidro Dr., Beverly Hills CA 90210-1548. (800)764-0012. Fax (888)378-8917. E-mail: prezwfl@earthlink.net. Website: http://www.11B-Report.com. Cliff Ford, pres. Publishes 4 titles/yr. Receives 30 submissions annually. 10% of books from first-time authors. No mss through agents. Reprints books. Prefers 320 pgs. Royalty 13-18% of net; no advance. Average first printing 15,000. Publication within 1 yr. No simultaneous submissions. Prefers e-mail submissions. Responds in 2-3 mos. No guidelines/catalog.

Nonfiction: Query only; phone/e-query OK.

Fiction: Query only. For adults.

WESTMINSTER JOHN KNOX PRESS, 100 Witherspoon St., Louisville KY 40202-1396. (502)569-5043. Fax (502)569-5113. E-mail: segnotov@2ctr. pcusa.org. Website: http://www. pcusa.org/ppc. Presbyterian Church (USA). Dr. Richard E. Brown, dir.; Stephanie Egnotovich, mng ed; G. Nick Street, Mark Ledbetter, and Cynthia Thompson, eds. Publishes 80-100 titles/yr. Prefers 200 pgs. Royalty 7-10%; negotiable advance. Responds in 2-3 mos. Requires disk. Guidelines (also on Website); free catalog.

Nonfiction: Proposal/chapters; fax query OK. Emphasizes Bible, ethics, spirituality, inspiration, biography, and theology.

+WHITE STONE CIRCLE, 1718 E. Speedway Blvd. Ste. 319, Tucson AZ 85719. (877)424-7253. Fax 011(526)226.1380. Independent. Wayne A. Ewing, Ph.D., ed. To provide fresh, high-quality, inspirational material on any variety of real-life living and concerns. Publishes 1-3 titles/yr. New publisher. 100% of books from first-time authors. Prefers 120-180 pgs. Will contract on individual basis; no advance. Average first printing 3,000. Publication within 18 mos. Considers simultaneous submissions. Requires disk. Responds in 2 mos. Guidelines; no catalog yet.

Nonfiction: Query only; fax query OK. "We are already booked through mid-2000. We will entertain queries in July 2000."

Also Does: Calligraphy poetry suitable for hanging.

Tips: "Most open to absolutely startling; creative; controversial; useful in the practicalities of life; hopeful and healing books. "

WOOD LAKE BOOKS, INC., 9025 Jim Bailey Rd., Kelowna BC V4V 1R2 Canada. (250)766-2778. Fax (250)766-2736. E-mail: info@woodlake.com. Website: http://www.joinhands.com. Ecumenical/mainline; Wood Lake Books, Inc. Cheryl Perry, series ed. Publishes quality resources that respond to the needs of the ecumenical church and promote spiritual growth and commitment to God. Publishes 5 titles/yr. Receives 100 submissions annually. 50% of books from first-time authors. Reprints books. Prefers 200-250 pgs. Royalty on net; compiler's fee (for compilations) $1,000-3,000; some advances $1,000-1,500. Average first printing 3,000-4,000. Publication within 18-24 mos. Considers simultaneous submissions. Prefers disk. Responds in 6-12 wks. Free guidelines/catalog.

Nonfiction: Query or proposal/2 chapters; fax/e-query OK. "Books with inclusive language and mainline, Protestant interest."

Tips: "We publish books, curriculum and resources for the mainline church. All queries and submissions should reflect this in their theological approach and use of inclusive language for God."

WORD PUBLISHING, 545 Marriott Dr., Ste 750, Nashville TN 37214. (615)902-3400. Fax (615)902-3200. E-mail: WRDPUB@aol.com. Website: http://www.thomasnelson.com. Joey Paul, sr VP; submit to Mark Sweeney. Query/outline and sample chapters. Does not accept unsolicited manuscripts. Prefers 65,000-95,000 wds. Royalty. No guidelines; free catalog.

   Nonfiction: Proposal/3 chapters. "Nonfiction dealing with the relationship and/or application of biblical principles to everyday life; 65,000-95,000 words."

   Fiction: Complete ms. Adult.

   **Note: This publisher serviced by The Writer's Edge.

WORLD BIBLE PUBLISHERS, 2976 Ivanrest Ave., Grandville MI 49418. (616)531-9110. Fax (616)531-9120. E-mail: WorldPub@aol.com. Riverside Book & Bible (Jordan Industries). Shari TeSlaa, ed.; submit to Carol A. Ochs, pub asst. Publishes Bibles and Bible-related products. Imprints: World and World Audio. Publishes 5-10 bks/yr; 15-20 Bibles. Receives 200-300 submissions annually. 1% of books from first-time authors. Prefers 200-375 pgs. Royalty 5-12% of net; advance $1,000. Average first printing 5,000-10,000. Publication within 18 mos. Considers simultaneous submissions. Responds in 3 mos. Requires disk. Guidelines; catalog for 9x12 SAE/5 stamps.

   Nonfiction: Proposal/3 chapters; no phone/fax/e-query. "Looking for devotional/inspirational books with a unique approach that are well-written."

   Ethnic Books: African-American.

   Tips: "Most open to books that are Bible-based; non-technical reference; devotional; books that can incorporate God's Word translation."

   **Note: This publisher serviced by The Writer's Edge.

YALE UNIVERSITY PRESS, PO Box 209040, New Haven CT 06520-9040. (203)432-0900. Fax (203)432-2394. Website: http//www.yale.edu/yup. Charles Grench, ed-in-chief. Publishes 10 religious titles/yr. Receives 200 submissions annually. 15% of books from first-time authors. Reprints books. Prefers up to 100,000 wds or 400 pgs. Royalty to 15% on net or retail; advance $500-30,000. Average first printing 1,500. Publication within 1 yr. Considers simultaneous submissions. Requires disk; no e-mail. Responds in 1-3 mos. Free guidelines (also on Website under FAQs)/catalog.

   Nonfiction: Proposal/1-2 chapters; fax query OK. "Excellent and salable scholarly books."

YOUNG READER'S CHRISTIAN LIBRARY, 1810 Barbour Dr., PO Box 719, Uhrichsville OH 44683. (614)922-6045. Fax (614)922-5948. E-mail: info@ barbourbooks.com. Website: http://www.barbourbooks.com. Susan Johnson, sr ed. Children's imprint of Barbour Publishing, Inc. 75% of books from first-time authors. No mss through agents. Reprints books. Prefers about 16,000 wds. Makes outright purchases $1,000. Publication within 2 yrs. Considers simultaneous submissions. Responds in 10 wks. Guidelines; catalog for 9x12 SAE/4 stamps.

   Nonfiction & Fiction: Proposal/3-4 chapters.

Tips: "We prefer action-oriented, fast-paced style at a sixth-grade reading level. The subject of the manuscript can be contemporary (post-World War II to today), a Bible character, or an historical figure."

YWAM PUBLISHING, PO Box 55787, Seattle WA 98155. (425)771-1153. Fax (425)775-2383. E-mail: 75701.2772@compuserve.com. Youth With a Mission. James Drake, sr ed. Provides missions-based materials to assist the Body of Christ worldwide in fulfilling the great commission. Publishes 15 titles/yr. Receives 100 submissions annually. 20% of books from first-time authors. Reprints books. Prefers 190 pgs. Royalty on net; advance. Average first printing 10,000. Publication within 5 mos . Considers simultaneous submissions. Responds in 3 mos. Accepts disk, no e-mail. Guidelines; catalog for 9x12 SAE/3 stamps.

Nonfiction: Query only; e-query OK. "Needs non-fiction missionary stories from different countries."

Fiction: Query only. For children and teens. "Especially historical mission stories with evangelism themes."

Also Does: Personal prayer diary—daily planner.

ZONDERVAN PUBLISHING HOUSE, General Trade Books; Academic and professional Books, 5300 Patterson SE, Grand Rapids MI 49530-0002. (616)698-6900. Fax (616)698-3454. E-mail: zpub@zph.com. Website: http://www. zondervan.com. HarperCollins. Scott Bolinder, sr VP; submit to Trade Manuscript Review Editor (A-1); Gwen Ellis, gift books. Seeks to meet the needs of people with resources that glorify Jesus Christ and promote biblical principles. Publishes 150 trade titles/yr. Receives about 2,000 submissions annually. 1% of books from first-time authors. Prefers 50,000 wds. Royalty on net; variable advance. Publication within 1 yr. Considers simultaneous submissions. Responds in 8-12 wks. Prefers NIV. Prefers disk. Free guidelines (also on Website at http://www.zondervan.com/subguide.htm) and catalog.

Nonfiction: Query only/outline & 1 chapter; no phone/fax/e-query.

Fiction: Query only.

Ethnic Books: Vida Publishers division: Spanish, Portuguese, and French.

Tips: "Absolutely stellar prose that meets demonstrated needs of our market always receives a fair and sympathetic hearing."

**Note: This publisher serviced by The Writer's Edge.

BOOK PUBLISHERS NOT INCLUDED

This information is now included in the General Index. See introduction to that section.

SUBSIDY PUBLISHERS

WHAT YOU NEED TO KNOW ABOUT SUBSIDY PUBLISHERS

Again this year, I am listing here any publishers who do 50% or more subsidy publishing. For our purposes here, I am defining a subsidy publisher as any publisher that requires the author to pay for any part of the publishing costs. They may call themselves by a variety of names, such as a book packager, a cooperative publisher, self-publisher, or simply someone who helps authors get their books published. Note that some of these also do at least some royalty publishing.

In the last couple of years, with the refinement of desk-top publishing, more subsidy publishers have sprung up, and there has been an increase in confusion over who or what type of subsidy publishing is legitimate, and what publishers fall in with what we call "vanity publishers." As many of the legitimate publishers (and even some questionable ones) try to distance themselves from the notoriety of the vanity publisher, they have come up with a variety of names to try to form definite lines of distinction. Unfortunately, it has only served to confuse the authors who might use their services. It is my hope in offering this separate listing that I can help you understand what this side of publishing entails, what to look for in a subsidy publisher, as well as what to look out for. To my knowledge the following publishers are legitimate subsidy publishers and are not vanity publishers. It is important that as a writer you understand that any time you are asked to send money for any part of the production of your book, you are entering into a non-traditional relationship with a publisher. In this constantly changing field it becomes a matter of buyer beware.

Realize, too, that some of these publishers will publish any book, as long as the author can afford to pay for it. Others are as selective about what they publish as a royalty publisher would be, or they publish only certain types of books. Many will do only nonfiction, no novels or children's books. These distinctions will be important as you seek the right publisher for your project.

Because there is so much confusion about subsidy publishing, with many authors going into agreements with these publishers having little or no knowledge of what to expect or even what is typical in this situation, many have come away unhappy or disillusioned. For that reason I frequently get complaints from authors who feel they have been cheated or taken advantage of. (Of course, I often get similar complaints about the royalty publishers listed in this book.) Each complaint brings with it an expectation that I should drop that publisher from the book. Although I am sensitive to their complaints, I also have come to the realization that I am not in a position to pass judgment on which publishers should be dropped. It has been my experience in publishing that for every complaint I get on a publisher, I can usually find several other authors who will sing the praises of the same publisher. For that reason, I feel I can serve the needs of authors better by giving them some insight into what to expect from a subsidy publisher and that kinds of terms should send up a red flag.

Because I am not an expert in this field, and because of space limitations, I will keep this brief and to the point. Let me clarify first that unless you know your book has a limited audience or you have your own method of distribution (such as being a speaker who can sell your own books when you speak), I recommend that you try all the appropriate royalty publishers first. If you are unsuccessful with the royalty publishers, but feel strongly about seeing your book published and have the financial resources to do so (or have your own distribution), one of the publishers listed below may be able to help you.

You can go to a local printer and take your book through all the necessary steps yourself, but a legitimate subsidy publisher has the contacts, know-how and resources to make the task easier and often less expensive. It is always good to get more than one bid to determine whether the terms you are being offered are fair and competitive with other such publishers.

There is not currently any kind of watchdog organization for subsidy publishers, but one is in the works. Until that group is in place, and since I do not have direct knowledge about all of the publishers listed below, I would recommend that no matter who makes you a first offer, you get a second one from Wine Press Publishing, Longwood Communications, or ACW Press (ones I can personally recommend).

As with any contract, have someone review it before signing anything. I do such reviews, as do a number of others listed in the Editorial Services section of this book. Be sure that any terms agreed upon are IN WRITING. Verbal agreements won't be binding. A legitimate subsidy publisher will be happy to provide you with a list of former clients as references (if they aren't, watch out). Don't just ask for that list; follow through and contact more than one of those references. Get a catalog of their books or a list of books they have published and try to find them or ask them to send you a review copy of one or two books they have published. Use those to check the quality of their work, the bindings, etc. Get answers to all your questions before you commit yourself to anything.

Keep in mind that the more copies of a book that are printed, the lower the cost per copy, but never let a publisher talk you into publishing more (or fewer) copies than you think is reasonable. Also find out up front, and have included in the contract, whether and how much promotion the publisher is going to do. Some will do as much as a royalty publisher; others do none at all. If they are not doing promotion, and you don't have any means of distribution yourself, it may not be a good idea to pursue publication. You don't want to end up with a garage full of books you can't sell. At the end of this section I am including the names and addresses of some of the main Christian book distributors. I don't know which ones will consider distributing a subsidy published book, so you will want to contact them to find out before you sign a contract.

LISTING OF SUBSIDY PUBLISHERS

Below is a listing of any publishers that do 50% or more subsidy publishing (where author pays some or all of the production costs). Before entering into dealings with any of these publishers, be sure to read the preceding section on what you need to know.

(*) An asterisk before a listing indicates no or unconfirmed information update.

(#) A number symbol before a listing indicates it was updated from their guidelines or other current sources.

(+) A plus sign before a listing indicates it is a new listing this year or was not included last year.

ACW PRESS, 5501 N. 7th Ave., Ste. 502, Phoenix AZ 85013. (800)931-BOOK. (602)336-8910. Fax (602)532-7123. E-mail: editor@acwpress.com. Website: http://www.acwpress.com. Steven R. Laube, exec ed. A self-publishing book packager. Publishes 12-18 titles/yr. Reprints books. **SUBSIDY PUBLISHES 95%.** Average first printing 500 minimum. Publication within 5-6 mos. Prefers e-mail submissions. Responds in 1 wk. Guideline booklet (also on Website). Not in topical listings; will consider any topic but picture books.

> **Tips:** "We offer a high quality publishing alternative to help Christian authors get their material into print. High standards, high quality."

AMBASSADOR HOUSE, PO Box 1153, Westminster CO 80030. (303)469-4056. Fax (303)469-4049. E-mail: ambhouse@hotmail.com. Non-denominational. Sandra Myers, pub. Publishes 2-6 titles/yr. Receives 10+ submissions annually. 90% of books from first-time authors. No Mss through agents. **SUBSIDY PUBLISHES 95%.** Royalty 35-95%; no advance. Average first printing 1,000. Publication within 2 mos. Considers simultaneous submissions. No disk or e-mail submissions. Responds in 1 mo. Guidelines (also by e-mail); free catalog.

> **Nonfiction:** Query or proposal/3 chapters; phone/fax/e-query OK."Especially want political, prophecy, end-times."

> **Fiction:** Query or proposal/3 chapters. "Purposeful advancement of situational, historical, prophetic, political and end-times education."

> **Tips:** " Our goal is to help individuals with important messages self-publish their books, and get the marketing, public relations and distribution they need. We will strive to insure that bookstores, and ultimately bookstore customers, know that these crucial books exist. "

BLACK FOREST PRESS, 539 Telegraph Canyon Rd. #521, Chula Vista CA 91910. (619)656-8048. Fax (619)482-8704. E-mail: dahk@blackforest press.com. Website: http://www.blackforestpress.com. Keith Pearson, acq ed. A self-publishing company. Imprints: Kinder Books (children's); Dichter Books (black and Hispanic); Abenteyer Books; Sonnenschein Books. Publishes 15 titles/yr. Receives 1,400+ submissions annually. 90-95% of books from first-time authors. **SUBSIDY PUBLISHES 50%** (helps people get published). Reprints books. Prefers 75+ pgs. Royalty 35% on retail; outright purchases; no advance. Average first printing 2,000-3,000. Publication within 5-6 months. Considers simultaneous submissions. Requires disk. Responds in 2-3 wks. Free guidelines/catalog (also on Website).

Nonfiction: Query/phone number; phone/fax/e-query OK. "Looking for true testimonials and books on angels."

Fiction: Query. "Looking for war novels and prophecy novels; 150-350 pages."

Ethnic Books: Publishes for Black and Hispanic markets.

Tips: "Looking for books on vital Christian issues; books with literary merit and significant lessons for life."

BRENTWOOD CHRISTIAN PRESS, 4000 Beallwood Ave., Columbus GA 31904. (404)576-5787. (800) 334-8861. E-mail: Brentwood@aol.com. Website: http://www.publishmybook.com. Mainline. Jerry L. Luquire, exec ed. Publishes 267 titles/yr. Receives 2,000 submissions annually. Reprints books. **SUBSIDY PUBLISHES 95%.** Prefers 120 pgs. Average first printing 500. Publication within 2 mos. Considers simultaneous submissions. Responds in 2 days. Guidelines.

Nonfiction: Complete ms. "Collection of sermons on family topics; poetry; relation of Bible to current day."

Fiction: Complete ms. "Stories that show how faith helps overcome small, day-to-day problems. Prefer under 200 pgs."

Tips: "Keep it short; support facts with reference." This publisher specializes in small print runs of 300-1,000.

COMMENTS PUBLISHING, PO Box 819, Assonet MA 02702. (508)763-8050. E-mail: editor@cftf.com. Website: http://www.webshowplace.com/Comm entsPublishing. David A. Reed, ed. A Christian outreach to Jehovah's Witnesses; cult exposés. Publishes 1 title/yr. Receives 3 submissions annually. 33% of books from first-time authors. **SUBSIDY PUBLISHES 100%.** Reprints books. Prefers 40,000 wds or 150 pgs. In most cases author pays for books; average cost $2-4/bk. Average first printing 1,000. Publication within 2 mos. Considers simultaneous submissions. Responds in 1 mo. No guidelines; catalog for #10 SAE/2 stamps.

Nonfiction: Query only first. E-query OK.

Fiction: Query only. For teens and adults.

Also Does: Booklets on Jehovah's Witnesses, 40-60 pages. Publisher pays for production and royalties.

Tips: "Our marketing and distribution are limited; we sell mostly via direct mail-order to evangelicals in counter-cult work. Authors in other fields should plan to distribute most of their own books."

CROSS WAY PUBLICATIONS, 1351 Morgan Ave., Williamsport PA 17701-2849. (717)323-3921. E-mail: crosspub@mail.microserve.net. Website: http://www. microserve.net/~crosspub/Crossway.html. Jerry Hoffman, ed. Produces poetry books which proclaim Christ as King. Publishes 2 titles/yr. Receives 15 submissions annually. 100% of books from first-time authors. No mss through agents. Prefers 75-100 pgs. No royalty/advance. Does all pre- and post-press preparation at no cost. Printing is done out of house. All copies are shipped to author. Also does web advertising for free. Average first printing 1,000. Publication within 6 mos. No simultaneous submissions. Responds in 2 wks. Requires disk (.txt format desired). No guidelines/catalog.

Nonfiction: Complete ms; e-query OK. "We accept only Christian poetry. Although we accept all forms, ideas must be clearly stated and openly point to Christ. Not interested in vague ideas which leave the reader wondering."

Also Does: Pamphlets; booklets.

ESSENCE PUBLISHING CO., INC., 44 Moira St. W., Belleville ON K8P 1S3 Canada. (613)962-3294. Fax (613)962-3055. E-mail: info@essence.on.ca. Website: http://www.essence.on.ca. Essence, Inc. Deborah Visser, ed. Provides affordable, short-run book publishing to the Christian community. Publishes 100 titles/yr. Receives 250+ submissions annually. 85% of books from first-time authors. **SUBSIDY PUBLISHES 90%.** Reprints books. Prefers 80-400 pgs. Average first printing 250-2,000. Publication within 3-5 mos. Considers simultaneous submissions. Responds in 2-4 wks. Accepts disk or e-mail. Guidelines (also by e-mail/Website)/free catalog.

Nonfiction: Complete ms; phone/fax/e-query OK.

Fiction: Complete ms. For all ages. Also picture books.

Also Does: Pamphlets, booklets and tracts.

FAIRWAY PRESS, Subsidy Division for C.S.S. Publishing Company, 517 S. Main St., Box 4503, Lima OH 45802-4503. (419)227-1818. Fax (419)228-9184. E-mail: csspub@csspub.com. Website: http://www.csspub.com. Teresa Rhoads, ed; submit to Thomas Lentz. Publishes 100 titles/yr. Receives 200-300 submissions annually. 80% of books from first-time authors. Reprints books. **SUBSIDY PUBLISHES 100%.** Royalty to 50%; no advance. Average first printing 500-1,000. Publication within 6-9 mos. Considers simultaneous submissions. Responds in up to 1 month. Prefers disk. Free guidelines/catalog for 9x12 SAE.

Nonfiction: Complete ms; phone/fax/e-query OK. "Looking for mss with a Christian theme, and seasonal material."

Fiction: Complete ms. For adults, teens, or children; all types.

FAME PUBLISHING, INC., 820 S. MacArthur Blvd., Ste. 105-220, Coppell TX 75019. (972)393-1467. Fax (972)462-9350. E-mail: FamePub@aol.com. Nondenominational. Margaret J. Kinney, pres. Publishes 3-5 titles/yr. **SUBSIDY PUBLISHER.** Not in topical listings.

Nonfiction & Fiction: Proposal/chapters.

GESHER, PO Box 33373, Philadelphia PA 19142-3373. (215)365-3350. Fax (215)365-3325. E-mail: info@gesher.org. Website: http://www.gesher.org. Helping people walk in all that God intends for them. Robert Winer, pres. Publishes 4 titles/yr. **SUBSIDY PUBLISHES 90%.** Reprints books. Prefers 150-250 pgs. Royalty 3-10% on retail; advance $250-500. Average first printing 3,000-5,000. Publication within 6-8 mos. Considers simultaneous submissions. Requires disk (Word, WordPerfect, or RTF format). Responds in 1-2 mos. Guidelines on Website soon; no catalog.

Nonfiction: Proposal with 2-3 chapters; e-query OK. "Books on deeper spirituality to help people mature in the Lord."

Special Needs: Messianic Jewish in addition to general Christianity.
Tips: "Most open to books that fulfill our mission statement."

IMPACT CHRISTIAN BOOKS, INC., 332 Leffingwell Ave. Ste. 101, Kirkwood MO 63122. (314)822-3309. Fax (314)822-3325. Website: http://www.impactchristianbooks.com. William D. Banks, pres. Books of healing, miraculous deliverance, and spiritual warfare; drawing individuals into a deeper walk with God. Publishes 20+ titles/yr. Receives 20-50 submissions annually. 50-70% of books from first-time authors. No mss through agents. **SUBSIDY PUBLISHES 50-70%.** Reprints books. Average first printing 5,000. Publication within 2 mos. Considers simultaneous submissions. Responds by prior arrangement in 30 days. Requires disk. Guidelines; catalog for 9x12 SAE/5 stamps. Not in topical listings.

Nonfiction: Query only; phone/fax query OK. Outstanding personal testimonies, and Christ-centered books.

LONGWOOD COMMUNICATIONS, 397 Kingslake Dr., DeBary FL 32713. (904)774-1991. Fax (904)774-8181. E-mail: longwood@totcon.com. Murray Fisher, VP. A service for authors who cannot get their books accepted by a traditional house. Publishes 8-12 titles/yr. Receives 80 submissions annually. 85% of books from first-time authors. No mss through agents. **100% SUBSIDY.** Reprints books. Average first printing 5,000. Publication within 3-5 mos. Considers simultaneous submissions. Responds in 1-2 wks. Requires disk. No guidelines; catalog for 2 stamps.

Nonfiction: Complete ms; phone query OK. Any topic as long as it's Christian. Also does booklets. Not in topical listings.

Fiction: Complete ms. For all ages. Any genre.

Tips: Looking for basic Christian books.

+THE MASTER DESIGN, PO Box 751663, Memphis TN 38175-1663. Fax (901)367-2677. E-mail: info@masterdesign.org. Website: http://www.masterdesign.org. Faithe Finley, submissions ed. To help publish the Gospel in all the world before Christ returns. Publishes 3-5 titles/yr. Receives 10 submissions annually. 75% of books from first-time authors. No mss through agents. **100% SUBSIDY.** Prefers 48-120 pgs. Author pays all costs plus 10% retail, keeps all other income from sales. Average first printing 500-2,000. Publication within 3 mos. Considers simultaneous submissions. Accepts disk or e-mail. Responds in 2 wks. Guidelines by e-mail; no catalog.

Nonfiction: Proposal/3 chapters; e-query OK.

Tips: "A writer who writes books expounding truth from the Word of God has the best chance of getting published."

MOONLETTERS PRESS, 7210 W. 57th Pl., Summit IL 60501. E-mail: ShaunaSkye@aol.com. Website: http://members.aol.com/ShaunaSkye/index.html. Shauna Skye, ed. This publisher on hold for now.

Nonfiction: Small poetry chapbooks. Send completed poems.

Fiction: Small fiction chapbooks; 8,000 wds total (one story or several short ones).

Tips: "Author will receive 10 copies of their chapbook, plus 25% off additional copies. Chapbooks will also be made available through our catalog."

OMEGA HOUSE PUBLISHING, PO Box 68, Three Rivers MI 49093. (616)278-3075. Fax (616)273-7026. Non-denominational. Zendra Manley, ed. To distribute and increase knowledge in the body of Christ (Hosea 4:6). Publishes 5 titles/yr. Receives 60 submissions annually. 75% of books from first-time authors. No mss through agents. **90% SUBSIDY.** Reprints books. Prefers 80-500 pgs. Royalty 8-10% of net; no advance. Average first printing 2,000-5,000. Publication within 6 mos. Considers simultaneous submissions. Responds in 2 wks. No disk. Guidelines; no catalog.

  Nonfiction: Proposal/3 chapters; no phone/fax query.

  Special Needs: Renewal, inspirational, healing.

  Also Does: Booklets, pamphlets.

  Tips: "We prefer small booklets. Develop a proposal that will grab our interest. Manuscripts are turned down that do not bring glory to God, and that are less than marketable."

PARTNERSHIP BOOK SERVICES, 212 N. Ash, Hillsboro KS 67063. (316)947-3966. Fax (316)947-3392. Hearth Publishing, Inc. Stan Thiessen, ed. Publishes 12 religious titles/yr (70 total). Receives 1,500 submissions annually. 85% of books from first-time authors. No mss through agents. **100% SUBSIDY.** Reprints books. Prefers 20,000-150,000 wds or 96-352 pgs. Average first printing 100-20,000. Publication within 6 mos. Considers simultaneous submissions. Responds in 2 wks-3 mos. No disk. Guidelines; no catalog. Not included in topical listings; considers any topic.

  Nonfiction/Fiction: Proposal/3-4 chapters; no phone/fax query. Send $35/SASE for manuscript evaluation. "Response includes suggestions for improvement."

  Also Does: Booklets, pamphlets, tracts and chapbooks.

  Tips: "PBS services include evaluation, editing, cover design, formatting, disk to film, printing, promotions and marketing."

PASTOR'S CHOICE PRESS, 4000 Beallwood Ave., Columbus GA 31904. (404/706)576-5787. E-mail: Brentwood@aol.com. Website: http://www. publishmybook.com. Subsidiary of Brentwood Publishers Group. Jerry Luquire, exec dir. **SUBSIDY OR CUSTOM PUBLISHES 100%.** Focus is on sermon notes, outlines, illustrations, plus news that pastors would find interesting. Publishes 300-500 copies. Cost of about $3-4/book. Publication in 45 days. Same day response.

POET'S COVE PRESS, 4000 Beallwood Ave., Columbus GA 31904. (404/706)576-5787. (800) 334-8861. E-mail: Brentwood@aol.com. Website: http://www.publishmybook.com. Subsidiary of Brentwood Publishers Group. Jerry Luquire, exec dir. Publishes 125 titles/yr. **SUBSIDY OR CUSTOM PUBLISHES 100%.** Specializes in self-publishing books of religious or inspirational poetry, in small press runs of under 500 copies. Publication in 45 days. Same day response.

  Tips: "Type one poem per page; include short bio and photo with first submission."

PROMISE PUBLISHING, 2324 N. Batavia #105, Orange CA 92865. (714)282-1199. Fax (714)997-5545. E-mail: ed-mary@ix.netcom.com. M.B. Steele, ed./ V.P. Publishes 6 titles/yr. 50% of books from first-time authors. **100%**

COOPERATIVE PUBLISHING in support of ministry organizations. Royalty 10% on net (negotiable); no advance. Average first printing 5,000. Publication within 6 mos. Considers simultaneous submissions. Preacceptance talks determine acceptance. Prefers disk or e-mail.

Nonfiction: Proposal/3 chapters; phone/fax/e-query OK.

Special Needs: "We are interested in whatever topics fall within the parameters of our 'cooperative publishing' approach, if it is not contradictory to the Bible."

Tips: "Most open to established ministries that will use the books for their constituency."

+**RECONCILIATION PRESS**, PO Box 209, Manassas VA 20108. (703)330-3262. E-mail: publisher@reconciliation.com. Website: http://www.reconciliation.com. Explores the historical roots of America's blessings and troubles. Guidelines (query@reconciliation.com);   catalog for 9x12 SAE/5 stamps.

*****RECOVERY COMMUNICATIONS, INC.**, PO Box 19910, Baltimore MD 21211. Fax (410)243-8558. Toby R. Drews, ed. Publishes 4-6 titles/yr. No mss through agents. **SUBSIDY PUBLISHER.** Prefers 110 pgs. Co-op projects; no royalty or advance. Average first printing 5,000. Publication within 11 mos. Excellent nationwide distribution and marketing in book stores.

Nonfiction or Fiction: Query only.

+**S AND S PRESS**, 25 Fullerton St., Boothbay Harbor MA 04538. (207)633-9739. Fax (207)633-7865. Website: http://www.cspublishing.com. Imprint of Christopher Scott Publishing, Ltd. Chris H. Scott, mng ed. A contract publisher; author pays 15-20% of cost.

Nonfiction: Complete ms/cover letter & synopsis.

SHEER JOY! PRESS/PROMOTIONS, 5502 Murphy Rd., Pink Hill NC 28572. (252)568-6101. Fax (252)568-4171. E-mail: sheerjoy@eastlink.net. Protestant. James R. Adams, pres.; submit to Patricia Adams, ed. Publishes 1-2 titles/yr. Receives 5-10 submissions annually. No mss through agents. **SUBSIDY PUBLISHES 85%.** Prefers 20,000-30,000 wds (200 pgs). Royalty on retail; no advance. Average first printing 1,000. Publication within 6 mos. Considers simultaneous submissions. Responds in 3-4 wks.

Nonfiction: Complete ms. "Need Bible-based dramatic readings."

Fiction: Complete ms. "Need Bible-based puppet skits."

Tips: "Be very illustrative and forceful in writing Christian drama."

SON-RISE PUBLICATIONS, 143 Greenfield Rd., New Wilmington PA 16142. (800)358-0777. Fax (412)946-8700. Florence W. Biros, acq ed. Publishes 5-6 titles/yr. Receives 20 submissions annually. 50% of books from first-time authors. **SUBSIDY PUBLISHES 50%.** Prefers 25,000-40,000 wds or 90-196 pgs. Royalty 7½-10% on retail; no advance. Average first printing 3,000. Publication within 8-9 mos. Responds ASAP.

Nonfiction: Query. "Most open to Christian teaching and testimony combined."

Fiction: Query only; overstocked.

Tips: "We are overstocked with royalty manuscripts. The only ones I can consider for now are subsidy manuscripts."

SOUTHERN BAPTIST PRESS, 4000 Beallwood, Columbus GA 31904. (404)576-5787. (800) 334-8861. E-mail: Brentwood@aol.com. Website: http://www.publishmybook.com. Jerry L. Luquire, exec ed. Publishes 42 books/yr. Receives 600 submissions annually. Reprints books. **SUBSIDY OR CUSTOM PUBLISHES 95%**. Prefers 120 pgs. Average first printing 500. Publication within 2 mos. Considers simultaneous submissions. Responds in 1 week. Guidelines.

> **Nonfiction:** Complete ms. "Collections of sermons on family topics; poetry; relation of Bible to current day."
>
> **Fiction:** Complete ms. "Stories that show how faith helps overcome small, day-to-day problems. Prefers under 200 wds."
>
> **Tips:** "Keep it short; support facts with reference."

TEACH SERVICES, INC., 254 Donovan Rd., Brushton NY 12916. (518)358-2125. Fax (518)358-3028. Timothy Hullquist, pres.; submit to Wayne Reid, acq ed. To publish uplifting books for the lowest price. Publishes 70-75 titles/yr. Receives 130 submissions annually. 35% of books from first-time authors. No mss through agents. **SUBSIDY PUBLISHES 50%** (author has to pay for first printing, then publisher keeps it in print). Reprints books. Prefers 45,000 wds or 96 pgs. Royalty 10% on retail; no advance. Average first printing 2,000. Publication within 4 mos. Disk required. Responds in 2 wks. Guidelines/catalog for #10 SAE/2 stamps.

> **Nonfiction:** Query only; no phone/fax query. "Looking for books on nutrition."
>
> **Also Does:** Pamphlets, booklets.

TYLER PRESS, 1221 W.S.W. Loop 323, Tyler TX 75701. (903)581-2255. Fax (903)581-7841. E-mail: tylerpress@electro-image.com. J. A. Johnson, sr ed. A self-publisher's service bureau that will lend its imprint to selected titles. Publishes 20 titles/yr. Receives 250+ submissions annually. 60% of books from first-time authors. **SUBSIDY PUBLISHES 100%**. Reprints books. Prefers 120 pgs & up. Provides full editing and design services, if needed. Average first printing 500-5,000. Publication within 2 mos.

> **Nonfiction:** Query; fax query OK. "We enthusiastically promote self-help/how-to, historical, creation science, current social and political issues, biographies, autobiographies, marriage and family, and women's issues."
>
> **Fiction:** Query. For children only.
>
> **Also Does:** Booklets.

*VESTA PUBLICATIONS, LTD., Box 1641, Cornwall ON K6H 5V6 Canada. (613)932-2135. Fax (613)932-7735. E-mail: sg@glen-net.ca. General trade publisher that does a few religious titles; focus is on world peace. Stephen Gill, ed. Publishes 4 titles/yr. Receives 20-60 submissions annually. 95% of books from first-time authors. No mss through agents. **SUBSIDY PUBLISHES 90%** (author pays about 50% of cost). Reprints books. Any length. Royalty 15% of net; no advance. Average first printing 1,500. Publication within 3 mos. No simultaneous submissions. Responds in 4-7 wks. Requires disk. Catalog for SAE/IRCs.

> **Nonfiction:** Proposal/1 chapter; phone query OK.
>
> **Tips:** "Most open to scholarly/religious books."

WELLNESS PUBLICATIONS, Box 2397, Holland MI 49423. (616)335-5553 or (800)543-0815. Darrell Franken, pres. Specializes in health and faith books. Publishes 3 titles/yr. Receives 200 submissions annually. All books from first-time authors. **100% SUBSIDY.** Prefers 250 pgs. Royalty 10% on retail; no advance; minimum subsidy $3,000. Average first printing 2,000. Publication within 6 mos. Considers simultaneous submissions. Responds in 2-4 wks. Free catalog.

> **Nonfiction:** Complete ms.

> **Tips:** "Most open to health/healing, stress management and psychological concerns."

+WEST COAST PARADISE PUBLISHING, #5 9060 Tronson Rd., Vernon BC V1H 1E7 Canada. (250)545-4186. Fax (250)545-4194. Robert G. Anstey, ed. Publishes 3 titles/yr. Receives 3 submissions annually. 100% of books from first-time authors. **100% SUBSIDY.** Reprints books. Prefers 200 pgs. Average first printing 100. Publication within 3 mos. Considers simultaneous submissions. Prefers disk. Responds in 1 wk. Guidelines.

> **Nonfiction:** Query only; phone/fax query OK. "Looking for poetry books."

> **Fiction:** Query only. For all ages.

> **Also Does:** Pamphlets and booklets.

WINDFLOWER COMMUNICATIONS, 844-K McLeod Ave., Winnipeg MB R2G 2T7 Canada. (204)668-7475. Fax (204)661-8530. E-mail: windflower@ brandtfamily.com. Website: http://www.infobahn.mb.ca/brandtfamily. Brandt Family Enterprises. Gilbert Brandt, pres. Publishes quality, wholesome literature for family reading, pleasure and learning. Publishes 4-6 titles/yr. Receives 125 submissions annually. 90% of books from first-time authors. **SUBSIDY PUBLISHES 95%.** Reprints books. Prefers 200 pgs. Royalty 10-20% on net; no advance. Average first printing 2,500. Publication within 14 mos. Considers simultaneous submissions. Responds in 6 mos. Prefers disk. Free guidelines/catalog.

> **Nonfiction:** Query or proposal/1-2 chapters; fax/e-query OK.

> **Fiction:** Proposal/1-2 chapters. All ages.

> **Tips:** "We are currently focusing on historical fiction."

WINE PRESS PUBLISHING, 12108 Mukilteo Speedway, PO Box 1406, Mukilteo WA 98275. (800)326-4674. Fax (206)353-4402. E-mail: info@ winepresspub.com. Website: http://www.winepresspub.com. Vic Lipsey, ed; submit to Rob Noland. Publishes 100+ titles/yr. Receives 500+ submissions annually. 70% of books from first-time authors. No mss through agents. **BOOK PACKAGERS 85%.** Reprints books. Prefers 40,000 wds or 150 pgs. Author pays production costs, keeps all income from sales. Average first printing 1,000-2,500. Publication in 3 mos. Considers simultaneous submissions. Responds in 48-72 hrs. Accepts disk. Free guidelines/ catalog. Not included in topical listings because they consider any topic or genre.

> **Nonfiction:** Complete ms; phone/fax/e-query OK. Publishes any topic as long as it's biblical or glorifies God.

> **Fiction:** Complete ms. All ages and all genres.

> **Also Does:** Booklets, gift books, calendars.

Tips: "We offer professional, yet affordable, book packaging for Christian writers, with unique marketing, distribution and fulfillment services available for qualifying projects. We don't purchase rights to books, but we still turn down manuscripts that don't glorify God or have a reasonably good chance of selling at least 1,000 copies."

LISTING OF CHRISTIAN BOOK DISTRIBUTORS

ANCHOR DISTRIBUTORS (formerly Whitaker Distributors), 30 Hunt Valley Cir., New Kensington PA 15068. (724)334-7000. (800)444-4484. Fax (800)765-1960 or (724)334-1200. E-mail: marketing@anchordistributors. com.

*APPALACHIAN, INC., PO Box 1573, 506 Princeton Rd., Johnson City TN 37601. (800)289-2772.

BEACON COOK CANADA, 55 Woodslee Ave., Box 98, Paris ON N3L 3E5 Canada. (800)263-2664. Fax (800)461-8575. Web site: http:// www.cook.ca. Can distribute only in Canada.

+BLESSINGWAY BOOKS, 134 E. Lupita St., Santa Fe NM 87505. (505)983-2647. Fax (505)983-2005. E-mail: blessingwy@aol.com. Website: http:// www.blessingway.com. Co-op distributor for self-published books. Authors pay $1,500 in two installments and then make 100% profit after that. Request a prospectus by phone or fax, or download from their Website.

+CELA DISTRIBUTION, 9818 Bluebonnet Blvd. Ste. B, Baton Rouge LA 70810. (888)607-2346.

+DICKSONS, PO Box 368, Seymour IN 47274. (800)457-9885.

*INGRAM BOOK COMPANY, 1125 Heil Quaker Rd., Nashville TN 37217. (615)793-5000. (800)937-8000.

R.G. MICHELL, 565 Gordon Baker Rd., Willowdale ON M2H 2W2, Canada. (416)499-4615. Fax (416)499-6340. Website: http://www.rgm.ca.

+MIDNIGHT CALL, PO Box 280008, Columbia SC 29228. (800)845-2420. Fax (803)755-6002.

MISSION PUBLISHING, 8015 Jim Court SE, Olympia WA 98503-4122. E-mail: artist@missionpub.com. Website: http://www.missionpub.com. Submit to Artist Relations. Distributes Christian music and drama on the Internet. Details on Website.

*NEW DAY CHRISTIAN DISTRIBUTORS, 126 Shivel Dr., Hendersonville TN 37075. (800)251-3633.

+PINEHILL DISTRIBUTION, Website: http://www.pinehillweb.com.

ACCESS PUBLISHERS NETWORK (formerly Publishers Distribution Service), 6893 Sullivan Rd., Grawn MI 49637. (616)276-5196. Fax (616)276-5197. Contact: John Lindberg, Acquisitions Coordinator. Works with 170 small presses and selected self publishers in distribution to the US bookstore and library trade.

#QUALITY BOOKS, 1003 W. Pines Rd., Oregon IL 61061. (815)732-4450.Fax (815)732-4499. E-mail: jim.hicks@dawson.com or carolyn.olson@ dawson.com. Contact: Jim Hicks or Carolyn Olson. Distributes small press books, videos, audios and CD-ROMS to secular libraries. Requires

55% discount. Payment 90 days after sales. Asks for 5 copies of the book, plus 30 covers.

+RAINBOW HOUSE DISTRIBUTORS, 60 Frobisher Dr., Unit 10, Waterloo ON N2V 2B1 Canada. (519)746-8921. (800)265-8887. Fax (519)746-5244. Canadian distributor.

*RIVERSIDE DISTRIBUTORS, PO Box 370, Iowa Falls IA 50126-0370. (515)648-4271. (800)247-5111. Fax (800)822-4271. Website: http://www.firstnetchristian.com.

*SLEEPER, DICK, DISTRIBUTION, 18680-B Langensand Rd., Sandy OR 97055-6426. (503)668-3454. Fax (503)668-5314. E-mail: sleepydick@ipns.com. Represents small press authors.

*SPRING ARBOR DISTRIBUTORS, 10885 Textile Rd., Belleville MI 48111. (313)481-0900. (800)395-5599. Fax (800)395-2682. Website: http://www. springarbor.com/index.htm.

+STREAMWOOD DISTRIBUTION), PO Box 91011, Mobile AL 36691. (888)670-7463.

*WARNER CHRISTIAN DISTRIBUTION, 24 Music Square East, Nashville TN 37203. (615)248-3300. Distributes records.

MARKET ANALYSIS

ALL PUBLISHERS IN ORDER OF MOST BOOKS PUBLISHED PER YEAR

CSS Publishing 200
Eerdmans 200
Standard Publishing 150
Zondervan 150
Bethany House 120-150
Baker Books 120
Concordia 120
Multnomah 120
United Methodist 120
Christian Univ Press 100
Element Books 100
Harvest House 100
Starburst Publishers 100
Tyndale House 100
Paulist Press 90-100
Westmin./John Knox 80-100
Christian Ed Publishers 80
InterVarsity Press 80
Barbour Publishing 75
Crossway 70
Liturgical Press 70
Moody Press 65-70
Tommy Nelson 65
HarperSanFrancisco 60-80
Honor Books 60+
Oxford University 60
Broadman & Holman 60
Kregel 60
Joshua Morris 60
Revell 60
Heartsong Presents 52
Brown/ROA 50-100
Custom Commun. 50-75
Review and Herald 50-60
Orbis Books 50-55
Boyds Mills Press 50
Crossroad Publishing 50
GROUP Publishing 50
Liguori Publications 50
Univ Press of America 50
Chariot Victor Books 45-50
Chalice Press 40-50
Destiny Image 40-45
Shaw 40-45
Christian Publications 40
Health Communications 40
Doubleday 36-40
Love Inspired 36
Eldridge 35 (plays)

Morehouse Publishing 35
Pilgrim Press 35
Smyth & Helwys 35
Summit Pub. Group 35
Trinity Press Intl. 35
Hendrickson 30-40
Beacon Hill Press 30
College Press 30
Conari Press 30
Good News Publishers 30
   (tracts)
Judson Press 30
Light and Life 30
McDougal Publishing 30
Our Sunday Visitor 30
Pacific Press 30
Sheed & Ward 30
Pauline Books 25-35
Creation House 25-30
Huntington House 25-30
Vital Issues Press 25-30
Mel Bay Publications 25
Meriwether 25 (plays)
Bridge/Logos 25
Hunt and Thorpe 25
Liturgy Training 25
Thomas More 25
Alba House 24
Lightwave Publishing 24
Peter Pauper Press 24
Sword Of The Lord 24
Baker's Plays 20-25 (plays)
Counterpoint 20-25
Saint Mary's Press 20-25
Loyola Press 20+
Gold 'n' Honey 20
Monument Press 20
Openbook Publishers 20
Rainbow Pub/Rainbow Books
   20
Resource Publications 20
Shining Star 20
Sovereign/Appaloosa 20
St. Anthony Mess. Press 18-20
Lillenas 18
Preservation Press 16
United Church Press 15-25
Catholic Book Publishing 15-
   20

Focus on the Family 15-20
J Countryman 15-20
New Leaf Press 15-20
Libros Liguori 15
Living the Good News 15
Paraclete Press 15
Still Waters 15
YWAM Publishing 15
Palisades 14
Howard Publishing 12-18
Blue Dolphin 12-15
New Hope 12-15
Albury Publishing 12
Dimension Books 12
Forward Movement 12
New City Press 12
Carey Library, Wm. 10-15
Loizeaux 10-15
Lydia Press 10-15
Ragged Edge 10-15
Warner Press 10-15
Gospel Publishing House 10-14
Eerdmans/Young Readers 10-
   12
Resurrection Press 10-12
ACTA Publications 10
ACU Press 10
Alban Institute 10
Haworth Press 10
Perigee Books 10
PREP Publishing 10
Rainbow Pub/Legacy Press 10
Treasure Learning Systems 10
United Church Publishing 10
Yale University Press 10
Daybreak Books/Rodale 9-12
Cistercian Publications 8-14
Northstone Publishing 8-12
St. Bede's Publications 8-12
Alexander Books 8-10
Holy Cross Orthodox 8-10
Journey Books 8-10
Master Books 8-10
One World 8-10
Presbyterian/Reformed 8-10
Chosen Books 8
ICS Publications 8
Innisfree Press 8
Neibauer Press 8

Royal Productions 8
Touch Publications 8
Franciscan Univ Press 7
Kaleidoscope Press 7
Lowenbrown Publishing 6-12
Messianic Jewish Publishers 6-12
Pace Publications 6-12
Elder Books 6-10
Accent Publications 6-8
Christopher Pub Hs 6-8
Cornell University Press 6-8
Catholic Univ of America 6
Church & Synagogue Libraries 6
Magnus Press 6
Trinity Foundation 6
Scarecrow Press 5-15
Erica House 5-10
Hensley Publishing 5-10
Regina Press 5-10
Wadsworth Publishing 5-10
World Bible 5-10
Cross Cultural 5-8
Religious Education Press 5-6
FOG Publishing 5
Christian Media 5
 Morrow 5
Mt. Olive College Press 5
Paradise Research 5
Rainbow Books (FL) 5
Rose Publishing 5
Wood Lake Books 5
Paragon House 4-7
Church Growth Institute 4-6
Focus Publishing 4-6
Friends United Press 4-6
Hearth Publishing 4-6

Victory House 4-5
American Catholic Press 4
Baylor Univ. Press 4
Bristol House 4
Hay House 4
Intl. Awakening Press 4
Langmarc Publishing 4
Open Court 4
Schocken Books 4
Toccoa Falls College Press 4
Western Front 4
Cerdic Publications 3-5
Facts on File 3-5
Cornerstone Press 3-4
Kindred Productions 3-4
Marlton Publishers 3
Meriwether 3
Art Can Drama 2-5
Conciliar Press 2-5
Tekna Books 2-5
Lifetime Books 2-4
Rainbow's End 2-4
Regnery Publishing 2-4
Univ. of Ottawa Press 2-4
Dry Bones Press 2-3
Sower's Press 2-3
Logion Press 2
Pelican Publishing 2
Read 'N Run Books 2
Barclay Press 1-5
Sonstar Publishing 1-5
Life Cycle Books 1-3
Middle Atlantic 1-3
White Stone Circle 1-3
Accent Books & Video 1-2
New Canaan 1-2
Gilgal Publications 1
Goetz 1

Good Book 1
Guernica Editions 1
Misty Hill Press 1
Small Helm Press 1

SUBSIDY PUBLISHERS

Brentwood 267
Poet's Cove 125
Essence Publishing 100
Fairway Press 100
Wine Press 100
TEACH Services 70-75
Southern Baptist Press 42
Impact Books 20
Tyler Press 20
Black Forest Press 15
ACW Press 12-18
Partnership Book Services 12
Longwood Communications 8-12
Promise Publishing 6
Son-Rise 5-6
Omega House 5
Recovery Communications 4-6
Windflower Communications 4-6
VESTA Publications 4
Fame Publishing 3-5
Master Design 3-5
Wellness Publications 3
West Coast Paradise 3
Ambassador House 2-6
Cross Way Publications 2
Sheer Joy! Press 1-2
Comments Publishing 1

BOOK PUBLISHERS WITH THE MOST BOOKS ON THE BESTSELLER LIST FOR THE LAST YEAR

Note: This tally is based on actual sales in Christian bookstores for October 1997-September 1998 (most recent information available). The list is broken down by types of books, i.e., children's, teen, fiction, nonfiction in paperback and cloth, mass-market paperbacks, and a new one this year, gift books. Numbers behind the names indicate the number of titles each publisher had on that bestseller list during the year. The combined list indicates the total number a particular publisher had on all the lists combined. If a particular publisher has more than one imprint listed, they are sometimes combined for these totals. It is interesting to note that each year the number of publishers appearing on the list has increased—26 publishers in 1993; 35 publishers in 1994; 43 in 1995, and 60 in 1996 until last year and this year when it has dropped back to 48.

FICTION BOOKS
1. Bethany House 20

2. Tyndale House 10
3. Multnomah 9

4. Harvest House 7
5. Thomas Nelson 5

6. Zondervan 5
7. Crossway 4
8. Chariot Victor 2
9. Moody Press 2
10. Palisades (Multnomah) 2
11. WaterBrook 2
12. Barbour 1
13. Broadman & Holman 1
14. Budget Book Service 1
15. Inspirational Press 1
16. Revell 1
17. Word 1

NONFICTION—CLOTH

1. Zondervan 13
2. Word 12
3. Thomas Nelson 7
4. J. Countryman/Word 5
5. Multnomah 4
6. Harrison House 3
7. Broadman & Holman 2
8. Creation House 2
9. Honor Books 2
10. Albury 1
11. Discovery House 1
12. Doubleday 1
13. Focus on the Family/ Tyndale 1
14. Harvest House 1
15. Hendrickson 1
16. Howard Publishing 1
17. Inspirational Press 1
18. Putnam 1
19. Regal Books 1
20. Regnery 1
21. WaterBrook 1

NONFICTION— PAPERBACK

1. Creation House 10
2. Multnomah 10
3. Honor Books 8
4. Frontier Research 4
5. Albury 3
6. Harrison House 3
7. Harvest House 3
8. Standard 3
9. Word 3
10. Chariot Victor 2
11. Thomas Nelson 2
12. Regal Books 2
13. Baker 1
14. Bob Siemon 1
15. Broadman & Holman 1
16. Christian Publications 1
17. Chosen Books 1

18. Moody Press 1
19. Revell 1
20. Treasure House 1
21. Western Front 1
22. Zondervan 1

MASS-MARKET PAPERBACKS

1. Barbour Books 12
2. Harrison House 6
3. Tyndale House 5
4. J. Countryman/Word 3
5. Hendrickson 3
6. Zondervan 3
7. Broadman & Holman 2
8. World Publishers 2
9. Fortress Press 1
10. InterVarsity 1
11. Thomas Nelson 1
12. Revell 1
13. Simon & Schuster 1
14. Whitaker House 1

CHILDREN'S BOOKS

1. Tommy Nelson 17
2. Concordia 6
3. Standard 6
4. Zondervan 6
5. Gold 'N' Honey/Mult. 5
6. Tyndale House 4
7. Chariot Victor 3
8. Baker 2
9. Crossway 2
10. Honor Books 2
11. Word/Everland 2
12. Barbour 1
13. Firefly 1
14. Lion/Chariot 1

YOUTH/TEEN BOOKS

1. Tyndale House 5
2. Zondervan 3
3. Baker 1
4. Broadman & Holman 1
5. Chariot Victor 1
6. Honor Books 1
7. Thomas Nelson 1
8. Regal Books 1
9. Standard 1

GIFT BOOKS

1. Honor Books 5
2. J. Countryman/Word 4
3. Multnomah 4
4. Word 2
5. Bob Siemon 1

6. Broadman & Holman 1
7. Howard 1
8. Thomas Nelson 1
9. Simon & Schuster 1

Combined Bestseller Lists (Combination of seven lists above)

1. Zondervan 31
2. Multnomah 27
3. Tyndale House 24
4. Bethany House 20
5. Word 20
6. Honor Books 18
7. Thomas Nelson 17
8. Tommy Nelson 17
9. Barbour 14
10. Creation House 12
11. Harrison House 12
12. J. Countryman 12
13. Harvest House 11
14. Standard 10
15. Broadman & Holman 8
16. Chariot Victor 8
17. Concordia 6
18. Crossway 6
19. Gold 'N' Honey 5
20. Albury 4
21. Baker 4
22. Frontier Research 4
23. Hendrickson 4
24. Regal 4
25. Moody Press 3
26. Revell 3
27. WaterBrook 3
28. Bob Siemon 2
29. Howard 2
30. Inspirational 2
31. Palisades/Multnomah 2
32. Simon & Schuster 2
33. World 2
34. Budget Book 1
35. Chosen 1
36. Christian Publ. 1
37. Discovery 1
38. Doubleday 1
39. Firefly 1
40. Focus on the Family 1
41. Fortress Press 1
42. InterVarsity 1
43. Lion 1
44. Putnam 1
45. Regnery 1
46. Treasure 1
47. Western Front 1
48. Whitaker 1

BOOK TOPICS MOST POPULAR WITH PUBLISHERS

Note: The numbers following the topics indicate how many publishers said they were interested in seeing a book on that topic. To find the list of publishers interested in each topic, go to the Topical Listings for books (see Table of Contents).

1. Prayer 108
2. Inspirational 107
3. Christian Living 106
4. Bible/Biblical Studies 103
5. Religion 103
6. Spirituality 102
7. Women's Issues 96
8. Family Life 93
9. Devotional Books 85
10. Theology 85
11. Marriage 84
12. Current Social Issues 79
13. Ethics 79
14. Christian Education 77
15. Parenting 77
16. Biography 75
17. Evangelism/Witnessing 75
18. Discipleship 74
19. How-To 74
20. Historical 72
21. Church Renewal 70
22. Fiction: Adult 65
23. Healing 63
24. Church Life 62
25. Ethnic/Cultural 61
26. Health 60
27. Youth Books 60
28. Men's Books 59
29. Psychology 59
30. Doctrinal 57
31. Pastor's Helps 56
32. Apologetics 55
33. Gift Books 55
34. Leadership 55
35. Self-Help 55
36. Controversial Issues 53
37. Fiction: Contemporary 53
38. Fiction: Historical 52
39. Reference Books 51
40. Social Justice Issues 51
41. Death/Dying 50

42. Humor 50
43. Fiction: Biblical 49
44. Fiction: Juvenile 47
45. Counseling Aids 46
46. Environmental Issues 46
47. Missionaries 46
48. Philosophy 46
49. Personal Renewal 45
50. Fiction: Adventure 44
51. Scholarly 44
52. Christian Home Schooling 43
53. Personal Experience 41
54. Autobiography 40
55. Liturgical Studies 40
56. Worship Resources 40
57. World Issues 39
58. Miracles 38
59. Booklets 37
60. Divorce 37
61. Prophecy 37
62. Group Study Books 36
63. *Personal Growth 35
64. Recovery 35
65. Stewardship 35
66. Children's Picture Books 34
67. Fiction: Mystery 34
68. Fiction: Teen/YA 34
69. Money Management 34
70. Cults/Occult 32
71. Poetry 32
72. Political Theory 32
73. Sr. Adult Concerns 32
74. Games/Crafts 31
75. Music-Related Books 31
76. Science 31
77. Spiritual Warfare 31
78. Sermons 30
79. Fiction: Humorous 29
80. Archaeology 28

81. Cookbooks 28
82. Singles Issues 28
83. Curriculum 27
84. Drama 27
85. Retirement 27
86. Economics 26
87. Fiction: Historical/Romance 26
88. Pamphlets 26
89. Sociology 25
90. Fiction: Romance 24
91. Fiction: Allegory 23
92. Youth Programs 22
93. Creation Science 21
94. Fiction: Frontier/Romance 22
95. Fiction: Frontier 21
96. Fiction: Mystery/Romance 21
97. Fiction: Ethnic 20
98. Fiction: Literary 20
99. Fiction: Short Story Coll. 20
100. Travel 20
101. *Church Traditions 19
102. Fiction: Plays 19
103. Sports/Recreation 19
104. Celebrity Profiles 18
105. Christian School Books 18
106. *Homiletics 18
107. Fiction: Fantasy 16
108. *Exegesis 13
109. Exposes 13
110. Fiction: Science Fiction 13
111. Tracts 13
112. *Time Management 12
113. Writing How-To 12
114. *Children's Easy Readers 11

Comments:

If you are a fiction writer, you are more likely to sell adult fiction (65 possible publishers—5 more than last year) than you are juvenile fiction (47 publishers—7 less than last year) or teen fiction (34 publishers—2 less than last year). These figures indicate that fiction is improving for adults, but is leveling off or dropping for children and teens.

The most popular fiction genres with publishers are (1) Contemporary Fiction, 53 markets (same position as last year), (2) Historical Fiction, 52 markets, (3) Biblical Fiction (moved ahead of Adventure Fiction since last year), 49 markets, (4) Adventure Fiction, 44 markets, (5) Mystery, 34 markets, and (6) Humorous (moved ahead of Historical/Romance since last year), 29 markets. All the numbers above show an increase in actual markets for each genre.

Last year the book market for poets dropped by three, this year it picked up two of those, putting us at 32. That compares to only 16 in 1994, doubling the market in the last five years. Even though the market is improving, many will still want to consider self-publishing (look for subsidy publishers listed in another section of this book), or sell to periodicals. Go to the periodical topical listings in this book to find 230 markets for poetry.

Compared to last year, Prayer has stayed in #1, but Christian Living has dropped from second to third, with Inspirational moving from fourth into second place, and Bible Studies moving from third to fourth. The biggest move is for Marriage, moving from seventh into 11th place. However, we find the same topics among the top 12, with most staying in the same position or moving only slightly. Among the next 10 topics, Youth Books dropped out of that section from #20 to #27, and Adult Fiction moved up from #26, into the #22 spot. The rest stayed fairly close to last year's position, except for Ethics which moved up 5 places, reflecting the country's renewed interest in that area.

In a general comparison to last year, their were not a lot of significant changes. In order from most to least, these topics increased in interest: Biblical Fiction, Youth Programs, Death/Dying, Cookbooks*, Politics, Divorce, and Self-help*. Those dropping the most in interest were: Picture Books, Christian School Books, Juvenile Fiction, Senior Adult Issues*, Liturgical Studies, Singles Issues*, and Social Justice Issues*. An asterisk (*) after these topics indicates that the increase or decrease has continued from last year.

SUMMARY OF INFORMATION ON CHRISTIAN BOOK PUBLISHERS FOUND IN THE ALPHABETICAL LISTINGS

Note: The following numbers are based on the maximum total estimate for each company. For example, if a company gave a range of 5-10, the averages were based on the higher number, 10. This information will be valuable in determining if the contract offered by your publisher is in line with other publishers in some of these areas. For further help, check the section on editorial services to find those who offer contract evaluations, which are most valuable.

TOTAL MANUSCRIPTS RECEIVED:
Two hundred seventeen publishers indicated they received a combined total of over 115,580 manuscripts during the year. That is an average of 533 manuscripts per editor, per year, a decrease from last year. The actual number of manuscripts received ranged from 3 to 10,000 per editor.

NUMBER OF BOOKS PUBLISHED:
Two hundred forty-nine publishers reported that they will publish a combined total of 6,948 titles during the coming year. That is an average of nearly 28 books per publisher (just slightly more per publisher than last year). The actual number per publisher ranges from 1 to 200. Last year the maximum number of titles for one publisher was 268. This drop to 200 is an indication that many publishers are dropping back on the number of titles done per year. If each publisher actually publishes his maximum estimate of books for the year, over 6% of the manuscripts submitted will be published (up about ½% over last year).

AVERAGE FIRST PRINT RUN:
Based on 188 book publishers who indicated their average first print run, the average first printing of a book for a new author is about 6,400 books. That's a decrease of almost 5% from last year. Actual print runs ranged from 100 to 250,000 copies.

ROYALTIES:
Of the 130 publishers who reported actual amounts that they paid for royalties, 53 (41%) pay on the retail price; 77 (59%) pay on the wholesale price or net. The average royalty based on the retail price of the book was 7.6% to 11.5% (compared to 7.8% to 11.3% last year). Actual royalties varied from 2% to 30%. The average royalty based on net varied from 8.6% to 13.1% (compared to 7.8%-11.3% last year). Actual royalties varied from 1/2% to 30%. The recommended royalty based on net is 18%, but only 9% of the Christian publishers counted here are paying up to 18% or higher (that is down 3% from last year).

Some publishers indicate they pay royalties, but don't give specific amounts. Of the 215 that fall into that category (includes those above), 31% pay on the retail price, 48% pay on net, and 21% don't say which.

ADVANCES:
One hundred ninety-one publishers responded to the question about whether or not they paid advances. Of those, 108 paid advances and 83 did not—which means those who do are still ahead of those who don't. Of those who pay advances, only 23% (44 publishers) gave a specific amount. The average advance for those 44 was $2,109-6,739 (about a 45% increase over last year). This large an increase after a 34% increase last year is more than encouraging, and an indication that advances are improving in the Christian market. The actual range is still from $100 to $50,000, so ask for the amount that you need or deserve based on past publishing history. Most publishers pay more for established authors or potentially best-selling books. It is not unusual for a first-time author to get no advance or a small one. Once you have one or more books published, feel free to ask for an advance, and raise the amount for each book. Don't be afraid to ask for an advance, even on a first book, if you need the money to support you while you finish the manuscript. Although more publishers are saying they don't give an advance or are reluctant to name an amount, the truth is many publishers do give advances when warranted but are reluctant to advertise that fact or to divulge an amount.

REPORTING TIME:
Waiting for a response from an editor is often the hardest part of the writing business. Of the 339 editors who indicated how long you should have to wait for a response from them, the average time was just over 7 weeks (3 weeks less than last year). However, since the times they actually gave ranged from 1 to 52 weeks, be sure to check the listing for the publisher you are interested in. Give them a 2-week grace period; then feel free to write a polite letter asking about the current status of your manuscript. Give them another month to respond, and if you don't hear anything, you can call as a last resort.

E-MAIL AND WEBSITES:
Last year the number of publishers with e-mail and Website almost doubled over the previous year. This year, out of 301 book publishers listed, 169 have e-mail (25% over last year), and 165 have Websites (43% more than last year). To connect to any of their Websites, visit my Website at http://www.stuartmarket.com.

TOPICAL LISTINGS OF PERIODICALS

As soon as you have an article or story idea, look up that topic in the following topical listings (see Table of Contents for a full list of topics). Study the appropriate periodicals in the primary/alphabetical listings (as well as their writers' guidelines and sample copies)nd select those that are most likely targets for the piece you are writing.

Note that most ideas can be written for more than one periodical if you slant them to the needs of different audiences; for example, current events for teens, or pastors, or women. Have a target periodical and audience in mind before you start writing. Each topic is divided by age group/audience, so you can pick appropriate markets for your particular slant.

If the magazine prefers or requires a query letter, be sure to write that letter firstnd then follow any guidelines or suggestions they make if they give you a go-ahead.

R—Takes reprints.
(*)—Indicates new topic this year.

BIBLE STUDIES

ADULT/GENERAL

America
Arlington Catholic
Atlantic Baptist
Banner
Baptist Informer
Bible Advocate—R
Bread of Life—R
Breakthrough Intercessor—R
Canadian Catholic
Catholic Rural Life
CGA World—R
Christian Computing (MO)—R
Christian Motorsports
Christian Ranchman
Christian Standard—R
Christianity Today—R
Church Herald/Holiness—R
Company—R
Companions—R
Connecting Point—R
Culture Wars—R
Day Star Tribune—R
Dovetail—R
Emphasis/Faith & Living—R
Fellowship Link—R
Family Network—R
First Things
Foursquare World—R
God's Revivalist

Grail
Green Cross—R
Hallelujah! (CAN)—R
Head to Head—R
Healing Inn—R
Hearing Hearts
Heartlight Internet—R
Hidden Manna—R
Indian Life—R
Inspirer—R
John Milton—R
Life Gate—R
L.I.G.H.T News—R
Lookout—R
Lutheran—R
Lutheran Journal—R
Lutheran Witness—R
Mennonite—R
Messenger/St. Anthony
Methodist History
North American Voice
Our Family—R
Our Sunday Visitor
Pentecostal Testimony—R
Peoples Magazine—R
Perspectives
Plain Truth—R
Pourastan—R
PrayerWorks—R
Presbyterian Outlook
Presbyterians Today—R
St. Anthony Messenger

St. Willibrord Journal
Silver Wings—R
Sojourners
Spiritual Life
Stand Firm—R
Star of Zion
TEAK Roundup—R
Times of Refreshing
Today's Christian Senior—R
Touchstone—R
Trumpeter—R
United Church Observer
U.S. Catholic
Way of St. Francis—R
Weavings—R
Wesleyan Advocate—R

CHILDREN

Discovery (NY)—R
Listen

*CHRISTIAN
EDUCATION/LIBRARY*

Children's Ministry
Christian School
Church & Synagogue Lib.
Church Educator—R
GROUP
Leader/Church School
   Today—R
Religion Teacher's Journal
Shining Star

Teacher's Interaction

MISSIONS

Catholic Near East
Quiet Hour Echoes
Urban Mission—R
Women of the Harvest

PASTORS/LEADERS

African American Pulpit
Catholic Servant
Celebration
Emmanuel
Five Stones—R
Journal/Christian Healing—R
Ministries Today
Preacher's Magazine—R
Priest
PROCLAIM—R
Pulpit Helps—R
Quarterly Review
Reaching Children at Risk
Resource—R
Single Adult Ministries
Today's Christian Preacher—R
Word & World

TEEN/YOUNG ADULT

Challenge (GA) —R
Conqueror—R
Cross Walk
Devo'Zine—R
Student Leadership—R
Teens on Target—R
YOU!—R
Young Adult Today
Young Salvationist—R
Youth Challenge—R
With—R

WOMEN

Adam's Rib—R
Church Woman
Horizons—R
Just Between Us—R
Lutheran Woman Today
Proverbs 31 Homemaker—R
True Woman
Woman's Touch—R

WRITERS

Inklings

BOOK EXCERPTS

ADULT/GENERAL

AXIOS—R

Bible Advocate—R
Canadian Catholic
Charisma/Christian Life
Chicken Soup/Mother—R
Chicken Soup/Single—R
Chicken Soup/Woman—R
Christian Arts Review
Christian Chronicle—R
Christian Edge—R
Christian Motorsports
Christian Renewal—R
Comments from the Friends—R
Common Boundary
Covenant Companion—R
Culture Wars—R
Day Star Tribune—R
Door
Dovetail—R
Family Network—R
Fellowship Link—R
Good News Journal (TX)
Hearing Hearts
Hidden Manna—R
Homeschooling Today—R
Home Times—R
Indian Life—R
Jewel Among Jewels—R
Living—R
Living Light News—R
MESSAGE/Open Bible—R
Metro Voice—R
Michigan Christian
New Covenant
New Heart—R
On Mission
Parent Paper—R
Perspectives
Plus—R
Power for Living—R
Presbyterian Outlook
Presbyterian Record—R
Prism—R
Re:generation
Religious Broadcasting—R
SCP Journal—R
Sojourners
Stand Firm—R
Star of Zion
Sursum Corda!—R
TEAK Roundup—R
Together—R
Trumpeter—R
United Church Observer
Upscale Magazine
U.S. Catholic
Weavings—R

CHILDREN

GUIDE—R

CHRISTIAN EDUCATION/LIBRARY

Christian School

MISSIONS

Areopagus—R
East-West Church
Intl. Journal/Frontier—R

PASTORS/LEADERS

African American Pulpit
Christian Century
Church Bytes—R
Clergy Journal—R
Five Stones—R
Ivy Jungle Report—R
Journal/Christian Healing—R
Ministries Today
Ministry & Liturgy—R
Networks—R
Sharing the Practice—R
Voice of the Vineyard —R
Worldwide Challenge
Youthworker—R

TEEN/YOUNG ADULTS

Breakaway—R
Challenge (GA) —R
Teen Life—R
Teens on Target—R
YOU!—R
Young Salvationist—R
Youth Challenge—R

WOMEN

Conscience—R
Horizons—R
Link & Visitor—R
Woman's Touch—R

WRITERS

Inklings

BOOK REVIEWS

ADULT/GENERAL

About Such Things—R
AGAIN—R
A.M.E. Christian Recorder—R
Anglican Journal—R
Arkansas Catholic
Arlington Catholic
AXIOS—R
Believer—R
Canadian Catholic

Cathedral Age
Catholic Insight
Catholic Rural Life
CBA Marketplace
Charisma/Christian Life
Christian Arts Review
Christian Century
Christian Chronicle—R
Christian Computing (MO)—R
Christian Courier (CAN)—R
Christian Edge—R
Christian Media—R
Christian Motorsports
Christian Poet—R
Christian Ranchman
Christian Research
Christianity/Arts
Christianity Today—R
Christians in Business
Comments /Friends—R
Common Boundary
Commonweal
Company—R
Connecting Point—R
Cornerstone—R
Creation Ex Nihilo
Cresset
Crisis Point
Culture Wars—R
Day Star Tribune—R
Discovery—R
Dovetail—R
Expression Christian
Family Network—R
Fellowship Link—R
First Things
Forefront
Good News Journal (MO)
Good News Journal (TX)
Grail
Green Cross—R
Head to Head—R
Hearing Hearts
Hidden Manna—R
Homeschooling Today—R
Home Times—R
Impact Magazine—R
Inland NW Christian
Interim—R
Jewel Among Jewels—R
John Milton—R
Joyful Noise
Life@Work
Life Gate—R
Light and Life
Living Light News—R
Mature Years—R
Mennonite Historian—R

Methodist History
Michigan Christian
MovieGuide
Narrow Gate
National Catholic
New Creation
New Moon—R
No-Debt Living—R
On Mission
Parent Paper—R
Perspectives
Poetry Forum—R
Pourastan—R
Prairie Messenger—R
Presbyterian Layman
Presbyterian Outlook
Presbyterian Record—R
Presbyterians Today—R
Prism—R
ProLife News—R
Re:generation
Religious Education
Right Road—R
Sacred Journey—R
SCP Journal—R
Single Connection—R
Social Justice
Sojourners
Something Better—R
Southwestern Writers—R
Spiritual Life
Stand Firm—R
Star of Zion
TEAK Roundup—R
Trumpeter—R
United Church Observer
Upscale Magazine
Upsouth—R
Way of St. Francis—R
Weavings—R

CHILDREN

Skipping Stones

CHRISTIAN EDUCATION/LIBRARY
Caravan
Catholic Library World
Christian Librarian—R
Christian Library Jour.—R
Christian School
Church & Synagogue Lib.
Church Libraries—R
Journal/Adventist Educ.—R
Religion Teacher's Journal
Vision—R

MISSIONS

Areopagus—R

East-West Church
Evangelical Missions—R
World Christian—R

MUSIC
CCM Magazine
Lighthouse Electronic
Songwriter—R

PASTORS/LEADERS—R
African American Pulpit
Catechumenate
Christian Century—R
Christian Management—R
Church Bytes—R
Clergy Journal—R
Diocesan Dialogue—R
Enrichment—R
Five Stones—R
Ivy Jungle Report—R
Journal/Christian Healing—R
Jour/Amer Soc/Chur Growth—
  R
Lutheran Partners—R
Ministries Today
Ministry Now
Networks—R
Preacher—R
Preacher's Magazine—R
Pulpit Helps—R
Reaching Children at Risk
Resource—R
Sharing the Practice—R
Single Adult Ministries
Theology Today (rarely)
Voice of the Vineyard —R
WCA News—R
Word & World
Worship Leader

TEEN/YOUNG ADULT
Challenge (GA) —R
Real Time—R
Student Leadership—R
Young Christian—R

WOMEN
Anna's Journal—R
Conscience—R
Esprit—R
Helping Hand—R
Horizons—R
Just Between Us—R
Kansas City Woman
Proverbs 31 Homemaker—R
True Woman
Virtuous Woman
Wesleyan Woman

Woman's Touch—R

WRITERS

Advanced Chris. Writer—R
Canadian Writer's Jour—R
Cross & Quill—R
Fellowscript—R
Gotta Write
Inklings
WIN-Informer
Writer On Line—R
Writer's Exchange—R
Writer's Guidelines/News
Writer's Ink—R
Writer's Potpourri—R
Southwestern Writers—R
Tickled by Thunder
VA Christian Writer—R

CANADIAN/FOREIGN MARKETS

ADULT/GENERAL

Anglican Arts
Anglican Journal
Annals of St. Anne
Atlantic Baptist
BC Catholic
Believer
Bread of Life
Canada Lutheran
Canadian Catholic Review
Canadian Mennonite
Catholic Insight
Christian Courier
Companion
Creation Ex Nihilo
Crossway/Newsline
Dreams & Visions
Faith Today
Fellowship Link
Fellowship Today
Grail
Hallelujah!
Impact
Indian Life
Interim
Living Light News
Mennonite Brethren Herald
Mennonite Historian
Messenger of the Sacred Heart
Messenger of St. Anthony
Our Family
Pentecostal Testimony
Peoples Magazine
Plowman
Pourastan
Prairie Messenger

Presbyterian Record
ProLife News
Shantyman
Spirit
TEAK Roundup
Time for Rhyme
Times of Refreshing
United Church Observer

CHRISTIAN EDUCATION/LIBRARY

Caravan

DAILY DEVOTIONALS

Words of Life

MISSIONS

Areopagus

PASTORS/LEADERS

Cell Life FORUM
Evangelical Baptist
Reaching Children at Risk
Resource
Technologies for Worship

TEEN/YOUNG ADULT

HYPE

WOMEN

Esprit
Link & Visitor
Women Today
Women Today Online

WRITERS

Canadian Writer's Journal
Exchange
Fellowscript
Tickled by Thunder
Writer's Lifeline

CELEBRITY PIECES

ADULT/GENERAL

American Tract Soc.—R
Angels on Earth
Arlington Catholic
AXIOS—R
Breakthrough Intercessor—R
Canadian Catholic
Catholic Digest—R
CBA Frontline
Celebrate Life—R
CGA World—R
Charisma/Christian Life
Chicken Soup/Mother—R
Chicken Soup/Single—R
Chicken Soup/Woman—R

Christian Arts Review
Christian Chronicle—R
Christian Edge—R
Christian Motorsports
Christian Ranchman
Christian Reader—R
Columbia
Companion
Day Star Tribune—R
Door
Expression Christian
Fellowship Link—R
Focus on the Family
Good News (AL)—R
Good News, Etc—R
Good News Journal (MO)—R
Good News Journal (TX)
Gospel Today
Gospel Tract—R
Guideposts
Head to Head—R
Hearing Hearts
Heartlight Internet—R
Home Times—R
Indian Life—R
Inside Journal—R
Jewel Among Jewels—R
Liguorian
Life Gate—R
Lifeglow—R
Light and Life
Living—R
Living Light News—R
Living with Teenagers—R
Marriage Partnership
Mature Years—R
Messenger/St. Anthony
Metro Voice—R
Michigan Christian
Minnesota Christian—R
New Writing—R
Our Sunday Visitor
ParentLife—R
Pentecostal Testimony—R
Plain Truth—R
Plus—R
Power for Living—R
PrayerWorks—R
Presbyterian Record—R
Prism—R
ProLife News—R
Pursuit—R
Religious Broadcasting—R
Right Road—R
Sacred Journey—R
Single Connection—R
Sports Spectrum
Standard—R

Stand Firm—R
TEAK Roundup—R
Trumpeter—R
Vibrant Life—R
War Cry—R

CHILDREN

Counselor—R
GUIDE—R
Guideposts for Kids
Live Wire—R
Power Station—R
Touch—R

CHRISTIAN EDUCATION/LIBRARY

Christian Library Jour.—R

MISSIONS

So All May Hear—R
Teachers in Focus—R
Worldwide Challenge

MUSIC

Christian Country—R
Gospel Industry Today
Songwriter—R

PASTORS/LEADERS

Catholic Servant
Christian Camp—R

TEEN/YOUNG ADULT

Breakaway—R
Brio
Challenge (GA) —R
Essential Connection—R
Insight—R
Listen—R
Sharing the VICTORY (sports)
    —R
Spirit
Straight—R
Teen Life—R
YOU!—R
Young Salvationist—R

WOMEN

Aspire
Virtue—R

WRITERS

Christian Communicator—R
Gotta Write
Inklings
WIN-Informer
Writer's Guidelines/News

CHRISTIAN BUSINESS

ADULT/GENERAL

A.M.E. Christian Recorder—R
Angels on Earth
AXIOS—R
Banner
Believer—R
Breakthrough Intercessor—R
Bridal Guides—R
Catholic Sentinel—R
CBA Marketplace
CGA World—R
Christian Businessman
Christian Chronicle—R
Christian Courier (CAN)—R
Christian Edge—R
Christian Living—R
Christian News NW—R
Christian Motorsports
Christian Ranchman
Christian Edge—R
Christians in Business
Company—R
Day Star Tribune—R
Disciple's Journal—R
Discovery—R
Evangel—R
Expression Christian
Faith Today
Family Network—R
Good News (AL)—R
Good News Journal (MO)—R
Good News Journal (TX)
Gospel Today
Grail
Guideposts
Heartlight Internet—R
Home Times—R
Indian Life—R
Life@Work
Life Gate—R
Light and Life
Living—R
Living Light News—R
Lutheran Journal—R
Marketplace
Mennonite—R
MESSAGE
Metro Voice

Michigan Christian
Minnesota Christian—R
New Covenant
On Mission
Parent Paper—R
Pentecostal Testimony—R
Peoples Magazine—R

Power for Living—R
PrayerWorks—R
Presbyterian Record—R
Prism—R
Re:generation
Religious Broadcasting—R
Single Connection—R
Social Justice
Something Better—R
Standard—R
Stand Firm—R
Star of Zion
TEAK Roundup—R
Today's Christian Senior—R
Together—R
Trumpeter—R
2-Soar—R
United Church Observer
War Cry—R

MISSIONS

Worldwide Challenge

PASTORS/LEADERS

African American Pulpit
Catholic Servant
Christian Camp—R
Christian Management—R
Preacher's Magazine—R
Reaching Children at Risk
Today's Christian Preacher—R
Today's Parish
Your Church—R

TEEN/YOUNG ADULT

Challenge (GA) —R
Young Christian—R

WOMEN

Aspire
Hearth
Horizons—R
Lutheran Woman Today
Proverbs 31 Homemaker—R
Women Today—R
Women Today Online—R

WRITERS

Inklings

CHRISTIAN EDUCATION

A.M.E. Christian Recorder—R
America
Anglican Journal—R
Arkansas Catholic
Arlington Catholic
Atlantic Baptist

AXIOS—R
Banner
Baptist Informer
B.C. Catholic—R
Believer—R
Bible Advocate—R
Breakthrough Intercessor—R
Canada Lutheran—R
Canadian Catholic
Catholic Digest—R
Catholic Parent
Catholic Sentinel—R
CGA World—R
Christian C.L. RECORD—R
Christian Courier (CAN)—R
Christian Edge—R
Christian Home & School
Christian Motorsports
Christian Ranchman
Christian Renewal—R
Church Herald/Holiness—R
Columbia
Companions—R
Company—R
Covenant Companion—R
Culture Wars—R
Day Star Tribune—R
Discovery—R
Emphasis/Faith & Living—R
Evangel—R
Expression Christian
Faith Today
Family Network—R
Focus on the Family
Foursquare World—R
God's Revivalist
Good News (AL)—R
Good News, Etc—R
Good News Journal (TX)
Gospel Today
Grail
Hearing Hearts
Heartlight Internet—R
Homeschooling Today—R
Home Times—R
Inland NW Christian
Interchange
Jewel Among Jewels—R
John Milton—R

Joyful Noise
Life Gate—R
Light and Life
Living Church
Living Light News—R
Living with Teenagers—R
Lutheran Digest—R
Lutheran Journal—R

Mennonite—R
Messenger/St. Anthony
Messenger of the Sacred Heart
Methodist History
Metro Voice—R
Michigan Christian
Minnesota Christian—R
Montana Catholic—R
New Covenant
North American Voice
NW Christian Journal—R
On Mission
Our Family—R
Our Sunday Visitor
Parent Paper—R
Peoples Magazine—R
Perspectives
Plain Truth—R
Pourastan—R
PrayerWorks—R
Presbyterian Layman
Presbyterian Outlook
Presbyterian Record—R
Preserving Christian Homes—
   R
Prism—R
Religious Education
Right Road—R
SCP Journal—R
Single Connection—R
Social Justice
Something Better—R
Stand Firm—R
Star of Zion
TEAK Roundup—R
Together—R
Trumpeter—R
United Church Observer
U.S. Catholic
War Cry—R
Way of St. Francis—R

CHILDREN

Discovery (NY)—R
My Friend
Together Time

CHRISTIAN EDUCATION/LIBRARY
(See alphabetical listings)

MISSIONS

East-West Church
So All May Hear—R

PASTORS/LEADERS

African American Pulpit
Art+Plus
Catholic Servant

Christian Camp—R
Christian Ministry
Church Administration
Church Bytes—R
Clergy Journal—R
Enrichment—R
Five Stones—R
Lutheran Partners—R
Ministries Today
Ministry & Liturgy—R
Networks—R
Preacher's Magazine—R
Reaching Children at Risk
Resource—R
Sabbath School Leadership
Sharing the Practice—R
Theology Today
Today's Christian Preacher—R
Today's Parish
Word & World
Youthworker—R

TEEN/YOUNG ADULT

Challenge (GA) —R
Conqueror—R
Cross Walk
Essential Connection—R
Insight—R
Teen Life—R
YOU!—R
Young Christian—R

WOMEN

Adam's Rib—R
Esprit—R
Horizons—R
Just Between Us—R
Lutheran Woman Today
Proverbs 31 Homemaker—R

WRITERS

Inklings

CHRISTIAN LIVING

ADULT/GENERAL

Advent Christian Witness—R
Alive!—R

alive now!
A.M.E. Christian Recorder—R
America
American Tract Soc.—R
Angels on Earth
Annals of St. Anne
Arkansas Catholic
Arlington Catholic
AXIOS—R

Banner
B.C. Catholic—R
Believer—R
Bible Advocate—R
Bible Advocate Online—R
Bread of Life—R
Breakthrough Intercessor—R
Brethren Evangelist
Bridal Guides—R
Canada Lutheran—R
Canadian Catholic
Catholic Digest—R
Catholic New York
Catholic Parent
Catholic Rural Life
Catholic Sentinel—R
CGA World—R
Charisma/Christian Life
Christian Century
Christian Chronicle—R
Christian Courier (WI)—R
Christian Courier (CAN)—R
Christian Edge—R
Christian Home & School
Christian Living—R
Christian Motorsports
Christian Poet—R
Christian Ranchman
Christian Reader—R
Christian Standard—R
Christianity Today—R
Church Advocate—R
Church Herald/Holiness—R
Church of God EVANGEL
Columbia
Commonweal
Companion
Companions—R
Company—R
Connecting Point—R
Conquest
Covenant Companion—R
Crisis Point
Crossway/Newsline—R
Culture Wars—R
Day Star Tribune—R
Decision
Discipleship Journal
Emphasis/Faith & Living—R
Evangel—R
Faith Today
Family Digest
Family Journal—R
Family Network—R
Fellowship Link—R
Focus on the Family
Forefront
Foursquare World—R

Gem—R
God's Revivalist
Good News (AL)—R
Good News(KY)—R
Good News, Etc—R
Good News Journal (MO)—R
Good News Journal (TX)
Gospel Tidings—R
Gospel Today
Gospel Tract—R
Grail
Guideposts
Hallelujah! (CAN)—R
Head to Head—R
Healing Inn—R
Hearing Hearts
Heartlight Internet—R
Highway News—R
Home Times—R
Impact Magazine—R
Indian Life—R
Inland NW Christian
Inspirer—R
Jewel Among Jewels—R
John Milton—R
Jour/Christian Nursing—R
Keys to Living—R
Life Gate—R
Lifeglow—R
Light and Life
L.I.G.H.T News—R
Liguorian
Live—R
Living—R
Living Light News—R
Living with Teenagers—R
Lookout—R
Lutheran—R
Lutheran Digest—R
Lutheran Journal—R
Marian Helpers—R
Marriage Partnership
Mature Years—R
Mennonite—R
Mennonite Brethren—R
MESSAGE
Messenger/St. Anthony
Messenger of the Sacred Heart
Methodist History
Metro Voice—R
Michigan Christian
Montana Catholic—R
Moody—R
New Covenant
New Heart—R
North American Voice
Northwestern Lutheran—R
Oblates

On Mission
Our Family—R
Our Sunday Visitor
ParentLife—R
Parent Paper—R
Pentecostal Evangel
Pentecostal Testimony—R
Peoples Magazine—R
Physician
Plain Truth—R
Plus—R
Pourastan—R
Power for Living—R
PrayerWorks—R
Presbyterian Layman
Presbyterian Record—R
Presbyterians Today—R
Progress—R
Purpose—R
Pursuit—R
Religious Broadcasting—R
Right Road—R
Romantic—R
SCP Journal—R
Seek—R
Signs of the Times—R
Single Connection—R
Smart Families
Social Justice
Something Better—R
Spiritual Life
Sports Spectrum (through
     sports)
Standard—R
Standard—R
Stand Firm—R
TEAK Roundup—R
Time of Singing—R
Times of Refreshing
Today's Christian Senior—R
Together—R
Touchstone—R
United Church Observer
U.S. Catholic
Upsouth—R
Vibrant Life—R
Vision—R
War Cry—R
Way of St. Francis—R
Weavings—R
Wesleyan Advocate—R

CHILDREN

Club Connection—R
CLUBHOUSE—R
Courage
Discoveries—R
Discovery (NY)—R

Discovery Trails—R
High Adventure—R
Lad
My Friend
Partners—R
Touch—R
Wonder Time

CHRISTIAN EDUCATION/LIBRARY

Brigade Leader—R
CE Connection—R
Children's Ministry
Church & Synagogue Lib.
Church Educator—R
GROUP
Leader/Church School
    Today—R
Religion Teacher's Journal
Resource—R
Shining Star
Teacher's Interaction

MISSIONS

American Horizon—R
Latin American Evangelist
Quiet Hour Echoes
Worldwide Challenge

MUSIC

Christian Country—R

PASTORS/LEADERS

African American Pulpit
Art+Plus
Catholic Servant
Cell Church—R
Cell Life FORUM
Christian Camp—R
Christian Management—R
Current Thoughts & Trends
Emmanuel
Eucharistic Minister—R
Five Stones—R
Journal/Christian Healing—R
Let's Worship
Lutheran Partners—R
Minister's Family
Preacher—R
Preacher's Illus. Service—R
Preacher's Magazine—R
Reaching Children at Risk
Resource—R
Review for Religious
Today's Christian Preacher—R
Word & World

TEEN/YOUNG ADULT

Certainty

Challenge (GA) —R
Challenge (IL)
Conqueror—R
Devo'Zine—R
Essential Connection—R
Insight—R
Real Time—R
Straight—R
Student Leadership—R
Teen Life—R
Teens on Target—R
Today's Christian Teen—R
With—R
YOU!—R
Young Adult Today
Young Christian—R
Young Salvationist—R
Youth Challenge—R

WOMEN

Adam's Rib—R
Aspire
CoLaborer—R
Esprit—R
Helping Hand—R
Horizons—R
Journey—R
Joyful Woman—R
Just Between Us—R
Keepers at Home
Link & Visitor—R
Lutheran Woman Today
Lutheran Woman's Quar.
Proverbs 31 Homemaker—R
Southwestern Writers—R
Today's Christian Woman
True Woman
Virtue—R
Wesleyan Woman—R
Woman's Touch—R
Women of Spirit—R

WRITERS

Inklings
Writers' Intl. Forum

CHURCH GROWTH

ADULT/GENERAL

A.M.E. Christian Recorder—R
Banner
Believer—R
Bible Advocate—R
Breakthrough Intercessor—R
Canada Lutheran—R
CGA World—R
Charisma/Christian Life
Christian Edge—R

Christian Motorsports
Christianity Today—R
Church Herald/Holiness—R
Church of God EVANGEL
Company—R
Covenant Companion—R
Culture Wars—R
Day Star Tribune—R
Emphasis/Faith & Living—R
Evangel—R
Faith Today
Fellowship Link—R
Good News(KY)—R
Good News, Etc—R
Gospel Tidings—R
Gospel Today
Grail
Hallelujah! (CAN)—R
Inside Journal—R
Interchange
Jewel Among Jewels—R
John Milton—R
Lutheran Journal—R
Mennonite—R
MESSAGE/Open Bible—R
Messenger of the Sacred Heart
Michigan Christian
Montana Catholic—R
On Mission
Peoples Magazine—R
Plain Truth—R
Presbyterian Layman
Presbyterian Outlook
Presbyterian Record—R
Preserving Christian Homes—
    R
Pursuit—R
Re:generation
Signs of the Times—R
Star of Zion
Together—R
United Church Observer
Upsouth—R

CHRISTIAN EDUCATION/LIBRARY

Baptist Leader—R
CE Leadership—R
Children's Ministry
Church & Synagogue Lib.
GROUP
Leader/Church School
    Today—R
Resource—R

MISSIONS

Latin American Evangelist
Missiology
P.I.M.E. World

World Pulse—R

PASTORS/LEADERS

African American Pulpit
Art+Plus
Catholic Servant
Cell Life FORUM—R
Church Growth Network—R
Clergy Journal—R
Creator—R
Current Thoughts & Trends
Emmanuel
Enrichment—R
Evangelical Baptist—R
Jour/Amer Soc/Chur
    Growth —R
Five Stones—R
Let's Worship
Lutheran Forum—R
Lutheran Partners—R
Ministries Today
Ministry
Ministry & Liturgy—R
Ministry Now
Preacher's Magazine—R
Pulpit Helps—R
Resource—R
Sharing the Practice—R
Technologies/Worship—R
Theology Today
Today's Christian Preacher—R
Vital Ministry
Voice of the Vineyard —R
Worship Leader
Your Church—R

TEEN/YOUNG ADULT

Challenge (GA) —R
Essential Connection—R
YOU!—R
Young Christian—R

WOMEN

Esprit—R
Just Between Us—R

WRITERS

Inklings
Writers' Intl. Forum

CHURCH LIFE

ADULT/GENERAL

A.M.E. Christian Recorder—R
Arkansas Catholic
Banner
Believer—R
Bible Advocate—R

Bread of Life—R
Breakthrough Intercessor—R
Brethren Evangelist
Canada Lutheran—R
Catholic Courier
Catholic Digest—R
CGA World—R
Christian Edge—R
Christian Living—R
Christian Motorsports
Christian News NW—R
Christian Reader—R
Church Herald/Holiness—R
Church of God EVANGEL
Companion
Conquest
Covenant Companion—R
Day Star Tribune—R
Decision
Discipleship Journal
Discovery—R
Emphasis/Faith & Living—R
Evangel—R
Faith Today
Family Digest
Family Journal—R
Family Network—R
Good News(KY)—R
Good News, Etc.—R
Gospel Tidings—R
Gospel Today
Grail
Jewel Among Jewels—R
John Milton—R
Liguorian
Live—R
Living Church
Lookout—R
Lutheran Digest—R
Lutheran Journal—R
Marriage Partnership
Mennonite—R
Messenger/St. Anthony
Michigan Christian
Montana Catholic—R
Moody—R
New Writing—R
North American Voice
On Mission
Our Family—R
Peoples Magazine—R
Presbyterian Outlook
Presbyterian Record—R
Re:generation
St. Willibrord Journal
Signs of the Times—R
Star of Zion
Times of Refreshing

Today's Christian Senior—R
Trumpeter—R
United Church Observer
Upsouth—R
Way of St. Francis—R
Weavings—R

CHILDREN

Discovery (NY)—R

CHRISTIAN EDUCATION/LIBRARY

CE Connection—R
CE Leadership—R
Children's Ministry
Church Educator—R
GROUP

MISSIONS

Catholic Near East
Latin American Evangelist
Quiet Hour Echoes

PASTORS/LEADERS

African American Pulpit
Catholic Servant
Cell Church—R
Christian Ministry
Clergy Journal—R
Current Thoughts & Trends
Enrichment—R
Evangelical Baptist—R
Five Stones—R
Leadership Journal—R
Let's Worship
Lutheran Partners—R
Minister's Family
Ministry
Ministry & Liturgy—R
Preacher—R
Preacher's Magazine—R
Pulpit Helps—R
Resource—R
Review for Religious
Sabbath School Leadership
Sharing the Practice—R
Technologies/Worship—R
Theology Today
Today's Christian Preacher—R
Vital Ministry
Voice of the Vineyard —R
WCA News—R

TEEN/YOUNG ADULT

Challenge (GA) —R
Essential Connection—R
Insight—R
Straight—R
Teen Life—R

Young Christian—R

WOMEN

Esprit—R
Horizons—R
Wesleyan Woman—R

WRITERS

Inklings
Writers' Intl. Forum

CHURCH MANAGEMENT

ADULT/GENERAL

A.M.E. Christian Recorder—R
AXIOS—R
Banner
Believer—R
Biblical Reflections—R
Breakthrough Intercessor—R
Canada Lutheran—R
Canadian Catholic
CGA World—R
Christian Computing (MO)—R
Christian Edge—R
Christian News NW—R
Church Herald/Holiness—R
Church of God EVANGEL
Covenant Companion—R
Culture Wars—R
Day Star Tribune—R
Disciple's Journal—R
Expression Christian
Faith Today
Good News, Etc—R
Gospel Tidings—R
Gospel Today
Grail
Hearing Hearts
Joyful Noise
Living Church
Lutheran Digest—R
Lutheran Journal—R
MESSAGE/Open Bible—R
Metro Voice—R
Michigan Christian
On Mission
Signs of the Times—R
Star of Zion
U.S. Catholic
Our Sunday Visitor
Presbyterian Layman
Presbyterian Outlook
Presbyterian Record—R
United Church Observer
Wesleyan Advocate—R

CHRISTIAN EDUCATION/LIBRARY

Baptist Leader—R
Children's Ministry
Church Educator—R
GROUP
Latin American Evangelist
Resource—R

PASTORS/LEADERS

African American Pulpit
Catholic Servant
Celebration
Christian Management—R
Christian Ministry
Church Bytes—R
Church Growth Network—R
Clergy Journal—R
Current Thoughts & Trends
Enrichment—R
Evangelical Baptist—R
Five Stones—R
Jour/Amer Soc/Chur Growth—R
Leadership Journal—R
Lutheran Forum—R
Lutheran Partners—R
Ministries Today
Ministry
Pastoral Life
Preacher's Magazine—R
Priest
Pulpit Helps—R
Resource—R
Sharing the Practice—R
Technologies/Worship—R
Theology Today
Today's Christian Preacher—R
Vital Ministry
Voice of the Vineyard—R
WCA News—R
Word & World
Worship Leader
Your Church—R

Youthworker—R

WOMEN

Just Between Us—R

WRITERS

Inklings

CHURCH OUTREACH

ADULT/GENERAL

Alive!—R

A.M.E. Christian Recorder—R
America
Arkansas Catholic
AXIOS—R
Banner
Baptist Informer
Believer—R
Bible Advocate—R
Bread of Life—R
Breakthrough Intercessor—R
Brethren Evangelist
Canadian Catholic
Canadian Mennonite
Cathedral Age
Catholic Digest—R
Catholic Rural Life
Catholic Sentinel—R
CGA World—R
Charisma/Christian Life
Christian Edge—R
Christian Motorsports
Christian Reader—R
Church Herald/Holiness—R
Church of God EVANGEL
Companion
Companions—R
Conquest
Covenant Companion—R
Culture Wars—R
Day Star Tribune—R
Decision
Emphasis/Faith & Living—R
Episcopal Life—R
Evangel—R
Faith Today
Family Network—R
God's Revivalist
Good News(KY)—R
Good News, Etc—R
Gospel Tidings—R
Grail
Indian Life—R
Inspirer—R
Jewel Among Jewels—R
John Milton—R
Liguorian
Living Church
Lookout—R
Lutheran—R
Lutheran Journal—R
MESSAGE/Open Bible—R
Metro Voice—R
Michigan Christian
Moody—R
New Covenant
North American Voice
Northwestern Lutheran—R

On Mission
Our Family—R
Our Sunday Visitor
Peoples Magazine—R
Plain Truth—R
Presbyterian Layman
Presbyterian Outlook
Presbyterian Record—R
Presbyterians Today—R
Prism—R
Purpose—R
Re:generation
Religious Education
St. Joseph's Messenger—R
SCP Journal—R
Signs of the Times—R
Single Connection—R
Social Justice
Something Better—R
Stand Firm—R
TEAK Roundup—R
2-Soar—R
United Church Observer
U.S. Catholic
Wesleyan Advocate—R

CHILDREN
Discovery (NY)—R
Focus/Clubhouse
Kids' Ministry Ideas—R

CHRISTIAN EDUCATION/LIBRARY
Brigade Leader—R
Caravan
CE Connection—R
CE Counselor—R
CE Leadership—R
Children's Ministry
Church Educator—R
GROUP
Insight—R
Journal/Adventist Educ.—R
Leader/Church School
   Today—R
Perspective—R
Religion Teacher's Journal
Resource—R

MISSIONS
American Horizon—R
East-West Church
Evangelical Missions—R
Latin American Evangelist
Urban Mission—R
World Pulse—R
Worldwide Challenge

PASTORS/LEADERS
African American Pulpit
Catholic Servant
Cell Church—R
Cell Life FORUM—R
Christian Management—R
Christian Ministry
Church Administration
Church Growth Network—R
Clergy Journal—R
Current Thoughts & Trends
Enrichment—R
Evangelical Baptist—R
Five Stones—R
Jour/Amer Soc/Chur Growth—R
Leadership Journal—R
Let's Worship
Lutheran Forum—R
Lutheran Partners—R
Ministries Today
Ministry
Ministry & Liturgy—R
Pastoral Life
Preacher—R
Preacher's Magazine—R
Priest
Pulpit Helps—R
Resource—R
Sharing the Practice—R
Technologies/Worship—R
Theology Today
Today's Christian Preacher—R
Today's Parish
Vital Ministry
WCA News—R
Word & World
Worship Leader
Your Church—R

TEEN/YOUNG ADULT
Challenge (GA)—R
Essential Connection—R
Insight—R
Teen Life—R
YOU!—R
Young Adult Today
Young Christian—R

WOMEN
Just Between Us—R
Lutheran Woman Today
Wesleyan Woman

WRITERS
Inklings
Writers' Intl. Forum

CHURCH TRADITIONS*

ADULT/GENERAL
A.M.E. Christian Recorder—R
Believer—R
Breakthrough Intercessor—R
Bridal Guides—R
Catholic Digest—R
Christian Renewal—R
Covenant Companion—R
Day Star Tribune—R
Decision
Dovetail—R
Faith Today
Family Digest
Forefront
Jewel Among Jewels—R
Light and Life
Lifeglow—R
Liguorian
John Milton—R
Montana Catholic—R
Pentecostal Testimony—R
Presbyterian Outlook
Presbyterian Record—R
Right Road—R
Sacred Journey—R
St. Willibrord Journal
United Church Observer
Way of St. Francis—R
Weavings—R

CHILDREN
Discovery (NY)—R
Listen

CHRISTIAN EDUCATION/LIBRARY
Baptist Leader—R

MISSIONS
Latin American Evangelist

PASTORS/LEADERS
African American Pulpit
Evangelical Baptist—R
Five Stones—R
Lutheran Partners—R
Quarterly Review
Resource—R
Sharing the Practice—R

TEEN/YOUNG ADULT
Young & Alive—R
Young Christian—R
Young Salvationist—R

WRITERS
Inklings
Writers' Intl. Forum

CONTESTS

Alberta Christian Writers
  (Canadian group)
Anglican Arts
Blue Mountain Arts (cards)
Bridal Guides
Byline
Canadian Writer's Jour
Catholic Digest
CEHUC Spanish Group (CA)
Celebration
China Lake Conference (ME)
Christian Arts Review
Christian Ministry
Christian Reader
Christianity and the Arts
Co-Laborer
Common Boundary
Company
Creation Illustrated
Day Star Tribune
Disciple's Journal
Dream Weaver
Faith Today
Fellowscript
Frontiers in Writing (TX conf.)
Glorieta Writers Conference
  (NM)
Greater Philadelphia Chr. Writ.
  (group)
Guideposts
Guideposts for Teens
Insight (teen)
Inspirational Writers Alive! (TX
  group)
Intl. Black Writers (IL group)
Intl. Network (conf./ID)
Jour/Christian Nursing
Maine Fellowship (group)
MESSAGE
Ministry & Liturgy
MN Christian Writers (group)
New Writing
NW Christian Author
Plowman
Pockets
Poetry Connection
Poetry Forum
Poets' Page
Poets' Paper
Presbyterian Writers
Right Road
San Diego Writers (CA)

Sharing the Practice
Silver Wings
Skipping Stones
Smile
Songwriter
Southwest Writers Wkshp
  (NM)
State of Maine Conference
TEAK Roundup
Tickled by Thunder
Time of Singing
Today's Christian Teen
2-Soar
West-Dayton Christian Writers
  (OH)
With (for teens)
Writer's Digest—R
Writer's Exchange
Writer's Ink
Writers' Intl. Forum
Writers' Journal
Writing World
Young Christian
Young Salvationist

CONTROVERSIAL ISSUES

ADULT/GENERAL

Accent on Living—R
A.M.E. Christian Recorder—R
American Tract Soc.—R
AXIOS—R
Bible Advocate—R
Bible Advocate Online—R
Bridal Guides—R
Canadian Catholic
Catholic Insight
Catholic Rural Life
CGA World—R
Charisma/Christian Life
Christian Arts Review
Christian Century
Christian Chronicle—R
Christian Courier (CAN)—R
Christian Living—R
Christian Media—R
Christian Motorsports
Christian Reader—R
Christian Renewal—R
Christian Research
Christian Social Action—R
Christianity Today—R
Church Advocate—R
Church Herald/Holiness—R
Comments/Friends—R
Common Boundary
Commonweal
Cornerstone—R

Covenant Companion—R
Creation Ex Nihilo
Cresset
Culture Wars—R
Day Star Tribune—R
Discipleship Journal
Door
Dovetail—R
Emphasis/Faith & Living—R
Episcopal Life—R
Expression Christian
Faith Today
Family Network—R
Gem—R
Good News(KY)—R
Good News, Etc—R
Good News Journal (MO)—R
Grail
Hallelujah! (CAN)—R
Head to Head—R
Healing Inn—R
Hearing Hearts
Highway News—R
Home Times—R
Indian Life—R
Interim—R
Jewel Among Jewels—R
John Milton—R
Jour/Christian Nursing—R
Joyful Noise
Light and Life
Living—R
Living Church
Living with Teenagers—R
Lutheran—R
Lutheran Witness—R
MESSAGE (limited)
Messenger/St. Anthony
Metro Voice—R
Michigan Christian
Minnesota Christian—R
Moody—R
MovieGuide
Newsline—R
New Writing—R
On Mission
Our Family—R
Pentecostal Testimony—R
Perspectives
Prairie Messenger—R
Presbyterian Layman
Presbyterian Outlook
Presbyterian Record—R
Presbyterians Today—R
Prism—R
ProLife News—R
Re:generation
Religious Education

Religious Broadcasting—R
Sacred Journey—R
SCP Journal—R
Seek—R
Signs of the Times—R
Single Connection—R
Social Justice
Something Better—R
Standard—R
Stand Firm—R
TEAK Roundup—R
United Church Observer
Upsouth—R
U.S. Catholic
War Cry—R
Weavings—R
Wesleyan Advocate—R

CHILDREN
Discovery (NY)—R

CHRISTIAN EDUCATION/LIBRARY
Children's Ministry
CE Counselor—R
Church Educator—R
GROUP
Guideposts for Kids
Today's Catholic Teacher—R

MISSIONS
American Horizon—R
Intl. Journal/Frontier—R
So All May Hear—R
Worldwide Challenge

PASTORS/LEADERS
African American Pulpit
Art+Plus
Christian Century
Christian Ministry
Cross Currents—R
Current Thoughts & Trends
Journal/Pastoral Care
Lutheran Forum—R
Lutheran Partners—R
Ministries Today
Ministry & Liturgy—R
Networks—R
Preacher—R
Pulpit Helps—R
Reaching Children at Risk
Resource—R
Single Adult Ministries
Word & World
Youthworker—R

TEEN/YOUNG ADULT
Brio

Challenge (GA)—R
Conqueror—R
Essential Connection—R
Student Leadership—R
Teen Life—R
With—R
YOU!—R
Young Adult Today
Young Christian—R
Young Salvationist—R

WOMEN
Aspire
Conscience—R
Hearth
Horizons—R
Virtue—R
Women of Spirit—R

WRITERS
Christian Response—R
WIN-Informer
Writers' Intl. Forum

CREATION SCIENCE

ADULT/GENERAL
Banner
Bible Advocate—R
Christian Chronicle—R
Christian Reader—R
Christian Renewal—R
Chrysalis Reader
Church Herald/Holiness—R
Companions—R
Conquest
Cornerstone—R
Creation Ex Nihilo
Day Star Tribune—R
Faith Today
Good News Journal (TX)
Gospel Today
Hallelujah! (CAN)—R
Homeschooling Today—R
Lifeglow—R
Live—R
Living—R
MESSAGE/Open Bible—R
MovieGuide
Peoples Magazine—R
Plain Truth—R
PrayerWorks—R
Signs of the Times—R
Something Better—R
Standard—R
Upsouth—R
War Cry—R

CHILDREN
Courage
Focus/Clubhouse
Nature Friend—R
Partners—R
Power & Light—R
Power Station—R
Primary Pal (IL)

CHRISTIAN EDUCATION/LIBRARY
Journal/Adventist Educ.—R

PASTORS/LEADERS
Christian Camp—R
Pulpit Helps—R

TEEN/YOUNG ADULT
Certainty
Challenge (IL)
Essential Connection—R
Insight—R
Straight—R
Teen Life—R
Teens on Target—R
Young & Alive—R
Youth Challenge—R

CULTS/OCCULT

ADULT/GENERAL
America
American Tract Soc.—R
AXIOS—R
Banner
Bible Advocate—R
Bible Advocate Online—R
CBA Marketplace
Charisma/Christian Life
Christian Chronicle—R
Christian Edge—R
Christian Ranchman
Christian Reader—R
Christian Renewal—R
Christian Research
Church Advocate—R
Comments from the Friends—R
Common Boundary
Companions—R
Conquest
Cornerstone—R
Culture Wars—R
Day Star Tribune—R
God's Revivalist
Good News, Etc—R
Gospel Tract—R
Grail
Healing Inn—R
Indian Life—R

Jour/Christian Nursing—R
Light and Life
Living with Teenagers—R
MESSAGE/Open Bible—R
Metro Voice—R
Michigan Christian
Minnesota Christian—R
New Heart—R
New Writing—R
Our Sunday Visitor
Plain Truth—R
SCP Journal—R
Social Justice
Something Better—R
Standard—R
Trumpeter—R

CHILDREN

High Adventure—R
Power & Light—R

CHRISTIAN EDUCATION/LIBRARY

CE Connection—R
Children's Ministry
GROUP
Team—R

MISSIONS

American Horizon—R
Areopagus—R
East-West Church
Intl. Journal/Frontier—R
World Christian—R
World Pulse—R

PASTORS/LEADERS

Journal/Christian Healing—R
Journal/Pastoral Care
Ministries Today
Today's Christian Preacher—R
Word & World

TEEN/YOUNG ADULT

Brio
Certainty
Challenge (GA) —R
Essential Connection—R
Insight—R
Straight—R
Teenage Christian—R
Teen Life—R
Teens on Target—R
YOU!—R
Young Adult Today
Young Christian—R
Youth Challenge—R
Youth Update

CURRENT/SOCIAL ISSUES

ADULT/GENERAL

About Such Things—R
Accent on Living—R
AGAIN—R
Alive!—R
alive now!
A.M.E. Christian Recorder—R
America
American Tract Soc.—R
Anglican Journal—R
Arlington Catholic
Atlantic Baptist
AXIOS—R
Banner
Baptist Informer
B.C. Catholic—R
Believer—R
Bible Advocate—R
Bible Advocate Online—R
Brethren Evangelist
Bridal Guides—R
Canadian Catholic
Canadian Mennonite
Catholic Courier
Catholic Digest—R
Catholic Insight
Catholic New York
Catholic Rural Life
Catholic Sentinel—R
CBA Marketplace
CGA World—R
Celebrate Life—R
Charisma/Christian Life
Christian American
Christian Arts Review
Christian Chronicle—R
Christian Courier (WI)—R
Christian Courier (CAN)—R
Christian Crusade
Christian Edge—R
Christian Home & School
Christian Living—R
Christian Motorsports
Christian News NW—R
Christian Ranchman
Christian Reader—R
Christian Renewal—R
Christian Social Action—R
Christian Standard—R
Christianity Today—R
Chrysalis Reader
Church Advocate—R
Church & State—R
Church Herald/Holiness—R
Columbia
Common Boundary

Commonweal
Company—R
Cornerstone—R
Covenant Companion—R
Creation Ex Nihilo
Cresset
Crisis Point
Culture Wars—R
Day Star Tribune—R
Discipleship Journal
Door
Dovetail—R
Emphasis/Faith & Living—R
Episcopal Life—R
Evangel—R
Faith Today
Family Journal—R
Fellowship Link—R
First Things
Focus on the Family
Foursquare World—R
Gem—R
Good News(KY)—R
Good News, Etc—R
Good News Journal (MO)—R
Good News Journal (TX)
Grail
Hallelujah! (CAN)—R
Head to Head—R
Healing Inn—R
Hearing Hearts
Heartlight Internet—R
Hidden Manna—R
Highway News—R
Homeschooling Today—R
Home Times—R
Impact Magazine—R
Indian Life—R
Inland NW Christian
Interim—R
John Milton—R
Jour/Christian Nursing—R
Journal of Church & State
Liberty—R
Life Gate—R
Light and Life
Liguorian
Living—R
Living Church
Living Light News—R
Living with Teenagers—R
Lookout—R
Lutheran—R
Lutheran Journal—R
Marian Helpers Bulletin
Marriage Partnership
Mennonite—R
Mennonite Brethren—R

MESSAGE
MESSAGE/Open Bible—R
Messenger/St. Anthony
Metro Voice—R
Michigan Christian
Minnesota Christian—R
Moody—R
New Covenant
New Heart—R
North American Voice
Northwestern Lutheran—R
New Writing—R
On Mission
Our Family—R
Our Sunday Visitor
Parent Paper—R
Pentecostal Evangel
Pentecostal Testimony—R
Peoples Magazine—R
Perspectives
Plain Truth—R
PrayerWorks—R
Presbyterian Layman
Presbyterian Outlook
Presbyterian Record—R
Presbyterians Today—R
Prism—R
ProLife News—R
Purpose—R
Quest
Quiet Revolution—R
Re:generation
Religious Broadcasting—R
Religious Education
St. Joseph's Messenger—R
SCP Journal—R
Signs of the Times—R
Single Connection—R
Social Justice
Sojourners
Something Better—R
Standard—R
Stand Firm—R
Together—R
Trumpeter—R
2-Soar—R
United Church Observer
Upsouth—R
War Cry—R
Way of St. Francis—R
Wesleyan Advocate—R

CHILDREN

Club Connection—R
Discovery Trails—R
God's World News—R
Guideposts for Kids
High Adventure—R

Skipping Stones

CHRISTIAN EDUCATION/LIBRARY

Catechist
Children's Ministry
Christian Classroom
Christian School Admin.
Church Educator—R
GROUP
Team—R
Today's Catholic Teacher—R
Vision—R

MISSIONS

American Horizon—R
Areopagus—R
East-West Church
Latin American Evangelist
New World Outlook
Urban Mission—R
Women of the Harvest
World Christian—R
Worldwide Challenge

MUSIC

CCM Magazine

PASTORS/LEADERS

African American Pulpit
Art+Plus
Catholic Servant
Christian Camp—R
Christian Century
Christian Ministry
Cross Currents—R
Current Thoughts & Trends
Ivy Jungle Report—R
Journal/Pastoral Care
Lutheran Forum—R
Lutheran Partners—R
Ministries Today
Pastoral Life
Pulpit Helps—R
Reaching Children at Risk
Resource—R
Single Adult Ministries
Vital Ministry
Word & World
Youthworker—R

TEEN/YOUNG ADULT

Brio
Challenge (GA)—R
Conqueror—R
Devo'Zine—R
Essential Connection—R
Insight—R
Real Time—R

Straight—R
Student Leadership—R
Teenage Christian—R
Teen Life—R
Teens on Target—R
Today's Christian Teen—R
With—R
YOU!—R
Young Adult Today
Young Christian—R
Young Salvationist—R
Youth Challenge—R
Youth Update

WOMEN

Aspire
Conscience—R
Esprit—R
Hearth
Helping Hand—R
Jour/Women's Ministries
Journey—R
Link & Visitor—R
Lutheran Woman Today
Today's Christian Woman
Virtue—R
Wesleyan Woman
Woman's Touch—R
Women of Spirit—R

WRITERS

Inklings
Writer
Writers' Intl. Forum

DEATH/DYING

ADULT/GENERAL

Alive!—R
American Tract Soc.—R
Arlington Catholic
Banner
Bible Advocate—R
Bible Advocate Online—R
Biblical Reflections—R
Bread of Life—R
Breakthrough Intercessor—R
Canada Lutheran—R
Catholic Courier
Catholic Digest—R
Celebrate Life—R
CGA World—R
Christian Living—R
Christian Reader—R
Christianity Today—R
Church Herald/Holiness—R
Columbia
Common Boundary

Cornerstone—R
Covenant Companion—R
Creation Ex Nihilo
Day Star Tribune—R
Discipleship Journal
Dovetail—R
Evangel—R
Family Digest
Family Network—R
Fellowship Link—R
Grail
Guideposts
Heartlight Internet—R
Interim—R
John Milton—R
Jour/Christian Nursing—R
Liguorian
Living Light News—R
Lutheran Journal—R
Mature Living
Mature Years—R
Mennonite—R
MESSAGE
Messenger/St. Anthony
Messenger of the Sacred Heart
Michigan Christian
Montana Catholic—R
New Heart—R
New Writing—R
Pentecostal Evangel
Pentecostal Testimony—R
Peoples Magazine—R
Physician
Plain Truth—R
Presbyterian Outlook
Presbyterian Record—R
Prism—R
ProLife News—R
Re:generation
Sacred Journey—R
Signs of the Times—R
Social Justice
Something Better—R
Star of Zion
Today's Christian Senior—R
United Church Observer
Upsouth—R
War Cry—R
Way of St. Francis—R
Weavings—R

CHILDREN

Skipping Stones

CHRISTIAN EDUCATION/LIBRARY

Church Educator—R
Leader/Church School
    Today—R

PASTORS/LEADERS

Catholic Servant
Celebration
Christian Ministry
Journal/Pastoral Care
Lutheran Partners—R
Pastoral Life
Preacher's Magazine—R
Pulpit Helps—R
Today's Christian Preacher—R
Vital Ministry

TEEN/YOUNG ADULT

Challenge (GA) —R
Devo'Zine—R
Essential Connection—R
Insight—R
Straight—R
Teen Life—R
Today's Christian Teen—R
With—R
Young Salvationist—R

WOMEN

Aspire
Esprit—R
Helping Hand—R
Horizons—R
Joyful Woman—R
Women of Spirit—R

WRITERS

Inklings

DEVOTIONALS/ MEDITATIONS

ADULT/GENERAL

About Such Things—R
alive now!
Annals of St. Anne
Arlington Catholic
Banner
Baptist Informer
Believer—R
Bread of Life—R
Breakthrough Intercessor—R
Bridal Guides—R
Canadian Catholic
Catholic Rural Life
Charisma/Christian Life
Christian Century
Christian Motorsports
Christian Reader—R
Christianity Today—R
Church Herald/Holiness—R
Common Boundary
Companion

Companions—R
Conquest (meditations)
Covenant Companion—R
Day Star Tribune—R
Decision
Emphasis/Faith & Living—R
Evangel—R
Family Network—R
Fellowship Link—R
Foursquare World—R
Gem—R
God's Revivalist
Good News(KY)—R
Good News Journal (MO)—R
Good News Journal (TX)
Gospel Tract—R
Green Cross—R
Head to Head—R
Healing Inn—R
Hearing Hearts
Heartlight Internet—R
Highway News—R
Ideals—R
Indian Life—R
Inspirer—R
John Milton—R
Keys to Living—R
Life Gate—R
L.I.G.H.T News—R
Liguorian
Living—R
Living Church
Lutheran Journal—R
Lutheran Witness—R
Mature Years—R
Mennonite Brethren—R
MESSAGE/Open Bible—R
Messenger/Sacred Heart
Messenger/St. Anthony
Metro Voice—R
New Covenant
New Heart—R
North American Voice
Northwestern Lutheran—R
Our Sunday Visitor
Pentecostal Evangel
Pentecostal Testimony—R
Peoples Magazine—R
Perspectives
Plain Truth—R
Plowman—R
Pourastan—R
PrayerWorks—R
Presbyterian Outlook
Presbyterian Record—R
Presbyterians Today—R
Preserving Christian Homes—
    R

Prism—R
Progress—R (meditations)
Right Road—R
Sacred Journey—R
St. Willibrord Journal
Silver Wings—R
Single Connection—R
Smile—R
Sojourners
Standard—R
Stand Firm—R
Star of Zion
TEAK Roundup—R
Today's Christian Senior—R
Together—R
Upsouth—R
U.S. Catholic
War Cry—R
Way of St. Francis—R
Weavings—R

CHILDREN

Club Connection—R
Courage
Discovery (NY)—R
High Adventure—R
Keys for Kids—R
Partners—R
Pockets—R
Power & Light—R
Primary Pal (IL)
Touch—R

CHRISTIAN EDUCATION/LIBRARY

CE Connection—R
Children's Ministry
Christian Classroom
Church & Synagogue Lib.
Church Educator—R
GROUP
Leader/Church School
    Today—R
Religion Teacher's Journal
Shining Star
Teacher's Interaction
Today's Catholic Teacher—R

DAILY DEVOTIONAL

(See alphabetical list)

MISSIONS

Areopagus—R
Latin American Evangelist
Quiet Hour Echoes
So All May Hear—R
Women of the Harvest

PASTORS/LEADERS

Art+Plus
Catholic Servant
Christian Century
Church Worship
Emmanuel
Evangelical Baptist—R
Five Stones—R
Journal/Christian Healing—R
Journal/Pastoral Care
Let's Worship
Minister's Family
Priest
Pulpit Helps—R
Reaching Children at Risk
Today's Christian Preacher—R
Voice of the Vineyard —R

TEEN/YOUNG ADULT

Breakaway—R
Brio
Certainty
Challenge (GA) —R
Challenge (IL)
Conqueror—R
Cross Walk
Devo'Zine—R
Essential Connection—R
Insight—R
Take Five
Teens on Target—R
Today's Christian Teen—R
YOU!—R
Young Adult Today
Young Christian—R
Young Salvationist—R
Youth Challenge—R

WOMEN

Adam's Rib—R
Helping Hand—R
Horizons—R
Jour/Women's Ministries
Joyful Woman—R
Just Between Us—R
Lutheran Woman Today
Proverbs 31 Homemaker—R
Woman's Touch—R
Women of Spirit—R

WRITERS

Cross & Quill—R
Fellowscript—R
Inklings
Southwestern Writers—R
Writers' Intl. Forum

DISCIPLESHIP

ADULT/GENERAL

Advent Christian Witness—R
A.M.E. Christian Recorder—R
Arlington Catholic
Atlantic Baptist
Banner
Believer—R
Bible Advocate—R
Bread of Life—R
Breakthrough Intercessor—R
Brethren Evangelist
Canada Lutheran—R
Canadian Catholic
Catholic Digest—R
Charisma/Christian Life
Christian Century
Christian Living—R
Christian Motorsports
Christian Parenting—R
Christian Ranchman
Christian Reader—R
Christianity Today—R
Church Herald/Holiness—R
Companion
Companions—R
Conquest
Covenant Companion—R
Cresset
Day Star Tribune—R
Decision
Discipleship Journal
Emphasis/Faith & Living—R
Evangel—R
Faith Today
Family Network—R
Focus on the Family
Gem—R
Good News(KY)—R
Good News, Etc—R
Good News Journal (MO)—R
Good News Journal (TX)
Gospel Tidings—R
Green Cross—R
Hallelujah! (CAN)—R
Head to Head—R
Healing Inn—R
Hearing Hearts
Heartlight Internet—R
Highway News—R
Inland NW Christian
Inspirer—R
John Milton—R
Life Gate—R
Light and Life

L.I.G.H.T News—R
Live—R
Living with Teenagers—R
Lookout—R
Lutheran Journal—R
Mennonite—R
MESSAGE/Open Bible—R
Metro Voice—R
Michigan Christian
Moody—R
New Covenant
New Heart—R
North American Voice
On Mission
Our Family—R
Pentecostal Testimony—R
Peoples Magazine—R
Plain Truth—R
PrayerWorks—R
Presbyterian Layman
Presbyterian Outlook
Presbyterian Record—R
Prism—R
Purpose—R
Re:generation
Religious Education
Right Road—R
St. Joseph's Messenger—R
Signs of the Times—R
Silver Wings—R
Sojourners
Standard—R
Stand Firm—R
TEAK Roundup—R
Times of Refreshing
Touchstone—R
Upsouth—R
U.S. Catholic
Vision—R
War Cry—R
Way of St. Francis—R
Weavings—R
Wesleyan Advocate—R

CHILDREN

BREAD/God's Children—R
Club Connection—R
Courage
Evangelizing Today's Child—R

CHRISTIAN EDUCATION/LIBRARY

Brigade Leader—R
Caravan
CE Connection—R
CE Counselor—R
CE Leadership—R
Children's Ministry
Christian School

Christian School Admin.
Church Educator—R
Evangelizing Today's Child—R
GROUP
Leader/Church School
    Today—R
Teacher's Interaction
Team—R

MISSIONS

American Horizon—R
Latin American Evangelist
Urban Mission—R
Worldwide Challenge

PASTORS/LEADERS

African American Pulpit
Art+Plus
Catholic Servant
Cell Church—R
Cell Life FORUM—R
Christian Camp—R
Christian Century
Christian Management—R
Christian Ministry
Church Growth Network—R
Current Thoughts & Trends
Emmanuel
Evangelical Baptist—R
Five Stones—R
Ivy Jungle Report—R
Journal/Christian Healing—R
Let's Worship
Lutheran Forum—R
Lutheran Partners—R
Ministries Today
Ministry
Ministry & Liturgy—R
Preacher—R
Preacher's Magazine—R
PROCLAIM—R
Pulpit Helps—R
Reaching Children at Risk
Review for Religious
Sharing the Practice—R
Today's Christian Preacher—R
Vital Ministry
Word & World
Youthworker—R

TEEN/YOUNG ADULT

Certainty
Challenge (GA)—R
Challenge (IL)
Conqueror—R
Essential Connection—R
Insight—R
Real Time—R

Straight—R
Student Leadership—R
Teenage Christian—R
Teen Life—R
Teens on Target—R
Today's Christian Teen—R
With—R
YOU!—R
Young Christian—R
Young Salvationist—R
Youth Challenge—R

WOMEN

Adam's Rib—R
CoLaborer—R
Esprit—R
Helping Hand—R
Horizons—R
Journey—R
Joyful Woman—R
Just Between Us—R
Link & Visitor—R
Sisters Today
Today's Christian Woman
Virtue—R
Virtuous Woman
Wesleyan Woman—R
Woman's Touch—R
Women of Spirit—R
Women Today—R
Women Today Online—R

WRITERS

Inklings

DIVORCE

ADULT/GENERAL

America
Angels on Earth
Arlington Catholic
Banner
Bible Advocate—R
Bible Advocate Online—R
Breakthrough Intercessor—R
Bridal Guides—R
Canada Lutheran—R
Catholic Digest—R
Charisma/Christian Life
Chicken Soup/Mother—R
Chicken Soup/Single—R
Christian Chronicle—R
Christian Edge—R
Christian Home & School
Christian Living—R
Christian Motorsports
Christian Parenting—R
Christian Ranchman

Creation Ex Nihilo
Culture Wars—R
Day Star Tribune—R
Decision
Dovetail—R
Evangel—R
Expression Christian
Faith Today
Focus on the Family
Gem—R
Good News, Etc—R
Good News Journal (MO)—R
Guideposts
Highway News—R
Home Times—R
Impact Magazine—R
Interim—R
Life Gate—R
Liguorian
Living—R
Living Light News—R
Lutheran Journal—R
Mature Living
MESSAGE
MESSAGE/Open Bible—R
Metro Voice—R
Michigan Christian
Minnesota Christian—R
New Covenant
New Heart—R
New Writing—R
On Mission
Our Family—R
Parent Paper—R
Peoples Magazine—R
Physician
Plain Truth—R
PrayerWorks—R
Presbyterian Outlook
Presbyterian Record—R
Presbyterians Today—R
Prism—R
Purpose—R
Single Connection—R
Single-Parent Family
Smart Families
Social Justice
Standard—R
Stand Firm—R
Star of Zion
2-Soar—R
TEAK Roundup—R
Upsouth—R
U.S. Catholic
War Cry—R

CHILDREN

Discovery Trails—R

Guideposts for Kids
Touch—R

CHRISTIAN EDUCATION/LIBRARY
Christian Classroom
Christian School Admin.
Leader/Church School
    Today—R

MISSIONS

Worldwide Challenge

PASTORS/LEADERS
Art+Plus
Current Thoughts & Trends
Journal/Pastoral Care
Lutheran Partners—R
Ministries Today
Ministry
Pastoral Life
PROCLAIM—R
Sharing the Practice—R
Single Adult Ministries
Word & World

TEEN/YOUNG ADULT
Challenge (GA)—R
Insight—R
Straight—R
Teenage Christian—R
Young Adult Today
Youth Update

WOMEN
Aspire
Esprit—R
Helping Hand—R
Journey—R
Joyful Woman—R
Lutheran Woman Today
Virtuous Woman
Woman's Touch—R
Women of Spirit—R

DOCTRINAL

ADULT/GENERAL
America
Anglican Journal—R
Banner
Baptist Informer
B.C. Catholic—R
Bible Advocate—R
Bread of Life—R
Breakthrough Intercessor—R
Canadian Catholic
Catholic Insight
CGA World—R

Charisma/Christian Life
Christian Century
Christian Media—R
Christian Motorsports
Christianity Today—R
Church Herald/Holiness—R
Comments/Friends—R
Companions—R
Conquest
Cresset
Culture Wars—R
Dovetail—R
Fellowship Link—R
Gospel Today
Hallelujah! (CAN)—R
Hearing Hearts
Indian Life—R
John Milton—R
Light and Life
Lutheran Witness—R
Mennonite—R
MESSAGE
Metro Voice—R
Montana Catholic—R
New Writing—R
North American Voice
On Mission
Our Family—R
Our Sunday Visitor
Pentecostal Testimony—R
Peoples Magazine—R
Perspectives
Plain Truth—R
PrayerWorks—R
Presbyterian Layman
Presbyterian Outlook
Presbyterian Record—R
Presbyterians Today—R
Queen of All Hearts
Re:generation
St. Anthony Messenger
St. Willibrord Journal
SCP Journal—R
Silver Wings—R
Social Justice
Star of Zion
TEAK Roundup—R
This Rock
United Church Observer
U.S. Catholic
Upsouth—R
Weavings—R

CHILDREN

Discovery Trails—R

CHRISTIAN EDUCATION/LIBRARY
Catechist

Shining Star
Teacher's Interaction

MISSION

Intl Jour/Frontier—R
Quiet Hour Echoes
Urban Mission—R
Worldwide Challenge

PASTORS/LEADERS

Catholic Servant
Christian Century
Current Thoughts & Trends
Emmanuel
Lutheran Partners—R
Ministries Today
Ministry
Preacher's Magazine—R
Priest
PROCLAIM—R
Quarterly Review
Reaching Children at Risk
Resource—R
Theology Today
Today's Christian Preacher—R
Word & World

TEEN/YOUNG ADULT

Certainty
Challenge (GA)—R
Essential Connection—R
Teenage Christian—R
Teen Life—R
YOU!—R
Young Adult Today
Youth Update

WOMEN

Lutheran Woman Today

WRITERS

Inklings

ECONOMICS

ADULT/GENERAL

America
AXIOS—R
Banner
Believer—R
Canadian Catholic
Catholic Rural Life
CBA Marketplace
CGA World—R
Christian C.L. RECORD—R
Christian Century
Christian Courier (CAN)—R
Christian Motorsports

Christian Ranchman
Christian Renewal—R
Christian Social Action—R
Christianity Today—R
Christians in Business
Covenant Companion—R
Cresset
Culture Wars—R
Day Star Tribune—R
Discovery—R
Faith Today
Family Network—R
First Things
Good News, Etc—R
Home Times—R
Life Gate—R
Light and Life
Mennonite—R
Metro Voice—R
Michigan Christian
Minnesota Christian—R
MovieGuide
No-Debt Living—R
Our Sunday Visitor
Parent Paper—R
Perspectives
Prairie Messenger—R
Presbyterian Layman
Prism—R
Quiet Revolution—R
Re:generation
SCP Journal—R
Single Connection—R
Single-Parent Family
Social Justice
Sojourners
Something Better—R
Stand Firm—R
Today's Christian Senior—R
2-Soar—R
U.S. Catholic

CHRISTIAN EDUCATION/LIBRARY

Christian School Admin.

MISSIONS

Urban Mission—R

PASTORS/LEADERS

Christian Century
Current Thoughts & Trends
Lutheran Partners—R
Reaching Children at Risk
Technologies/Worship—R
Today's Christian Preacher—R
Today's Parish
Word & World
Your Church—R

TEEN/YOUNG ADULT

Challenge (GA) —R
Young Adult Today
Youth Update

WOMEN

Helping Hand—R
Horizons—R

WRITERS

Inklings

ENVIRONMENTAL ISSUES

ADULT/GENERAL

Anglican Journal—R
AXIOS—R
Banner
Bible Advocate—R
Bible Advocate Online—R
Brethren Evangelist
Canada Lutheran—R
Canadian Catholic
Catholic Forester—R
Catholic Rural Life
Catholic Sentinel—R
CGA World—R
Christian Century
Christian Courier (CAN)—R
Christian Living—R
Christian Motorsports
Christian Social Action—R
Christianity Today—R
Chrysalis Reader
Common Boundary
Commonweal
Companion
Covenant Companion—R
Cresset
Day Star Tribune—R
Faith Today
Fellowship Link—R
Forefront
Grail
Green Cross—R
John Milton—R
Keys to Living—R
Light and Life
Living Light News—R
Lutheran—R
Mennonite—R
Messenger/St. Anthony
Metro Voice—R
Michigan Christian
Minnesota Christian—R
NW Christian Journal—R
Our Family—R
Our Sunday Visitor

Parent Paper—R
Pegasus Review—R
Peoples Magazine—R
Perspectives
Plain Truth—R
PrayerWorks—R
Presbyterian Layman
Presbyterian Outlook
Presbyterian Record—R
Presbyterians Today—R
Prism—R
Purpose—R
Re:generation
Right Road—R
SCP Journal—R
Sojourners
Something Better—R
Star of Zion
TEAK Roundup—R
Time of Singing—R
Total Health
Touchstone—R
United Church Observer
Upsouth—R
War Cry—R
Way of St. Francis—R

CHILDREN

Discovery (NY)—R
Guideposts for Kids
Kidz Chat—R
Live Wire—R
My Friend
On the Line—R
Pockets—R
Power & Light—R
Skipping Stones

CHRISTIAN EDUCATION/LIBRARY

Christian School
Leader/Church School
    Today—R

PASTORS/LEADERS

Christian Camp—R
Christian Century
Christian Ministry
Cross Currents—R
Current Thoughts & Trends
Lutheran Partners—R
Quarterly Review
Reaching Children at Risk
Word & World

TEEN/YOUNG ADULT

Challenge (GA) —R
Devo'Zine—R
Essential Connection—R

Insight—R
Real Time—R
Student Leadership—R
Teen Life—R
With—R
YOU!—R
Young Adult Today
Young Christian—R
Young Salvationist—R
Youth Update

WOMEN

Aspire
Esprit—R
Helping Hand—R
Horizons—R

WRITERS

Inklings
Writers' Intl. Forum

ESSAYS

ADULT/GENERAL

About Such Things—R
alive now!
A.M.E. Christian Recorder—R
Annals of St. Anne
Arlington Catholic
AXIOS—R
Banner
Breakthrough Intercessor—R
Catholic Answer
Catholic Insight
Catholic Parent
Christian Arts Review
Christian Century
Christian Motorsports
Christian Poet—R
Christian Renewal—R
Christian Traveler—R
Christianity/Arts
Chrysalis Reader
Church Advocate—R
Church & State—R
Common Boundary
Commonweal
Companions—R
Company—R
Cornerstone—R
Cresset
Crisis Point
Culture Wars—R
Day Star Tribune—R
Door—R
Faith Today
Family Journal—R
First Things

Forefront
Good News (AL)—R
Good News Journal (TX)
Grail
Green Cross—R
Head to Head—R
Healing Inn—R
Hidden Manna—R
Home Times—R
Inspirer—R
Interim—R
John Milton—R
Light and Life
Marriage Partnership
Messenger/St. Anthony
Metro Voice—R
Michigan Christian
National Catholic
New Moon—R
New Writing—R
Over the Back Fence—R
Parent Paper—R
Pegasus Review—R
Perspectives
Plenty Good Room
Poetry Forum—R
Poet's Page
PrayerWorks—R
Presbyterian Outlook
Presbyterians Today—R
Prism—R
ProLife News—R
Re:generation
Religious Education
Right Road—R
SCP Journal—R
Smile—R
Sojourners
Spiritual Life
TEAK Roundup—R
Upsouth—R
Visitation
War Cry—R
Weavings—R

CHILDREN

Discovery(NY)—R
Nature Friend—R

MISSIONS

Areopagus—R
PFI World Report—R
Women of the Harvest

MUSIC

Creator—R
Songwriter—R

PASTORS/LEADERS

African American Pulpit
Catholic Servant
Christian Century
Christian Ministry
Church Bytes—R
Journal/Pastoral Care
Reaching Children at Risk
Word & World
Youthworker—R

TEEN/YOUNG ADULT

Challenge (GA) —R
Essential Connection—R
Student Leadership—R
Teen Life—R
YOU!—R
Young Adult Today

WOMEN

Anna's Journal—R
Aspire
Helping Hand—R
Horizons—R
Lutheran Woman Today
Proverbs 31 Homemaker—R

WRITERS

Byline
Canadian Writer's Jour—R
Inklings
Once Upon a Time—R
WIN-Informer
Writer's Digest—R
Writer's Guidelines/News
Writer's Ink—R
Writers' Intl. Forum

ETHICS

ADULT/GENERAL

A.M.E. Christian Recorder—R
Angels on Earth
Atlantic Baptist
AXIOS—R
Banner
Bible Advocate—R
Bible Advocate Online—R
Biblical Reflections—R
Breakthrough Intercessor—R
Canada Lutheran—R
Canadian Catholic
Catholic Insight
Catholic Parent
Catholic Rural Life
CGA World—R
Christian Century
Christian Courier (CAN)—R

Christian Edge—R
Christian Media—R
Christian Motorsports
Christian Renewal—R
Christian Research
Christianity Today—R
Christians in Business
Chrysalis Reader
Church Herald/Holiness—R
Columbia
Commonweal
Companions—R
Company—R
Conquest
Cornerstone—R
Covenant Companion—R
Creation Ex Nihilo
Culture Wars—R
Day Star Tribune—R
Dovetail—R
Faith Today
Fellowship Link—R
First Things
Good News (AL)—R
Good News, Etc—R
Good News Journal (TX)
Grail
Head to Head—R
Homeschooling Today—R
Home Times—R
Impact Magazine—R
Indian Life—R
Interim—R
John Milton—R
Jour/Christian Nursing—R
Journal of Church & State
Life@Work
Light and Life
Living Light News—R
Lutheran Journal—R
Mennonite Brethren—R
Messenger/St. Anthony
Metro Voice—R
Michigan Christian
Minnesota Christian—R
Moody—R
New Covenant
New Heart—R
On Mission
Our Family—R
Our Sunday Visitor
Pegasus Review—R
Pentecostal Testimony—R
Peoples Magazine—R
Perspectives
Physician
Pourastan—R
Prairie Messenger—R

PrayerWorks—R
Presbyterian Layman
Presbyterian Outlook
Presbyterian Record—R
Prism—R
Purpose—R
Re:generation
Religious Broadcasting—R
Religious Education
St. Anthony Messenger
St. Willibrord Journal
Signs of the Times—R
Social Justice
Sojourners
Something Better—R
Stand Firm—R
TEAK Roundup—R
2-Soar—R
United Church Observer
Upsouth—R
War Cry—R

CHILDREN

BREAD/God's Children—R
CLUBHOUSE—R
Discovery(NY)—R
Guideposts for Kids
High Adventure—R
Power & Light—R
Skipping Stones
Wonder Time

CHRISTIAN EDUCATION/LIBRARY

Christian Classroom
Christian School Admin.
Vision—R

MISSIONS

Areopagus—R
East-West Church
Teacher's Interaction
Urban Mission—R
Worldwide Challenge

PASTORS/LEADERS

African American Pulpit
Art+Plus
Christian Century
Christian Management—R
Christian Ministry
Church Bytes—R
Cross Currents—R
Current Thoughts & Trends
Ivy Jungle Report—R
Journal/Christian Healing—R
Journal/Pastoral Care
Lutheran Partners—R
Priest

PROCLAIM—R
Quarterly Review
Reaching Children at Risk
Sharing the Practice—R
Theology Today
Today's Christian Preacher—R
Word & World
Youthworker—R

TEEN/YOUNG ADULT
Certainty
Challenge (GA)—R
Conqueror—R
Essential Connection—R
Insight—R
Student Leadership—R
Teenage Christian—R
YOU!—R
Young Salvationist—R
Youth Update

WOMEN
Adam's Rib—R
Aspire
Conscience—R
Esprit—R
Hearth
Helping Hand—R
Horizons—R
Wesleyan Woman—R

WRITERS
Canadian Writer's Jour—R
Inklings
Writers' Intl. Forum

ETHNIC/CULTURAL PIECES

ADULT/GENERAL
A.M.E. Christian Recorder—R
American Tract Soc.—R
Arlington Catholic
Banner
Baptist Informer
Bible Advocate—R
Bible Advocate Online—R
Breakthrough Intercessor—R
Bridal Guides—R
Catholic Digest—R
Catholic Insight
CBA Marketplace
CGA World—R
Christian Century
Christian Edge—R
Christian Living—R
Christian Motorsports
Christian News NW—R
Christian Ranchman

Christian Reader—R
Christian Social Action—R
Christianity Today—R
Church Herald/Holiness—R
Common Boundary
Company—R
Cornerstone—R
Covenant Companion—R
Creation Ex Nihilo
Day Star Tribune—R
Dovetail—R
Emphasis/Faith & Living—R
Faith Today
Fellowship Link—R
First Things
Foursquare World—R
Good News(KY)—R
Good News, Etc.—R
Gospel Today
Grail
Green Cross—R
Hallelujah! (CAN)—R
Healing Inn—R
Homeschooling Today—R
Home Times—R
Impact Magazine—R
Indian Life—R
John Milton—R
Jour/Christian Nursing—R
Journal of Church & State
Light and Life
Living—R
Living Light News—R
Lookout—R
Joyful Noise
Living with Teenagers—R
Mennonite—R
MESSAGE
MESSAGE/Open Bible—R
Messenger/St. Anthony
Michigan Christian
Moody—R
New Writing—R
On Mission
Pentecostal Evangel
Perspectives
Plenty Good Room
PrayerWorks—R
Presbyterian Outlook
Presbyterian Record—R
Prism—R
ProLife News—R
Purpose—R
Pursuit—R
Re:generation
Religious Broadcasting—R
Sacred Journey—R
Sojourners

Something Better—R
Standard—R
TEAK Roundup—R
Together—R
Trumpeter—R
2-Soar—R
Upscale Magazine
Upsouth—R
War Cry—R

CHILDREN
Discovery(NY)—R
On the Line—R
Skipping Stones
Story Friends—R

CHRISTIAN EDUCATION/LIBRARY
Catechist
Leader/Church School
    Today—R
Vision—R

MISSIONS
Missiology
Urban Mission

PASTORS/LEADERS
African American Pulpit
Cell Life FORUM—R
Christian Ministry
Current Thoughts & Trends
Five Stones—R
Journal/Pastoral Care—R
Lutheran Partners—R
Ministries Today
Quarterly Review
Reaching Children at Risk
Sharing the Practice—R

TEEN/YOUNG ADULT
Certainty
Challenge (GA)—R
Devo'Zine—R
Essential Connection—R
Student Leadership—R
Take Five (photos)
Teen Life—R
Young Adult Today
Young Christian—R
Young Salvationist—R

WOMEN
Aspire
Horizons—R
Link & Visitor—R
Virtue—R
Women of Spirit—R

WRITERS

Inklings
Writers' Intl. Forum

EVANGELISM/ WITNESSING

ADULT/GENERAL

Alive!—R
A.M.E. Christian Recorder—R
American Tract Soc.—R
Anglican Journal—R
Annals of St. Anne
Atlantic Baptist
Banner
Baptist Informer
Believer—R
Bible Advocate—R
Bread of Life—R
Breakthrough Intercessor—R
Brethren Evangelist
Canadian Catholic
Canadian Lutheran—R
Catholic Digest—R
Catholic Insight
Charisma/Christian Life
Christian Century
Christian Courier (WI)—R
Christian Edge—R
Christian Motorsports
Christian Poet—R
Christian Ranchman
Christian Reader—R
Christian Research
Christianity Today—R
Church Herald/Holiness—R
Comments/Friends—R
Companion
Companions—R
Conquest
Cornerstone—R
Covenant Companion—R
Creation Ex Nihilo
Crossway/Newsline—R
Day Star Tribune—R
Decision
Discipleship Journal
Emphasis/Faith & Living—R
Evangel—R
Faith Today
Fellowship Link—R
Gem—R
God's Revivalist
Good News(KY)—R
Good News, Etc—R
Good News Journal (MO)—R
Good News Journal (TX)
Gospel Today
Gospel Tract—R

Green Cross—R
Hallelujah! (CAN)—R
Healing Inn—R
Hearing Hearts
Highway News—R
Indian Life—R
Inland NW Christian
Inspirer—R
John Milton—R
Journal/Christian Nursing—R
Life Gate—R
Light and Life
Liguorian
Live—R
Lookout—R
Lutheran—R
Lutheran Digest—R
Lutheran Journal—R
Lutheran Witness—R
Marriage Partnership
Mennonite Brethren—R
MESSAGE/Open Bible—R
Metro Voice—R
Michigan Christian
Moody—R
New Covenant
New Heart—R
New Writing—R
Northwestern Lutheran—R
Oblates
On Mission
Our Family—R
Pentecostal Evangel
Pentecostal Testimony—R
Peoples Magazine—R
Plain Truth—R
Power for Living—R
PrayerWorks—R
Presbyterian Layman
Presbyterian Record—R
Presbyterians Today—R
Prism—R
Purpose—R
Queen of All Hearts
Re:generation
Religious Education
St. Anthony Messenger
SCP Journal—R
Shantyman—R
Sharing—R
Signs of the Times—R
Silver Wings—R
Sojourners
Something Better—R
Standard—R
Standard—R
Stand Firm—R
TEAK Roundup—R

This Rock
Trumpeter—R
United Church Observer
Upsouth—R
U.S. Catholic
Vision—R
Vision—R
War Cry—R
Way of St. Francis—R
Wesleyan Advocate—R

CHILDREN

Club Connection—R
Counselor—R
Courage
Discovery(NY)—R
Focus/Clubhouse
Kids' Ministry Ideas—R
Live Wire—R
Power & Light—R
Power Station—R
Primary Pal (IL)
Touch—R

CHRISTIAN EDUCATION/LIBRARY

Brigade Leader—R
CE Connection—R
Children's Ministry
Church Educator—R
Church Media Library—R
Evangelizing Today's Child—R
GROUP
Leader/Church School
    Today—R
Resource—R
Shining Star—R
Teacher's Interaction

MISSIONS

American Horizon—R
Evangelical Missions—R
Intl Jour/Frontier—R
Latin American Evangelist
Leaders for Today
Message of the Cross—R
Missiology
Quiet Hour Echoes
So All May Hear—R
Urban Mission—R
World Christian—R
World Pulse—R
Worldwide Challenge

MUSIC

Quest—R

PASTORS/LEADERS

African American Pulpit

Art+Plus
Cell Church—R
Cell Life FORUM—R
Christian Camp—R
Church Administration
Church Growth Network—R
Current Thoughts & Trends
Emmanuel
Eucharistic Minister—R
Evangelical Baptist—R
Five Stones—R
Jour/Amer Soc/Chur Growth—R
Journal/Christian Healing—R
Let's Worship
Lutheran Forum—R
Lutheran Partners—R
Ministries Today
Ministry Now
Networks—R
Preacher—R
Preacher's Magazine—R
Priest
PROCLAIM—R
Pulpit Helps—R
Reaching Children at Risk
Resource—R
Review for Religious
Sharing the Practice—R
Today's Christian Preacher—R
Vital Ministry
Voice of the Vineyard —R
Youthworker—R

TEEN/YOUNG ADULT

Certainty
Challenge (GA)—R
Challenge (IL)
Conqueror—R
Devo'Zine—R
Essential Connection—R
Real Time—R
Straight—R
Student Leadership—R
Teenage Christian—R
Teen Life—R
Teens on Target—R
Today's Christian Teen—R
With—R
YOU!—R
Young Adult Today
Young Christian—R
Young Salvationist—R
Youth Challenge—R

WOMEN

Adam's Rib—R
Aspire

CoLaborer—R
Esprit—R
Helping Hand—R
Horizons—R
Joyful Woman—R
Just Between Us—R
Lutheran Woman Today
Proverbs 31 Homemaker—R
Today's Christian Woman
Wesleyan Woman—R
Woman's Touch—R
Women of Spirit—R

WRITERS

Inklings

EXEGESIS*

ADULT/GENERAL

A.M.E. Christian Recorder—R
Bible Advocate—R
Church Herald/Holiness—R
Cornerstone—R
Day Star Tribune—R
Hidden Manna—R
John Milton—R
L.I.G.H.T News—R
Pentecostal Testimony—R
Presbyterian Outlook
St. Willibrord Journal
Weavings—R

CHRISTIAN EDUCATION/LIBRARY

Shining Star

PASTORS/LEADERS

African American Pulpit
Enrichment—R
Jour/Amer Soc/Chur Growth—R
Preacher—R
Pulpit Helps—R
Quarterly Review
Reaching Children at Risk
Sharing the Practice—R

WRITERS

Inklings

FAMILY LIFE

ADULT/GENERAL

Accent on Living—R
Alive!—R
A.M.E. Christian Recorder—R
America
Angels on Earth
Annals of St. Anne

Arlington Catholic
Atlantic Baptist
AXIOS—R
Banner
Baptist Informer
B.C. Catholic—R
Believer—R
Bible Advocate—R
Bible Advocate Online—R
Bread of Life—R
Breakthrough Intercessor—R
Brethren Evangelist
Bridal Guides—R
Canada Lutheran—R
Canadian Catholic
Catholic Digest—R
Catholic Forester—R
Catholic Insight
Catholic Parent
Celebrate Life—R
CGA World—R
Charisma/Christian Life
Chicken Soup/Mother—R
Chicken Soup/Woman—R
Christian C.L. RECORD—R
Christian Courier (WI)—R
Christian Courier (CAN)—R
Christian Edge—R
Christian Home & School
Christian Living—R
Christian Motorsports
Christian Parenting—R
Christian Ranchman
Christian Reader—R
Christian Renewal—R
Christian Social Action—R
Church Advocate—R
Church Herald/Holiness—R
Columbia
Companion
Companions—R
Connecting Point—R
Conquest
Covenant Companion—R
Creation Ex Nihilo
Culture Wars—R
Day Star Tribune—R
Disciple's Journal—R
Decision
Dovetail—R
Emphasis/Faith & Living—R
Evangel—R
Expression Christian
Family Digest
Family Journal—R
Family Network—R
Fellowship Link—R
Focus on the Family

Foursquare World—R
Gem—R
God's Revivalist
Good News (AL)—R
Good News, Etc—R
Good News Journal (MO)—R
Good News Journal (TX)
Gospel Tidings—R
Guideposts
Head to Head—R
Healing Inn—R
Hearing Hearts
Heartlight Internet—R
Highway News—R
Homeschooling Today—R
Home Times—R
Ideals—R
Impact Magazine—R
Indian Life—R
Inland NW Christian
Interim—R
Jewel Among Jewels—R
John Milton—R
Keys to Living—R
LA Catholic Agitator
Life Gate—R
Light and Life
L.I.G.H.T News—R
Liguorian
Live—R
Living—R
Living Light News—R
Living with Teenagers—R
Lookout—R
Lutheran—R
Lutheran Digest—R
Lutheran Journal—R
Lutheran Witness—R
Marriage Partnership
Mennonite—R
MESSAGE
MESSAGE/Open Bible—R
Messenger
Messenger/St. Anthony
Metro Voice—R
Michigan Christian
Minnesota Christian—R
Moody—R
North American Voice
Oblates
On Mission
Our Family—R
Our Sunday Visitor
Over the Back Fence—R
ParentLife—R
Parent Paper—R
Pegasus Review—R
Pentecostal Evangel

Pentecostal Testimony—R
Peoples Magazine—R
Physician
Plain Truth—R
Plus—R
Pourastan—R
Power for Living—R
Prairie Messenger—R
PrayerWorks—R
Presbyterian Layman
Presbyterian Record—R
Presbyterians Today—R
Preserving Christian Homes—
   R
Progress—R
ProLife News—R
Purpose—R
Pursuit—R
Real FamilyLife
Re:generation
Religious Education
Right Road—R
Romantic—R
Sacred Journey—R
Signs of the Times—R
Smart Families
Social Justice
Sojourners
Something Better—R
Standard—R
Standard—R
Stand Firm—R
Star of Zion
TEAK Roundup—R
Time of Singing—R
Today's Christian Senior—R
   (grandparenting)
Together—R
Trumpeter—R
United Church Observer
Upsouth—R
U.S. Catholic
Vibrant Life—R
Vision—R
War Cry—R
Way of St. Francis—R
Wesleyan Advocate—R

CHILDREN

BREAD/God's Children—R
Club Connection—R
CLUBHOUSE—R
Courage
Discoveries—R
Discovery (NY)—R
Discovery Trails—R
High Adventure—R
Listen

My Friend
Nature Friend—R
Pockets—R
Skipping Stones
Touch—R
Wonder Time

CHRISTIAN EDUCATION/LIBRARY

Caravan
CE Connection—R
CE Counselor—R
Children's Ministry
Church Educator—R
GROUP
Leader/Church School
   Today—R
Shining Star
Teacher's Interaction

MISSIONS

American Horizon—R
Quiet Hour Echoes
World Christian—R
Worldwide Challenge

PASTORS/LEADERS

African American Pulpit
Art+Plus
Catholic Servant
Cell Life FORUM—R
Christian Camp—R
Current Thoughts & Trends
Evangelical Baptist—R
Journal/Christian Healing—R
Journal/Pastoral Care
Lutheran Partners—R
Minister's Family
Ministries Today
Networks—R
Policy Review
Preacher's Illus. Service—R
PROCLAIM—R
Reaching Children at Risk
Sharing the Practice—R
Today's Christian Preacher—R
Today's Parish
Vital Ministry
Voice of the Vineyard —R
Word & World
Youthworker—R

TEEN/YOUNG ADULT

Breakaway—R
Certainty
Challenge (IL)
Conqueror—R
Devo'Zine—R
Essential Connection—R

Insight—R
Straight—R
Teens on Target—R
Today's Christian Teen—R
YOU!—R
Young Adult Today
Young Christian—R
Youth Challenge—R

WOMEN

Adam's Rib—R
Aspire
Esprit—R
Hearth
Helping Hand—R
Horizons—R
Journey—R
Joyful Woman—R
Kansas City Woman
Keepers at Home
Just Between Us—R
Lutheran Woman's Quar.
Lutheran Woman Today
Proverbs 31 Homemaker—R
Today's Christian Woman
Virtue—R
Virtuous Woman
Welcome Home
Wesleyan Woman—R
Woman's Touch—R
Women of Spirit—R

WRITERS

Inklings
Writers' Intl. Forum

FILLERS: ANECDOTES

ADULT/GENERAL

Alive!—R
Angels on Earth
AXIOS—R
Bible Advocate Online—R
Bridal Guides—R
Catholic Digest—R
Chicken Soup/Mother—R
Chicken Soup/Single—R
Chicken Soup/Woman—R
Christian Arts Review
Christian Chronicle—R
Christian Courier (WI)—R
Christian Edge—R
Christian Motorsports
Christian Ranchman
Christian Reader—R
Christian Traveler—R
Church Herald/Holiness—R
Church of God EVANGEL

Companion
Companions—R
Conquest
Day Star Tribune—R
Decision
Disciple's Journal—R
Family Digest
Family Network—R
Forefront
Foursquare World—R
Gem—R
Good News (AL)—R
Good News Journal (TX)
Gospel Tract—R
Guideposts
Head to Head—R
Healing Inn—R
Heartlight Internet—R
Home Times—R
Impact Magazine—R
Inspirer—R
Jewel Among Jewels—R
John Milton—R
Legions of Light—R
Life Gate—R
L.I.G.H.T News—R
Liguorian
Living—R
Lutheran Digest—R
Lutheran Journal—R
Mature Living
Mennonite—R
Messenger/St. Anthony
Metro Voice—R
MovieGuide
New Heart—R
Our Family—R
ParentLife—R
Peoples Magazine—R
Pourastan—R
Presbyterian Record—R
Presbyterians Today—R
Purpose—R
Smile—R
TEAK Roundup—R
Visitation
War Cry—R
Way of St. Francis—R

CHILDREN

Club Connection—R
CLUBHOUSE—R
Discovery (NY)—R
High Adventure—R
Skipping Stones

CHRISTIAN EDUCATION/LIBRARY

Christian Classroom

Christian Librarian—R
Christian School
Christian School Admin.
Religion Teacher's Journal
Shining Star
Teachers in Focus—R
Vision—R

MUSIC

Church Musician
Church Pianist, etc.
Creator—R
Songwriter—R

PASTORS/LEADERS

Art+Plus
Cell Life FORUM—R
Christian Management—R
Christian Ministry
Eucharistic Minister—R
Five Stones—R
Ivy Jungle Report—R
Journal/Christian Healing—R
Joyful Noiseletter
Leadership Journal—R
Preacher's Magazine—R
Pulpit Helps—R
Resource—R
Sharing the Practice—R
Voice of the Vineyard—R
Worship Leader—R

TEEN/YOUNG ADULT

Guideposts for Teens—R
Young Christian—R
Young Salvationist—R

WOMEN

Anna's Journal—R
CoLaborer—R
Just Between Us—R
Proverbs 31 Homemaker—R
Today's Christian Woman
Virtuous Woman
Wesleyan Woman—R
Woman's Touch—R
Women of the Harvest

WRITERS

Byline
Cross & Quill—R
Canadian Writer's Jour—R
Christian Response—R
Fellowscript—R
Once Upon a Time—R
Southwestern Writers—R
Tickled by Thunder
Writer's Digest—R

Writer's Exchange—R
Writer's Guidelines/News
Writers' Journal—R
Write Touch—R

FILLERS: CARTOONS

ADULT/GENERAL

Advent Christian Witness—R
Alive!—R
alive now!
Angels on Earth
AXIOS—R
Banner
Bridal Guides—R
Catholic Digest—R
Catholic Forester—R
CBA Frontline
CBA Marketplace
Chicken Soup/Mother—R
Chicken Soup/Single—R
Chicken Soup/Woman—R
Christian Chronicle—R
Christian Computing (MO)—R
Christian Edge—R
Christian Motorsports
Christian Ranchman
Church Herald/Holiness—R
Commonweal
Companion
Computing Today
Connecting Point—R
Cornerstone—R
Covenant Companion—R
Culture Wars—R
Day Star Tribune—R
Disciple's Journal—R
Door
Evangel—R
Expression Christian
Family Network—R
Foursquare World—R
Gem—R
Good News (AL)—R
Good News Journal (MO)—R
Good News Journal (TX)
Green Cross—R
Head to Head—R
Hearing Hearts
Heartlight Internet—R
Home Times—R
Impact Magazine—R
Inside Journal
Inspirer—R
Jewel Among Jewels—R
John Milton—R
Keys to Living—R
Liguorian

Light and Life
Lookout—R
Lutheran—R
Lutheran Digest—R
Lutheran Journal—R
Lutheran Witness—R
Mature Living
Mature Years—R
Mennonite—R
MESSAGE/Open Bible—R
Messenger/St. Anthony
Metro Voice—R
Michigan Christian
MovieGuide
New Creation
New Heart—R
NW Christian Journal—R
Our Family—R
Pegasus Review—R
Peoples Magazine—R
Physician
Power for Living—R
Presbyterian Record—R
Presbyterians Today—R
Purpose—R
Pursuit—R
Right Road—R
Single Connection—R
Smile—R
Sojourners
TEAK Roundup—R
Today's Christian Senior—R
Touchstone—R
United Church Observer
Way of St. Francis—R

CHILDREN

Club Connection—R
CLUBHOUSE—R
Counselor—R
Discoveries—R
Focus/Clubhouse Jr
High Adventure—R
My Friend
On the Line—R
Power Station—R
Skipping Stones
Story Friends—R

CHRISTIAN EDUCATION/LIBRARY

Baptist Leader—R
CE Connection—R
CE Counselor—R
Children's Ministry
Christian Classroom
Christian Librarian—R
Christian School Admin.
GROUP

Journal/Adventist Educ.—R
Team—R
Today's Catholic Teacher—R
Vision—R

MUSIC

Christian Country—R
Church Musician
Church Pianist, etc.
Creator—R
Glory Songs—R
Senior Musician—R
Songwriter—R

PASTORS/LEADERS

Art+Plus
Catholic Servant
Cell Life FORUM—R
Christian Century
Christian Management—R
Christian Ministry
Clergy Journal—R
Diocesan Dialogue—R
Eucharistic Minister—R
Five Stones—R
Ivy Jungle Report—R
Joyful Noiseletter
Leadership Journal—R
Lutheran Partners—R
Ministry Now
Preacher's Magazine—R
Preaching
Priest
Reformed Worship
Resource—R
Small Group Dynamics
Vital Ministry
Voice of the Vineyard—R
WCA News—R
Your Church—R

TEEN/YOUNG ADULT

Breakaway—R
Brio
Campus Life—R
Guideposts for Teens—R
Listen—R
Real Time—R
Teen Life—R
With—R
YOU!—R
Young Christian—R
Young Salvationist—R

WOMEN

Horizons—R
Joyful Woman—R
Just Between Us—R

Proverbs 31 Homemaker—R
Today's Christian Woman
Virtuous Woman
Wesleyan Woman—R
Women Alive!—R

WRITERS
Byline
Canadian Writer's Jour—R
Cross & Quill—R
Dream Weaver
Fellowscript—R
Heaven—R
NW Christian Author—R
Once Upon a Time—R
Writer's Exchange—R
Writer's Guidelines/News
Writers' Journal—R

FILLERS: FACTS

ADULT/GENERAL
Alive!—R
Angels on Earth
AXIOS—R
Bible Advocate—R
Bible Advocate Online—R
Bread of Life—R
Bridal Guides—R
Catholic Digest—R
CBA Marketplace
Christian Arts Review
Christian Chronicle—R
Christian Courier (WI)—R
Christian Edge—R
Christian Motorsports
Christian Ranchman
Christian Reader—R
Christian Traveler—R
Day Star Tribune—R
Disciple's Journal—R
Family Network—R
God's Revivalist
Good News (AL)—R
Good News Journal (TX)
Gospel Tract—R
Hallelujah! (CAN)—R
Head to Head—R
Healing Inn—R
Inspirer—R
Jewel Among Jewels—R
John Milton—R
Legions of Light—R
Life Gate—R
L.I.G.H.T News—R
Lutheran Digest—R
Lutheran Journal—R
Mature Living

Mennonite—R
MESSAGE
MESSAGE/Open Bible—R
Messenger/St. Anthony
MovieGuide
Peoples Magazine—R
PrayerWorks—R
Presbyterian Record—R
Single Connection—R
Visitation
Way of St. Francis—R

CHILDREN
Club Connection—R
Discoveries—R
Discovery Trails—R
Focus/Clubhouse
Guideposts for Kids
High Adventure—R
Live Wire—R
On the Line—R
Power Station—R

CHRISTIAN EDUCATION/LIBRARY
Christian Classroom
Christian School Admin.
Shining Star
Today's Catholic Teacher—R
Vision—R

MISSIONS
So All May Hear—R

MUSIC
Songwriter—R

PASTORS/LEADERS
Christian Ministry
Church Management—R
Ivy Jungle Report—R
Journal/Christian Healing—R
Single Adult Ministries
Voice of the Vineyard—R

TEEN/YOUNG ADULT
Breakaway—R
Brio
Campus Life—R
Certainty
Guideposts for Teens—R
Student Leadership—R
Teen Life—R
Young Christian—R
Young Salvationist—R

WOMEN
Anna's Journal—R

WRITERS
Christian Response—R
Dream Weaver
Fellowscript—R
Writer's Exchange—R
Writers' Journal—R
Write Touch—R

FILLERS: GAMES

ADULT/GENERAL
Alive!—R
Angels on Earth
Bridal Guides—R
Catholic Digest—R
Catholic Forester—R
CGA World—R
Christian Edge—R
Christian Motorsports
Christian Ranchman
Connecting Point—R
Day Star Tribune—R
Disciple's Journal—R
Family Network—R
Good News Journal (MO)—R
Good News Journal (TX)
Gospel Tract—R
Head to Head—R
Healing Inn—R
Hearing Hearts
Heartlight Internet—R
Inspirer—R
Keys to Living—R
Liguorian
Lutheran Journal—R
Mature Living
MESSAGE
MovieGuide
ParentLife—R
Peoples Magazine—R
Right Road—R

CHILDREN
Club Connection—R
CLUBHOUSE—R
Courage
Discoveries—R
Discovery (NY)—R
Focus/Clubhouse
Focus/Clubhouse Jr
GUIDE—R
Guideposts for Kids
High Adventure—R
Kidz Chat—R
Listen
Live Wire—R
On the Line—R
Pockets—R

Power Station—R
Primary Pal (IL)
Together Time
Touch—R

CHRISTIAN EDUCATION/LIBRARY

Children's Ministry
CE Counselor—R
Christian Classroom
Christian School Admin.
GROUP
Leader/Church School
   Today—R
Perspective—R
Religion Teacher's Journal
Shining Star
Voice of the Vineyard —R

MUSIC

Songwriter—R

PASTORS/LEADERS

Vital Ministry

TEEN/YOUNG ADULT

Challenge (IL)
Conqueror—R
Listen—R
Minister's Family
Student Leadership—R
YOU!—R
Young Christian—R
Young Salvationist—R

FILLERS: IDEAS

ADULT/GENERAL

Angels on Earth
Bridal Guides—R
Catholic Parent
CBA Marketplace
CGA World—R
Christian Chronicle—R
Christian Edge—R
Christian Home & School
Christian Motorsports
Christian Ranchman
Christian Traveler—R
Church of God EVANGEL
Conquest
Day Star Tribune—R
Disciple's Journal—R
Family Network—R
God's Revivalist
Good News (AL)—R
Good News Journal (TX)
Head to Head—R
Healing Inn—R

Hearing Hearts
Heartlight Internet—R
Inspirer—R
Jewel Among Jewels—R
John Milton—R
L.I.G.H.T News—R
Messenger/St. Anthony
Metro Voice—R
MovieGuide
ParentLife—R
Pourastan—R
Presbyterian Record—R
St. Joseph's Messenger—R
Seek—R
TEAK Roundup—R

CHILDREN

Club Connection—R
Discovery (NY)—R
High Adventure—R
Listen
Live Wire—R
Pockets—R
Together Time

CHRISTIAN EDUCATION/LIBRARY

CE Connection—R
CE Counselor—R
Children's Ministry
Christian Classroom
Christian School Admin.
GROUP
Leader/Church School
   Today—R
Parish Teacher
Religion Teacher's Journal
Shining Star
Teacher's Interaction
Team—R
Vision—R

MUSIC

Creator—R
Glory Songs—R
Senior Musician—R
Songwriter—R

PASTORS/LEADERS

Church Worship
Cell Life FORUM—R
Enrichment—R
Five Stones—R
Journal/Christian Healing—R
Leadership Journal—R
Lutheran Partners—R
Minister's Family
Pray!—R
Preacher's Illus. Service—R

Preacher's Magazine—R
Single Adult Ministries
Small Group Dynamics
Vital Ministry
Voice of the Vineyard —R
WCA News—R

TEEN/YOUNG ADULT

Brio
Campus Life—R
Certainty
Young Christian—R

WOMEN

Keepers at Home
Proverbs 31 Homemaker—R
Wesleyan Woman—R
Woman's Touch—R

WRITERS

Fellowscript—R
Just Between Us—R
Tickled by Thunder
VA Christian Writer—R
Writer's Exchange—R
Writer's Ink—R
Writers' Journal—R
Write Touch—R

FILLERS: JOKES

ADULT/GENERAL

Angels on Earth
Catholic Digest—R
Christian Motorsports
Christian Ranchman
Day Star Tribune—R
Disciple's Journal—R
Family Network—R
Good News (AL)—R
Good News Journal (MO)—R
Good News Journal (TX)
Healing Inn—R
Heartlight Internet—R
Home Times—R
Impact Magazine—R
Inspirer—R
Keys to Living—R
Liguorian
Lutheran—R
Lutheran Digest—R
Mature Years—R
MovieGuide
New Heart—R
Our Family—R
PrayerWorks—R
Right Road—R
Seek—R

Single Connection—R
Smile—R
Today's Christian Senior—R

CHILDREN

Club Connection—R
CLUBHOUSE—R
Discovery (NY)—R
Flicker
Guideposts for Kids
High Adventure—R
Live Wire—R
My Friend
On the Line—R
Pockets—R (& riddles)

CHRISTIAN EDUCATION/LIBRARY

Baptist Leader—R
Christian Classroom
Christian School Admin.

MUSIC

Creator—R

PASTORS/LEADERS

Cell Life FORUM—R
Five Stones—R
Ivy Jungle Report—R
Journal/Christian Healing—R
Joyful Noiseletter
Preacher's Illus. Service—R
Voice of the Vineyard —R

TEEN/YOUNG ADULT

Guideposts for Teens—R
Real Time—R
YOU!—R

WOMEN

Joyful Woman—R

WRITERS

Writer's Exchange—R
Writer's Guidelines/News
Writers' Journal—R

FILLERS: NEWSBREAKS

ADULT/GENERAL

Angels on Earth
Anglican Journal—R
Arkansas Catholic
B.C. Catholic—R
Bridal Guides—R
Canada Lutheran—R
Catholic Telegraph
CBA Marketplace
Celebrate Life—R

Christian Arts Review
Christian Courier (WI)—R
Christian Edge—R
Christian Living—R
Christian Motorsports
Christian Ranchman
Christian Renewal—R
Christian Traveler—R
Common Boundary
Day Star Tribune—R
Disciple's Journal—R
Family Network—R
Good News Journal (TX)
Hallelujah! (CAN)—R
Head to Head—R
Healing Inn—R
Heartlight Internet—R
Home Times—R
Indian Life—R
Inspirer—R
Jewel Among Jewels—R
Legions of Light—R
Living Light News—R
Mennonite Weekly
Metro Voice—R
MovieGuide
Religious Broadcasting—R
TEAK Roundup—R

CHILDREN

Club Connection—R

CHRISTIAN EDUCATION/LIBRARY

Christian Librarian—R
Vision—R

MISSIONS

So All May Hear—R

MUSIC

Songwriter—R

PASTORS/LEADERS

Christian Ministry
Ivy Jungle Report—R
Journal/Christian Healing—R
Preacher's Illus. Service—R
Single Adult Ministries
Voice of the Vineyard —R

TEEN/YOUNG ADULT

Certainty
Teen Life—R
Young Christian—R

WOMEN

Anna's Journal—R
Conscience—R

Joyful Woman—R
Women Today—R
Women Today Online—R

WRITERS

Writer's Exchange—R
Writer's Ink—R

FILLERS: PARTY IDEAS

ADULT/GENERAL

Bridal Guides—R
Christian Ranchman
Day Star Tribune—R
Disciple's Journal—R
Good News Journal (TX)
Family Network—R
Head to Head—R
Hearing Hearts
Living with Teenagers—R
MovieGuide
ParentLife—R
Single Connection—R
TEAK Roundup—R

CHILDREN

Club Connection—R
Focus/Clubhouse
Live Wire—R
On the Line—R
Young Christian—R

CHRISTIAN EDUCATION/LIBRARY

Perspective—R
Team—R

MUSIC

Creator—R
Glory Songs
Senior Musician—R

TEEN/YOUNG ADULT

Conqueror—R
Student Leadership—R
Young Christian—R

WOMEN

CoLaborer—R
Proverbs 31 Homemaker—R
Wesleyan Woman—R

FILLERS: PRAYERS

ADULT/GENERAL

alive now!
Angels on Earth
Bridal Guides—R
CGA World—R

Christian Living—R
Christian Motorsports
Christian Ranchman
Church Herald/Holiness—R
Cornerstone—R
Disciple's Journal—R
Family Network—R
Forefront
Good News Journal (TX)
Green Cross—R
Head to Head—R
Healing Inn—R
Heartlight Internet—R
Inspirer—R
Jewel Among Jewels—R
John Milton—R
L.I.G.H.T News—R
Mature Years—R
MovieGuide
Our Family—R
Plowman—R
Pourastan—R
PrayerWorks—R
Presbyterian Record—R
Right Road—R
Way of St. Francis—R

CHILDREN

Kidz Chat—R
Pockets—R
Primary Pal (IL)
Touch—R

CHRISTIAN EDUCATION/LIBRARY

Baptist Leader—R
Christian Classroom
Religion Teacher's Journal
Teacher's Interaction
Vision—R

PASTORS/LEADERS

Church Management—R
Clergy Journal—R
Preacher—R
Reformed Worship

TEEN/YOUNG ADULT

Straight—R
YOU!—R
Young Christian—R
Young Salvationist—R

WOMEN

Anna's Journal—R
Horizons—R
Journey—R
Joyful Woman—R
Just Between Us—R

Proverbs 31 Homemaker—R
Virtuous Woman

WRITERS

Cross & Quill—R
Southwestern Writers—R
WIN-Informer

FILLERS: PROSE

ADULT/GENERAL

Angels on Earth
Bible Advocate—R
Bible Advocate Online—R
Bread of Life—R
Christian Motorsports
Christian Ranchman
Church Herald/Holiness—R
Companions—R
Conquest
Decision
Disciple's Journal—R
Discovery—R
Family Network—R
Forefront
Gem—R
God's Revivalist
Good News Journal (TX)
Hallelujah! (CAN)—R
Head to Head—R
Healing Inn—R
Heartlight Internet—R
Hidden Manna—R
Inspirer—R
Jewel Among Jewels—R
John Milton—R
Lutheran Journal—R
MovieGuide
Pegasus Review—R
Pentecostal Evangel
Plowman—R
Presbyterian Record—R
Presbyterians Today—R
TEAK Roundup—R
Way of St. Francis—R
Wesleyan Advocate—R

CHILDREN

CLUBHOUSE—R
Courage

CHRISTIAN EDUCATION/LIBRARY

Vision—R

PASTORS/LEADERS

Preacher's Illus. Service—R
Pulpit Helps—R

TEEN/YOUNG ADULT

Brio
Certainty
Conqueror—R
Guideposts for Teens—R
Real Time—R
Young Christian—R

WOMEN

Anna's Journal—R
Keepers at Home
Proverbs 31 Homemaker—R
Today's Christian Woman
Virtuous Woman

WRITERS

Chip Off Writer's Block—R
Dream Weaver
Once Upon a Time—R
The Writer
Writer's Exchange—R
Write Touch—R

FILLERS: QUIZZES

ADULT/GENERAL

Alive!—R
Angels on Earth
Bridal Guides—R
Catholic Digest—R
Christian Motorsports
Christian Ranchman
Day Star Tribune—R
Door
Disciple's Journal—R
Family Network—R
Good News (AL)—R
Good News Journal (MO)—R
Good News Journal (TX)
Healing Inn—R
Hearing Hearts
Impact Magazine—R
Inspirer—R
Jewel Among Jewels—R
Keys to Living—R
Lutheran Journal—R
Mature Living
MESSAGE
MovieGuide
Peoples Magazine—R
Right Road—R
St. Willibrord Journal
Single Connection—R
Today's Christian Senior—R

CHILDREN

Club Connection—R
Counselor—R

Crusader—R
Discoveries—R
Discovery (NY)—R
Focus/Clubhouse
GUIDE—R
Guideposts for Kids
High Adventure—R
Kidz Chat—R
Nature Friend—R
On the Line—R
Partners—R
Power Station—R
Skipping Stones
Story Mates—R
Touch—R
Young Christian—R

CHRISTIAN EDUCATION/LIBRARY
CE Counselor—R

MUSIC
Glory Songs—R
Senior Musician—R

PASTORS/LEADERS
Ivy Jungle Report—R
Voice of the Vineyard —R

TEEN/YOUNG ADULT
Breakaway—R
Brio
Certainty
Conqueror—R
Guideposts for Teens—R
Listen—R
Real Time—R
Student Leadership—R
Teens on Target—R
YOU!—R
Young Christian—R
Young Salvationist—R
Youth Challenge—R

WOMEN
Anna's Journal—R
Virtuous Woman
Women Today—R
Women Today Online—R

WRITERS
Fellowscript—R
Once Upon a Time—R
WIN-Informer
Writer's Ink—R

FILLERS: QUOTES

ADULT/GENERAL
Angels on Earth
Bible Advocate—R
Bible Advocate Online—R
Bread of Life—R
Catholic Digest—R
Christian Arts Review
Christian Chronicle—R
Christian Edge—R
Christian Motorsports
Christian Ranchman
Christian Traveler—R
Companion
Culture Wars—R
Day Star Tribune—R
Disciple's Journal—R
Family Network—R
Good News (AL)—R
Good News Journal (TX)
Gospel Tract—R
Guideposts
Hallelujah! (CAN)—R
Head to Head—R
Healing Inn—R
Heartlight Internet—R
Hidden Manna—R
Home Times—R
Inspirer—R
Jewel Among Jewels—R
John Milton—R
Keys to Living—R
L.I.G.H.T News—R
Lutheran Journal—R
MESSAGE/Open Bible—R
Messenger/St. Anthony
Metro Voice—R
MovieGuide
Our Family—R
Pegasus Review—R
Poets' Paper—R
Pourastan—R
PrayerWorks—R
Seek—R
Smile—R

CHILDREN
Discovery (NY)—R
Live Wire—R
Skipping Stones

CHRISTIAN EDUCATION/LIBRARY
Christian Library Jour.—R
Shining Star

MUSIC
Songwriter—R

PASTORS/LEADERS
Christian Management—R
Ivy Jungle Report—R
Journal/Christian Healing—R
Pulpit Helps—R
Single Adult Ministries
Voice of the Vineyard —R
Worship Leader

TEENS/YOUNG ADULTS
YOU!—R
Young Christian—R

WOMEN
Anna's Journal—R
Joyful Woman—R
Just Between Us—R
Proverbs 31 Homemaker—R
Virtuous Woman
Wesleyan Woman—R

WRITERS
Christian Response—R
Southwestern Writers—R
WIN-Informer
Writer's Exchange—R
Writer's Guidelines/News
Writer's Ink—R

FILLERS: SHORT HUMOR

ADULT/GENERAL
Alive!—R
Angels on Earth
Catholic Digest—R
Chicken Soup/Mother—R
Chicken Soup/Single—R
Chicken Soup/Woman—R
Christian Chronicle—R
Christian Edge—R
Christian Motorsports
Christian Ranchman
Christian Reader—R
Christian Traveler—R
Church Herald/Holiness—R
Companion
Covenant Companion—R
Day Star Tribune—R
Disciple's Journal—R
Door
Evangel—R
Family Network—R
Gem
God's Revivalist
Good News (AL)—R
Good News Journal (TX)
Gospel Tract—R
Green Cross—R

Guideposts
Head to Head—R
Healing Inn—R
Hidden Manna—R
Highway News—R
Heartlight Internet—R
Home Times—R
Impact Magazine—R
Inspirer—R
Jewel Among Jewels—R
John Milton—R
Keys to Living—R
Legions of Light—R
Liguorian
Living—R
Living with Teenagers—R
Lutheran—R
Lutheran Digest—R
Lutheran Journal—R
Lutheran Witness—R
Mature Living
MESSAGE/Open Bible—R
Metro Voice—R
MovieGuide
New Heart—R
Our Family—R
Peoples Magazine—R
Pourastan—R
PrayerWorks—R
Presbyterian Record—R
Presbyterians Today—R
Purpose—R
St. Willibrord Journal
Seek—R
Single Connection—R
Smile—R
Star of Zion
TEAK Roundup—R
Visitation

CHILDREN

Club Connection—R
Discovery (NY)—R
Discovery Trails—R
Guideposts for Kids
Touch—R

CHRISTIAN EDUCATION/LIBRARY

Christian Classroom
Christian Librarian—R
Christian School Admin.
Teachers in Focus
Team—R

MUSIC

Christian Country—R
Creator—R
Glory Songs—R

Senior Musician—R
Songwriter—R

PASTORS/LEADERS

Catholic Servant
Christian Management—R
Enrichment—R
Eucharistic Minister—R
Five Stones—R
Ivy Jungle Report—R
Journal/Christian Healing—R
Joyful Noiseletter
Leadership Journal—R
Ministry Now
Preacher's Illus. Service—R
Resource—R
Sharing the Practice—R
Voice of the Vineyard —R

TEEN/YOUNG ADULT

Brio
Campus Life—R
Certainty
Guideposts for Teens—R
Real Time—R
Straight—R
Young Christian—R
Young Salvationist—R

WOMEN

Journey—R
Joyful Woman—R
Just Between Us—R
Proverbs 31 Homemaker—R
Wesleyan Woman—R
Women of the Harvest

WRITERS

Byline
Dream Weaver
Once Upon a Time—R
Tickled by Thunder
Writer's Digest—R
Writer's Exchange—R
Writer's Guidelines/News
Writers' Journal—R
Write Touch—R

FILLERS: WORD PUZZLES

ADULT/GENERAL

Alive!—R
Bridal Guides—R
CGA World—R
Christian Edge—R
Christian Ranchman
Companion
Connecting Point—R

Conquest
Day Star Tribune—R
Disciple's Journal—R
Family Network—R
Good News (AL)—R
Good News Journal (TX)
Gospel Tract—R
Head to Head—R
Healing Inn—R
Hearing Hearts
Heartlight Internet—R
Impact Magazine—R
Inspirer—R
Jewel Among Jewels—R
Liguorian
Mature Living
Mature Years—R
MESSAGE
Michigan Christian
MovieGuide
Power for Living—R
Right Road—R
Single Connection—R
Smile—R
Standard—R
Today's Christian Senior—R

CHILDREN

Club Connection—R
CLUBHOUSE—R
Counselor—R
Courage
Crusader—R
Discoveries—R
Discovery (NY)—R
Flicker
Focus/Clubhouse
Focus/Clubhouse Jr
GUIDE—R
Guideposts for Kids
High Adventure—R
Kidz Chat—R
Nature Friend—R
On the Line—R
Our Little Friend—R
Partners—R
Pockets—R
Power Station—R
Primary Pal (IL)
Skipping Stones
Story Friends—R
Story Mates—R
Young Christian—R

CHRISTIAN EDUCATION/LIBRARY

Christian Classroom
Leader/Church School
  Today—R

Parish Teacher
Shining Star
Voice of the Vineyard —R

TEEN/YOUNG ADULT

Certainty
Challenge (IL)
Conqueror—R
Listen—R
Real Time—R
Teens on Target—R
YOU!—R
Young Christian—R
Young Salvationist—R
Youth Challenge—R

WRITERS

Heaven—R

FOOD/RECIPES

ADULT/GENERAL

AXIOS—R
Believer—R (maybe)
Bridal Guides—R
Catholic Digest—R
Catholic Forester—R
Catholic Parent
CGA World—R
Christian C.L. RECORD—R
Day Star Tribune—R
Dovetail—R
Family Network—R
Fellowship Link—R
Good News Journal (TX)
Healing Inn—R
Home Times—R
Ideals—R
John Milton—R
Living—R
Lutheran Digest—R
Lutheran Journal—R
Mature Living
MESSAGE
Over the Back Fence—R
ParentLife—R
Parent Paper—R
Peoples Magazine—R
Poetry Forum—R
Progress—R
Single Connection—R
Today's Christian Senior—R
Vibrant Life—R

CHILDREN

Club Connection—R
CLUBHOUSE—R
Discovery (NY)—R

Focus/Clubhouse
Focus/Clubhouse Jr.
Listen
Live Wire—R
On the Line—R
Pockets—R (recipes)
Skipping Stones
Together Time
Touch—R

MISSIONS

World Mission People—R
Young Christian—R

PASTORS/LEADERS

Minister's Family

WOMEN

Aspire
Helping Hand—R
Joyful Woman—R
Kansas City Woman
Proverbs 31 Homemaker—R
True Woman
Virtue—R
Welcome Home
Women Today—R
Women Today Online—R

HEALING

ADULT/GENERAL

A.M.E. Christian Recorder—R
Angels on Earth
Banner
Bible Advocate—R
Bible Advocate Online—R
Biblical Reflections—R
Bread of Life—R
Breakthrough Intercessor—R
Canada Lutheran—R
Catholic Digest—R
Celebrate Life—R
CGA World—R
Charisma/Christian Life
Chicken Soup/Mother—R
Chicken Soup/Woman—R
Christian Chronicle—R
Christian Motorsports
Christian Ranchman
Chrysalis Reader
Common Boundary
Connecting Point—R
Day Star Tribune—R
Family Network—R
Foursquare World—R
Gem—R
Good News(KY)—R

Good News, Etc—R
Good News Journal (MO)—R
Guideposts
Head to Head—R
Healing Inn—R
John Milton—R
Jour/Christian Nursing—R
Life Gate—R
Light and Life
L.I.G.H.T News—R
Liguorian
Mature Years—R
Mennonite—R
Metro Voice—R
Michigan Christian
New Covenant
New Heart—R
New Writing—R
Our Family—R
Pentecostal Testimony—R
Peoples Magazine—R
PrayerWorks—R
Presbyterian Record—R
Presbyterians Today—R
Preserving Christian Homes—
   R
Purpose—R
Sacred Journey—R
SCP Journal—R
Sharing—R
Single Connection—R
Smile—R
Sojourners
Something Better—R
Spiritual Life
Total Health
United Church Observer
Upsouth—R
Vision—R
Way of St. Francis—R
Weavings—R

CHILDREN

BREAD/God's Children—R
Discovery (NY)—R
Discovery Trails—R
High Adventure—R

MISSIONS

American Horizon—R
Areopagus—R

PASTORS/LEADERS

African American Pulpit
Art+Plus
Eucharistic Minister—R
Journal/Christian Healing—R
Journal/Pastoral Care

Lutheran Partners—R
Ministries Today
Ministry
Networks—R
Priest
Sharing the Practice—R
Voice of the Vineyard—R
Word & World

TEEN/YOUNG ADULT

Conqueror—R
Devo'Zine—R
Teen Life—R
Young Adult Today
Young Christian—R

WOMEN

Adam's Rib—R
Aspire
Helping Hand—R
Lutheran Woman Today
Virtuous Woman
Woman's Touch—R

WRITERS

Writers' Intl. Forum

HEALTH

ADULT/GENERAL

Accent on Living—R
Alive!—R
A.M.E. Christian Recorder—R
And He Will Give
Angels on Earth
Anglican Journal—R
Banner
B.C. Catholic—R
Believer—R
Bible Advocate—R
Biblical Reflections—R
Breakthrough Intercessor—R
Canada Lutheran—R
Catholic Digest—R
Catholic Forester—R
Celebrate Life—R
CGA World—R
Charisma/Christian Life
Christian Chronicle—R
Christian Courier (WI)—R
Christian Courier (CAN)—R
Christian Living—R
Christian Motorsports
Christian Ranchman
Christian Reader—R
Christian Social Action—R
Common Boundary
Companion

Day Star Tribune—R
Disciple's Journal—R
Discovery—R
Expression Christian
Faith Today
Family Network—R
Fellowship Link—R
Good News Journal (MO)—R
Good News Journal (TX)
Gospel Today
Green Cross—R
Guideposts
Head to Head—R
Healing Inn—R
Home Times—R
Inland NW Christian
Inside Journal—R
John Milton—R
Jour/Christian Nursing—R
Lifeglow—R
Light and Life
Living—R
Living Light News—R
Living with Teenagers—R
Lutheran Digest—R
Lutheran Journal—R
Lutheran Witness—R
Marriage Partnership
Mature Years—R
Mennonite—R
MESSAGE
Metro Voice—R
Michigan Christian
New Heart—R
No-Debt Living—R
ParentLife—R
Parent Paper—R
Peoples Magazine—R
Physician
Plus—R
Poetry Forum—R
Pourastan—R
PrayerWorks—R
ProLife News—R
Right Road—R
Sacred Journey—R
SCP Journal—R
Single Connection—R
Single-Parent Family
Smart Families
Something Better—R
Standard—R
Stand Firm—R
TEAK Roundup—R
Today's Christian Senior—R
Total Health
Trumpeter—R
Upscale Magazine

Upsouth—R
Vibrant Life—R
War Cry—R

CHILDREN

BREAD/God's Children—R
Club Connection—R
Focus/Clubhouse Jr
High Adventure—R
Live Wire—R
On the Line—R
Power Station—R
Skipping Stones
Touch—R
Young Christian—R

CHRISTIAN EDUCATION/LIBRARY

Leader/Church School
   Today—R

MISSIONS

Areopagus—R
Quiet Hour Echoes

PASTORS/LEADERS

Christian Camp—R
Journal/Christian Healing—R
Journal/Pastoral Care
Lutheran Partners—R
Minister's Family
Ministries Today
Reaching Children at Risk
Word & World

TEEN/YOUNG ADULT

Challenge (GA) —R
Conqueror—R
Essential Connection—R
Today's Christian Teen—R
Young Adult Today
Young & Alive—R
Young Christian—R

WOMEN

Adam's Rib—R
Aspire
Esprit—R
Hearth
Helping Hand—R
Journey—R
Lutheran Woman's Quar.
Lutheran Woman Today
Proverbs 31 Homemaker—R
Today's Christian Woman
Virtue—R
Virtuous Woman
Welcome Home
Woman's Touch—R

Women Today—R
Women Today Online—R

HISTORICAL

ADULT/GENERAL

AGAIN—R
America
Angels on Earth
Arlington Catholic
AXIOS—R
Banner
Baptist History
Canadian Catholic
Cathedral Age
Catholic Answer
Catholic Digest—R
Catholic Dossier
Catholic Heritage—R
Catholic Insight
Catholic Sentinel—R
Celebrate Life—R
Christian C.L. RECORD—R
Christian Courier (CAN)—R
Christian History—R
Christian Motorsports
Christian Ranchman
Christian Reader—R
Christian Renewal—R
Christianity Today—R
Chrysalis Reader
Church & State—R
Columbia
Comments/Friends—R
Companions—R (church)
Company—R (of Jesuits)
Conquest
Covenant Companion—R
Creation Ex Nihilo
Cresset
Dallas/Ft. Worth Heritage
Day Star Tribune—R
Dovetail—R
Faith Today
Fellowship Link—R
Good News, Etc—R
Good News Journal (TX)
Gospel Today
Healing Inn—R
Hidden Manna—R
Homeschooling Today—R
Home Times—R
Indian Life—R
John Milton—R
Jour/Christian Nursing—R
Journal of Church & State
Legions of Light—R
Lifeglow—R

Light and Life
Lutheran Journal—R
Lutheran Witness—R
Mennonite Historian—R
Messenger/St. Anthony
Methodist History
Michigan Christian
Minnesota Christian—R
New Moon—R
Our Sunday Visitor
Over the Back Fence—R
Peoples Magazine—R
Poet's Page
Presbyterian Layman
Presbyterian Outlook
Presbyterians Today—R
Pourastan—R
Power for Living—R
PrayerWorks—R
Purpose—R
Re:generation
Religious Education
Sacred Journey—R
SCP Journal—R
Sharing—R
Single Connection—R
Social Justice
Something Better—R
TEAK Roundup—R
Today's Christian Senior—R
Upscale Magazine
Upsouth—R

CHILDREN

Courage
Discovery(NY)—R
Focus/Clubhouse
Guideposts for Kids
My Friend
Nature Friend—R
On the Line—R
Partners—R
Power & Light—R
Trails 'N' Treasures—R
Young Christian—R

CHRISTIAN EDUCATION/LIBRARY

Christian School Admin.
Vision—R

MISSIONS

American Horizon—R
Areopagus—R
East-West Church
Missiology
So All May Hear—R
Urban Mission—R
Women of the Harvest

Worldwide Challenge

MUSIC

Church Pianist, etc.
Creator—R

PASTORS/LEADERS

African American Pulpit
Five Stones—R
Journal/Christian Healing—R
Lutheran Partners—R
Ministry
Preacher's Magazine—R
Reaching Children at Risk
Sharing the Practice—R
Today's Parish—R
Word & World

TEEN/YOUNG ADULT

Certainty
Challenge (GA) —R
Challenge (IL)
Essential Connection—R
Listen—R
Student Leadership—R
Teen Life—R
Young Adult Today
Young & Alive—R
Young Christian—R

WOMEN

Just Between Us—R

WRITERS

Writers' Intl. Forum

HOLIDAY/SEASONAL

ADULT/GENERAL

Accent on Living—R
Advent Christian Witness—R
Alive!—R
alive now!
American Tract Soc.—R
Angels on Earth
Annals of St. Anne
Arlington Catholic
AXIOS—R
Banner
Believer—R
Bread of Life—R
Breakthrough Intercessor—R
Bridal Guides—R
Canada Lutheran—R
Canadian Catholic
Cathedral Age
Catholic Digest—R
Catholic Faith & Family—R

Catholic Forester—R
Catholic New York
Catholic Parent
Catholic Sentinel—R
CGA World—R
Charisma/Christian Life
Chicken Soup/Mother—R
Chicken Soup/Single—R
Chicken Soup/Woman—R
Christian Century
Christian Chronicle—R
Christian C.L. RECORD—R
Christian Courier (WI)—R
Christian Edge—R
Christian Home & School
Christian Living—R
Christian Motorsports
Christian Parenting—R
Christian Ranchman
Christian Reader—R
Christian Renewal—R
Christian Standard—R
Christian Traveler—R
Christianity Today—R
Church Herald/Holiness—R
Companions—R
Connecting Point—R
Conquest
Covenant Companion—R
Day Star Tribune—R
Decision
Discovery—R
Dovetail—R
Emphasis/Faith & Living—R
Evangel—R
Expression Christian
Family Digest
Family Network—R
Fellowship Link—R
Focus on the Family
Forefront
Foursquare World—R
Gem—R
God's Revivalist
Good News (AL)—R
Good News Journal (TX)
Good News, Etc—R
Gospel Tidings—R
Gospel Today
Gospel Tract—R
Guideposts
Healing Inn—R
Hearing Hearts
Heartlight Internet—R
Homeschooling Today—R
Home Times—R
Ideals—R
Indian Life—R

Inside Journal—R
Inspirer—R
John Milton—R
Jour/Christian Nursing—R
Keys to Living—R
Life Gate—R
Lifeglow—R
Light and Life
Liguorian
Live—R
Living—R
Living Church
Living Light News—R
Living with Teenagers—R
Lutheran Digest—R
Lutheran Journal—R
Lutheran Witness—R
Marriage Partnership
Mature Living
Mennonite—R
MESSAGE
Messenger
Messenger/St. Anthony
Michigan Christian
Minnesota Christian—R
Montana Catholic—R
North American Voice
NW Christian Journal—R
Oblates
On Mission
Our Sunday Visitor
Over the Back Fence—R
ParentLife—R
Parent Paper—R
Pegasus Review—R
Pentecostal Evangel
Pentecostal Testimony—R
Peoples Magazine—R
Plain Truth—R
Plenty Good Room
Plus—R
Power for Living—R
PrayerWorks—R
Presbyterian Outlook
Presbyterian Record—R
Presbyterians Today—R
Preserving Christian Homes—
    R
Progress—R
Purpose—R
Religious Broadcasting—R
Right Road—R
Romantic—R
St. Joseph's Messenger—R
Sharing—R
Signs of the Times—R
Single Connection—R
Smart Families

Smile—R
Sojourners
Something Better—R
Standard—R
Standard—R
Stand Firm—R
TEAK Roundup—R
Time of Singing—R
Today's Christian Senior—R
Together—R
Trumpeter—R
United Church Observer
U.S. Catholic
Vibrant Life—R
War Cry—R
Way of St. Francis—R
Weavings—R
Wesleyan Advocate—R

CHILDREN

Club Connection—R
CLUBHOUSE—R
Counselor—R
Courage
Discovery (NY)—R
Discovery Trails—R
Focus/Clubhouse
Focus/Clubhouse Jr
Guideposts for Kids
Live Wire—R
On the Line—R
Partners—R
Pockets—R
Power Station—R
Primary Pal (IL)
Skipping Stones
Together Time
Touch—R
Trails 'N' Treasures—R
Wonder Time
Young Christian—R

CHRISTIAN EDUCATION/LIBRARY

Baptist Leader—R
CE Connection—R
Children's Ministry
Church Educator—R
Evangelizing Today's Child—R
GROUP
Leader/Church School
    Today—R
Parish Teacher
Shining Star
Teacher's Interaction
Vision—R

MISSIONS

Worldwide Challenge

MUSIC
Church Pianist
Creator—R
Quest—R
Songwriter—R

PASTORS/LEADERS
African American Pulpit
Art+Plus
Catholic Servant
Celebration
Christian Camp—R
Christian Management—R
Church Bytes—R
Enrichment—R
Five Stones—R
Let's Worship
Lutheran Forum—R
Lutheran Partners—R
Ministry & Liturgy—R
Preacher's Magazine—R
Proclaim
Pulpit Helps—R
Vital Ministry

TEEN/YOUNG ADULT
Breakaway—R
Certainty
Challenge (GA) —R
Challenge (IL)
Conqueror—R
Cornerstone—R
Devo'Zine—R
Essential Connection—R
Insight—R
Listen—R
Real Time—R
Straight—R
Teenage Christian—R
YOU!—R
Young & Alive—R
Young Christian—R
Young Salvationist—R

WOMEN
Anna's Journal—R
Aspire
Esprit—R
Helping Hand—R
Horizons—R
Journey—R
Joyful Woman—R
Lutheran Woman's Quar.
Proverbs 31 Homemaker—R
Today's Christian Woman
Virtue—R
Woman's Touch—R
Women of Spirit—R

Women Today—R
Women Today Online—R

WRITERS
Inklings
Southwestern Writers—R
Writers' Intl. Forum

HOME SCHOOLING

ADULT/GENERAL
Anglican Journal—R
Arlington Catholic
AXIOS—R
Banner
Believer—R
Bible Advocate—R
Breakthrough Intercessor—R
Catholic Faith & Family—R
Catholic Insight
CBA Marketplace
Charisma/Christian Life
Christian Chronicle—R
Christian C.L. RECORD—R
Christian Computing—R
Christian Edge—R
Christian Motorsports
Christian Parenting—R
Christian Ranchman
Crisis Point
Day Star Tribune—R
Disciple's Journal—R
Discovery—R
Expression Christian
Family Journal—R
Family Network—R
Focus on the Family
Good News (AL)—R
Good News, Etc—R
Good News Journal (MO)—R
Good News Journal (TX)
Green Cross—R
Homeschooling Today—R
Home Times—R
Inspirer—R
Interim—R
Life Gate—R
Living Light News—R
Lutheran Life—R
MESSAGE/Open Bible—R
Metro Voice—R
Michigan Christian
Minnesota Christian—R
NW Christian Journal—R
ParentLife—R
Parent Paper—R
Preserving Christian Homes—
   R

Religious Education
Single Connection—R
Social Justice
Something Better—R
Sursum Corda!—R
Trumpeter—R
Wesleyan Advocate—R

CHILDREN
BREAD/God's Children—R
Skipping Stones
Young Christian—R

CHRISTIAN EDUCATION/LIBRARY
CE Counselor—R
Christian Educators Jour—R
Christian Library Jour.—R
Christian School

PASTORS/LEADERS
Church Bytes—R
Pastoral Life
Reaching Children at Risk
Today's Christian Preacher—R

TEEN/YOUNG ADULT
Conqueror—R
Insight—R
YOU!—R

WOMEN
Esprit—R
Helping Hand—R
Proverbs 31 Homemaker—R

HOMILETICS*

ADULT/GENERAL
A.M.E. Christian Recorder—R
Bible Advocate—R
Church Herald/Holiness—R
Day Star Tribune—R
Light and Life
Pentecostal Testimony—R
Presbyterian Outlook
St. Willibrord Journal

PASTORS/LEADERS
African American Pulpit
Christian Ministry
Clergy Journal—R
Current Thoughts & Trends
Leadership Journal—R
Lutheran Partners—R
Preacher—R
Pulpit Helps—R
Quarterly Review
Sharing the Practice—R

HOW-TO ACTIVITIES (JUV.)

ADULT/GENERAL

Christian Edge—R
Christian Ranchman
Church Herald/Holiness—R
Day Star Tribune—R
Family Network—R
Good News (AL)—R
Good News Journal (MO)—R
Green Cross—R
Homeschooling Today—R
Living—R
Living Light News—R
Living with Teenagers—R
Lutheran Life—R
Michigan Christian
ParentLife—R
Right Road—R
TEAK Roundup—R

CHILDREN

BREAD/God's Children—R
Club Connection—R
Counselor—R
Courage
Crusader—R
Discovery (NY)—R
Discovery Trails—R
Focus/Clubhouse
Focus/Clubhouse Jr.
God's World News—R
GUIDE—R
High Adventure—R
Kids' Ministry Ideas—R
Kidz Chat—R
Listen
Live Wire—R
My Friend
Nature Friend—R
On the Line—R
Partners—R
Pockets—R
Power & Light—R
Power Station—R
Primary Pal (IL)
Together Time
Touch—R
Wonder Time
Young Christian—R

CHRISTIAN EDUCATION/LIBRARY

CE Connection—R
Christian School Admin.
Church Educator—R
Evangelizing Today's Child—R
Junior Teacher—R

Leader/Church School
    Today—R
Perspective—R
Shining Star
Today's Catholic Teacher—R

PASTORS/LEADERS

Let's Worship
Networks—R
Reaching Children at Risk

TEEN/YOUNG ADULT

Breakaway—R
Challenge (GA) —R
Essential Connection—R
Insight—R
Real Time—R
Teen Life—R
Young Christian—R
Young Salvationist—R

WOMEN

Esprit—R
Proverbs 31 Homemaker—R
Wesleyan Woman—R

HOW-TO

ADULT/GENERAL

Accent on Living—R
Baptist Informer
Bridal Guides—R
CBA Frontline
CBA Marketplace
Celebrate Life—R
CGA World—R
Charisma/Christian Life
Christian Arts Review
Christian Chronicle—R
Christian Edge—R
Christian Home & School
Christian Living—R
Christian Motorsports
Christian Parenting—R
Christian Ranchman
Christian Reader—R
Christian Standard—R
Christian Traveler—R
Church of God EVANGEL
Companion
Connecting Point—R
Conquest
Day Star Tribune—R
Discipleship Journal
Discovery—R
Expression Christian
Family Digest
Family Network—R

Fellowship Link—R
Good News (AL)—R
Good News, Etc.—R
Gospel Today
Green Cross—R
Growing in Christ
Hallelujah! (CAN)—R
Head to Head—R
Healing Inn—R
Hearing Hearts
Homeschooling Today—R
Inland NW Christian
Jour/Christian Nursing—R
Life@Work
Light and Life
Live—R
Living Light News—R
Living with Teenagers—R
Lutheran Digest—R
Marriage Partnership
Mature Living
Mennonite—R
MESSAGE
Michigan Christian
Narrow Gate
New Writing—R
Our Sunday Visitor
ParentLife—R
Physician
Plain Truth—R
Plus—R
Poet's Page
PrayerWorks—R
Preserving Christian Homes—
    R
Pursuit—R
Quiet Revolution—R
Religious Broadcasting—R
Romantic—R
Smart Families
Standard—R
Standard—R
TEAK Roundup—R
Total Health
TEAK Roundup—R
2-Soar—R
Vibrant Life—R
Visitation

CHILDREN

Discovery (NY)—R
Focus/Clubhouse
High Adventure—R
Kids' Ministry Ideas—R

CHRISTIAN EDUCATION/LIBRARY

Brigade Leader—R
Catechist

Catholic Library World
CE Connection—R
CE Connection
    Communique—R
CE Counselor—R
CE Leadership—R
Christian Classroom
Children's Ministry
Christian School
Christian School Admin.
Church & Synagogue Lib.—R
Church Educator—R
Church Libraries—R
GROUP
Leader/Church School
    Today—R
Lollipops
Perspective—R
Shining Star
Teacher's Interaction
Vision—R

MISSIONS

PFI World Report—R
Quiet Hour Echoes
Women of the Harvest
World Mission People—R

MUSIC

Church Music Report
Gospel Industry Today
Songwriter—R

PASTORS/LEADERS

Art+Plus
Christian Camp—R
Church Administration
Church Bytes—R
Clergy Journal—R
Ivy Jungle Report—R
Journal/Christian Healing—R
Lutheran Partners—R
Ministry & Liturgy—R
Newsletter Newsletter
Networks—R
Priest
Reaching Children at Risk
Sharing the Practice—R
Small Group Dynamics
Vital Ministry
Youthworker—R

TEEN/YOUNG ADULT

Breakaway—R
Certainty
Challenge (GA) —R
Challenge (IL)
Essential Connection—R

Guideposts for Teens—R
Insight—R
Real Time—R
Straight—R
Student Leadership—R
Teens on Target—R
YOU!—R
Young Christian—R
Youth Challenge—R

WOMEN

Esprit—R
Helping Hand—R
Just Between Us—R
Kansas City Woman
Keepers at Home
Lutheran Woman Today
Today's Christian Woman
Wesleyan Woman—R
Women Today—R
Women Today Online—R

WRITERS

Byline
Canadian Writer's Jour—R
Christian Communicator—R
Cross & Quill—R
Exchange—R
NW Christian Author
Once Upon a Time
Songwriter—R
Southwestern Writers—R
VA Christian Writer—R
WIN-Informer
Writer's Digest—R
Writer's Exchange—R
Writer's Forum (OH)—R
Writer's Guidelines/News
Writer's Ink—R

HUMOR

ADULT/GENERAL

About Such Things—R
Accent on Living—R
Alive!—R
alive now!
Angels on Earth
AXIOS—R
Catholic Digest—R
Catholic Forester—R
Catholic Parent
CBA Frontline
CGA World—R
Charisma/Christian Life
Chicken Soup/Mother—R
Chicken Soup/Single—R
Chicken Soup/Woman—R

Christian Chronicle—R
Christian C.L. RECORD—R
Christian Computing—R
Christian Edge—R
Christian Home & School
Christian Living—R
Christian Motorsports
Christian Parenting—R
Christian Ranchman
Christian Reader—R
Church Herald/Holiness—R
Church of God EVANGEL
Companion
Connecting Point—R
Covenant Companion—R
Day Star Tribune—R
Disciple's Journal—R
Door—R(satire)
Dovetail—R
Emphasis/Faith & Living—R
Faith Today
Family Digest
Family Journal—R
Family Network—R
Fellowship Link—R
Gem—R
Good News (AL)—R
Good News, Etc.—R
Good News Journal (MO)—R
Good News Journal (TX)
Gospel Today
Growing in Christ
Head to Head—R
Healing Inn—R
Hearing Hearts
Home Times—R
Impact Magazine—R
Indian Life—R
Inland NW Christian
John Milton—R
Jour/Christian Nursing—R
Legions of Light—R
Life Gate—R
Light and Life
Lifeglow—R
Liguorian
Live—R
Living—R
Living Light News—R
Living with Teenagers—R
Lookout—R
Lutheran—R
Lutheran Digest—R
Lutheran Journal—R
Lutheran Witness—R
Marriage Partnership
Mature Living
Mennonite—R

MESSAGE/Open Bible—R
Messenger/St. Anthony
Michigan Christian
Minnesota Christian—R
New Moon—R
Our Family—R
Over the Back Fence—R
ParentLife—R
Pegasus Review—R
Pentecostal Testimony—R
Peoples Magazine—R
PrayerWorks—R
Presbyterian Record—R
Presbyterians Today—R
Preserving Christian Homes—
    R
Pursuit—R
Religious Broadcasting—R
Right Road—R
Seek—R
Single Connection—R
Single-Parent Family
Smart Families
Smile—R
Sojourners
Something Better—R
Standard—R
Stand Firm—R
Today's Christian Senior—R
Upsouth—R
Visitation
War Cry—R
Weavings—R

CHILDREN

Club Connection—R
Courage
Discovery (NY)—R
Focus/Clubhouse
Focus/Clubhouse Jr
GUIDE—R
High Adventure—R
Live Wire—R
My Friend
On the Line—R
Power & Light—R
Touch—R
Trails 'N' Treasures—R
Wonder Time

CHRISTIAN EDUCATION/LIBRARY

CE Connection—R
Children's Ministry
Christian Classroom
Christian School
Christian School Admin.
GROUP

Leader/Church School
    Today—R
Teachers in Focus—R
Teacher's Interaction
Team—R
Vision—R

MISSIONS

Areopagus—R
Women of the Harvest
World Christian—R
World Mission People—R
Worldwide Challenge

MUSIC

Church Pianist, etc.
Creator—R
Quest—R
Songwriter—R

PASTORS/LEADERS

Art+Plus
Catholic Servant
Cell Life FORUM—R
Christian Camp—R
Christian Ministry
Clergy Journal—R
Enrichment—R
Evangelical Baptist—R
Five Stones—R
Journal/Christian Healing—R
Leadership Journal—R
Let's Worship
Minister's Family
Ministries Today
Ministry & Liturgy—R
Ministry Now
Networks—R
Preacher's Illus. Service—R
Priest
Sharing the Practice—R
Small Group Dynamics
Today's Parish
Vital Ministry
WCA News—R

TEEN/YOUNG ADULT

Breakaway—R
Brio
Certainty
Challenge (IL)
Conqueror—R
Devo'Zine—R
Essential Connection—R
Guideposts for Teens—R
Insight—R
Listen—R
Real Time—R

Straight—R
Teen Life—R
With—R
YOU!—R
Young Adult Today
Young & Alive—R
Young Salvationist—R

WOMEN

Aspire
Esprit—R
Helping Hand—R
Horizons—R
Joyful Woman—R
Just Between Us—R
Lutheran Woman's Quar.
Lutheran Woman Today
Proverbs 31 Homemaker—R
Today's Christian Woman
Virtue—R
Virtuous Woman
Wesleyan Woman—R
Woman's Touch—R
Women of Spirit—R

WRITERS

Byline
Canadian Writer's Jour—R
Exchange—R
Once Upon a Time—R
WIN-Informer
Writer's Guidelines/News
Writers' Intl. Forum
Writer's Potpourri—R

INSPIRATIONAL

ADULT/GENERAL

A.M.E. Christian Recorder—R
Angels on Earth
Annals of St. Anne
Arlington Catholic
Banner
Believer—R
Bible Advocate—R
Bible Advocate Online—R
Bread of Life—R
Breakthrough Intercessor—R
Bridal Guides—R
Catholic Answer
Catholic Digest—R
Catholic Faith & Family—R
Catholic Forester—R
Catholic Parent
CBA Frontline
Celebrate Life—R
CGA World—R
Charisma/Christian Life

Chicken Soup/Mother—R
Chicken Soup/Single—R
Chicken Soup/Woman—R
Christian Arts Review
Christian Chronicle—R
Christian Edge—R
Christian Living—R
Christian Motorsports
Christian Parenting—R
Christian Reader—R
Church Advocate—R
Church Herald/Holiness—R
Church of God EVANGEL
Common Boundary
Companion
Companions—R
Connecting Point—R
Covenant Companion—R
Day Star Tribune—R
Decision
Emphasis/Faith & Living—R
Evangel—R
Family Digest
Fellowship Link—R
Family Network—R
Forefront
Foursquare World—R
Gem—R
God's Revivalist
Good News (AL)—R
Good News(KY)—R
Good News Journal (MO)—R
Good News Journal (TX)
Gospel Today
Gospel Tract—R
Guideposts
Head to Head—R
Healing Inn—R
Hearing Hearts
Heartlight Internet—R
Highway News—R
Home Times—R
Ideals—R
Indian Life—R
Inland NW Christian
Inspirer—R
Jewel Among Jewels—R
John Milton—R
Jour/Christian Nursing—R
Keys to Living—R
Legions of Light—R
Life Gate—R
Lifeglow—R
Light and Life
L.I.G.H.T News—R
Liguorian
Live—R
Living—R

Living Light News—R
Living with Teenagers—R
Lookout—R
Lutheran—R
Lutheran Digest—R
Lutheran Journal—R
Lutheran Witness—R
Marian Helpers—R
Marriage Partnership
Mature Living
Mature Years—R
Mennonite Brethren—R
MESSAGE
MESSAGE/Open Bible—R
Messenger/Sacred Heart
Messenger/St. Anthony
Michigan Christian
New Covenant
New Heart—R
New Moon—R
New Writing—R
Northwestern Lutheran—R
Oblates
On Mission
Our Sunday Visitor
Over the Back Fence—R
ParentLife—R
Pegasus Review—R
Pentecostal Evangel
Pentecostal Testimony—R
Peoples Magazine—R
Plain Truth—R
Plenty Good Room
Plowman—R
Plus—R
Pourastan—R
Power for Living—R
PrayerWorks—R
Presbyterian Record—R
Presbyterians Today—R
Preserving Christian Homes—
      R
Purpose—R
Queen of All Hearts
Right Road—R
Romantic—R
Sacred Journey—R
St. Joseph's Messenger—R
Seek—R
Shantyman—R
Smart Families
Smile—R
Sojourners
Something Better—R
Standard—R
Stand Firm—R
Sursum Corda!—R
TEAK Roundup—R

Time of Singing—R
Today's Christian Senior—R
Together—R
Total Health
2-Soar—R
United Church Observer
Upscale Magazine
Upsouth—R
U.S. Catholic
Vision—R
Visitation
War Cry—R
Way of St. Francis—R
Weavings—R
Wesleyan Advocate—R
Worldwide Challenge

CHILDREN

BREAD/God's Children—R
Club Connection—R
CLUBHOUSE—R
Discovery (NY)—R
Guideposts for Kids
High Adventure—R
Partners—R
Power & Light—R
Touch—R
Wonder Time

CHRISTIAN EDUCATION/LIBRARY

Brigade Leader—R
CE Connection—R
CE Counselor—R
Children's Ministry
Christian Classroom
Christian School
Christian School Admin.
Church & Synagogue Lib.
GROUP
Journal/Adventist Educ.—R
Junior Teacher—R
Leader/Church School
      Today—R
Perspective—R
Shining Star
Teacher's Interaction
Vision—R

MISSIONS

American Horizon—R
Areopagus—R
Latin American Evangelist
Message of the Cross—R
Quiet Hour Echoes

MUSIC

Creator—R
Quest—R

Senior Musician—R
Songwriter—R

PASTORS/LEADERS
African American Pulpit
Art+Plus
Catholic Servant
Cell Church—R
Cell Life FORUM—R
Christian Camp—R
Christian Management—R
Eucharistic Minister—R
Evangelical Baptist—R
Journal/Christian Healing—R
Journal/Pastoral Care
Leadership Journal—R
Minister's Family
Ministry
Networks—R
Preacher's Magazine—R
Priest
PROCLAIM—R
Reaching Children at Risk
Resource—R
Sharing the Practice—R
Today's Christian Preacher—R
Voice of the Vineyard —R

TEEN/YOUNG ADULT
Breakaway—R
Challenge (GA) —R
Conqueror—R
Devo'Zine—R
Essential Connection—R
Guideposts for Teens—R
Insight—R
Real Time—R
Straight—R
Teenage Christian—R
Teen Life—R
Teens on Target—R
Today's Christian Teen—R
With—R
YOU!—R
Young Adult Today
Young & Alive—R
Young Christian—R
Youth Challenge—R

WOMEN
Adam's Rib—R
Aspire
Esprit—R
Helping Hand—R
Horizons—R
Journey—R
Joyful Woman—R
Just Between Us

Kansas City Woman
Keepers at Home
Lutheran Woman's Quar.
Lutheran Woman Today
Proverbs 31 Homemaker—R
Sisters Today
Today's Christian Woman
Virtue—R
Virtuous Woman
Wesleyan Woman—R
Woman's Touch—R
Women Alive!—R
Women of Spirit—R
Women Today—R
Women Today Online—R

WRITERS
Byline
Canadian Writer's Jour—R
Fellowscript—R
Once Upon a Time—R
VA Christian Writer—R
Writer's Digest—R
Writer's Forum (OH)—R
Writer's Guidelines/News
Writers' Intl. Forum

INTERVIEWS/PROFILES

ADULT/GENERAL
About Such Things—R
Accent on Living—R
AGAIN—R
Alive!—R
A.M.E. Christian Recorder—R
American Tract Soc.—R
Anglican Journal—R
Arkansas Catholic
Arlington Catholic
AXIOS—R
Breakthrough Intercessor—R
Canadian Catholic
Canadian Mennonite
Catholic Digest—R
Catholic Faith & Family—R
Catholic New York
Catholic Parent
Catholic Sentinel—R
Celebrate Life—R
Charisma/Christian Life
Christian Arts Review
Christian Chronicle—R
Christian C.L. RECORD—R
Christian Courier (WI)—R
Christian Courier (CAN)—R
Christian Edge—R
Christian Motorsports
Christian News NW—R

Christian Parenting—R
Christian Ranchman
Christian Reader—R
Christianity Today—R
Church Advocate—R
Church & State—R
Columbia
Companion
Cornerstone—R (music)
Creation Ex Nihilo
Culture Wars—R
Day Star Tribune—R
Discipleship Journal
Door
Episcopal Life—R
Expression Christian
Faith Today
Family Digest
Focus on the Family
Forefront
Good News (AL)—R
Good News(KY)—R
Good News, Etc—R
Good News Journal (MO)—R
Good News Journal (TX)
Gospel Today
Grail
Green Cross—R
Guideposts
Head to Head—R
Healing Inn—R
Hearing Hearts
Heartlight Internet—R
Hidden Manna—R
Homeschooling Today—R
Home Times—R
Impact Magazine—R
Indian Life—R
Inside Journal—R
Interim—R
John Milton—R
Jour/Christian Nursing—R
Joyful Noise
Legions of Light—R
Life@Work
Lifeglow—R
Light and Life
Liguorian
Living—R
Living Church
Living Light News—R
Living with Teenagers—R
Lookout—R
Lutheran—R
Lutheran Journal—R
Lutheran Witness—R
Marriage Partnership
Mature Years—R

Mennonite—R
Mennonite Historian—R
MESSAGE
Messenger
Messenger/St. Anthony
Metro Voice—R
Michigan Christian
Minnesota Christian—R
Montana Catholic—R
New Covenant
New Creation
New Heart—R
New Moon—R
New Writing—R
NW Christian Journal—R
On Mission
Our Sunday Visitor
Over the Back Fence—R
Physician
Plain Truth—R
Plenty Good Room
Poetry Forum—R
Poet's Page
Power for Living—R
Presbyterian Layman
Presbyterian Outlook
Presbyterian Record—R
Presbyterians Today—R
Prism—R
ProLife News—R
Pursuit—R
Quiet Revolution—R
Re:generation
Religious Broadcasting—R
Sacred Journey—R
St. Anthony Messenger
SCP Journal—R
Signs of the Times—R
Single Connection—R
Single-Parent Family
Sojourners
Something Better—R
Standard—R
Stand Firm—R
Stewardship
Sursum Corda!—R
TEAK Roundup—R
Today's Christian Senior—R
Together—R
Trumpeter—R
United Church Observer
Upscale Magazine
Upsouth—R
U.S. Catholic
Visitation
War Cry—R

CHILDREN
Discovery(NY)—R
Focus/Clubhouse
Guideposts for Kids
Live Wire—R
Pockets—R
Skipping Stones
Touch—R

CHRISTIAN EDUCATION/LIBRARY
Brigade Leader—R
Children's Ministry
CE Counselor—R
Christian Educators Jour—R
Christian School
Church Libraries—R
GROUP
Leader/Church School
   Today—R
Perspective—R
Teachers in Focus—R
Vision—R

MISSIONS
American Horizon—R
Catholic Near East
East-West Church
Evangelical Missions—R
Latin American Evangelist
Leaders for Today
PFI World Report—R
So All May Hear—R
Urban Mission—R
Women of the Harvest
World Christian—R
World Mission People—R
Worldwide Challenge

MUSIC
Church Music World
Gospel Industry Today
Lighthouse Electronic
Quest—R
Songwriter—R

PASTORS/LEADERS
Catholic Servant
Cell Church—R
Christian Camp—R
Christian Management—R
Church Bytes—R
Clergy Journal—R
Cross Currents—R
Five Stones—R
Ivy Jungle Report—R
Journal/Christian Healing—R
Jour/Amer Soc/Chur Growth—
   R

Leadership Journal—R
Lutheran Partners—R
Ministries Today
Ministry & Liturgy—R
Ministry Now
Networks—R
Preacher—R
Preacher's Magazine—R
PROCLAIM—R
Reaching Children at Risk
Sabbath School Leadership
Technologies/Worship—R
Voice of the Vineyard —R
WCA News—R
Youthworker—R

TEEN/YOUNG ADULT
Breakaway—R
Challenge (GA) —R
Devo'Zine—R
Essential Connection—R
Guideposts for Teens—R
Insight—R
Real Time—R
Sharing the VICTORY—R
Spirit
Straight—R
Teenage Christian—R
Teen Life—R
YOU!—R
Young Adult Today
Young & Alive—R
Young Salvationist—R

WOMEN
Aspire
Church Woman
Esprit—R
Horizons—R
Jour/Women's Ministries
Journey—R
Kansas City Woman
Lutheran Woman Today
Proverbs 31 Homemaker—R
Virtue—R

WRITERS
Advanced Christian Writer—R
Canadian Writer's Jour—R
Christian Communicator—R
Cross & Quill—R
Exchange—R
Fellowscript—R
Inklings
NW Christian Author—R
Once Upon a Time—R
Songwriter—R
Southwestern Writers—R

WIN-Informer
Writer On Line—R
Writer's Guidelines/News
Writer's Info
Writer's Ink—R
Writer's Potpourri—R

LEADERSHIP

ADULT/GENERAL

A.M.E. Christian Recorder—R
Angels on Earth
Atlantic Baptist
Banner
Believer—R
Bible Advocate—R
Breakthrough Intercessor—R
Catholic Forester—R
CGA World—R
Christian Century
Christian Chronicle—R
Christian Edge—R
Christian Living—R
Christian Motorsports
Christian Ranchman
Christians in Business
Church Advocate—R
Church Herald/Holiness—R
Companion
Covenant Companion—R
Culture Wars—R
Day Star Tribune—R
Decision
Discipleship Journal
Disciple's Journal—R
Dovetail—R
Emphasis/Faith & Living—R
Evangel—R
Expression Christian
Faith Today
Family Network—R
Forefront
Foursquare World—R
Good News(KY)—R
Good News, Etc—R
Good News Journal (TX)
Gospel Tidings—R
Gospel Today
Hearing Hearts
Heartlight Internet—R
Home Times—R
Inland NW Christian
John Milton—R
Jour/Christian Nursing—R
Light and Life
Living Church
Living Light News—R
Lookout—R

Lutheran Journal—R
Michigan Christian
NW Christian Journal—R
Our Family—R
Our Sunday Visitor
Perspectives
Pourastan—R
Presbyterian Layman
Presbyterian Outlook
Presbyterian Record—R
Prism—R
Purpose—R
Re:generation
Religious Broadcasting—R
Religious Education
Single Connection—R
Something Better—R
Stand Firm—R
Trumpeter—R
United Church Observer
Way of St. Francis—R
Weavings—R

CHILDREN

BREAD/God's Children—R
Club Connection—R
Discovery(NY)—R
Guideposts for Kids

CHRISTIAN EDUCATION/LIBRARY

Baptist Leader—R
Brigade Leader—R
CE Connection—R
CE Connection
  Communique—R
CE Counselor—R
CE Leadership—R
Children's Ministry
Christian Classroom
Christian School Admin.
Church Educator—R
GROUP
Leader/Church School
  Today—R
Perspective—R
Resource—R
Teacher's Interaction
Team—R
Vision—R

MISSIONS

American Horizon—R
Catholic Near East
East-West Church
Latin American Evangelist
Leaders for Today
Missiology
Urban Mission—R

Worldwide Challenge

PASTORS/LEADERS

African American Pulpit
Catholic Servant
Cell Church—R
Cell Life FORUM—R
Christian Camp—R
Christian Century
Christian Management—R
Christian Ministry
Church Bytes—R
Church Growth Network—R
Church Management—R
Church Worship
Clergy Journal—R
Current Thoughts & Trends
Emmanuel
Enrichment—R
Evangelical Baptist—R
Five Stones—R
Ivy Jungle Report—R
Journal/Christian Healing—R
Jour/Amer Soc/Chur Growth—
  R
Leadership Journal—R
Lutheran Partners—R
Minister's Family
Ministries Today
Ministry
Ministry Now
Pastoral Life
Preacher—R
Preacher's Magazine—R
Priest
Reaching Children at Risk
Resource—R
Sabbath School Leadership
Sharing the Practice—R
Today's Christian Preacher—R
Vital Ministry
Voice of the Vineyard —R
WCA News—R
Word & World
Worship Leader
Your Church—R
Youthworker—R

TEEN/YOUNG ADULT

Challenge (GA) —R
Essential Connection—R
Student Leadership—R
Teenage Christian—R
YOU!—R
Young Christian—R

WOMEN

Aspire

Esprit—R
Helping Hand—R
Horizons—R
Insight—R
Just Between Us—R
Sisters Today
Virtuous Woman
Woman's Touch—R
Women of Spirit—R

LITURGICAL

ADULT/GENERAL

AGAIN—R
alive now!
A.M.E. Christian Recorder—R
Arkansas Catholic
Arlington Catholic
Banner
Breakthrough Intercessor—R
Canadian Catholic
Catholic Digest—R
Catholic Insight
Catholic Parent
CGA World—R
Christian Century
Christian Motorsports
Commonweal
Companion
Company—R
Cresset
Culture Wars—R
Episcopal Life—R
John Milton—R
Living Church
Lutheran Journal—R
Messenger (KY)
Messenger/ Sacred Heart
Messenger/St. Anthony
New Writing—R
North American Voice
Our Family—R
Our Sunday Visitor
Perspectives
Prairie Messenger—R
St. Anthony Messenger
St. Willibrord Journal
Silver Wings—R
Standard—R
Touchstone—R
U.S. Catholic
Way of St. Francis—R
Weavings—R

CHRISTIAN EDUCATION/LIBRARY

Catechist
Church Educator—R
Parish Teacher

Religion Teacher's Journal

MISSIONS

Areopagus—R
Catholic Near East

MUSIC

Church Pianist, etc.
Gospel Industry Today
Hymn

PASTORS/LEADERS

Catholic Servant
Catechumenate
Celebration
Christian Century
Christian Ministry
Church Administration
Church Bytes—R
Church Worship
Current Thoughts & Trends
Diocesan Dialogue—R
Emmanuel
Eucharistic Minister—R
Journal/Christian Healing—R
Leadership Journal—R
Let's Worship
Lutheran Forum—R
Lutheran Partners—R
Ministries Today
Ministry & Liturgy—R
Parish Liturgy
Pastoral Life
Preacher's Illus. Service—R
Preacher's Magazine—R
Priest
PROCLAIM—R
Quarterly Review
Reformed Worship
Theology Today
Today's Parish
Word & World
Worship Leader

TEENS/YOUNG ADULT

YOU!—R
Youth Update

WOMEN

Lutheran Woman Today
Sisters Today

MARRIAGE

ADULT/GENERAL

Accent on Living—R
Alive!—R
A.M.E. Christian Recorder—R

America
American Tract Soc.—R
Angels on Earth
Arkansas Catholic
Arlington Catholic
Atlantic Baptist
AXIOS—R
Banner
Believer—R
Bible Advocate—R
Bread of Life—R
Breakthrough Intercessor—R
Bridal Guides—R
Canadian Catholic
Catholic Digest—R
Catholic Faith & Family—R
Catholic Forester—R
Catholic Parent
Celebrate Life—R
Charisma/Christian Life
Chicken Soup/Mother—R
Chicken Soup/Woman—R
Christian C.L. RECORD—R
Christian Courier (CAN)—R
Christian Edge—R
Christian Home & School
Christian Living—R
Christian Motorsports
Christian Parenting—R
Christian Ranchman
Christian Reader—R
Church Advocate—R
Church Herald/Holiness—R
Columbia
Common Boundary
Companion
Companions—R
Cornerstone—R
Covenant Companion—R
Culture Wars—R
Day Star Tribune—R
Decision
Discipleship Journal
Disciple's Journal—R
Dovetail—R
Emphasis/Faith & Living—R
Evangel—R
Expression Christian
Faith Today
Family Digest
Family Network—R
Focus on the Family
Foursquare World—R
Gem—R
Good News (AL)—R
Good News, Etc—R
Good News Journal (MO)—R
Good News Journal (TX)

Gospel Tidings—R
Gospel Today
Guideposts
Head to Head—R
Hearing Hearts
Heartlight Internet—R
Highway News—R
Home Times—R
Impact Magazine—R
Indian Life—R
Inside Journal—R
Interim—R
Joyful Noise
Life Gate—R
Lifeglow—R
Light and Life
Liguorian
Live—R
Living—R
Living Light News—R
Lookout—R
Lutheran—R
Lutheran Digest—R
Lutheran Journal—R
Lutheran Witness—R
Marriage Partnership
Mennonite—R
Mennonite Brethren—R
MESSAGE
MESSAGE/Open Bible—R
Messenger/St. Anthony
Metro Voice—R
Michigan Christian
Minnesota Christian—R
Montana Catholic—R
Moody—R
New Covenant
North American Voice
Northwestern Lutheran—R
NW Christian Journal—R
On Mission
Our Family—R
Our Sunday Visitor
Pegasus Review—R
Pentecostal Evangel
Pentecostal Testimony—R
Peoples Magazine—R
Physician
Plain Truth—R
Plus—R
Pourastan—R
Prairie Messenger—R
PrayerWorks—R
Presbyterian Layman
Presbyterian Record—R
Presbyterians Today—R
Preserving Christian Homes—
   R

Prism—R
Progress—R
Purpose—R
Re:generation
Right Road—R
Romantic—R
St. Anthony Messenger
Seek—R
Signs of the Times—R
Social Justice
Something Better—R
Standard—R
Standard—R
Stand Firm—R
Star of Zion
Together—R
Trumpeter—R
2-Soar—R
Upsouth—R
U.S. Catholic
Vibrant Life—R
Vision—R
War Cry—R
Wesleyan Advocate—R

CHRISTIAN EDUCATION/LIBRARY

CE Connection—R
Children's Ministry
GROUP

MISSIONS

Quiet Hour Echoes
Worldwide Challenge

PASTORS/LEADERS

African American Pulpit
Art+Plus
Catholic Servant
Cell Church—R
Current Thoughts & Trends
Five Stones—R
Journal/Christian Healing—R
Journal/Pastoral Care
Let's Worship
Lutheran Forum—R
Lutheran Partners—R
Minister's Family
Ministries Today
Networks—R
Pastoral Life
Preacher—R
Preacher's Illus. Service—R
PROCLAIM—R
Pulpit Helps—R
Sharing the Practice—R
Today's Christian Preacher—R
Today's Parish
Vital Ministry

Voice of the Vineyard —R
Word & World

TEEN/YOUNG ADULT

Insight—R
Today's Christian Teen—R
YOU!—R
Young Adult Today
Young & Alive—R
Young Christian—R
Youth Update

WOMEN

Adam's Rib—R
Aspire
Anna's Journal—R
Esprit—R
Hearth
Helping Hand—R
Horizons—R
Journey—R
Joyful Woman—R
Just Between Us—R
Lutheran Woman's Quar.
Lutheran Woman Today
Proverbs 31 Homemaker—R
Today's Christian Woman
True Woman
Virtue—R
Virtuous Woman
Welcome Home
Woman's Touch—R
Women Alive!—R
Women of Spirit—R

WRITERS

Writers' Intl. Forum

MEN'S ISSUES

ADULT/GENERAL

Advent Christian Witness—R
A.M.E. Christian Recorder—R
American Tract Soc.—R
Annals of St. Anne
Arlington Catholic
Atlantic Baptist
AXIOS—R
Banner
Bible Advocate—R
Bread of Life—R
Breakthrough Intercessor—R
Catholic Digest—R
Catholic Forester—R
Catholic Parent
CBA Marketplace
Charisma/Christian Life
Christian Edge—R

Christian Living—R
Christian Motorsports
Christian News NW—R
Christian Ranchman
Christian Social Action—R
Chrysalis Reader
Church Herald/Holiness—R
Church of God EVANGEL
Columbia
Common Boundary
Companion
Day Star Tribune—R
Decision
Discipleship Journal
Disciple's Journal—R
Discovery—R
Emphasis/Faith & Living—R
Evangel—R
Expression Christian
Family Network—R
Focus on the Family
Foursquare World—R
Gem—R
Good News (AL)—R
Good News, Etc—R
Good News Journal (MO)—R
Gospel Today
Healing Inn—R
Hearing Hearts
Heartlight Internet—R
Highway News—R
Home Times—R
Indian Life—R
Inland NW Christian
Inside Journal—R
Interim—R
Jour/Christian Nursing—R
Joyful Noise
Life Gate—R
Liguorian
Light and Life
Living—R
Living Light News—R
Lookout—R
Marriage Partnership
Mennonite—R
Messenger/St. Anthony
Metro Voice—R
Michigan Christian
Moody—R
Newsline—R
Northwestern Lutheran—R
Our Family—R
Pentecostal Testimony—R
Peoples Magazine—R
Physician
Plain Truth—R
Plus—R

PrayerWorks—R
Presbyterian Outlook
Preserving Christian Homes—R
Prism—R
Purpose—R
Re:generation
Romantic—R
Single Connection—R
Smart Families
Something Better—R
Standard—R
Stand Firm—R
Star of Zion
Together—R
Touchstone—R
Trumpeter—R
2-Soar—R
United Church Observer
Upsouth—R
Vibrant Life—R (health)

CHRISTIAN EDUCATION/LIBRARY

Brigade Leader—R
CE Connection—R

MISSIONS

American Horizon—R
Brigade Leader—R
Worldwide Challenge

MUSIC

Quest—R

PASTORS/LEADERS

Art+Plus
Christian Ministry
Current Thoughts & Trends
Journal/Pastoral Care
Lutheran Partners—R
Ministries Today
Preacher—R
Preacher's Magazine—R
Pulpit Helps—R
Sharing the Practice—R
Today's Christian Preacher—R
Voice of the Vineyard —R
Word & World

TEEN/YOUNG ADULT

Challenge (GA) —R
YOU!—R

WOMEN

Aspire
Horizons—R
Virtue—R

WRITERS
Writers' Intl. Forum

MIRACLES

ADULT/GENERAL

A.M.E. Christian Recorder—R
America
Angels on Earth
Bible Advocate—R
Bread of Life—R
Breakthrough Intercessor—R
Canadian Catholic
Catholic Digest—R
CGA World—R
Charisma/Christian Life
Christian Chronicle—R
Christian Edge—R
Christian Motorsports
Christian Ranchman
Church Advocate—R
Church Herald/Holiness—R
Church of God EVANGEL
Common Boundary
Companion
Connecting Point—R
Day Star Tribune—R
Creation Ex Nihilo
Culture Wars—R
Family Network—R
God's Revivalist
Good News (AL)—R
Good News, Etc—R
Good News Journal (MO)—R
Gospel Today
Guideposts
Hallelujah! (CAN)—R
Healing Inn—R
Home Times—R
Impact Magazine—R
John Milton—R
Lifeglow—R
Light and Life
Liguorian
Lutheran Digest—R
Messenger/St. Anthony
Michigan Christian
North American Voice
Pegasus Review—R
Plain Truth—R
PrayerWorks—R
Preserving Christian Homes—R
Queen of All Hearts
Right Road—R
Single Connection—R
Something Better—R
Standard—R

Total Health
2-Soar—R
Upsouth—R
Vision—R
Weavings—R

CHILDREN

BREAD/God's Children—R
Discovery (NY)—R
GUIDE—R
Guideposts for Kids
Leader/Church School
    Today—R

MISSIONS

American Horizon—R
Areopagus—R
So All May Hear—R

PASTORS/LEADERS

Art+Plus
Journal/Christian Healing—R
Lutheran Partners—R
Ministries Today
Networks—R
Voice of the Vineyard —R
Word & World

TEEN/YOUNG ADULT

Conqueror—R
Guideposts for Teens—R
Insight—R
With—R
YOU!—R
Young Adult Today
Young & Alive—R
Young Christian—R

WOMEN

Helping Hand—R
Lutheran Woman Today
Woman's Touch—R

MISSIONS

ADULT/GENERAL

Alive!—R
A.M.E. Christian Recorder—R
Anglican Journal—R
Banner
Baptist Informer
B.C. Catholic—R
Believer—R
Bible Advocate—R
Breakthrough Intercessor—R
Canadian Catholic
Canadian Mennonite
Catholic Digest—R

Charisma/Christian Life
Christian Chronicle—R
Christian Edge—R
Christian Motorsports
Christian News NW—R
Christian Ranchman
Christian Reader—R
Christianity Today—R
Church Advocate—R
Church Herald/Holiness—R
Church of God EVANGEL
Companion
Companions—R
Connecting Point—R
Conquest
Culture Wars—R
Day Star Tribune—R
Discipleship Journal
Decision
Emphasis/Faith & Living—R
Episcopal Life—R
Faith Today
Family Network—R
Gem—R
Good News (AL)—R
Good News (KY)—R
Good News, Etc—R
Good News Journal (MO)—R
Gospel Today
Hallelujah! (CAN)—R
Healing Inn—R
Indian Life—R
John Milton—R
Jour/Christian Nursing—R
Life Gate—R
Light and Life
Live—R
Living Church
Lookout—R
Lutheran—R
Lutheran Journal—R
Lutheran Witness—R
MESSAGE/Open Bible—R
Messenger/St. Anthony
Michigan Christian
New Heart—R (medical)
North American Voice
On Mission
Our Family—R
Our Sunday Visitor
Pentecostal Testimony—R
Peoples Magazine—R
Power for Living—R
PrayerWorks—R
Presbyterian Layman
Presbyterian Outlook
Presbyterian Record—R
Presbyterians Today—R

Prism—R
Purpose—R
Queen of All Hearts
Re:generation
Right Road—R
Single Connection—R
Something Better—R
Standard—R
Standard—R
Stand Firm—R
TEAK Roundup—R
2-Soar—R
Upsouth—R
Vision—R

CHILDREN

BREAD/God's Children—R
Discovery(NY)—R
Counselor—R
Lad
Partners—R
Power Station—R

CHRISTIAN EDUCATION/LIBRARY

Brigade Leader—R
Children's Ministry
Church Educator—R
Courage
Evangelizing Today's Child—R
GROUP
Leader/Church School
    Today—R
Perspective—R
Shining Star

MISSIONS

(See alphabetical listings)

MUSIC

Quest—R

PASTORS/LEADERS

Art+Plus
Christian Management—R
Christian Ministry
Church Administration
Current Thoughts & Trends
Emmanuel
Enrichment—R
Evangelical Baptist—R
Journal/Christian Healing—R
Lutheran Partners—R
Ministries Today
Networks—R
Preacher's Magazine—R
Priest
PROCLAIM—R
Pulpit Helps—R

Quarterly Review
Resource—R
Sharing the Practice—R
Today's Christian Preacher—R
Vital Ministry
Voice of the Vineyard —R
Word & World
Youthworker—R

TEEN/YOUNG ADULT

Certainty
Challenge (GA) —R
Challenge (IL)
Conqueror—R
Devo'Zine—R
Essential Connection—R
Insight—R
Real Time—R
Student Leadership—R
With—R
YOU!—R
Young Adult Today
Young Salvationist—R

WOMEN

Aspire
CoLaborer—R
Esprit—R
Horizons—R
Joyful Woman—R
Just Between Us—R
Lutheran Woman Today
WIN-Informer

MONEY MANAGEMENT

ADULT/GENERAL

A.M.E. Christian Recorder—R
Anglican Journal—R
AXIOS—R
Banner
Believer—R
Brethren Evangelist
Bridal Guides—R
Catholic Forester—R
Catholic Parent
CBA Marketplace
CGA World—R
Christian C.L. RECORD—R
Christian Edge—R
Christian Living—R
Christian Motorsports
Christian Parenting—R
Christian Ranchman
Christians in Business
Church Advocate—R
Church Herald/Holiness—R
Connecting Point—R

Conquest
Day Star Tribune—R
Decision
Disciple's Journal—R
Discovery—R
Evangel—R
Expression Christian
Family Network—R
Good News (AL)—R
Good News Journal (MO)—R
Gospel Today
Head to Head—R
Healing Inn—R
Heartlight Internet—R
Home Times—R
Indian Life—R
Inland NW Christian
Life Gate—R
Lifeglow—R
Light and Life
Living—R
Living Light News—R
Lookout—R
Lutheran Journal—R
Marriage Partnership
MESSAGE
MESSAGE/Open Bible—R
Michigan Christian
No-Debt Living—R
Parent Paper—R
Peoples Magazine—R
Physician
Presbyterian Layman
Preserving Christian Homes—
   R
Religious Broadcasting—R
Right Road—R
Signs of the Times—R
Single Connection—R
Smart Families
Something Better—R
Stand Firm—R
Star of Zion
Stewardship
Today's Christian Senior—R
2-Soar—R
Visitation
War Cry—R

CHILDREN

Courage
Young Christian—R

CHRISTIAN EDUCATION/LIBRARY

CE Connection—R
Children's Ministry
Christian School
Christian School Admin.

Church Educator—R
GROUP

MISSIONS

Quiet Hour Echoes
World Christian—R

PASTORS/LEADERS

Cell Church—R
Christian Ministry
Church Bytes—R
Clergy Journal—R
Enrichment—R
Evangelical Baptist—R
Journal/Christian Healing—R
Ministries Today
Networks—R
Pastor's Tax & Money
Reaching Children at Risk
Sharing the Practice—R
Today's Christian Preacher—R
Today's Parish
Vital Ministry
Your Church—R
Youthworker—R

TEEN/YOUNG ADULT

Certainty
Challenge (GA)—R
Challenge (IL)
Essential Connection—R
Today's Christian Teen—R
Young Adult Today
Young Christian—R

WOMEN

Adam's Rib—R
Aspire
Esprit—R
Horizons—R
Journey—R
Just Between Us—R
Lutheran Woman Today
Proverbs 31 Homemaker—R
True Woman
Virtuous Woman
Woman's Touch—R
Women Today—R
Women Today Online—R

MUSIC REVIEWS

ADULT/GENERAL

Arlington Catholic
Atlantic Baptist
Banner
Canadian Catholic
Catholic Faith & Family—R

CBA Marketplace
Charisma/Christian Life
Christian Arts Review
Christian Edge—R
Christian Media—R
Christian Parenting—R
Christian Renewal—R
Christianity/Arts
Commonweal
Cornerstone—R
Crisis Point
Day Star Tribune—R
Expression Christian
Good News (AL)—R
Good News Journal (MO)—R
Head to Head—R
Heartlight Internet—R
Homeschooling Today—R
Home Times—R
Impact Magazine—R
Interim—R
Life Gate—R
Light and Life
Living Light News—R
Living with Teenagers—R
Mature Years—R
Michigan Christian
MovieGuide
Narrow Gate
On Mission
ParentLife—R
Pentecostal Testimony—R
Plowman—R
Presbyterian Record—R
Prism—R
Re:generation
Single Connection—R
Sojourners
Something Better—R
Stand Firm—R
Star of Zion
TEAK Roundup—R
Trumpeter—R
Upsouth—R

CHILDREN

Club Connection—R

CHRISTIAN EDUCATION/LIBRARY

CE Counselor—R
Church Libraries—R

MUSIC

CCM Magazine
Christian Country—R
Creator—R
Gospel Industry Today
Hymn

Lighthouse Electronic
Quest—R
Release

PASTORS/LEADERS

Ivy Jungle Report—R
Ministries Today
Technologies/Worship—R
WCA News—R
Reformed Worship

TEEN/YOUNG ADULT

Challenge (GA) —R
Devo'Zine—R
Essential Connection—R
Real Time—R
Teenage Christian—R
With—R
YOU!—R
Young Christian—R
Young Salvationist—R

WOMEN

Horizons—R
Kansas City Woman

WRITERS

Inklings

NATURE

ADULT/GENERAL

Alive!—R
AXIOS—R
Canadian Catholic
Catholic Digest—R
Catholic Forester—R
Christian Reader—R
Christian Traveler—R
Chrysalis Reader
Christian Renewal—R
Companion
Creation Ex Nihilo
Day Star Tribune—R
Fellowship Link—R
Good News (AL)—R
Green Cross—R
Ideals—R
Keys to Living—R
Lifeglow—R
Light and Life
Lutheran Digest—R
Messenger/St. Anthony
Over the Back Fence—R
Pegasus Review—R
Pourastan—R
PrayerWorks—R
Right Road—R

Smile—R
TEAK Roundup—R
Time of Singing—R
Today's Christian Senior—R
2-Soar—R
Upsouth—R

CHILDREN

Club Connection—R
Counselor—R
Courage
Crusader—R
Discovery(NY)—R
Discovery Trails—R
GUIDE—R
Guideposts for Kids
Live Wire—R
My Friend
Nature Friend—R
On the Line
Partners—R
Power Station—R
Skipping Stones
Story Friends—R
Touch—R
Young Christian—R

CHRISTIAN EDUCATION/LIBRARY

Leader/Church School
  Today—R
Shining Star

PASTORS/LEADERS

Art+Plus
Christian Camp—R
Journal/Christian Healing—R
Word & World

TEEN/YOUNG ADULT

Challenge (GA) —R
Essential Connection—R
Insight—R
Teenage Christian—R
YOU!—R
Young & Alive—R

WOMEN

Aspire
Esprit—R
Proverbs 31 Homemaker—R

WRITERS

Writers' Intl. Forum

NEWSPAPERS

Alabama Baptist
Anglican Journal

Arkansas Catholic
Arlington Catholic
Awareness TN Christian
Baptist Informer
B.C. Catholic
Believer
Catholic Courier
Catholic Faith & Family
Catholic New York
Catholic Peace Voice
Catholic Sentinel
Catholic Servant
Catholic Telegraph
Christian American
Christian Courier (WI)
Christian Courier (CAN)
Christian Crusade
Christian Edge
Christian Media
Christian News NW
Christian Observer
Christian Ranchman
Christian Renewal
Church Advocate
Dallas/Ft. Worth Heritage
Day Star Tribune
Disciple's Journal
Discovery
Episcopal Life
Expression Christian
Family Journal
Good News (AL)
Good News, Etc.
Good News Journal (MO)
Good News Journal (TX)
Harvest Press
Home Times
Indian Life
Inland NW Christian
Inside Journal
Interchange
Interim
John Milton
Kentucky Christian
Life Gate
Live Wire
Living
Living Light News
Mennonite Weekly
Messenger
Metro Voice
Michigan Christian
Minnesota Christian
Montana Catholic
National Catholic Reporter
Network
NW Christian Journal
Our Sunday Visitor

Parent Paper
PrayerWorks
Presbyterian Layman
Pulpit Helps
Shantyman
Single Connection
So All May Hear
Something Better News
So. CA Christian
Star of Zion
Together
YOU! (teen)

ONLINE MAGAZINES

ADULT/GENERAL
Believer
Bible Advocate Online
Books & Culture
Cathedral Age
Catholic Courier
Catholic Digest
Christian Arts Review
Christian Computing
Christian Home & School
Christian Reader
Christian Single Online
Christianity & the Arts
Comments From the Friends
Company
Cornerstone
Decision
Disaster News Network
Disciple's Journal
Discovery
Head to Head
Heartlight
Interim
Narrow Gate
National Catholic
New Writing
On Mission
Pentecostal Evangel
Pentecostal Testimony
Presbyterians-Week
Prism
Quest
Religious Broadcasting
 St. Anthony Messenger
Seeds
 Sports Spectrum Online
Trumpeter
Uplook
Visions of Glory

CHILDREN
Keys for Kids

MISSIONS
Latin America Evangelist

MUSIC
CCM Magazine
Lighthouse Electronic

PASTORS/LEADERS
Evangelical Baptist
Leadership Journal
Ministry Now
Preacher
Pulpit Helps
Sermon Notes
WCA News
Youthworker

TEEN/YOUNG ADULT
Student Leadership
Young Salvationist

WOMEN
True Woman
Virtuous Woman
Women Today Online

WRITERS
Teachers & Writers
Writers On Line
Writers' Intl. Forum

OPINION PIECES

ADULT/GENERAL
About Such Things—R
Annals of St. Anne
Arlington Catholic
AXIOS—R
Banner
B.C. Catholic—R
Bible Advocate—R
Bridal Guides—R
Canadian Catholic
Canadian Mennonite
Catholic Faith & Family—R
Catholic New York
Charisma/Christian Life
Christian Arts Review
Christian Chronicle—R
Christian Edge—R
Christian Living—R
Christian Motorsports
Christian News NW—R
Christian Renewal—R
Christian Social Action—R
Christianity Today—R
Commonweal
Company—R

Cornerstone—R
Covenant Companion—R
Culture Wars—R
Day Star Tribune—R
Door
Episcopal Life—R
Faith Today
Family Journal—R
Family Network—R
First Things
Good News, Etc—R
Good News Journal (MO)—R
Gospel Today
Grail
Head to Head—R
Healing Inn—R
Home Times—R
Indian Life—R
Inland NW Christian
Interim—R
Jewel Among Jewels—R
Jour/Christian Nursing—R
Light and Life
Living Light News—R
Lutheran—R
Mennonite Brethren—R
Mennonite Weekly
MESSAGE/Open Bible—R
Messenger
Messenger/St. Anthony
Metro Voice—R
Michigan Christian
Minnesota Christian—R
New Creation
New Moon—R
Perspectives
Plain Truth—R
PrayerWorks—R
Presbyterian Outlook
Presbyterian Record—R
Presbyterians Today—R
ProLife News—R
Quiet Revolution—R
Re:generation
Single Connection—R
Social Justice
Sojourners
TEAK Roundup—R
Touchstone—R
United Church Observer
Upsouth—R
U.S. Catholic
Visitation
Way of St. Francis—R

CHRISTIAN EDUCATION/LIBRARY

Christian School Admin.
Today's Catholic Teacher—R

MISSIONS

American Horizon—R
Areopagus—R
East-West Church
So All May Hear—R

MUSIC

Songwriter—R

PASTORS/LEADERS

Cell Life FORUM—R
Christian Century
Christian Ministry
Journal/Christian Healing—R
Journal/Pastoral Care
Lutheran Forum—R
Lutheran Partners—R
Priest
Pulpit Helps—R
Word & World
Worship Leader

TEEN/YOUNG ADULT

Essential Connection—R
Insight—R
YOU!—R
Young Adult Today
Young Christian—R

WOMEN

Anna's Journal—R
Conscience—R
Horizons—R
Lutheran Woman Today

WRITERS

Advanced Christian Writer—R
Canadian Writer's Jour—R
Exchange—R
Once Upon a Time—R
WIN-Informer
Writer's Exchange—R
Writer's Guidelines/News
Writer's Ink—R
Writers' Intl. Forum

PARENTING

ADULT/GENERAL

American Tract Soc.—R
Angels on Earth
Annals of St. Anne
Arkansas Catholic
Arlington Catholic
Atlantic Baptist
AXIOS—R
Banner
Believer—R

Bible Advocate—R
Bread of Life—R
Breakthrough Intercessor—R
Catholic Digest—R
Catholic Faith & Family—R
Catholic Forester—R
Catholic Parent
Catholic Sentinel—R
Celebrate Life—R
Charisma/Christian Life
Chicken Soup/Mother—R
Chicken Soup/Single—R
Chicken Soup/Woman—R
Christian Courier (CAN)—R
Christian Home & School
Christian Living—R
Christian Motorsports
Christian Parenting—R
Christian Ranchman
Christian Renewal—R
Church Advocate—R
Church Herald/Holiness—R
Columbia
Companion
Companions—R
Covenant Companion—R
Crisis Point
Culture Wars—R
Day Star Tribune—R
Decision
Discipleship Journal
Disciple's Journal—R
Dovetail—R
Emphasis/Faith & Living—R
Evangel—R
Expression Christian
Family Digest
Family Network—R
Focus on the Family
Foursquare World—R
Gem—R
God's Revivalist
Good News (AL)—R
Good News, Etc—R
Good News Journal (MO)—R
Good News Journal (TX)
Gospel Tidings—R
Gospel Today
Green Cross—R
Hearing Hearts
Heartlight Internet—R
Highway News—R
Homeschooling Today—R
Home Times—R
Impact Magazine—R
Indian Life—R
Inside Journal—R
Interim—R

Jewel Among Jewels—R
Life Gate—R
Light and Life
Liguorian
Live—R
Living—R
Living Light News—R
Living with Teenagers—R
Lookout—R
Lutheran—R
Lutheran Digest—R
Lutheran Journal—R
Marriage Partnership
Mennonite—R
Mennonite Brethren—R
MESSAGE
Messenger/St. Anthony
Metro Voice—R
Michigan Christian
Moody—R
MovieGuide
New Covenant
New Moon—R
On Mission
Our Family—R
Our Sunday Visitor
ParentLife—R
Parent Paper—R
Pegasus Review—R
Pentecostal Evangel
Peoples Magazine—R
Plain Truth—R
Plus—R
Pourastan—R
Power for Living—R
PrayerWorks—R
Presbyterians Today—R
Preserving Christian Homes—R
Progress—R
Purpose—R
Pursuit—R
Real FamilyLife
Religious Education
Right Road—R
Sacred Journey—R
St. Anthony Messenger
St. Joseph's Messenger—R
Seek—R
Single-Parent Family
Smart Families
Social Justice
Sojourners
Standard—R
Standard—R
Stand Firm—R
Together—R
Trumpeter—R

2-Soar—R
Upsouth—R
U.S. Catholic
Vibrant Life—R
Vision—R
War Cry—R
Way of St. Francis—R
Wesleyan Advocate—R

CHRISTIAN EDUCATION/LIBRARY

CE Connection—R
CE Counselor—R
Children's Ministry
Christian School
GROUP
Leader/Church School
   Today—R

MISSIONS

Quiet Hour Echoes
Worldwide Challenge

PASTORS/LEADERS

Art+Plus
Catholic Servant
Church Bytes—R
Journal/Christian Healing—R
Lutheran Partners—R
Minister's Family
Networks—R
Preacher's Illus. Service—R
Pulpit Helps—R
Reaching Children at Risk
Sharing the Practice—R
Single Adult Ministries
Today's Christian Preacher—R
Youthworker—R

WOMEN

Adam's Rib—R
Aspire
Esprit—R
Helping Hand—R
Horizons—R
Joyful Woman—R
Just Between Us—R
Keepers at Home
Link & Visitor—R
Lutheran Woman's Quar.
Lutheran Woman Today
Proverbs 31 Homemaker—R
Today's Christian Woman
True Woman
Virtue—R
Virtuous Woman
Welcome Home
Wesleyan Woman—R
Woman's Touch—R

Women Alive!—R
Women of Spirit—R

WRITERS

Writers' Intl. Forum

PERSONAL EXPERIENCE

ADULT/GENERAL

AGAIN—R
alive now!
Angels on Earth
Annals of St. Anne
Banner
B.C. Catholic—R
Believer—R
Bible Advocate—R
Bible Advocate Online—R
Breakthrough Intercessor—R
Bridal Guides—R
Canadian Mennonite
Catholic Digest—R
Catholic New York
Catholic Sentinel—R
Celebrate Life—R
CGA World—R
Chicken Soup/Mother—R
Chicken Soup/Woman—R
Christian Chronicle—R
Christian Courier (CAN)—R
Christian Edge—R
Christian Home & School
Christian Motorsports
Christian Ranchman
Christian Reader—R
Christian Traveler—R
Chrysalis Reader
Church Advocate—R
Church Herald/Holiness—R
Church of God EVANGEL
Comments/Friends—R
Common Boundary
Commonweal
Companion
Company—R
Conquest
Cornerstone—R
Covenant Companion—R
Crossway/Newsline—R
Day Star Tribune—R
Decision
Door
Dovetail—R
Emphasis/Faith & Living—R
Evangel—R
Family Network—R
Gem—R
God's Revivalist

Good News (AL)—R
Good News, Etc—R
Good News Journal (MO)—R
Good News Journal (TX)
Gospel Today
Gospel Tract—R
Grail
Guideposts
Hallelujah! (CAN)—R
Head to Head—R
Healing Inn—R
Hearing Heart—R
Hidden Manna—R
Highway News—R
Home Times—R
Ideals
Impact Magazine—R
Indian Life—R
Inland NW Christian
Inspirer—R
Inside Journal—R
Interim—R
Jewel Among Jewels—R
John Milton—R
Jour/Christian Nursing—R
Keys to Living—R
Legions of Light—R
Light and Life
L.I.G.H.T News—R
Liguorian
Live—R
Living—R
Living with Teenagers—R
Lookout—R
Lutheran—R
Lutheran Digest—R
Lutheran Journal—R
Marian Helpers—R
Marriage Partnership
Mennonite—R
Mennonite Brethren—R
MESSAGE
Messenger/St. Anthony
Michigan Christian
Minnesota Christian—R
Moody—R
MovieGuide
Narrow Gate
New Covenant
New Heart—R
New Moon—R
Newsline—R
New Writing—R
North American Voice
Oblates
Our Family—R
Over the Back Fence—R
Pentecostal Evangel

Plain Truth—R
Plenty Good Room
Plus—R
PrayerWorks—R
Presbyterians Today—R
Progress—R
ProLife News—R
Purpose—R
Quest
Religious Broadcasting—R
Romantic—R
Sacred Journey—R
St. Anthony Messenger
SCP Journal—R
Seek—R
Shantyman—R
Sharing—R
Single Connection—R
Single-Parent Family
Smile—R
Sojourners
Spiritual Life
Standard—R
Stand Firm—R
Stewardship
Sursum Corda!—R
TEAK Roundup—R
Time of Singing—R
Together—R
Upscale Magazine
Upsouth—R
VISION—R
Vision—R
Visitation
War Cry—R
Way of St. Francis—R
Weavings—R
Wesleyan Advocate—R

CHILDREN

Club Connection—R
Counselor—R
Courage
Discovery (NY)—R
GUIDE—R
Guideposts for Kids
Live Wire—R
Partners—R
Power & Light—R
Skipping Stones
Touch—R
Venture

CHRISTIAN EDUCATION/LIBRARY

Brigade Leader—R
CE Connection—R
CE Counselor—R
Children's Ministry

Christian Classroom
GROUP
Journal/Adventist Educ.—R
Perspective—R
Religion Teacher's Journal
Today's Catholic Teacher—R

MISSIONS

American Horizon—R
Areopagus—R
Heartbeat—R
P.I.M.E. World
Quiet Hour Echoes
So All May Hear—R
Women of the Harvest
World Christian—R
World Mission People—R
Worldwide Challenge

MUSIC

Songwriter—R

PASTORS/LEADERS

Art+Plus
Catholic Servant
Cell Church—R
Cell Life FORUM—R
Christian Camp—R
Christian Century
Christian Ministry
Church Bytes—R
Eucharistic Minister—R
Five Stones—R
Journal/Christian Healing—R
Journal/Pastoral Care
Minister's Family
Networks—R
Preacher's Illus. Service—R
Preacher's Magazine—R
Reaching Children at Risk
Sabbath School Leadership
Sharing the Practice—R
Single Adult Ministries
Theology Today (rarely)
Today's Parish
Youthworker—R

TEEN/YOUNG ADULT

Breakaway—R
Campus Life—R
Certainty
Challenge (GA) —R
Challenge (IL)
Conqueror—R
Devo'Zine—R
Essential Connection—R
Guideposts for Teens—R
Insight—R

Listen—R
Real Time—R
Sharing the VICTORY—R
Spirit
Straight—R
Teen Life—R
Teens on Target—R
Today's Christian Teen—R
With—R (1st person teen)
YOU!—R
Young Adult Today
Young & Alive—R
Young Christian—R
Young Salvationist—R
Youth Challenge—R

WOMEN

Anna's Journal—R
Aspire
Esprit—R
Hearth
Helping Hand—R
Horizons—R
Journey—R
Jour/Women's Ministries
Joyful Woman—R
Just Between Us—R
Kansas City Woman
Keepers at Home
Lutheran Woman Today
Proverbs 31 Homemaker—R
Today's Christian Woman
Virtue—R
Welcome Home
Wesleyan Woman—R
Woman's Touch—R
Women Alive!—R
Women of Spirit—R

WRITERS

Byline
Exchange—R
Fellowscript—R
Inklings
Once Upon a Time—R
WIN-Informer
Writer's Guidelines/News
Writer's Ink—R
Writers' Intl. Forum
Writer's Potpourri—R

PERSONAL GROWTH*

ADULT/GENERAL

A.M.E. Christian Recorder—R
Annals of St. Anne
Believer—R
Bible Advocate—R

Breakthrough Intercessor—R
Bridal Guides—R
Chicken Soup/Mother—R
Chicken Soup/Woman—R
Church Herald/Holiness—R
Common Boundary
Cornerstone—R
Covenant Companion—R
Day Star Tribune—R
Decision
Discipleship Journal
Dovetail—R
Evangel—R
Growing in Christ
Home Times—R
Jewel Among Jewels—R
John Milton—R
Light and Life
L.I.G.H.T News—R
Liguorian
Live—R
Living Light News—R
Lookout—R
Mennonite—R
Northwestern Lutheran—R
On Mission
Peoples Magazine—R
Preserving Christian Homes—R
Pursuit—R
Romantic—R
Seek—R
TEAK Roundup—R
Way of St. Francis—R
Weavings—R

CHILDREN

Discovery(NY)—R
GUIDE—R
Power & Light—R

CHRISTIAN EDUCATION/LIBRARY

CE Connection—R
Shining Star

PASTORS/LEADERS

Lutheran Partners—R
Reaching Children at Risk
Sharing the Practice—R
Vital Ministry

TEEN/YOUNG ADULT

Essential Connection—R
Insight—R
Teen Life—R
With—R
Young Christian—R
Young Salvationist—R

WOMEN

Anna's Journal—R
Hearth
Horizons—R
Joyful Woman—R
Sisters Today
Today's Christian Woman
Women of Spirit—R

WRITERS

Writers' Intl. Forum

PHOTOGRAPHS

Note: "Reprint" indicators (R) have been deleted from this section and "B" for black & white glossy prints or "C" for color transparencies inserted. An asterisk (*) before a listing indicates they buy photos with articles only.

ADULT/GENERAL

ABS RECORD
*Accent on Living—B/C
Alive!—B
alive now!—B
American Tract Soc.
Anglican Journal—B/C
*Annals of St. Anne—B/C
Arlington Catholic—B
Banner
Bible Advocate—C
Bridal Guides—B/C
Calvinist Contact—B/C
Canada Lutheran—B
Canadian Mennonite —B/C
*Cathedral Age—B
Catholic Courier—B
*Catholic Digest—B/C
Catholic Faith & Family
Catholic Forester—B/C
Catholic Heritage
Catholic New York—B
Catholic Parent
Catholic Rural Life—B
*Catholic Sentinel—B/C
Catholic Telegraph—B
CBA Frontline—C
CBA Marketplace—C
*Celebrate Life—C
Charisma/Christian Life—C
Christian Century—B
Christian Courier—B
Christian Crusade—B
*Christian Edge—B
*Christian History—B/C

Christian Home & School—C
Christian Living—B
*Christian Motorsports—B
Christian Parenting Today—B/C
*Christian Reader—B/C
Christian Social Action—B
Christian Standard—B/C
Christian Traveler—C
*Christianity Today—C
Church Advocate
Church & State
Church of God EVANGEL—C
Columbia—C
Comments/Friends—B
*Commonweal—B/C
Companion—B
*Company
Connecting Point—B
*Conquest—B/C
Cornerstone—B/C
Covenant Companion—B/C
Culture Wars—B/C
Day Star Tribune—B/C
Episcopal Life—B
*Evangel—B
Faith Today—B
Focus on the Family—B/C
Foursquare World—C
Good News (AL)—B
Good News, Etc—C
*Good News Journal (MO)—B
Good News Journal (TX)
Gospel Tidings—B
Gospel Tract—C
Grail—B/C
*Guideposts—B/C
Hallelujah—B
Head to Head—B/C
Highway News—B
Homeschooling Today—B/C
*Home Times—B/C
Impact Magazine—C
Inland NW Christian—B
*Inside Journal—B
Inspirer—B
Interchange—B
*Interim—B/C
*Journal/Christian Nursing—
    B/C
Joyful Noise
Liberty—B/C
*Lifeglow—B/C
Light and Life—B/C
*Liguorian—B/C
Live—C
Living—B/C
Living Church—B/C

Living Light News—B/C
Lookout—B/C
Lutheran—B
*Lutheran Journal—B/C
Lutheran Witness—B/C
Marian Helpers—B/C
Mature Living
*Mature Years—C
Mennonite—B/C
Mennonite Brethren—B
Mennonite Weekly—B
MESSAGE—B/C
Messenger—B
*Messenger/St. Anthony—B/C
Michigan Christian—B
*Montana Catholic—B
Nat. Christian Reporter—B/C/
    prints
*New Heart—C
New Moon—B
Northwestern Lutheran
*On Mission—C
Our Family—B/C
Our Sunday Visitor—B/C
Over the Back Fence—C
Pentecostal Evangel—B/C
*Pentecostal Testimony—B/C
*Plain Truth—B/C (few)
Plenty Good Room—B
Poetry Forum—B
Poets' Paper
*Power for Living—B
*Prairie Messenger—C
*Presbyterian Layman—B
Presbyterian Outlook—B/C
Presbyterian Record—B/C
Presbyterians Today—B/C
Prism—B/C
Progress—C
*Purpose—B
*Pursuit—B
Quiet Revolution—B
Re:generation
Right Road—C
Sacred Journey—B
*St. Anthony Messenger—B/C
SCP Journal—B/C
Signs of the Times—C
Sojourners—B/C
*Something Better
Spiritual Life—B
Sports Spectrum—C
Standard—B
Standard
Stand Firm—C
*Star of Zion
*Sursum Corda!—R
Together—B/C

Total Health—B/C
Twin Cities Christian—B
*United Church Observer—B/
    C
Upscale Magazine
*Vibrant Life—C
VISION—B/C
*Visitation
War Cry—B/C
Way of St. Francis—B
Wesleyan Advocate—C

CHILDREN

*Counselor—B/C
*Courage
Crusader
Discovery Trails—C
*Focus/Clubhouse Jr.—C
God's World News—C
Guideposts for Kids—C
Kidz Chat—C
Listen—C
Live Wire—C
Nature Friend—B/C
My Friend
On the Line—B/C
*Pockets—B/C
Power & Light—B
*Power Station
*Primary Pal (IL)
*Skipping Stones—B
Story Friends—B
Together Time—C
Touch—C
Venture—C
Wonder Time—B/C

CHRISTIAN EDUCATION/LIBRARY

Baptist Leader—B/C
Brigade Leader—B
CE Counselor—B/C
CE Leadership—B/C
Children's Ministry—C
Christian Classroom—C
Christian Librarian—B
Christian School—C
Christian School Admin.—C/C
*Church Educator—B
*Church Libraries—B/C
Evangelizing Today's Child—
    B/C
GROUP—C
Journal/Adventist Education—
    B
Junior Teacher—B/C
*Leader/Church School
    Today—B
Lollipops

Parish Teacher—B
Religion Teacher's Journal—B/
   C
Teachers in Focus—C
*Teachers Interaction—B
Team—B/C
*Today's Catholic Teacher—C

DAILY DEVOTIONALS

Daily Dev for Deaf—C
Secret Place—B/C
Words of Life—B/C

MISSIONS

American Horizon
Areopagus—B/C
*Catholic Near East—C
Evangelical Missions
PFI World Report
*P.I.M.E. World—C
Intl Jour/Frontier—R
Message of the Cross—B/C
*New World Outlook—C
World Christian—B/C
*World Pulse

MUSIC

Christian Country—B
Church Musician—B
*Creator—B/C
*Songwriter

PASTORS/LEADERS

Catholic Servant
*Cell Life FORUM—B/C
Christian Camp—B/C
Christian Century—B/C
Christian Ministry—B
Clergy Journal—B
Environment & Art—B/C
Evangelical Baptist—B/C
Leadership Journal—B
Lutheran Forum—B
*Lutheran Partners—B (rarely)
Ministry—B
Networks—B
Pray!
*Preacher—B
Preacher's Magazine—B/C
Resource—B/C
Sharing the Practice
Today's Parish—B/C
Vital Ministry - C
WCA News—C
*Worship Leader—C
*Your Church—B/C

TEEN/YOUNG ADULT

Breakaway—C
Brio—C
Campus Life—C
*Certainty—B
*Challenge (GA)—B/C
*Challenge (IL)
The Conqueror—B/C
Essential Connection—B/C
Guideposts for Teens—R
*Insight
Lighted Pathway—B/C
*Listen—B/C
*Real Time—B
*Sharing the VICTORY—C
Spirit—B/C
Straight—C
Student Leadership—B/C
Take Five—B/C
Teen Life—C
Venture—B
With—B
Young Adult Today—B
*Young & Alive—B
Young Christian—B/C

WOMEN

Anna's Journal—B
Conscience—B
*Esprit—B
Helping Hand—B
*Horizons—B/C
Jour/Women's Ministries—B
*Journey
Joyful Woman—B/C
Kansas City Woman—B
*Link & Visitor—B
Lutheran Woman Today—B
Sisters Today—for covers
Today's Christian Woman—C
Virtue—B/C
Wesleyan Woman
Women Alive!—B

WRITERS

*Byline
Gotta Write—B
Tickled by Thunder
*Writer's Digest—R
Writer's Guidelines/News—B/C

POETRY

ADULT/GENERAL

About Such Things—R
alive now!
America
AXIOS—R

Banner
Bible Advocate—R
Bread of Life—R
Breakthrough Intercessor—R
Bridal Guides—R
Christian Century
Christian Courier (CAN)—R
Christian Living—R
Christian Motorsports
Christian Poet—R
Christian Ranchman
Christianity/Arts
Church Herald/Holiness—R
Commonweal
Companion
Connecting Point—R
Cornerstone—R
Covenant Companion—R
Creatively Yours
Cresset
Culture Wars—R
Decision
Disciple's Journal—R
Door
Dovetail—R
Evangel—R
Family Journal—R
Family Network—R
First Things
Forefront
Foursquare World—R
Gems of Truth—R
Good News (AL)—R
Good News Journal (TX)
Gospel Tract—R
Grail
Green Cross—R
Guideposts
Hallelujah! (CAN)—R
Head to Head—R
Healing Inn—R
Hearing Hearts
Heartlight Internet—R
Hidden Manna—R
Home Times—R
Ideals—R
Impact Magazine—R
Inspirer—R
Jewel Among Jewels—R
John Milton—R
Jour/Christian Nursing—R
Keys to Living—R
Liberty (little)—R
Life Gate—R
Light and Life
Lighthouse Fiction
Live—R
Living Church

Lutheran Digest—R
Lutheran Journal—R
Mature Living
Mature Years—R
Mennonite—R
Mennonite Brethren—R
Miraculous Medal
Narrow Gate
New Heart—R
New Writing—R
North American Voice
Oblates
Our Family—R
Over the Back Fence—R
Parent Paper—R
Pegasus Review—R
Pentecostal Testimony—R
Perspectives
Plowman—R
Poetry Forum—R
Poet's Page
Poets' Paper—R
Pourastan—R
Prairie Messenger—R
PrayerWorks—R
Presbyterian Layman
Presbyterian Record—R
Presbyterians Today—R
Purpose—R
Queen of All Hearts
Re:generation
Sacred Journey—R
St. Anthony Messenger
St. Joseph's Messenger—R
San Diego Co. Christian
Sharing—R
Silver Wings—R
Smile—R
Sojourners
Standard—R
Star of Zion
TEAK Roundup—R
Time for Rhyme
Time of Singing—R
Today's Christian Senior—R
2-Soar—R
Upsouth—R
U.S. Catholic
Vision—R
War Cry—R
Weavings—R
Wesleyan Advocate—R

CHILDREN

Club Connection—R
CLUBHOUSE—R
Creatively Yours
Discovery (NY)—R

Discovery Trails—R
Flicker
Focus/Clubhouse Jr
Guideposts for Kids
Kidz Chat—R
Listen
Mission
Nature Friend—R
On the Line—R
Our Little Friend—R
Partners—R
Pockets—R
Primary Treasure—R
Skipping Stones
Story Friends—R
Story Mates—R
Together Time
Touch—R
Young Christian—R

CHRISTIAN EDUCATION/LIBRARY

Baptist Leader—R
Christian Educators Jour—R
Christian School
Church Educator—R
Lollipops
Resource—R
Shining Star
Today's Catholic Teacher—R
Vision—R

DAILY DEVOTIONALS

Living Words—R
Secret Place
These Days

MISSIONS

Quiet Hour Echoes
Women of the Harvest

MUSIC

Choir Herald, etc.
Church Pianist, etc.
Glory Songs—R
Hymn (hymns only)
Quest—R
Senior Musician—R

PASTORS/LEADERS

Art+Plus
Catechumenate
Cell Life FORUM—R
Christian Century
Cross Currents—R
Emmanuel
Journal/Christian Healing—R
Journal/Pastoral Care
Let's Worship

Lutheran Forum—R
Lutheran Partners—R
Minister's Family
Networks—R
Preacher—R
Preacher's Illus. Service—R
Pulpit Helps—R
Review for Religious
Sharing the Practice—R
Theology Today

TEEN/YOUNG ADULT

Campus Life
Devo'Zine—R
Essential Connection—R (by teens)
Guideposts for Teens—R
Insight—R
Real Time—R (by teens)
Sharing the VICTORY—R
Straight—R
Student Leadership—R
Take Five—R
Teenage Christian—R
Teen Life—R
YOU!—R
Young Adult Today
Young Christian—R
Young Salvationist—R

WOMEN

Adam's Rib—R
Anna's Journal—R
Conscience—R
Esprit—R
Horizons—R
Jour/Women's Ministries
Joyful Woman—R
Keepers at Home
Link & Visitor—R
Lutheran Woman Today
Proverbs 31 Homemaker—R
Sisters Today
Virtue—R
Virtuous Woman
Welcome Home
Wesleyan Woman—R

WRITERS

Byline
Canadian Writer's Jour—R
Christian Communicator—R
Cross & Quill—R
Dream Weaver
Gotta Write
Heaven—R
Inklings
My Legacy—R

Omnific—R
Once Upon a Time—R
Poetry Connection
Southwestern Writers—R
Tickled by Thunder
WIN-Informer
Writer's Digest—R
Writer's Exchange—R
Writer's Guidelines/News
Writer's Ink—R
Writers' Journal—R
Write Touch—R

POLITICAL

ADULT/GENERAL

Anglican Journal—R
Arkansas Catholic
Arlington Catholic
AXIOS—R
Banner
Bible Advocate—R
Canadian Catholic
Catholic Courier
Catholic Insight
Christian American
Christian Chronicle—R
Christian C.L. RECORD—R
Christian Courier (WI)—R
Christian Courier (CAN)—R
Christian Crusade
Christian Edge—R
Christian Motorsports
Christian Renewal—R
Christian Social Action—R
Christianity Today—R
Commonweal
Company—R
Cresset
Crisis Point
Day Star Tribune—R
Faith Today
First Things
Good News, Etc—R
Gospel Today
Green Cross—R
Head to Head—R
Home Times—R
Indian Life—R
Inland NW Christian
Interim—R
Journal of Church & State
Light and Life
Metro Voice—R
Michigan Christian
Minnesota Christian—R
Perspectives
Presbyterian Outlook

Presbyterians Today—R
Prism—R
Re:generation
Religious Broadcasting—R
Religious Education
SCP Journal—R
Social Justice
Sojourners
Stand Firm—R
Trumpeter—R
Upsouth—R

CHRISTIAN EDUCATION/LIBRARY

Christian School Admin.
Today's Catholic Teacher—R

MISSIONS

Areopagus—R
East-West Church

PASTORS/LEADERS

Christian Century
Current Thoughts & Trends
Lutheran Partners—R
Networks—R
Policy Review
Preacher's Illus. Service—R
Word & World

TEEN/YOUNG ADULT

Challenge (GA) —R
Essential Connection—R
Inteen
With—R
Young Adult Today

WOMEN

Conscience—R

PRAYER

ADULT/GENERAL
alive now!
A.M.E. Christian Recorder—R
Angels on Earth
Annals of St. Anne
Atlantic Baptist
Banner
Baptist Informer
Believer—R
Bible Advocate—R
Bible Advocate Online—R
Bread of Life—R
Breakthrough Intercessor—R
Brethren Evangelist
Canadian Catholic
Catholic Digest—R
Celebrate Life—R

CGA World—R
Charisma/Christian Life
Christian Chronicle—R
Christian Edge—R
Christianity Today—R
Christian Living—R
Christian Motorsports
Christian Parenting—R
Christian Poet—R
Christian Ranchman
Christian Reader—R
Church Advocate—R
Church Herald/Holiness—R
Church of God EVANGEL
Columbia
Common Boundary
Companion
Companions—R
Company—R
Connecting Point—R
Conquest
Cornerstone—R
Covenant Companion—R
Culture Wars—R
Day Star Tribune—R
Decision
Discipleship Journal
Dovetail—R
Emphasis/Faith & Living—R
Episcopal life—R
Evangel—R
Faith Today
Family Digest
Family Network—R
Fellowship Link—R
Focus on the Family
Forefront
Foursquare World—R
God's Revivalist
Good News (KY)—R
Good News, Etc—R
Good News Journal (MO)—R
Good News Journal (TX)
Gospel Today
Green Cross—R
Head to Head—R
Healing Inn—R
Hearing Hearts
Heartlight Internet—R
Highway News—R
Home Times—R
Indian Life—R
Inland NW Christian
Inspirer—R
Jewel Among Jewels—R
John Milton—R
Jour/Christian Nursing—R
Life Gate—R

Lifeglow—R
Light and Life
L.I.G.H.T News—R
Liguorian
Live—R
Living Church
Lookout—R
Lutheran—R
Lutheran Digest—R
Lutheran Journal—R
Lutheran Witness—R
Marian Helpers—R
Marriage Partnership
Mature Years—R
Mennonite—R
Mennonite Brethren—R
MESSAGE
MESSAGE/Open Bible—R
Messenger/St. Anthony
Metro Voice—R
Michigan Christian
Montana Catholic—R
Moody—R
New Covenant
New Heart—R
North American Voice
Northwestern Lutheran—R
On Mission
Our Family—R
Our Sunday Visitor
ParentLife—R
Pegasus Review—R
Peoples Magazine—R
Plain Truth—R
Plowman—R
Plus—R
Pourastan—R
Prairie Messenger—R
PrayerWorks—R
Presbyterian Outlook
Presbyterian Record—R
Presbyterians Today—R
Purpose—R
Queen of All Hearts
Re:generation
Right Road—R
Sacred Journey—R
St. Anthony Messenger
St. Willibrord Journal
Seek—R
Silver Wings—R
Social Justice
Sojourners
Something Better—R
Spiritual Life
Standard—R
Standard—R
Stand Firm—R

Time of Singing—R
Today's Christian Senior—R
Together—R
Trumpeter—R
Upsouth—R
U.S. Catholic
Vision—R
War Cry—R
Way of St. Francis—R
Weavings—R
Wesleyan Advocate—R

CHILDREN

BREAD/God's Children—R
Club Connection—R
Counselor—R
Courage
Discovery (NY)—R
GUIDE—R
High Adventure—R
Power Station—R
Touch—R
Wonder Time
Young Christian—R

CHRISTIAN EDUCATION/LIBRARY

CE Counselor—R
Children's Ministry
Church Educator—R
Evangelizing Today's Child—R
GROUP
Leader/Church School
   Today—R
Religion Teacher's Journal
Shining Star
Teacher's Interaction
Vision—R

MISSIONS

American Horizon—R
Areopagus—R
Intl Jour/Frontier—R
Latin American Evangelist
Message of the Cross—R
PFI World Report—R
So All May Hear—R
Worldwide Challenge

MUSIC

Creator—R
Quest—R
Quiet Hour Echoes

PASTORS/LEADERS

African American Pulpit
Art+Plus
Catholic Servant
Celebration

Cell Life FORUM—R
Christian Ministry
Church Growth Network—R
Church Worship
Current Thoughts & Trends
Diocesan Dialogue—R
Emmanuel
Enrichment—R
Five Stones—R
Journal/Christian Healing—R
Jour/Amer Soc/Chur Growth—
   R
Leadership Journal—R
Let's Worship
Lutheran Partners—R
Minister's Family
Ministries Today
Ministry
Ministry & Liturgy—R
Networks—R
Pastoral Life
Pray!—R
Preacher—R
Preacher's Illus. Service—R
Preacher's Magazine—R
Priest
PROCLAIM—R
Reaching Children at Risk
Reformed Worship
Sharing the Practice—R
Theology Today
Today's Christian Preacher—R
Today's Parish
Word & World
Worship Leader

TEEN/YOUNG ADULT

Certainty
Challenge (GA) —R
Challenge (IL)
Conqueror—R
Devo'Zine—R
Essential Connection—R
Insight—R
Inteen
Real Time—R
Straight—R
Student Leadership—R
Teenage Christian—R
Teen Life—R
Teens on Target—R
Today's Christian Teen—R
Vision—R
With—R
YOU!—R
Young Adult Today
Young & Alive—R
Young Christian—R

Young Salvationist—R
Youth Challenge—R
Youth Update

WOMEN
Adam's Rib—R
Aspire
CoLaborer—R
Esprit—R
Helping Hand—R
Horizons—R
Journey—R
Joyful Woman—R
Just Between Us—R
Lutheran Woman's Quar.
Lutheran Woman Today
Proverbs 31 Homemaker—R
Sisters Today
Today's Christian Woman
Virtue—R
Virtuous Woman
Women Alive!—R
Women of Spirit—R

PROPHECY

ADULT/GENERAL
A.M.E. Christian Recorder—R
Apocalypse Chronicles—R
Banner
Bible Advocate—R
Bread of Life—R
Breakthrough Intercessor—R
Charisma/Christian Life
Christian Edge—R
Christian Motorsports
Conquest
Creation Ex Nihilo
Day Star Tribune—R
Fellowship Link—R
Foursquare World—R
God's Revivalist
Good News, Etc—R
Good News Journal (MO)—R
Gospel Tract—R
Hallelujah! (CAN)—R
John Milton—R
MESSAGE
Metro Voice—R
Michigan Christian
New Writing—R
Our Family—R
Plain Truth—R
Queen of All Hearts
SCP Journal—R
Signs of the Times—R
Silver Wings—R
Single Connection—R

Today's Christian Senior—R
Trumpeter—R
2-Soar—R
Upsouth—R

MISSIONS
Quiet Hour Echoes

PASTORS/LEADERS
Current Thoughts & Trends
Journal/Christian Healing—R
Ministries Today
PROCLAIM—R
Today's Christian Preacher—R
Voice of the Vineyard —R
Word & World

TEEN/YOUNG ADULT
Certainty
Inteen
Young Adult Today
Young Christian—R

WOMEN
Woman's Touch—R

PSYCHOLOGY

ADULT/GENERAL
A.M.E. Christian Recorder—R
AXIOS—R
Banner
Biblical Reflections—R
Bridal Guides—R
Christian Chronicle—R
Christian Motorsports
Chrysalis Reader
Church Advocate—R
Common Boundary
Companion
Company—R
Day Star Tribune—R
Good News (AL)—R
Good News, Etc—R
Good News Journal (MO)—R
Jewel Among Jewels—R
John Milton—R
Jour/Christian Nursing—R
Light and Life
Michigan Christian
New Covenant
Our Family—R
ParentLife—R
Peoples Magazine—R
Religious Education
SCP Journal—R
Single Connection—R
Social Justice

Spiritual Life
Total Health
Upsouth—R

CHRISTIAN EDUCATION/LIBRARY
Catechist
Church Educator—R

PASTORAL/LEADERS
Cell Church—R
Christian Ministry
Current Thoughts & Trends
Eucharistic Minister—R
Five Stones—R
Journal/Christian Healing—R
Journal/Pastoral Care
Lutheran Partners—R
Ministries Today
Priest
Reaching Children at Risk
Sharing the Practice—R
Word & World

WRITERS
Writers' Intl. Forum

PUPPET PLAYS

CE Connection—R
Children's Ministry
Christian Parenting—R
Christianity/Arts
Church Street Press
Club Connection—R
Creatively Yours
Evangelizing Today's Child—R
Focus/Clubhouse Jr
Good News Journal (MO)—R
Good News Journal (TX)
Kids' Ministry Ideas—R
Leader/Church School
    Today—R
Let's Worship
Lillenas
Reaching Children at Risk
Sheer Joy! Press
Shining Star
Touch—R

RELATIONSHIPS

ADULT/GENERAL
Accent on Living—R
A.M.E. Christian Recorder—R
Angels on Earth
Annals of St. Anne
AXIOS—R
Banner

Believer—R
Bible Advocate—R
Bible Advocate Online—R
Breakthrough Intercessor—R
Bridal Guides—R
Catholic Digest—R
Catholic Forester—R
Celebrate Life—R
Charisma/Christian Life
Chicken Soup/Mother—R
Chicken Soup/Woman—R
Christian Edge—R
Christian Living—R
Christian Motorsports
Christian Parenting—R
Christian Ranchman
Christian Reader—R
Chrysalis Reader
Church Advocate—R
Church Herald/Holiness—R
Church of God EVANGEL
Columbia
Common Boundary
Companion
Companions—R
Conquest
Cornerstone—R
Day Star Tribune—R
Decision
Discipleship Journal
Dovetail—R
Emphasis/Faith & Living—R
Evangel—R
Faith Today
Family Digest
Family Network—R
Fellowship Link—R
Forefront
Foursquare World—R
Gem—R
Good News (AL)—R
Good News, Etc—R
Good News Journal (MO)—R
Good News Journal (TX)
Gospel Today
Guideposts
Head to Head—R
Healing Inn—R
Hearing Hearts
Heartlight Internet—R
Highway News—R
Home Times—R
Inside Journal—R
Jewel Among Jewels—R
John Milton—R
Jour/Christian Nursing—R
Life Gate—R
Light and Life

Liguorian
Live—R
Living—R
Living Light News—R
Living with Teenagers—R
Lookout—R
Lutheran Digest—R
Lutheran Journal—R
Marriage Partnership
MESSAGE
Messenger/St. Anthony
Metro Voice—R
Michigan Christian
Moody—R
New Heart—R
New Writing—R
On Mission
ParentLife—R
Pegasus Review—R
Pentecostal Testimony—R
Peoples Magazine—R
Plain Truth—R
Plus—R
Pourastan—R
PrayerWorks—R
Preserving Christian Homes—R
Progress—R
Purpose—R
Pursuit—R
Real FamilyLife
Romantic—R
Seek—B
Silver Wings—R
Single-Parent Family
Standard—R
Stand Firm—R
TEAK Roundup—R
Time of Singing—R
Together—R
Trumpeter—R
Upscale Magazine
Upsouth—R
U.S. Catholic
War Cry—R

CHILDREN

BREAD for God's Children
Club Connection—R
Discovery (NY)—R
Focus/Clubhouse Jr
High Adventure—R
My Friend
Touch—R
Young Christian—R

CHRISTIAN EDUCATION/LIBRARY

CE Connection—R

Children's Ministry
Christian School Admin.
GROUP
Leader/Church School
   Today—R
Perspective—R

MISSIONS

American Horizon—R
Message of the Cross—R
Quiet Hour Echoes
World Mission People—R
Worldwide Challenge

PASTORS/LEADERS

Art+Plus
Cell Church—R
Cell Life FORUM—R
Christian Camp—R
Current Thoughts & Trends
Five Stones—R
Lutheran Partners—R
Minister's Family
Ministries Today
Ministry
Preacher's Magazine—R
Pulpit Helps—R
Reaching Children at Risk
Sharing the Practice—R
Single Adult Ministries
Today's Christian Preacher—R
Youthworker—R
Vital Ministry
Voice of the Vineyard —R
Word & World

TEEN/YOUNG ADULT

Certainty
Challenge (GA) —R
Challenge (IL)
Devo'Zine—R
Essential Connection—R
Insight—R
Listen—R
Real Time—R
Straight—R
Student Leadership—R
Teenage Christian—R
Teen Life—R
Teens on Target—R
Today's Christian Teen—R
With—R
YOU!—R
Young Christian—R
Young Salvationist—R
Youth Challenge—R
Youth Update

WOMEN
Adam's Rib—R
Aspire
Esprit—R
Helping Hand—R
Horizons—R
Journey—R
Joyful Woman—R
Just Between Us—R
Link & Visitor—R
Lutheran Woman's Quar.
Proverbs 31 Homemaker—R
Today's Christian Woman
Virtue—R
Virtuous Woman
Welcome Home
Wesleyan Woman—R
Woman's Touch—R
Women of Spirit—R

WRITERS
Writers' Intl. Forum

RELIGIOUS FREEDOM

ADULT/GENERAL
AGAIN—R
A.M.E. Christian Recorder—R
America
Arlington Catholic
AXIOS—R
Banner
Bible Advocate—R
Bread of Life—R
Breakthrough Intercessor—R
Charisma/Christian Life
Christian Arts Review
Christian Chronicle—R
Christian C.L. RECORD—R
Christian Courier (WI)—R
Christian Courier (CAN)—R
Christian Edge—R
Christian Motorsports
Christian Ranchman
Christianity Today—R
Church & State—R
Church Herald/Holiness—R
Columbia
Comments/Friends—R
Connecting Point—R
Cornerstone—R
Covenant Companion—R
Cresset
Day Star Tribune—R
Dovetail—R
Episcopal Life—R
Faith Today
First Things

God's Revivalist
Good News, Etc—R
Good News Journal (TX)
Grail
Hallelujah! (CAN)—R
Home Times—R
Interim—R
John Milton—R
Journal of Church & State
Liberty—R
Life Gate—R
MESSAGE
Messenger/St. Anthony
Metro Voice—R
Michigan Christian
Minnesota Christian—R
Moody—R
On Mission
Our Family—R
Our Sunday Visitor
Pegasus Review—R
Pentecostal Testimony—R
Pourastan—R
Presbyterian Layman
Presbyterian Outlook
Presbyterians Today—R
Prism—R
Re:generation
Religious Broadcasting—R
Religious Education
SCP Journal—R
Single Connection—R
Social Justice
Something Better—R
Spiritual Life
Standard—R
Stand Firm—R
TEAK Roundup—R
Touchstone—R
U.S. Catholic
Upsouth—R

CHILDREN
High Adventure—R

CHRISTIAN EDUCATION/LIBRARY
Christian School Admin.
Vision—R

MISSIONS
Areopagus—R
East-West Church
Evangelical Missions—R
Quiet Hour Echoes
World Pulse—R
Worldwide Challenge

MUSIC
Quest—R

PASTORS/LEADERS
Art+Plus
Catholic Servant
Cell Church—R
Christian Century
Christian Ministry
Church Worship
Current Thoughts & Trends
Five Stones—R
Journal/Christian Healing—R
Lutheran Partners—R
Ministry
Networks—R
Theology Today
Today's Christian Preacher—R
Word & World

TEEN/YOUNG ADULT
Challenge (GA) —R
Conqueror—R
Essential Connection—R
Inteen
Young Adult Today
Young Christian—R

WOMEN
Esprit—R

WRITERS
Christian Response—R
Writers' Intl. Forum

SALVATION TESTIMONIES

ADULT/GENERAL
AGAIN—R
American Tract Soc.—R
Banner
Believer—R
Bible Advocate—R
Breakthrough Intercessor—R
Christian Chronicle—R
Christian Motorsports
Christian Ranchman
Christian Reader—R
Church Herald/Holiness—R
Church of God EVANGEL
Companions—R
Connecting Point—R
Conquest
Crossway/Newsline—R
Day Star Tribune—R
Decision
Evangel—R
Family Network—R

Fellowship Link—R
Gem—R
God's Revivalist
Good News, Etc—R
Good News Journal (TX)
Gospel Tract—R
Guideposts
Hallelujah! (CAN)—R
Head to Head—R
Healing Inn—R
Hearing Hearts
Indian Life—R
Inside Journal—R
Inspirer—R
Live—R
Lutheran Journal—R
Mennonite Brethren—R
MESSAGE/Open Bible—R
Michigan Christian
Moody—R
New Covenant
New Heart—R
On Mission
Peoples Magazine—R
Plain Truth—R
Power for Living—R
PrayerWorks—R
Quest
SCP Journal—R
Seek—B
Shantyman—R
Silver Wings—R
Single Connection—R
Something Better—R
Standard—R
Stand Firm—R
TEAK Roundup—R
Together—R
Upsouth—R
Wesleyan Advocate—R

CHILDREN

BREAD/God's Children—R
Club Connection—R
Counselor—R
Courage
Discovery(NY)—R
GUIDE—R
Power & Light—R
Power Station—R

CHRISTIAN EDUCATION/LIBRARY

Evangelizing Today's Child—R

MISSIONS

American Horizon—R
Latin American Evangelist
So All May Hear—R

Women of the Harvest
Worldwide Challenge

PASTORS/LEADERS

Art+Plus
Cell Church—R
Christian Camp—R
Journal/Christian Healing—R
Ministry
Networks—R
Preacher's Magazine—R
Small Group Dynamics

TEEN/YOUNG ADULT

Challenge (GA) —R
Challenge (IL)
Conqueror—R
Essential Connection—R
Insight—R
Inteen
Real Time—R
Today's Christian Teen—R
Young Adult Today
Young Salvationist—R

WOMEN

Esprit—R
Helping Hand—R
Journey—R
Joyful Woman—R
Wesleyan Woman—R
Woman's Touch—R

SCIENCE

ADULT/GENERAL

AXIOS—R
Banner
Biblical Reflections—R
Canadian Catholic
Catholic Dossier
Christian C.L. RECORD—R
Christian Courier (CAN)—R
Christian Motorsports
Christian Reader—R
Christianity Today—R
Companions—R
Creation Ex Nihilo
Day Star Tribune—R
Faith Today
First Things
Good News (AL)—R
Home Times—R
Lifeglow—R
Light and Life
Messenger/St. Anthony
Metro Voice—R
Michigan Christian

PrayerWorks—R
Religious Education
SCP Journal—R
Something Better—R
Standard—R
Upsouth—R

CHILDREN

Discovery (AL)
Guideposts for Kids
Live Wire—R
My Friend
Nature Friend—R
Power Station—R

CHRISTIAN EDUCATION/LIBRARY

Christian Classroom
Christian School Admin.
Shining Star
Vision—R

PASTORS/LEADERS

Journal/Christian Healing—R
Lutheran Partners—R
Pulpit Helps—R
Technologies/Worship—R
Word & World

TEEN/YOUNG ADULT

Challenge (GA) —R
Essential Connection—R
Inteen
Young Adult Today

WOMEN

Aspire
Esprit—R

SELF-HELP

ADULT/GENERAL

Bridal Guides—R
Catholic Forester—R
CGA World—R
Chicken Soup/Mother—R
Chicken Soup/Single—R
Chicken Soup/Woman—R
Christian Edge—R
Christian Living—R
Christian Motorsports
Christian Ranchman
Common Boundary
Companion
Covenant Companion—R
Day Star Tribune—R
Disciple's Journal—R
Discovery—R
Expression Christian

Fellowship Link—R
Good News (AL)—R
Good News Journal (MO)—R
John Milton—R
Living—R
Living Light News—R
Living with Teenagers—R
Marriage Partnership
MESSAGE
Messenger/St. Anthony
Michigan Christian
New Writing—R
Our Family—R
Peoples Magazine—R
St. Anthony Messenger
Single Connection—R
Social Justice
Standard—R
Stand Firm—R
TEAK Roundup—R
Touchstone—R
2-Soar—R
Vibrant Life—R

PASTORS/LEADERS

Art+Plus
Cell Church—R
Reaching Children at Risk

TEEN/YOUNG ADULT

Challenge (GA) —R
Essential Connection—R
Insight—R
Listen—R
Straight—R
Teenage Christian—B/C
Young Christian—R
Young Salvationist—R

WOMEN

Esprit—R
Journey—R
Today's Christian Woman
Wesleyan Woman—R
Women of Spirit—R
Women of the Harvest

SENIOR ADULT ISSUES

ADULT/GENERAL

Alive!—R
Angels on Earth
Anglican Journal—R
Annals of St. Anne
Atlantic Baptist
AXIOS—R
Banner
B.C. Catholic—R

Believer—R
Breakthrough Intercessor—R
Canada Lutheran—R
Catholic Digest—R
Catholic Forester—R
CGA World—R
Christian Courier (CAN)—R
Christian Edge—R
Christian Home & School
Christian Living—R
Christian Motorsports
Church Advocate—R
Church Herald/Holiness—R
Church of God EVANGEL
Companion
Conquest
Covenant Companion—R
Day Star Tribune—R
Decision
Discovery—R
Dovetail—R
Emphasis/Faith & Living—R
Evangel—R
Family Digest
Family Network—R
Fellowship Link—R
Gem—R
Good News (AL)—R
Good News, Etc—R
Good News Journal (MO)—R
Good News Journal (TX)
Hearing Hearts
Home Times—R
Inspirer—R
John Milton—R
Jour/Christian Nursing—R
Life Gate—R
Lifeglow—R
Liguorian
Live—R
Living—R
Living Light News—R
Lookout—R
Lutheran—R
Lutheran Digest—R
Mature Living
Mature Years—R
Metro Voice—R
Michigan Christian
Minnesota Christian—R
Moody—R
NW Christian Journal—R
On Mission
Our Family—R
Our Sunday Visitor
Pentecostal Evangel
Peoples Magazine—R
Plain Truth—R

Plus—R
Power for Living—R
PrayerWorks—R
Presbyterians Today—R
Purpose—R
Resource—R
Sacred Journey—R
Smile—R
Sojourners
Something Better—R
Standard—R
Star of Zion
Today's Christian Senior—R
U.S. Catholic
War Cry—R
Wesleyan Advocate—R

CHRISTIAN EDUCATION/LIBRARY

Baptist Leader—R
CE Counselor—R
CE Leadership—R
Church Educator—R

MISSIONS

Worldwide Challenge

MUSIC

Senior Musician—R

PASTORS/LEADERS

Art+Plus
Christian Ministry
Diocesan Dialogue—R
Evangelical Baptist—R
Five Stones—R
Journal/Christian
   Healing—R
Lutheran Partners—R
Pastoral Life
Sharing the Practice—R
Vital Ministry
Word & World

WOMEN

Adam's Rib—R
Aspire
Esprit—R
Today's Christian Woman
Wesleyan Woman—R
Woman's Touch—R

WRITERS

Canadian Writer's Jour—R
Writers' Intl. Forum

SERMONS

ADULT/GENERAL

A.M.E. Christian Recorder—R
Arlington Catholic
Banner
Breakthrough Intercessor—R
Cathedral Age
Christian Chronicle—R
Christian Motorsports
Church Herald/Holiness—R
Cresset
God's Revivalist
Good News, Etc—R
Green Cross—R
Hallelujah! (CAN)—R
Healing Inn—R
Inspirer—R
John Milton—R
Joyful Noise
Presbyterians Today—R
Sojourners
Star of Zion
Trumpeter—R
Upsouth—R
Weavings—R

MISSIONS

Quiet Hour Echoes

PASTORS/LEADERS

African American Pulpit
Celebration
Christian Ministry
Church Worship
Clergy Journal—R
Enrichment—R
In Season
Journal/Christian Healing—R
Ministry Now
Preacher's Illus. Service—R
Preacher's Magazine—R
Preaching
PROCLAIM—R
Pulpit Helps—R
Sharing the Practice—R
Today's Parish

SHORT STORY: ADULT/ RELIGIOUS

About Such Things—R
Adam's Rib—R
Alive!—R
alive now!
Annals of St. Anne
Anna's Journal—R
Banner

Baptist Informer
Believer—R
Bridal Guides—R
Canadian Writer's Jour—R
Catholic Forester—R
CGA World—R
Chip Off Writer's Block—R
Christian Century
Christian Chronicle—R
Christian Classroom
Christian Courier (CAN)—R
Christian Educators Journal
Christian Living—R
Christian Motorsports
Christian Reader—R
Christian Renewal—R
Christian School
Christian School Admin.
Christianity/Arts
Church & Synagogue Lib.
Companion
Companions—R
Connecting Point—R
Conquest
Cornerstone—R
Covenant Companion—R
Creation Ex Nihilo
Day Star Tribune—R
Discovery—R
Dreams & Visions—R
Dream Weaver
Emphasis/Faith & Living—R
Esprit—R
Evangel—R
Family Network—R
Fellowship Link—R
Five Stones—R
Gem—R
Gems of Truth—R
God's Revivalist
Good News (AL)—R
Good News Journal (MO)—R
Good Story
Gospel Tidings—R
Gospel Tract—R
Growing in Christ
Head to Head—R
Healing Inn—R
Hearing Hearts
Heartlight Internet—R
Heaven
Helping Hand—R
Hidden Manna—R
Highway News—R
Home Times—R
Horizons—R
Impact Magazine—R
Inklings

Inspirer—R
John Milton—R
Journal/Christian Healing—R
Journal/Pastoral Care
Joyful Woman—R
Legions of Light—R
Lighthouse Fiction
Liguorian
Live—R
Living—R
Living Light News—R
Lookout—R
Lutheran Digest
Lutheran Partners—R
Lutheran Witness—R
Lutheran Woman's Quar.
Lutheran Woman Today
Mature Living
Mature Years—R
Mennonite Brethren—R
Messenger/Sacred Heart
Messenger/St. Anthony
Miraculous Medal
Moody—R
My Legacy—R
Narrow Gate
New Writing—R
North American Voice
Pegasus Review—R
Pentecostal Testimony—R
Peoples Magazine—R
Perspectives
Plowman—R
Poetry Forum—R
PrayerWorks—R
Presbyterian Record—R
Preserving Christian Homes—R
Queen of All Hearts
Quest—R
Re:generation
St. Anthony Messenger
St. Joseph's Messenger—R
San Diego Co. Christian
Seek—R
Single Connection—R
Sojourners
Standard—R
Star of Zion
Sursum Corda!—R
TEAK Roundup—R
Tickled by Thunder
Today's Christian Senior—R
Today's Christian Woman
Upsouth—R
U.S. Catholic
Virtue—R
Vision—R

War Cry—R
Weavings—R
Women Alive!—R
Writers' Intl. Forum
Write Touch—R
YOU!—R

SHORT STORY: ADVENTURE

ADULT

Alive!—R
Annals of St. Anne
Bridal Guides—R
Byline
Chip Off Writer's Block—R
Christian Courier (CAN)—R
Christianity/Arts
Day Star Tribune—R
Dreams & Visions—R
Dream Weaver
Good News (AL)—R
Healing Inn—R
Heartlight Internet—R
Legions of Light—R
Lighthouse Fiction
Liguorian
Live—R
Miraculous Medal
My Legacy—R
Narrow Gate
New Writing—R
Peoples Magazine—R
Standard—R
TEAK Roundup—R
Today's Christian Senior—R
Upsouth—R
Vision—R
Writers' Intl. Forum

CHILDREN

Annals of St. Anne
BREAD/God's Children—R
CLUBHOUSE—R
Connecting Point—R
Counselor—R
CourageCrusader—R
Discoveries—R
Discovery (NY)—R
Discovery Trails—R
Focus/Clubhouse
Focus/Clubhouse Jr
Guideposts for Kids
Kidz Chat—R
Lighthouse Fiction
Listen
Lollipops (young)
My Friend
Power Station—R

Primary Pal (IL)
Story Friends—R
Trails 'N' Treasures—R
Writers' Intl. Forum
Young Christian—R

TEEN/YOUNG ADULT

Annals of St. Anne
Breakaway—R
Challenge (GA)—R
Challenge (IL)
Discovery—R
Dream Weaver
Essential Connection—R
Inteen
Lighthouse Fiction
Straight—R
Teenage Christian—R
Teen Life—R
Teens on Target—R
Teens Today—R
Writers' Intl. Forum
Young Adult Today
Young Christian—R
Young Salvationist—R
Youth Challenge—R

SHORT STORY: ALLEGORY

ADULT

About Such Things—R
Byline
Chip Off Writer's Block—R
Christianity/Arts
Covenant Companion—R
Discovery—R
Dreams & Visions—R
Dream Weaver
Emphasis/Faith & Living—R
Family Network—R
Good News (AL)—R
Grail
Head to Head—R
Healing Inn—R
Hearing Hearts
Heartlight Internet—R
Highway News—R
Home Times—R
Horizons—R
Inklings
Inspirer—R
Mennonite Brethren—R
Messenger/St. Anthony
My Legacy—R
Narrow Gate
New Writing—R
Peoples Magazine—R
Prism—R

Vision—R
Weavings—R

CHILDREN

Discovery (NY)—R
Head to Head—R
Nature Friend—R
Pockets—R
Touch—R

TEENS/YOUNG ADULT

Conqueror—R
Discovery—R
Dream Weaver
Essential Connection—R
Head to Head—R
John Milton—R
Student Leadership—R
Teen Life—R
With—R
YOU!—R
Young Salvationist—R

SHORT STORY: BIBLICAL

ADULT

Annals of St. Anne
Bridal Guides—R
CGA World—R
Christian Courier (CAN)—R
Christianity/Arts
Church & Synagogue Lib.
Church Worship
Connecting Point—R
Day Star Tribune—R
Discovery—R
Dreams & Visions—R
Dream Weaver
Esprit—R
Emphasis/Faith & Living—R
Evangel—R
Family Network—R
Fellowship Link—R
Five Stones—R
Good News (AL)—R
Gospel Tract—R
Grail
Head to Head—R
Healing Inn—R
Hearing Hearts
Heartlight Internet—R
Helping Hand—R
Hidden Manna—R
Highway News—R
Home Times—R
Impact Magazine—R
Inspirer—R

Joyful Woman—R
Lutheran Woman's Quar.
Lutheran Woman Today
Mature Years—R
Mennonite Brethren—R
Miraculous Medal
My Legacy—R
Narrow Gate
New Writing—R
Peoples Magazine—R
Perspectives
Plowman—R
Preacher's Illus. Service—R
Presbyterian Record—R
Preserving Christian Homes—R
Seek—B
Sojourners
TEAK Roundup—R
Today's Christian Senior—R
Upsouth—R
U.S. Catholic
Virtue—R
War Cry—R
Weavings—R
Writers' Intl. Forum

CHILDREN

Annals of St. Anne
BREAD/God's Children—R
Discoveries—R
Discovery (NY)—R
Focus/Clubhouse
Focus/Clubhouse Jr
Head to Head—R
Kidz Chat—R
MESSAGE
John Milton—R
Nature Friend—R
North American Voice
Pockets—R
Preacher's Illus. Service—R
Trails 'N' Treasures—R
Writers' Intl. Forum
Young Christian—R

TEEN/YOUNG ADULT

Annals of St. Anne
Challenge (GA) —R
Conqueror—R
Discovery—R
Dream Weaver
Essential Connection—R
Head to Head—R
Inteen
John Milton—R
Preacher's Illus. Service—R
Real Time—R

Student Leadership—R
Teenage Christian—R
Teen Life—R
Teens on Target—R
Writers' Intl. Forum
YOU!—R
Young Adult Today
Young Christian—R
Youth Challenge—R

SHORT STORY: CONTEMPORARY

ADULT

About Such Things—R
Annals of St. Anne
Bridal Guides—R
Byline
Canadian Lutheran—R
Chip Off Writer's Block—R
Christian Century
Christian Living—R
Christian Renewal—R
Christianity/Arts
Companion
Connecting Point—R
Conquest
Cornerstone—R
Covenant Companion—R
Dreams & Visions—R
Dream Weaver
Emphasis/Faith & Living—R
Esprit—R
Evangel—R
Good News (AL)—R
Head to Head—R
Healing Inn—R
Hearing Hearts
Heartlight Internet—R
Hidden Manna—R
Horizons—R
Inklings
Inspirer—R
Legions of Light—R
Lighthouse Fiction
Liguorian
Living Light News—R
Lookout—R
Mature Living
Messenger/St. Anthony
Miraculous Medal
Moody—R
My Legacy—R
Narrow Gate
New Moon—R
New Writing—R
Peoples Magazine—R
Perspectives

Poetry Forum—R
St. Anthony Messenger
St. Joseph's Messenger—R
Seek—B
Standard—R
TEAK Roundup—R
Tickled by Thunder
Upsouth—R
U.S. Catholic
Virtue—R
War Cry—R
Writers' Intl. Forum

CHILDREN

Annals of St. Anne
BREAD/God's Children—R
Canada Lutheran—R
Discoveries—R
Discovery (NY)—R
Discovery Trails—R
Focus/Clubhouse
Focus/Clubhouse Jr
Guideposts for Kids
Head to Head—R
Kidz Chat—R
Lighthouse Fiction
Listen
On the Line—R
Partners—R
Pockets—R
Right Road—R
Story Friends—R
Together Time
Touch—R
Writers' Intl. Forum
Young Christian—R

TEEN/YOUNG ADULT

Annals of St. Anne
BREAD/God's Children—R
Certainty
Challenge (IL)
Discovery—R
Dream Weaver
Essential Connection—R
Head to Head—R
Lighthouse Fiction
Listen—R
Real Time—R
Spirit
Straight—R
Teenage Christian—R
Teen Life—R
Writers' Intl. Forum
Young Christian—R

SHORT STORY: ETHNIC

ADULT

Bridal Guides—R
Byline
Christian Living—R
Dreams & Visions—R
Dream Weaver
Fellowship Link—R
Good News (AL)—R
Hidden Manna—R
Inklings
Legions of Light—R
Live—R
Seek—B
Upsouth—R
Writers' Intl. Forum

CHILDREN

Counselor—R
Discovery (NY)—R
Discovery Trails—R
Guideposts for Kids
Skipping Stones
Writers' Intl. Forum

TEEN/YOUNG ADULT

Discovery—R
Dream Weaver
Essential Connection—R
Straight—R
Teen Life—R
Writers' Intl. Forum
Young Christian—R
Young Salvationist—R

SHORT STORY: FANTASY

ADULT

About Such Things—R
Byline
Chip Off Writer's Block—R
Christian Courier (CAN)—R
Christianity/Arts
Connecting Point—R
Dreams & Visions—R
Dream Weaver
Esprit—R
Good News Journal (MO)—R
Inklings
Legions of Light—R
Messenger/St. Anthony
My Legacy—R
Narrow Gate
New Creation
Presbyterian Record—R
Tickled by Thunder
Writers' Intl. Forum

CHILDREN

Discovery (NY)—R
Guideposts for Kids
Lollipops (young)
Touch—R
Trails 'N' Treasures—R
Venture
Writers' Intl. Forum
Young Christian—R

TEEN/YOUNG ADULT

Discovery—R
Dream Weaver
Essential Connection—R
Inteen
New Creation
Spirit
Teen Life—R
With—R
Writers' Intl. Forum
Young Adult Today
Young Christian—R
Young Salvationist—R

SHORT STORY: FRONTIER

ADULT

About Such Things—R
Bridal Guides—R
Byline
Chip Off Writer's Block—R
Christianity/Arts
Connecting Point—R
Dreams & Visions—R
Dream Weaver
Good News (AL)—R
Inspirer—R
Legions of Light—R
Lighthouse Fiction
Miraculous Medal
My Legacy—R
Narrow Gate
TEAK Roundup—R
Upsouth—R
Writers' Intl. Forum

CHILDREN

Discovery Trails—R
Focus/Clubhouse
Focus/Clubhouse Jr
Guideposts for Kids
High Adventure—R
Lighthouse Fiction
Touch—R
Writers' Intl. Forum
Young Christian—R

TEEN/YOUNG ADULT

Dream Weaver
Essential Connection—R
Lighthouse Fiction
Writers' Intl. Forum
Young Christian—R

SHORT STORY: FRONTIER/ ROMANCE

About Such Things—R
Bridal Guides—R
Byline
Chip Off Writer's Block—R
Christianity/Arts
Connecting Point—R
Dreams & Visions—R
Dream Weaver
Essential Connection—R
Healing Inn—R
Helping Hand—R
Lighthouse Fiction
Miraculous Medal
My Legacy—R
Narrow Gate
TEAK Roundup—R
Writers' Intl. Forum
Young Christian—R

SHORT STORY: HISTORICAL

ADULT

About Such Things—R
Alive!—R
Bridal Guides—R
Byline
Chip Off Writer's Block—R
Christian Classroom
Christian Courier (CAN)—R
Christian Living—R
Christian Renewal—R
Christianity/Arts
Companions—R
Connecting Point—R
Conquest
Dreams & Visions—R
Dream Weaver
Esprit—R
Family Network—R
Fellowship Link—R
Good News (AL)—R
Healing Inn—R
Heartlight Internet—R
Hidden Manna—R
Home Times—R
Inklings
Legions of Light—R
Lighthouse Fiction

Live—R
Lutheran Woman's Quar.
Messenger/St. Anthony
Miraculous Medal
My Legacy—R
Narrow Gate
New Writing—R
North American Voice
Peoples Magazine—R
Perspectives
Presbyterian Record—R
TEAK Roundup—R
Today's Christian Senior—R
Upsouth—R
Writers' Intl. Forum

CHILDREN

CLUBHOUSE—R
Counselor—R
Courage
Discovery (NY)—R
Discovery Trails—R
Focus/Clubhouse
Focus/Clubhouse Jr
Guideposts for Kids
High Adventure—R
Kidz Chat—R
Lighthouse Fiction
Friend
Nature Friend—R
On the Line—R
Touch—R
Writers' Intl. Forum
Young Christian—R

TEEN/YOUNG ADULT

BREAD/God's Children—R
Challenge (GA) —R
Challenge (IL)
Discovery—R
Dream Weaver
Essential Connection—R
Inteen
John Milton—R
Lighthouse Fiction
Teen Life—R
Writers' Intl. Forum
Young Adult Today
Young Christian—R
Youth—R

SHORT STORY: HISTORICAL/ ROMANCE

About Such Things—R
Bridal Guides—R
Byline
Christianity/Arts

Connecting Point—R
Dreams & Visions—R
Dream Weaver
Essential Connection—R
Healing Inn—R
Lighthouse Fiction
Messenger/St. Anthony
Miraculous Medal
My Legacy—R
Narrow Gate
TEAK Roundup—R
Writers' Intl. Forum
Young Christian—R

SHORT STORY: HUMOROUS

ADULT

About Such Things—R
Alive!—R
Byline
Canada Lutheran—R
Catholic Forester—R
Chip Off Writer's Block—R
Christian Chronicle—R
Christian Courier (CAN)—R
Christianity/Arts
Christian School Admin.
Church & Synagogue Lib.
Clergy Journal—R
Companion
Connecting Point—R
Conquest
Covenant Companion—R
Day Star Tribune—R
Dreams & Visions—R
Dream Weaver
Esprit—R
Five Stones—R
Gem—R
Good News (AL)—R
Gospel Tract—R
Growing in Christ
Healing Inn—R
Helping Hand—R
Heartlight Internet—R
Hidden Manna—R
Highway News—R
Home Times—R
Horizons—R
Impact—R
Inspirer—R
John Milton—R
Legions of Light—R
Lighthouse Fiction
Liguorian
Live—R
Living—R
Living Light News—R

Mature Living
Mature Years—R
Messenger/St. Anthony
Miraculous Medal
My Legacy—R
Narrow Gate
New Writing—R
ParentLife—R
Peoples Magazine—R
Preacher's Illus. Service—R
Presbyterian Record—R
Preserving Christian Homes— R
St. Joseph's Messenger—R
Seek—R
Single Connection—R
Sojourners
TEAK Roundup—R
Tickled by Thunder
Today's Christian Senior—R
Upsouth—R
Virtue—R
Writer's Guidelines/News
Writers' Intl. Forum

CHILDREN

Crusader—R
Discovery (NY)—R
Discovery Trails—R
Focus/Clubhouse
Focus/Clubhouse Jr
Guideposts for Kids
High Adventure—R
Kidz Chat—R
Lighthouse Fiction
Living—R
My Friend
On the Line—R
Preacher's Illus. Service—R
Right Road—R
Story Friends—R
Touch—R
Wonder Time
Writers' Intl. Forum

TEEN/YOUNG ADULT

Breakaway—R
Brio—R
Campus Life—R
Challenge (GA) —R
Challenge (IL)
Discovery—R
Dream Weaver
Essential Connection—R
Inteen
Lighthouse Fiction
Listen—R
Preacher's Illus. Service—R

Real Time—R
Right Road—R
Straight—R
Student Leadership—R
Teenage Christian—R
Teen Life—R
Teens Today—R
With—R
Writers' Intl. Forum
YOU!—R
Young Adult Today
Young Salvationist—R

SHORT STORY: JUVENILE

Annals of St. Anne
Beginner's Friend—R
BREAD/God's Children—R
Catholic Forester—R
Challenge (GA) —R
Children's Church—R (6-8)
Christian Home & School
   (few)
Christian Renewal—R
Church Educator—R
Church & Synagogue Lib.
Counselor—R
Courage
Crusader—R
Day Star Tribune—R
Discoveries—R
Discovery (NY)—R
Discovery Trails—R
Evangelizing Today's Child—R
Flicker
Focus/Clubhouse
Focus/Clubhouse Jr
Good News (AL)—R
Good News Journal (MO)—R
Guideposts for Kids
Head to Head—R
High Adventure—R
Junior Companion—R
Kidz Chat—R
Lighthouse Fiction
Listen (3-4's)
Living—R
Lollipops
Lutheran Woman Today
MESSAGE (5-8 yrs)
Messenger/St. Anthony
My Friend
My Legacy—R
On the Line—R
Parent Paper—R
Partners—R
Pockets—R
Presbyterian Record—R

Primary Pal (IL)
Primary Pal (KS)—R
Right Road—R
Skipping Stones
Story Friends—R
Today's Catholic Teacher—R
Together Time (3-4)
Touch—R
Trails 'N' Treasures—R
United Church Observer
Venture
Visitation
War Cry—R
Wonder Time
Write Touch
Writers' Intl. Forum
Young Christian—R
Young Salvationist—R

SHORT STORY: LITERARY

ADULT

About Such Things—R
Byline
Chip Off Writer's Block—R
Christian Century
Christian Classroom
Christian Courier (CAN)—R
Christian Living—R
Christianity/Arts
Christian School Admin.
Conquest
Cornerstone—R
Covenant Companion—R
Chrysalis Reader
Dreams & Visions—R
Dream Weaver
Esprit—R
Good News (AL)—R
Healing Inn—R
Hidden Manna—R
Horizons—R
Inklings
Mennonite Brethren Herald—
   R
Messenger/St. Anthony
Miraculous Medal
My Legacy—R
Narrow Gate
New Writing—R
Perspectives
Poetry Forum—R
Re:generation
Seek—R
Sojourners
Standard—R
TEAK Roundup—R
Tickled by Thunder

Upsouth—R
Virtue—R
War Cry—R
Weavings—R
Writer's Guidelines/News
Writers' Intl. Forum

CHILDREN

Discovery (NY)—R
Story Friends—R
Writers' Intl. Forum

TEEN/YOUNG ADULT

Dream Weaver
Essential Connection—R
Writers' Intl. Forum
Young Salvationist—R

SHORT STORY: MYSTERY

ADULT

About Such Things—R
Bridal Guides—R
Byline
Chip Off Writer's Block—R
Christian Courier (CAN)—R
Christianity/Arts
Connecting Point—R
Day Star Tribune—R
Dreams & Visions—R
Dream Weaver
Healing Inn—R
Heartlight Internet—R
Inklings
Legions of Light—R
Lighthouse Fiction
Messenger/St. Anthony
Miraculous Medal
My Legacy—R
Narrow Gate
New Writing—R
Quest
TEAK Roundup—R
Tickled by Thunder
Writers' Intl. Forum

CHILDREN

Courage
Discovery (NY)—R
Discovery Trails—R
Focus/Clubhouse
Focus/Clubhouse Jr
Kidz Chat—R
Lighthouse Fiction
On the Line—R
Touch—R
Trails 'N' Treasures—R
Writers' Intl. Forum

Young Christian—R

TEEN/YOUNG ADULT

Challenge (IL)
Discovery—R
Dream Weaver
Essential Connection—R
Inteen
Lighthouse Fiction
Straight—R
Teen Life—R
Writers' Intl. Forum
Young Adult Today
Young Christian—R
Young Salvationist—R

SHORT STORY: MYSTERY/ROMANCE

About Such Things—R
Bridal Guides—R
Byline
Chip Off Writer's Block—R
Christianity/Arts
Connecting Point—R
Dreams & Visions—R
Dream Weaver
Essential Connection—R
Healing Inn—R
Lighthouse Fiction
Messenger/St. Anthony
Miraculous Medal
Narrow Gate
Standard—R
Writers' Intl. Forum
Young Christian—R

SHORT STORY: PARABLES

ADULT

alive now!
America
Annals of St. Anne
Bridal Guides—R
Christian Chronicle—R
Christian Classroom
Christian Courier (CAN)—R
Christian Living—R
Christianity/Arts
Christian School Admin.
Church Worship
Companion
Covenant Companion—R
Day Star Tribune—R
Discovery—R
Dreams & Visions—R
Dream Weaver
Esprit—R

Family Network—R
Fellowship Link—R
Five Stones—R
God's Revivalist
Good News (AL)—R
Good News Journal (MO)—R
Gospel Tract—R
Grail
Healing Inn—R
Hearing Hearts
Heartlight Internet—R
Helping Hand—R
Hidden Manna—R
Highway News—R
Home Times—R
Horizons—R
Impact Magazine—R
Inklings
Inspirer—R
LA Catholic
Lutheran
Mennonite Brethren—R
MESSAGE
Messenger/St. Anthony
Narrow Gate
New Writing—R
Pentecostal Testimony—R
Peoples Magazine—R
Perspectives
Preacher's Illus. Service—R
Presbyterian Record—R
Sojourners
Star of Zion
Upsouth—R
U.S. Catholic
Weavings—R

CHILDREN

Annals of St. Anne
Church Educator—R
Courage
Discovery (NY)—R
High Adventure—R
Kidz Chat—R
MESSAGE
John Milton—R
Pockets—R
Preacher's Illus. Service—R
Touch—R
Young Christian—R

TEEN/YOUNG ADULT

Annals of St. Anne
Church Educator—R
Discovery—R
Dream Weaver
Essential Connection—R
Inteen

John Milton—R
Pentecostal Testimony—R
Preacher's Illus. Service—R
Student Leadership—R
Teen Life—R
With—R
YOU!—R
Young Adult Today
Young Christian—R

SHORT STORY: PLAYS

Baptist Leader—R
Bridal Guides—R
Challenge (IL)
Church Worship
Courage (short short)
Creatively Yours
Day Star Tribune—R
Discovery (NY)—R
Esprit—R
Fellowship Link—R
Five Stones—R
Focus/Clubhouse Jr
Guideposts for Kids
Head to Head—R
Hidden Manna—R
Horizons—R
Inklings
Lutheran Digest
Messenger/St. Anthony
National Drama Service
New Writing—R
Peoples Magazine—R
Shining Star
TEAK Roundup—R
Touch—R
YOU!—R
Young Christian—R

SHORT STORY: ROMANCE

ADULT

About Such Things—R
Alive!—R
Bridal Guides—R
Byline
Chip Off Writer's Block—R
Christianity/Arts
Connecting Point—R
Dreams & Visions—R
Dream Weaver
Helping Hand—R
Inklings
Kansas City Woman
Legions of Light—R
Lighthouse Fiction
Mature Living

Messenger/St. Anthony
Miraculous Medal
Narrow Gate
Preserving Christian Homes—
    R
St. Joseph's Messenger—R
Virtue—R
Writers' Intl. Forum

TEEN/YOUNG ADULT

Brio
Discovery—R
Dream Weaver
Essential Connection—R
Healing Inn—R
Lighthouse Fiction
Straight—R
Teens Today—R
With—R
Writers' Intl. Forum
Young Christian—R
Young Salvationist—R

SHORT STORY: SCIENCE FICTION

ADULT

About Such Things—R
Byline
Chip Off Writer's Block—R
Christian Courier (CAN)—R
Christianity/Arts
Connecting Point—R
Dreams & Visions—R
Dream Weaver
Impact Magazine—R
Inklings
Legions of Light—R
Narrow Gate
Tickled by Thunder
Writers' Intl. Forum

CHILDREN

Focus/Clubhouse Jr
Writers' Intl. Forum

TEEN/YOUNG ADULT

Breakaway—R
Dream Weaver
Essential Connection—R
Inteen
Teen Life—R
With—R
Writers' Intl. Forum
Young Adult Today
Young Salvationist—R

SHORT STORY: SKITS

ADULT

Baptist Leader—R
Church Worship
Day Star Tribune—R
Esprit—R
Five Stones—R
Head to Head—R
Helping Hand—R
Horizons—R
New Writing—R
Wesleyan Woman—R

CHILDREN

Discovery (NY)—R
Head to Head—R
Shining Star
Touch—R

TEEN/YOUNG ADULT

Discovery—R
Head to Head—R
Student Leadership—R
YOU!—R

SHORT STORY: TEEN/YOUNG ADULT

Annals of St. Anne
Beautiful Christian Teen
BREAD/God's Children—R
Breakaway—R
Bridal Guides—R
Brio
Campus Life—R
Canada Lutheran—R
Catholic Forester—R
Certainty
Challenge (GA)—R
Challenge (IL)
Church & Synagogue Lib.
Church Educator—R
CLUBHOUSE—R
CoLaborer—R
Companions—R
Conqueror—R
Day Star Tribune—R
Discovery—R
Dream Weaver
Essential Connection—R
Evangel—R
Five Stones—R
Good News Journal (MO)—R
Gospel Tidings—R
Head to Head—R
High Adventure—R
Inteen

Lighthouse Fiction
Liguorian
Listen—R
Parent Paper—R
Partners—R
Pentecostal Testimony—R
Presbyterian Record—R
Quest—R
Real Time—R
Right Road—R
Skipping Stones
Sojourners
Spirit
Star of Zion
Straight—R
Student Leadership
Teenage Christian—R
Teen Life—R
Teens on Target—R
Touch—R
War Cry—R
With—R
Write Touch—R
Writers' Intl. Forum
YOU!—R
Young Adult Today
Young Christian—R
Young Salvationist—R
Youth Challenge—R
Youth Compass—R

SINGLES ISSUES

ADULT/GENERAL

A.M.E. Christian Recorder—R
Annals of St. Anne
Banner
Bible Advocate Online—R
Breakthrough Intercessor—R
Bridal Guides—R
Catholic Digest—R
Chicken Soup/Single—R
Christian Courier (CAN)—R
Christian Living—R
Christian Motorsports
Church Advocate—R
Companion
Conquest
Covenant Companion—R
Day Star Tribune—R
Discipleship Journal
Dovetail—R
Evangel—R
Family Network—R
Foursquare World—R
Gem—R
Good News (AL)—R
Good News, Etc.—R

Gospel Today
Hearing Hearts
Heartlight Internet—R
Home Times—R
Indian Life—R
Light and Life
Liguorian
Live—R
Living—R
Living Light News—R
Lookout—R
Lutheran—R
Lutheran Digest—R
Mennonite—R
MESSAGE
Metro Voice—R
Michigan Christian
Minnesota Christian—R
Moody—R
Newsline—R
Northwestern Lutheran—R
NW Christian Journal—R
On Mission
Pentecostal Testimony—R
Peoples Magazine—R
Plain Truth—R
Power for Living—R
Presbyterian Layman
Presbyterians Today—R
Purpose—R
Right Road—R
Romantic—R
Seek—R
Signs of the Times—R
Single Connection—R
Single-Parent Family
Sojourners
Something Better—R
Standard—R
Trumpeter—R
2-Soar—R
U.S. Catholic
War Cry—R
Wesleyan Advocate—R

CHRISTIAN EDUCATION/LIBRARY

Baptist Leader—R
CE Connection—R
CE Leadership—R
Leader/Church School
   Today—R

MISSIONS

Worldwide Challenge

MUSIC

Quest—R

PASTORS/LEADERS

Art+Plus
Church Administration
Five Stones—R
Journal/Christian Healing—R
Lutheran Partners—R
Ministries Today
Pastoral Life
Sharing the Practice—R
Single Adult Ministries
Vital Ministry
Word & World

TEEN/YOUNG ADULT

Conqueror—R
Inteen
YOU!—R
Young Adult Today
Young Christian—R

WOMEN

Adam's Rib—R
Anna's Journal—R
Aspire
Esprit—R
Horizons—R
Joyful Woman—R
Today's Christian Woman
True Woman
Virtue—R
Virtuous Woman
Wesleyan Woman—R
Women of Spirit—R
Women Today —R
Women Today Online—R

WRITERS

Writers' Intl. Forum

SOCIAL JUSTICE

ADULT/GENERAL

A.M.E. Christian Recorder—R
Arkansas Catholic
Arlington Catholic
Banner
Brethren Evangelist
Canadian Catholic
Catholic Digest—R
Catholic Insight
Catholic Rural Life
Catholic Sentinel—R
Charisma/Christian Life
Christian Century
Christian Chronicle—R
Christian Edge—R
Christian Living—R
Christian Motorsports

Christian Social Action—R
Christianity Today—R
Church Advocate—R
Commonweal
Company—R
Covenant Companion—R
Cresset
Culture Wars—R
Day Star Tribune—R
Faith Today
Family Network—R
Forefront
Foursquare World—R
Good News, Etc—R
Grail
Hallelujah! (CAN)—R
Head to Head—R
Hidden Manna—R
Home Times—R
Indian Life—R
Inland NW Christian
John Milton—R
Jour/Christian Nursing—R
Light and Life
Liguorian
Living—R
Mennonite—R
Mennonite Brethren—R
Messenger/St. Anthony
Michigan Christian
Montana Catholic—R
Moody—R
North American Voice
Our Family—R
Peoples Magazine—R
Perspectives
Pourastan—R
Prairie Messenger—R
Presbyterian Layman
Prism—R
ProLife News—R
Purpose—R
Re:generation
Religious Broadcasting—R
Single Connection—R
Social Justice
Sojourners
Something Better—R
Spiritual Life
United Church Observer
Upsouth—R
Way of St. Francis—R

CHILDREN

Skipping Stones

CHRISTIAN EDUCATION/LIBRARY

Church Educator—R

Journal/Adventist Educ.—R
Religion Teacher's Journal

MISSIONS

Catholic Near East
Missiology
P.I.M.E. World

PASTORS/LEADERS

African American Pulpit
Art+Plus
Celebration
Current Thoughts & Trends
Emmanuel
Five Stones—R
Lutheran Partners—R
Ministries Today
Reaching Children at Risk
Sharing the Practice—R
Voice of the Vineyard —R

TEEN/YOUNG ADULT

Devo'Zine—R
Essential Connection—R
Teenage Christian—B/C
YOU!—R
Young Salvationist—R

WOMEN

Aspire
Horizons—R
Woman's Touch—R

SOCIOLOGY

ADULT/GENERAL

Anglican Journal—R
Catholic Rural Life
Christian Courier (CAN)—R
Christian Edge—R
Common Boundary
Commonweal
Culture Wars—R
Day Star Tribune—R
Faith Today
Family Network—R
Fellowship Link—R
Good News, Etc—R
Good News Journal (MO)—R
Grail
Home Times—R
John Milton—R
Journal of Church & State
Light and Life
Michigan Christian
Quiet Revolution—R
Re:generation
SCP Journal—R

Social Justice
Standard—R
Upsouth—R

CHRISTIAN EDUCATION/LIBRARY

Catechist
Church Educator—R

MISSIONS

Areopagus—R
Missiology
Urban Mission—R

PASTORS/LEADERS

African American Pulpit
Current Thoughts & Trends
Eucharistic Minister—R
Five Stones—R
Journal/Christian Healing—R
Reaching Children at Risk
Word & World

TEEN/YOUNG ADULT

Inteen
Young Adult Today

WOMEN

Aspire

SPIRITUALITY

ADULT/GENERAL

Acts 2
Advent Christian Witness—R
alive now!
A.M.E. Christian Recorder—R
American Tract Soc.—R
Angels on Earth
Annals of St. Anne
Arlington Catholic
Banner
Believer—R
Bible Advocate—R
Bible Advocate Online—R
Bread of Life—R
Breakthrough Intercessor—R
Brethren Evangelist
Canada Lutheran—R
Canadian Catholic
Cathedral Age
Catholic Digest—R
Catholic Insight
Catholic Parent
Catholic Rural Life
CGA World—R
Charisma/Christian Life
Christian Century
Christian Chronicle—R

Christian Home & School
Christian Living—R
Christian Motorsports
Christian Parenting—R
Christian Poet—R
Christian Reader—R
Christianity Today—R
Chrysalis Reader
Church Advocate—R
Church of God EVANGEL
Columbia
Common Boundary
Commonweal
Companion
Companions—R
Company—R
Conquest
Covenant Companion—R
Cresset
Chrysalis Reader
Culture Wars—R
Day Star Tribune—R
Decision
Door
Dovetail—R
Emphasis/Faith & Living—R
Episcopal Life—R
Faith Today
Family Digest
Family Network—R
Fellowship Link—R
Forefront
Gem—R
God's Revivalist
Good News (KY)—R
Good News, Etc—R
Good News Journal (MO)—R
Gospel Today
Grail
Guideposts
Healing Inn—R
Hearing Hearts
Heartlight Internet—R
Hidden Manna—R
Highway News—R
Inland NW Christian
John Milton—R
Jour/Christian Nursing—R
Life Gate—R
Lifeglow—R
Light and Life
L.I.G.H.T News—R
Liguorian
Living Church
Living Light News—R
Living with Teenagers—R
Lookout—R
Lutheran—R

Lutheran Journal—R
Marriage Partnership
Mature Years—R
Mennonite—R
Mennonite Brethren—R
Messenger/St. Anthony
Messenger of the Sacred Heart
Michigan Christian
Montana Catholic—R
New Covenant
New Heart—R
Newsline—R
New Writing—R
North American Voice
Oblates
On Mission
Our Family—R
Our Sunday Visitor
Pegasus Review—R
Pentecostal Testimony—R
Peoples Magazine—R
Perspectives
Plowman—R
Prairie Messenger—R
Presbyterian Outlook
Presbyterians Today—R
Preserving Christian Homes—
   R
Prism—R
Purpose—R
Queen of All Hearts
Re:generation
Religious Education
Sacred Journey—R
St. Anthony Messenger
SCP Journal—R
Seek—R
Signs of the Times—R
Single Connection—R
Smile—R
Social Justice
Sojourners
Spiritual Life
Standard—R
Standard—R
Stand Firm—R
TEAK Roundup—R
Touchstone—R
2-Soar—R
Upsouth—R
U.S. Catholic
Vision—R
War Cry—R
Way of St. Francis—R
Weavings—R
Wesleyan Advocate—R

CHILDREN

BREAD/God's Children—R
Discoveries—R
Discovery (NY)—R
Pockets—R
Skipping Stones
Wonder Time

CHRISTIAN EDUCATION/LIBRARY

CE Connection—R
Christian School
Church Educator—R
Leader/Church School
   Today—R
Religion Teacher's Journal
Teacher's Interaction
Vision—R

MISSIONS

Areopagus—R
Catholic Near East
Evangelical Missions—R
Latin American Evangelist
Message of the Cross—R
Quiet Hour Echoes
Worldwide Challenge

MUSIC

Quest—R

PASTORS/LEADERS

African American Pulpit
Art+Plus
Celebration
Christian Century
Christian Ministry
Church Worship
Clergy Journal—R
Cross Currents—R
Current Thoughts & Trends
Diocesan Dialogue—R
Emmanuel
Eucharistic Minister—R
Five Stones—R
Journal/Christian Healing—R
Journal/Pastoral Care
Let's Worship
Lutheran Partners—R
Ministries Today
Ministry
Pastoral Life
Preacher's Illus. Service—R
Priest
PROCLAIM—R
Pulpit Helps—R
Reaching Children at Risk
Reformed Worship
Review for Religious

Sharing the Practice—R
Theology Today
Today's Christian Preacher—R
Today's Parish
Word & World
Youthworker—R

TEEN/YOUNG ADULT

Challenge (GA) —R
Conqueror—R
Devo'Zine—R
Essential Connection—R
Insight—R
Inteen
Student Leadership—R
Teenage Christian—R
Teen Life—R
YOU!—R
Young Adult Today
Young & Alive—R
Young Christian—R
Young Salvationist—R
Youth Update

WOMEN

Adam's Rib—R
Aspire
Esprit—R
Horizons—R
Joyful Woman—R
Just Between Us—R
Lutheran Woman's Quar.
Lutheran Woman Today
Sisters Today
Virtue—R
Virtuous Woman
Wesleyan Woman—R
Women of Spirit—R

WRITERS

Writers' Intl. Forum

SPIRITUAL WARFARE

ADULT/GENERAL

A.M.E. Christian Recorder—R
Angels on Earth
Banner
Bible Advocate—R
Bible Advocate Online—R
Bread of Life—R
Breakthrough Intercessor—R
Celebrate Life—R
CGA World—R
Charisma/Christian Life
Christian Chronicle—R
Christian Edge—R
Christian Motorsports

Christian Ranchman
Church Herald/Holiness—R
Church of God EVANGEL
Common Boundary
Day Star Tribune—R
Discipleship Journal
Emphasis/Faith & Living—R
Family Network—R
Fellowship Link—R
Good News (KY)—R
Good News, Etc—R
Good News Journal (MO)—R
Hallelujah! (CAN)—R
Healing Inn—R
Hearing Hearts
Heartlight Internet—R
Indian Life—R
John Milton—R
Life Gate—R
Light and Life
Lutheran Journal—R
MESSAGE
New Heart—R
On Mission
Pentecostal Evangel
Peoples Magazine—R
PrayerWorks—R
Preserving Christian Homes—
    R
Single Connection—R
Something Better—R
Stand Firm—R
Times of Refreshing
Trumpeter—R
2-Soar—R
Upsouth—R

CHILDREN
BREAD/God's Children—R
Discovery (NY)—R
High Adventure—R
Shining Star

MISSIONS
Latin American Evangelist
Quiet Hour Echoes
World Mission People—R

PASTORS/LEADERS
Art+Plus
Cell Church—R
Cell Life FORUM—R
Christian Camp—R
Current Thoughts & Trends
Jour/Amer Soc/Chur
    Growth—R
Ministries Today
Reaching Children at Risk

Today's Christian Preacher—R

TEEN/YOUNG ADULT
Challenge (GA) —R
Essential Connection—R
Insight—R
Real Time—R
Teen Life—R
Young Christian—R

WOMEN
Adam's Rib—R
Joyful Woman—R
Just Between Us—R
Virtuous Woman
Women of Spirit—R

WRITERS
Writers' Intl. Forum

SPORTS/RECREATION

ADULT/GENERAL
Accent on Living—R
A.M.E. Christian Recorder—R
American Tract Soc.—R
Angels on Earth
Arlington Catholic
AXIOS—R
Banner
Catholic Digest—R
Christian Courier (WI)—R
Christian Courier (CAN)—R
Christian Living—R
Christian Motorsports
Christian Ranchman
Christian Reader—R
Christian Renewal—R
Columbia
Connecting Point—R (Special
    Olympics)
Day Star Tribune—R
Discovery—R
Expression Christian
Family Journal—R
Gem—R
Good News (AL)—R
Good News, Etc—R
Good News Journal (TX)
Guideposts
Home Times—R
Indian Life—R
Lifeglow—R
Light and Life
Living Light News—R
Living with Teenagers—R
Lutheran Witness—R
Messenger/St. Anthony

Metro Voice—R
Minnesota Christian—R
New Writing—R
NW Christian Journal—R
Over the Back Fence—R
ParentLife—R
Right Road—R
Single Connection—R
Something Better—R
Sports Spectrum
Standard—R
Stand Firm—R
TEAK Roundup—R
Trumpeter—R
Vibrant Life—R

CHILDREN
BREAD/God's Children—R
Club Connection—R
Courage
Crusader—R
Discovery (NY)—R
Focus/Clubhouse
Guideposts for Kids
High Adventure—R
Live Wire—R
On the Line—R
Power & Light—R
Power Station—R
Touch—R
Young Christian—R

CHRISTIAN EDUCATION/LIBRARY
CE Leadership—R
Christian Classroom
Christian School

MISSIONS
Worldwide Challenge

MUSIC
Quest—R

PASTORS/LEADERS
Preacher's Illus. Service—R
Reaching Children at Risk

TEEN/YOUNG ADULT
Breakaway—R
Certainty
Challenge (GA) —R
Challenge (IL)
Devo'Zine—R
Essential Connection—R
Insight—R
Inteen
Real Time—R
Sharing the VICTORY—R

Straight—R
Teen Life—R
Today's Christian Teen—R
YOU!—R
Young Adult Today
Young & Alive—R
Young Christian—R
Young Salvationist—R

WOMEN

Aspire
Esprit—R

WRITERS

Writers' Intl. Forum

STEWARDSHIP

ADULT/GENERAL

A.M.E. Christian Recorder—R
Angels on Earth
Banner
Believer—R
Bible Advocate—R
Breakthrough Intercessor—R
Canada Lutheran—R
Canadian Catholic
Catholic Rural Life
Celebrate Life—R
Christian Edge—R
Christian Living—R
Christian Motorsports
Christian Ranchman
Church Advocate—R
Church of God EVANGEL
Companions—R
Covenant Companion—R
Day Star Tribune—R
Decision
Discipleship Journal
Evangel—R
Faith Today
Family Network—R
Gem—R
Good News, Etc—R
Gospel Tidings—R
Gospel Today
Gospel Tract—R
Green Cross—R
Healing Inn—R
Life Gate—R
Liguorian
Lutheran Digest—R
Lutheran Journal—R
Mennonite—R
MESSAGE
Michigan Christian
Montana Catholic—R

Moody—R
Northwestern Lutheran—R
Pentecostal Testimony—R
Peoples Magazine—R
Plain Truth—R
Power for Living—R
Presbyterian Layman
Presbyterian Outlook
Prism—R
Re:generation
Religious Broadcasting—R
Stand Firm—R
Stewardship
Today's Christian Senior—R
United Church Observer
U.S. Catholic

CHILDREN

BREAD/God's Children—R
Lad

CHRISTIAN EDUCATION/LIBRARY

Children's Ministry
Christian School Admin.
Church Educator—R
GROUP
Leader/Church School
   Today—R

MISSIONS

Quiet Hour Echoes
So All May Hear—R
World Mission People—R

PASTORS/LEADERS

African American Pulpit
Art+Plus
Cell Church—R
Clergy Journal—R
Five Stones—R
Let's Worship
Lutheran Partners—R
Ministries Today
Ministry
Preacher's Magazine—R
Pulpit Helps—R
Reaching Children at Risk
Resource—R
Sharing the Practice—R
Theology Today
Today's Christian Preacher—R
Your Church—R

TEEN/YOUNG ADULT

Challenge (GA)—R
Essential Connection—R
Teen Life—R
Teens on Target—R

Today's Christian Teen—R
With—R
YOU!—R
Youth Challenge—R

WOMEN

Aspire
Esprit—R
Virtuous Woman
Wesleyan Woman—R

WRITERS

Writers' Intl. Forum

TAKE-HOME PAPERS

ADULT/GENERAL

Companions
Conquest
Evangel
Gems of Truth
Gem
Live
Lookout
Power for Living
Purpose
Seek
Standard
Vision

CHILDREN

Beginner's Friend
Counselor
Courage
Discoveries
Discovery Trails
Good News for Children
Guide
Junior Companion
Kidz Chat
Our Little Friend
Partners
Power & Light
Power Station
Primary Pal (IL)
Primary Pal (KS)
Primary Treasure
Promise
Seeds
Story Mates
Together Time
Venture
Wonder Time

TEEN/YOUNG ADULT

Certainty
Challenge (IL)
Cross Walk

I.D.
Insight
Real Time
Straight
Teens on Target
Visions
Young Christian
Youth Challenge
Youth Compass (KS)

THEOLOGICAL

ADULT/GENERAL

AGAIN—R
A.M.E. Christian Recorder—R
America
Anglican Journal—R
Arlington Catholic
Banner
Baptist Informer
B.C. Catholic—R
Annals of St. Anne
Breakthrough Intercessor—R
Canadian Catholic
Catholic Insight
Catholic Rural Life
Charisma/Christian Life
Christian Century
Christian Motorsports
Christian Renewal—R
Christian Research
Christian Social Action—R
Christianity Today—R
Church Herald/Holiness—R
Church of God EVANGEL
Commonweal
Companion
Companions—R
Company—R
Conquest
Cornerstone—R
Creation Ex Nihilo
Cresset
Crisis Point
Culture Wars—R
Day Star Tribune—R
Dovetail—R
Episcopal Life—R
Faith Today
Fellowship Link—R
First Things
Good News (KY)—R
Grail
Green Cross—R
Hidden Manna—R
John Milton—R
Journal of Church & State
Light and Life

L.I.G.H.T News—R
Living Church
Lutheran—R
Messenger/St. Anthony
Messenger of the Sacred Heart
Michigan Christian
Montana Catholic—R
North American Voice
On Mission
Our Family—R
Our Sunday Visitor
Pentecostal Testimony—R
Peoples Magazine—R
Perspectives
Prairie Messenger—R
Presbyterian Layman
Presbyterian Outlook
Presbyterians Today—R
Queen of All Hearts
Re:generation
Religious Education
St. Anthony Messenger
St. Willibrord Journal
SCP Journal—R
Silver Wings—R
Social Justice
Sojourners
Spiritual Life
Touchstone—R
United Church Observer
U.S. Catholic
Way of St. Francis—R
Weavings—R

CHRISTIAN EDUCATION/LIBRARY

Catholic Library World
Church Educator—R
Shining Star
Teacher's Interaction

MISSIONS

Areopagus—R
Catholic Near East
East-West Church
Latin American Evangelist
Missiology
Quiet Hour Echoes
Urban Mission—R
Women of the Harvest
Worldwide Challenge

PASTORS/LEADERS

African American Pulpit
Catechumenate
Celebration
Christian Camp—R
Christian Century
Christian Ministry

Church Worship
Cross Currents—R
Current Thoughts & Trends
Diocesan Dialogue—R
Emmanuel
Eucharistic Minister—R
Five Stones—R
Journal/Christian Healing—R
Journal/Pastoral Care
Jour/Amer Soc/Chur Growth—R
Let's Worship
Lutheran Forum—R
Lutheran Partners—R
Ministries Today
Ministry
Ministry & Liturgy—R
Networks—R
Preacher's Illus. Service—R
Preacher's Magazine—R
Priest
PROCLAIM—R
Pulpit Helps—R
Quarterly Review
Reaching Children at Risk
Review for Religious
Sharing the Practice—R
Theology Today
Today's Christian Preacher—R
Today's Parish
Word & World
Youthworker—R

TEEN/YOUNG ADULT

Challenge (GA) —R
Essential Connection—R
Inteen
YOU!—R
Young Adult Today
Youth Update

WOMEN

Aspire
Conscience—R
Esprit—R
Horizons—R
Jour/Women's Ministries
Lutheran Woman Today
Sisters Today

WRITERS

Writers' Intl. Forum

THINK PIECES

ADULT/GENERAL

Alive!—R
Annals of St. Anne

AXIOS—R
Banner
Believer—R
Bible Advocate—R
Bible Advocate Online—R
Bridal Guides—R
Canadian Catholic
Catholic Digest—R
Catholic Forester—R
Catholic Rural Life
CGA World—R
Christian Chronicle—R
Christian C.L. RECORD—R
Christian Courier (CAN)—R
Christian Edge—R
Christian Living—R
Christian Poet—R
Christian Social Action—R
Common Boundary
Commonweal
Companion
Conquest
Covenant Companion—R
Day Star Tribune—R
Door
Dovetail—R
Episcopal Life—R
Expression Christian
Family Journal—R
First Things
Forefront
Good News (AL)—R
Good News, Etc—R
Good News Journal (MO)—R
Good News Journal (TX)
Green Cross—R
Head to Head—R
Healing Inn—R
Hearing Hearts
Heartlight Internet—R
Hidden Manna—R
Home Times—R
Inspirer—R
John Milton—R
Living Light News—R
Lutheran—R
Lutheran Journal—R
MESSAGE
Metro Voice—R
Michigan Christian
Minnesota Christian—R
New Writing—R
Pegasus Review—R
Pentecostal Testimony—R
Peoples Magazine—R
PrayerWorks—R
Presbyterian Layman
Presbyterian Outlook

Presbyterians Today—R
Purpose—R
Re:generation
Religious Broadcasting—R
Religious Education
San Diego Co. Christian
Single Connection—R
Sojourners
Stand Firm—R
Star of Zion
TEAK Roundup—R
Upsouth—R
Way of St. Francis—R
Wesleyan Advocate—R

CHILDREN

Discovery (NY)—R
Touch—R

CHRISTIAN EDUCATION/LIBRARY

CE Connection—R
Christian Classroom
Christian School Admin.
Resource—R
Vision—R

MISSIONS

Areopagus—R

MUSIC

Quest—R
Songwriter—R

PASTORS/LEADERS

Art+Plus
Catholic Servant
Celebration
Church Bytes—R
Eucharistic Minister—R
Five Stones—R
Journal/Christian Healing—R
Journal/Pastoral Care
Lutheran Partners—R
Ministries Today
Networks—R
Priest
Pulpit Helps—R
Reaching Children at Risk
Sharing the Practice—R
Single Adult Ministries
Technologies/Worship—R
Word & World

TEEN/YOUNG ADULT

Certainty
Challenge (GA) —R
Conqueror—R
Essential Connection—R

Vision—R
YOU!—R
Young Christian—R

WOMEN

Anna's Journal—R
Aspire
Horizons—R
Lutheran Woman Today
Virtue—R
Wesleyan Woman—R

WRITERS

Writer's Exchange—R
Writers' Intl. Forum

TIME MANAGEMENT*

ADULT/GENERAL

A.M.E. Christian Recorder—R
Believer—R
Breakthrough Intercessor—R
Bridal Guides—R
Day Star Tribune—R
Decision
Disciple's Journal—R
Discipleship Journal
Good News Journal (TX)
Homeschooling Today—R
Home Times—R
Standard—R

CHILDREN

Power & Light—R

CHRISTIAN EDUCATION/LIBRARY

Christian Classroom

MISSIONS

Latin American Evangelist

PASTORS/LEADERS

Christian Ministry
Enrichment—R
Five Stones—R
Lutheran Partners—R
Reaching Children at Risk
Sharing the Practice—R
Vital Ministry

TEEN/YOUNG ADULT

Essential Connection—R
Insight—R
Young Christian—R

WOMEN

Women of Spirit—R

WRITERS
WIN-Informer
Writer
Writers' Intl. Forum

TRAVEL

ADULT/GENERAL
Accent on Living—R
Alive!—R
Angels on Earth
Arlington Catholic
Bridal Guides—R
Catholic Digest—R
Charisma/Christian Life
Christian Courier (CAN)—R
Christian Ranchman
Christian Reader—R
Christian Traveler—R
Companion
Day Star Tribune—R
Family Digest
Fellowship Link—R
Good News (AL)—R
Good News Journal (TX)
Home Times—R
John Milton—R
Joyful Noise
Living with Teenagers—R
Lutheran Journal—R
Mature Living
Mature Years—R
Mennonite Historian—R
Messenger/St. Anthony
Michigan Christian
MovieGuide
Over the Back Fence—R
ParentLife—R
Right Road—R
Single Connection—R
Southwestern Writers—R
TEAK Roundup—R
Time of Singing—R
Today's Christian Senior—R
Upscale Magazine
Upsouth—R
Visitation

CHILDREN
Discovery (NY)—R
High Adventure—R
Skipping Stones
Touch—R

MISSIONS
Areopagus—R
East-West Church
Latin American Evangelist

World Mission People—R

PASTORS/LEADERS
Preacher's Illus. Service—R

TEEN/YOUNG ADULT
Conqueror—R
Teenage Christian—R
Young Christian—R

WOMEN
Aspire

WRITERS
Writers' Intl. Forum

TRUE STORIES

ADULT/GENERAL
AGAIN—R
Alive!—R
Angels on Earth
Believer—R
Bible Advocate—R
Bible Advocate Online—R
Breakthrough Intercessor—R
Bridal Guides—R
Catholic Digest—R
CBA Frontline
Chicken Soup/Mother—R
Chicken Soup/Single—R
Chicken Soup/Woman—R
Christian Chronicle—R
Christian Edge—R
Christian Living—R
Christian Motorsports
Christian Ranchman
Christian Reader—R
Church Advocate—R
Church of God EVANGEL
Companion
Conquest
Covenant Companion—R
Crossway/Newsline—R
Culture Wars—R
Day Star Tribune—R
Emphasis/Faith & Living—R
Family Network—R
Fellowship Link—R
Foursquare World—R
Gem—R
God's Revivalist
Good News (AL)—R
Good News, Etc—R
Good News Journal (MO)
Good News Journal (TX)
Gospel Today
Green Cross—R

Guideposts
Head to Head—R
Healing Inn—R
Hearing Hearts
Heartlight Internet—R
Hidden Manna—R
Home Times—R
Impact Magazine—R
Indian Life—R
Inspirer—R
John Milton—R
Jour/Christian Nursing—R
Keys to Living—R
Lifeglow—R
Liguorian
Living—R
Living Light News—R
Lutheran—R
Lutheran Journal—R
Lutheran Witness—R
Messenger/St. Anthony
Metro Voice—R
Michigan Christian
Minnesota Christian—R
Moody—R
New Heart—R
New Writing—R
Our Family—R
Pentecostal Evangel
Peoples Magazine—R
Physician
Plain Truth—R
Plus—R
Poetry Forum—R
Power for Living—R
PrayerWorks—R
Preserving Christian Homes—R
ProLife News—R
Quiet Revolution—R
Religious Broadcasting—R
SCP Journal—R
Signs of the Times—R
Single Connection—R
Something Better—R
Standard—R
Stand Firm—R
TEAK Roundup—R
Today's Christian Senior—R
Trumpeter—R
2-Soar—R
Vision—R
War Cry—R
Wesleyan Advocate—R

CHILDREN
Club Connection—R
CLUBHOUSE—R

Counselor—R
Courage
Discovery (NY)—R
Discovery Trails—R
Focus/Clubhouse
Focus/Clubhouse Jr
GUIDE—R
Guideposts for Kids
High Adventure—R
Listen
Live Wire—R
Mission
Nature Friend—R
Our Little Friend—R
Partners—R
Pockets—R
Power & Light—R
Power Station—R
Primary Treasure—R
Skipping Stones
Story Friends—R
Touch—R

CHRISTIAN EDUCATION/LIBRARY

CE Connection—R
Christian Classroom
Christian School Admin.
Church Media Library—R
Perspective—R

MISSIONS

American Horizon—R
Areopagus—R
Heartbeat—R
Leaders for Today
Quiet Hour Echoes
So All May Hear—R
Urban Mission—R
World Christian—R
World Mission People—R
Worldwide Challenge

MUSIC

Quest—R

PASTORS/LEADERS

Cell Church—R
Cell Life FORUM—R
Eucharistic Minister—R
Five Stones—R
Minister's Family
Networks—R
Preacher's Illus. Service—R
Sharing the Practice—R

TEEN/YOUNG ADULT

Certainty
Challenge (GA)—R

Challenge (IL)
Conqueror—R
Essential Connection—R
Guideposts for Teens—R
Insight—R
Real Time—R
Straight—R
Teen Life—R
Teens on Target—R
Today's Christian Teen—R
With—R
YOU!—R
Young & Alive—R
Young Christian—R
Young Salvationist—R
Youth Challenge—R

WOMEN

Aspire
Esprit—R
Helping Hand—R
Journey—R
Joyful Woman—R
Just Between Us—R
Lutheran Woman Today
Proverbs 31 Homemaker—R
Virtue—R
Wesleyan Woman—R
Woman's Touch—R
Women of Spirit—R

WRITERS

Writers' Intl. Forum

VIDEO REVIEWS

ADULT/GENERAL

Arlington Catholic
Bridal Guides—R
CBA Marketplace
Christian Arts Review
Christian Edge—R
Christian Renewal—R
Christianity/Arts
Companion
Day Star Tribune—R
Discovery—R
Expression Christian
Good News (AL)—R
Good News Journal (MO)—R
Hidden Manna—R
Homeschooling Today—R
Interim—R
Living Light News—R
Michigan Christian
MovieGuide
Pentecostal Testimony—R
ProLife News—R

Something Better—R
Stand Firm—R
TEAK Roundup—R
Upsouth—R

CHILDREN

Club Connection—R

CHRISTIAN EDUCATION/LIBRARY

Catholic Library World
Church Libraries—R

PASTORS/LEADERS

Five Stones—R
Lutheran Partners—R
Ministries Today
Sharing the Practice—R

TEEN/YOUNG ADULT

Challenge (GA) —R
Devo'Zine—R
With—R

WOMEN

Esprit—R

WOMEN'S ISSUES

ADULT/GENERAL

Advent Christian Witness—R
American Tract Soc.—R
Anglican Journal—R
Annals of St. Anne
Arlington Catholic
Atlantic Baptist
Banner
Bread of Life—R
Breakthrough Intercessor—R
Bridal Guides—R
Canadian Catholic
Catholic Digest—R
Catholic Faith & Family—R
Catholic Forester—R
Catholic Insight
Catholic Parent
Catholic Rural Life
CBA Marketplace
Celebrate Life—R
CGA World—R
Charisma/Christian Life
Chicken Soup/Mother—R
Christian C.L. RECORD—R
Christian Courier (CAN)—R
Christian Edge—R
Christian Living—R
Christian News NW—R
Christian Ranchman
Christian Social Action—R

Christians in Business
Chrysalis Reader
Church Advocate—R
Church of God EVANGEL
Columbia
Common Boundary
Companion
Day Star Tribune—R
Decision
Discipleship Journal
Disciple's Journal—R
Discovery—R
Dovetail—R
Emphasis/Faith & Living—R
Episcopal Life—R
Evangel—R
Expression Christian
Faith Today
Family Journal—R
Family Network—R
Focus on the Family
Foursquare World—R
Gem—R
Good News (AL)—R
Good News, Etc—R
Good News Journal (MO)—R
Good News Journal (TX)
Hallelujah! (CAN)—R
Healing Inn—R
Heartlight Internet—R
Homeschooling Today—R
Home Times—R
Indian Life—R
Interim—R
John Milton—R
Jour/Christian Nursing—R
Joyful Noise
Keys to Living—R
Life Gate—R
Light and Life
Liguorian
Live—R
Living—R
Living Light News—R
Living with Teenagers—R
Lookout—R
Lutheran—R
Marriage Partnership
Mennonite—R
Mennonite Brethren—R
MESSAGE
Messenger/St. Anthony
Metro Voice—R
Michigan Christian
Minnesota Christian—R
Moody—R
Newsline—R
New Writing—R

On Mission
Our Sunday Visitor
ParentLife—R
Pentecostal Evangel
Peoples Magazine—R
Perspectives
Plain Truth—R
Plus—R
Presbyterian Layman
Presbyterian Outlook
Presbyterians Today—R
ProLife News—R
Purpose—R
Romantic—R
St. Joseph's Messenger—R
Signs of the Times—R
Single Connection—R
Sojourners
Something Better—R
Standard—R
Together—R
Total Health
Touchstone—R
Trumpeter—R
2-Soar—R
United Church Observer
War Cry—R

CHRISTIAN EDUCATION/LIBRARY

Baptist Leader—R
Resource—R

MISSIONS

American Horizon—R
East-West Church
Urban Mission—R
World Mission People—R
Worldwide Challenge

PASTORS/LEADERS

Art+Plus
Cell Church—R
Christian Century
Christian Ministry (feminist)
Enrichment—R
Journal/Christian Healing—R
Lutheran Partners—R
Ministries Today (little)
Ministry
Preacher's Magazine—R
Pulpit Helps—R
Reaching Children at Risk
Sharing the Practice—R
Youthworker—R
Word & World

TEEN/YOUNG ADULT

Brio

Vision—R
YOU!—R

WOMEN

(See alphabetical listing)

WRITERS

Writers' Intl. Forum

WORLD ISSUES

ADULT/GENERAL

Alive!
A.M.E. Christian Recorder—R
America
Annals of St. Anne
Arlington Catholic
Atlantic Baptist
AXIOS—R
Banner
Baptist Informer
Believer—R
Bible Advocate—R
Bible Advocate Online—R
Breakthrough Intercessor—R
Bridal Guides—R
Canadian Catholic
CGA World—R
Charisma/Christian Life
Christian Century
Christian Courier (CAN)—R
Christian Crusade
Christian Edge—R
Christian Living—R
Christian Motorsports
Christian Ranchman
Christian Renewal—R
Christian Social Action—R
Church of God EVANGEL
Commonweal
Companion
Covenant Companion—R
Creation Ex Nihilo
Culture Wars—R
Day Star Tribune—R
Decision
Discipleship Journal
Evangel—R
Expression Christian
Faith Today
Family Network—R
First Things
God's Revivalist
Good News (AL)—R
Good News, Etc.—R
Good News Journal (MO)—R
Good News Journal (TX)
Gotta Write

Grail
Green Cross—R
Hallelujah! (CAN)—R
Healing Inn—R
Heartlight Internet—R
Home Times—R
Inland NW Christian
Interchange
Interim—R
John Milton—R
Journal of Church & State
Liberty—R
Light and Life
Living Light News—R
Lookout—R
Lutheran—R
Lutheran Journal—R
Mennonite—R
MESSAGE
Messenger
Messenger/St. Anthony
Metro Voice—R
Michigan Christian
Minnesota Christian—R
Moody—R
Our Sunday Visitor
Pentecostal Testimony—R
Peoples Magazine—R
Presbyterian Layman
Presbyterian Outlook
Presbyterians Today—R
ProLife News—R
Quiet Revolution—R
Re:generation
Religious Broadcasting—R
SCP Journal—R
Single Connection—R
Sojourners
Something Better—R
Stand Firm—R
TEAK Roundup—R
2-Soar—R
United Church Observer
Vision—R
War Cry—R

CHILDREN

Counselor—R
Discovery (NY)—R
God's World News—R
Skipping Stones

MISSIONS

Areopagus—R
Catholic Near East
East-West Church
Latin American Evangelist
Missiology

New World Outlook
P.I.M.E. World
So All May Hear—R
Urban Mission—R
World Christian—R
World Mission People—R
World Pulse—R
Worldwide Challenge

PASTORS/LEADERS

African American Pulpit
Cell Church—R
Christian Century
Current Thoughts & Trends
Lutheran Partners—R
Ministries Today
Networks—R
Preacher's Illus. Service—R
Preacher's Magazine—R
Quarterly Review
Reaching Children at Risk
Word & World
Youthworker—R

TEEN/YOUNG ADULT

Challenge (GA)—R
Conqueror—R
Essential Connection—R
Student Leadership—R
Teenage Christian—R
YOU!—R
Young Christian—R

WOMEN

Aspire
Esprit—R
Helping Hand—R
Horizons—R
Lutheran Woman Today
Wesleyan Woman—R

WRITERS

Writers' Intl. Forum

WORSHIP

ADULT/GENERAL

Advent Christian Witness—R
alive now!
A.M.E. Christian Recorder—R
Angels on Earth
Annals of St. Anne
Arlington Catholic
Atlantic Baptist
Baptist Informer
Believer—R
Bible Advocate—R
Bread of Life—R

Breakthrough Intercessor—R
Brethren Evangelist
Canadian Catholic
Canadian Mennonite
Cathedral Age
Catholic Digest—R
CGA World—R
Charisma/Christian Life
Christian Century
Christian Edge—R
Christian Motorsports
Christianity Today—R
Church Herald/Holiness—R
Church of God EVANGEL
Commonweal
Companion
Companions—R
Conquest
Cornerstone—R
Covenant Companion—R
Cresset
Culture Wars—R
Day Star Tribune—R
Decision
Discipleship Journal
Dovetail—R
Emphasis/Faith & Living—R
Evangel—R
Faith Today
Family Digest
Family Network—R
Fellowship Link—R
Foursquare World—R
Good News, Etc—R
Good News Journal (MO)—R
Green Cross—R
Healing Inn—R
Inspirer—R
John Milton—R
Joyful Noise
Life Gate—R
Lifeglow—R
Light and Life
L.I.G.H.T News—R
Liguorian
Live—R
Living Church
Living with Teenagers—R
Lutheran—R
Lutheran Journal—R
Mennonite—R
Messenger/St. Anthony
Michigan Christian
Montana Catholic—R
Moody—R
North American Voice
NW Christian Journal—R
On Mission

Our Family—R
Our Sunday Visitor
Pentecostal Testimony—R
Peoples Magazine—R
Perspectives
Plain Truth—R
Plenty Good Room
Power for Living—R
Prairie Messenger—R
PrayerWorks—R
Presbyterian Outlook
Presbyterian Record—R
Presbyterians Today—R
St. Anthony Messenger
St. Willibrord Journal
Silver Wings—R
Spiritual Life
Standard—R
Time of Singing—R
Touchstone—R
Trumpeter—R
United Church Observer
U.S. Catholic
War Cry—R
Way of St. Francis—R
Weavings—R
Wesleyan Advocate—R

CHILDREN

BREAD/God's Children—R
Wonder Time

CHRISTIAN EDUCATION/LIBRARY

Children's Ministry
Christian Ed Journal—R
CE Leadership—R
Christian School Admin.
Church Educator—R
Church Media Library—R
Evangelizing Today's Child—R
GROUP
Leader/Church School
    Today—R
Shining Star

MISSIONS

American Horizon—R
Areopagus—R
Latin American Evangelist
Quiet Hour Echoes
Worldwide Challenge

MUSIC

Church Pianist, etc.
Creator—R
Glory Songs—R
Gospel Industry Today
Hymn

PASTORS/LEADERS

African American Pulpit
Celebration
Cell Church—R
Cell Life FORUM—R
Christian Century
Christian Management—R
Church Bytes—R
Church Growth Network—R
Church Worship
Clergy Journal—R
Emmanuel
Enrichment—R
Environment & Art
Evangelical Baptist—R
Five Stones—R
Journal/Christian Healing—R
Leadership Journal—R
Let's Worship
Lutheran Forum—R
Lutheran Partners—R
Ministries Today
Ministry
Ministry & Liturgy—R
Networks—R
Preacher's Illus. Service—R
Preacher's Magazine—R
Preaching
Priest
PROCLAIM—R
Reaching Children at Risk
Reformed Worship
Resource—R
Today's Christian Preacher—R
Today's Parish
Vital Ministry
WCA News—R
Word & World
Worship Leader
Youthworker—R

TEEN/YOUNG ADULT

Challenge (GA) —R
Conqueror—R
Essential Connection—R
Insight—R
Real Time—R
Straight—R
Student Leadership—R
Teenage Christian—R
Teen Life—R
Teens on Target—R
Today's Christian Teen—R
With—R
YOU!—R
Youth Challenge—R
Youth Update

WOMEN

Adam's Rib—R
Aspire
Esprit—R
Horizons—R
Joyful Woman—R
Lutheran Woman Today
Proverbs 31 Homemaker—R
Sisters Today
Virtue—R
Virtuous Woman
Wesleyan Woman—R

WRITERS

Writers' Intl. Forum

WRITING HOW-TO

ADULT/GENERAL

CBA Marketplace
Christian Edge—R
Day Star Tribune—R
Home Times—R
Michigan Christian
Narrow Gate
New Writing—R
Poetry Forum—R
Poet's Page
Poets' Paper—R
TEAK Roundup—R
2-Soar—R

CHILDREN

Challenge (GA)—R
Discovery (NY)—R

CHRISTIAN EDUCATION/LIBRARY

Children's Ministry
GROUP
Leader/Church School
    Today—R

PASTORS/LEADERS

Newsletter Newsletter
Reaching Children at Risk
Sharing the Practice—R
Technologies/Worship—R

TEEN/YOUNG ADULT

Challenge (GA)—R
Insight—R
Young Christian—R

WOMEN

Esprit—R

WRITERS

Advanced Chris. Writer—R

Byline
Canadian Writer's Jour—R
Cross & Quill—R
Dream Weaver
Exchange—R
Fellowscript—R
NW Christian Author—R
Once Upon a Time—R
Songwriter—R
Southwestern Writers—R
Teachers & Writers
Tickled by Thunder
WIN-Informer
Writer
Writer On Line—R
Writer's Digest—R
Writer's Exchange—R
Writer's Forum—R
Writer's Guidelines/News
Writers' Journal—R
Writer's Potpourri—R
Writing World

YOUTH ISSUES

ADULT/GENERAL

American Tract Soc.—R
Annals of St. Anne
Arlington Catholic
AXIOS—R
Banner
Believer—R
Breakthrough Intercessor—R
Canadian Catholic
Catholic Faith & Family—R
Catholic Rural Life
Charisma/Christian Life
Christian Courier (CAN)—R
Christian Edge—R
Christian Living—R
Christian Motorsports
Christian Ranchman
Christian Renewal—R
Christian Social Action—R
Church Herald/Holiness—R
Columbia
Companion
Covenant Companion—R
Culture Wars—R
Day Star Tribune—R
Decision
Emphasis/Faith & Living—R
Evangel—R
Expression Christian
Faith Today

Foursquare World—R
Good News (AL)—R
Good News, Etc—R
Good News Journal (TX)
Gospel Today
Hallelujah! (CAN)—R
Homeschooling Today—R
Indian Life—R
John Milton—R
Life Gate—R
Living Light News—R
Living with Teenagers—R
Lutheran—R
MESSAGE
Messenger/St. Anthony
Metro Voice—R
Michigan Christian
On Mission
Our Family—R
ParentLife—R
Prairie Messenger—R
Presbyterian Outlook
Presbyterian Record—R
Presbyterians Today—R
Prism—R
ProLife News—R
Real FamilyLife
Religious Education
Right Road—R
Sojourners
Something Better—R
TEAK Roundup—R
Trumpeter—R
2-Soar—R
U.S. Catholic

CHILDREN

BREAD/God's Children—R
Children's Ministry
Club Connection—R
CLUBHOUSE—R
Courage
Crusader—R
Discovery (NY)—R
Focus/Clubhouse Jr
Guideposts for Kids
My Friend
On the Line—R
Power & Light—R
Skipping Stones
Touch—R

CHRISTIAN EDUCATION/LIBRARY

Baptist Leader—R
CE Connection—R

CE Counselor—R
CE Leadership—R
Christian Classroom
Christian School Admin.
Church Educator—R
Enrichment—R
GROUP
Journal/Adventist Educ.—R
Leader/Church School
   Today—R
Parish Teacher
Perspective—R
Resource—R
Shining Star
Team—R
Vision—R

MISSIONS

American Horizon—R
Quiet Hour Echoes
Worldwide Challenge

MUSIC

Quest—R

PASTORS/LEADERS

Art+Plus
Catholic Servant
Cell Church—R
Cell Life FORUM—R
Christian Camp—R
Current Thoughts & Trends
Five Stones—R
Ivy Jungle Report—R
Journal/Christian Healing
Lutheran Partners—R
Minister's Family
Ministries Today
Pastoral Life
Reaching Children at Risk
Sharing the Practice—R
Word & World
Youthworker—R

TEEN/YOUNG ADULT

(See alphabetical listing)

WOMEN

Esprit—R
Proverbs 31 Homemaker—R
Wesleyan Woman—R

WRITERS

Writers' Intl. Forum

ALPHABETICAL LISTINGS OF PERIODICALS

Following are the listings of periodicals. They are arranged alphabetically by type of periodical (see Table of Contents for a list of types). Nonpaying markets are indicated in bold letters within those listings, e.g., **NO PAYMENT**.

If a listing is preceded by an asterisk (*), it indicates that publisher did not send updated information. If it is preceded by a number symbol (#) it was updated from current guidelines or available sources. If it is preceded by a (+) it is a new listing. It is important that freelance writers request writer's guidelines and a recent sample copy before submitting to any of these publications, but especially to those with the * and # symbols.

If you do not find the publication you are looking for, look in the General Index. See the introduction of that index for the codes used to identify the current status of each unlisted publication.

For a detailed explanation of how to understand and get the most out of these listings, as well as solid marketing tips, see the "How to Use This Book" section at the front of the book. Unfamiliar terms are explained in the Glossary at the back of the book.

(*) An asterisk before a listing indicates no or unconfirmed information update.

(#) A number symbol before a listing means it was updated from the current writer's guidelines or other sources.

(+) A plus sign means it is a new listing.

ADULT/GENERAL MARKETS

ACCENT ON LIVING, PO Box 700, Bloomington IL 61702. (309)378-2961. Fax (309)378-4420. E-mail: acntlvng@aol.com. Website: http://www.blvd. com/accent. Cheever Publishing. Betty Garee, ed. Provides information on new devices and easier ways to do things, so people with physical disabilities can enjoy a better and more satisfying lifestyle. Quarterly mag; 112 pgs; circ 18,000. Subscription $12. 80% freelance. Query; phone/fax/e-query OK. Pays .10/wd on publication for one-time rts. Articles (30-40/yr) to 800 wds. Responds in 4 wks. Seasonal 6 mos ahead. Accepts simultaneous submissions & reprints (tell when/where appeared). Accepts disk or e-mail submission (copied into message). Some sidebars. Guidelines (also by e-mail); copy $3.50. (Ads)

> **Fillers:** Cartoons; $20.
>
> **Tips:** "We prefer an informal, rather than academic approach. We want to show individuals with disabilities getting involved in all aspects of life."

+ABOUT SUCH THINGS, Tenth Presbyterian Church, 1701 Delancey St., Philadelphia PA 19103. E-mail: aboutsuch@juno.com. Website: Http://

www.world.std.com/pduggan/ast/astoot.html. Laurel W. Carver, mng ed. Readership seeks to interact with culture at large in a thoughtful, morally-grounded manner. Biannual mag (deadlines are January 2 and July 20 each year). **PAYS 2 COPIES** for one-time rts. Articles to 2,500 wds; fiction to 3,000 wds. Prefers disk. Guidelines (also by e-mail/Website); copy $3.

Poetry: Free verse; 4-80 lines. Submit max 5 poems.

Tips: "In nonfiction, we are particularly interested in articles that evaluate popular culture and the arts from a Christian perspective. In fiction, emphasize character development and theme. Characters should be multi-faceted and should change or grow during the course of the story."

ADVENT CHRISTIAN WITNESS, PO Box 23152, Charlotte NC 28227. (704)545-6161. Fax (704)573-0712. E-mail: ACPub@adventchristian.org. Advent Christian General Conference. Keith D. Wheaton, ed. Denominational. Monthly mag; 16 pgs; circ 3,200. Subscription $13. Query; e-query OK. **NO PAYMENT** for one-time rts. Articles 1,500-2,000 wds (3-4/yr). Responds in 6-10 wks. Seasonal 7 mos ahead. Accepts simultaneous submissions & reprints. Accepts disk. Regular sidebars. Prefers NIV. No guidelines; copy for 9x12 SAE/4 stamps. (No ads)

Fillers: Cartoons.

AGAIN MAGAZINE, PO Box 76, Ben Lomond CA 95005. (408)338-3644. Fax (408)336-8882. E-mail: shouston@conciliarpress.com. Website: http://www. conciliarpress.com. Orthodox/Conciliar Press. Raymond Zell, mng ed. A call to the people of God to return to their roots of historical orthodoxy once AGAIN. Quarterly mag; 32 pgs; circ 5,000. Subscription $14.50. 1% freelance. Query. **PAYS IN COPIES.** Accepts simultaneous submissions & reprints. Articles 1,500-2,500 wds; fiction 1,500-2,500 wds; book reviews 500-700 wds. Responds in 16 wks. Seasonal 2 mos ahead. Serials 2 parts. Prefers disk. Copy $2.50/9x12 SAE/5 stamps.

THE ALABAMA BAPTIST, 3310 Independence Dr., Birmingham AL 35209-5602. (205)870-4720. Fax (205)870-8957. E-mail: 70420.127@ compu serve.com. Dr. Bob Terry, ed. Shares news and information relevant to members of Baptist churches in Alabama. Weekly newspaper; circ 110,000. Subscription $10. Open to freelance. Query. Not in topical listings. (Ads)

ALIVE! A MAGAZINE FOR CHRISTIAN SENIOR ADULTS, PO Box 46464, Cincinnati OH 45246-0464. (513)825-3681. E-mail: jcLangl@aol.com. Christian Seniors Fellowship. June Lang, office ed. Focuses on activities and opportunities for active, Christian senior adults, 55 and older; upbeat rather than nostalgic. Bimonthly mag; 28 pgs; circ 3,000. Subscription/membership $15. 70% freelance. Complete ms/cover letter. Pays .04-.06/wd on publication for one-time or reprint rts. Articles 600-1,200 wds (35-40/yr); fiction 600-1,200 wds (6-8/yr). Responds in 6-8 wks. Seasonal 4 mos ahead. Accepts reprints (tell when/where appeared). No disk. Some sidebars. Guidelines; copy for 9x12 SAE/3 stamps. (Ads)

Poetry: Rarely use. Free verse, light verse, traditional; $3-10. Submit max 3 poems.

Fillers: Buys 20/yr. Anecdotes, cartoons, quizzes, short humor, and word puzzles, 50-500 wds; $5-25.

Columns/Departments: Buys 35/yr. Heart Medicine (humor, grandparent/grandchild anecdotes), to 100 wds, $5-10.

Tips: "Most open to fresh material of special appeal to Christian senior adults. Avoid nostalgia. Our market is seniors interested in living in the present, not dwelling on the past. We pay little attention to credits/bios. Articles stand on their own merit."

ALIVE NOW! PO Box 189, Nashville TN 37202-0189. (615)340-7218. Fax (615)340-7267. E-mail: alivenow@upperroom.org. Website: http://www.upperroom.org. United Methodist/The Upper Room. George R. Graham, ed. Short theme-based writings in attractive graphic setting for reflection and meditation. Bimonthly mag; 64 pgs; circ 65,000. 30% freelance. Complete ms/cover letter. Pays $20-30 or more on publication for newspaper, periodical and electronic rts. Articles 250-400 wds; fiction 250-750 wds. Responds 13 wks before issue date. Seasonal 6-8 mos ahead. Accepts disk. Guidelines/theme list; free copy.

   Poetry: Free verse, traditional; to 25 lines or one page.

   Fillers: Cartoons, prayers.

+A.M.E. CHRISTIAN RECORDER, 500 8th Ave. S, Ste 213, Nashville TN 37203. (615)256-8548. Fax (615)244-1833. African Methodist Episcopal Church. Ricky Spain, ed. Denominational. Bimonthly tabloid; 8-12 pgs; circ 10,000. Subscription $20. 100% freelance. Complete ms/cover letter. **PAYS IN COPIES** for all rts. Articles to 2,500 wds. Responds in 3 wks. Seasonal 2 mos ahead. Accepts simultaneous submissions & reprints. Accepts disk. No sidebars. Guidelines; copy for 9x12 SAE/3 stamps.

AMERICA, 106 W. 56th St., New York NY 10019-3893. (212)581-4640. Fax (212)399-3596. E-mail: articles@americapress.org. Website: http://www.americapress.org. Catholic. Thomas J. Reese, S.J., ed-in-chief. For thinking Catholics and those who want to know what Catholics are thinking. Weekly mag; 32+ pgs; circ 40,000. 100% freelance. Complete ms/cover letter; fax/e-query OK. Pays $100-200 on acceptance for first and electronic rts. Articles 1,500-2,000 wds. Responds in 6 wks. Seasonal 3 mos ahead. Guidelines; (also on Website) copy for 9x12 SAE. (Ads)

   Poetry: Patrick Samway, S.J. Light verse, serious poetry, unrhymed; 15-30 lines; $7.50-25 or $1.40/line (on publication). Submit max 3 poems.

AMERICAN TRACT SOCIETY, Box 462008, Garland TX 75046. (972)276-9408. Fax (972)272-9642. E-mail: PBatzing@ATSTracts.org. Website: http://www.gospelcom.net/AmericanTractSociety. Peter Batzing, tract ed. Majority of tracts written to win unbelievers. Bimonthly tracts; 25 million produced annually. 5% freelance. Complete ms/cover letter; e-query OK. **PAYS IN COPIES** on publication for exclusive tract rts. Tracts 900-1,200 wds (5/yr). Responds in 6-8 wks. Seasonal 1 yr ahead. Accepts simultaneous submissions & reprints (tell when/where appeared). Prefers disk, no e-mail submission. Prefers NIV or KJV. Guidelines/free samples for #10 SAE/1 stamp. (No ads)

   Special Needs: Youth issues, Hispanic, African-American.

Tips: "Read our current tracts; submit polished writing; relate to people's needs and experiences."

+AND HE WILL GIVE YOU REST, PO Box 502886, San Diego CA 92150. (619)237-1698. E-mail: rest@ixpress.com. Website: http://www.ixpress.com/jlcopen. Rest Ministries, Inc. Lisa Copen, ed. For people who live with chronic illness or pain; offers encouragement, support and hope dealing with everyday issues. Monthly mag. Estab 1997. 60% freelance. **PAYS IN COPIES.** Articles. Guidelines; copy $1. Not in topical listings.

Tips: "Avoid articles about physical healing and people who have physically overcome their illness. Write for people who will live with their illness indefinitely, but who are searching for how to live joyfully despite the 'thorn.'"

*ANGEL TIMES, PO Box 1325, Duluth GA 30096-1325. Angelic Realms Unlimited, Inc. Linda Whitman Vephula, pub. Stories of true, angelic experiences. Quarterly mag. **NO PAYMENT.** Articles 1,500 wds. Not in topical listings.

#ANGELS ON EARTH, 16 E. 34th St., New York NY 10016. (212)251-8100. Fax (212)684-0679.E-mail: angelsedtr@guideposts.org. Website: http://www.guideposts.org. Guideposts. Colleen Hughes, mng ed.; Celeste McCauley, ed. for features and fillers. Presents true stories about God's angels and humans who have played angelic roles on earth. Bimonthly mag; circ 800,000. Subscription $15.95. 90% freelance. Complete ms/cover letter. Pays $25-400 on publication for all rts. Articles 100-2,000 wds (80-100/yr; all stories must be true). Responds in 13 wks. Seasonal 6 mos ahead. Regular sidebars. No disk. Guidelines; copy for 7x10 SAE/4 stamps.

Fillers: Buys many. Anecdotal shorts of similar nature; to 250 wds; $25-100.

Columns/Departments: Accepts 25/yr. Earning Their Wings (good deeds), 150 wds; Only Human? (human or angel?/mystery), 250 wds; $50-100.

+ANGLICAN ARTS (AngliCan), 14845-6 Yonge St., Ste 158, Aurora ON L4G 6H8 Canada. Phone/Fax (905)841-1802. E-mail: mwleach@yorku.ca. Michael Leach, ed. For those with an above average interest in the artistic and aesthetic aspects of their spiritual lives as practitioners or observers and how the sacred arts help or hinder them. Monthly journal. Estab 1998.

*ANGLICAN JOURNAL, 600 Jarvis St., Toronto ON M4Y 2J6 Canada. (416)924-9192. Anglican Church of Canada. Carolyn Purden, ed; submit to Vianney Carriere, news ed. Informs Canadian Anglicans about the church at home and overseas. Newspaper (10x/yr); 24 pgs; circ 272,000. 25% freelance. Query only; phone query OK. Pays $50-300 CAN, on acceptance for 1st rts. Articles to 1,000 wds. Responds in 2 wks. Seasonal 2 mos ahead. Accepts reprints. Guidelines.

THE ANNALS OF SAINT ANNE DE BEAUPRE, PO Box 1000, St. Anne de Beaupre QC G0A 3C0 Canada. (418)827-4538. Fax (418)827-4530. Catholic/Redemptorist Fathers. Father Roch Achard, C.ss.R., ed. Promotes Catholic family values. Monthly mag; 32 pgs; circ 45,000. Subscription $9 US,

$10.25 CAN. 35% freelance. Complete ms/cover letter; no phone/fax query. Pays .03-.04/wd on acceptance for 1st rts. Articles & fiction (250/yr); 500-1,500 wds. Responds in 4 wks. Seasonal 4-5 mos ahead. No disk. No sidebars. Prefers NRSV. Guidelines; copy for 9x12 SAE/IRC. (No ads)

> **Tips:** "Writing must be uplifting and inspirational; clearly written, not filled with long quotations. We tend to stay away from extreme controversy and focus on the family, good family values, devotion and Christianity."

*THE APOCALYPSE CHRONICLES, Box 448, Jacksonville OR 97530. (541)899-8888. Christian Media. James Lloyd, ed/pub. Deals with the apocalypse exclusively. Quarterly newsletter; circ 2,000-3,000. Query; prefers phone query. Payment negotiable for reprint rts. Articles. Responds in 3 wks. KJV only. Copy for #10 SAE/2 stamps.

> **Tips:** "It's helpful if you understand your own prophetic position and are aware of its name, i.e., Futurist, Historicist, etc."

ARKANSAS CATHOLIC, PO Box 7417, Little Rock AR 72217. (501)664-0125. Fax (501)664-9075. E-mail: malea@alltel.net. Catholic Diocese of Little Rock. Malea Walters, ed. Regional newspaper for the local Diocese. Weekly tabloid; 12 pgs; circ 7,000. Subscription $15. 10% freelance. Query/clips; fax query OK. Pays on acceptance or publication for 1st rts. Articles (2/yr) 400-800 wds. Accepts simultaneous submissions. Accepts disk. Regular sidebars. Prefers Catholic Bible. Guidelines; copy for 7x10 SAE/2 stamps. (Ads)

> **Columns/Departments:** Kathy Neal. Accepts 2/yr. Seeds of Faith (education).

> **Tips:** "Make stories as localized as possible."

ARLINGTON CATHOLIC HERALD, 200 N. Glebe Rd., Ste. 607, Arlington VA 22203. (703)841-2590. Fax (703)524-2782. E-mail: achflach@aol.com, or editorial@cathilicherald.com. Website: http://catholicherald.com/index.htm. Catholic Diocese of Arlington. Michael Flach, ed. Regional newspaper for the local Diocese. Weekly newspaper; 28 pgs; circ 53,000. Subscription $14. 10% freelance. Query; phone/fax/e-query OK. Pays $50-150 on publication for one-time rts. Articles 500-1,500 wds. Responds in 2 wks. Seasonal 3 mos ahead. Accepts simultaneous submissions. Prefers disk. Regular sidebars. Guidelines (also on Website); copy for 11x17 SAE. (Ads)

> **Columns/Departments:** Sports; School News; Local Entertainment; 500 wds.

> **Tips:** "All submissions must be Catholic-related. Avoid controversial issues within the Church."

*ATLANTIC BAPTIST, PO Box 756, Kentville NS B4N 3X9 Canada. (902)681-6868. Fax (902)681-0315. Atlantic Baptist Convention. Michael A. Lipe, ed. Denominational. Monthly; 32-48 pgs; circ 7,500. Subscription $27.50. 25% freelance. Query or complete ms; fax query OK. Pays $15-30 on publication for one-time rts. Articles 750-1,500 wds. Responds in 2-5 wks. Guidelines.

*AWARENESS TENNESSEE CHRISTIAN COMMUNICATOR, PO Box 100415, Nashville TN 37224. Phone/fax (615)889-1791. Nondenominational.

Karynthia Phillips, pub/ed. Provides national, international and local news. Monthly newspaper; 8 pgs; circ 10,000. Free subscription. 100% freelance. Query/clips. **PAYS IN COPIES.**

*AXIOS, 1501 E. Chapman Ave. #345, Fullerton CA 92631-4000. Orthodox Christian. Fr. Daniel John Gorham, ed. Review of public affairs, religion, literature and the arts, and is especially interested in the Orthodox Catholic Church and its world view. Bimonthly newsletter; 32 pgs; circ 15,672. Subscription $25. 90% freelance. Complete ms/cover letter. Pays .04/wd & up ($25-500) on publication for 1st rts. Articles any length (29/yr); book reviews 2,000 wds. Responds in 4-8 wks. Seasonal 4 mos ahead. Accepts simultaneous submissions & reprints. Kill fee 25%. Copy $4.20/9x12 SAE/$1.20 currency.

   Poetry: Buys 6/yr. Traditional; any length; $5-25. Submit max 3 poems.

   Fillers: Buys 25/yr. Anecdotes, cartoons, facts.

   Columns/Departments: Buys 80 religious book and film reviews/yr. Query.

   Tips: "Most open to articles. Be sure you have an idea of who and what an orthodox Christian is."

   ** This periodical was #58 on the 1994 Top 50 Christian Publishers list.

THE BANNER, 2850 Kalamazoo Ave. SE, Grand Rapids MI 49560. (616)224-0732. Fax (616)224-0834. E-mail: banner@crcna.org. Christian Reformed Church. John D. Suk, ed; Malcolm McBryde, assoc ed. Denominational; to inform, challenge, educate, comfort, and inspire members of the church. Biweekly mag; 39 pgs; circ. 30,000. Subscription $34.95. 10% freelance. Query or complete ms/cover letter; phone/fax/e-query OK. Pays $125-200 on acceptance for all rts. Articles 850 or 1,200-1,800 wds (5/yr); fiction to 2,500 wds; book/music/video reviews, 850 wds, $50. Responds in 8 wks. Seasonal 6-8 mos ahead. Requires disk. Kill fee 50%. Regular sidebars. Prefers NIV. Guidelines/theme list; copy for 9x12 SAE/4 stamps. (Ads)

   Poetry: Buys 10/yr. Any type; 5-50 lines; $40. Submit max 5 poems.

   Fillers: Buys 48/yr. Church related cartoons; $40.

   Columns/Departments: Tuned In (critical critiques of movies, music, TV, etc.), 800 wds; $50.

   Tips: "One must really get to know the Christian Reformed Church. All of our articles are geared to this expression of faith."

   ** 1997 EPA Award of Merit—Denominational.

*BANNER NEWS SERVICE, 7127 Little River Turnpike, Ste. 205, Annandale VA 22003. (703)750-3078. Fax (703)916-7773. E-mail: TWMgroup@ipo. net. World-wide, nondenominational news organization. Fidelis Iyebote, ed. Provides companies, church organizations and individuals with news, information, ideas, innovations, and facts to promote business and individual growth. Subscription $150. Buys 20 articles/day; 2 typed, double-spaced pages. Query/clips or complete ms; fax query OK (prefers mail). Payment is attractive, but depends on quality. Responds in 4 wks. House style book available to accredited contributors and correspondents.

Tips: "Most open to exclusive, authentic, well-researched stories on topical current issues."

BAPTIST HISTORY AND HERITAGE, Editor's address: Carson-Newman College, 1646 Russell Ave., Jefferson City TN 37760. (431)471-3200. Southern Baptist Historical Society (Oklahoma Baptist University, Box 61838, 500 W. Shawnee, Shawnee OK 74801-2590, (800)966-2278). Mel Hawkins, mng ed. A scholarly journal focusing on Baptist history. Quarterly journal; 64 pgs; circ 2,000. 15-20% freelance. Query. Pays $192 (for assigned only) for all rts. Articles to 4,000 wds. Responds in 9 wks. Prefers disk. Guidelines.

Tips: "Most open to lesser known aspects of Baptist history based on primary sources."

***THE BAPTIST INFORMER**, 603 S. Wilmington St., Raleigh NC 27601. (919)821-7466. Fax (919)836-0061. General Baptist. Archie D. Logan, ed. Regional African-American publication. Monthly tabloid; 16 pgs; circ 10,000. 10% freelance. Query or complete ms/cover letter; fax query OK. **PAYS IN COPIES** for one-time rts. Articles & fiction. Responds in 13 wks. Accepts simultaneous submissions. Prefers disk. Free copy.

THE B.C. CATHOLIC, 150 Robson St., Vancouver BC V6B 2A7 Canada. (604)683-0281. Fax (604)683-8117. E-mail: bcc@axion.net. Website: Http://www.rcav.bc.ca. Catholic. Paul Schratz, ed. News, education and inspiration for Canadian Catholics. Weekly (47X) newspaper; 20 pgs; circ 20,000. 70% freelance. Query; phone query OK. Pays variable rate on publication for 1st rts. Articles 400-500 wds. Responds in 6 wks. Seasonal 4 wks ahead. Accepts simultaneous submissions & reprints. Accepts e-mail submission (attached file). (Ads)

Tips: "We prefer to use Catholic writers."

THE BELIEVER, 5375 Alderley Rd., Victoria BC V8Y 1X9 Canada. (250)658-8508. Fax (250)658-8481. E-mail: msbowes@islandnet.com or believer@islandnet.com. Website: http://www.islandnet.com/~believer. Tidewater Publishing Co. Madge S. Bowes, ed. Easy-to-read Christian/mission news and inspiration for churches and businesses. Online newspaper. Query; fax/e-query OK. Not copyrighted. **NO PAYMENT**. Articles 300-750 wds; fiction to 750 wds; a few book/music reviews, 400 wds. Seasonal 2 mos ahead. Accepts simultaneous submissions & reprints. Accepts disk (Mac only) or e-mail submission (copied into message). No sidebars. Prefers NIV. Copy for 9x12 SAE/IRCs or $1. (No ads)

Poetry: Accepts very little.

Fillers: Anecdotes; accepts few.

Tips: "Need material for Believer's News, Mission News, Book Reviews, Of Interest (with Christian view), and All in the Family. If I get enough good short stories, I might add a section for that." Prefers not to have to return mss.

BIBLE ADVOCATE, Box 33677, Denver CO 80233. (303)452-7973. Fax (303)452-0657. E-mail: cofgsd@denver.net. Church of God (Seventh Day). Calvin Burrell, ed; Sherri Langton, assoc ed. Mostly older adult readers; 50% not members of the denomination. Monthly (10X) mag; 24

pgs; circ 13,500. Free subscription. 25% freelance. Complete ms/cover letter; e-query OK. Query for electronic submissions. Pays $15-35 on publication for 1st, one-time, reprint & simultaneous rts. Articles 1,000-1,800 wds (20-25/yr). Responds in 4-8 wks. Seasonal 9 mos ahead. Accepts simultaneous submissions & reprints (tell when/where appeared). Accepts disk or e-mail submission. Kill fee up to 50%. Regular sidebars. Prefers NIV, NKJV. Guidelines/theme list (also on Website); copy for 9x12 SAE/4 stamps. (No ads)

Poetry: Buys 6-10/yr. Free verse, traditional; 5-20 lines; $10. Submit max 5 poems.

Fillers: Buys 5-10/yr. Facts, prose, quotes; 100-400 wds; $5-10.

Columns/Departments: Accepts 6-10/yr. Viewpoint (social or religious issues), 600-650 wds, pays copies.

Special Needs: Articles centering on theme for 1999: Winding Down and Amazing Century (see theme list).

Tips: "If you write well, all areas are open to freelance, especially personal experiences that tie in with the monthly themes. Fresh writing with keen insight is most readily accepted. "

BIBLE ADVOCATE ONLINE, Box 33677, Denver CO 80233. (303)452-7973. Fax (303)452-0657. E-mail: cofgsd@denver.net. Website: http://www.denver.net/ ~baonline. Church of God (Seventh Day). Calvin Burrell, ed; Sherri Langton, assoc ed. Articles on salvation, Jesus, social issues, life problems that are inclusive of non-Christians. Monthly online mag; available only online. Estab 1996. 25-75% freelance. Complete ms/cover letter; phone/e-query OK. Pays $15-35 on publication for first, one-time rts, simultaneous & reprint rts. Articles 1,200-1,500 wds (20/yr). Responds in 4-8 wks. Seasonal 6 mos ahead. Accepts simultaneous submissions & reprints (tell when/where appeared). Accepts disk or e-mail submission. Regular sidebars. Prefers NIV. Guidelines/theme list (also on Website); copy of online article for 9x12 SAE/2 stamps. (No ads)

Fillers: Buys 5-10/yr. Anecdotes, facts, prose, quotes; 50-100 wds. Pays $5-10.

Special Needs: Always need personal experience pieces showing a person's struggle that either brought him/her to Christ or deepened faith in God. Also need more articles on social issues.

Tips: "Think of your topic in terms of the unchurched. How would you write your piece for a non-Christian? Looking for contemporary style and topics: ethics, morality, violence, and the future."

BIBLICAL REFLECTIONS ON MODERN MEDICINE, PO Box 14488, Augusta GA 30919. (706)736-0161. Fax (706)721-0758. Website: http://www.usit. net/public/capo/friendly/jbem. Dr. Ed Payne, ed. For all Christians interested in medical-ethical issues. Bimonthly newsletter; 8 pgs; circ 1,100. Subscription $19. 20% freelance. Complete ms/cover letter. **PAYS IN COPIES & SUBSCRIPTION**, for 1st rts. Articles to 1,500 wds (5/yr). Responds in 1-4 wks. Accepts simultaneous submissions & reprints. No sidebars. Prefers NAS. Guidelines/copy for #10 SAE/1 stamp. (No ads)

Tips: "Most open to careful biblical/critical analysis of medicine and medical ethics."

BOOKS & CULTURE, 465 Gundersen Dr., Carol Stream IL 60188. (630)260-6200. Fax (630)260-0114. E-mail: WilsonBKS@aol.com. Website: http://www.booksandculture.net. Christianity Today, Inc. John Wilson, ed. To edify, sharpen, and nurture the evangelical intellectual community by engaging the world from all its complexity from a distinctly Christian perspective. Bimonthly & online mag; circ 12,000. Subscription $24.95. Open to freelance. Query. Not in topical listings. (Ads)

*****THE BREAD OF LIFE**, 209 Macnab St. N., Box 395, Hamilton ON L8N 3H8 Canada. (905)529-4496. Fax (905)529-5373. Catholic. Fr. Peter Coughlin, ed. Catholic Charismatic; to encourage spiritual growth in areas of renewal in the catholic church today. Bimonthly mag; 32 pgs; circ 5,200. Subscription $30. 10% freelance. Complete ms/cover letter; fax query OK. **PAYS IN COPIES.** Articles 1,200-1,400 wds; book reviews 250 wds. Responds in 2-3 wks. Seasonal 6 mos ahead. Accepts reprints (tell when/where appeared). No disk. No sidebars. Prefers NAB or NJB. Guidelines; copy for 9x12 SAE/6 stamps. (Ads)

>   **Poetry:** Accepts 12-15/yr. Traditional; 10-25 lines. Submit max 2 poems.

>   **Fillers:** Accepts 10-12/yr. Facts, prose, quotes; to 250 wds.

+THE BREAKTHROUGH INTERCESSOR, PO Box 121, Lincoln VA 20160. (540)338-4131. Fax (540)338-1934. E-mail: breakthrough@intercessors.com. Nondenominational. Andrea Doudera Duncan, ed. For intercessors and those in need of prayer; teaching and equipping.. Quarterly mag; 28 pgs; circ 10,000. Subscription $15. 100% freelance. Complete ms/cover letter; phone/fax/e-query OK. **NO PAYMENT.** Articles (50/yr). Responds in 6 wks. Seasonal 2 mos ahead. Accepts reprints (tell when/where appeared). Accepts disk or e-mail submission. Regular sidebars. Any version. No guidelines; copy for 6x9 SAE/2 stamps. (No ads)

>   **Poetry:** Accepts 5/yr. Traditional.

>   **Special Needs:** All articles must have to do with prayer.

THE BRETHREN EVANGELIST, 524 College Ave., Ashland OH 44805. (419)289-1708. Fax (419)281-0450. E-mail: Brethren@bright.net. The Brethren Church. Richard C. Winfield, ed. Denominational. Monthly newsletter; 12 pgs; circ 8,150. Free to members/$15 to non-members. 5% freelance. Complete ms/cover letter; no phone/fax/e-query. Pays to $50 on publication for one-time rts. Articles 750 wds (6/yr). Responds in 6 wks. Seasonal 3 mos ahead. Accepts simultaneous submissions. No disk. Some sidebars. Prefers NIV. No guidelines; copy for 9x12 SAE/3 stamps. (No ads)

+BRIDAL GUIDES, PO Box 1264, Huntington WV 25714. (304)523-2162. Tellstar Productions/Interdenominational. Shannon Bridget Murphy, ed. A GUIDE FOR PLANNING Christian weddings, formals, and receptions. Bimonthly mag; 80-100 pgs; circ 50,000. Subscription $42. Estab 1998. 75-90% freelance. Complete ms/cover letter. Pays variable rates on publication for 1st or one-time rts. Articles 500+ wds or features 800-2,000 wds (50/yr); fiction 500+ wds (50/yr); book review (exchange for the book or product). Responds in 4-8 wks. Seasonal 2-6 mos ahead. Accepts reprints (tell when/where appeared). No disk. Regular sidebars. Guidelines; copy $7. (Ads)

Poetry: Buys many/yr. Any type or length. Pays variable rates. Submit any number.

Fillers: Buys many/yr. Anecdotes, cartoons, facts, games, ideas, news-breaks, party ideas, prayers, quizzes, word puzzles. Pays variable rates.

Special Needs: Christian business pieces from owners of businesses of interest to readers or how-to pieces.

Contest: Send SASE for contest information.

Tips: "Most open to personal experiences of weddings, formals, receptions and planning for events; how-to articles. Functional wedding, formal and reception creations and patterns. Photographs from events."

CANADA LUTHERAN, 302-393 Portage Ave., Winnipeg MB R3B 3H6 Canada. (204)984-9150. Fax (204)984-9185. E-mail: canaluth@elcic.ca. Evangelical Lutheran Church in Canada. Kenn Ward, ed. Denominational. Monthly (9X) mag; 48 pgs; circ 20,000. Subscription $17 US. Up to 50% freelance. Query or complete ms/cover letter; fax/e-query OK. Pays $40-110 CAN on publication for one-time rts. Articles 800-1,500 wds (15/yr); fiction 850-1,200 wds (4/yr). Responds in 5 wks. Seasonal 10 mos ahead. Accepts simultaneous submissions & reprints. Prefers e-mail submission (copied into message). Some sidebars. Prefers NRSV. Guidelines (also by e-mail). (Ads)

Tips: "Canadians/Lutherans receive priority, but not the only consideration. Want material that is clear, concise and fresh. Articles that talk about real life experiences of faith receive our best reader response."

CANADIAN CATHOLIC REVIEW, St. Joseph's College, University of Alberta, Edmonton AB T6G 2J5 Canada. (403)492-7681x246. Fax (403)492-8145. E-mail: ccr@gpu.srv.ualberta.ca. Canadian Catholic Review Corporation. Rev. Jeff Thompson, CSB, ed; Marc J. Ratusz, bk review ed. Promotes Canadian views on religious, social and cultural topics. Magazine (5X/yr); 50 pgs; circ 1,000. Subscription $26.75CAN, $25 US. 50% freelance. Query; phone/fax/e-query OK. Pays to $300 on publication for 1st NASR. Articles 3,000-4,000 wds (10/yr); book reviews 300-700 wds/$25. Responds immediately. Seasonal 3 mos ahead. Prefers disk or e-mail submission (attached file). Some sidebars. Prefers RSV. Guidelines/theme list (also by e-mail); copy $6/9x12 SAE/$3 in IRCs. (Ads)

Tips: "Most open to columns and general articles. Be lucid, articulate, faithful and brief. Also letters to the editor, 200 wds."

*CANADIAN MENNONITE , 3-312 Marsland Dr., Waterloo ON N2J 3Z1 Canada. (519)884-3810. Fax (519)884-3331. Mennonite. Ron Rempel, ed. Denominational. Biweekly mag; 40 pgs; circ 20,000. 20% freelance. Query; fax query OK. Pays .10/wd on publication for 1st rts. Articles 750-1,250 wds; news 400-600 wds. Responds in 4 wks. Accepts simultaneous submissions. Guidelines; free copy.

Tips: "Most of our readers are Canadians; give us a Canadian perspective."

CATHEDRAL AGE, Mount St. Alban, Massachusetts & Wisconsin Aves NW, Washington DC 20016-5098. (202)537-5681. Fax (202)364-6600. E-mail: Cathedral_Age@cathedral.org. Website: http://www.cathedral.org/cathedral. Washington National Cathedral (Episcopal). Craig W. Stapert, ed. About what's happening in and to cathedrals and their programs. Quarterly & online mag; 36 pgs; circ 29,000. Subscription $15. 20% freelance. Query/clips; phone/fax query OK. Pays to $500 on acceptance for all rts. Articles 1,000-1,500 wds (10/yr); book reviews 600 wds, $100. Responds in 4 wks. Seasonal 6 mos ahead. Requires disk or e-mail submission (attached file). Kill fee 50%. Regular sidebars. Prefers NRSV. No guidelines; copy $5/9x12 SAE/5 stamps. (No ads)

> **Special Needs:** Art, architecture, music.
>
> **Tips:** "We assign all articles, so query/clips first. Always write from the viewpoint of an individual first, then move into a more general discussion of the topic. Human interest angle important."

*THE CATHOLIC ANSWER, 207 Adams St., Newark NJ 07105. (219)356-8400. Website: http://www.osc.com. Our Sunday Visitor/Catholic. Father Peter Stravinskas, mng ed. Answers to questions of belief for orthodox Catholics. Bimonthly mag; 64 pgs; circ 60,000. 50% freelance. Query/clips. Pays $100 on publication for 1st rts. Articles 1,200-2,200 wds (80/yr). Seasonal 6 mos ahead. Guidelines; free copy (from 200 Noll Plaza, Huntington IN 46750).

CATHOLIC COURIER, 1150 Buffalo Rd., Rochester NY 14624. (716)328-4340. Fax (716)328-8640. Website: http://www.catholiccourier.com. Catholic. Karen M. Franz, gen mng ed. Newspaper for the Diocese of Rochester NY. Weekly & online newspaper; 20 pgs; circ 48,000. Subscription $20. Less than 1% freelance. Query/clips or complete ms/cover letter. Pays $30-100 on publication for one-time rts. Articles 1,200 wds. Responds in 4-9 wks. Accepts simultaneous submissions. Prefers disk. (Ads)

> **Columns/Departments:** News; Leisure; Opinion; Youth; 750 wds.
>
> **Tips:** "We publish very little freelance and virtually none from non-local writers."

CATHOLIC DIGEST, 2115 Summit Ave., St. Paul MN 55105-1081. (651)962-6739. Fax (651)962-6758. E-mail: cdigest@stthomas.edu. Website: http://www.CatholicDigest.org. Catholic/University of St. Thomas. Submit to Articles Editor. Readers have a stake in being Catholic and a wide range of interests: religion, family, health, human relationships, good works, nostalgia, and more. Monthly & online mag; 128 pgs; circ 501,025. Subscription $19.95. 25% freelance. Complete ms (for original material)/cover letter, tear sheets for reprints. Pays $200-400 ($100 for reprints) on acceptance for one-time rts. Online only articles receive $100, plus half of any traceable revenue. Articles 1,000-3,500 wds (90-100/yr). Responds in 6-8 wks. Seasonal 4 mos ahead. Accepts reprints (tell when/where appeared). Accepts disk or e-mail submission (copied into message). Regular sidebars. Prefers NAB. Guidelines (also on Website); copy for 7x10 SAE/2 stamps. (Ads)

> **Fillers:** Buys 200-300/yr. Anecdotes, cartoons, facts, games, jokes, quizzes, quotes, short humor; to 500 wds; $2/published line.
>
> **Columns/Departments:** Buys 100-150/yr. Open Door (personal stories of conversion to Catholicism); 200-500 wds; pays $2/published line. See guidelines for full list.

Special Needs: Family and career concerns of Baby Boomers who have a stake in being Catholic.

Contest: See Website for current contest, or send an SASE.

Tips: "We favor the anecdotal approach. Stories must be strongly focused on a definitive topic that is illustrated for the reader with a well-developed series of true-life, interconnected vignettes."

** This periodical was #9 on the 1998 Top 50 Christian Publishers list (#27 in 1997, #29 in 1996, #30 in 1995, #25 in 1994).

+CATHOLIC DOSSIER, PO Box 591120, San Francisco CA 94159-1120. (800)651-1531. Website: http://www.ignatius.com/mags/cd.htm. Examines Catholic beliefs from many perspectives, including philosophy, history, science, art and even fiction. New bimonthly magazine. Subscription $24.95. Incomplete topical listings.

CATHOLIC FAITH & FAMILY(formerly Catholic Twin Circle) 33 Rossotto Dr., Hamden CT 06514. (203)288-5600. Fax (203)288-5157. E-mail: editor@twincircle.com. Catholic/Circle Media. Loretta G. Seyer, ed.; Mary Zurolo, asst ed, mzurolo@twincircle.com. Features writing for Catholics and/or Christian families of all ages. Weekly newspaper; 20 pgs; circ 30,000. 45% freelance. Complete ms/cover letter; fax/e-query OK. Pays $75 for opinion pcs; $74, $150, or $300 for features, on publication for all rts. Opinion pieces, 600 or 825 wds; features 600, 1,100, or 2,000 wds. Responds in 13 wks. Seasonal 2 mos ahead. Serials 3 parts. Prefers e-mail submission. Kill fee. No sidebars. Prefers Catholic Bible. Guidelines/theme list; copy for 9x12 SAE/2 stamps or $2. (Ads)

Fillers: Cartoons.

Columns/Departments: Point of View (opinion on various Catholic issues), 600-800 wds, $50.

Tips: "We are interested in articles focusing on Catholic family life and daily living as a Catholic family."

CATHOLIC FORESTER, Box 3012, Naperville IL 60566-7012. (630)983-3381. Fax (630)983-3384. Catholic Order of Foresters. Mary Anne File, assoc ed. For mixed audience, primarily parents and grandparents between the ages of 30 and 80. Bimonthly mag; 36 pgs; circ 100,000+. Free/membership. 10% freelance. Complete ms/cover letter; no phone/fax/e-query. Pays .10/wd (.25/wd for fiction), on acceptance for all, 1st, one-time rts. Articles 1,200-1,500 wds (5/yr); fiction for all ages 500-1,200 wds (5/yr). Responds in 8-12 wks. Seasonal 4-6 mos ahead. Accepts simultaneous submissions & reprints (tell when/where appeared). Accepts disk; no e-mail submission. Kill fee 20-25%. Regular sidebars. Prefers Catholic version. Guidelines; copy for 9x12 SAE/4 stamps. (No ads)

Poetry: Free verse, light verse, traditional. Pay varies. Submit max 5 poems.

Fillers: Keith Halla. Cartoons, games. Pays $30.

Tips: "Looking for informational, inspirational articles. Writing should be energetic with good style and rhythm."

** This periodical was #45 on the 1998 Top 50 Christian Publishers list (#28 in 1997, #50 in 1996).

CATHOLIC HERITAGE, 200 Noll Plaza, Huntington IN 46750. (219)356-

8400. Fax (219)356-9117. E-mail: cheritage@osv.com. Website: http:// www.osv.com. Catholic/Our Sunday Visitor. Bill Dodds, ed. For those interested in Catholic history. Bimonthly mag; 43 pgs; circ 25,000. 75% freelance. Query; e-query OK. Query for electronic submissions. Pays $200 on acceptance for 1st rts. Articles 1,000-1,200 wds (30/yr). Responds in 3-5 wks. Seasonal 6 mos ahead. Accepts reprints (payment negotiable). Kill fee 33% or $50-75. Prefers disk or e-mail submission. Regular sidebars. Prefers NAB or RSV. Guidelines; free copy.

> **Tips:** "Most open to general features."

*CATHOLIC INSIGHT, PO Box 625, Adelaide Sta., 36 Adelaide St. E., Toronto ON M5C 2J8 Canada. (416)368-4558. Fax (416)368-8575. E-mail: interim@direct.com. Life Ethics Information Center. Alphonse de Valk, ed/ pub. News, analysis and commentary on social, ethical, political, and moral issues from a Catholic perspective. Monthly (10X) mag; 20-24 pgs; circ 3,100. Subscription $25 CAN, $28 US. 30-40% freelance. Query/clips; phone/fax query OK. Pays variable rates on publication for all rts. Articles 750-1,500 wds (20-30/yr); book/music/video reviews 750 wds. Responds in 6-8 wks. Seasonal 2 mos ahead. Accepts disk. Regular sidebars. Prefers RSV (Catholic). Copy $2.50 CAN/9x12 SAE/.90 postage or IRC. (Ads)

> **Tips:** "We are interested in political/social/current affairs—Canadian—from viewpoint of informed readership and encouraging involvement in the political process as essential to social change."

CATHOLIC NEW YORK, 1011 1st Ave., 17th Fl., New York NY 10022. (212)688-2399. Fax (212)688-2642. Catholic. Anne Buckley, ed-in-chief. To inform New York Catholics. Weekly newspaper; 44 pgs; circ 130,000. Subscription $20. 10% freelance. Query or complete ms/cover letter. Pays $15-100 on publication for one-time rts. Articles 500-800 wds. Responds in 5 wks. Copy $1.

> **Columns/Departments:** Comment; Catholic New Yorkers (profiles of unique individuals); 325 wds.

> **Tips:** "Most open to articles that show how to integrate Catholic faith into work, hobbies or special interests."

#CATHOLIC PARENT, 200 Noll Plaza, Huntington IN 46750. (800)348-2440 or (219)356-8400. Catholic. Woodeene Koenig-Bricker, ed. Practical advice for Catholic parents, with a specifically Catholic slant. Bimonthly mag; 52 pgs; circ 32,000. Subscription $18. 95% freelance. Query/clips or complete ms/cover letter; fax query OK. Pays $100-200 on acceptance for 1st rts. Articles 250-1,000 wds (50/yr). Responds in 9 wks. Seasonal 6 mos ahead. Kill fee. Considers simultaneous submissions. Accepts disk. Regular sidebars. Guidelines; copy $3.

> **Fillers:** Mary Bazzett. Accepts 40/yr. Parenting tips, 100-200 wds, $25.

> **Columns/Departments:** This Works! (short parenting tips), 200 wds. Pays $15-25.

> **Tips:** "We need true-life, heart-warming stories dealing with family life and parenting."

> ** This periodical was #17 on the 1998 Top 50 Christian Publishers list (#20 in 1997, #51 in 1996, #25 in 1995, #26 in 1994).

CATHOLIC PEACE VOICE, 532 W. 8th, Erie PA 16502-1343. (814)453-4955.

Fax (814)452-4784. E-mail: peacevoice@paxchristiusa.org. Website: http://www.nonviolence.org/~nvweb/pcusa. Dave Robinson, ed. For members of US Catholic Peace Movement. Quarterly newspaper; 16 pgs; circ 20,000. Distributed free. 5% freelance. Query; phone/fax/e-query OK. Pays on publication for one-time rts. Accepts simultaneous submissions & reprints. Prefers disk. Guidelines; copy for 9x12 SAE/2 stamps. Not in topical listings. (Ads)

> **Tips:** "Emphasis is on nonviolence. No sexist language."

CATHOLIC RURAL LIFE, 4625 Beaver Ave., Des Moines IA 50310-2199. (515)270-2634. Fax (515)270-9447. E-mail: ncrlc@aol.com. Website: http://www.ncrlc.com. Catholic. Sandra A. LaBlanc, commun dir. Semiannual mag; 40 pgs; circ 3,000. Membership $25. 50% freelance. Query/clips; phone/fax/e-query OK. Pays for 1st rts. Articles 1,000-1,500 wds. Responds in 6 wks. Seasonal 6 mos ahead. Prefers disk. Regular sidebars. Guidelines/theme list; copy for 9x12 SAE/3 stamps.

> **Columns/Departments:** Building Community, 350 wds; Closer Look (think piece), 750-1,000 wds; no payment.

#CATHOLIC SENTINEL, PO Box 18030, Portland OR 97218-0030. (503)281-1191. Fax (503)282-3486. E-mail: casentinel@aol.com. Catholic. Robert Pfohman, ed. For Catholics in the Archdiocese of western and eastern Oregon. Weekly tabloid; 16-24 pgs; circ 15,000. Subscription $22. 25% freelance. Query; phone/fax query OK (if timely). Pays $25-150 on publication for one-time rts. Not copyrighted. Articles 800-1,800 wds (15/yr). Responds in 6 wks. Seasonal 1 month ahead. Accepts reprints (on columns, not news or features; tell them). Prefers disk or modem. Kill fee 100%. Regular sidebars. Copy 50 cents/9x12 SAE/2 stamps.

> **Columns/Departments:** Buys about 30/yr. Opinion Page, 600 wds, $10. Send complete ms.

> **Tips:** "Find active Catholics living their faith in specific, interesting, upbeat, positive ways."

*CATHOLIC TELEGRAPH, 100 E. 8th St., Cincinnati OH 45202. (513)421-3131. Fax (513)381-2242. Catholic. Tricia Hempel, gen. mng Diocese newspaper for Cincinnati area. Weekly newspaper; 20 pgs; circ 27,000. 10% freelance. Send resume and writing samples for assignment. Pays varying rates on publication for all rts. Articles. Responds in 2-3 wks. Kill fee. Guidelines sent on acceptance; free copy.

> **Fillers:** Newsbreaks (local).

CATHOLIC WORLD REPORT, PO Box 591300, San Francisco CA 94159-1300. (800)651-1531. Website: http://ignatius.com/mags/cwr.htm. Catholic. A news magazine that not only reports on important events in the Church, but helps to shape them. Monthly mag. Subscription $39.95. Not in topical listings.

CBA FRONTLINE, PO Box 200, Colorado Springs CO 80901-0200. (719)576-7880. Fax 719)576-0795. E-mail: publications@cba-intl.org. Website: http://www.cbaonline.org. Christian Booksellers Assn. Steve Parolini, ed. To give product knowledge and inspiration to the frontline staff in Christian retail stores. Monthly trade journal; 32 pgs; circ 10,000. Estab 1997. 10-20% freelance. Query/clips; phone/fax/e-query OK. Pays .16-.25/wd. on acceptance for all rts. Articles. Responds in 4 wks. Seasonal 4-5 mos ahead. Accepts simultaneous submissions. Accepts disk. Kill fee. Regular sidebars. Prefers NIV. Guidelines/theme list.

Columns/Departments: Buys many/yr. Humor (true retail-oriented anecdotes & cartoons), 25-100 wds. Pays $25.

Tips: "We rarely accept unsolicited mss, but assign 2-5 articles per month to freelancers based on our agenda. Send cover letter, including experience and areas of interest, plus clips. Also looking for retail and product anecdotes."

CBA MARKETPLACE, PO Box 200, Colorado Springs CO 80901-0200. (719)576-7880. Fax (719)576-0795. E-mail: publications@cba-intl.org. Website: http://www.cbaonline.org. Christian Booksellers Assn. Sue Grise, ed. To provide Christian bookstore owners and managers with professional retail skills, product information, and industry news. Monthly trade journal; 110-260 pgs; circ 8,000. Subscription $50. 50% freelance. Query/clips; phone/fax query OK. Pays .16-.25/wd on acceptance for all rts. Articles 800-2,500 wds (30/yr assigned); book reviews 100-150 wds, $30; music/video reviews 100-150 wds, $25. Responds in 8 wks. Seasonal 4-5 mos ahead. Prefers disk. Regular sidebars. Accepts any modern version. Theme list; copy $5/9x12 SAE/6 stamps. (Ads)

Fillers: Buys 12/yr. Cartoons ($100), retail facts, ideas, trends, newsbreaks.

Columns/Departments: Buys 10-20/yr. Industry Watch; Music News; Gift News; Video & software News; Book News; all 100-800 wds. Pays .16-.25/wd. Query.

Tips: "All our articles are by assignment and focus on producing and selling Christian products or conducting retail business. Send cover letter, including related experience and areas of interest, plus samples. We also assign reviews of books, music, videos, Spanish products, kids products, and software."

CELEBRATE LIFE, Box 1350, Stafford VA 22555. (540)659-4171. Fax (540)659-2586. E-mail: clmag@all.org. Website: http://www.all.org. American Life League. Cathy Kenyon, assoc ed. A pro-life, pro-family magazine for Christian audience. Bimonthly mag; 48 pgs; circ 80,000. Subscription $12.95. 50% freelance. Complete ms/cover letter; fax/e-query OK. Pays .10/wd on publication for 1st, one-time, or reprint rts. Articles 300-1,200 wds (2/yr). Responds in 8 wks. Seasonal 4-6 mos ahead. Accepts simultaneous submissions & reprints (tell when/where appeared). Prefers e-mail submission. Kill fee 25%. Some sidebars. Prefers NIV,NASB, RSV. Guidelines/theme list (also by e-mail); copy for 9x12 SAE/5 stamps. (Ads)

Fillers: Buys 6/yr. Newsbreaks (local or special pro-life news); 50-100 wds; $10.

Columns/Departments: Buys 3/yr. Prayer and Fasting (personal spirituality), 500 wds, $25-50. Query.

Special Needs: Personal experience about abortion, activism, death/dying, post abortion stress/healing, euthanasia, natural family planning.

Tips: "We are No-Exceptions pro-life. Emphasizing the importance of that philosophy is a great help. A spiritual slant is necessary in all our articles. A scriptural application or conversion experience will help the article. If the article lacks these, reference to scripture or a scriptural principle is mandatory. Human interest stories with accompanying photos are best."

**This periodical was #66 on the 1994 Top 50 Christian Publishers list.

*CGA WORLD, 430 Penn Ave., Scranton PA 18503. (717)342-3294. Fax (717)963-0149. Catholic Golden Age. Barbara Pegula, ed. For Catholics 50+. Quarterly mag; 32 pgs; circ. 100,000. Subscription/membership $8. Query. Pays .10/wd on publication for 1st, one-time, or reprint rts. Articles & fiction. Responds in 6 wks. Seasonal 6 mos ahead. Accepts reprints (tell when/where appeared). Accepts disk. Guidelines; copy for 9x12 SAE/3 stamps. (Ads)

   Fillers: Games, ideas, prayers, word puzzles.

CHARISMA & CHRISTIAN LIFE, 600 Rinehart Rd., Lake Mary FL 32746. (407)333-0600. Fax (407)333-7133. E-mail: grady@strang.com. Website: http://charismamagcom/index.htm. Strang Communications. Lee Grady, exec ed.; Billy Bruce, news ed; Jimmy Stewart, book & music review ed. Primarily for the Pentecostal and Charismatic Christian community. Monthly mag; 100+ pgs; circ 220,000. Subscription $21.97. 75% freelance. Query; no phone/fax/e-query. Pays $100-800 on publication for 1st rts. Articles 2,000 wds (120/yr); book/music reviews, 200 wds, $20. Responds in 8-12 wks. Seasonal 4 mos ahead. Kill fee $50. Prefers disk. Regular sidebars. Guidelines; copy $3. (Ads)

   Tips: "Most open to news section, reviews or features. Query (published clips help a lot)."

+CHICKEN SOUP FOR THE MOTHER'S SOUL #2, Dept. CW, PO Box 1959, Fairfield IA 52556. (515)472-4047. Fax (515)472-7288. E-mail: chicken soup@lisco.com. Website: http://www.chickensoup-womanssoul.com. Chicken Soup for the Soul. Submit to Editor. 101 stories to open the hearts and rekindle the spirits of mothers. Stories go into a book. Sales of 2 million. Release date: May 2000. 100% freelance. Complete ms/cover letter. Pays $300/story (plus 1 copy of bk) on publication for one-time rts. Articles 200-1,200 wds (101/bk). Responds in 16 wks. Accepts simultaneous submissions & reprints (tell when/where appeared). Accepts e-mail submission (copied into message). Guidelines (also by e-mail/Website); sample stories for #10 SAE/1 stamp.

   Fillers: Buys 25/book. Anecdotes, cartoons, short humor; 100-200 wds. Pays $250.

   Special Needs: Looks for true stories about motherhood that inspire and touch mothers. The stories are universal and non-denominational.

   Tips: "Read some of our Chicken Soup for the Soul Books." DEADLINE FOR THIS BOOK IS JUNE 30, 1999.

+CHICKEN SOUP FOR THE SINGLE SOUL, Dept. CW, PO Box 1959, Fairfield IA 52556. (515)472-4047. Fax (515)472-7288. E-mail: chicken soup@lisco.com. Website: http://www.chickensoup-womanssoul. com. Chicken Soup for the Soul. Submit to Editor. 101 stories to open the hearts and rekindle the spirits of the single or single again. Stories go into a book. Sales of 1million (projected). Release date: October 1999. 100% freelance. Complete ms/cover letter. Pays $300/story (plus 1 copy of bk) on publication for one-time rts. Articles 200-1,200 wds (101/bk). Responds in 16 wks. Accepts simultaneous submissions & reprints (tell when/where appeared). Accepts e-mail submission (copied into message). Guidelines (also by e-mail/Website); sample stories for #10 SAE/1 stamp.

Fillers: Buys 25/book. Anecdotes, cartoons, short humor; 100-200 wds. Pays $250.

Special Needs: Looking for true stories about singles that inspire, uplift and touch other singles. The stories are universal and non-denominational.

Tips: "Read some of our Chicken Soup for the Soul Books." DEADLINE FOR THIS BOOK IS FEBRUARY 28, 1999.

+**CHICKEN SOUP FOR THE WOMAN'S SOUL #3**, Dept. CW, PO Box 1959, Fairfield IA 52556. (515)472-4047. Fax (515)472-7288. E-mail: chicken soup@lisco.com. Website: http://www.chickensoup-womanssoul.com. Chicken Soup for the Soul. Submit to Editor. 101 stories to open the hearts and rekindle the spirits of women. Stories go into a book. Sales of 4 million. Release date: 2000. 100% freelance. Complete ms/cover letter. Pays $300/story (plus 1 copy of bk) on publication for one-time rts. Articles 200-1,200 wds (101/bk). Responds in 16 wks. Accepts simultaneous submissions & reprints (tell when/where appeared). Accepts e-mail submission (copied into message). Guidelines (also by e-mail/Website); sample stories for #10 SAE/1 stamp.

Fillers: Buys 25/book. Anecdotes, cartoons, short humor; 100-200 wds. Pays $250.

Special Needs: Looking for true stories about women that inspire, uplift and touch other women. The stories are universal and non-denominational.

Tips: "Read some of our Chicken Soup for the Soul Books." DEADLINE FOR THIS BOOK IS DECEMBER 31, 1999.

***CHRISTIAN AMERICAN NEWSPAPER**, 1801-L Sara Dr., Chesapeake VA 23320. (757)424-2630. Fax (757)424-4326. Christian Coalition, Inc. Michael Ebert, ed. To provide a Christian perspective on the news, enabling readers to be more effective citizens by being better informed. Bimonthly newspaper; circ 400,000. Subscription $14.95. Open to freelance. Query. (Ads)

***THE CHRISTIAN ARTS REVIEW**, 803 Hwy. 90E., Chipley FL 32428. (908)638-0643. E-mail: BRIGHT@aol.com. Website: http://www.christian link.com/ home/arts. Brightwater Communications Group. William Curtis Bridenback, ed. For evangelical Christians, 25-55, who enjoy Christian books and music. Quarterly newsletter; online edition updated monthly, and 2 special editions/yr; 6-8 pgs; circ 1,500. Subscription $12. 50% freelance. Query/clips; e-query OK. Pays $5-25 on publication for 1st & electronic rts. Articles 175-350 wds (10-15/yr); book/music/video reviews 75-150 wds, $5/product. Responds in 2 wks. Seasonal 4-5 mos ahead. Prefers disk. Kill fee. Regular sidebars. Guidelines/theme list; copy for #10 SAE/1 stamp. (Ads)

Fillers: Buys 50/yr. Anecdotes, facts, newsbreaks, quotes; 75-150 wds; $5-25.

Columns/Departments: Buys 10-15/yr. Feature Artist (celebrity interview/profile), 350 wds; Spotlight (new product), 275 wds; Etcetera (news & information soundbites), 75-150 wds. Pays $5-25.

Special Needs: Bible reviews, essays on Christian media. Always looking for good reviewers who have the time and enjoy the work.

Contest: At end of year, gives $25 certificates to best writers in each area.

Tips: "Short items are a good way to go. We'd like to do more issues-oriented stories and op/ed pieces on Christian media. Our summer special issue is also a good place to start; write for topic information."

+**THE CHRISTIAN BUSINESSMAN**, 7001 SW 24th Ave., Gainesville FL 32607-3704. Carlson Communications. Rob Dilbone, ed. To equip and empower working men with the tools they need to become successful spiritually, personally, and financially, while advancing gospel of Christ. Query only. Incomplete topical listings.

*__THE CHRISTIAN CHRONICLE__, PO Box 12623, Reading PA 19612-2623. (610)378-1245. Fax (610)378-1378. Nondenominational. Alice Swoyer-Smolkowicz, pub. For non-Charismatic Christians. Bimonthly newsletter; 8 pgs; circ. 2,000. Subscription $12. 90% freelance. Complete ms/cover letter; phone/fax/e-query OK. **NO PAYMENT** for one-time rts. Articles 100-500 wds (18/yr); fiction (2/yr). Seasonal 3 mos ahead. Accepts reprints. Prefers disk. Prefers NIV. Copy for #10 SAE/1 stamp.

Fillers: Accepts 24/yr. Anecdotes, cartoons, facts, ideas, quotes, short humor; 50-200 wds.

THE CHRISTIAN CIVIC LEAGUE OF MAINE RECORD, Box 5459, Augusta ME 04332. (207)622-7634. Fax (207)621-0035. E-mail: email@cclmaine. org. Website: http://www.cclmaine.org/ethics5.htm. Cyndee Randall, ed. Focuses on church, public service and political action. Monthly newsletter; 4 pgs; circ 4,600. 10% freelance. Query. **NO PAYMENT** for one-time rts. Articles (10-12/yr). Responds in 4-8 wks. Accepts simultaneous query & reprints. Free copy. Not in topical listings. (No ads)

CHRISTIAN COMPUTING MAGAZINE, PO Box 198, 309 S. Washington, Raymore MO 64083. (816)331-3881. Fax (816)331-5510. E-mail: steve @ccmagcom. Website: http://www.ccmagcom. Steve Hewitt, ed-in-chief; Michael C. Hastings, online ed (michael@ccmag.com). For Christian/church computer users. Monthly (11X) & online mag; 2 pgs; circ. 90,000. Subscription $14.95. 40% freelance. Query/clips; fax/e-query OK. **NO PAYMENT** for all rts. Articles 1,000-1,800 wds (12/yr). Responds in 4 wks. Seasonal 2 mos ahead. Accepts reprints. Requires disk. Regular sidebars. Guidelines; copy for 9x12 SAE.

Fillers: Accepts 6 cartoons/yr.

Columns/Departments: Accepts 12/yr. Telecommunications (computer), 1,500-1,800 wds.

Special Needs: Articles on Internet, DTP, computing.

THE CHRISTIAN COURIER, 1933 W. Wisconsin Ave., Milwaukee WI 53233. (414)344-7300. Fax (414)344-7375. E-mail: probucolls@juno.com. ProBuColls Assn. John M. Fisco, Jr., pub. To propagate the Gospel of Jesus Christ in the Midwest. Monthly newspaper; circ 10,000. 10% freelance. Query. **PAYS IN COPIES**, for one-time rts. Not copyrighted. Articles 300-1,500 wds (6/yr). Responds in 2-4 wks. Seasonal 2 mos ahead. Accepts reprints. Guidelines; free copy.

> **Fillers:** Anecdotes, facts, newsbreaks; 10-100 wds.

#CHRISTIAN COURIER, 4-261 Martindale Rd., St. Catherines ON L2W 1A1 Canada. (US address: Box 110, Lewiston NY 14092-0110.) (905)682-8311. Fax (905)682-8313. E-mail: cceditor@aol.com. Independent (Protestant Reformed). Bert Witvoet, ed; Bob Vander Vennen, book review ed. To present Canadian and international news, both religious and secular, from a Reformed Christian perspective. Weekly (44X) newspaper; 20 pgs; circ 5,000. 20% freelance. Complete ms/cover letter; phone query OK. Pays $35-60 (assigned), or $25-50 (unsolicited). after publication for one-time rts. Articles 500-1,200 wds (40/yr); fiction 1,000-2,000 wds (10/yr); book reviews 100-500 wds. Responds in 3 wks. Seasonal 6 mos ahead. Accepts simultaneous submissions & reprints. Kill fee 50%. Guidelines; copy for 9x12 SAE/IRC.

> **Poetry:** Buys 20/yr. Avant-garde, free verse, traditional; 10-30 lines; $15-30. Submit max 5 poems.

*CHRISTIAN CRUSADE NEWSPAPER, PO Box 279, Neosho MO 64850. (918)438-4234. Fax (417)451-4319. Interdenominational. Billy James Hargis, pub. A Christian, pro-American approach to current social and political issues. Monthly newspaper; 24 pgs; circ 25,000. 50% freelance. Query. Pays varying rates on publication for all rts. Articles (any length). Responds in 9 wks. Free copy.

*CHRISTIAN DRAMA MAGAZINE, 1824 Celestia Blvd., Walla Walla WA 99362-3619. (509)522-5242. Suspending publication until March 1999.

*THE CHRISTIAN EDGE, 6501 Bronson Ln., Bakersfield CA 93309. Phone/fax (805)837-1378. Chase Productions/evangelical. Don Chase, pub. Activity and resources guide; not an issues-driven publication. Monthly newspaper; 8-12 pgs; circ 15,000. Subscription $18. 10% freelance. Query/clips; e-query OK. **NO PAYMENT** for one-time rts. Articles 350-1,000 wds (10/yr); book/music/video reviews 150 wds. Responds in 3 wks. Seasonal 2 mos ahead. Accepts simultaneous submissions & reprints (tell when/where appeared). Prefers disk. Regular sidebars. Copy for 9x12 SAE/4 stamps. (Ads)

*CHRISTIAN ENTERTAINMENT, PO Box 314, Anniston AL 36202. (205)238-8336. Fax (205)238-8336. Darryal W. Ray, ed. To highlight options for the Christian family in various forms of entertainment. Weekly news-page distributed by Universal Press Syndicate; circ 100,000. Subscription $30. Query. Not in topical listings. (Ads)

CHRISTIAN HISTORY, 465 Gundersen Dr., Carol Stream IL 60188. (630)260-6200. Fax (630)260-0114. E-mail: CHedit@aol.com. Website: http://www.christianity.net/christianhistory. Christianity Today, Inc. Mark

Galli, ed. To teach Christian history to educated readers in an engaging manner. Quarterly mag; 52 pgs; circ 70,000. Subscription $19.95. 75% freelance. Query; fax/e-query OK. Pays .10/wd on acceptance for 1st, electronic & some ancillary rts. Articles 1,000-3,000 wds (1/yr). Responds in 2 wks. Accepts reprints (tell when/where appeared). Requires disk. Kill fee 50%. Regular sidebars. Guidelines/theme list; copy $5.50. (Ads)

> **Tips:** "Let us know your particular areas of specialization and any books or papers you have written in the area of Christian history."
> ** 1997 & 1995 EPA Award of Merit—General.

CHRISTIAN HOME & SCHOOL, 3350 East Paris Ave. SE, Grand Rapids MI 49512. (616)957-1070x239. Fax (616)957-5022. E-mail: ChrSchInt@aol. com. Website: http://www.ChristianSchoolsInt.org. Christian Schools Intl. Roger Schmurr, sr. ed. Focuses on parenting and Christian education; for parents who send their children to Christian schools. Bimonthly & online mag; 32 pgs; circ 64,000. Subscription $11.95. 60% freelance. Complete ms. Pays $125-200 on publication for 1st rts. Articles 750-2,000 wds (30/yr); fiction 1,200-2,000 wds (5/yr); book reviews $25 (assigned). Responds in 1 wk. Seasonal 5 mos ahead. Accepts simultaneous query. Accepts disk (prefers clean copy they can scan). Regular sidebars. Prefers NIV. Guidelines/theme list (also on Website); copy for 9x12 SAE/4 stamps. (Ads)

> **Fillers:** Ideas; 75-100 wds. Pays $25-40.
> **Tips:** Most open to features (check back issues on our Website). Needs Christmas fiction.
> ** 1998, 1997 & 1995 EPA Award of Merit—Organizational.

#THE CHRISTIAN LEADER, PO Box V, Hillsboro KS 67063. (316)947-5543. Fax (316)947-3266. E-mail: chleader@southwind.net. U.S. Conference of Mennonite Brethren. Don Ratzlaff, ed. Denominational. Monthly mag; circ. 9,800. Subscription $16. Query. Open to freelance. Not in topical listings.

#CHRISTIAN LIVING, 616 Walnut Ave., Scottdale PA 15683-1999. (724)887-8500. Fax (724)887-3111. E-mail: levi%MPH@mcimail.com. Mennonite Publishing House. Levi Miller, interim ed. Denominational with focus on contemporary stories of faith in action in a variety of contexts. Monthly (8X) mag; 28-36 pgs; circ 4,900. Subscription $20. 95% freelance. Query or complete ms/cover letter; no electronic submissions. Pays .04-.06/wd on publication for 1st, one-time, reprint or simultaneous rts. Articles 700-1,500 wds (25/yr); fiction 800-1,500 wds (1-2/yr). Responds in 6-8 wks. Seasonal 4-6 mos ahead. Accepts simultaneous submissions & reprints (tell when/where appeared). Accepts disk. Regular sidebars. Prefers NRSV. Guidelines/theme list; copy for 9x12 SAE/3 stamps. (Ads)

> **Poetry:** Buys 15-20/yr. Free verse, haiku; 3-25 lines; pays $1/line. Submit max 5 poems.
> **Fillers:** Buys 2-3/yr. Newsbreaks, prayers; 50-30 wds; $5-20.
> **Ethnic:** Targets all ethnic groups involved in the Mennonite religion. Needs articles on issues of race.
> **Tips:** "Looking for good articles on peace issues. A good understand-

ing of issues related to our emphasis and community, family and peace and justice will help the writer."

** This periodical was #51 on the 1995 Top 50 Christian Publishers list (#56 in 1994).

*CHRISTIAN MEDIA, Box 448, Jacksonville OR 97530. (541)899-8888. James Lloyd, ed./pub. For emerging Christian songwriters, artists, and other professionals involved in music, video, film, print, and broadcasting. Bimonthly tabloid; 16 pgs; circ 2,000-6,000. Query; prefers phone query. NO PAYMENT for negotiable rts. Articles; book & music reviews, 3 paragraphs. Accepts simultaneous submissions & reprints. Prefers disk. KJV only. Copy for 9x12 SAE/2 stamps.

Special Needs: Particularly interested in stories that expose dirty practices in the industry—royalty rip-offs, misleading ads, financial misconduct, etc. No flowery pieces on celebrities; wants well-documented articles on abuse in the media.

*CHRISTIAN MOTORSPORTS ILLUSTRATED, PO Box 129, Mansfield PA 16933. (717)549-2282. Fax (717)549-3366. E-mail: cpo@epix.net. CPO Publishing. Roland Osborne, pub. Covers Christian involved in motorsports. Bimonthly mag; 64 pgs; circ 40,000. Subscription $19.96. 50% freelance. Complete ms; no phone/fax/e-query. Pays .20/wd on publication for 1st rts. Articles 500-2,000 wds (30/yr). Seasonal 4 mos ahead. Requires disk. Regular sidebars. Free copy. (Ads)

Poetry: Buys 10/yr. Any type. Pays .20/wd. Submit max 10 poems.

Fillers: Buys 100/yr. Anecdotes, cartoons, facts, games, ideas, jokes, newsbreaks, prayers, prose, quizzes, quotes, short humor. Pays .20/wd.

Columns/Departments: Buys 10/yr.

Tips: "Send a story on a Christian involved in motorsports."

CHRISTIAN NEWS NORTHWEST, PO Box 974, Newberg OR 97132. Phone/fax (503)537-9220. E-mail: cnnw@juno.com. Website: http://www.cnnw.com. John Fortmeyer, ed. News of ministry in the evangelical Christian community in western and central Oregon and southwest Washington; distributed primarily through evangelical churches. Monthly newspaper; 28-36 pgs; circ 25,000. Subscription $15. 10-15% freelance. Query; phone/fax/e-query OK. NO PAYMENT. Not copyrighted. Articles 300-400 wds (100/yr). Responds in 4 wks. Seasonal 3 mos ahead. Accepts reprints (tell when/where appeared). Accepts e-mail submission. Regular sidebars. Guidelines; copy $1.50. (Ads)

Tips: "Emphasis is on news in our local area."

THE CHRISTIAN OBSERVER, 9400 Fairview Ave., Ste. 200, Manassas VA 22110. (703)335-2844. Fax (703)368-4817. E-mail: Elliott@xc.org. Christian Observer Foundation; Presbyterian Reformed. Edwin P. Elliott, ed. To encourage and edify God's people and families. Monthly newspaper; circ 2,000. Subscription $27. Query. NO PAYMENT. Not in topical listings. (Ads)

CHRISTIAN PARENTING TODAY, 465 Gundersen Dr., Carol Stream IL 60188-2498. (630)260-6200. Fax (630)260-0114. E-mail: CPTmag@aol. com.Christianity Today, Inc. Ron R. Lee, exec ed. Practical advice for parents (of kids birth-14), from a Christian perspective, that runs the whole gamut of needs: social, educational, spiritual, medical, etc. Bimonthly mag; 76-92 pgs; circ 100,000. Subscription $17.95. 80-90% freelance. Query; fax/e-query OK. Pays $30-350 on acceptance for assigned for 1st & reprint rts. Articles 400-1,800 wds (150/yr); product reviews (games, toys, etc.), 150 wds, $25-35. Responds in 10 wks. Seasonal 8-12 mos ahead. Accepts reprints (tell when/where appeared). Accepts disk. Kill fee 25%. Regular sidebars. Prefers NIV. Guidelines; copy for 9x12 SAE/$3 postage. (Ads)

> **Columns/Departments:** Buys 50/yr. Your Child Today, 500 wds, $150; Healthy & Safe, 450 wds, $150; Can You Help? (parenting tips) 100 wds; Life in Our House (humorous anecdotes), 100 wds, $30.
>
> **Tips:** "Study past issues. Cultivate journalism skills. Be selective in sending clips that demonstrate the kind of writing we publish. Demonstrate that you can identify with our readers."
>
> ** This periodical was #1 on the 1997 Top 50 Christian Publishers list (#20 in 1996, #2 in 1995, #27 in 1994). 1996 EPA Award for Most Improved Publication.

CHRISTIAN POET (formerly Poet's Park), 2745 Monterey Hwy #76, San Jose CA 95111-3129. E-mail: poet@soos.com. Website: http://www.soos.com/poetpark. Redwood Family Chapel. Submit to The Editor as e-mail submission. Quarterly mag; 32 pgs; circ 350. Subscription $20. 100% freelance. Complete ms. **PAYS 3 COPIES** for one-time rts. Articles 350-2,500 wds (12/yr). Responds in 4 wks. Seasonal 6 mos ahead. Accepts simultaneous submissions & reprints (tell when/where appeared). Requires disk or e-mail submission. Regular sidebars. Guidelines. (Ads)

> **Poetry:** Accepts 160/yr. Any type; 1-60 lines. Submit max 3 poems.

THE CHRISTIAN RANCHMAN, 7022-A Lake County Dr., Fort Worth TX 76179. (817)236-0023. Fax (817)236-0024. E-mail: cowboysforchrist@juno.com. Interdenominational. Ted Pressley, ed. Monthly tabloid; 12 pgs; circ 28,000. No subscription. Open to freelance. Complete ms/cover letter. **NO PAYMENT** for all rts. Articles; book/video reviews (length open). No sidebars.

> **Poetry:** Accepts 40/yr. Free verse. Submit max 3 poems.
>
> **Fillers:** Accepts all types.

CHRISTIAN READER, 465 Gundersen Dr., Carol Stream IL 60188-2498. (630)260-6200. Fax (630)260-0114. E-mail: creditoria@aol.com. Website: http://www.christianreader.net. Christianity Today, Inc. Bonne Steffen, ed. A Christian "Reader's Digest" that uses both reprints and original material. Bimonthly & online mag; 108 pgs; circ 210,000. Subscription $17.50. 35% freelance. Complete ms/cover letter; phone/fax/e-query OK. Pays $100-250 (.10/wd) on acceptance for 1st rts. Articles 500-1,500 wds (50/yr). Responds in 3 wks. Seasonal 9 mos ahead. Accepts reprints ($50-100, tell when/where appeared). Accepts e-mail submission (copied into message). Kill fee. No sidebars. Prefers NIV. Guidelines/theme list (also on Website); copy for 6x9 SAE/4 stamps. (Ads)

> **Fillers:** Buys 25-35/yr. Anecdotes, facts, short humor (see Lite Fare); 25-400 wds; pays $15-35.

Columns/Departments: Cynthia Thomas. Buys 150/yr. Lite Fare (adult church humor); Kids of the Kingdom (kids say and do funny things); Rolling Down the Aisle (true humor from weddings/rehearsals); all to 250 wds; $25-35.

Contest: Annual contest, March 1 deadline. Prizes $1,000, $500, $250. Send SASE for contest fact sheet.

Tips: "Most open to fillers, end-of-article vignettes, annual writing contest, humor anecdotes." Online version uses original material, or reprints with permission.

** This periodical was #4 on the 1998 Top 50 Christian Publishers list (#29 in 1997, #7 in 1996, #63 in 1995).

CHRISTIAN RENEWAL, Box 770, Lewiston NY 14092-0770. (905)562-5719. Fax (905)562-7828. E-mail: JVANDYK@aol.com. Reformed (Conservative). John Van Dyk, mng ed. Church-related and world news for members of the Reformed community of churches in North America. Biweekly newspaper; 20 pgs; circ 4,000. Subscription $29. 5% freelance. Query/ clips; e-query OK. Pays $25-100 for one-time rts. Articles 500-3,000 wds; fiction 2,000 wds (6/yr); book reviews 50-200 wds. Responds in 9 wks. Seasonal 3 mos ahead. Accepts simultaneous submissions & reprints. Prefers e-mail submission (copied into message). Some sidebars. Prefers NIV or NKJV. No guidelines; copy $1. (Ads)

#CHRISTIAN RESEARCH JOURNAL, PO Box 7000, Rancho Santa Margarita, CA 92688-7000. (714)858-6100. Fax (714)858-6111. E-mail: CRITALK @equip.org. Christian Research Institute. Elliot Miller, ed-in-chief. For those who have been affected by cults and the occult. Quarterly journal; 56 pgs; circ 35,000. Subscription $20. 1% freelance. Query or complete ms/cover letter; fax query OK. Pays .15/wd on publication for 1st rts. Articles to 5,000 wds (1/yr); book reviews 1,800-2,500 wds. Responds in 16-20 wks. Accepts simultaneous submissions. Kill fee to 50%. Requires disk. Sidebars assigned. Guidelines; copy $6. (Ads)

Columns/Departments: Witnessing Tips (evangelism), 1,000 wds; Viewpoint (opinion on cults, ethics, etc.), 875 wds.

Tips: "Be patient; we sometimes review mss only twice a year, but we will get back to you. Most open to features (on cults), book reviews, opinion pieces and witnessing tips."

** 1997 & 1996 EPA Award of Merit—Organizational.

CHRISTIAN RETAILING, 600 Rinehart Rd., Lake Mary FL 32746. (407)333-0600. Fax (407)333-7133. E-mail: retailing@strang.com. Website: http://www.christianretailing.com. Strang Communications Co. Melissa Bogdany, mng ed. This publisher is now using only assignment writers and has more writers than they can use.

CHRISTIAN SINGLE, 127 9th Ave. N, Nashville TN 37234-0140. (615)251-2230. Fax (615)251-5008. E-mail: christiansingle@bssb.com. Website: http://www.bssb.com. No freelance.

+CHRISTIAN SINGLE ONLINE, 127 9th Ave. N, Nashville TN 37234-0140. (615)251-2230. Fax (615)251-5008. E-mail: christiansingle@bssb.com or wgibson@bssb.com. Website: http://www.christiansingle.com.

CHRISTIAN SOCIAL ACTION, 100 Maryland Ave. NE, Washington DC 20002. (202)488-5621. Fax (202)488-1617. E-mail: ealsgaard@umc-gbcs.org. Website: http://www.umc-gbcs.org. United Methodist. Eric Alsgaard, ed. Information and analysis of critical social issues from the perspective of Christian faith. Monthly (11X) mag; 40 pgs; circ 2,000. Subscription $15. 20% freelance. Query/clips or complete ms/cover letter. Pays $75-150 on publication for all rts (negotiable). Articles 2,000 wds (12/yr); book reviews 500 wds, $25. Responds in 4 wks. Consider simultaneous submissions & reprints (tell when/where appeared). Prefers disk. Regular sidebars. Prefers RSV. Guidelines; copy for 9x12 SAE/2 stamps. (Ads)

> **Columns/Departments:** Buys 10/yr. Talking (reader's write), 1,000 wds; Media Watch (reviews), 500 wds. Pays $25-50.
> **Special Needs:** Urban issues, children's issues, environment.
> **Tips:** "Most open to regular articles on issues."

#CHRISTIAN STANDARD, 8121 Hamilton Ave., Cincinnati OH 45231. (513)931-4050. Fax (513)931-0950. E-mail: STANDARDMAIL@attmail.com. Standard Publishing/Christian Churches/Churches of Christ. Sam E. Stone, ed. Devoted to the restoration of New Testament Christianity, its doctrines, its ordinances, and its fruits. Weekly mag; 24 pgs; circ 58,000. Subscription $22.50. 50% freelance. Complete ms/cover letter. Pays $10-80 on publication for 1st or one-time rts. Articles 400-1,600 wds (200/yr). Responds in 9 wks. Seasonal 8-12 mos ahead. Accepts reprints. Guidelines; copy for 9x12 SAE/3 stamps or $1. (Ads)

THE CHRISTIAN TRAVELER, PO Box 1736, Holland MI 49422. (616)494-0907. Fax (616)494-0912. E-mail: tct@iserv.net. Amy Eckert, ed. Features travel destinations of significance to Christians. Bimonthly mag 85% freelance. Query; fax/e-query OK. Query for electronic submissions. Pays .30/wd on publication for 1st, one-time, reprint & electronic rts. Articles 1,000-2,500 wds. Responds in 4-6 wks. Seasonal 6 mos ahead. Accepts reprints (tell when/where appeared). Prefers disk. Regular sidebars. Prefers NIV. Guidelines; copy for 9x12 SAE/2 stamps. (Ads)

> **Fillers:** Anecdotes, facts, ideas, newsbreaks, quotes, short humor, tips on healthy travel or travel budgeting. Pay negotiable.
> **Columns/Departments:** Buys 12/yr. Emmaus Road (personal experience essay) 800 wds; Working Vacations (missions/outreach projects) 1,000 wds; Wilderness Wanderings (outdoor nature traveling) 1,000 wds; Family (destinations of interest to all ages) 1,000 wds; and Retreats (great retreat/get-aways) 1,000 wds.
> **Tips:** "Looking for destinations outside the US and Europe. Take time to learn the art of travel writing, which is different from other types of non-fiction. We look for writers who are talented and willing to grow with us as we become a better established publication." Pays $75/color photo.

CHRISTIANITY AND THE ARTS, PO Box 118088, Chicago IL 60611. (312)642-8606. Fax (312)266-7719. E-mail: submit@christianarts.net. Website: http://www.christianarts.net. Nondenominational. Marci Whitney-Schenck, ed/pub. Celebrates the revelation of God through the arts and encourages Christian artistic expression. Quarterly & online mag; 72 pgs; circ 4,000. Subscription $21. 75% freelance. Query or complete ms/cover letter; phone/fax/e-query OK. Sometimes pays $100 on acceptance or publication for 1st rts. Articles 2,000 wds (20/yr); fiction 2,000 wds (uses little); book, music, video reviews 500 wds. Responds in 3 wks. Seasonal 6 mos ahead. Accepts simultaneous submissions. Accepts disk. Regular sidebars. Theme list; copy $6.(Ads)

Poetry: Poetry Editor, 901 S. Plymouth Ct. #1801, Chicago IL 60605. Accepts 12/yr. Avant-garde, free verse, haiku, traditional. No payment.

Special Needs: Visual arts, dance, music, literature, drama.

Contest: Poetry contests with cash prizes. Deadlines vary. Entry free is discounted subscription to the magazine at $15.

Tips: "Interested in features and interviews that focus on ethnic celebration of Christian arts, social problems and the arts, and Jewish-Christian links. I need three contributors to write on drama, dance, and film (four articles a year—No payment). Be knowledgeable, but readable to mass market."

CHRISTIANITY TODAY, 465 Gundersen Dr., Carol Stream IL 60188-2498. (630)260-6200. Fax (630)260-0114. E-mail: ctedit@aol.com or carolthi @aol.com. Website: http://www.christianitytoday.net. Kevin D. Miller, assoc ed. For evangelical Christian thought leaders who seek to integrate their faith commitment with responsible action. Magazine published 14X/yr; 80-120 pgs; circ 178,000. Subscription $24.95. 80% (little unassigned) freelance. Query only; phone/fax/e-query OK. Pays $100-1,000 (.10/wd) on acceptance for 1st rts. Articles 1,000-4,000 wds (60/yr); book reviews 800-1,000 wds, pays per-page rate. Responds in 13 wks. Seasonal 8 mos ahead. Accepts reprints (tell when/where appeared—payment 25% of regular rate). Kill fee 25%. No sidebars. Prefers NIV. Guidelines; copy for 9x12 SAE/3 stamps. (Ads)

*CHRISTIANS IN BUSINESS, 3595 Webb Bridge Rd., Alphretta GA 30203. (770)442-1500. Fax (770)442-1844. Aslan Group Publishing, Inc. Os Hillman, ed. To reflect Christ in the marketplace. Estab 1997. Bimonthly mag; 32 pgs. Subscription $16.95. Complete ms; phone/fax/e-query/submissions OK. (Ads)

Tips: "If you have a story in which Christ was reflected in your marketplace, we want to hear about it."

CHRYSALIS READER, Rte. 1 Box 184, Dillwyn VA 23936. (804)983-3021. Fax (804)983-1074. Swedenborg Foundation. Carol S. Lawson, ed. Focuses on spiritual life and literature. An annual collection of stories, articles and poetry in book form; 192 pgs; circ. 3,000. $13.95/issue. 60% freelance. Query. Pays $50-150 (plus 3 copies) on publication for one-time rts. Articles and short stories (15-25/yr) 2,000-3,500 wds. Responds in 8 wks. Prefers disk. No sidebars. Guidelines/theme list; copy $10/7x10 SAE/5 stamps. (No ads)

Poetry: Robert Lawson. Buys 15/yr. Avant-garde, free verse, haiku; $25 plus 2 copies. Submit max 6 poems.

Tips: "Each issue is on a theme, so we always need essays on those themes; also literary fiction."

THE CHURCH ADVOCATE, Box 926, 700 E. Melrose Ave., Findlay OH 45839. (419)424-1961. Fax (419)424-3433. E-mail: ejs@brt.bright.net. Website: http://www.cggc.org. Churches of God General Conference. Evelyn J. Sloat, ed. Denominational. Quarterly tabloid; 16 pgs; circ 13,000. Subscription free to denomination. Little freelance. Complete ms. Pays $10/printed pg. on publication for one-time rts. Articles 750 wds & up (6/yr). Seasonal 6 mos ahead. Accepts simultaneous submissions & reprints. Accepts e-mail submission. Regular sidebars. Prefers NIV. Guidelines; copy for 9x12 SAE.

> **Tips:** Uses little freelance. Most open to personal experience.

#CHURCH & STATE, 1816 Jefferson Pl. NW, Washington DC 20036. (202)466-3234. Fax (202)466-2587. Website: http://www.au.org. Americans United for Separation of Church and State. Joseph L. Conn, mng ed. Emphasizes religious liberty and church/state relations matters. Monthly mag; 24-32 pgs; circ 33,000. 10% freelance. Query. Pays $150-300 on acceptance for all rts. Articles 800-1,600 wds (11/yr), prefers 800-1,600. Responds in 9 wks. Accepts simultaneous query & reprints. Guidelines; copy for 9x12 SAE/3 stamps.

> **Tips:** "We are not a religious magazine. You need to see our magazine before you try to write for it."

CHURCH HERALD AND HOLINESS BANNER, 7415 Metcalf, Box 4060, Overland Park KS 66204. (913)432-0331. Fax (913)722-0351. E-mail: HBeditor@juno.com.   Website: http://www.sunflower.org/~kccbslib. Church of God (Holiness)/Herald and Banner Press. Mark D. Avery, ed. Denominational; conservative/ Wesleyan/evangelical people. Biweekly mag; 20 pgs; circ 1,700. Subscription $12.50. 50% freelance. Complete ms/cover letter. **NO PAYMENT** for one-time, reprint or simultaneous rts. Not copyrighted. Articles 200-600 wds (40/yr). Responds in 4 wks. Seasonal 3 mos ahead. Accepts simultaneous submissions & reprints (tell when/where appeared). Accepts disk or e-mail submission (copied into message). Some sidebars. Prefers KJV. Guidelines (also by e-mail); copy for 6/9 SAE/2 stamps. (No ads)

> **Poetry:** Buys few. Traditional; 8-24 lines. Submit max 4 poems.
> **Fillers:** Anecdotes, facts, prose, quotes; 150-400 wds.
> **Tips:** "Most open to devotional articles. Must be concise, well-written, and get one main point across; 200-600 wds."

CHURCH OF GOD EVANGEL, PO Box 2250, Cleveland TN 37320-2250. (423)478-7589. Fax (423)478-7521. Church of God (Cleveland, TN). Wilma Amison, mng ed. Denominational. Monthly mag; 36 pgs; circ 51,000. Subscription $12. 10% freelance. Complete ms/cover letter only. Pays $10-50 on acceptance for 1st, one-time, simultaneous rts. Articles 300-1,200 wds (50/yr). Responds in 2-3 wks. Seasonal 4 mos ahead. Accepts simultaneous submissions. Accepts disk. Some sidebars. Prefers KJV, NKVJ, NIV. Free guidelines/copy. (No ads)

> **Fillers:** Anecdotes & ideas.
> **Tips:** "Need human interest articles. Always willing to buy thoughtful, well-written pieces that speak to people where they live. Always need humor with a point."

COLUMBIA, PO Box 1670, 1 Columbus Plaza, New Haven CT 06510. (203)772-2130. Fax (203)777-0114. Knights of Columbus (Catholic). Richard McMunn, ed. Geared to a general Catholic family audience. Monthly mag; 32 pgs; circ 1.5 million. Subscription $6; foreign add $2. 25% freelance. Query. Pays to $250-500 on acceptance for 1st rts. Articles 1,000-1,500 wds (20/yr). Responds in 3-4 wks. Seasonal 6 mos ahead. Prefers disk. Kill fee $100. Some sidebars. Free guidelines/copy.

> **Tips:** "Keep eye out for K of C activity in local area and send a query letter about it. Also articles on Catholic family life. Articles must be accompanied by photos or transparencies."
> ** This periodical was #55 on the 1998 Top 50 Christian Publishers list (#38 in 1997, #25 in 1996, #32 in 1995, #19 in 1994).

COMMENTS FROM THE FRIENDS, Box 819, Assonet MA 02702. (508)763-8050. E-mail: editor@cftf.com. Website: http://www.cftf.com. David A. Reed, ed. For ex-Jehovah's Witnesses, their relatives, Christians reaching out to them, and dissident Witnesses. Quarterly & online newsletter; 16 pgs; circ 1,200. Also online edition. Subscription $11. 5% freelance. Complete ms/cover letter; e-query OK. Pays $20 (sometimes copies or subscription) on publication for all rts. Articles 100-1,000 wds (4/yr); book reviews 50-1,000 wds. Responds in 4-8 wks. Seasonal 3 mos ahead. Accepts simultaneous submissions & reprints. Macintosh disks or e-mail submission (copied into message). No sidebars. Any version. Guidelines (also by e-mail); copy $1/ 8x10 SAE/2 stamps or see Website for online edition.

> **Columns/Departments:** Witnessing Tips, 500-1,000 wds.
> **Tips:** "Acquaint us with why you are qualified to write about J.W.'s. Write well-documented, concise articles relevant to J.W.'s today. We automatically reject all material not specifically about Jehovah's Witnesses."

COMMON BOUNDARY, 4905 Del Ray Ave. Ste. 210, Bethesda MD 20814. (301)652-9495. Fax (301)652-0579. E-mail: editor@commonboundary. org. Website: http://www.commonboundary.org. Ecumenical/Common Boundary, Inc. Charles Simpkinson, pub. For spiritual seekers searching for a way to integrate spirituality with psychology and the creative arts. Bimonthly mag; 64 pgs; circ 26,000. 50% freelance. Query. Pays varying rates on publication for 1st rts. Articles 3,000-4,000 wds. Responds in 13-26 wks. Accepts simultaneous submissions. Prefers e-mail submission (attached file). Kill fee 1/3. Some sidebars. Guidelines; copy $5. (Ads)

> **Fillers:** Newsbreaks, 200-600 wds.
> **Contest:** Annual $1,000 Dissertation/Thesis award for best psychospiritual topic. Also Annual Green Dove Award of $5,000 for project integrating spirituality, psychology, and ecology offered in conjunction with the Simple Abundance Charitable Fund.
> **Tips:** "Read articles on our Website to see the style and kinds of topics covered."

COMMONWEAL, 475 Riverside Dr., Room 405, New York NY 10115-0499. (212)662-4200. Fax (212)662-4183. E-mail: commonweal@msn.com. Website: http://www.commonwealmagazine.org. Commonweal Foundation/Catholic. Patrick Jordan, mng ed. A review of public affairs, religion, literature and the arts, for an intellectually engaged readership. Biweekly mag; 32 pgs; circ 19,000. Subscription $44. 20% freelance. Query/clips; phone query OK. Pays $50-100 (.03/wd) on acceptance or publication for all rts. Articles 1,000 or 3,000 wds (20/yr). Responds 4 wks. Seasonal 2 mos ahead. Prefers disk or e-mail submission. Kill fee 2%. Some sidebars. Guidelines; copy for 9x12 SAE/4 stamps. (Ads)

Poetry: Rosemary Deen. Buys 20/yr. Free verse, traditional; to 75 lines; .75/line. Submit max 5 poems. Submit October-May.

Columns/Departments: Upfronts (brief, newsy facts and information behind the headlines), 750-1,000 wds; The Last Word (commentary based on insight from personal experience or reflection), 700 wds.

Tips: "Most open to meaningful articles on social, political, religious and cultural topics; or columns."

COMPANION MAGAZINE, 695 Coxwell Ave., Ste 600, Toronto ON M4C 5R6 Canada. (800)461-1619 or (416)690-5611. Fax (416)690-3320. E-mail: 102532.1737@compuserve.com. Website: http://www.cmpa.ca.no10. html. Catholic/Franciscan. Fr. R. Riccioli, ed; submit to Betty McCrimmon, mng ed. An adult, Catholic, inspirational, devotional family magazine. Monthly (11X) mag; 32 pgs; circ 5,000. Subscription $16 CAN or $18 US & foreign. 50% freelance. Complete ms/cover letter; phone/fax/e-query OK. Pays .06/wd CAN on publication for 1st rts. Articles 500-1,000 wds (35/yr); fiction 500-1,000 wds (7/yr). Responds in 6 wks. Seasonal 5 mos ahead. Accepts disk (Mac). Guidelines; copy for 7x10 SAE with IRCs. (Ads)

Poetry: Free verse, light verse, traditional. Pays .60/line CAN.

Fillers: Anecdotes, cartoons, prayers, quotes, short humor, word puzzles.

Special Needs: Articles on St. Francis, Franciscan spirituality, and social justice.

Tips: Most open to human interest.

COMPANIONS, PO Box 555, Seymour MO 65746. (417)935-4639. Mennonite/Christian Light Publications. Roger L. Berry, ed. Consistent with conservative Mennonite doctrine: believer baptism, nonresistance, and nonconformity. Monthly take-home paper; 4 pgs; circ 9,000. Subscription $9.70. 75% freelance. Complete ms only. Pays .02-.05/wd on acceptance for all, 1st, one-time, simultaneous or reprint rts. Articles 100-750 wds (150/yr); true stories 800-2,000 wds (50/yr). Responds in 6-8 wks. Seasonal 6 mos ahead. Accepts simultaneous submissions & reprints (tell when/where appeared). No disk. No sidebars. KJV only. Guidelines; copy for 9x12 SAE/2 stamps. (No ads)

Fillers: Buys 20/yr. Anecdotes, prose; 30-100 wds.

Columns/Departments: Buys 12/yr. Science and Scripture (creationist/Biblicist), 400-700; Archaeology and Scripture (archaeology that supports biblical truths); 400-700 wds.

Tips: "We are most open to freelancers in our columns, or short inspirational articles. Pay close attention to our list of do's and dont's. Because of lifestyle differences, stories are the most difficult for non-Mennonite freelancers to write for us."

** This periodical was #49 on the 1998 Top 50 Christian Publishers list (#51 in 1997, #45 in 1996, #14 in 1995, #28 in 1994).

+**COMPANY: A Magazine of the American Jesuits**, 3441 N. Ashland Ave., Chicago IL 60657. (773)281-1534. Fax (773)281-2667. E-mail: company mag@luc.edu. Website: Http://www.companysj.com. Rita George, asst ed. For people interested in or involved with Jesuit ministries. Quarterly & online mag; 32 pgs; circ 124,000. Subscription for donation. Complete ms/cover letter; fax/e-query OK. Pays $150-350 on publication for one-time rts. Articles 500-2,000 wds (20/yr). Responds in 6 wks. Seasonal 3 mos ahead. Accepts simultaneous submissions & reprints (tell when/where appeared). Prefers disk or e-mail submission (attached file). Kill fee $50. Regular sidebars. Prefers NRSV, NAB, NJB. Guidelines; copy for 9x12 SAE/4 stamps. (No ads)

> **Columns/Departments:** Buys 24-32/yr. Books with a Jesuit connection; Minims and Maxims (short items of interest to Jesuit world), 100-150 wds/photo; Letters to the Editor; Obituaries. No payment (usually).
>
> **Tips:** "We welcome manuscripts as well as outlines of story ideas and indication of willingness to accept free-lance assignments (please include resume and writing samples with the latter two)."

COMPUTING TODAY, 465 Gundersen Dr., Carol Stream IL 60189-2498. (630)260-6200. Fax (630)260-0114. E-mail: computingt@aol.com. Website: http://www.computingtoday.net. Christianity Today, Inc. Mark Moring, ed. To provide Christian computer users with practical information to help them in their ministries and personal use. Bimonthly mag; 50 pgs; circ 100,000. Subscription $9.95. 75% freelance. Query; fax/e-query OK. Pays variable rates on acceptance publication for 1st rts. Articles 1,000-1,500 wds (15/yr). Responds in 4 wks. Seasonal 9 mos ahead. Accepts reprints (tell when/where appeared). Requires disk or e-mail submission. Kill fee 50%. Regular sidebars. Prefers NIV. Guidelines; copy for 9x12 SAE. Limited reference in topical listings (accepts all types of articles).

> **Fillers:** Buys10/yr. Cartoons, short humor; $125 for cartoons.

*__CONNECTING POINT,__ Box 685, Cocoa FL 32923. (407)632-0130. Linda G. Howard, ed. For and by the mentally challenged (retarded) community; primarily deals with spiritual and self-advocacy issues. Monthly mag; circ 1,000. 75% freelance. Complete ms. **NO PAYMENT** for 1st rts. Articles (24/yr) & fiction (12/yr), 250-750 wds; book reviews 150 wds. Responds in 3-6 wks. Seasonal 3 mos ahead. Accepts simultaneous submissions & reprints. Guidelines; copy for 9x12 SAE/6 stamps.

> **Poetry:** Accepts 4/yr. Any type; 4-66 lines. Submit max 10 poems.
>
> **Fillers:** Accepts 12/yr. Cartoons, games, word puzzles; 50-250 wds.
>
> **Columns/Departments:** Accepts 24/yr. Devotion Page, 1,000 wds; Bible Study, 500 wds. Query.
>
> **Special Needs:** Record reviews, self-advocacy, integration/normalization, justice system.
>
> **Tips:** "All mss need to be in primary vocabulary."

*CONQUEST, 1300 N Meacham Rd., Schaumburg IL 60173-4888. (847)843-1600. Fax (847)843-3757. Regular Baptist. Joan E. Alexander, ed. For adults associated with fundamental Baptist Churches. Weekly take-home paper. Note: This periodical is being redesigned as we go to press. Send for new guidelines before submitting.

CORNERSTONE, 939 W. Wilson Ave., Chicago IL 60640-5706. (773)561-2450. Fax (773)989-2076. Website: http://www.cornerstonemagcom. Cornerstone Communications, Inc. Submissions ed. For young adults, 18-35; to communicate doctrinal truth based on Scripture and to break the "normal Christian" mold with a stance that has cultural relevancy. Quarterly (3-4 issues) & online mag; 64-72 pgs; circ 38,000. Subscription free. 10% freelance. Complete ms/cover letter; fax query OK. Pays .08-.10/wd on publication for 1st, one-time, reprint & simultaneous rts. Articles to 4,000 wds (20/yr); fiction 250-4,000 wds (1-4/yr); book/music reviews 500-1,000 wds. Responds in 13-26 wks to accepted mss only (discards others, don't send SASE). Seasonal 6 mos ahead. Accepts simultaneous submissions & reprints (tell when/where appeared). Prefers disk, no e-mail submission. Regular sidebars. Guidelines (also on Website); copy for 9x12 SAE/5 stamps. (Ads)

> **Poetry:** Poetry Editor. Buys 15-24/yr. Avant-garde, free verse, haiku, light verse; $10-25. Submit any number.
>
> **Fillers:** Buys 1-4/yr. Cartoons, prayers; 500-1,000 wds. Pays .08-.10/wd
> **Columns/Departments:** Buys 3-4/yr. News items, 500-1,000 wds; Music Interviews (Christian & secular artists) to 2,700 wds; Music & Book Reviews (Christian & secular).
>
> **Tips:** "Most open to avant-garde, creative, thought-provoking, original fiction with a Christian worldview."

THE COVENANT COMPANION, 5101 N. Francisco Ave., Chicago IL 60625. (773)784-3000x328. Fax (773)784-4366. E-mail: CovCom@compuserve.com. Website: http://www.npcts.edu/cov. Evangelical Covenant Church. Suzanne K. Swanson-Nystrom, ed. Informs, stimulates thought, and encourages dialogue on issues that impact the denomination. Monthly mag; 40 pgs; circ 20,000. Subscription $29.95. 10-15% freelance. Complete ms/cover letter; fax/e-query OK. Pays $25-75 after publication for one-time or simultaneous rts. Articles 500-1,500 wds (15/yr), fiction 750-1,200 (3/yr). Prefers e-mail submission. Responds in 4 wks. Seasonal 3 mos ahead. Accepts simultaneous submissions & reprints (tell when/where appeared). Some kill fees. Regular sidebars. Prefers NRSV. Guidelines/theme list (also by e-mail); copy for 9x12 SAE/5 stamps; or $2.50. (Ads)

> **Fillers:** Cartoons, short humor.

+CREATION EX NIHILO, PO Box 6302, Acacia Ridge Qld 4110 Australia. Phone: 07 3273 7650. Fax 07 3273 7672. E-mail: admin@ answer singenesis.com. Website: Http://www.answers in genesis.org. Answers in Genesis. Carl Weiland, ed. A family, nature, science magazine focusing on creation/evolution issues. Quarterly mag; 56 pgs; circ 50,000. 50% freelance. Complete ms/cover letter; phone/fax/e-query OK. Query for electronic submissions. **NO PAYMENT**for all rts. Articles to 1,500wds (20/yr);

fiction 1,000-1,500 wds (1/yr). Responds in 2-3 wks. Prefers disk or e-mail submission (attached file). Regular sidebars. Prefers KJV. Guidelines; copy $6.95. (No ads)

+CREATION ILLUSTRATED, PO Box 7955, Auburn CA 95604. (916)637-5568. Fax (916)637-5170. E-mail: creation@foothill.net. Tom Ish, ed. A Christian nature magazine that is uplifting, Bible-based, and glorifies God; for ages 9-99. Quarterly mag; 68 pgs; circ 9,000. Subscription $19.95. 99% freelance. Query or query/clips; fax/e-query OK. Pays $75-125 on publication for 1st rts. Articles 1,500-2,500 words (25/yr). Responds in 3 weeks. Seasonal 6 mos ahead. Accepts simultaneous submissions & reprints (tell when/where appeared). Prefers disk. Some kill fees. Some sidebars. Prefers KJV. Guidelines/theme list; copy $3/9x12 SAE/ $1.75 postage. (No ads)

> **Poetry:** Buys 8/yr. Light verse, traditional; 10-20 lines. Pays $15. Submit max 4 poems.
>
> **Fillers:** Games, 100-200 wds. Pays variable rates.
>
> **Contest:** Photography contest in each issue for best nature, animal and creation shots.
>
> **Tips:** "Most open to an experience with nature/creation that brought you closer to God and will inspire the reader to do the same."

THE CRESSET, A Review of Arts, Literature & Public Affairs, Huegli Hall #29, Valparaiso IN 46383. (219)464-5274. Fax (219)464-5496. E-mail: Gail.Eifrig@valpo.edu. Valparaiso University/Lutheran. Gail McGrew Eifrig, ed. For college educated, professors, pastors, lay people; serious review essays on religious-cultural affairs. Bimonthly (7X) mag; 36 pgs; circ 4,700. Subscription $8.50. 50% freelance. Complete ms/cover letter. Pays $35 on publication for 1st rts. Articles 2,500-5,000 wds (20-30/ yr). Responds in 12 wks. Seasonal 3 mos ahead. Prefers disk. No sidebars. Copy for 9x12 SAE/5 stamps.

> **Poetry:** John Ruff. Buys 15-20/yr. Avant-garde, free verse, traditional; to 40 lines; $15. Submit max 5 poems.

+CRISIS POINT, PO Box 24703, Omaha NE 68124. E-mail: editor@ crisispoint.com. Bimonthly newsletter (hard copy or e-mail submission version).

> **Tips:** "If you are interested in contributing, reply to the above e-mail submission address with the word 'interest' in the subject box and your name and postal address in the body of the message. We will send copies of both versions of the next issue."

*CROSSWAY/NEWSLINE/FAIRFORD NEWS, PO Box 10, Lightwater, Surrey GU18 SJS England. Phone/fax 012764 72724. Airline Aviation & Aerospace Christian Fellowship. J. Brown, gen. sec. For non-Christians working in aviation. Crossway is an annual magazine; Newsline a quarterly newsletter; 16 pgs. Free subscription. 100% freelance. Complete ms/cover letter. **NO PAYMENT.** Sometimes copyrighted. Articles on aviation to 2,000 wds. Accepts simultaneous submissions & reprints.

CULTURE WARS, 206 Marquette Ave., South Bend IN 46617. (219)289-9786. Fax (219)289-1461. E-mail: 71554.445@ compuserve.com. Ultramontagne Associates, Inc. Dr. E. Michael Jones, ed. Issues relating to

Catholic families and issues affecting America that impact all people. Monthly (11X) mag; 35 pgs; circ. 3,500. Subscription $25. 20% freelance. Complete ms/cover letter; fax/e-query OK. Pays $100 & up on publication for all rts. Articles (25/yr); book reviews $50. Responds in 12-24 wks. Query about reprints. Prefers disk. Some sidebars. Developing guidelines; copy for 9x12 SAE/5 stamps.

> **Poetry:** Buys 15/yr. Free verse, light verse, traditional; 10-50 lines; $25. Submit max 2 poems.
>
> **Fillers:** Buys 15/yr. Cartoons, quotes; 25 wds & up; variable payment.
>
> **Columns/Departments:** Buys 25/yr. Commentary, 2,500 wds; Feature, 5,000 wds; $100-250.
>
> **Tips:** "All fairly open except cartoons. Single-spaced preferred; avoid dot matrix; photocopies must be clear."

THE DALLAS/FORT WORTH HERITAGE, PO Box 1424, Ennis TX 75120. (972)846-2900. Fax (972)846-2800. E-mail: DFWHER@fni.com. Website: http://www.fni.com/heritage/index.html. John J. Dwyer, ed. To help preserve and sustain America's Christian heritage and pass it on to the nation's children. Monthly newspaper; 50-70 pgs; circ 45,000. Subscription $25. Open to freelance. No e-mail submission. Query. (Ads)

+DAY STAR TRIBUNE, PO Box 2082, Fairmont WV 26554. (304)367-6556. Fax (304)367-8939. E-mail: daystartribune@prodigy.net. Power Publishing. Craig A. Richards, pub. Conservative Christian newspaper providing Christian views on the world of news. Monthly newspaper; 16-24 pgs; circ 3,000. Subscription $16. Estab 1998. 10% freelance. Query; e-query OK. Query for electronic submissions. Pays based on writer & topic on publication or acceptance for variable rts. Not copyrighted. Articles 500-1,000 wds; fiction 500-2,000 wds; book/music/video reviews, 20-250 wds. Responds in 2 wks (usually). Seasonal 2 mos ahead. Accepts simultaneous submissions & reprints (tell when/where appeared). Prefers disk or e-mail submission (copied into message). Regular sidebars. Any version. No guidelines; copy for 9x12 SAE/4 stamps. (Ads)

> **Fillers:** Buys some. Anecdotes, cartoons, facts, games, ideas, jokes, newsbreaks, party ideas, quizzes, quotes, short humor, word puzzles, to 500 wds. Pays variable rates.
>
> **Columns/Departments:** Barbara Toler-Marsh, lifestyle ed. Query. Pays variable rates.
>
> **Special Needs:** Wants to add more freelance writers and feature columns and departments.
>
> **Contest:** Currently considering.
>
> **Tips:** "Looking for creative, original, very useful, practical freelance material."

DECISION, PO Box 779, Minneapolis MN 55440-0779. (612)338-0500. Fax (612)335-1299. E-mail: submissions@bgea.org. Website: http://www.decisionmag.org. Billy Graham Evangelistic Assn. Bob Paulson, assoc ed. Evangelism/Christian nurture. Monthly & online mag; 44 pgs; circ 1,800,000. Subscription $9. 25% freelance. Complete ms/cover letter (no queries); no phone/fax/e-query. Pays $55-230 on publication for all or 1st rts. Articles 1,000-1,400 wds (40/yr). Responds 10-12 wks. Seasonal 10-12 mos ahead. Accepts disk; prefers e-mail submission (copied into message). Kill fee. Regular sidebars. Prefers NIV. Guidelines/ theme list (also by e-mail/Website); copy for 10x13 SAE/3 stamps. (No ads)

Poetry: Buys 6/yr. Free verse, light verse, traditional; 4-16 lines; .60/ wd. Submit max 7 poems.

Fillers: Buys 50/yr. Anecdotes, prose; 300-600 wds; $25-75.

Columns/Departments: Buys 12/yr. Where Are They Now? (people who have become Christian through Billy Graham ministries); 600-800 wds; $85.

Tips: "We want first-person, personal experience articles that show how you learned and grew in a specific situation. What have you experienced that has caused you to grow closer to Christ? How have you applied biblical principles in a difficult situation? Let us see what you did—let us learn with you."

** This periodical was #59 on the 1994 Top 50 Christian Publishers list.

DISASTER NEWS NETWORK (formerly Village Life), PO Box 816, Ellicott City MD 21041-0816. Fax (410)203-9063. E-mail: news@disasternews. net. Website: http://www.disasternews.net. Villagelife.org, Inc. Submit to The Editor. An interactive daily news site on the World Wide Web. Query; phone/fax/e-query (preferred) OK. Pays $85-100 after publication for 1st & global electronic rts. Articles; book reviews, $30-40. Accepts few reprints (tell when/where appeared). Requires e-mail submission. Guidelines on the Website. Not in topical listings.

Tips: "Authors are expected to have an e-mail submission address, which will be included in the credits of published articles."

DISCIPLESHIP JOURNAL, Box 35004, Colorado Springs CO 80935. (719)531-3529. Fax (719)598-7128. E-mail: susan.nikaido@navpress. com. Website: http://www.gospelcom.net/navs/NP/djhome.html. The Navigators. Susan Nikaido, ed. For motivated, maturing Christians desiring to grow spiritually and to help others grow; biblical and practical. Bimonthly mag; 96+ pgs; circ 110,000. Subscription $21.97. 95% freelance. Query; query for electronic submissions. Pays .25/wd (.05/wd for reprints) on acceptance for 1st & electronic rts. Articles 1,500-2,500 wds (60/yr); fiction 1,500-2,500 wds (1-2/yr). Responds in 6-8 wks. Accepts simultaneous submissions. Prefers disk or e-mail submission (attached file). Kill fee 50%. Regular sidebars. Prefers NIV. Guidelines/theme list (also by e-mail/Website). (Ads)

Columns/Departments: Buys 15+/yr. On the Home Front (Q & A regarding family issues); 1,000 wds; Bible Study Methods (how-to), to 1,000 wds; DJ Plus (ministry how-to on missions, evangelism, serving, discipling, teaching & small groups), to 500 wds. Pays .25/wd.

Tips: "Most open to non-theme articles, departments, DJ Plus and sidebars. Our articles focus on biblical passages or topics. Articles should derive main principles from a thorough study of Scripture; should illustrate each principle; should show how to put each principle into practice; and should demonstrate with personal illustrations

and vulnerability that the author has wrestled with the subject in his or her life."
** This periodical was #5 on the 1998 Top 50 Christian Publishers list. (#10 in 1997, #2 in 1996 , #15 in 1995, #8 in 1994). Also 1998 & 1997 EPA Award of Excellence—General (1996 EPA Award of Merit—General.)

DISCIPLE'S JOURNAL, 10 Fiorenza Dr., Wilmington MA 01887-4421. (978)657-7373. Fax (978)657-5411. E-mail: dddj@disciplesdirectory.com. Website: http://www.disciplesdirectory.com. Kenneth A. Dorothy, ed. To strengthen, edify, inform and unite the body of Christ. Monthly & online newspaper; 16-32 pgs; circ 10,000. Subscription $9.95. 25% freelance. Query; fax/e-query OK. **NO PAYMENT** for one-time rts. Articles 400 wds (24/yr); book/music/video reviews 200 wds. Responds in 2 wks. Seasonal 2 mos ahead. Accepts simultaneous submissions & reprints (tell when/where appeared). Prefers disk or e-mail submission (attached file). Some sidebars. Prefers NIV. Guidelines/theme list (also by e-mail); copy for 9x12 SAE/$1.70 postage. (Ads)
   Poetry: Accepts 12/yr. All types; 12-24 lines. Submit max 6 poems.
   Fillers: Accepts 12/yr. All types; 100-400 wds.
   Columns/Departments: Financial; Singles; Men; Women; Business; Parenting. 400 wds.
   Contest: Poetry contest.
   Tips: "Most open to men's, women's or singles' issues; missions; or home schooling. Send sample of articles for review."

DISCOVERY, 400 W. Lake Brantley Rd., Altamonte Springs FL 32714-2715. (407)682-9494. Fax (407)682-7005. E-mail: joyful953@aol.com. Website: http://www.wtln.com. Radio Station WTLN FM/AM. John Adams, ed. For Christian community in Central Florida. Monthly & online newspaper; circ 25,000. Subscription free/$9 for home delivery. 20% freelance. Complete ms; phone/fax query OK. **NO PAYMENT**. Not copyrighted. News driven & informative articles under 500 wds. Seasonal 1+ mos ahead. Accepts reprints. Regular sidebars. No disk. Theme list. (Ads)
   Columns/Departments: Local/National News, Local Ministries, Broadcaster's Information, Sports, Christian Living, Seasonal themed features.
   Tips: "We may submit articles to our other publications in Knoxville and Philadelphia."

THE DOOR, PO Box 1444, Waco TX 76703-1444. (817)752-1468. Fax (817)752-4915. E-mail (submissions): rfd3@flash.net. Website: http://www.the-door.org. Trinity Foundation. Robert Darden, ed. Satire of evangelical church plus issue-oriented interviews. Bimonthly mag; 66 pgs; circ 16,000. Subscription $29.95. 90% freelance. Complete ms. Pays $40-200 after publication for 1st rts. Not copyrighted. Articles 750-1,500 wds (25/yr). Responds in 6 wks. Accepts simultaneous submissions & reprints (if from non-competing markets). Kill fee $40-50. Regular sidebars. Guidelines (also by e-mail); copy $5.
   Tips: "We look for biting satire/humor—National Lampoon not

Reader's Digest. You must understand our satirical slant. Read more than one issue to understand our 'wavelength.' We desperately need genuinely funny articles with a smart, satiric bent." This is the old Wittenburg Door, only the name has changed.

DOVETAIL: A Journal by and for Jewish/Christian Families, 775 Simon Greenwell Ln., Boston KY 40107. (502)549-5440. Fax (549)540-3543. E-mail: di-ifr@bardstown.com. Website: http://www.mich.com/dovetail. Dovetail Institute for Interfaith Family Resources. Mary Rosenbaum, ed. Offers balanced, non-judgmental articles for interfaith families and the professionals who serve them. Bimonthly mag; 12-16 pgs; circ 1,500. Subscription $25. 50-80% freelance. Complete ms/cover letter; phone/fax/e-query OK. Pays $10-20 on publication for all rts. Articles 800-1,000 wds (18-20/yr); book reviews 500 wds, $10. Responds in 4 wks. Seasonal 4 mos ahead. Accepts simultaneous submissions & reprints (tell when/where appeared). Prefers disk or e-mail submission (copied into message). Some sidebars. Prefers KJV. Guidelines/theme list (also by e-mail); copy for 9x12 SAE/3 stamps. (Ads)

> **Columns/Departments:** Buys 3-6/yr. Food & Family (Jewish & Christian), 500 wds, $20. Complete ms.
> **Special Needs:** The extended family.
> **Poetry:** Buys 1-2/yr. Traditional; $10. Submit max 4 poems.
> **Tips:** "Please do not send articles that deal with Christian theology or beliefs. Our audience is families with two faiths, and articles should address this specific situation."

DREAMS & VISIONS, 35 Peter St. S., Orillia ON L3V 5A8 Canada. Fax (705)329-1770. E-mail: skysong@bconnex.net. Website: http://www.bconnex.net/ ~skysong. Skysong Press. Steve Stanton, ed. An international showcase for short literary fiction written from a Christian perspective. Irregular journal; 56 pgs; circ 200. Subscription $12. 100% freelance. Complete ms/cover letter; fax/e-query OK. Pays .005/wd on publication for 1st rts & one non-exclusive reprint. Fiction 2,000-6,000 wds (10/yr). Responds in 4-6 wks. Seasonal 6 mos ahead. Accepts simultaneous submissions & reprints (tell when/where appeared). Accepts disk. Guidelines; copy $4.95 (4 back issues to writers $10).

EMPHASIS ON FAITH AND LIVING, Box 9127, Fort Wayne IN 46899-9127. (219)747-2027. Fax (219)747-5331. E-mail: mcdenomusa@aol.com. Website: http://www.mcusa.org. Missionary Church. Robert Ransom, mng ed. Denominational; for adults 40 and older. Bimonthly mag; 16 pgs; circ 13,000. Subscription free. 10% freelance. Query or complete ms/cover letter; no phone/fax/e-query. Pays .03-.04/wd on publication for 1st, one-time, reprint or simultaneous rts. Not copyrighted. Articles 200-800 wds (3/yr); fiction 200-1,600 wds (1-2/yr). Responds in 4-8 wks. Seasonal 4 mos ahead. Accepts simultaneous submissions & reprints. Accepts disk; no e-mail submission. Some sidebars. Guidelines (also by e-mail); copy for 9x12 SAE/2 stamps. (Ads)

> **Tips:** "Our publication provides church news, missions information, and spiritual reading for members and friends of the Missionary

Church denomination. We seek material that is compatible with our Wesleyan-Armenian church doctrine. Need articles on prayer."

EPISCOPAL LIFE, 815 2nd Ave., New York NY 10017. (212)922-5398. Fax (212)949-8059. E-mail: episcopal.life@ecunet.org. Website: http://www.dfms.org/episcopal-life. Episcopal Church. Jerrold F. Hames, ed; Edward P. Stannard, mng ed. Denominational. Monthly newspaper; 32 pgs; circ 180,000. Subscription $7. 35% freelance. Query/clips or complete ms/cover letter; phone query on breaking news only. Pays $50-300 on publication for 1st, one-time or simultaneous rts. Articles 250-1,200 wds (12/yr); assigned book reviews 400 wds ($35). Responds in 5 wks. Seasonal 4 mos ahead. Accepts simultaneous submissions & reprints. Accepts e-mail submission. Kill fee 50%. Free copy.

> **Columns/Departments:** Nan Cobbey. Buys 36/yr. Commentary on political/religious topics; 300-600 wds; $35-75. Query.
>
> **Tips:** "All articles must have Episcopal Church slant or specifics. We need topical/issues, not devotional stuff. Most open to feature stories about Episcopalians—clergy, lay, churches, involvement in local efforts, movements, ministries."

EVANGEL, Box 535002, Indianapolis IN 46253-5002. (317)244-3660. Fax (317)244-1247. Free Methodist/Light and Life Communications. Julie Innes, ed. For young to middle-aged adults; encourages spiritual growth. Weekly take-home paper; 8 pgs; circ 19,000-20,000. Subscription $7.40. 100% freelance. Query. Pays .04/wd on publication for one-time rts. Articles to 1,200 wds (100/yr); fiction to 1,200 wds (100/yr). Responds in 6-8 wks. Seasonal 9-12 mos ahead. Accepts simultaneous submissions & reprints (tell when/where appeared). Accepts disk. Some sidebars. Prefers NIV. Guidelines; copy for #10 SAE/1 stamp.

> **Poetry:** Buys 30/yr. Free verse, light verse; 3-16 lines; $10. Submit max 5 poems. Rhyming poetry not usually taken too seriously.
>
> **Fillers:** Buys 20/yr. Cartoons, short humor; to 100 wds; humor $10, cartoons $20.
>
> **Tips:** "Write about a topic that is new and fresh. Avoid redundancy and focus on thesis for clarity of submission."

*THE EVANGEL, PO Box 348, Marlow OK 73055. (405)658-5631. Fax (405)658-2867. Home Mission Board, Southern Baptist Church. Michael H. Reynolds, ed. To expose Mormonism and explain its views of doctrine, history and current events. Bimonthly; circ 20,000. Subscription free. Open to freelance. Complete ms. Not in topical listings. (Ads)

#THE EVANGELICAL ADVOCATE, 1426 Lancaster Pike, Circleville OH 43113. (740)474-8856. Fax (740)477-7766. Churches of Christ in Christian Union. Ralph Hux, ed. Denominational; emphasizing fundamental evangelical holiness. Monthly mag; circ 5,000. Subscription $12. Open to freelance. Query. Not in topical listings. (Ads)

EXPRESSION CHRISTIAN NEWSPAPER, 200 Dinsmore Ave., Pittsburgh PA 15205. (412)921-1300. Fax (412)921-1537. E-mail: express@nauticom. net. Website: http://www.expressionnews.com. The Sonshine Foundation. Cathy Hickling, ed. Geared toward bringing unity among the churches in the Pittsburgh and west PA area. Monthly newspaper; 24-32 pgs; circ

15,000. Subscription $20 (first year free). 75% freelance. Query; fax/e-query OK. Pays $25-100 on publication for one-time rts. Not copyrighted. Articles 300-500 or 750-1,000 wds; book/music/video reviews 300 wds (no pay). Responds in 3-4 wks. Seasonal 2 mos ahead. Accepts simultaneous submissions. Kill fee. Regular sidebars. Accepts disk. Guidelines/theme list; copy for 9x12 SAE/3 stamps. (Ads)

> **Fillers:** Buys 4-6/yr. Cartoons; $10-25.

> **Tips:** "Send local/state stories, for example: Interview with local guy, Mel Blount (ex-Steeler), who has a half-way house for boys. Most open to editorials; PA stories of interest."

+FAITH IN ACTION, PO Box 1, Yakima WA 98907. (509)575-1965. Fax (509)575-4732. E-mail: kengaub@kengaub.com. Website: Http://www.kengaub.com. Ken Gaub Worldwide Ministry/radio ministry. Ken Gaub, pres. Quarterly mag; 12-16 pgs; circ 50,000. Free subscription . Buys all rts. Articles. Not in topical listings. (No ads)

FAITH TODAY, M.I.P. Box 3745, Markham ON L3R 0Y4 Canada. (905)479-5885. Fax (905)479-4742. E-mail: ft@efc-canada.com. Website: http://www.efc-canada.com. Evangelical Fellowship of Canada. Marianne Meed Ward, mng ed. Informing Canadian evangelicals on thoughts, trends, issues and events. Bimonthly mag; 62-80 pgs; circ 18,000. Subscription $17.65 CAN. 80% freelance. Query; fax/e-query OK. Query for electronic submissions. Pays $50-800 on publication for 1st rts. Articles (90/yr) 400-3,000 wds; news stories 400 wds; profiles 900 wds. Responds in 2 wks. Prefers disk or e-mail submission. Kill fee 30-50%. Regular sidebars. Any version. Guidelines/theme list (also by e-mail, eventually on Website); copy for 9x12 SAE/$2.05 in Canadian funds. (Ads)

> **Columns/Departments:** Buys 6/yr. Other Voices (current social/political/religious issues of concern to Canadian church); Guest Column; 600 wds; $90.

> **Special Needs:** "Canadian news. All topics to be approached in a journalistic—not personal viewpoint—style (except for 'Other Voices'). "The Century in Review" pieces; uniting science and faith."

> **Contest:** The God Uses Ink '99 Writer's Contest is open to work published in 1998. Deadline for entries is February 7, 1999. Contest guidelines and entry forms available from Faith Today.

> **Tips:** "Feature/Cover section is most open to freelancers. Be sure to submit analytical journalistic articles on a Canadian event, trend or issue of current interest. Keep cover and feature articles 1,200-5,000 words."

> ** This periodical was #42 on the 1998 Top 50 Christian Publishers List.(#4 in 1997, #65 in 1996, #43 in 1994).

THE FAMILY DIGEST, PO Box 40137, Fort Wayne IN 46804. Catholic. Corine B. Erlandson, ed. Dedicated to the joy and fulfillment of Catholic family life and its relationship to the Catholic parish. Bimonthly journal/booklet; 48 pgs; circ 150,000. Distributed through parishes. 90% freelance. Complete ms/cover letter; no phone/fax/e-query. Pays $40-60, 4-8 wks after acceptance, for 1st rts. Articles 700-1,200 wds (60/yr). Responds in 4-8 wks. Seasonal 7 mos ahead. Occasionally buys reprints. No disk. No sidebars.

Prefers NAB. Guidelines; copy for 6x9 SAE/2 stamps. (Ads—Call 612-929-6765)

Fillers: Buys 24/yr. Anecdotes drawn from experience, 20-100 wds, $20.

Tips: "Prospective freelance writers should be familiar with the types of articles we accept and publish. Need upbeat articles which affirm simple ways in which the Catholic faith is expressed in daily life. Articles on family life, parish life, seasonal articles, how-to pieces, inspirational, prayer, spiritual life and Church traditions will be gladly reviewed for possible acceptance and publication."

** This periodical was #52 on the 1995 Top 50 Christian Publishers list (#57 in 1994).

THE FAMILY JOURNAL, PO Box 506, Bath NY 14810-0506. (607)776-4151. Fax (607)776-6929. E-mail: famlife@aol.com Interdenominational/Family Life Ministries. Jack Hager, ed. A ministry center and 8 radio stations in northern PA and southern NY. Bimonthly newspaper; 24 pgs; circ 34,000. Free to donors. 5% freelance. Complete ms/cover letter; no phone/fax/e-query. **NO PAYMENT.** Not copyrighted. Articles 250 wds (3/yr). Responds in wks. Seasonal 3 mos ahead. Accepts simultaneous submissions & reprints. Requires disk. No sidebars. Prefers NIV. No guidelines; copy for 10x13 SAE/2 stamps. (Ads)

Tips: "Virtually all out writing is done in-house or by writers living in our listening area (western NY and northern PA)."

*THE FAMILY NETWORK, RR1 Box 354, Claude TX 79019. Phone/fax (806)944-5414. Stacy Lewis, ed. To encourage Christian living, purity, modesty, home education, trusting God in family planning, home birth, and prayer. Bimonthly newsletter; 12 pgs; circ 150. Subscription $15. 100% freelance. Complete ms; phone query OK. **NO PAYMENT.** Not copyrighted. Articles 50-800 wds (50/yr); fiction to 800 wds (15/yr). Responds in 3 wks. Seasonal 4 mos ahead. Accepts simultaneous submissions & reprints. Accepts disk. Regular sidebars. Guidelines; copy $3. (Ads)

Poetry: Accepts 12-20/yr. Any type; any length. Submit max 5 poems.

Fillers: Accepts 30/yr. All types.

Columns/Departments: Accepts 6/yr. Herbs (how to grow, dry, prepare own medicinals) 50-200; Child Training 50-1,000 wds; Marriage 50-1,000 wds.

Special Needs: Organizational helps and large family concerns.

Tips: "Any family/marriage/serving-God type articles. We love testimonies, articles that glorify God and encourage the believer."

*THE FELLOWSHIP LINK, 679 Southgate Dr., Guelph ON N1G 4S2 Canada. (519)821-4830. Fax (519)821-9829. Fellowship of Evangelical Baptist Churches in Canada. Dr. T. Starr, ed. To edify and strengthen people 55+ through the various stages of aging. Quarterly mag; 24 pgs; circ. 2,000. Subscription $12. 90% freelance. Query w/wo clips. **NO PAYMENT** for all rts. Not copyrighted. Articles 300-350 wds (12/yr); fiction 300-350 wds (12/yr); book reviews 100 wds. Responds in 2 weeks. Seasonal 3 mos ahead. Accepts simultaneous submissions & reprints (tell when/where appeared). Guidelines; copy for 9x12 SAE/.90 postage or IRCs. (Ads)

Poetry: Accepts 3/yr. Traditional; short. Submit max 2 poems.

Fillers: Accepts 6/yr. Anecdotes, cartoons, games, ideas, jokes, quizzes, short humor; to 250 wds.

Tips: "Most open to devotional articles or short stories, true or fictional."

*FELLOWSHIP TODAY, Box 237, Barrie ON L4M 4T2, Canada. (705)737-0114. United Church Renewal Fellowship. Gail Reid, mng ed. Not in topical listings.

FIRST THINGS: A Monthly Journal of Religion and Public Life, 156 Fifth Ave., Ste. 400, New York NY 10010. (212)627-1985. Fax (212)627-2184. E-mail: ft@firstthings.com. Website: http://www.firstthings.com. Institute on Religion & Public Life. James Nuechterlein, ed. Shows relation of religion and religious insights to contemporary issues of public life. Monthly (10X) mag; 64-84 pgs; circ 31,500. Subscription $29. 70% freelance. Complete ms/cover letter. Pays $250-700 on publication for all rts. Articles 4,000-6,000 wds, opinion 1,500 wds; (50-60/yr); book reviews, 1,500 wds, $125. Responds in 2 wks. Seasonal 4-5 mos ahead. Prefers disk or e-mail submission (attached file). Kill fee. No sidebars. Any version. Guidelines; copy for 9x12 SAE/9 stamps. (Ads)

Poetry: Poetry Editor. Buys 30/yr. Traditional; to 40 lines; $50.

Columns/Departments: Opinion, 1,000-2,000 wds.

Tips: "Most open to opinion and articles."

FOCUS ON THE FAMILY MAGAZINE, 8605 Explorer Dr., Colorado Springs CO 80920. (719)548-5881. Fax (719)531-3499. Website: http://www.family.org. Focus on the Family. Tom Neven, ed. To help families utilize Christian principles to strengthen their marriages, improve their child-rearing and to help in the problems of everyday life. Monthly mag; 16 pgs; circ 2,500,000. Free to donors. 1% freelance. Query/clip; no phone/fax query. Pays $100-500 on publication for 1st rts. Articles 700-1,000 wds (8/yr). Responds in 4-6 wks. Seasonal 6 mos ahead. Accepts disk. Kill fee 25%. Regular sidebars. Prefers NIV. Guidelines; copy for 9x12 SAE/2 stamps.

Tips: "This magazine is 99% generated from within our ministry. It's very hard to break in. Must be a unique look at a subject or very interesting topic not usually seen in our magazine, but still fitting the audience."

**This periodical was #51 on the 1998 Top 50 Christian Publishers list (#11 in 1997, #54 in 1994).

+**FOREFRONT**, Box 219, Crestone CO 81131. (719)256-4778. Spiritual Life Institute/Catholic. Fr. David Denny, ed. Practical Spirituality and contemplative prayer; inter-religious dialogue and culture. Quarterly mag; 32 pgs; circ 2,000. Subscription $16. 40% freelance. Query; no phone query. **PAYS 3 COPIES** for one-time rts. Articles 1,000-1,500 wds (6/yr). Responds in 12 wks. Seasonal 8 mos ahead. No disk. Some sidebars. No guidelines; copy $5/10x13 SAE. (No ads)

Poetry: Accepts 4/yr. Any type; to 20 lines. Submit 2 max poems.

Fillers: Accepts 3/yr. Anecdotes, prayers, prose, 300-500 wds.

Special Needs: Contemplation and Mysticism; interreligious dialogue.

Tips: "Most open to articles commenting on how to live one's faith in today's world; articles of biographical nature about faith/cultural models, out of the ordinary examples. No autobiographical material."

FOURSQUARE WORLD ADVANCE, 1910 W. Sunset Blvd., Ste. 200, Los Angeles CA 90026-0176. (213)484-2400. Fax (213)413-3824. E-mail: comm@foursquare.org. Website: http://www.foursquare.org/advmag. International Church of the Foursquare Gospel. Dr. Ronald Williams, ed. Denominational. Bimonthly magazine; 23 pgs; circ 98,000. Subscription free. 5% freelance. Complete ms/cover letter; phone/fax/e-query OK. Pays $75 on publication for 1st, one-time, simultaneous, or reprint rts. Not copyrighted. Articles 1,000-1,200 wds (2-3/yr); fiction. Responds in 2 wks. Seasonal 6 mos ahead. Accepts simultaneous submissions & reprints. Accepts e-mail submission (attached file). Regular sidebars. Free guidelines/theme list (also on Website)/copy. (Ads)

Poetry: Buys 1-2/yr. Pays $50.

Fillers: Buys 1-2/yr. Anecdotes, cartoons; 250-300 wds; $50.

THE GEM, 700 E. Melrose Ave., Box 926, Findlay OH 45839-0926. (419)424-1961. Fax (419)424-3433. E-mail: ejs@brt.bright.net. Website: http://www.cggc.org. Churches of God, General Conference. Evelyn J. Sloat, ed. Weekly take-home paper for adults; 8 pgs; circ 7,000. Subscription $9. 90% freelance. Complete ms. Pays $7.50-15 on publication for one-time rts. Not copyrighted. Articles 100-1,500 wds (125/yr); fiction 100-1,500 wds. Responds slowly. Seasonal 6 mos ahead. Accepts simultaneous submissions & reprints (tell when/where appeared). Accepts disk or e-mail submission. No sidebars. Prefers NIV. Guidelines/copy for #10 SAE/1 stamp.

Poetry: Buys 5/yr. Free verse, traditional. Pays $7.50. Submit max 5 poems.

Fillers: Buys 15/yr. Anecdotes, cartoons, prose, short humor; 100-200 wds. Pays $7.50.

Tips: "We are accepting more material that is 400 wds or less as fillers (pays $5-10). Holiday material always welcome, although often we don't use it the first year we have it."

*GEMS OF TRUTH, PO Box 4060, Overland Park KS 66204. (913)432-0331. Fax (913)722-0351. Church of God (holiness)/Herald & Banner Press. Arlene McGehee, Sunday school ed. Denominational. Weekly adult take-home paper; 8 pgs; circ 14,000. Subscription $1.90. Complete ms/cover letter; phone/fax query OK. Pays .005/wd on publication for 1st rts. Fiction 1,000-2,000 wds. Seasonal 6-8 mos ahead. Accepts simultaneous submissions & reprints (tell when/where appeared). Prefers KJV. Guidelines/theme list; copy. Not in topical listings.

Poetry: Traditional; pays .25/line.

*GOD'S REVIVALIST, 1810 Young St., Cincinnati OH 45210. (513)721-7944x296. Fax (513)721-3971. Larry Smith, ed. Salvation theme; Wesleyan persuasion. Monthly mag; 24 pgs; circ 20,000. Subscription $8. 75% freelance (currently overstocked). Complete ms/cover letter. **NO PAYMENT** for one-time rts. Articles 600-1,400 wds (3/yr). Responds in 9 wks. Seasonal 2 mos ahead. Accepts simultaneous submissions. Guidelines; copy $1/9x12 SAE.

Poetry: Accepts 5/yr. Free verse, light verse, traditional; 8-20 lines. Submit max 10 poems.

Fillers: Accepts 5/yr. Facts, ideas, prose, short humor; 50-90 wds.

Tips: "We need some information about the author."

*GOOD NEWS (AL), PO Box 26617, Hoover AL 35260-6617. (205)978-6008. Fax (205)823-5263. E-mail: FJBritton@aol.com. Shades Mountain Independent Church. Jackie Britton, ed. Community newspaper with a Christian slant; not preachy. Bimonthly tabloid; 24 pgs; circ 20,000. Subscription free. 100% freelance. Complete ms/cover letter; phone/fax/e-query OK. **PAYS 3 COPIES** for one-time rts. Articles 300-600 wds (30/yr); fiction 500 wds (6/yr); book/music/video reviews, 300 wds (no pay). Responds in 3-4 wks. Seasonal 3 mos ahead. Accepts simultaneous submissions & reprints (tell when/where appeared). Accepts disk. Regular sidebars. Guidelines; copy for 9x12 SAE/2 stamps. (Ads)

Poetry: Accepts 3-4/yr. Light verse, traditional; 8-12 lines.

Fillers: Anecdotes, cartoons, facts, ideas, jokes, quizzes, quotes, short humor, word puzzles; 100-200 wds.

Tips: "We especially like articles dealing with Alabamians and/or life-changing situations."

GOOD NEWS (KY), 308 E. Main St., PO Box 150, Wilmore KY 40390. (606)858-4661. Fax (606)858-4972. E-mail: andrea@goodnewsmag.org. Website: http://www.goodnewsmag.org. United Methodist/Forum for Scriptural Christianity, Inc. Steve Beard, ed; submit to Andrea Nasfell, ed asst. Focus is evangelical renewal within the denomination. Bimonthly mag; 44 pgs; circ 65,000. Subscription free. 20% freelance. Query; no phone/fax/e-query. Pays $100-150 on publication for one-time rts. Articles 1,500-1,850 wds (25/yr). Responds in 24 wks. Seasonal 4-6 mos ahead. Accepts simultaneous submissions & reprints (tell when/where appeared). Accepts disk. Kill fee. Regular sidebars. Prefers NIV. Guidelines (also on Website); copy $2.75/9x12 SAE. (Ads)

Tips: "Most open to features."

GOOD NEWS, ETC., PO Box 2660, Vista CA 92085. (760)724-3075. Fax (760)724-8311. E-mail: rmonroe@goodnewsetc.com. Website: http://www.goodnewsetc.com. Good News Publishers, Inc. of California. Rick Monroe, ed. Feature stories and local news of interest to Christians in San Diego County. Monthly tabloid; 24-32 pgs; circ 40,000. Subscription $15. 2% freelance. Query; e-query OK. Pays $20 on publication for all, 1st, one-time or reprint rts. Articles 500-700 wds (15/yr). Responds in 2 wks. Seasonal 2 mos ahead. Accepts simultaneous submissions & reprints (tell when/where appeared). Prefers disk. Regular sidebars. Prefers NIV. Guidelines/theme list; copy for 9x12 SAE/4 stamps. (Ads)

Tips: "Most open to local, personality-type articles."

** 1994 EPA Award of Merit—Newspaper.

#GOOD NEWS JOURNAL (MO), Box 1882, Columbia MO 65205. (573)875-8755. Fax (573)874-4964. E-mail: goodnews@digmo.org. Good News

Publishers. Teresa Parker, ed. Christian newspaper for mid-Missouri area. Monthly tabloid; 12-16 pgs; circ 25,000-50,000. Subscription $20. 10% freelance. Query; complete ms for fiction. **NO PAYMENT** for one-time rts. Articles 500 wds (2/yr); fiction 750 wds (5/yr); book/music/video reviews, 50 wds. Responds in 6-8 wks. Seasonal 3 mos ahead. Accepts simultaneous submissions & reprints (tell when/where appeared). Accepts disk. Some sidebars. Prefers NIV. Copy $1/ 9x12 SAE. (Ads)

>**Fillers:** Accepts 1-6/yr. Cartoons, games, jokes, quizzes, no pay.

>**Columns/Departments:** Accepts 12/yr. Good News Kids (fiction for kids up to 12 yrs), 500-750 wds; Golden Digest (testimonies or devotionals for those over 55), 1,000 wds.

>**Special Needs:** Testimonies of healing with verification of physician.

>**Tips:** "Interested in testimonies and personal experience stories that illustrate Christian growth or Christian principles."

+GOOD NEWS JOURNAL (TX), 1901 S. Hwy 183, Leander TX 78641. (512)260-1800. Fax (512)259-0892. E-mail:goodnews98@aol.com. Website: Http://www.goodnewsjournal.com. Evelyn W. Davison, pub. Christian paper for the Austin, Texas area. Monthly newspaper; 16-20 pgs; circ 60,000. Subscription $29.95. Estab 1997. 50% freelance. Query; fax query OK.   **NO PAYMENT** for one-time rts. Articles 200-400 wds. Accepts reprints. Prefers disk. Guidelines (also by e-mail/Website); copy for 9x12SAE/2 stamps. (Ads)

>**Poetry:** Accepts 4-6/yr. Traditional.

>**Fillers:** Accepts many. All types; 10-50 wds.

THE GOOD SHEPHERD, 171 White Plains Rd., Bronxville NY 10708. (914)337-5172. Fax (914)779-5274. E-mail: shepherd@concordia-ny.edu. Website: http://www.shepherdcenter.org. A publication for Christian families. No freelance for now.

+GOOD STORY, 8037 Jeanes St., Philadelphia PA 19111. (215)379-1931. Fax (215)379-1936. E-mail: story777@aol.com. Tom Sims, ed/pub. Showcases real-world fiction from a Christian perspective. Quarterly mag Free subscription. Complete ms; e-mail submission OK. **PAYS IN COPIES** Fiction to 2,500 wds.

>**Tips:** "Stories definitely must not be preachy."

GOSPEL TIDINGS, 5800 S. 14th St., Omaha NE 68104-3584. (402)731-4780. Fax (402)731-1173. E-mail: febcoma@aol.com. Fellowship of Evangelical Bible Churches. Robert L. Frey, ed. To inform, educate and edify members of affiliate churches. Bimonthly mag; 20 pgs; circ 2,300. Subscription $8. 5% freelance. Complete ms/cover letter; fax/e-query OK. Pays to $15-35 on publication for all rts. Articles (2/yr) & fiction (1/yr); 1,500/2,500 wds. Responds ASAP. Seasonal 3 mos ahead. Accepts simultaneous submissions & reprints (tell when/ where appeared). Accepts disk or e-mail submission (copied into message). Some sidebars. Prefers NIV. Guidelines (also by e-mail); copy for 9x12 SAE/3 stamps. (No ads)

GOSPEL TODAY MAGAZINE, 761 Old Hickory Blvd. Ste. 205, Brentwood TN 37027. (615)376-5656. Fax (615)376-0882. E-mail: gospel@usit.net. Websites: http://www.gospeltoday.com, and http://www.gospeltoday magcom. Horizon Concepts, Inc. Teresa Harris, pub. Ministry and Christian/gospel music; Christian lifestyles directed toward African Americans. Bimonthly (8X) mag; 60 pgs; circ 50,000. Subscription $20. 50% freelance. Query; fax query OK. Pays $150-250 on publication for all, one-time or simultaneous rts. Articles 1,000-3,500 wds (4/yr); book reviews 1,00-1,500 wds. Responds in 4 wks. Seasonal 4 mos ahead. Requires disk. Kill fee 15%. Regular sidebars. Prefers KJV. Guidelines/theme list; copy for 10x13 SAE/8 stamps. (Ads)

Columns/Departments: Precious Memories (historic overview of renowned personality), 1,500-2,000 wds; From the Pulpit (issue-oriented observation from clergy), 2,500-3,000 wds; Life & Style (travel, health, beauty, fashion tip, etc.), 1,500-2,500 wds. **NO PAYMENT.**

Tips: "Looking for more human-interest pieces—ordinary people doing extraordinary things."

+GOSPEL TRACT HARVESTER, 1105 S. Fuller St., Independence MO 64050. (816)461-6086. Fax (816)461-4305. E-mail: gospel@qni.com. Gospel Tract Society, Inc. David Buttram, ed. For Christians of all ages (few unchurched readers). Monthly mag; 15 pgs; circ 70,000. Subscription free (donations). 10 % freelance. Query. **PAYS UP TO 20 COPIES** for all rts. Not copyrighted. Articles 1,000 wds (10/yr); fiction 1,000 wds. Responds in 2-3 wks. Seasonal 4 mos ahead. Accepts reprints (tell when/where appeared). Some sidebars. Prefers KJV. Guidelines; copy for 6x9 SAE/2 stamps. (No ads)

Poetry: Accepts 8-12/yr. Free verse, traditional; 5-25 lines. Submit max 5 poems.

Fillers: Accepts 15-20/yr. Anecdotes, facts, games, quotes, short humor, word puzzles, 10-100 wds.

Special Needs: Good, fresh, well-written tracts.

Tips: "Most open to personal testimonies if well-written and documented; children's games (cross-word puzzles, etc.). Have a message to share and a sincere desire to share the message of salvation."

*GRAIL: An Ecumenical Journal, 223 Main St., Ottawa ON K1S 1C4 Canada. (613)782-3036. Fax (613)751-4020. E-mail: cgreen@spu.stpaul.uottawa. ca. Novalis–St. Paul University. Caryl Green, mng ed. A contemporary and ecumenical journal. Quarterly journal; 100 pgs; circ 1,300. Subscription $22 CAN & $25 US. 80% freelance. Complete ms/cover letter; phone/fax/e-query OK. Pays an honorarium on publication for all rts. Articles 1,000-2,000 wds (12/yr); fiction 1,000-1,500 wds (4/yr); book reviews, 1,000 wds, $50. Responds in 3-4 wks. Prefers disk. Regular sidebars. Prefers NRSV or Jerusalem. Copy for 7x10 SASE.

Poetry: Buys 16-20/yr. Free verse, traditional; $25.

+GREAT FAMILIES, PO Box 270616, San Diego CA 92198-2616. (619)487-7099. Fax (619)487-7356. E-mail: FamilyU@aol.com. Family University. Mike Yorkey, ed. Helpful, how-to advice and humorous "slice-of-life" anecdotes on matters concerning the family. Pays $50-300 for one-time and electronic rts. Articles 200-1,000 wds. Responds in 1-3 wks. Accepts reprints. Not in topical listings.

*GREEN CROSS MAGAZINE, 10 E. Lancaster Ave., Wynnewood PA 19096. (610)645-9390. Fax (610)649-8090.Evangelicals for Social Action. Michael Crook, ed. For Christians who care about earth stewardship. Quarterly mag; 20 pgs; circ 5,000. Subscription $25. 90% freelance. Query; fax/e-query OK. Query for electronic submissions (crook@esa.online.org). Pays to $150 on publication for one-time & electronic rts. Articles 500-1,200 wds (20/yr); book reviews 200 wds (no payment). Responds in 6-8 wks. Seasonal 4 mos ahead. Accepts reprints (tell when/where appeared). Prefers disk. Regular sidebars. Prefers NRSV or NIV. Guidelines; copy for 10x13 SAE/4 stamps. (Ads)

> **Poetry:** All types; 5-30 lines. No payment. Submit max 3 poems.
>
> **Fillers:** Buys 10-12/yr. Cartoons, newsbreaks, prayers, short humor; 50-250 wds; $10-25.
>
> **Tips:** "Looking for well-written personal testimony on writer's discovery of Christian/biblical basis for conservation. Other than that, we don't need articles that say 'What a surprise! The Bible says to care for God's creation.'"

+GROWING IN CHRIST, 1451 Putnam Dr., Charleston SC 29412. Phone/fax (843)795-1983. E-mail: cannpeifer@aol.com. Cori Peifer, ed/pub. ed. Targets new believers in Christ. Monthly mag Pays variable rates on publication for 1st or reprint rts. Articles 1,000-1,500 wds; fiction 1,000-1,500 wds.

> **Columns/Departments:** Has a number of columns; 250-500 wds. See guidelines.

#GUIDEPOSTS, 16 E 34th St., New York NY 10016. (212)251-8100. Website: http://www.guideposts.org. Interfaith. Submit to The Editor. Personal faith stories showing how faith in God helps each person cope with life in some particular way. Monthly mag; 48 pgs; circ 3.8 million. Subscription $13.94. 30% freelance. Complete ms/cover letter. Pays $100-500 on acceptance for all rts. Articles 750-1,500 wds (40-60/yr). Responds 8-9 wks. Seasonal 6 mos ahead. Accepts simultaneous submissions. Kill fee 25%. Some sidebars. Free guidelines/copy.

> **Poetry:** Celeste McCauley. Buys 6/yr. Free verse, light verse, traditional; 2-12 lines; $15-25. Submit max 2 poems.
>
> **Fillers:** Celeste McCauley. Buys 15-20/yr. Anecdotes; quotes, short humor; 10-200 wds; $25-100.
>
> **Columns/Departments:** Celeste McCauley. Buys 24/yr. His Mysterious Ways (divine intervention), 250 wds; What Prayer Can Do, 250 wds; Angels Among Us, 400 wds; Divine Touch (tangible evidence of God's help), 400 wds. ("This is our most open area. Write in 3rd person."); $100.
>
> **Contest:** Writers Workshop Contest held on even years with a late June deadline. Winners attend a week-long seminar (all expenses paid) on how to write for Guideposts. Also Young Writers Contest; $25,000 college scholarship; best stories to 1,200 wds; deadline November 30.
>
> **Tips:** "Be able to tell a good story, with drama, suspense, description and dialogue. The point of the story should be some practical spiri-

tual help the reader receives from what the author learned through his experience." First person only.

** This periodical was #22 on the 1998 Top 50 Christian Publishers list. (#47 in 1996, #54 in 1995, #44 in 1994)

HALLELUJAH! PO Box 223, Postal Stn. A, Vancouver BC V6C 2M3 Canada. (604)498-3895. Cable: Hallelujah. Bible Holiness Movement. Wesley H. Wakefield, ed. For evangelism and promotion of holiness revivals; readership mostly ethnic, non-white minorities. Bimonthly mag; 32-40 pgs; circ 5,000. Subscription $5. Very little freelance. Query or complete ms; no phone query. Pays $10-50 on acceptance for one-time or simultaneous rts. Articles 300-2,500 wds (4/yr). Responds in 5 wks. Accepts simultaneous submissions & reprints (tell when/where appeared). No disk. No sidebars. Prefers KJV. Guidelines; copy for 6x9 SAE/$1 postage.

> **Poetry:** Buys 4/yr. Traditional, hymn length (5 stanzas). Pays $5 or royalties. Submit max 5 poems. Prefers poetry of hymn or song quality with identifiable meter.
>
> **Fillers:** Buys few. Prefers striking quotes from early Methodism or salvationers; 10-50 wds; $5.
>
> **Special Needs:** Spiritual warfare; religious conditions in southern Sudan; child labor/slavery; and Christian revival movements.
>
> **Ethnic:** Distributes to Nigeria, Canada and US
>
> **Tips:** "Avoid Americanisms. No Calvinistic articles or premillenialism. Be very familiar with evangelistic emphasis, doctrines, life standards, social stands of holiness churches." works 6-8 months ahead.

*HARVEST PRESS, PO Box 2876, Newport News VA 23609. (757)886-0713. Fax (757)886-1295. Tyrone Campbell, ed. To proclaim the gospel of Jesus Christ, to reach the unreached and promote unity within the body of Christ. Monthly newspaper; circ 20,000. Subscription $25. Open to freelance. Query. Not in topical listings. (Ads)

HEAD TO HEAD, PO Box 711, St. Johnsbury VT 05819-0711. Phone/fax (802)748-8000. E-mail: pwebb@plainfield.bypass.com. Website: http://www.bypass.com/~pwebb/hth.htm. The Lambs in Mission. Paul A. Webb, ed-in-chief. Shows Christ as the greatest hope for brain-injury survivors and caretakers. Online mag; circ world-wide on the Internet. Subscription free on the Internet. 50% freelance. Complete ms/cover letter; fax query OK. **PAYS IN COPIES** for 1st rts. Articles 250-1,200 wds (to 36/yr); fiction for all ages 500-1,000 wds; book/music/video reviews, 500 wds. Responds in 8 wks. Seasonal 6 mos ahead. Accepts reprints. Prefers disk. Guidelines/theme list for #10 SAE/2 stamps.

> **Poetry:** Accepts 12/yr. All types, 4-60 lines. Submit max 5 poems.
>
> **Fillers:** Most types; 50-250 wds.
>
> **Columns/Departments:** Tips & Hints; Caregiver Concerns & Family Matters, 250 wds.
>
> **Special Needs:** All topics should relate to brain injury, traumatic or congenital brain injury, cerebral palsy, encephalitis, multiple sclerosis, strokes, or alcohol/drug-induced brain injury.
>
> **New Features:** Articles and stories about (1) Christian Evangelism,

(2) Prophetic exhortation and admonition to the Christian church, its leadership and parishioners, (3) Current issues and the biblical view. **Tips:** "Need how-tos on survival, coping skills, cognitive strategies, social skills, job skills, and communication."

*THE HEALING INN, 3908 NE 140th St., Seattle WA 98125-3840. Phone/fax (206)542-0210. Christian Airline Personnel Missionary Outreach. June Shafhid, ed. Offers healing for Christians wounded by a church or religious cult. Semiannual mag; 20 pgs; circ. 5,000. No subscriptions. 100% freelance. Complete ms; phone/fax query OK. **PAYS IN COPIES** for 1st or reprint rts. Articles 500-2,500 wds; fiction 500-3,000 wds. Responds in 3-4 wks. Seasonal 6 mos ahead. Accepts simultaneous submissions & reprints (tell when/where appeared). No disk. Some sidebars. Prefers KJV, NIV or NAS. Theme list; free copy. (Ads)

Poetry: All types; 5-20 lines. Accepts 10-20/yr. Submit max 10 poems.

Fillers: Accepts 20/yr. Anecdotes, facts, games, ideas, jokes, newsbreaks, prose, quizzes, prayers, quotes, short humor, word puzzles.

Tips: "All areas open. Looking for stories that will woo the lost back to Christ."

HEARING HEARTS, 4 Silo Mill Ct., Sterling VA 20164. Phone/fax (703)430-7387. American Ministries to the Deaf. Beverly Cox, ed. For deaf adults and those with whom they live, work and worship. Quarterly mag; 24 pgs; circ 500. Subscription $12. 75% freelance. Query/clips; phone/fax query OK. **PAYS IN COPIES.** Articles 100-600 wds (50-100/yr). Responds in 2 wks. Seasonal 3 mos ahead. Regular sidebars. Theme list; copy for 9x12 SAE/4 stamps.

Poetry: Accepts 100/yr. Free verse, haiku, light verse, traditional; 5-30 lines. Submit max 5 poems.

Fillers: Cartoons, games, ideas, party ideas, quizzes, word puzzles.

Special Needs: Wants interviews with interesting deaf Christians.

Tips: "Needs Bible-application articles—lively & brief. Best if it can have a deaf twist—not using standard verses that refer to deaf. Show creativity to touch people within the 'don't fix me; I ain't broke' deaf culture."

HEARTLIGHT INTERNET MAGAZINE, 8332 Mesa Dr., Austin TX 78759. (514)345-6386. Fax (512)345-6634. E-mail: phil@heartlight.org. Website: http://www.heartlight.org. Phil Ware & Paul Lee, co-eds. Offers positive Christian resources for living in today's world. Weekly online mag (see Website above); 20+ pgs; circ 6,000. Subscription free. Estab 1996. 20% freelance. E-query. **NO PAYMENT** for electronic rts. Articles 300-450 wds (25-35/yr); fiction 500-700 wds (12-15/yr). Responds in 3 wks. Seasonal 2 mos ahead. Accepts simultaneous submissions & reprints (tell when/ where appeared). Prefers disk or e-mail submission. Regular sidebars. Prefers NIV. Copy available on the Internet.

Poetry: Accepts 10/yr. Free verse, light verse, traditional. Submit max 10 poems.

Fillers: Accepts 12/yr. Anecdotes, cartoons, games, ideas, jokes, newsbreaks, prayers, prose, quotes, short humor, word puzzles; to 350 wds.

Tips: "Most open to feature articles, Just for Men or Just for Women, or Heartlight for Children."

+**HIDDEN MANNA**, 17914 Valley Knoll, Houston TX 77084. E-mail: hiddenmanna@triquetra.org. Website: Http://www.triquetra.org. Triquetra Publishing. Daniel C. Massey, ed. For thoughtful Christians who believe that faith nurtured by story is a faith that endures. Quarterly journal; 40 pgs; circ 500. Subscription $15. Estab 1998. 90% freelance. Complete ms/cover letter; e-query OK. **PAYS IN COPIES & SUBSCRIPTION** for 1st or reprint rts. Articles 500-2,000 wds (12/yr); fiction 500-3,000 wds (12/yr); book/video reviews 500 wds.. Responds in 6 wks. Accepts simultaneous submissions & reprints (tell when/where appeared). Requires disk or e-mail submission. No sidebars. Any version. Guidelines (also on Website); copy $4 (check to Triquetra Publishing)/6x9 SAE. (No ads)

 Poetry: Accepts 6-20/yr. Avant-garde, free verse, traditional, literary; to 40 lines (few longer). Submit max 3 poems.

 Fillers: Accepts to 20/yr. Prose, quotes, short humor 25-250 wds. Also excerpts from other publications, with permission.

 Columns/Departments: Accepts 12/yr. Dialogues (interviews with everyday Christians with great stories) 1,500-2,500 wds; Essays (creative, scholarly essays on narrative theology, with emphasis on Biblical narrative; also analysis of fiction) 500-2,000 wds.

 Special Needs: Unconventional Christian fiction with a literary bent; fiction with an uncommon Christian voice.

 Tips: "All submissions must celebrate paradox, leave more questions than answers. Write fiction with mature Christian themes from everyday life, and tell the story on several levels. Don't interview famous people, but the lonely, the outcast, the quiet forgotten ones with great untold stories. Send essays that show how narrative points to a complex incarnate God."

HIGHWAY NEWS AND GOOD NEWS, PO. Box 303, Denver PA 17517-0303. (717)721-9800. Fax (717)721-9351. E-mail: GoTFC@aol.com. Lisa Graham, ed. For truck drivers and their families; evangelistic, with articles for Christian growth. Monthly mag; 16 pgs; circ 35,000. Subscription $25. 75% freelance. Complete ms/cover letter; phone, fax, e-query OK. **PAYS IN COPIES** for rights offered. Articles 600 or 1,200 wds & fiction 1,200-1,400 wds. Seasonal 4 mos ahead. Accepts simultaneous submissions & reprints (tell when/where appeared). Accepts disk. Some sidebars. Prefers NIV. Guidelines/theme list; free copy for 9x12 SAE.

 Fillers: Short humor, 100 wds.

 Tips: "All articles/stories must relate to truckers; need pieces on marriage, parenting, and fatherhood. Most open to features."

HOLINESS TODAY(formerly Herald of Holiness and World Mission), 6401 The Paseo, Kansas City MO 64131. (816)333-7000 x2302. Fax (816)333-1748. Church of the Nazarene. Gay L. Leonard, exec ed. No freelance.

HOMESCHOOLING TODAY, PO Box 1608, Fort Collins CO 80522-1608. (970)493-3793. Fax (970)493-8781. E-mail: publisher@homeschooltoday.com. Website: http://www.homeschooltoday.com. S. Squared Productions. Maureen McCaffrey, ed-in-chief. Practical articles and lessons for homeschoolers. Bimonthly mag; 68 pgs; circ 25,000. Subscription $19.99. 90% freelance. Query/clips; fax/e-query OK. Pays .08/wd on publication for 1st rts. Articles 500-2,000 wds (20/yr). Responds in 6 wks. Accepts simultaneous submissions & reprints (tell when/where appeared. Requires disk, no e-mail submission. Regular sidebars. Any version. Guidelines; copy for 9x12 SAE. (Ads)

> **Columns/Departments:** Buys 10-12/yr. Parents Speak Out, 500-700 wds. (See guidelines for other departments.) Query. Pays .08/wd.

HOME TIMES, 3676 Collins Dr. #12, West Palm Beach FL 33406. (561)439-3509. E-mail: hometimes@aol.com. Neighbor News, Inc. Dennis Lombard, ed/pub. Conservative, pro-Christian community newspaper. Monthly tabloid; 24 pgs; circ 4,000. Subscription $12. 50% freelance. Complete ms only/cover letter; no phone/e-query. Pays $5-25 on publication for one-time rts. Articles 200-800 wds (20/yr); fiction 200-600 wds (5/yr). Responds in 3-4 wks. Seasonal 6 wks ahead. Accepts simultaneous submissions & reprints (tell when/where appeared). No disk or e-mail submission (unless requested).
Regular sidebars. Prefers NIV. Guidelines; copy $3. (Ads)

> **Poetry:** Buys 12/yr. Light verse, traditional; 2-32 lines; $5. Submit max 3 poems.

> **Fillers:** Accepts 15-20/yr. Anecdotes, cartoons, jokes, newsbreaks, quotes, short humor; 25-100 wds; pays 6 issues.

> **Columns/Departments:** Buys 35/yr. See guidelines for columns, to 600 wds; $5-15.

> **Tips:** "Very open to new writers, but study guidelines and sample first; we are different. Published by Christians, but not religious. Looking for more positive articles and stories."

IDEALS MAGAZINE, Ideals Publishing, Inc., PO Box 305300, Nashville TN 37230-5300. (615)333-0478. Pat Pingry, ed. Seasonal, inspirational, nostalgic magazine for mature men and women of traditional values. Mag published 6 times/yr; 88 pgs; circ 180,000. Subscription $19.95. 95% freelance. Complete ms/cover letter; no phone query. Pays .10/wd on publication for one-time rts. Articles 800-1,000 wds (20/yr). Responds in 13 wks. Seasonal 8 mos ahead. Accepts simultaneous submissions & reprints (tell when/where appeared). No disk. No sidebars. Prefers KJV. Guidelines; copy $4.

> **Poetry:** Buys 100+/yr. Free verse, light verse, traditional; 8-40 lines; $10. Submit max 5 poems.

> **Tips:** "Most open to optimistic poetry oriented around a season or theme."

*IMMACULATE HEART MESSENGER, 240 5th St. W., Alexandria SD 57311-0158. Catholic/Fatima Family Apostate. Fr. Robert J. Fox, ed. Bimonthly mag; circ. 10,000. Subscription $13. 50% freelance. **NO PAYMENT** for one-time rts. Articles 5 double-spaced pgs. Seasonal 6 mos ahead. Not in topical listings.

IMPACT MAGAZINE, 301 Geyland Centre, #03-04 Geyland Rd., Singapore 389 344. 65-748-1244. Fax 65-748-3744. E-mail: impact@pacific.net.sg. Evangelical Fellowship of Singapore. Andrew Goh, ed. To help young working adults apply Christian principles to contemporary issues. Bimonthly mag; 56 pgs; circ 6,000. Subscription $12. 10-15% freelance. Query or complete ms/cover letter; phone query OK. **NO PAYMENT** up to $20/pg, for all rts. Articles (12/yr) & fiction (6/yr); 1,000-2,000 wds. Seasonal 2 mos ahead. Accepts reprints. Accepts e-mail submission (attached file). Some sidebars. Prefers NIV. Guidelines (also by e-mail); copy for $3 & $1.70 postage (surface mail). (Ads)

Poetry: Accepts 2-3 poems/yr. Free verse, 20-40 lines. Submit max 3 poems.

Fillers: Accepts 6/yr. Anecdotes, cartoons, jokes, quizzes, short humor, and word puzzles.

Columns/Departments: Closing Thoughts (current social issues), 600-800 wds; Testimony (personal experience), 1,500-2,000 wds; Parenting (Asian context), 1,000-1,500 wds.

Tips: "We're most open to fillers."

INDIAN LIFE, PO Box 3765, RPO Redwood Center, Winnipeg MB R2W 3R6 Canada. US address: Box 32, Pembina ND 58271. (204)661-9333. Fax (204)661-3982. E-mail: indianlife@compuserve.com. Website: http://www.indianlife.org. Indian Life Ministries. Jim Uttley, ed; Viola Fehr, asst ed. An evangelistic publication for English-speaking aboriginal people in North America. Bimonthly newspaper; 16 pgs; circ 32,000. Subscription $7. 20% freelance. Query; fax/e-query OK. **NO PAYMENT** for 1st rts. Articles 1,000-1,200 wds (6/yr). Responds in 4 wks. Seasonal 6 mos ahead. Accepts reprints. Regular sidebars. Accepts disk. Guidelines; copy $1. (Ads)

Columns/Departments: Jim Uttley. Accepts 12/yr. Family Life (native families); Native Business (natives in business); Crossword Puzzles; native pastor's column; all 500 wds.

Tips: "Most open to historical pieces, news items and personal experience. Native authors preferred, but some others are published. Aim at an 8th grade reading level; short paragraphs; avoid multi-syllable words and long sentences."

#INLAND NORTHWEST CHRISTIAN NEWS, 222 W. Mission #132, Spokane WA 99201. (509)328-0820. Fax (509)326-4921. Zeda Leonard, ed. To inform, motivate and encourage evangelical Christians in Spokane and the inland Northwest. Newspaper published 18X/yr; 12 pgs; circ 2,500. Subscription $17.95. 30% freelance. Query; phone query OK. Pays $1/column inch on publication for 1st rts. Articles 500 wds. Responds in 9 wks. Copy $1.50. (Ads)

INSIDE JOURNAL, PO Box 17429, Washington DC 20041-0429. (703)478-0100x560. Fax (703)318-0235. E-mail: Jeff_Peck@pfm.org. Website: http://www.pfm.org. Prison Fellowship Ministries. Terry White, ed; submit to Jeff Peck, mng ed. To proclaim the gospel to non-Christian prisoners within the context of a prison newspaper. Bimonthly (8X) tabloid;8 pgs; circ 400,000. Subscription $10. 60% freelance. Query; phone/fax/e-query OK. Modest payment, depending on situation, on acceptance for one-time rts. Articles to 1,200 wds (25/yr). Responds in 4 wks. Seasonal 4 mos ahead. Accepts disk or e-mail submission. Regular sidebars. Guidelines (also by e-mail); free copy. (Ads)

Columns/Departments: Buys 15-20/yr. Shortimer (those preparing for release within 6 wks), 500 wds; Especially for Women (issues for incarcerated women), 600-800 wds. Variable payment.

Tips: "Always need seasonal material for Christmas, Easter and Thanksgiving. Also celebrity stories that demonstrate triumph over adversity."

** 1995 EPA Award of Merit—Newspaper.

*INSPIRATIONAL NEWS NETWORK, 20 Main St., Shenandoah PA 17976-2016. (717)628-2166. Fax (717)628-2167. Shirley C. Cicioni, pres/ed. A syndication that distributes articles dealing with news from an inspirational point of view. Not in topical listings.

*THE INSPIRER, 737 Kimsey Ln. #620, Henderson KY 42420-4917. (502)826-5720. Billy Edwards, ed. To encourage believers in their Christian life. (Especially open to writers who are physically disabled.) Quarterly newsletter; 8 pgs; circ 2,500. Subscription for donation. 50% freelance. Query. Articles 250-700 wds (15/yr); fiction 250-500 wds (5/yr); book reviews, 500 wds. **PAYS IN COPIES/SUBSCRIPTION.** Not copyrighted. Responds in 2 wks. Seasonal 2 mos ahead. Accepts simultaneous submissions & reprints. No sidebars. Prefers KJV. Guidelines; copy for #10 SASE/2 stamps.

Poetry: Accepts 5-10/yr. Traditional, 10-50 lines. Submit max 3 poems.

Fillers: Accepts 10-15/yr. Anecdotes, cartoons, facts, games, ideas, jokes, newsbreaks, prose, quizzes, prayers, quotes, short humor, word puzzles; 50-250 wds.

Columns/Departments: Accepts 10/yr. Let the Redeemed Say So (testimonies), 250-500 wds; The Lighter Side (humor), to 300 wds.

Special Needs: Issues of interest to (and from) the physically disabled; biblically based and Christ-centered.

*INTERCHANGE, 412 Sycamore St., Cincinnati OH 45202. (513)421-0311. Fax (513)421-0315. Episcopal. Michael R. Barwell, ed. Regional paper for the Episcopal and Anglican Church in southern Ohio. Bimonthly tabloid; 28 pgs; circ 12,600. Free. 5% freelance. Query or complete ms/cover letter. Pays $35-50 on publication for all rts. Articles 500-2,000 wds (1-2/yr). Responds in 9 wks. Accepts simultaneous submissions. Prefers disk (Mac compatible). Regular sidebars. Copy for 9x12 SASE.

Tips: "Most open to features, especially with a local angle."

THE INTERIM, 306-53 Dundas St. E., Toronto ON M5B 1C6 Canada. (416)368-0250. Fax (416)368-8575. E-mail: interim@globalserve.net. Website: http://www.lifesite.net. The Interim Publishing Co. Ltd. David Curtin, ed-in-chief. Abortion, euthanasia, pornography, feminism and religion from a pro-life perspective; Catholic and evangelical Protestant audience. Monthly & online newspaper; 24 pgs; circ 30,000. Subscription $25 CAN or US. 60% freelance. Query; phone/fax/e-query OK. Pays $50-150 CAN, on publication. Articles 400-750 wds; book, music, video reviews, 500wds ($50-75 CAN). Responds in 2 wks. Seasonal 2 mos ahead. Accepts simultaneous submissions & reprints (tell when/where appeared). Prefers e-mail submission (copied into message). Kill fee. Some sidebars. Prefers RSV & others. No guidelines; catalog. (Ads)

Tips: "We are most interested in articles relating to issues of human life and the family."

JEWEL AMONG JEWELS ADOPTION NEWS, PO Box 502065, Indianapolis IN 46256. Phone/fax (317)849-5651. E-mail: adoptjewel@aol.com. Website: http://members.aol.com/adoptjewel. Nondenominational. Sherrie Eldridge, ed. To advocate for the adoptee by educating birth parents, adoptive parents, and mental health professionals about the special needs of adoptees. Quarterly newsletter; 8 pgs; circ. 1,500. Free subscription in US. 100% freelance. Complete ms/cover letter; fax/e-query OK. **NO PAYMENT.** Articles 750 wds. Responds in 2 wks. Seasonal 3 mos ahead. Accepts simultaneous submissions & reprints. Prefers disk or e-mail submission (attached file). Regular sidebars. Prefers NIV. Guidelines/theme list; copy for 1 stamp. (No ads)

Poetry: Free verse, traditional. Submit any number.

Fillers: Accepts 10/yr. Anecdotes, cartoons, facts, ideas, newsbreaks, prose, quizzes, prayers, quotes, short humor, word puzzles; 100-150 wds.

Columns/Departments: Common Threads, Passages of Adoption, The Great Awakening, Trigger Points, Reframing the Loss, The Blessings of Adoption; all 250 wds. See guidelines for descriptions.

Special Needs: Adoptive parenting, adoption, grief & loss, identity in Christ, bonding & attachment perspectives, 12-step writing about adoption, how to find therapist who understands adoption issues. Articles by birth mothers.

Tips: "Most open to real-life testimonials from all members of the adoption triad, giving hope that healing is possible through Jesus Christ."

JOHN MILTON MAGAZINE, 475 Riverside Dr., Rm. 455, New York NY 10115. (212)870-3335. Fax (212)870-3229. E-mail: order@jmsblind.org. Website: http://www.jmsblind.org. John Milton Society for the Blind/nonsectarian. Darcy Quigley, exec dir. Reprints material from over 60 religious periodicals in a large-type digest for the visually impaired. Quarterly tabloid; 24 pgs; circ 5,188. Free to visually impaired. 1% freelance. Complete ms/cover letter; fax query OK. **NO PAYMENT** for reprint rts. Not copyrighted. Articles 750-1,500 (1/yr); fiction 750-1,500 (1/yr). Responds in 6 wks. Seasonal 9-12 mos ahead. Accepts simultaneous submissions & reprints (tell when/where appeared). Accepts disk. Some sidebars. Any version. Guidelines (also on Website); copy for 9x12 SAE/3 stamps. (No ads)

Poetry: Accepts 4/yr. Any type; 5-30 lines. Submit max 3 poems. Seasonal/holiday.

Fillers: Accepts 1/yr. Anecdotes, cartoons, facts, games, prayers, prose, quotes, short humor; 10-150 wds.

Tips: "Most open to poems, prayers and personal inspirational pieces about more timeless themes: Christian holidays, overcoming challenges like visual impairment, love, forgiveness, etc. If writing about blindness, don't be patronizing. Send complete manuscripts requiring little or no editing. Look at the magazines we typically reprint from (see guidelines)."

JOURNAL OF CHRISTIAN NURSING, PO Box 1650, Downers Grove IL 60515-1650. (630)734-4030. Fax (630)734-4200. E-mail: jcn@ivpress. com. Website: www.gospelcom.net/iv/ncf/jcn. Nurses Christian Fellowship of InterVarsity Christian Fellowship. Melodee Yohe, mng ed. Personal, professional, practical articles to help nurses view nursing through the eyes of faith. Quarterly mag; 48 pgs; circ 9,000. Subscription $19.95. 35% freelance. Complete ms/cover letter; phone/fax query OK. Pays $25-80 on publication for all (rarely), one-time or reprint rts (few). Not copyrighted. Articles 6-12 pgs (20/yr). Responds in 4-6 wks. Seasonal 1 yr ahead. Accepts some reprints (tell when/where appeared). Accepts disk. Kill fee 50%. Regular sidebars. Prefers NRSV. Guidelines/theme list (also on Website); copy $4.50/9x12 SAE/6 stamps. (Ads)

Columns/Departments: Pulse Beats (this and that).

Special Needs: Healing prayer, missions/cross-cultural nursing, standards in nursing/advanced practice, and feeding our faith.

Contests: Sponsors an occasional contest. None planned for now.

Tips: "All topics must relate to nursing, or contain illustrations using nurses. freelancers can interview and write about Christian nurses involved in creative ministry (include pictures). Interview/profile a Christian nurse involved in a creative ministry."

** 1996 EPA Award of Merit—Christian Ministry.

JOURNAL OF CHURCH AND STATE, Baylor University, PO Box 97308, Waco TX 76798-7308. (254)710-1510. Fax (254)710-1571. E-mail: Derek_Davis@Baylor.edu. Website: http://www.baylor.edu/academics. Baylor University/Interdenominational. Dr. Derek H. Davis, dir. Provides a forum for the critical examination of the interaction of religion and government worldwide. Quarterly journal; 225 pgs; circ 1,700. Subscription $20. 50% freelance. Complete ms (3 copies)/cover letter; phone/fax/e-query OK. **NO PAYMENT** for all rights. Articles 25-30 pgs/footnotes (24/yr). Responds in 6-8 wks. Prefers disk, no e-mail submission. No sidebars. Prefers KJV. Guidelines; copy $8 + $1.50 postage. (Ads)

Special Needs: Church-state issues.

*JOYFUL NOISE**, 4259 Elkcam Blvd. SE, St. Petersburg FL 33705-4216. Nondenominational. William W. Maxwell, ed. Deals with African-American life and religious culture. Bimonthly mag Complete ms/cover letter or query/ clips. Pays $50-250 on acceptance for 1st rts. Articles 700-3,000 wds. Guidelines.

THE KANSAS CHRISTIAN, PO Box 47003, Topeka KS 66647. (913)273-4424. Fax (913)272-5595. E-mail: ChrstnNews@aol.com. Eagle Christians, Inc. Everett R. Daves, ed. To promote the gospel of Jesus Christ. Weekly; circ 2,700. Subscription free (donation $20). Open to freelance. Query or complete ms. Not in topical listings. (Ads)

*KENTUCKY CHRISTIAN NEWS**, 3270 Blazer Pkwy #101, Lexington KY 40509-1847. Beverly Byrd, ed. Christian Newspaper. Not in topical listings.

KEYS TO LIVING, PO Box 154, Washingtonville PA 17884. (717)437-2891. E-mail: owcam@sunlink.net. Connie Mertz, ed/pub. Educates and encourages readers through inspirational writings while presenting an appreciation for God's natural world. Quarterly newsletter; 10 pgs; circ 125. Subscription $7. 40% freelance. Complete ms/cover letter; no phone query. **PAYS 3 COPIES** for one-time or reprint rts. Articles 350-500 wds. Responds in 4 wks. Seasonal 2-4 mos ahead. Accepts reprints. No disk; e-mail submission OK (copied into message). Prefers NIV. Guidelines/ theme list; copy for 7x10 SAE/2 stamps. (No ads)

> **Poetry:** Any type; to 20 lines. Religious or nature.
>
> **Fillers:** Cartoons, games, jokes, quizzes, quotes, short humor; to 100 wds.
>
> **Tips:** "Always looking for personal experiences or devotions on themes (get theme list). Seasonal poetry on nature is open for all issues. Teens encouraged to submit."

+LEGIONS OF LIGHT, Box 874, Margaretville NY 12455. Phone/fax (914)586-2759. E-mail: beth@stepahead.net. Website: http://www.step ahead.net/lol/legions.htm. Art By Beth. Elizabeth Mami, ed. A literary magazine for readers of all ages. Bimonthly mag; length varies; circ 3,000. Subscription $15. 100% freelance. Query or complete ms/cover letter. Pays .$5-10 on publication for one-time rts. Not copyrighted. Articles 500-1,500 wds (40/yr); fiction 1,500 wds (70/yr). Responds in 8 wks. Seasonal 6 mos ahead. Accepts simultaneous submissions & reprints (tell when/ where appeared). Prefers e-mail submission (copied into message). Some sidebars. Guidelines (also by e-mail/Website); copy $3.

> **Poetry:** Buys 15-30/yr. All types; any length Pays $5-10.
>
> **Fillers:** Buys 5-10/yr. Anecdotes, cartoons, facts, ideas, jokes, newsbreaks, prayers, prose, quotes, short humor. Pays $5-10.
>
> **Tips:** "We are especially open to unpublished writers, particularly children. Be open and honest in your writing. We accept about 90% of submissions."

*LIBERTY, Religious Liberty Dept., 12501 Old Columbia Pike, Silver Springs MD 20904. (301)680-6448. Fax (301)680-6695. E-mail: 74617.263@ compuserve.com. Seventh-day Adventist. Clifford R. Goldstein, ed. Deals with religious liberty issues for government officials, civic leaders, and laymen. Bimonthly mag; 32 pgs; circ 250,000. 90% freelance. Query; phone/fax/e-query OK. Pays $500-750 on acceptance for 1st rts. Articles & essays to 2,500 wds. Responds in 4 wks. Requires disk. Guidelines.

+LIFE@WORK JOURNAL, PO Box 1928, Fayetteville AR 72702. (501)444-0664. Fax (501)443-4125. E-mail: scaldwell@lifeatwork.com. Submissions to: submissions@lifeatwork.com. The Life@Work Company. Stephen Caldwell, mng ed. Features Christian professionals addressing such issues as faith in the workplace, skill development, and implementing biblical values at work. Monthly mag; circ 3,500. Subscription $49.95. Query; fax/equery OK. Copy $9.95. Articles 200-3,000 wds. Pays .20/wd for 1st rts. Incomplete topical listings. (Ads)

> **Special Needs:** Book reviews, commentaries, and profiles of leaders and companies that successfully apply biblical wisdom for business excellence.

Tips: "Help business leaders link their faith and their work."

*LIFE GATE, 2026 Boulder Run Dr., Richmond VA 23233. Phone/fax (804)750-1504. By His Design, Inc. Randy Moore, ed. Positive news for Protestant Christians. Monthly tabloid; circ. 23,000. 40% freelance. Query; fax/e-query OK. **NO PAYMENT.** Articles 250-500 wds (12/yr); book/music reviews 350 wds. Seasonal 4 mos ahead. Accepts simultaneous submissions & reprints. Prefers disk. Prefers NIV. Copy $1.50.

Poetry: Accepts 8-10/yr. Avant-garde, free verse, light verse, traditional; 100-500 wds. Submit max 5 poems.

Fillers: Anecdotes, facts.

LIFEGLOW, Box 6097, Lincoln NE 68506. (402)448-0981. Fax (402)488-7582. E-mail: 74617,236@compuserve.com. Christian Record Services. Richard J. Kaiser, mng ed. For sight-impaired adults over 25; interdenominational Christian audience. Quarterly mag; 65-70 pgs (lg. print); circ 30,000. Free to sight-impaired. 95% freelance. Complete ms; no phone/e-query. Pays .04-.05/wd on acceptance for one-time rts. Articles & true stories 750-1,400 wds. Responds in 12 wks. Seasonal 18 mos ahead. Accepts simultaneous submissions & reprints. Accepts disk. No sidebars. Guidelines; copy for 9x12 SAE/5 stamps.

Special Needs: Handicapped experiences. Overstocked on Christianity, relationships.

Tips: "Remember the readers are sight impaired or physically handicapped. Would the topics be relevant to them? Follow guidelines and write quality work."

LIGHT AND LIFE, Box 535002, Indianapolis IN 46253-5002. (317)244-3660. Fax (317)248-9055. E-mail: llmeditor@aol.com. Free Methodist Church of North America. Doug Newton, ed. Christian growth, ministry to saved and unsaved, denominational news; thought-provoking Wesleyan-Arminian perspective. Bimonthly mag; 72 pgs; circ 20,000. Subscription $16. 40% freelance. Query; fax/e-query OK. Pays .04-.05/wd on publication for 1st or one-time rts. Articles 500-600 or 800-1,800 wds (30/yr). Responds in 6-8 wks. Seasonal 8 mos ahead. Accepts simultaneous submissions. Prefers disk or e-mail submission (attached file). Kill fee 50%. Some sidebars. Prefers NIV. Guidelines; copy $4. (Ads)

Poetry: Buys 6-10/yr. Free verse, traditional; 4-16 lines; $10. Send max 5 poems. Uses as sidebars to articles.

Fillers: Cartoons.

Columns/Departments: Buys 6-10/yr. Personal Opinion; Young Voice (ages 16-22); 500-600 wds.

Tips: "Best to write a query letter. We are emphasizing contemporary issues articles, well researched. Ask the question, 'What topics are not receiving adequate coverage in the church and Christian periodicals?'"
** 1994 EPA Award of Excellence—Denominational.

*LIGHTHOUSE FICTION COLLECTION, PO Box 1377, Auburn WA 98071-1377. Tim Clinton, ed/pub. Timeless fiction for the whole family. Quarterly mag; 56 pgs; circ 300. Subscription $7.95 for 6/$14.95 for 12. 100% freelance. Complete ms/cover letter. Pays to $5-50 on publication for 1st or one-time rts. Fiction for all ages 250-5,000 wds (40-50/yr). Responds in 6-18 wks. Seasonal any time. Guidelines; copy $3.

Poetry: Buys 12-20/yr. Free-verse, light verse, traditional; 6-80 lines; $1-5. Submit max 5 poems.

Tips: "Read and follow guidelines. Basic need is for good stories and poems—well-written, interesting, new plot."

+L.I.G.H.T. NEWS, PO Box 1330, South Holland IL 60473. (708)596-5774. House of L.I.G.H.T (Love Is God's Healing Truth). Robert Fier, ed. Dedicated to complete healing available in Jesus Christ. Monthly newsletter; 4-10 pgs. Subscription $15. 5% freelance. Query/clips. Pays $10 for one-time or reprint rts. Articles 200-500 wds. Responds in 2-4 wks. Seasonal 2 mos ahead. Accepts reprints (tell when/where appeared). No sidebars. Prefers KJV. Guidelines; copy for 9x12 SAE/3 stamps. (No ads)

Fillers: Anecdotes, facts, ideas, prayers, quotes, scripture commentary, 25-100 wds. Pays $10.

Tips: "Filler section most open, but main section also open. Relate your relationship with the Lord in a way that is both invigorating and edifying."

LIGUORIAN, One Liguori Dr., Liguori MO 63057-9999. (314)464-2500. Fax (314)464-8449. E-mail: aweinert@liguori.org. Website: http://www. liguori.org. Catholic/Liguori Publications. Allan Weinert, CSSR, ed. To help readers lead a fuller Christian life through the sharing of experiences, scriptural knowledge, and a better understanding of the church. Monthly (10X)mag; 40 pgs; circ 250,000. Subscription $20. 15% freelance. Query or complete ms/cover letter; phone/fax/e-query OK. Pays .10-.12/wd (to $200) on acceptance for all rts. Articles 400-2,000 wds (8/yr); fiction 2,000 wds (10/yr). Responds in up to 26 wks. Seasonal 6 mos ahead. Prefers disk. No e-mail submission. Some sidebars. Prefers NAS (St. Joseph edition). Guidelines; copy for 9x12 SAE/3 stamps. (Ads)

Fillers: Anecdotes, cartoons, games, jokes, short humor, word puzzles; .10/wd.

Columns/Departments: Buys 12/yr. Five-Minute Meditation (reflective essay), 750 wds. Complete ms.

Tips: "Polish your own ms. Need personal testimonies, beware of limited subjectivity. Also needs fiction and humor."

LIVE, 1445 Boonville Ave., Springfield MO 65802-1894. (417)862-2781x4356. Fax (417)862-6059. E-mail: psmith@ag.org. Assemblies of God. Paul W. Smith, adult ed. Inspiration and encouragement for adults. Weekly take-home paper; 8 pgs; circ 130,000. Subscription $9.20. 100% freelance. Complete ms; no phone/fax query. Pays .10/wd (.07/wd for reprints) on acceptance for 1st, one-time simultaneous or reprint rts. Articles 700-1,600 wds (75/yr); fiction 700-1,600 wds (30/yr). Responds in 6-8 wks. Seasonal 1 yr ahead. Accepts simultaneous submissions & reprints (tell when/where appeared). No disk. Some sidebars. Prefers NIV. Guidelines/copy for 6x9 SAE/2 stamps. (No ads)

Poetry: Buys 15-25/yr. Free verse, traditional; 12-24 lines; $60 when scheduled. Submit max 3 poems.

Fillers: Buys 30/yr; 200-700 wds; pays by the word.

Tips: "Encourage our readers to live more productive Christian lives. We want them to be uplifted, not preached at or merely informed. Our purpose is mainly Christian inspiration and encouragement. Send no more than two articles in the same envelope and send an SASE. We always need holiday articles, other than Christmas."

** This periodical was #23 on the 1998 Top 50 Christian Publishers list. (#31 in 1997, #26 in 1996, #16 in 1995, #20 in 1994)

LIVING, 13241 Port Republic Rd., Grottoes VA 24441. Phone/fax (540)249-3177. E-mail: Tgether@aol.com. Shalom Foundation, Inc. Melodie Davis, ed. A positive, practical and uplifting publication for the whole family; mass distribution. Quarterly tabloid; 32 pgs; circ 250,000. Free. 80% freelance. Query or complete ms/cover letter; e-query OK. Pays $25-50 on publication for one-time rts. Articles 500-1,000 wds (36/yr); fiction (4/yr). Responds in 12-16 wks. Seasonal 4 mos ahead. Accepts simultaneous submissions & reprints (tell when/where appeared). Accepts disk or e-mail submission (copied into message). Some sidebars. Prefers NIV. Guidelines/theme list (also by e-mail); copy for 9x12 SAE/4 stamps. (Ads)

Fillers: Buys 4-8/yr. Anecdotes, short humor; 100-200 wds; $20-25.

Tips: "We are directed toward the general public, many of whom have no Christian interests, and we're trying to publish high-quality writing on family issues/concerns from a Christian perspective. That means religious language must be low key. Too much of what we receive is directed toward a Christian reader. We use fiction for adults or children, 6-14 (has to be emotionally moving/involving)."

THE LIVING CHURCH, PO Box 514036, Milwaukee WI 53203-3436. (414)276-5420. Fax (414)276-7483. E-mail: tlc@livingchurch.org. Website: http://www.livingchurch.org. Episcopal/The Living Church Foundation, Inc. John Schuessler, mng ed. Independent news coverage of the Episcopal Church for clergy and lay leaders. Weekly mag; 16+ pgs; circ 9,000. Subscription $39.50. 50% freelance. Query or complete ms/cover letter; phone/fax/e-query OK. Pays $25-100 (for solicited articles, nothing for unsolicited) for one-time rts. Articles 1,000 wds (10/yr). Responds in 2-4 wks. Seasonal 2 mos ahead. Accepts disk or e-mail submission. Regular sidebars. Free copy. (Ads)

Poetry: Accepts 5-10/yr. Light verse, traditional; 4-15 lines. Submit max 3 poems.

Columns/Departments: Accepts 10/yr. Benediction (devotional/inspirational), 200 wds.

Tips: "Most open to features, as long as they have something to do with the Episcopal Church."

LIVING LIGHT NEWS, #200, 5304-89 St., Edmonton AB T6E 5P9 Canada. (403)468-6397. Fax (403)468-6872. E-mail: livinglight@enabel.ab.ca. Website: http://www.livinglightnews.org. Living Light Ministries. Jeff Caporale, ed. To motivate and encourage Christians; witnessing tool to the lost. Bimonthly tabloid; 28 pgs; circ 20,000. Subscription $19.95 US. 75% freelance. Query; phone/fax/e-query OK. Pays $20-125 (.05-.10/wd), $20-50 for fiction, on publication for all, 1st, one-time, simultaneous or reprint rts. Articles 300-750 wds (20/yr); fiction to 1,500 wds (3/yr for Christmas only); book reviews 350 wds, music reviews 165 wds, & video reviews 300 wds; .10/wd. Responds in 4 wks. Seasonal 3-4 mos ahead. Accepts simultaneous submissions & reprints. Accepts disk. Regular sidebars. Prefers NIV. Guidelines/theme list; copy for 10x13 SAE/$2.25 CAN postage or IRCs. (Ads)

Fillers: Newsbreaks.

Columns/Departments: Buys 20/yr., 450-600 wds, $10-30. Parenting; Relationships; Finance (helpful, Godly advice in entertaining style). Query.

Special Needs: Celebrity interviews/testimonials of well-known personalities; interesting fiction and nonfiction stories related to Christmas; unique ministries.

Tips: "Most open to a timely article about someone who is well known in North America, say in sports, entertainment, or politics. They may or may not be Christian, but the article focuses on a Christian perspective."

** 1996 EPA Award of Excellence—Newspaper.

*LIVING WITH TEENAGERS, 127 Ninth Ave. N, Nashville TN 37234-0140. (615)251-2229. Fax (615)251-5008. E-mail: lwt@bssb.com. Website: http://www.bssb.com. LifeWay Press. Jeff Large, mng ed. Christian parenting for parents of teenagers. Monthly mag; 36 pgs; circ. 42,000. Subscription $18.95. 30% freelance. Query/clips; fax/e-query OK. Pays $100-500 on acceptance for all, 1st, one-time, or electronic rts. Articles 400-1,000 wds (35/yr). Responds in 6-8 wks. Seasonal 8 mos ahead. Accepts simultaneous submissions & reprints rarely (tell when/where appeared). Accepts disk. Regular sidebars. Prefers NIV. Guidelines; copy for 9x12 SAE/3 stamps.

Fillers: Buys 25/yr. Party ideas, short humor, parent/teen devotional ideas; 100-500 wds; $25-150.

Tips: "Most open to articles."

** This periodical was #11 on the 1998 Top 50 Christian Publishers list (#15 in 1997).

THE LOOKOUT, 8121 Hamilton Ave., Cincinnati OH 45231-9981. (513)931-4050. Fax (513)931-0950. Standard Publishing. Patricia McCarty, asst ed. For adults in Sunday school who are interested in learning more about applying the gospel to their lives. Weekly take-home paper; 16 pgs; circ 105,000. Subscription $23.50. 40-50% freelance. Query only; no phone/fax/e-query. Pays .05-.15/wd on acceptance for 1st, one-time, simultaneous or reprint rts. Articles 400-1,800 wds or 400-700 wds(50/yr). Responds in 18 wks. Seasonal 6 mos ahead. Accepts simultaneous submissions & reprints (tell when/where appeared). Accepts disk, no e-mail submission. Kill fee 33%. Regular sidebars. Prefers NIV. Guidelines/theme list; copy for .75. (No ads)

Fillers: Cartoons, $50.

Columns/Departments: Buys 24/yr. Outlook (personal opinion), 500-900 wds; Salt & Light (innovative ways to reach out into the community), 500-900 wds. Pays .05-.07/wd.

Tips: "Get a copy of our theme list and query (by letter) about a theme-related article at least six months in advance."

** This periodical was #37on the 1998 Top 50 Christian Publishers list (#40 in 1997, #1 in 1996, #3 in 1993 & 1995). Also EPA 1996 Award of Excellence—Sunday School Take-Home.

THE LUTHERAN, 8765 W. Higgins Rd., Chicago IL 60631-4183. (773)380-2540. Fax (773)380-2751. E-mail: lutheran@elca.org. Website: http://www.thelutheran.org. Evangelical Lutheran Church in America. Edgar R. Trexler, ed.; Roger R. Kahle, mng ed.; submit to David L. Miller, sr. ed. Addresses broad constituency of the church. Monthly mag; 68 pgs; circ 150,000. 10% freelance. Query only; fax/e-query OK. Pays $150-600 (assigned), $75-500 (unsolicited) on acceptance for 1st rts. Articles 400-1,500 wds (40/yr). Responds in 4-9 wks. Seasonal 4 mos ahead. Accepts reprints. Disk or E-mail submission OK. Kill fee 50%. Guidelines/theme list; free copy.

Fillers: Roger Kahle. Buys 50/yr. Cartoons, jokes, short humor. Uses only true anecdotes from ELCA congregations.

Columns/Departments: Roger Kahle. Lite Side (church and religious humor), 25-100 wds; $10.

Tips: "Most open to feature articles."

** This periodical was #2 on the 1998 Top 50 Christian Publishers list. (#12 in 1997, #31 in 1996, #7 in 1995, #9 in 1994)

THE LUTHERAN DIGEST, Box 4250, Hopkins MN 55343. (612)933-2820. Fax (612)933-5708. Lutheran. David L. Tank, ed. Blend of secular and light theological material used to win non-believers to the Lutheran faith. Quarterly mag; 72 pgs; circ 155,000. Subscription $22/2 yrs. 100% freelance. Query/clips or complete ms/cover letter; no phone/fax query. Pays $25 on acceptance for one-time rts. Articles to 1,000 wds (25-30/yr). Responds in 4-9 wks. Seasonal 6-9 mos ahead. Accepts reprints (70% is reprints). No disk. Some sidebars. Guidelines; copy $3/6x9 SAE/3 stamps. (Ads)

Poetry: Accepts 45-50/yr. Light verse, traditional; any length; no payment. Submit max 3 poems.

Fillers: Anecdotes, cartoons, facts, jokes, short humor; to 100 wds; no payment.

Tips: "Compose well-written, short pieces that would be of interest to middle-age and senior Christians-and also acceptable to Lutheran church pastors. (The word Hope is frequently associated with our publication.)."

**This periodical was #50 on the 1994 Top 50 Christian Publishers list.

#THE LUTHERAN JOURNAL, 7317 Cahill Rd., Ste. 201, Minneapolis MN 55439-2081. (612)941-6830. Fax (612)941-3010. Macalester Park Publishing. Rev. Armin Deye, ed; submit to Stephani Karges, ed asst Family magazine for church members, middle age and older. Triannual mag; 32 pgs; circ 130,000. Subscription $6. 60% freelance. Complete ms/cover letter; fax query OK. Pays .01-.04/wd on publication for one-time rts. Articles 400-1,500 wds (25-30/yr); book reviews, 150 wds, $5. Responds in 18 wks. Seasonal 4-5 mos ahead. Accepts simultaneous submissions & reprints. Regular sidebars. Prefers NIV, NAS or KJV. Accepts disk. Guidelines; copy for 9x12 SAE/3 stamps. (Ads)

Poetry: Buys 6-9/yr. Free verse, haiku, light verse, traditional; to 2 pgs. Pays $5-30. Submit max 5 poems.

Fillers: Buys 5/yr. Anecdotes, cartoons, facts, games, prose, quizzes, quotes, short humor; to 100 wds; $5-30.

Columns/Departments: Buys 40/yr. Apron Strings (short recipes); About Books (reviews), 50-150 wds. Pays $5-25.

Tips: "Most open to Lutheran lifestyles or Lutherans in action."

LUTHERAN WITNESS, 1333 S. Kirkwood Rd., St. Louis MO 63122-7295. (314)965-9000. Fax (314)965-3396. E-mail: DAVID.STRAND@lcms.org. Website: http://www.lcms.org/services.html. Lutheran Church-Missouri Synod. Rev. David Mahsman, ed; submit to David L. Strand, mng ed. Denominational. Monthly mag; 26 pgs; circ 325,000. 50% freelance. Complete ms/cover letter. Pays $100-300 on acceptance for 1st rts. Articles 250-1,600 wds (40-50/yr); fiction 500-1,500 wds. Responds in 9 wks. Seasonal 6 mos ahead. Considers simultaneous submissions & reprints. Kill fee 50%. Free guidelines/copy.

Fillers: Accepts 60+/yr. Cartoons ($50), short humor; no payment.

Columns/Departments: Buys 60/yr. Bible Studies, Humor, Opinion; $50-100.

MARIAN HELPERS BULLETIN, PO Box 951, Stockbridge MA 01263. (413)298-3691. Catholic. Dave Kane, ed. Quarterly mag; circ 500,000. 20% freelance. Query/clips or complete ms/cover letter. Pays .10/wd on acceptance for all, 1st, or reprint rts. Articles 500-900 wds; book reviews. Responds in 3 wks. Seasonal 6 mos ahead. Accepts reprints. Kill fee 30%. Free guidelines/copy.

Tips: "Also needs articles on mercy in action or devotion to Blessed Virgin Mary."

+MARKETPLACE, 12900 Preston Rd., Ste. 1215, Dallas TX 75230. (972)385-7657. Fax (972)385-7307. E-mail: mmihq@marketplaceministries.com. Website: Http://www.marketministries.com. Marketplace Ministries. Art Stricklin, ed. Focus is on working in the corporate workplace. Semiannual mag; 12 pgs; circ 12,000. 5-10% freelance. Query; e-query OK. Pays variable rates on publication for all rts. Articles. Prefers e-mail submission. No copy. Incomplete topical listings. (No ads)

MARRIAGE PARTNERSHIP, 465 Gundersen Dr., Carol Stream IL 60188. (630)260-6200. Fax (630)260-0114. E-mail: MPedit@aol.com. Website: http://www.marriagepartnership.net. Christianity Today, Inc. Caryn D. Rivadeneira, assoc ed. To promote and strengthen Christian marriages. Quarterly mag; 74 pgs; circ 55,000. Subscription $19.95. 5% freelance. Query only; fax/e-query OK. Pays $50-300 (.15/wd) on acceptance for 1st rts. Articles 500-2,000 wds. Responds in 8-10 wks. Seasonal 6 mos ahead. Some sidebars. Guidelines; copy $5.

Columns/Departments: Work it Out (working out a marriage problem).

MATURE LIVING, 127 9th Ave. N., Nashville TN 37234-0140. (615)251-5955.

Fax (615)251-5008. Southern Baptist. Al Shackleford, ed; submit to Judy Pregel, mng ed. Christian leisure-reading for senior adults (50+) characterized by human interest and Christian warmth. Monthly mag; 52 pgs; circ 350,000. Subscription $17.95. 70% freelance. Complete ms. Pays .055/wd ($75 min.) on acceptance for all (preferred) or one-time rts. Articles 600-1,200 (100/yr); fiction 900-1,200 wds (12/yr). Responds in 13 wks. Seasonal 1 yr ahead. Serials. Some sidebars. Prefers KJV or NIV. Guidelines; copy for 9x12 SAE/4 stamps. (No ads)

Poetry: Buys 30/yr. Light verse, traditional; senior adult themes; any length; $13-20. Submit max 5 poems.

Fillers: Buys 120/yr. Anecdotes, facts, games, short humor; to 50 wds; $15.

Columns/Departments: Cracker Barrel (brief humor), $10; Grandparent's Brag Board, $15.

Tips: "Most open to human-interest stories. All articles and fiction must relate to senior adults."

** This periodical was #52 on the 1998 Top 50 Christian Publishers list (#53 in 1997).

MATURE YEARS, Box 801, Nashville TN 37202. (615)749-6292. Fax (615)749-6512. E-mail: mcropse@umpublishing.org. United Methodist. Marvin W. Cropsey, ed. Inspiration, information, and leisure reading for persons of retirement age. Quarterly mag; 112 pgs; circ 70,000. Subscription $12. 50% freelance. Complete ms/cover letter; fax/e-query OK. Pays .05/wd on acceptance for one-time rts. Articles 900-2,000 wds (60/yr); fiction 1,200-2,000 wds (4/yr). Responds in 3-8 wks. Seasonal 14 mos ahead. Accepts reprints. Prefers e-mail submission (copied into message). Regular sidebars. Prefers NRSV or NIV. Guidelines; copy $4.50. (No ads)

Poetry: Buys 24/yr. Free verse, haiku, light verse, traditional; 4-16 lines; pays $1/line. Submit max 6 poems.

Fillers: Buys 20/yr. Cartoons, jokes, prayers, word puzzles (religious only); to 30 wds; $5-25.

Columns/Departments: Buys 20/yr. Health Hints, 900-1,200 wds; Modern Revelations (inspirational), 900-1,100 wds; Fragments of Life (true life inspirational), 250-600 wds; Going Places (travel), 1,000-1,500 wds; Money Matters, 1,200-1,800 wds.

Special Needs: Articles on crafts and pets. Fiction on older adult situation.

** This periodical was #56 on the 1998 Top 50 Christian Publishers list. (#63 in 1997, #56 in 1996, #65 in 1995, #51 in 1994)

THE MENNONITE, Box 347, Newton KS 67114. (316)283-5100. Fax (316)283-0454. E-mail: TheMennonite@gcmc.org. Website: http://www. themennonite.org. General conference Mennonite Church. Gordon Houser, assoc ed (gordonh@gcmc.org). Practical articles on aspects of Christian living. Weekly mag; 16 pgs; circ 21,600. Subscription $34.95. Estab 1998. 10% freelance. Complete ms/cover letter; phone/fax/e-query OK. Pays .05/wd on publication for 1st rts. Articles 1,000-1,200 wds (10/yr). Responds in 1-2 wks. Seasonal 6 mos ahead. Accepts simultaneous submissions & reprints (tell when/where appeared). Accepts e-mail submission (copied into message). Kill fee 50%. Regular sidebars. Prefers NRSV. Guidelines/theme list (also on Website); copy for 9x12 SAE/4 stamps. (Ads)

Poetry: Buys 5-10/yr. Avant-garde, free verse; $30-50. Submit max 3 poems.

Fillers: Buys 5/yr. Anecdotes, ideas, short humor; 100-400 wds; $10-20.

Columns/Departments: Buys 10/yr. Speaking Out (opinion)700 wds. Pays $30-40.

Tips: "Most of our writers are Mennonite. Our freelance material is primarily features. We prefer unique stories with a point (not overstated). " Note: This is a new publication that resulted from a merge with Gospel Herald.

MENNONITE BRETHREN HERALD, 3-169 Riverton Ave., Winnipeg MB R2L 2E5 Canada. (204)669-6575. Fax (204)654-1865. E-mail: mbherald@ cdnmbconf.ca. Website: http://www.cdnmbconf.ca/mb/mbherald/htm. Canadian Conference of Mennonite Brethren Churches. Susan Brandt, mng ed. Denominational; for information, communication and spiritual enrichment. Biweekly mag; 32 pgs; circ 15,000. Subscription $30. 40% freelance. Complete ms/cover letter; phone query OK. Pays .07/wd on publication for 1st rts. Articles 1,200 wds (40/yr); fiction 1,000-2,000 wds (10/yr). Responds in 20 wks. Seasonal 5 mos ahead. Accepts reprints (tell when/where appeared). Prefers disk or e-mail submission. Regular sidebars. Prefers NIV. Guidelines/theme list; copy for 9x12 SAE/$1 Canadian postage. (Ads)

Poetry: Buys 15/yr. Avant-garde, free verse, traditional; any length; pays to $10.

Tips: "Most open to feature articles on relevant topics."

MENNONITE HISTORIAN, 600 Shaftesbury Blvd., Winnipeg MB R3P 0M4 Canada. (204)888-6781. Fax (204)831-5675. E-mail: kreddig@ con fmenno.ca. Website: http://www.mbnet.mb.ca/mhc. Conference of Mennonites in Canada. Ken Reddig, ed/dir. Gathers and shares historical material related to Mennonites; focus on North America, but also beyond. Quarterly newsletter; 8 pgs; circ. 2,600. Subscription $9. 60% freelance. Complete ms/cover letter; phone/fax query OK. **NO PAYMENT EXCEPT BY SPECIAL ARRANGEMENT** for 1st rts. Articles 250-1,000 wds (6/yr). Responds in 3 wks. Seasonal 3 mos ahead. Accepts simultaneous submissions & reprints (depending on where published). Prefers disk or e-mail submission (attached file). Guidelines (also by e-mail); copy $1/9x12 SAE. (Ads)

Tips: "Must be Mennonite related. Most open to lead articles. Write with your ideas. Also genealogical articles."

MENNONITE WEEKLY REVIEW, Box 568, Newton KS 67114-0568. (316)283-3670. Fax (316)283-6502. E-mail: menwkrv@southwind.net. Mennonite. Paul Schrag, ed. Features religious and Mennonite news. Weekly newspaper; 12-16 pgs; circ 11,000. Subscription $31. 5% freelance. Complete ms/ cover letter; e-query OK. Pays .07/wd on publication for one-time rts. Articles 400-500 wds. Responds in 5 wks. Accepts simultaneous submissions. Prefers NIV. Copy $1/SAE/2 stamps. (Ads)

Tips: "Topic must be Mennonite; we are exclusively a Mennonite publication."

MESSAGE, Review and Herald Pub. Assn., 55 W. Oak Ridge Dr., Hagerstown MD 21740. (301)791-7000. Fax (301)714-1753. E-mail: 74617.3047@compu serve.com. Seventh-day Adventist. Dwain N. Esmond, asst ed. Blacks and other minorities who have an interest in current issues and are seeking a better lifestyle. Bimonthly mag; 32 pgs; circ 125,000. Subscription $12.97. 25% freelance. Complete ms/cover letter; fax query OK. Pays $50-300 ($50-75 for fiction) on acceptance for 1st rts. Articles 700-1,200 wds (50/yr); parables; fiction (6/yr) for children (ages 5-8), 500 wds. Responds in 6-10 wks. Seasonal 6 mos ahead. Prefers disk, no e-mail submission. Regular sidebars. Prefers NIV. Guidelines; copy for 9x12 SAE/2 stamps. (Ads)

Fillers: Facts, games, quizzes, word puzzles; to 500 wds; $50-75.

Columns/Departments: Buys 12/yr. Healthspan (health issues), 700 wds; MESSAGE Jr. (biblical stories or stories with clear-cut moral for ages 5-8), 500 wds. Pays $75-150.

Contests: Sometimes has a black history contest and/or Bible-related contest.

Tips: "As with any publication, writers should have a working knowledge of MESSAGE. They should have some knowledge of our style and our readers."

** This periodical was #24 on the 1998 Top 50 Christian Publishers list. (#18 in 1997, #28 in 1995). Also 1996 EPA Award of Merit—Missionary.

MESSAGE OF THE OPEN BIBLE, 2020 Bell Ave., Des Moines IA 50315-1096. (515)288-6761. Fax (515)288-2510. E-mail: message@openbible.org. Open Bible Churches. Andrea Johnson, ed. To inspire, inform and educate the Open Bible family. Bimonthly mag; 16 pgs; circ 4,300. Subscription $9.75. 5% freelance. Complete ms/cover letter; e-query OK. **PAYS 5 COPIES**. Not copyrighted. Articles 750 wds (2/yr). Responds in 4 wks. Seasonal 4 mos ahead. Accepts simultaneous submissions & reprints (tell when/where appeared). Accepts disk or e-mail submission. Regular sidebars. Prefers NIV. Guidelines/theme list; copy for 9x12 SAE/2 stamps.

Fillers: Accepts 6/yr. Cartoons, facts, quotes, short humor; 50 wds.

Tips: "Most open to inspiration or evangelistic pieces. A writer can best break in by giving us something valuable for an upcoming theme or something that would inspire or uplift the average church member, specifically as they relate to Open Bible."

** 1996 EPA Award of Merit—Denominational.

MESSENGER, Box 18068, Covington KY 41018-0068. (606)283-6226. Catholic. Jean Bach, news ed. Diocese paper of Covington KY. Weekly (45X) newspaper; 24 pgs; circ 16,000. Subscription $18. 40% freelance. Query/clips. Pays $1.25/column inch on publication for 1st rts. Articles 500-800 wds. Responds in 1 wk. Seasonal 1 mo ahead. Accepts simultaneous submissions. Guidelines; free copy.

#MESSENGER OF THE SACRED HEART, 661 Greenwood Ave., Toronto ON M4J 4B3 Canada. (416)466-1195. Catholic/Apostleship of Prayer. Rev. F.J.

Power, S.J., ed. Help for daily living on a spiritual level. Monthly mag; 32 pgs; circ 15,000. Subscription $12. 20% freelance. Complete ms; no phone query. Pays .04/wd on acceptance for 1st rts. Articles 800-1,500 wds (30/yr); fiction 800-1,500 wds (12/yr). Responds in 5 wks. Seasonal 5 mos ahead. No disk. No sidebars. Guidelines; copy $1/9x12 SAE.

Tips: "Most open to inspirational stories and articles."

THE MESSENGER OF ST. ANTHONY, Via Orto Botanico, 11, 35123 Padova, Italy (US address: Anthonian Assn., 101 St. Anthony Dr., Mt. Saint Francis IN 47146). (812)923-6356. Fax (812)923-3200. E-mail: m.conte@mess-s-antonio.it. Website: http://www.mess-s-antonio.it. Catholic. Martin de Sa'Pinto, asst ed. For middle-age and older Catholics in English-speaking world; articles that address current issues. Monthly mag; 48 pgs; circ 23,000. Subscription $25 US. 80% freelance. Query (complete ms for fiction); phone/fax/e-query OK. Pays .10-.15/wd on publication for all rts. Not copyrighted. Articles 600-2,000 wds (150/yr); fiction 600-1,400 wds (11/yr). Responds in 6-8 wks. Seasonal 4 mos ahead. Prefers disk or e-mail submission. Regular sidebars. Prefers Liguori Faithware. Guidelines (also by e-mail); free copy for 10x13 SAE. (No ads)

Fillers: Buys 11/yr. Anecdotes, cartoons, facts, ideas, quotes; 600-800 wds. Pays $55.

Columns/Departments: Buys 50-60/yr. Documentary (issues), 600-2,000 wds; Spirituality, 600-2,000 wds; Church Life, 600-2,000 wds; Saint Anthony (devotional), 600-1,400 wds; Living Today (family life), 600-1,400 wds. Pays $55-200. Complete ms.

Tips: "We prefer articles on parishes dedicated to Saint Anthony with accompanying photos. Current affairs articles (not necessarily with a religious slant) are also encouraged."

METHODIST HISTORY, PO Box 127, Madison NJ 07940. (973)408-3189. Fax (973)408-3909. E-mail: cyrigoyen@gcah.org. Website: http://www.gcah. org. United Methodist. Charles Yrigoyen Jr., ed. History of the United Methodism and Methodist/Wesleyan churches. Quarterly journal; 64 pgs; circ 1,000. Subscription $15. 100% freelance. Query; phone query OK. **PAYS IN COPIES** for all rts. Historical articles to 5,000 wds (15/yr); book reviews 500 wds. Responds in 8 wks. Requires disk. No sidebars. Guidelines; copy $5. (Ads)

*****METRO VOICE,** 108 SE 3rd St., Lee's Summit MO 64063. (816)524-4522. Fax (816)525-4423. Non-denominational. Dwight & Anita Widaman, pubs; Melanie Miles, ed. To promote Christian business, ministries and organizations; provide thought-provoking commentary for edification of the body of Christ. Monthly newspaper; circ 35,000. Subscription $14. 50% freelance. Complete ms/cover letter; short phone query OK. **PAYS IN COPIES** or limited amount for well-researched pieces, for one-time or reprint rts. Not copyrighted. Articles to 1,200 wds (100/yr). Responds in 6 wks. Seasonal 6 mos ahead. Accepts reprints. Guidelines; copy for 9x12 SAE/$1 postage.

Fillers: Accepts 12/yr. Anecdotes, cartoons, ideas, newsbreaks, quotes, short humor; to 500 wds.

Tips: "We look for up-to-date information. Willing to work with new writers who want to learn."

*MICHIGAN CHRISTIAN ADVOCATE, 316 Springbrook Ave., Adrian MI 49221. (517)265-2075. Fax (517)263-7422. United Methodist. Erik Alsgaard, ed. For Michigan United Methodists. Biweekly tabloid; 16 pgs; circ 12,000. Subscription $12. 75% freelance. Complete ms/cover letter; fax query OK. Pays $30-50 on publication for one-time rts. Articles 400-550 wds; book/music/video reviews, 200 wds, $15. Responds in 4 wks. Seasonal 3 mos ahead. Accepts simultaneous submissions. Accepts disk. Regular sidebars. Prefers NRSV. Copy available. (Ads)

Fillers: Buys 30-35/yr. Cartoons, word puzzles. Pay varies.

Columns/Departments: Buys 20-26/yr. My Experience (true), 450-550 wds; In My Opinion (church topics), 400-500 wds. Pays $30.

Special Needs: Easter, My Experience columns, 350-450 wds.

Tips: "Always looking for touching true experience columns—be brief, not sappy. Always looking for good cartoonists—pay $25-50 depending on artist. Young cartoonists please apply."

MINNESOTA CHRISTIAN CHRONICLE, 7317 Cahill Rd., Minneapolis MN 55439. (612)562-1234. Fax (612)941-3010. E-mail: editor@mcchronicle. com. Website: http://www.mcchronicle.com. Beard Communications. Doug Trouten, ed. Local news and features of interest to the Christian community. Biweekly newspaper; 28 pgs; circ 7,000. Subscription $19.95. 10% freelance. Query; phone/e-query OK. Pays $50-150 after publication for one-time rts. Articles 500-1,500 wds (25/yr). Responds in 13 wks. Seasonal 2 mos ahead. Accepts simultaneous query & reprints. Guidelines; copy $2. (Ads)

Tips: "Not interested in anything without a Minnesota 'hook.' Tell us about people and ministries we're not aware of." Loves e-queries.

** 1997 EPA Award of Merit—Newspaper. (1996 EPA Award of Excellence—Newspaper.)

THE MIRACULOUS MEDAL, 475 E. Chelten Ave., Philadelphia PA 19144-5785. (215)848-1010. Catholic. Rev. William J. O'Brien C.M., ed. Fiction & poetry for Catholic adults, mostly women. Quarterly mag; 36 pgs; circ 340,000. 100% freelance. Complete ms/cover letter. Pays .02/wd on acceptance for 1st rts. Religious fiction 1,600-2,400 wds (6/yr). Responds in 26 wks. Seasonal anytime. Accepts simultaneous submissions. Guidelines; copy for 2 stamps. (No ads)

Poetry: Buys 6/yr. Free verse, traditional; to 20 lines; .50 & up/line. Send any number. "Must have religious theme, preferably about the Blessed Virgin Mary."

THE MONTANA CATHOLIC, PO Box 1729, Helena MT 59624-1729. (406)442-5820. Fax (406)442-5191. Catholic. Alex Lobdell, ed. News and features for the Catholic community of western Montana. Monthly tabloid; 20-24 pgs; circ 9,300. Subscription $12 (in state), $16 (out of state). 5% freelance. Complete ms/cover letter or query; e-query OK. Pays .05-.10/wd on acceptance for 1st, one-time, simultaneous or reprint rts. Articles 200-950 wds (12/yr). Responds in 3 wks. Seasonal 2 mos ahead. Accepts simultaneous submissions & reprints (tell when/where appeared). Accepts disk, no e-mail submission. Kill fee 35%. Regular sidebars. Prefers NAS or RSV. Guidelines; copy $2/9x12 SAE. (Ads)

>**Tips:** "Our greatest need is for freelance writers who reside in western Montana, have an understanding of the Catholic Church, and are willing to take on news and feature writing assignments of local interest. Photographic ability helpful. On rare occasions we use feature articles by other freelancers, particularly when geared toward seasons and days of the liturgical year or our semi-annual special sections on religious vocations."

MOODY MAGAZINE, 820 N. LaSalle Blvd., Chicago IL 60610. (312)329-2164. Fax (312)329-2149. E-mail: Moodyedit@aol.com, or moodyltrs@aol.com. Website: http://www.moody.edu/MOODYMAG. Moody Bible Institute. Andrew Scheer, mng ed. To encourage and equip evangelical Christians to think and live biblically. Bimonthly mag; 84-96 pgs; circ 112,000. Subscription $24. 62% freelance. Query only; no phone/fax/e-query. Query for electronic submissions. Pays $210-500 (.15-.20/wd) on acceptance for 1st & nonexclusive electronic rts. Articles 1,200-2,200 wds (55/yr); fiction 1,200-2,000 wds (1-3/yr). Responds in 9 wks. Seasonal 9 mos ahead. Accepts reprints (tell when/where appeared). Kill fee 50%. Requires disk. Regular sidebars. Prefers NIV. Guidelines; copy for 9x12 SASE/8 stamps. (Ads)

>**Columns/Departments:** Buys 12/yr. First Person (salvation testimonies—may be as-told-to), 800-900 wds; $150-225.

>**Tips:** "We want feature articles from freelancers for the second (non-cover) section of each issue. In generating article ideas, consider these questions: What has God been working on in my life the last few years? How am I applying a new realization of what the Bible is directing me to do? What difference has this obedience made? Answers should lead you to appropriate content for a Moody article." Continues to look for 1,500-word parenting pieces.

>** This periodical was #12 on the 1998 Top 50 Christian Publishers list. (#13 in 1997, #9 in 1996, #4 in 1995 & 1994)

MOVIEGUIDE, 2510-G Los Posas Rd. #502, Camarillo CA 93010. (805)383-2000. Fax (805)738-0715. E-mail: movieguide@compuserve.com. Website: http://movieguide.org. Good News Communications/Christian Film & TV Commission. Dr. Theodore Baehr, pub. Family guide to media entertainment from a biblical perspective. Biweekly mag; 30+ pgs.; circ 7,000. Subscription $40. 40% freelance. Query/clips. **NO PAYMENT** for all rts. Articles 1,200 wds (100/yr); book/music/video/movie reviews, 1,200 wds. Responds in 6 wks. Seasonal 6 mos ahead. Accepts disk. Regular sidebars. Guidelines/theme list; copy for SAE/4 stamps. (Ads)

>**Fillers:** Accepts 1,000/yr; all types; 20-50 wds.

>**Columns/Departments:** MovieGuide; TravelGuide; VideoGuide; CDGuide, etc.; 1,200 wds.

+THE NARROW GATE, E-mail: shaunaskye@aol.com. Website: Http://members.aol.com/shaunaskye/index.html. Shauna Skye, ed. Geared to Christian writers, musicians, and artists, as well as those who love music, literature and art. Free monthly online mag . Complete ms/cover letter by e-mail submission only (copied into message). **NO PAYMENT EXCEPT**

OPTION TO RUN PRE-APPROVED 50-WORD CLASSIFIED AD. Articles to 1,000 wds; fiction to 3,000 wds book/music reviews 500 wds. Guidelines on Website. Not in topical listings. (Ads)

Poetry: Free verse, light verse, traditional; any length.

Special Needs: Musical editorials, Artist/Illustrator editorials; articles about writers/poets/editors; reviews of Christian concerts, publications, artists

NATIONAL CATHOLIC REPORTER, 115 E. Armour Blvd., Kansas City MO 64111. (816)531-0538. Fax (816)968-2280. E-mail: natcath@aol.com. Website: http://www.natcath.com. Catholic. Thomas Fox, pub; Michael Farrell, ed. Independent. Weekly (44X) & online newspaper; 44-48 pgs; circ 48,000. Query/clips. Pays varying rates on publication. Articles any length. Responds in 9 wks. Accepts simultaneous submissions.

Columns/Departments: Query with ideas for columns.

***NETWORK**, PO Box 131165, Birmingham AL 35213-6165. (205)328-7112. Interdenominational. Dolores Milazzo Hicks, ed/pub. To encourage and nurture dialog, understanding and unity in Jewish and Christian communities. Monthly tabloid; 12-16 pgs; circ 15,000. 50% freelance. Negotiable payment. Not copyrighted. Accepts simultaneous submissions. Articles and news.

NEW COVENANT, 200 Noll Plaza, Huntington IN 46750. (219)356-8400. Fax (219)356-8472. E-mail: NewCov@aol.com. Website: http://www.osv.com. Catholic/Our Sunday Visitor. Mike Aquilina, ed. Serves readers interested in orthodox Catholic spirituality. Monthly mag; 36 pgs; circ 20,000. Subscription $18. 85% freelance. Query only; fax/e-query OK. Pays $100-200 on acceptance for 1st or one-time rts. Articles 1,000-1,200 wds (40/yr). Responds in 5 wks. Seasonal 5 mos ahead. Prefers disk. Guidelines; copy for 9x12 SAE/5 stamps. (Ads)

Tips: "Most open to practical, useful approaches to deepening one's spiritual life and relationship with Christ. Be familiar with New Covenant's style so you can speak to our audience."

** This periodical was #67 on the 1997 Top 50 Christian Publishers list. (#33 in 1996, #48 in 1995, #46 in 1994)

***NEW CREATION**, PO Box 254, Temple City CA 91780. (562)948-2008. E-mail: DEnsign888@aol.com. Christian Comics Arts Society. Ralph E. Miley, exec ed. Reports on the Christian comics movement. Bimonthly newsletter; 8-10 pgs; circ 64. Subscription $12. Estab 1996. 20-30% freelance. Query; phone/e-query OK. **NO PAYMENT** for all rts. Articles 700 wds (6/yr); book reviews 200 wds. Responds in 3 wks. Accepts reprints (tell when/where appeared). No sidebars. Prefers KJV. Guidelines/theme list; copy for SAE/ stamps. (Ads)

Fillers: Accepts 6 cartoons/yr.

Columns/Departments: Accepts 6/yr. Editorials, 700 wds; Forerunner reviews, 200 wds.

Special Needs: Comic book, cartoon strip and animation news, Christian oriented. Fantasy fiction.

A NEW HEART, Box 4004, San Clemente CA 92674-4004. (714)496-7655. Fax (714)496-8465. E-mail: HCFUSA@juno.com. Website: http://www.HCF

USA.com. Aubrey Beauchamp, ed. For Christian healthcare-givers; information regarding medical/Christian issues. Quarterly mag; 16 pgs; circ 5,000. Subscription $25. 20% freelance. Complete ms/cover letter; phone/fax query OK. **PAYS 2 COPIES** for one-time rts. Not copyrighted. Articles 600-1,800 wds (20-25/yr). Responds in 2-3 wks. Accepts simultaneous submissions & reprints. Accepts e-mail submission. No sidebars. Guidelines (also by fax); copy for 9x12 SAE/3 stamps. (Ads)

> **Poetry:** Accepts 1-2/yr. Submit max 1-3 poems.
>
> **Fillers:** Accepts 3-4/yr. Anecdotes, cartoons, facts, jokes, short humor; 100-120 wds.
>
> **Columns/Departments:** Accepts 20-25/yr. Chaplain's Corner, 200-250 wds; Physician's Corner, 200-250 wds.
>
> **Tips:** "Most open to real life situations which may benefit and encourage healthcare givers and patients."

+NEW MOON NETWORK, For Adults Who Care about Girls, PO Box 3620, Duluth MN 55803. (218)728-5507. Fax (218)728-0314. E-mail: newmoon@cp.duluth.mn.us. Website: http://www.newmoon.org. New Moon Publishing, Inc. Joe Kelly, ed. For adults (teachers, parents, etc.) who work with girls 8-14. Bimonthly mag; circ 3,000. 10% freelance. Query. Pays .04-.08/wd on publication for 1st & reprint rts. Articles 750-1,500 wds (6/yr); fiction 900-1,800 wds (1/yr); book reviews 900 wds. Responds in 5-9 wks. Seasonal 4 mos ahead. Accepts simultaneous submissions & reprints (tell when/where appeared). Guidelines/theme list; copy $6.50.

> **Columns/Departments:** Buys 3/yr. Mothering (personal experience), 900 wds; Fathering, 900 wds; Current Research (girl-related), 900-1,800 wds. Query.
>
> **Tips:** "Study our guidelines carefully, follow our themes, and understand our goals."

NEW WRITING MAGAZINE, Box 1812, Amherst NY 14226-7812. (716)834-1067. E-mail: newwriting@aol.com, or the bookdoc@aol.com. Website: http://1812.simplenet.com. New Writing Agency. Richard Lynch, co-ed. The best of new writing by beginning and established writers. Annual online mag. Free on the Internet. 95% freelance. Complete ms/cover letter; e-query OK. **NO PAYMENT** for 1st rts. Not copyrighted. Articles (5/yr); fiction (20/yr). Responds in 6-8 wks. Seasonal 6 mos ahead. Accepts simultaneous submissions & reprints (tell when/where appeared). Guidelines. (Ads)

> **Poetry:** Buys 20/yr. Avant-garde, free verse, traditional; any length. Submit max 5 poems.
>
> **Contest:** "We run a writing contest and literary agency. Visit http://members.aol.com/newwriting.contest.html."

NO-DEBT LIVING, Financial Management with a Christian Perspective, PO Box 282, Veradale WA 99037-0282. Phone/fax (509)927-1322 (call for fax). E-mail: rfrank@nodebtnews.com. Website: http://www.nodebtnews.com. Robert E. Frank, ed. Financial and home-management information from a Christian perspective. Monthly newsletter; 12 pgs; circ. 2,000. Subscription $25.95. 40% freelance. Query/clips or resume; fax/e-query OK.

Pays $30-70 on publication for 1st, one-time rts. Articles 300-1,200 wds (40/yr); 400-600 wds (vignettes); book reviews 300 wds. Responds in 2 wks. Seasonal 2 mos ahead. Accepts simultaneous submissions & reprints (tell when/where appeared). Prefers disk or e-mail submission in ASCII format. Regular sidebars. Prefers NAS. Guidelines/theme list; copy for 6x9 SAE/2 stamps.

Special Needs: Consumer-related news, investment, and taxes.

Tips: "Follow AP style. Use original quotes from two well-known professionals (preferably Christians). Link story to a current news trend or issue. Most open to money-management (if writer has experience and/or professional expertise)."

THE NORTH AMERICAN VOICE OF FATIMA, 1023 Swan Rd., Youngstown NY 14174. (716)754-7489. Fax (716)754-9130. E-mail: FatimaShr@aol. com. Barnabite Fathers, Inc./Catholic. Father Paul Keeling, ed. A Marian publication with emphasis on apparitions of Our Lady of Fatima. Bimonthly mag; 20 pgs; circ 3,000. Subscription $4.50. 50% freelance. Complete ms/cover letter. Pays .04/wd on publication for 1st rts. Not copyrighted. Articles & fiction 1,000 wds. Responds in 6 wks. Seasonal 4 mos ahead. Accepts simultaneous submissions & reprints. No disk. Regular sidebars. Guidelines/copy for #10 SAE.

Poetry: Buys 20/yr. Free verse, traditional. Pays $10.

NORTHWEST CHRISTIAN JOURNAL, Box 59014, Renton WA 98058. (425)255-3552. Fax (425)228-8749. E-mail: storysearc@aol.com. Tami Tedrow, ed. Local, national, and international news with an evangelical perspective. Monthly tabloid newspaper; 16-40 pgs; circ 27,000. Subscription $15. Little freelance. Query/clips; no phone queries. Pays $40 on publication for one-time or simultaneous rts. Articles 500-750 wds. Accepts simultaneous submissions & reprints. Accepts disk or e-mail submission. Some sidebars. Prefers NIV. Guidelines (2 stamps); copy $1.50. (Ads)

Fillers: Limited interest in cartoons.

Special Needs: Advertising themes: January—Marriage; March & October—Christian Education Guide.

Tips: "This is a news publication, which limits our interest to stories that are timely and localized for the Northwest. No devotional material, columns, poetry, personal testimonies (unless localized with a news angle) or promotions of business (contact our advertising dept.). Local writers preferred."

NORTHWESTERN LUTHERAN, 2929 N Mayfair Rd., Milwaukee WI 53222-4398. (414)256-3888. Fax (414)256-3899. E-mail: nl@sab.wels.net. Wisconsin Evangelical Lutheran Synod. Gary P. Baumler, ed. Denominational. Monthly mag; 36 pgs; circ 55,000. Subscription $9. 25% freelance. Complete ms/cover letter; no phone/fax/e-query. Pays $50/pg on publication for one-time rts. Articles 500-1,000 wds (50/yr). Responds in 4-6 wks. Seasonal 4 mos ahead. Accepts reprints (tell when/where appeared). Accepts disk or e-mail submission (copied into message). Regular sidebars. Prefers NIV. Guidelines; copy for 9x12 SAE/2 stamps. (No ads)

Tips: "Most of our writers belong to the denomination and write about our members, organizations or institutions. Most open to strong personal witness; strong inspirational example of Christian living."

OBLATES, 9480 N. De Mazenod Dr., Belleville IL 62223-1160. (618)398-4848. Fax (618)398-8788. Catholic/Missionary Assn. of Missionary Oblates of Mary Immaculate. Mary Mohrman, mss ed. To inspire, comfort, uplift, and motivate an older Catholic/Christian audience. Bimonthly mag; 20 pgs; circ 500,000. Free to members. 30% freelance. Complete ms only/cover letter; no phone/fax query. Pays $80 on acceptance for 1st rts. Articles 500-600 wds (40/yr). Responds in 9 wks. Seasonal 6 mos ahead. Considers simultaneous submissions. No disk. No sidebars. Prefers NAB. Guidelines; copy for 6x9 SAE/2 stamps. (No ads)

> **Poetry:** Buys 10-12/yr. Free verse, traditional; 8-16 lines; $30. Submit max 2 poems.
>
> **Tips:** "Need personal, inspirational articles with a strong spiritual theme firmly grounded to a particular incident and poetry. No Christmas issue."

+ON MISSION, 4200 North Point Pkwy, Alpharetta GA 30022-4176. (770)410-6286. Fax (770)410-6006. E-mail: ccurtis@namb.net. Website: http://www.onmission.com. North American Mission Board, Southern Baptist. Carolyn Curtis, ed. Helping readers share Christ in the real world. Bimonthly & online mag; 68 pgs; circ 130,000. Subscription, 1 yr free. 50% freelance. Query for assignments. Pays .20/wd & up on publication for all, 1st, one-time, reprint and electronic rts. Articles 250-3,000 wds (6/yr). Responds in 4-6 wks. Seasonal 8 mos ahead. Accepts e-mail submission (copied into message). Kill fee. Regular sidebars. Prefers NIV. Guidelines; copy for 9x12 SAE/8 stamps.

> **Tips:** "Our primary purpose is to help readers and churches become more 'on mission' in the area of personal evangelism. Send a resume, along with your best writing samples. We are an On Assignment magazine."

OUR FAMILY, Box 249, Battleford SK S0M 0E0 Canada. (306)937-7771. Fax (306)937-7644. E-mail: ourfamily@marianpress.sk.ca. Website: http:// marianpress.sk.ca/ourfamily. Catholic/Missionary Oblates of St. Mary's Province. Marie-Louise Ternier-Gommers, ed. All aspects of family life in the light of Christian faith. Monthly (11X) mag; 40 pgs; circ 8,000. Subscription $17.98 CAN. 95% freelance. Complete ms; phone query OK. Pays .07/wd US on acceptance for 1st & electronic rts. Articles 700-1,700 wds (100-135/yr). Responds in 5-6 wks. Seasonal 5-6 mos ahead. Accepts simultaneous submissions & reprints (tell when/where appeared). Accepts e-mail submission submissions (copied into message). Kill fee 100%. Some sidebars. Prefers NRSV. Guidelines/theme list (also on Website); copy $2.50/9x12 SAE./Canadian postage or IRCs. (No ads)

> **Poetry:** Buys 60-100/yr. Free verse, haiku, light verse, traditional, inspirational; 2-25 lines; $.75/line.
>
> **Fillers:** Buys 40-60/yr. Anecdotes, cartoons, jokes, short humor; to 100 wds. Pays .07/wd.
>
> **Tips:** "Your SASE must have Canadian postage. We aim at the average

reader. Looking for articles which deal with specific Catholic issues; articles that are rooted in social justice, service to others, and the Sunday liturgy. Articles need an experiential point of view with practical guidelines."

** This periodical was #30 on the 1998 Top 50 Christian Publishers list. (#47 in 1997, #39 in 1996 & 1995, #29 in 1994)

OUR SUNDAY VISITOR, 200 Noll Plaza, Huntington IN 46750. (219)356-8400. Fax (219)359-9117. Website: http://www.osc.com. Catholic. David Scott, ed. Vital news, spirituality for today's Catholic. Weekly newspaper; 24 pgs; circ 120,000. Subscription $36. 5% freelance. Query. Pays $150-250 on acceptance for 1st rts. Articles to 1,000 wds (25/yr). Responds in 5 wks. Seasonal 2 mos ahead. Kill fee. Guidelines; Copy for #10 SASE.

   Columns/Departments: Buys 50/yr. Viewpoint (editorial/op-ed), 750 wds, $100.

   Tips: "Need familiarity with Catholic Church issues and with Catholic Press—newspapers and magazines."

   **This publication was #1 on the 1994 Top 50 Christian Publishers list..

+OVER THE BACK FENCE/NORTHERN OHIO, 5311 Meadow Lane Ct., Ste. 3. Elvira OH 44035. (440)934-1812. Fax (440)934-1816. E-mail: kbsagert@ aol.com. Website: Http://www.backfence.com. Back Fence Publishing, Inc. Kelly Boyer Sagert, mng ed. Positive news about Northern Ohio. Quarterly mag; 64 pgs; circ 15,000. Subscription $9.97. 100% freelance. Query/clips; fax/e-query OK. Pays .10-.20/wd on publication for one-time rts. Articles 1,000 wds (56/yr). Responds in 4 wks. Seasonal 6-12 mos ahead. Accepts simultaneous submissions & reprints (tell when/where appeared). Requires disk or e-mail submission (copied into message). Regular sidebars. Guidelines (also by e-mail/Website); copy $4/9x12 SAE. (Ads)

   Poetry: Buys 4-8/yr. Free verse, light verse, traditional; 1 pg. Pays $25. Submit max 5 poems.

   Columns/Departments: Buys 12-20/yr. Profiles From the Past (interesting history that never made the headlines), 800-1,000 wds; Heartstrings (touching essays), 800 wds; Shorts (humorous essays), 800 wds. Complete ms. Pays $80-120.

   Special Needs: Think upbeat and positive. Articles on nature, history, travel, nostalgia and family.

   Tips: "Following tips on our Tip Sheet will help a writer break in. We work with writers to get their articles into publishable form."

+OVER THE BACK FENCE/SOUTHERN OHIO, 14 S. Paint St., Ste. 69, PO Box 756, Chillicothe OH 45601. (740)772-2165. Fax (740)773-7626. E-mail: backfenc@bright.net. Website: Http://www.backfence.com. Back Fence Publishing, Inc. Sarah Williamson, mng ed. Positive news about Southern Ohio. Quarterly mag; 64 pgs; circ 15,000. Subscription $9.97. 100% freelance. Query/clips; fax/e-query OK. Pays .10-.20/wd on publication for one-time rts. Articles 1,000 wds (56/yr). Responds in 4 wks. Seasonal 6-12 mos ahead. Accepts simultaneous submissions & reprints (tell when/where appeared). Requires disk or e-mail submission (copied into message). Regular sidebars. Guidelines (also by e-mail/Website); copy $4/9x12 SAE. (Ads)

Poetry: Buys 4-8/yr. Free verse, light verse, traditional; 1 pg. Pays $25. Submit max 5 poems.

Columns/Departments: Buys 12-20/yr. Profiles From the Past (interesting history that never made the headlines), 800-1,000 wds; Heartstrings (touching essays), 800 wds; Shorts (humorous essays), 800 wds. Complete ms. Pays $80-120.

Special Needs: Think upbeat and positive. Articles on nature, history, travel, nostalgia and family.

Tips: "Following tips on our Tip Sheet will help a writer break in. We work with writers to get their articles into publishable form."

PARENTLIFE, 127 Ninth Ave. N., Nashville TN 37234-0140. (615)251-2229. Fax (615)251-5008. E-mail: parentlife@bssb.com. Website: http://www.bssb.com/kidtrek/prntlife.htm#top. Southern Baptist/LifeWay Press. Jeff Large, mng ed. For parents of children—birth to 12 years. Monthly mag; 50 pgs; circ 115,000. Subscription $19.95. 30% freelance. Query/clips; fax/e-query OK. Pays $100-500 on acceptance for all, first, one-time & electronic rts. Articles 800-1,200 wds (75/yr). Responds in 6-8 wks. Seasonal 8 mos ahead. Considers simultaneous submissions. Accepts disk. Regular sidebars. Prefers NIV. Guidelines; copy for 9x12 SAE/3 stamps.

Fillers: Buys 50/yr. Anecdotes, games, ideas, party ideas; 75-100 wds; $25-100.

Tips: "Looking for articles on specific aspects of parenting. Good topics are developmental articles, school, home school, family life. You must send an SASE, or no response."

** This periodical was #7 on the 1998 Top 50 Christian Publishers list. (#3 in 1997, #27 in 1996, #40 in 1995)

THE PARENT PAPER, PO Box 1313, Manchester TN 37349. (931)728-8309. Fax (931)723-1902. E-mail: rhurst@edge.net. Rebekah Hurst, pub. A Christian perspective on topics that benefit the family. Monthly newspaper; 16-20 pgs; circ. 5,000. Subscription $15. Complete ms; e-query OK. **PAYS 3 COPIES** for 1st or reprint rts. Articles; fiction for children or teens (400-600 words). Seasonal 6 mos ahead. Accepts simultaneous submissions & reprints. Accepts e-mail submission (attached file). Some sidebars. Prefers NIV. Guidelines; copy for 9x12 SAE/4 stamps. (Ads)

Poetry: Accepts 6/yr; to 32 lines.

Tips: "Any area is open to freelancers. Freelancers can best break in by writing about issues that affect the family."

THE PEGASUS REVIEW, PO Box 88, Henderson MD 21640-0088. (410)482-6736. Art Bounds, ed. Theme-oriented poetry, short fiction & essays; not necessarily religious; in calligraphy. Bimonthly mag; 6-10 pgs; circ 115. Subscription $12. 100% freelance. Query; phone query OK. **PAYS 2 COPIES** for one-time rts. Fiction 2 1/2 pgs, single-spaced (6-10/yr); also one-page essays. Responds in 4 wks. Seasonal 2 mos ahead. Accepts simultaneous submissions & reprints (tell when/where appeared). No disk. No sidebars. Prefers KJV. Guidelines/theme list; copy $2.50. (No ads)

Poetry: Accepts 20-30/yr. Any type; to 24 lines (shorter the better). Theme oriented. Submit max 5 poems.

Fillers: Accepts 10-20/yr. Cartoons, prose, essays; short.

Special Needs: 1999 themes include Birth, Spring, The Planets, Summer, Fall, Winter.

Tips: "Believe in your craft and persevere. Become active in a local writer's group, especially one that does critiquing. Follow the theme, submit 3-5 poems or one story, and heed editor's suggestions."

PENTECOSTAL EVANGEL, 1445 Boonville, Springfield MO 65802-1894. (417)862-2781. Fax (417)862-0416. E-mail: pevangel@ag.org. Website: http://www.ag.org/evangel. Assemblies of God. Hal Donaldson, ed. Denominational; Pentecostal. Weekly mag (some articles online); 32 pgs; circ 265,000. Subscription $23.95. 10% freelance. Complete ms/cover letter; fax/e-query OK. Pays .06-.08/wd (.03/wd for reprints) on acceptance for 1st and electronic rts. Articles 800-1,000 wds. Responds in 6-8 wks. Seasonal 6-8 mos ahead. Kill fee 100%. Prefers disk (Word 5.1 or 6.0) or e-mail submission (attached file). Regular sidebars. Prefers NIV or KJV. Guidelines on Website; no copy. (Ads)

Fillers: Practical, how-to pieces on family life, devotions, evangelism, seasonal, current issues, Christian living; 50-200 wds. Pays $20.

Columns/Departments: Why I Serve.

Tips: Needs general inspirational articles with a strong focus; feature articles targeted to the unsaved; seasonal articles (major holidays). A large percentage of articles are now assigned.

** This periodical was #61 on the 1998 Top 50 Christian Publishers list. (#28 in 1996, #11 in 1995, #23 in 1994)

THE PENTECOSTAL TESTIMONY, 6745 Century Ave., Mississauga ON L5N 6P7 Canada. (905)542-7400. Fax (905)542-7313. E-mail: testimony@ paoc.org. Website: http://paoc.org. The Pentecostal Assemblies of Canada. Rick Hiebert, ed. Focus is inspirational and Christian living; Pentecostal holiness slant. Monthly & online mag; 28 pgs; circ 21,650. Subscription $24 US/$17 CAN. 20% freelance. Query; fax query OK. Pays $20-75 ($100 for fiction) on publication for 1st or reprint rts. Articles 800-1,200 wds (12/yr); fiction 1,000-1,500 wds (5/yr); book/music reviews, 400 wds ($20 or copy of book). Responds in 6-8 wks. Seasonal 4 mos ahead. Accepts reprints (tell when/where appeared). Prefers disk or e-mail submission (copied into message). Regular sidebars. Prefers NIV. Guidelines; copy $2/ 9x12 SAE. (Ads)

Special Needs: Youth-related articles; native issues. Looking for young writers able to write for young readers (teens through 20-something).

Tips: "Our readership is 98% Canadian. We prefer Canadian writers or at least writers who understand that Canadians are not Americans in long underwear."

+THE PEOPLES MAGAZINE, 374 Sheppard Ave. E., Willowdale ON L4G 6M1 Canada. (416)223-3341. Fax (416)222-3344.The Peoples Church/Toronto Canada. Dr. T. Starr, mng ed. Quarterly mag; 24 pgs; circ 12,000. Subscription $15. 80% freelance. Query or complete ms/cover letter. **NO PAYMENT.** Not copyrighted. Articles 350-500 wds (20/yr); fiction 350-500 wds; book/video reviews 350 wds. Responds in 2 wks. Seasonal 2 mos ahead. Accepts simultaneous submissions & reprints (tell when/where appeared). No disk. Some sidebars. Any version. Guidelines; copy for 10x13 SAE/$1.17 CAN postage. (Ads)

Fillers: Accepts 10-15/yr. Anecdotes, cartoons, facts, games, quizzes, short humor, 25-40 wds.

Columns/Departments: Accepts 20/yr.

PERSPECTIVES, A Journal of Reformed Thought, PO Box 470, Ada MI 49301-0470. (616)241-2053. Fax (616)285-9828. E-mail: boogaart@ macatawa.org. Reformed Church Press. Dr. Thomas A. Boogaart and Evelyn Diephouse, co eds. To express the Reformed faith theologically; to engage issues that Reformed Christians meet in personal, ecclesiastical, and societal life. Monthly (10X) mag; 24 pgs; circ. 3,000. Subscription $24.95. Query or complete ms/cover letter; fax/e-query OK. **PAYS IN COPIES** for all rts (usually). Articles (10/yr) and fiction (3/yr), 2,000-2,500 wds; book reviews 500-1,500 wds. Responds in 4-6 wks. Seasonal 4 mos ahead. Prefers disk. Sidebars rare. Prefers NRSV. Copy for 9x12 SAE/$1.50 postage. (Ads)

Poetry: Francis Fike. Free verse, traditional. Accepts 5-7/yr. Submit max 2 poems.

Columns/Departments: Accepts 20-24/yr. As We See It (editorial/ opinion) 750-1,500 wds; Inside Out (biblical exegesis) 750 wds. Complete ms.

PHYSICIAN, 8605 Explorer Dr., Colorado Springs CO 80920. (719)531-3400. Fax (719)531-3499. E-mail: stevensm@macmail.fotf.org. Website: http:// www.family.org. Focus on the Family. Susan Stevens, ed. To encourage physicians and their families. Bimonthly mag; 24 pgs; circ 74,000. Free to medical profession. 10% freelance. Complete ms/cover letter; fax/e-query OK. Pays $100-500 on publication for 1st rts. Articles 800-2,400 wds. Responds in 6 wks. Prefers disk. Kill fee. Regular sidebars. Prefers NIV. Copy available.

Fillers: Cartoons; $50.

Tips: "Call ahead. Be a physician. Understand the medical industry." ** 1997 EPA Award of Excellence—Christian Ministry.

THE PLAIN TRUTH, 300 W. Green St., Pasadena CA 91129. Fax (818)795-0107. E-mail: Monte_Wolverton@ptm.org. Website: http://www.ptm.org/ index.htm. Plain Truth Ministries. Monte Wolverton, mng ed. Proclaims the Gospel of Jesus Christ, emphasizing the central teachings of Christianity and making those teachings plain and clear. Bimonthly mag; 68 pgs; circ 135,000. Subscription $12.95. 60-70% freelance. Query/clips or complete ms/cover letter; fax/e-query OK. Pays .25/wd (.15/wd for reprints) on publication for 1st, one-time, reprint, and world (all languages) rts. Articles 750-2,000 wds (25/yr); book/music/video reviews 100 wds, $25. Responds in 4-6 wks. Seasonal 6-8 mos ahead. Accepts simultaneous submissions & reprints (tell when/where appeared). Requires disk. Kill fee 75%. Regular sidebars. Prefers NIV. Guidelines; copy for 9x12 SAE/4 stamps. (Ads)

Columns/Departments: Buys 18/yr. Family (family issues), 1,500 wds; Commentary (hot topic editorials), 550-650 wds; Christian People (testimonial/interviews), 1,500 wds. Query or complete ms.

Tips: "Best to send tear sheets of previously published articles and submit detailed query for standard articles."

PLENTY GOOD ROOM, 1800 N. Hermitage Ave., Chicago IL 60622-1101. (773)486-8970. Catholic. J. Glen Murray, ed. Focuses on African-American worship within the church. Bimonthly mag; 12 pgs. Query. Pays $25/pg, for all rts. Articles. Responds in 13 wks. Guidelines; free copy.

THE PLOWMAN, Box 414, Whitby ON L1N 4G7 Canada. (905)668-7803. The Plowman Ministries/Christian. Tony Scavetta, ed/pub. Poetry and prose of social commentary; any topics. Semiannual newsletter; 20 pgs; circ 5,000. Subscription $10 US. 90% freelance. Query; phone query OK. **NO PAYMENT.** Articles (10/yr) & fiction (50/yr), 1,000 wds. Responds in 2-4 wks. Accepts simultaneous submissions & reprints. No disk. No sidebars. Free guidelines/copy for 9x12 SAE. (Ads)

> **Poetry:** Accepts 100/yr. All types; to 38 lines (55 characters across max). Submit max 4 poems.
> **Fillers:** Accepts 25/yr. Cartoons, prayers, short humor; 25-30 wds.
> **Special Needs:** Also publishes chapbooks; 20% royalties.
> **Contest:** Sponsors monthly poetry contests; $2/poem entry fee.
> **Tips:** " All sections open, especially poetry and short stories."

PLUS, 66 E. Main St., Pawling NY 12564. (914)855-5000. Fax (914)855-1462. Peale Center for Christian Living. Pat Planeta, ed. Spiritually oriented, based on positive thinking and faith. Monthly (10X) mag; 36 pgs; circ 600,000. Subscription $10. 30% freelance. Complete ms/cover letter; phone/fax query OK. Pays $25/pg on publication for 1st or one-time rts. Articles 500-2,500 wds (8/yr). Responds in 3-4 wks. Seasonal 6 mos ahead. Accepts reprints. Some sidebars. Guidelines; copy for #10 SAE/1 stamp.

> **Tips:** "Have a deep, living knowledge of Christianity. Our audience is 65-70% female, average age is 55."
> ** This periodical was #31 on the 1995 Top 50 Christian Publishers list.

POETRY FORUM SHORT STORIES, 5713 Larchmont Dr., Erie PA 16509. Phone/fax (814)866-2543. E-mail: 75562.670@compuserve.com. Interdenominational. Gunvor Skogsholm, ed. Poetry and prose that takes an honest look at the human condition. Bimonthly mag; 20 pgs; circ 400. Subscription $22. 90% freelance. Complete ms/cover letter; fax/e-query OK. **NO PAYMENT** for one-time rts (buys only from subscribers). Articles 300 wds; fiction 3,000 wds (150/yr); book reviews 200 wds. Responds in 8 wks. Seasonal 2 mos ahead. Accepts simultaneous submissions & reprints (tell when/where appeared). Prefers disk or e-mail submission (attached file). Guidelines (also by e-mail); copy $4. (Ads)

> **Poetry:** Accepts 40/yr. Inspirational; any type; to 50 lines. Submit max 10 poems.
> **Contest:** Monthly poetry & short stories; $10 cash prizes. Entry fees, $1 for poetry, $2 for short story. Send SASE for information.

+THE POET'S PAGE, PO Box 372, Wyanet IL 61379. For poets, scholars, teachers and poetry lovers. Quarterly. Subscription $10. Complete ms. **PAYS IN COPIES** for one-time rts. Articles. Responds in 2-3 wks. Guidelines; copy $3.

> **Poetry:** Any style, any length.

Special Needs: Articles on poetry and/or poetic forms, biographical sketches of recognized poets, short essays on history and development of poetic styles, etc.

Contest: Annual poetry contest. Prizes of $25, $50 & $75. Entry fee $1/poem.

*POETS' PAPER , PO Box 85, Easton PA 18044-0085. (610)559-9287. Anderie Poetry Press. Carole J. Heffley, exec ed; submit to Michael Steffen, acq ed. For the publication of fine poetry. Quarterly journal; 56-60 pgs; circ 3,000. Subscription $24. Estab 12/96. 90% freelance. Complete ms/cover letter; phone/e-query OK. Query for electronic submissions. **NO PAYMENT** for one-time rts. Responds in 4-6 wks. Seasonal 6 mos ahead. Reprints if it's been more than a year (tell when/where appeared). Guidelines; copies $6.50. (Ads)

Poetry: Accepts 1,000+/yr; to 38 lines. Submit max 3 poems.

Fillers: Quotes: must pertain to poetry, poets or writing. Pays one copy.

Columns/Departments: Buys 20/yr. Pays $25. "Would accept a column on writing inspirational poetry; markets for inspirational poetry."

Contest: Sponsors several contests. Send for guidelines. Also collects poetry for an annual edition of praise poetry; 100 poems/edition.

Tips: "We do not accept overly religious poems. Use subtle images of our Creator—mostly in nature."

POURASTAN, 615 Stuart Ave., Outremont QB H2V 3H2 Canada. (514)279-3066. Fax (514)276-9960. Canadian Diocese of the Armenian Holy Apostolic Church. Mr. N. Ouzounian, ed. Denominational; religious, social and community oriented. Bimonthly mag; 32 pgs; circ 1,200. Free for donations. 100% freelance. Complete ms/cover letter; phone/fax query OK. **NO PAYMENT.** Not copyrighted. Articles 250-1,500 wds (10/yr); book reviews, 300 wds. Seasonal 1 mo ahead. Accepts simultaneous submissions & reprints. No sidebars. Accepts disk. Copy for 9x12 SAE/90 cents.

Poetry: Accepts 10/yr. Traditional, 4-40 lines. Submit max 2 poems.

Fillers: Anecdotes, ideas, prayers, quotes, short humor, 10-50 wds.

Note: This publication is published in Armenian with occasional English and French.

POWER FOR LIVING, Box 36640, Colorado Springs CO 80936. (719)536-0100. Fax (719)536-3243. E-mail: PFLeditor@sppublications.org. Cook Communications/Scripture Press Publications. Don Alban Jr., ed. To expressly demonstrate the relevance of specific biblical teachings to everyday life via reader-captivating profiles of exceptional Christians. Weekly take-home paper; 8 pgs; circ 250,000. Subscription $10. 25% freelance. Complete ms; no phone/fax/e-query. Pays up to .15/wd (reprints up to .10/wd) on acceptance for 1st or one-time rts. Articles 700-1,500 wds (20/yr). Responds in 4 wks. Seasonal 1 yr ahead. Accepts simultaneous submissions & reprints (tell when/where appeared). Accepts disk or e-mail submission (attached file in RTF format or copied into message if less than 2,000 wds). Kill fee. Some sidebars. Paraphrase Bible verses (avoids direct quotes). Guidelines/copy for #10 SAE/1 stamp.

Special Needs: Third-person profiles of truly out-of-the-ordinary Christians who express their faith uniquely. We use very little of anything else.

Tips: "Most open to vignettes, 450-1,000 wds, of prominent Christians with solid testimonies or profiles from church history. Focus on the unusual. Signed releases required." Does not return submissions (send no SASE).

** This periodical was #11 on the 1996 Top 50 Christian Publishers list. (#9 in 1995, #21 in 1994)

#PRAIRIE MESSENGER, Catholic Journal, PO Box 190, Muenster SK S0K 2Y0 Canada. (306)682-1772. Fax (306)682-5285. E-mail: pmessenger @sk.sympatico.ca. Catholic/Benedictine Monks of St. Peter's Abbey. Marion Noll, OSU, assoc ed. For Catholics in Saskatchewan & Manitoba, and Christians in other faith communities. Weekly journal; circ 7,300. Subscription $25 CAN. 10% freelance. Complete ms/cover letter; phone/ fax/e-query OK. Pays to $40-60 ($2/column inch for news items) on publication for 1st, one-time, simultaneous & reprint rts. Not copyrighted. Articles to 250-600 wds (15/yr). Responds in 9 wks. Seasonal 3 mos ahead. Accepts simultaneous submissions & reprints. Regular sidebars. Guidelines; copy for 9x12 SAE/$1 CAN/$1.24 US.

Poetry: Accepts 46/yr. Free verse; 6-25 lines.

Special Needs: Ecumenism; social justice; native concerns.

Tips: "Comment/feature section is most open. Send topic of concern or interest to Prairie readership. It's difficult to break into our publication."

** This periodical was selected #1 for general excellence by the Canadian Church Press (10 times during the last 16 years).

PRAYERWORKS, PO Box 301363, Portland OR 97294. (503)761-2072. Fax (503)760-1184. E-mail: 7653.3202@compuserve.com. V. Ann Mandeville, ed. For prayer warriors in retirement centers; focuses on prayer. Weekly newspaper; 4 pgs; circ 600. Free subscription. 100% freelance. Complete ms; phone/fax query OK. **PAYS IN COPIES** for one-time rts. Not copyrighted. Articles (30-40/yr) & fiction (30/yr); 300-500 wds. Responds in 3 wks. Seasonal 2 mos ahead. Accepts simultaneous submissions & reprints. No sidebars. Guidelines; copy for #10 SAE/1 stamp.

Poetry: Accepts 20-30/yr. Free verse, haiku, light verse, traditional. Submit max 10 poems.

Fillers: Accepts up to 50/yr. Facts, jokes, prayers, quotes, short humor; to 50 wds.

Tips: "Write tight. Half our audience is over 70, but 30% is young families. Subject matter isn't important as long as it is scriptural and designed to help people pray."

#THE PRESBYTERIAN LAYMAN, 136 Tremont Park, PO Box 2210, Lenoir NC 28645. (704)758-8716. Fax (704)758-0920. Presbyterian Lay Committee. Parker T. Williamson, exec ed. For the conservative/evangelical members of the Presbyterian Church (USA). Bimonthly newspaper; 24 pgs; circ. 575,000. No subscriptions. 10% freelance. Query. Pays negotiable rates on publication for 1st rts. Articles 800-1,200 wds (12/yr). Responds in 2 wks. Seasonal 2 mos ahead. Prefers disk. Regular sidebars. Copy for 9x12 SAE/3 stamps.

Poetry: Traditional; pay negotiable. Submit max 1 poem.

THE PRESBYTERIAN OUTLOOK, Box 85623, Richmond VA 23285-5623. (804)359-8442. Fax (804)353-6369. E-mail: outlook.parti@pcusa.org. Website: http://www.pres-outlook.com. Presbyterian Church (USA)/Independent. Robert H. Bullock Jr., ed. For ministers, members and staff of the denomination. Weekly (43X) mag; 16-40 pgs; circ 12,734. Subscription $28.85. 5% freelance. Query; phone/fax/e-query OK. **NO PAYMENT** for all rts. Not copyrighted. Articles to 1,000 wds; book reviews 1 1/2 pgs. Responds in 1-2 wks. Seasonal 2 mos ahead. Requires disk; accepts e-mail submission. (copied into message), save as ASCII or plain text). Some sidebars. Prefers NRSV. Guidelines; free copy. (Ads)

Tips: "Correspond with editor regarding current needs. Most material is commissioned; anything submitted should be of interest to Presbyterians."

PRESBYTERIAN RECORD, 50 Wynford Dr., North York ON M3C 1J7 Canada. (416)444-1111. Fax (416)441-2825. E-mail: pcrecord@presbyterian.ca. Website: http://www.presbycan.ca. The Presbyterian Church in Canada. Rev. John Congram, ed. Denominational. Monthly (11X) mag; 52 pgs; circ 55,000. 50% freelance. Query (preferred) or complete ms/cover letter; fax query OK. Pays $50 CAN on publication for 1st, one-time, reprint or simultaneous rts. Articles 1,000-1,500 wds (15-20/yr); book/music reviews, to 400 wds/no pay. Responds in 9-13 wks. Seasonal 3 mos ahead. Accepts simultaneous submissions & reprints. Accepts e-mail submission (attached file). Regular sidebars. Prefers NRSV. Guidelines (also by e-mail); copy for 9x12 SAE/$1 Canadian postage or IRCs from US writers. (Ads)

Poetry: Thomas Dickey. Buys 8-15/yr. Free verse, haiku, light verse, traditional; 10-30 lines preferred; $35. Send any number.

Fillers: Buys 6/yr. Anecdotes, cartoons, facts, ideas, prose, prayers, short humor; to 200 wds; $15-25.

Columns/Departments: Buys 12/yr. Vox Populi (controversial issues), 750 wds; $35-50.

Tips: "It helps if submissions have some connection to Canada and/ or the Presbyterian Church."

PRESBYTERIANS TODAY, 100 Witherspoon St., Louisville KY 40202-1396. (502)569-5637. Fax (502)569-8632. E-mail: today@pcusa.org. Website: http://www.pcusa.org/pcusa/today. Presbyterian Church (USA). Catherine Cottingham, mng ed.; submit to Eva Stimson, ed. Denominational; not as conservative or evangelical as some. Monthly (10X) mag; 44 pgs; circ 90,000. Subscription $12.95. 65% freelance. Complete ms/cover letter; fax/e-query OK. Pays $200 before publication for 1st rts. Articles 1,000-1,500 wds (20/yr). Responds in 4-5 wks. Seasonal 4 mos ahead. Some reprints. Kill fee. Guidelines; free copy. (Ads)

Fillers: Cartoons, $25, short humor to 100 wds, no payment.

Tips: "Most open to feature articles or news articles about Presbyterian people and programs (600-800 wds, $75). Do not often use inspirational or testimony-type articles."

** This periodical was #47 on the 1998 Top 50 Christian Publishers list. (#48 in 1997, #64 in 1996, #41 in 1995)

+PRESBYTERIANS-WEEK, 9400 Fairview Ave., Ste. 200, Manassas VA 22110. (703)335-2844. Fax (703)368-4817. E-mail: Elliott@xc.org. Christian Observer Foundation; Presbyterian Reformed. Edwin P. Elliott, ed. To encourage and edify God's people and families. Free online electronic weekly newspaper. Query. **NO PAYMENT.** Not in topical listings. (Ads)

PRESERVING CHRISTIAN HOMES, 8855 Dunn Rd., Hazelwood MO 63042-2299. (314)837-7300. Fax (314)837-4503. E-mail: Gyouth8855@aol.com. Website: http://www.upci.org. United Pentecostal Church. Scott Graham, ed. Addresses relevant topics for the Christian family. Bimonthly mag; 16 pgs; circ 4,000. Subscription $9. 40% freelance. Complete ms/cover letter; phone/fax/e-query OK. Pays $30 on publication for one-time or simultaneous rts. Articles 500-1,500 wds (12/yr); fiction 500-1,500 wds (12/yr). Responds in 3-4 wks. Seasonal 6 mos ahead. Accepts simultaneous submissions & reprints (tell when/where appeared). No disk; accepts e-mail submission. Some sidebars. Prefers KJV. Guidelines; copy for 10x13 SAE. (No ads)

Poetry: Buys 3-4/yr. Light verse, traditional; 4-50 lines. Pays $15-30. Submit max 2 poems.

Fillers: Buys 2/yr. Cartoons, games, quizzes, word puzzles. Pays $15-30.

Tips: "Most open to fiction and relationships. Be relevant and practical."

#PRISM, 10 Lancaster Ave., Wynnewood PA 19096-3495. (610)645-9390. Fax (610)649-8090. E-mail: prism@esa-online.org. Website: http://www.libertynet.org/esa/prism. Evangelicals for Social Action. Dwight Ozard, ed. For Christians who are interested in the social and political dimensions of the gospel. Bimonthly mag; 44 pgs; circ 9,000. Subscription $25. 15% freelance. Query/clips; fax/e-query OK. Pays $200 ($100 for fiction) 6 wks after publication for 1st or reprint rts. Articles 500-2,800 wds (5/yr); fiction, 700-1,600 wds (1/yr); book/video reviews, 500 wds, $0-100. Responds in 8-12 wks. Seasonal 6 mos ahead. Accepts reprints (tell when/where appeared). Prefers disk. Regular sidebars. Prefers NRSV. Guidelines; copy $3. (Ads)

Tips: "Looking for analysis on religious right; social justice fiction. Understand progressive evangelicals and E.S.A. Read Tony Campolo, Ron Sider and Richard Foster. Most open to features."

*PROGRESS, Box 9609, Kansas City MO 64134-0609. (816)763-7800. Fax (816)765-2522. Stonecroft Ministries. Susan Collard, mng ed. For women and their families who are involved in some aspect of Stonecroft Ministries. Bimonthly mag; 64 pgs; circ 30,000. Subscription $8.50. 15% freelance. Complete ms/cover letter; phone/fax query OK. **PAYS IN COPIES**, for 1st rts. Not copyrighted. Articles 300-600 wds (15/yr). Responds in 2 wks. Seasonal 6 mos ahead. Accepts reprints (tell when/where appeared). Accepts disk. Some sidebars. Prefers NIV. Guidelines; copy for 6x9 SAE/4 stamps.

Columns/Departments: Buys 12/yr. Coping Series (how God helped through crisis or stress—prefers other than illness); Family Builders (help for families); 1,000-1,200 wds. These columns most open to freelance.

Tips: "We do not include controversial or doctrinal issues about which Christians disagree. Material should be Christ-centered and biblically based."

PROLIFE NEWS CANADA, B1 - 90 Garry St., Winnipeg MB R3C 4H1 Canada. (204)943-5273. Fax (204)943-9283. E-mail: lebow@escape.ca. Barbara LeBow, mng ed. For those who respect and protect life, from conception to natural death. Monthly (10X) mag;16 pgs; circ 30,000. Subscription $21.40 (GST incl.). Variable freelance. Complete ms/cover letter; phone/fax/e-query OK. Pays $50 CAN on publication for all rts. Articles 1,000-1,200 wds (10-20/yr); book or some video reviews, under 1,000 wds. Responds in 4 wks. Seasonal 2 mos ahead. Accepts simultaneous submissions & reprints (tell when/where appeared). No disk; accepts e-mail submission (copied into message). Some sidebars. Guidelines; copy for 9x12 SAE/.90 CAN postage. (Ads)

Special Needs: Human rights, rights of the child in the womb, euthanasia.

Tips: "All areas open. Send a sample of your work."

#PURPOSE, 616 Walnut Ave., Scottdale PA 15683-1999. (412)887-8500. Fax (412)887-3111. E-mail: horsch%mph@mcimail.com. Mennonite Church. James E. Horsch, ed. Denominational, for older youth and adults. Weekly take-home paper; 8 pgs; circ 13,000. Subscription $16.10. 95% freelance. Complete ms (only)/cover letter; phone query OK. Pays .05/wd on acceptance for one-time rts. Articles & fiction, to 750 wds (130/yr). Responds in 13 wks. Seasonal 6 mos ahead. Accepts simultaneous submissions & reprints (tell when/where appeared). Regular sidebars. Guidelines; copy for 6x9 SAE/2 stamps.

Poetry: Buys 130/yr. Free verse, light verse, traditional; 3-12 lines; up to $2/line ($7.50-20). Submit max 10 poems.

Fillers: Buys 15/yr. Anecdotes, cartoons, short humor; 200-500 wds; .04/wd.

Tips: "Articles must carry a strong story line. First person is preferred. Don't exceed maximum word length."

** This periodical was #39 on the 1998 Top 50 Christian Publishers list. (#49 in 1997, #48 in 1996, #20 in 1995, #22 in 1994)

PURSUIT, PO Box 315, Charlottesville VA 22902. (804)961-2500. Fax (804-961-2507. E-mail: DianeMc@JourneyGroup.com. Evangelical Free Church. Diane McDougall, ed. An evangelistic magazine aimed to help non-Christians address life issues while stimulating thought about spiritual answers. Quarterly mag; 32 pgs; circ 50,000. Subscription $15. 95% freelance. Query./clips; fax/e-query OK. Pays .20/wd, 45 days after final edit, for 1st, reprint or simultaneous rts. Articles 500-1,800 wds (2-4/yr); fiction 500-1,800 wds (1/yr). Responds in 8 wks. Seasonal 5 months ahead. Accepts simultaneous submissions & reprints (tell when/where appeared). Prefers e-mail submission (attached file). Kill fee 2%. Some sidebars. Prefers NIV. Guidelines/theme list; copy for 9x12 SAE/5 stamps. (Ads)

Columns/Departments: Cultural Comments (comments on issue/ book/music in current culture, drawing reader into asking questions on spiritual side of life—not religious; contemplative); 500-600 wds. Pays $100-120.

Tips: "Reading current issue is essential. Too many freelancers send overtly religious material or assume readers have an interest in Christianity. Need to assume they have questions/concerns about life but have never considered spiritual answers before."

QUEEN OF ALL HEARTS, 26 S. Saxon Ave., Bay Shore NY 11706-8993. (516)665-0726. Fax (516)665-4349. E-mail: Q.O.A.H.@aol.com. Catholic/ Montfort Missionaries. Rev. Roger M. Charest, SMM, mng ed. Focus is Mary, the Mother of Jesus. Bimonthly journal; 48 pgs; circ 2,800. Subscription $20. 80% freelance. Complete ms/cover letter; phone query OK. Pays $25-75 ($40-60 for fiction) on publication for 1st rts. Not copyrighted. Articles (40/yr) and fiction (6/yr) 1,500-2,000 wds; book reviews 100 wds. Responds in 3 wks. Seasonal 4 mos ahead. No disk. Some sidebars. Prefers NRSV. Guidelines; copy for $2.50/9x12 SAE. (No ads)

> **Poetry:** Buys 12/yr. Free verse; to 25 lines; Marian themes only. Pays 2 year subscription and 6 copies. Submit max 2 poems.

+QUEST, Santa Ynez Presbyterian Church, 1825 Alamo Pintado Rd., Solvang CA 93463. E-mail: quest@syv.com. Website: Http://QUEST.syv.com. Webpage with articles dealing with many life crises. Online magazine. **NO PAYMENT** for one-time or reprint rts. Articles about 500 wds (2 screens). Accepts simultaneous submissions & reprints. Prefers disk or e-mail submission (attached file, saved as text only). Guidelines (http:// syvpc.syv.com, under Evangelism); copy for 9x12 SAE/3 stamps. Incomplete topical listings.

*THE QUIET REVOLUTION, 1655 St. Charles St., Jackson MS 39209. (601)353-1635. Voice of Calvary Ministries. Cornelius J. Jones, ed. Interracial ministry to the poor; conservative/evangelical. Quarterly mag; 7 pgs; circ 3,000. 10% freelance. Query or complete ms/cover letter. **NO PAYMENT** for one-time rts. Articles 3-4 pgs. Responds in 5 wks. Accepts reprints. Free copy.

> **Tips:** "Most open to articles about ministering to the poor."

REAL FAMILY LIFE, 3900 N. Rodney Parham, Little Rock AR 72212. (501)223-8663. Fax (501)224-2529. E-mail: RFL@FamilyLife-ccc.org. Website: http:/ /www.familylife.com. FamilyLife/Campus Crusade for Christ. John Cooper, business mgr; David Boehi, ed. Provides practical, biblical help for families. Bimonthly (6X) mag; circ 165,000. Subscription free. Query only. Incomplete topical listings. (Ads)

+RE:GENERATION, PO Box 381042, Cambridge MA 02238-1042. (617)868-3659. Fax (617)249-0270. E-mail: editor@regeneration.com. Website: http://www.regeneration.com. The Regeneration Forum, Inc. Andrew Crouch, ed. Community transforming culture; Christians seeking to integrate faith and culture. Quarterly mag; 48 pgs; circ 2,000. Subscription $19.95. 80% freelance. Complete ms/cover letter; phone/fax/e-query OK. Pays up to $1,000 on publication for 1st, reprint and electronic rts. Articles 500-3,000 words (60/yr); fiction 500-3,000 wds (4/yr); book/music/ video reviews 800 words, pays up to $100. Responds in 12-16 wks. Requires disk. Some sidebars. Prefers NRSV. Guidelines; sample for 9x12 SAE/$1.75 postage. (Ads)

> **Poetry:** Buys 4/yr. Avant-garde, free verse; 4-30 lines. Pays up to $200. Submit max 4 poems.
>
> **Tips:** "We're looking for manuscripts that relate Christianity to modern culture, or interpret culture through the lens of Christianity. Articles that emphasize the role of/need for Christian community are particularly desirable. Urban issues, sociology, cultural trends, ecumenicisms, new perspectives/fresh ideas all welcome."

RELIGIOUS BROADCASTING, National Religious Broadcasters, 7839 Ashton Ave., Manassas VA 22109. (703)330-7000. Fax (703)330-6996. E-mail: ssmith@nrb.com. Website: http://www.nrb.com. Christine L. Pryor, assoc ed. Topics relate to Christian radio, television and satellite; promoting access excellence in religious broadcasting. Monthly (10X) mag, with online version; 84 pgs; circ 9,000. Subscription $24. 70% freelance. Complete ms/cover letter; fax/e-query OK. **PAYS 6 COPIES** ($75-150 for assigned) on publication for 1st or reprint rts. Articles 2,000-3,000 wds (30/yr). Responds in 2-5 wks. Seasonal 6 mos ahead. Accepts simultaneous submissions & reprints (tell when/where appeared). Prefers disk. Regular sidebars. Prefers NIV & KVJ. Free guidelines/theme list/copy. (Ads)

> **Columns/Departments:** Sarah E. Smith. Accepts 10/yr. Trade Talk or Media Focus (news items/events in religious broadcasting), 300 wds; Socially Speaking (social issues), 1,000 wds.
>
> **Special Needs:** Electronic media; education. All articles must relate in some way to broadcasting; radio, TV, programs on radio/TV.
>
> **Tips:** "Most open to feature articles relevant to religious broadcasters. Become acquainted with religious broadcasters in your area and note their struggles, concerns, and victories. Find out what they would like to know, research the topic, then write about it."

*RELIGIOUS EDUCATION**, 15600 Mulholland Dr., Los Angeles CA 90077. (310)476-9777. Fax (310)471-1278. University of Judaism. Dr. Hanan Alexander, ed-in-chief. Scholarly journal for professors of religious education of all faiths. Quarterly journal; 130-160 pgs; circ 2,000. Call for subscription/membership rate. 100% freelance. Complete ms/cover letter; phone/fax/e-query OK. **PAYS 3 COPIES** for all rts. Articles to 6,500 wds; book reviews, 250 wds. Responds in 8-12 wks. Requires disk. No sidebars. Guidelines; copy $3/9x12 SAE. (Ads)

> **Columns/Departments:** Insights from Scholarship; Insights from Practice; Forum (diverse points of view on topics of interest); and Critique (reviews of books, media and curricula).
>
> **Special Needs:** Spiritual, cultural & social issues; policy & practice; models & methods; traditions & trends; sacred texts, moral values, & character education, religious education, and educational theory.

+RIGHT ROAD, A Magazine for Encouragement**, 100 E. Main St., Easley SC 29640. (864)306-3005. Fax (864)306-0017. E-mail: RightRoad1@aol. com.

Right Road Ministry, Inc. Christi Morrison, ed. Seeks to provide inspiration, information and entertainment for the entire family from a Christian perspective. Bimonthly mag; 48 pgs; circ 1,000. Estab 1998. 100% freelance. Complete ms. Pays $5-150 on publication for one-time rts. Articles 850-2,000 wds (50/yr); children's (8-13/13-18) fiction (20/yr); book reviews 250 wds, $25. Responds in 8 wks. Seasonal 4 mos ahead. Accepts reprints (tell when/where appeared). Prefers e-mail submission (copied into message). Regular sidebars. Prefers NIV. Guidelines/theme list (also by e-mail); copy for 9x12 SAE/7 stamps. (No ads, but considering)

Fillers: Accepts 16-20/yr. Cartoons, games, jokes, prayers, quizzes, word puzzles, 25-50 wds. No payment.

Columns/Departments: Buys 200/yr. Family Fruits (parenting, marriage, finances), 250-500 wds; Singles Caf (singles issues), 250-500 wds; Kid's Corner (articles & games), 250-500 wds; and Devotions (daily meditation on scripture), 150-250 wds. Pays $25-50. Query.

Contest: Photography Contest, color photos by amateurs.

Tips: "We publish 365 devotions a year, so submissions in this area are always welcome. Best to contact us via e-mail submission and pitch your idea, then follow up with manuscript."

+**ROMANTIC TIMES, Hundreds of Fun & Creative Tips to Enrich Your Relationship**, 750 SE Maynard Rd. Ste. 108, Cary NC 27511. (919)462-0900. E-mail: romantc@aol.com. Website: Http://www.TheRomantic. com. Sterling Publications. Michael Webb, ed. For Christians and non-Christians who seek to constantly improve their relationship through more fun and romance; some practical advice on understanding your mate. Bimonthly newsletter; 12 pgs; circ 10,000. Subscription $15. 10% freelance. Complete ms or query by e-mail submission. **PAYS A SUBSCRIPTION.** for all rts. Articles 100-500 wds (20/yr). Responds in 1 wk. Seasonal 3 mos ahead. Accepts simultaneous submissions & reprints (tell when/where appeared). Prefers e-mail submission. Some sidebars. No guidelines; copy for 6x9 SAE/2 stamps. (Ads)

Tips: "Submit a first-hand account of a creative, romantic event. The more unique the better. Publication is Christian-based but not preachy or religious."

SACRED JOURNEY, The Journal of Fellowship in Prayer, 291 Witherspoon St., Princeton NJ 08542. (609)924-6863. Fax (609)924-6910. E-mail: via Website. Website: http://www.sacredjourney.org. Fellowship In Prayer, Inc. Rebecca Laird, ed. An interfaith spirituality journal. Bimonthly journal; 48 pgs; circ 10,000. Subscription $16. 100% freelance. Complete ms/cover letter; fax query OK. **PAYS IN COPIES & SUBSCRIPTION** for one-time & electronic rts. Articles to 1,500 wds (40/yr); book reviews 400 wds. Responds in 8 wks. Seasonal 4 mos ahead. Accepts simultaneous submissions & reprints (tell when/where appeared). Requires disk or e-mail submission. No sidebars. Guidelines; copy for 6x9 SAE/3 stamps. (No ads)

Poetry: Accepts 6-8/yr. Free-verse, haiku, light verse, traditional; 10-35 lines. Submit max 3 poems.

Columns/Departments: Buys 30/yr. A Transforming Experience (personal experience of spiritual significance); Pilgrimage (journey taken for spiritual growth of service); Spirituality and the Family; Spirituality and Aging; to 750 wds.

Special Needs: Meditation and service to others.

Tips: "Write well about your own spiritual experience and we'll consider it."

ST. ANTHONY MESSENGER, 1615 Republic St., Cincinnati OH 45210-1298. (513)241-5615. Fax (513)241-0399. E-mail: StAnthony@American Catholic.org. Website: http://www.AmericanCatholic.org. Norman Perry, O.F.M., ed. For Catholic adults and families. Monthly & online mag; 60 pgs; circ 345,000. Subscription $22. 40% freelance. Query; fax/e-query OK. Pays .15/wd on acceptance for 1st, reprint (right to reprint), & electronic rts. Articles 1,500-3,000 wds (45-50/yr); fiction 1,500-2,500 wds (12/yr); book reviews 500 wds, $25. Responds in 8 wks. Seasonal 6+ mos ahead. Kill fee. Some sidebars. Prefers NAB. Guidelines; copy for 9x12 SAE. (Ads)

Poetry: Susan Hines-Brigger. Buys 20/yr. Free verse, haiku, traditional; 3-25 lines; $2/line ($10 min.) Submit max 2 poems.

Fillers: Cartoons.

Special Needs: Fathership of God and Millennium preparation.

Tips: "Most open to articles, fiction, profiles, interviews of Catholic personalities, personal experiences and prayer. Writing must be professional, use Catholic terminology and vocabulary. Writing must be faithful to Catholic belief and teaching, life and experience."

** This periodical was #55 on the 1997 Top 50 Christian Publishers list (#40 in 1994).

ST. JOSEPH'S MESSENGER AND ADVOCATE OF THE BLIND, PO Box 288, Jersey City NJ 07303-0288. (201)798-4141. Catholic/Sisters of St. Joseph of Peace. Sister Mary Kuiken, CSJP, ed. For older Catholics interested in supporting ministry to the aged, young, blind, and needy. Semiannual mag; 16 pgs; circ 15,500. Subscription $5. 30% freelance. Complete ms. Pays $3-15 ($6-25 for fiction) on publication for 1st rts. Articles 500-1,000 wds (24/yr); fiction 1,000-1,500 wds (30/yr). Responds in 5 wks. Seasonal 3 mos ahead. Accepts simultaneous submissions & reprints. No sidebars. Guidelines; copy for 9x12 SAE/2 stamps.

Poetry: Buys 25/yr. Light verse, traditional; 4-40 lines; $5-20 on publication. Submit max 10 poems.

Fillers: Buys 20/yr. Ideas, 50-100 wds; $5-10.

Tips: "Most open to contemporary fiction."

ST. WILLIBRORD JOURNAL, Box 271751, Houston TX 77277-1751. (713)515-8206. Christ Catholic Church. Father Charles E. Harrison SWJ, ed. Strictly Catholic; concentrating on the unchurched. Quarterly journal; 40 pgs; circ 500. Subscription $8. 5% freelance. Complete ms/cover letter; no phone query. **NO PAYMENT** for one-time rts. Not copyrighted. Articles to 1,000 wds. Responds in 9 wks. Seasonal 6 mos ahead. Some sidebars. Any version. No guidelines; copy $2. (No ads)

Columns/Departments: Question Box; Q & A column on doctrinal and biblical questions.

Tips: "We will read anything if it is sincere and orthodox. Most open to what's happening in the Christian church: doctrinal changes, attitude adjustments, moral attitudes. Especially want essays. Keep it short. Spare us your personal opinions; and remember the virtue of the simple, declarative sentence."

SCP JOURNAL & NEWSLETTER, (Spiritual Counterfeits Project), PO Box 4308, Berkeley CA 94704-4308. (510)540-0300. Fax (510)540-1107. E-mail: scp@dnai.com. Website: http://www.scp-inc.org. Tal Brooke, ed. Christian apologetics for the college educated. Quarterly journal 55 pgs & newsletter; circ 18,000. Subscription $25. 5-10% freelance. Query/clips; phone query encouraged. Pays $20-35/typeset pg on publication for negotiable rts. Articles 2,500-3,500 wds (5/yr); book reviews 1,500 wds. Responds in 13 wks. Accepts simultaneous query & reprints. Requires disk or e-mail submission (attached file). Some sidebars. Guidelines (also by e-mail); copy $8.75. (No ads)

  Tips: "Must be an extremely good writer who is aware of the issues. Most of our writers come from the top 20 universities."

+SEEDS MAGAZINE, 602 James Ave., Waco TX 76706-1476. (817)755-7745. E-mail: SeedsHope@aol.com. Website: http://www.helwys.com/chliving. html. Seeds of Hope, Inc. L. Katherine Cook, ed. Committed to the healing of hunger and poverty in our world. Quarterly online mag Sprouts edition published 8X/yr. Subscription $20. Not in topical listings.

SEEK, 8121 Hamilton Ave., Cincinnati OH 45231. (513)931-4050x365. Standard Publishing. Eileen H. Wilmoth, ed. Light, inspirational, take-home reading for young and middle-aged adults. Weekly take-home paper; 8 pgs; circ 45,000. No subscriptions. 98% freelance. Complete ms/cover letter. Pays .05-.07/wd on acceptance for 1st or one-time rts, .035/wd for reprints. Articles 400-1,200 wds (150-200/yr); fiction 400-1,200 wds. No disk. Some sidebars. Responds in 13 wks. Seasonal 1 yr ahead. Accepts reprints (tell when/where appeared). Guidelines; copy for 6x9 SAE/2 stamps. (No ads)

  Fillers: Buys 50/yr. Ideas, jokes, short humor. Pays $15.

  ** This periodical was #54 on the 1998 Top 50 Christian Publishers list. (#56 in 1997, #49 in 1996, #57 in 1995, #36 in 1994)

THE SHANTYMAN, 2476 Argentia Rd., Ste. 213, Mississauga ON L5N 6M1 Canada. (905)821-6310. Fax (905)821-6311. E-mail: shanty@pathcom. com. Websites: http://www.netaccess.on.ca/fingertip, and http://www. cyberus.ca/gd/shantyman. Shantymen's Christian Assn. Phil Hood, mng ed. Distributed by their missionaries in remote areas of Canada and northern US as an evangelism tool. Bimonthly mini-tabloid; 16 pgs; circ 17,000. Subscription $6. 90% freelance. Complete ms/cover letter; no phone/fax query. Pays $20-50 CAN, on publication for one-time or reprint rts. Articles 800-1,600 wds (30/yr). Responds in 4-6 wks. Seasonal 6 mos ahead. Accepts reprints (tell when/where appeared). No disk. Some sidebars. Prefers NAS. Guidelines; copy for #10 SAE/2 stamps or IRCs.

  Columns/Departments: Accepts 6/yr. Way of Salvation (fresh look at gospel message), 300-400 wds.

  Tips: "We always have a need for salvation testimonies, first person (preferred) or as-told-to. We always have too many inspirational stories."

*SHARING, A Journal of Christian Healing, 6807 Forest Haven St., San Antonio TX 78240-3343. (210)681-5146. Fax (210)681-5146. Order of St. Luke the Physician. Marjorie George, ed. For Christians interested in spiritual and physical healing. Monthly journal; 32 pgs; circ 9,000. Subscription $12. 100% freelance. Complete ms/cover letter. **NO PAYMENT** for one-time or reprint rts. Articles 750-900 wds (50/yr). Responds in 3 wks. Seasonal 2 mos ahead. Accepts simultaneous submissions & reprints (tell when/where appeared). Prefers disk. Some kill fees. Some sidebars. Prefers RSV. Guidelines; copy for 8x10 SAE/2 stamps.

> **Poetry:** Accepts 10-12/yr. Free verse, traditional; 6-14 lines.
> **Tips:** "The entire magazine is open. We're looking for crisp, clear, well-written articles on the theology of healing and personal witness of healing. We do not return mss or poems, nor do we reply to inquiries regarding mss status."

SIGNS OF THE TIMES, Box 5353, Nampa ID 83653-5353. (208)465-2577. Fax (208)465-2531. E-mail: signs@pacificpress.com. Website: http://www.pacificpress.com. Seventh-day Adventist. Marvin Moore, ed. Biblical principles relevant to all of life; for general public. Monthly mag; 32 pgs; circ 245,000. Subscription $17.95. 40% freelance. Complete ms/no cover letter. Pays $100-400 (to .20/wd) on acceptance for 1st rts. Articles 500-2,000 wds (75/yr). Responds in 4-9 wks. Seasonal 8 mos ahead. Accepts reprints (tell when/where appeared). Prefers disk/hard copy. Kill fee 50%. Some sidebars. Guidelines (also by e-mail); copy for 9x12 SAE/3 stamps. (No ads)

> ** This periodical was #44 on the 1998 Top 50 Christian Publishers list. (#33 in 1997, #34 in 1996, #42 in 1995, #33 in 1994)

SILVER WINGS MAYFLOWER PULPIT, PO Box 1000, Pearblossom CA 93553. (805)264-3726. E-mail: poetwing@yahoo.com. Jackson Wilcox, ed. Christian understanding and uplift through poetry. Biweekly mag; 12 pgs; circ 200. Subscription $10. 50% freelance. Complete ms/cover letter; phone query OK. **PAYS 1 COPY** for 1st rts. Not copyrighted. Responds in 3 wks. Seasonal 4 mos ahead. Accepts simultaneous submissions & reprints (tell when/where appeared). No disk. No sidebars. Prefers KJV. Guidelines; copy $2/6x9 SAE/2 stamps. (No ads)

> **Poetry:** Accepts 200/yr. Free verse, haiku, light verse, traditional; 2-20 lines. Submit max 5 poems.
> **Contest:** Annual poetry contest; send SASE for details.

*SINGLE CONNECTION, PO Box 17519, Pittsburgh PA 15235. Phone/fax (412)856-1039. JoAnne McBriar, pub/ed. A resource and forum for single adults. Bimonthly newspaper; 12 pgs; circ 30,000. Subscription $12. Estab 1997. Complete ms. **NO PAYMENT.** Articles/fiction 600-800 wds (25/yr). Responds in 4-6 wks. Seasonal 4 mos ahead. Accepts simultaneous submissions & reprints (tell when/where appeared). Regular sidebars. Copy $3. (Ads)

> **Fillers:** Cartoons, facts, jokes, party ideas, quizzes, short humor, word puzzles.
> **Tips:** "Material used as space permits."

#SINGLE-PARENT FAMILY, 8605 Explorer Dr., Colorado Springs CO 80920. (719)548-4588. Fax (719)531-3499. Website: http://www.family.org. Focus on the Family. Dr. Lynda Hunter, ed. To encourage and equip single parents to do the best job they can at creating stable, godly homes for themselves and their children. Monthly mag; 24 pgs; circ. 36,000. Membership $15. 13% freelance. Query or complete ms. Pays .10-.15/wd. Articles 600-1,200 wds. (Ads)

SMART FAMILIES, Box 270616, San Diego CA 92198-2616. (619)487-7099. Fax (619)487-7356. E-mail: familyu@aol.com. Website: http://www.family university.com. Submit to The Editor. Christian parenting, with strong crossover to secular families. Quarterly newsletter; 16 pgs; circ 140,000. Subscription $24 (includes 2 tapes). Little freelance. Complete ms preferred; fax query OK. Pays $50-250 on publication for 1st rts. Articles 250-900 wds. Responds in 2-4 wks. Seasonal 4 mos ahead. Accepts simultaneous submissions. Prefers disk; accepts e-mail submission (attached file). Some sidebars. Prefers NIV. Guidelines (also by e-mail); copy for 10x13 SAE/4 stamps. (No ads)

> **Fillers:** Games, ideas, quotes.
>
> **Tips:** "We are not a magazine and have tight length requirements. Because of crossover audience, we do not regularly print Scripture references or use traditional God-word language."
>
> **Note:** Parent company having financial problems. Publication on hold.

SMILE, PO Box 5090, Brookfield CT 06804-5090. Joyce M. Johnson, ed. Poetry devoted to cheering up people. Quarterly mag; 32 pgs; circ 300. Subscription $12. 90% freelance. Complete ms/cover letter. **PAYS ONE COPY** for 1st or reprint rts. Not copyrighted. Articles 200 wds (essay or first-person reminiscences—8/yr.). Responds in 2 wks. Seasonal 2 mos ahead. Accepts reprints (tell when/where appeared). No disk or e-mail submission. No sidebars. Prefers NIV or NJB. Guidelines; copy $3.

> **Poetry:** Free verse, haiku, light verse, traditional (on Christian values); 3-24 lines; 40 characters wide maximum.
>
> **Fillers:** Accepts 18-20/yr. Anecdotes, cartoons, jokes, quotes (state source), short humor and word puzzles; 25-50 wds.
>
> **Contest:** You must be a subscriber to be eligible for poetry prizes awarded four times per year. Prizes of $15, $10 and $5. Send 3-32 cent stamps with submission.
>
> **Tips:** "We encourage new poets. We like light, humorous verse about facing the daily problems in life. Especially welcome older-aged poets and shut-ins, with their spiritual wisdom."

SOCIAL JUSTICE REVIEW, 3835 Westminster Pl., St. Louis MO 63108-3472. (314)371-1653. Catholic Central Union of America. Rev. John H. Miller, C.S.C., ed. For those interested in the social teaching of the Catholic Church. Bimonthly journal; 32 pgs; circ 4,750. Subscription $20. 90% freelance. Query or complete ms/cover letter. Pays .02/wd on publication for one-time rts. Not copyrighted. Articles to 3,000 wds (80/yr); book reviews 500 wds **(no pay)**. Responds in 1 wk. Seasonal 3 mos ahead. Accepts reprints (tell when/where appeared). No disk or e-mail submission. No sidebars. Guidelines; copy for 9x12 SAE/3 stamps. (No ads)

Columns/Departments: Virtue; Economic Justice; variable length. Query.

Tips: "Fidelity to papal teaching and clarity and simplicity of style; thoughtful and thought-provoking writing."

SOJOURNERS, 2401 15th St. NW, Washington DC 20009. (202)328-8842. Fax (202)328-8757. E-mail: sojourners@ari.net. Website: http://www.sojourners.com/sojourners/home.html. Jim Rice, mng ed. For those who seek to turn their lives toward the biblical vision of justice and peace. Bimonthly mag; 68 pgs; circ. 24,000. Subscription $30. 30% freelance. Query. Pays $75-200 on publication for variable rts (no reprints). Articles 600-3,600 wds (10/yr); book/music reviews, 650-1,300 wds, $50-100 (to Molly Marsh, asst ed). Responds in 6 wks. Seasonal 6 mos ahead. Kill fee. Prefers NRSV. Regular sidebars. Guidelines; copy for 9x12 SAE. (Ads)

Poetry: Rose Marie Berger. Accepts 6-10/yr. Free verse, haiku; $50.

Fillers: Accepts 6 cartoons/yr; also other unsolicited artwork and photographs.

Columns/Departments: Buys 15/yr. Culture Watch (reviews), 650-1,300 wds; Commentary (editorials), 650 wds; $50-75.

Tips: "Most open to features, Culture Watch reviews, and short pieces on groups working successfully in their communities to empower the poor, create jobs, and promote peace and reconciliation."

** 1997 EPA Award of Merit—General.

THE SOMETHING BETTER NEWS, 3300 28th St. SW #1, Grandville MI 49418-1423. (616)530-3957. Fax (616)530-0728. Something Better Publications, Inc. Jerry Fennell, ed. Christian Newspaper. Monthly newspaper; 16 pgs; circ 75,000. Subscription $20. 10% freelance. Query/clips; phone query OK. **NO PAYMENT** for 1st rts. Articles 500 wds (10-20/yr); book/music reviews 300 wds, music/video reviews 750-1,000 wds, $10. Responds in 4 wks. Seasonal 2 mos ahead. Accepts reprints (tell when/where appeared). Prefers disk. Regular sidebars. Prefers KJV. Guidelines/theme list; copy for 10x13 SAE/$1.50 postage. (Ads)

Columns/Departments: Accepts 10-20/yr. God & Money; Revival; Advice; all 1,000 wds. Query or complete ms.

Special Needs: Wants to expand their Christian entertainment section. Always looking for sports/recreation pieces.

Tips: "Most open to concert reviews and news stories."

+SOUTHERN CALIFORNIA CHRISTIAN TIMES, PO Box 2606, El Cajon CA 92021. (610)660-5500. Theresa Keener, ed. Monthly newspaper (in 7 editions). Free

+SPIRIT: THE CHRISTIAN WRITERS' SYMPOSIUM, PO Box 328, St. Eugene ON K0B 1P0 Canada. Providence Publishing. Bimonthly mag.

SPIRITUAL LIFE, 2131 Lincoln Rd. NE, Washington DC 20002-1199. (202)832-8489. Fax (202)832-8967. E-mail: edodonnell@aol.com. Website: http://www.spiritual-life.org. Catholic. Edward O'Donnell, O.C.D., ed. For college-educated Christians interested in spirituality. Quarterly mag; 64 pgs; circ 12,000. Subscription $15. 80% freelance. Complete ms/cover letter; phone/fax query OK. Pays $50-250 ($10/ms pg) on acceptance for 1st rts. Articles/essays 3,000-5,000 wds (20/yr); book reviews 1,500 wds, $15. Responds in 9 wks. Seasonal 9 mos ahead. Accepts simultaneous submissions. Requires disk. No sidebars. Prefers NAB. Guidelines; copy for 7x10 SAE/5 stamps.

Tips: "No stories of personal healing, conversion, miracles, etc."

SPORTS SPECTRUM and SPORTS SPECTRUM ONLINE, 3000 Kraft SE, Grand Rapids MI 49512. (616)974-2711. Fax (616)957-5741. E-mail: ssmag@sport.org. Website: http://www.sport.org. Discovery House Publishers. Dave Branon, mng ed. An evangelistic tool that sports fans can use to witness to non-Christian friends. Monthly (10X) mag (also online); 32 pgs; circ 50,000. Subscription $15.97. 65% freelance. Query/clips; fax/e-query OK. Pays .18/wd on acceptance for 1st & electronic rts. Not copyrighted. Articles 250-2,000 wds (70/yr). Responds in 3-4 wks. Accepts disk or e-mail submission. Kill fee 30-50%. Regular sidebars. Prefers NIV. Guidelines (also by e-mail); copy for 9x12 SAE/4 stamps. (No ads)

> **Columns/Departments:** Buys 30/yr. Leaderboard (Christian athletes serving others), 725 wds; Front Row (on the scene sports scenarios), 800-1,200 wds; Champions (lesser-known athletes), 250 wds. Pays .18/wd.
>
> **Tips:** "The best thing a writer can do is to be aware of the special niche Sports Spectrum has developed in sports ministry. Then, find athletes who fit that niche and who haven't been covered in the magazine."
>
> **This periodical was #69 on the 1994 Top 50 Christian Publishers list. 1996 EPA Award of Merit—General.

STANDARD, 6401 The Paseo, Kansas City MO 64131. (816)333-7000. Fax (816)333-4439. Website: http://www.nazarene.org. Nazarene. Rev. Everett Leadingham, ed. Examples of Christianity in everyday life for adults college-age through retirement. Weekly take-home paper; 8 pgs; circ 150,000. Subscription $8.95. 80% freelance. Complete ms. Pays .035/wd (.02/wd for reprints) on acceptance for 1st or reprint rts. Articles (20/yr) or fiction (200/yr) 800-1,200 wds. Responds in 8-12 wks. Seasonal 6 mos ahead. Accepts simultaneous submissions & reprints (tell when/where appeared). No disk. Kill fee. No sidebars. Prefers NIV. Guidelines/theme list/copy for #10 SAE/2 stamps.

> **Poetry:** Buys 100/yr. Free verse, haiku, traditional; to 25 lines; $5-12.50. Submit max 5 poems.
>
> **Fillers:** Buys 50/yr. Word puzzles; $20.
>
> **Tips:** "Fiction or true-experience stories must demonstrate Christianity in action. Show us, don't tell us. Action in stories must conform to Wesleyan-Armenian theology and practices."
>
> ** This periodical was #15 on the 1998 Top 50 Christian Publishers list. (#68 in 1997, #41 in 1996, #12 in 1995, #2 in 1994)

THE STANDARD, 2002 S. Arlington Hts. Rd., Arlington Hts. IL 60005. (847)228-0200. Fax (847)228-5376. E-mail: JodiLynnH@aol.com. Website: http://www.bgc.bethel.edu. Baptist General Conference. Jodi Hanning, mng ed. Denominational. Monthly (10X) mag; 32 pgs; circ. 9,300. Subscription $15.75. 60-70% freelance. Query or complete ms/no cover letter; e-query OK. Query for electronic submissions. Pays $15-200+ on publication for 1st & electronic rts. Articles 500-1,200 wds (20-30/yr). Responds in 6-8 wks. Seasonal 3 mos ahead. Accepts simultaneous submissions & reprints (tell when/where appeared). Kill fee 50%. Prefers disk or e-mail submission (copied into message). Kill fee 50%. Regular sidebars ($20). Prefers NIV. Guidelines/theme list (also by e-mail); copy for 9x12 SAE/4 stamps. (Ads)

Special Needs: Looking for reporters willing to work with editor on assignments about the Baptist General Conference. Open to denominational news, 30-150 words.

Tips: "When we use a general article, it has to be tailor-made to fit our themes."

** 1997 EPA Award of Merit—Denominational; 1995 & 1994 EPA Award of Excellence—Denominational.

#STAND FIRM, God's Challenge for Today's Man, 127 Ninth Ave. N., Nashville TN 37234-0140. (615)251-5955. Fax (615)251-5008. Website: http://www.bssb.com. Lifeway Press/Baptist Sunday School board. Valerie Hancock, copy ed. Addresses the unique and distinctive needs of men of the 90s. Monthly digest-size mag; 36 pgs; circ 60,000. Subscription $18.95. 25-30% freelance. Complete ms/cover letter or query; fax/e-query OK. Pays negotiable rates on acceptance for all (preferred), 1st, or electronic rts. Articles 50-400 wds; book/music/video reviews, 20-50 wds. Responds in 4-6 wks. Seasonal 6-8 mos ahead. Accepts simultaneous submissions & reprints (tell when/where appeared). Prefers disk. Regular sidebars. Prefers NIV. Guidelines/theme list; copy for 6x9 SAE/3 stamps. (No ads)

Tips: "Looking for feature articles for weekends; interviews with recognized Christian leaders, reviews of men's products/books/events, news/ideas/projects/activities for men, ministry news, and insights into sports, finances, and other topics of interest to men."

THE STAR OF ZION, 401 E. 2nd St., Charlotte NC 28231. (704)377-4329. Fax (704)377-2809. E-mail: starozion@juno.com. African Methodist Episcopal Zion Church. Dr. Marie P. Tann, assoc ed. Ethnic publication; moderate; conservative. Biweekly tabloid; 16-20 pgs; circ 8,000. Subscription $33. 90% freelance. Query; phone query OK. **PAYS 5 COPIES**. Articles & fiction to 600 wds. Responds in 9 wks. Seasonal 2 mos ahead. Accepts simultaneous submissions. No sidebars. Copy $1/10x14 SAE/2 stamps.

Poetry: African-American themes.

Fillers: Short humor.

*STEWARDSHIP, 32401 Industrial Dr., Madison Heights MI 48071. (248)585-7800. Fax (248)585-2193. Parish Publications, Inc. Richard Meurer, ed. To help church members understand stewardship. Monthly newsletter; 4 pgs. 50% freelance. Query or complete ms/cover letter; fax query OK. Pays $25-100 on publication for all rts. Articles 200-300 wds. Free copy.

+STUDIO CLASSROOM, 51 Wrangler Dr., Bozeman MT 59718. E-mail: ruth@imt.net. Overseas Radio & Television (a Christian ministry). Ruth Seamans Devli, sr ed. Used to teach English to the Chinese in Taiwan. Query or complete ms. Pays .25/wd on acceptance.

Fillers: Anecdotes, cartoons, quizzes, short humor, and word puzzles

Tips: "Most readers are not Christians, so articles shouldn't be religious (except material for the Christmas and Easter issues)."

*SURSUM CORDA! The Catholic Revival, PO Box 993, Ridgefield CT 06877. Fax (203)438-1305. E-mail: roger.mccaffrey@internetmci.com. Foundation for Catholic Reform. Roger McCaffrey, ed; submit to Tom Woods, mng ed. Covers the good things that happen in the Catholic Church; includes a 16-page homeschooling section. Quarterly mag; circ 16,000. Complete ms; fax query OK. Pays $150-500 on publication for one-time or reprint rts. Articles 2,000-5,000 wds (2/yr); religious fiction. Responds in 5-9 wks. Accepts simultaneous submissions & reprints. Free copy.

Tips: "Keep in mind that the theme of our magazine is the orthodox Catholic Revival. We are conservative."

TEAK ROUNDUP, #5 9060 Tronson Rd., Vernon BC V1H 1E7 Canada. (250)545-4186. Fax (250)545-4194. West Coast Paradise Publishing. Robert G. Anstey, ed. General, family-oriented poetry and prose. Quarterly mag; 52 pgs; circ. 200. Subscription $13 US, $17 CAN. Query; phone/fax query OK. **NO PAYMENT** for one-time rts. Articles (100/yr) & fiction to 1,000 wds; book reviews to 1,000 wds. Responds in 1 wk. Seasonal 2 mos ahead. Accepts reprints. Accepts disks. Regular sidebars. Prefers KJV. Guidelines; copy $3 US/$5 CAN/6x9 SAE/.90 CAN postage or $1.17 US. (Ads)

Poetry: Accepts 100/yr. Any type; to 40 lines. Submit max 5 poems.

Fillers: Anecdotes, cartoons, ideas, newsbreaks, party idea, prose, short humor. Also accepts line-art drawings.

Contest: For subscribers only.

Tips: Most open to poetry. Subscribers only are eligible for publication.

THIS ROCK, 7290 Engineer Rd. Ste. H, PO Box 17490, San Diego CA 92111. (619)541-1131. Fax (619)541-1154. E-mail: editor@catholic.com. Website: http://www.catholic.com. Catholic. Karl Keating, ed. Deals with doctrine, evangelization and apologetics. Monthly (11X) mag; 48 pgs; circ 12,000. Subscription $29.95. 70% freelance. Query. Pays $300 on publication for 1st rts. Articles 1,500-3,500 wds. Responds in 5-13 wks. Guidelines; copy $4.

TIME FOR RHYME, PO Box 1055, Battleford SK S0M 0E0 Canada. (306)445-5172. Family Books. Richard W. Unger, ed. Poetry only; not strictly Christian (but editor is). Quarterly mag; 32 pgs; circ less than 100. Subscription $12, US or CAN. 80% freelance. Complete ms/cover letter. **PAYS IN COPIES** for 1st rts. Seasonal 1 yr ahead. Accepts reprints (tell when/where appeared). Prefers KJV. Guidelines; copy $3.25 US or CAN. (Ads)

Poetry: Buys 60/yr; 2-32 lines. Rhyming only; light or serious. Submit max 5 poems. Not keen on holiday poems.

Tips: "Write experience, not philosophy; write so as to share that experience, appealing to as many senses as possible (making the reader feel he/she is really there); or write light verse (again in rhyme) if you have a good sense of humor."

TIME OF SINGING, A Magazine of Christian Poetry, PO Box 149, Conneaut Lake PA 16316. Fax(814)382-7159. E-mail: timesing@toolcity.

net. Lora Zill, mng ed. We try to appeal to all poets and lovers of poetry. Quarterly booklet; 44 pgs; circ 250. Subscription $15. 95% freelance. Complete ms/cover letter. **PAYS IN COPIES.** for 1st, one-time or reprint rts. Poetry only. Responds in 6-8 wks. Seasonal 6-8 mos ahead. Accepts simultaneous submissions & reprints (tell when/where appeared). Accepts e-mail submission (copied into message). Guidelines/theme list; copy $4. (No ads)

> **Poetry:** Buys 150-200/yr. Free verse, haiku, light verse, traditional forms; 3-50 lines. Submit max 5 poems.
>
> **Contest:** Sponsors 1-2 annual poetry contests on specific themes or forms ($2 entry fee/poem) with cash prizes (send SASE for rules).
>
> **Tips:** "Study poetry—read widely. Work at the craft. Editor will comment on work that is close to publication."

+TIMES OF REFRESHING, Box 6855, Fort St. John BC V1J 4J3 Canada. (250)785-7215. Daniel Yordy, ed. A deeper expression of the gospel for mature Christians. Monthly newsletter; 8 pgs; circ 60. Subscription $20 CAN, $18 US. Open to freelance. Complete ms. **PAYS A SUBSCRIPTION** for one-time rts. Articles 1,500-2,000 wds (3-4/yr). Prefers NKJV. Guidelines; copy for #10 SAE/1 stamp. (No ads)

> **Tips:** "We look for a fresh word from God for his church. Interested in pieces that point to a closer walk with God, based on the Scriptures."

TODAY'S CHRISTIAN SENIOR, 127 Webster Rd., Shelburne VT 05482. (802)985-5744. Fax (802)985-2811. E-mail: BryanBice@aol.com. Scepter Publication. Bryan Bice, ed. Geared to senior citizens in the areas of health, finances, ministry and travel. Quarterly mag; 16 pgs; circ 50,000. Free subscription. Estab 1996. 15% freelance. Complete ms/cover letter; e-query OK. Pays $150 on publication for 1st, one-time or simultaneous rts. Articles & fiction 900-1,000 wds. Responds in 4 wks. Seasonal 9 mos ahead. Accepts reprints (tell when/where appeared). Prefers disk. Regular sidebars. Prefers KJV. Guidelines/theme list; copy for 9x12 SAE/3stamps. (Ads)

> **Poetry:** Light verse, traditional. Pays $25. Submit max 3 poems.
>
> **Fillers:** Cartoons, jokes, quizzes, word puzzles; $10.

TOGETHER, 13241 Port Republic Rd., Grottoes VA 24441. (540)249-3900. Fax (540)249-3177. E-mail: Tgether@aol.com. Shalom Foundation, Inc. Melodie Davis, ed. An outreach magazine distributed by churches to attract the general public to Christian faith & life. Quarterly tabloid; 8 pgs; circ 150,000. Free. 90% freelance. Complete ms/cover letter; e-query OK. Pays $30-50 on publication for one-time rts. Articles 500-1,200 wds (16/yr). Responds in 12-16 wks. Seasonal 4 mos ahead. Accepts simultaneous submissions & reprints. Accepts disk or e-mail submission (copied into disk). Some sidebars. Prefers NIV. Guidelines/theme list (also by e-mail); copy for 9x12 SAE/4 stamps. (Ads)

+TOMORROW'S CHRISTIAN GRADUATE, PO Box 1357, Oak Park, IL 60304. (708)524-5070. Fax: (708) 524-5174. E-mail:kipland@juno.com. Website: http://www.christiangraduate.com. Kipland Publishing House/WINPress. Tonya Eichelberger, ed. Planning guide for adults pursuing a seminary or Christian graduate education. Annual mag; circ 150,000+. Free to prospective seminary or Christian graduate school students. 85% freelance. Prefers 1-page query; fax/e-query OK. Payment varies for all rts (usually). Articles 800-1,600 wds. Some sidebars. Guidelines/theme list; copy $3. (Ads)

Special Needs: First-person and how-to features that express the value of a seminary or Christian graduate education and focus on all topics of interest to adults pursuing graduate studies including: paying for graduate school, earning a degree at home, financial aid and scholarships, study tips, entrance requirements, Christian education for marketplace careers, spending time with God, selecting a school, interdisciplinary studies, applying for admission, time management, training for missions.

Tips: "We are open to working with new/unpublished authors, especially current graduate students, graduates, professors, admissions personnel, career counselors and financial aid officers. Visit our Website to view articles we've previously published."

*TOTAL HEALTH, 165 N. 100 E. Ste 2, St. George UT 84770-2505. Submit to Arpi Coliglow, asst ed. A family health magazine. Bimonthly mag; 70 pgs; circ 90,000. Subscription $16. 75% freelance. Query or complete ms. Pays $50-75 on publication for all and reprint rts. Articles 1,400-1,800 wds (48/yr). Responds in 4 wks. Seasonal 4 mos ahead. Accepts simultaneous submissions. Query or complete ms/cover letter. Regular sidebars. Requires disk (Mac). Guidelines; copy $1/9x12 SAE/5 stamps.

Columns/Departments: Contemporary Herbal, 1,000 wds, $50.

Tips: "Most open to self-help and prevention articles."

TOUCHSTONE, A Journal of Mere Christianity, PO Box 18109, Chicago IL 60618. (773)481-1090. Fax (773)481-1095. E-mail: touchstone@fsj.org. Website: http://www.fsj.org.   Fellowship of St. James. James Kushiner, ed. News and opinion devoted to a thoughtful appreciation of orthodox Christian faith. Bimonthly mag; 48 pgs; circ 1,800. 15% freelance. Query; fax/e-query OK. Pay $100/type-set pg on publication for one-time & electronic rts. Articles (6/yr) 3,000-6,000 wds; book/video reviews 2,000-3,000 wds. Responds in 4 wks. Seasonal 4 mos ahead. Accepts simultaneous submissions & reprints (tell when/where appeared). Prefers disk or e-mail submission (attached file). Regular sidebars. Prefers RSV or NIV. Guidelines; copy for 10x13 SAE/7 stamps. (Ads)

Fillers: Cartoons.

THE TRUMPETER, 6320 Sunset Dr., South Miami FL 33143-4823. (305)668-6462. Fax (305)668-3596. E-mail: info@thetrumpeter.com. Website: http://www.thetrumpeter.com. Non-denominational. Martiele Swanko, ed-in-chief. Unites all South Florida Christian denominations, ethnic groups, and cultures. Bimonthly & online mag; 60 pgs; circ 50,000. 100% freelance. Complete ms/cover letter; e-query OK. Features & sports, 900-1,000 wds; articles 700-1,500 wds; book/music reviews, 70 wds. **NO PAYMENT.** Accepts reprints (tell when/where appeared). Accepts disk or e-mail submission. Regular sidebars. Prefers NIV. Guidelines/theme list (on Website). (Ads)

Columns/Departments: Around town (local talk), 100-125 wds; Arts & Entertainment, 400 wds; Legal, 450 wds; Political/Viewpoint, 100-125 wds.

2-SOAR, PO Box 574, South Bend IN 46624. (219)289-8760. Church of God in Christ (Pentecost). Izola Bird, pub. Denominational. Quarterly newsletter; 8 pgs; circ 7,000. Subscription $15. 95% freelance. Complete ms/cover letter; no phone query. **PAYS IN COPIES** for one-time rts. Articles 4 pgs. Responds in 2 wks. Accepts reprints (tell when/where appeared). No disk. No sidebars. No guidelines; copy for #10 SAE/1 stamp. (Ads)

Poetry: Accepts 10/yr. Free verse, light verse, traditional, love, inspirational; to 21 lines. Submit max 4 poems.

Fillers: Newsbreaks.

Contest: Spring poetry contest; entry fee $10. Send SASE for details.

Tips: "All areas open to freelancers. We want to hear from African-American writers."

THE UNITED CHURCH OBSERVER, 478 Huron St., Toronto ON M5R 2R3 Canada. (416)960-8500. Fax (416)960-8477. E-mail: general@ucobserver. org. Website: http://www.ucobserver.org. United Church of Canada. Muriel Duncan, ed. Denominational news. Monthly (11X) mag; 60 pgs; circ 120,000. Subscription $20. 20% freelance. Query/clips or complete ms/cover letter; fax/e-query OK. Pays negotiable rates on publication for 1st rts. Articles to 1,200 wds (8/yr); juvenile fiction (6-12 yrs), query; book reviews (all assigned), $50. Responds in 12 wks. Seasonal 3-4 mos ahead. Kill fee 1%. Some sidebars. Guidelines; copy $1. (Ads)

Fillers: Buys 24 cartoons/yr; $25.

Columns/Departments: Buys 40-50/yr. Faith; Living; World; Ministry; Front Page (church-related opinion piece), 800 wds. Pays $200.

*UPLOOK MAGAZINE, PO Box 2041, Grand Rapids MI 49501-2041. E-mail: editor@uplook.org. Website: http://www.gospelcom.net/uplook/home.html. Uplook Ministries. Print and online magazine. Submit to e-mail submission address. Not in topical listings.

Columns/Departments: Accepts material for Frontlines or What's Going On columns.

UPSCALE MAGAZINE, The Successful Black Magazine, 600 Bronner Brothers Way SW, Atlanta GA 30310. (404)758-7467. Fax (404)755-9892. Upscale Communications, Inc. Sheila Bronner, ed-in-chief; submit to Paula M. White, assoc ed. To inspire, inform, and entertain African-Americans. Monthly mag; circ 242,000. 75-80% freelance. Query. Pays $150 & up for all rts. Articles (135/yr); novel excerpts. Seasonal 4 mos ahead. Accepts simultaneous submissions. Kill fee 25%. Guidelines; copy $2.

Columns/Departments: Lee Bliss. Buys 50/yr. Positively You, Viewpoint, Perspective (personal inspiration/perspective). Query. Pays $75. These columns most open to freelance.

Tips: "We are open to queries for exciting and informative nonfiction." Uses inspirational and religious articles.

UPSOUTH, PO Box 20133, Bowling Green KY 42102-6133. (502)843-8018. E-mail: galen.smith@BGAmug.org. Christian. Galen Smith, ed. By freelance poets and writers interested in spiritual and Southern life and issues. Quarterly newsletter; 12-16 pgs; circ 75. Subscription $8. 98% freelance. Query; e-query OK. **PAYS FREE COPY** for one-time rts. Articles & fiction to 500 wds; book/music/video reviews to 500 wds. Responds in 2-8 wks. Accepts simultaneous submissions & reprints. No disk or e-mail submission. No sidebars. Guidelines; copy $2/#10 SAE/1 stamp. (No ads)

> **Poetry:** Any type, to 25 lines. Submit max 3 poems.
>
> **Tips:** "Prefer short, concise pieces that are crisp, interesting and uplifting. Writing about the South should be culture-centered. Most open to good poetry—spiritual, inspirational and uplifting poems that can move a reader."

U.S. CATHOLIC, 205 W. Monroe St., Chicago IL 60606. (312)236-7782. Fax (312)236-8207. E-mail: editors@uscatholic.org. Website: http://www.uscatholic.org. The Claretians. Tom McGrath, exec ed.; Meinrad Schrer-Emunds, mng ed. Devoted to starting and continuing a dialogue with Catholics of diverse lifestyles and opinions about the way they live their faith. Monthly mag; 52 pgs; circ 40,000. Subscription $22. 95% freelance. Complete ms/cover letter; phone/fax/e-query OK. Pays $250-600 (fiction $300-400) on acceptance for all rts. Articles 2,500-4,000 wds; fiction 2,500-3,500 wds. Responds in 5 wks. Seasonal 6 mos ahead. Accepts disk or e-mail submission. Regular sidebars. Guidelines; free copy. (Ads - Dianne Wade, 312-236-7782x474)

> **Poetry:** Maureen Abood (312-236-7782x515). Buys poetry. Pays $100.
>
> **Columns/Departments:** (See guidelines first.) Sounding Board, 1,100-1,300 wds, $250; Gray Matter and A Modest Proposal, 1,100-1,800 wds, $250; Practicing Catholic, 750 wds, $150.
>
> **Tips:** "All articles (except for fiction or poetry) should have an explicit religious dimension that enables readers to see the interaction between their faith and the issue at hand. Fiction should be well-written, creative, with solid character development."

VIBRANT LIFE, 55 W. Oak Ridge Dr., Hagerstown MD 21740-7390. (301)393-4019. Fax (301)393-4055. E-mail: vleditor@rhpa.org. Website: http://www.rhpa.org/vibrantlife/index.html. Seventh-day Adventist/Review & Herald. Larry Becker, ed. Total health publication (physical, mental and spiritual); plus articles on family and marriage improvement; ages 30-50. Bimonthly mag; 48+ pgs; circ 40,000. Subscription $11.97. 80% freelance. Query/clips; fax/e-query OK. Pays $75-300 on acceptance for 1st, simultaneous or electronic rts. Not copyrighted. Articles 500-1,700 wds (35-40/yr). Responds in 2-4 wks. Seasonal 7 mos ahead. Accepts simultaneous submissions & reprints (tell when/where appeared). Accepts disk or e-mail submission (attached file). Kill fee 25-50%. Regular sidebars. Prefers NIV. Guidelines; copy $1/9x12 SAE. (Ads)

> **Columns/Departments:** Buys 6/yr. Fit People (people whose lives are changed for the better when applying timeless health principles/before & after photos), 500 wds; $100-150.

Tips: "Writers need to be practical, supply well-documented material, not be preachy. Sidebars help."
** This periodical was #48 on the 1998 Top 50 Christian Publishers List (#57 in 1997, #22 in 1996).

THE VISION, 8855 Dunn Rd., Hazelwood MO 63042-2299. (314)837-7300. Fax (314)837-4503. E-mail: WAPeditor@aol.com. Website: http://www.upci.org. United Pentecostal Church. Richard M. Davis, ed. Denominational. Weekly take-home paper; 4 pgs; circ 10,000. Subscription $4.40. 95% freelance. Complete ms/cover letter. Pays $18-25 on publication for 1st rts. Articles 1,200-1,600 wds (to 120/yr); fiction 1,200-1,600 wds (to 120/yr). Seasonal 9 months ahead. Accepts simultaneous submissions & reprints. Guidelines; free copy.

   Poetry: Buys 30/yr. Pays $3-12.

   Tips: "Most open to good stories and articles for a traditional, fundamental, conservative church." Accepts material primarily from members of the denomination.

+VISIONS OF GLORY, E-mail: editor@vog.org. Website: Http://www.visionsofgloryorg/guide.htm. Online mag. Submit by e-mail submission. Complete ms. **NO PAYMENT.** Articles to 1,000 wds. Guidelines on Website. Not included in topical listings.

   Tips: "Try to keep the focus of the article on one small moment or event in your life, or the life of someone close to you, which revealed part of the glorious nature of our Lord; His faithfulness, His mercy, His grace, His provision, etc."

WAR CRY, 615 Slaters Ln., Alexandria VA 22314. (703)684-5500. Fax (703)584-5539. E-mail: Warcry@USN.salvationarmy.org. Website: http://publications.salvationarmyusa.org. The Salvation Army. Lt. Col. Marlene Chase, ed-in-chief; Jeff McDonald, mng ed. Pluralistic readership reaching all socioeconomic strata and including distribution in institutions. Biweekly mag; 24 pgs; circ 500,000. Subscription $7.50. 20% freelance. Complete ms/brief cover letter; no phone/fax/e-query. Pays .15-.20/wd (.12-.15/wd for reprints) on acceptance for one-time or reprint rts. Articles & fiction 1,200-1,500 wds (58/yr). Responds in 4 wks. Seasonal 1 yr ahead. Accepts simultaneous submissions & reprints (tell when/where appeared). Requires disk or e-mail submission (attached file). Regular sidebars. Prefers NIV. Guidelines/theme list (also on Website); copy for 9x12 SAE/3 stamps. (No ads)

   Poetry: Buys 10-20/yr. Free verse, traditional; to 16 lines. Inspirational only. Pays by the word. Submit max 5 poems.

   Fillers: Buys 10-20/yr. Anecdotes (inspirational), 200-500 wds. Pays .15-.20/wd.

   Tips: "We are soliciting more short fiction, inspirational articles and poetry, interviews with Christian athletes, evangelical leaders and celebrities, and theme-focused articles. Always looking for theologically sound coverage of essential Christian doctrine and how it applies to daily living. Also short contemporary articles (400 wds) with an evangelical message."

** This periodical was #19 on the 1998 Top 50 Christian Publishers List. (#25 in 1997, #6 in 1996, #70 in 1994)

THE WAY OF ST. FRANCIS, 1500 34th Ave., Oakland CA 94601-3092. (916)443-5717. Fax (916)443-2019. E-mail: ofmcaway@att.net. Website: http://www.sbfranciscans.org. Franciscan Friars of California/Catholic. Camille Franicevich, ed. For those interested in the message of St. Francis of Assisi as lived out by contemporary people. Bimonthly mag; 48 pgs; circ 5,000. Subscription $12. 15% freelance. Complete ms/cover letter; no phone/fax/e-query. Pays $25-100 on publication for 1st rts. Articles 500-1,500 wds (4-6/yr). Responds in 6 wks. Seasonal 6 mos ahead. Accepts simultaneous submissions & reprints (tell when/where appeared). Prefers disk or e-mail submission. Regular sidebars. Any version. Guidelines/theme list (also by e-mail); copy for 6x9 SAE/6 stamps. (No ads)

> **Fillers:** Anecdotes, cartoons, facts, prayers, prose; to 100 wds. Pays $25-50.
>
> **Columns/Departments:** Buys 12/yr. First Person (opinion/issue), to 900 wds; Portrait (interview or personality), to 1,200 wds; Inspirations (spiritual), to 1,200 wds. Pays $25-50.
>
> **Tips:** "Most open to columns. Make direct connection to St. Francis St. Clare, or a recognizable aspect of their life and vision."

WEAVINGS, 1908 Grand Ave., PO Box 189, Nashville TN 37202-0189. (615)340-7254. Fax (615)340-7006. E-mail: weavings@upperroom.org. Website: http://www.upperroom.org. The Upper Room. John S. Mogabgab, ed.; submit to Kathleen Stephens, assoc ed. A thoughtful, thematic focus on the Christian spiritual life. Bimonthly journal; 48 pgs; circ. 40,000. Subscription $24. 75% freelance. Complete ms/cover letter; e-query OK. Pays .12 & up/wd on publication for all, one-time or reprint rts. Articles 1,250-2,500 wds (2/yr); fiction (6/yr) 2,000 wds (vignettes 500 wds); book reviews 750 wds (most open to). Responds in 8 wks. Seasonal 9 mos ahead. Accepts reprints (tell when/where appeared). Accept disk or e-mail submission (copied into message). Kill fee. No sidebars. Prefers NRSV. Guidelines/theme list (also by e-mail/Website); copy for 7x10 SAE/5stamps. (No ads)

> **Poetry:** Buys 1/yr. Free verse, light verse, traditional. Must have a spiritual focus; $75 & up.

WESLEYAN ADVOCATE, Box 50434, Indianapolis IN 46250-0434. (317)576-8156. Fax (317)842-1649. E-mail: communications@wesleyan.org. The Wesleyan Publishing House. Jerry Brecheisen, mng ed. A full salvation family mag; denominational. Monthly mag; 36 pgs; circ 20,000. Subscription $15. 50% freelance. Complete ms/cover letter; phone query OK. Pays $10-40 for assigned, $5-25 for unsolicited, .01-.02/wd for reprints on publication for 1st or simultaneous rts. Not copyrighted. Articles 250-650 wds (50/yr). Responds in 2 wks. Seasonal 6 mos ahead. Accepts simultaneous submissions & reprints. Guidelines; copy $2. (Ads)

> **Poetry:** Buys 30/yr. Free verse or traditional; 10-15 lines; $5-10. Send max 6 poems.
>
> **Fillers:** Prose, 100-300 wds. Pays $2-6.

Columns/Departments: Personal Experiences, 700 wds; Ministry Tips, 600 wds; $10.

*WHO CARES, 1511 K St. NW #412, Washington DC 20005. (202)628-1691. Fax (202)628-2063. Who Cares, Inc. Samantha Stainburn, mng ed. A business magazine for people who do good works (secular). Bimonthly mag; 48 pgs; circ 50,000. Subscription free. 80-100% freelance. Query/clips; fax query OK. Pays .10/wd on publication for first, reprint & electronic rts. Articles 700-3,000 wds (many/yr). Responds in 8 wks. Seasonal 3-4 mos ahead. Accepts reprints (tell when/where appeared). Prefers disk. Kill fee 25%. Regular sidebars. Guidelines; copy for 9x12 SAE/5 stamps.

Columns/Departments: Tool box, 700-1,200 wds; Civil Society, 700-1,200 wds. Pays $70-120. See guidelines for details.

Special Needs: May/June Legacy issue: The history of service.

Tips: "We have an ongoing need for writers who can discuss religion as an impetus for community service with a secular audience. We also seek case studies of churches and church leaders who take innovative approaches to service."

*THE WICHITA CHRONICLE, PO Box 781079, Wichita KS 67278. Karen McBride, ed.

CHILDREN'S MARKETS

*BEGINNER'S FRIEND, PO Box 4060, Overland Park KS 66204. (913)432-0331. Fax (913)722-0351. Church of God (holiness)/Herald and Banner Press. Arlene McGehee, Sunday school ed. Denominational; for young children. Weekly take-home paper; 4 pgs; circ 2,700. Subscription $1.30. Complete ms/cover letter; phone/fax query OK. Pays .005/wd on publication for 1st rts. Fiction 500-800 wds. Seasonal 6-8 mos ahead. Accepts simultaneous submissions & reprints (tell when/where appeared). Prefers KJV. Guidelines/theme list; copy. Not in topical listings.

BREAD FOR GOD'S CHILDREN, Box 1017, Arcadia FL 34265-1017. (941)494-6214. Fax (941)993-0154. E-mail: bread@desoto.net. Bread Ministries, Inc. Judith M. Gibbs, ed. A family magazine for serious Christians who are concerned about their children or grandchildren (ages 6-18). Monthly (8X) mag; 32 pgs; circ 10,000. Free subscription. 20-25% freelance. Complete ms. Pays $20-30 ($30-50 for fiction) on publication for 1st or one-time rts. Not copyrighted. Articles 600-800 wds (6/yr); fiction & true stories 600-900 wds for 4-10 yrs, 900-1,500 wds for teens (15/yr). Responds in 8-12 wks (may hold longer). Some simultaneous submissions & reprints (tell when/where appeared). Some sidebars. Prefers KJV. Guidelines; 3 copies for 9x12 SAE/5 stamps; 1 copy 3 stamps.

Columns/Departments: Buys 5-8/yr. Let's chat (discussion issues facing children), 500-800 wds; Teen Page (teen issues), 600-900 wds; and Idea Page (object lessons or crafts for children), 300-800 wds.. Pays $10-30.

Tips: "Most open to fiction. Stories should teach Christian values and lifestyle without preaching. No tag endings or adult solutions coming from children. Create realistic characters and situations. No 'sudden inspiration' solutions."

CLUB CONNECTION, 1445 Boonville Ave., Springfield MO 65802-1894. (417)862-2781. Fax (417)862-0503. E-mail: mettes@ag.org. Kerry Clarensau, ed. For girls grades 4-8 (with leader edition for Missionettes leaders). Estab 1997. Quarterly mag; 32 pgs; circ 18,000-20,000. Subscription $6.50 (leader's $7.50). 30-40% freelance. Complete ms/cover letter. Pays $10-50 on publication for 1st or one-time rts. Articles 500 wds (4-6/yr). Responds in 10 wks. Seasonal 10-12 mos ahead. Accepts simultaneous submissions & reprints (tell when/where appeared). Accepts disk. Kill fee. Regular sidebars. Prefers NIV. Guidelines/theme list; copy for 9x12 SAE/3 stamps.

> **Poetry:** Buys 1-2 /yr. Light verse; 4-20 lines; $5-10. Submit max 2 poems.
>
> **Fillers:** Buys 6-8/yr. Anecdotes, cartoons, facts, games, ideas, jokes, newsbreaks, party ideas, quizzes, short humor, word puzzles; 20-50 or 100 wds; $5-20.
>
> **Columns/Departments:** Buys 4-6/yr. Pays $10-50.
>
> **Tips:** "Articles with a Christian slant of interest to girls."

*CLUBHOUSE, c/o Your Story Hour, Box 15, Berrien Springs MI 49103. (616)471-3701. Fax (616)471-4661. Non-denominational. Krista Phillips, ed. To help young people (9-14) feel good about themselves. Monthly newsletter; 4 pgs; circ 8,000. Subscription $5. 75% freelance. Complete ms. Pays $12-35 on acceptance for one-time rts. Articles 25-1,200 wds (150/yr); fiction 100-1,200 wds (30/yr). Responds in 4-5 wks. Seasonal 6 mos ahead. Accepts simultaneous submissions & reprints. No disk. Guidelines; copy for 5x7 SAE/2 stamps.

> **Poetry:** Buys 60/yr. Free verse, light verse, traditional; to 12 lines; $12. Submit max 3 poems.
>
> **Fillers:** Buys 60/yr. Anecdotes, cartoons, games, jokes, word puzzles; 50-100 wds; $12.
>
> **Tips:** "Send all material once a year in March."
>
> ** This periodical was #50 on the 1996 Top 50 Christian Publishers List.

COUNSELOR, 4050 Lee Vance View, Colorado Springs CO 80918. (719)536-0100. Fax (719)533-3044. Cook Communications Ministries. Janice K. Burton, ed. Presents the way spiritual truths in the weekly lesson can be worked out in everyday life—a correlated teaching tool for 8-12 yr olds. Weekly take-home paper; 4 pgs. Subscription $11.50. 50% freelance. Complete ms/cover letter; no phone/fax query. Pays .10/wd on acceptance for all, 1st, one-time, or reprint rts. Articles 300 wds (12/yr); fiction/true stories 800-850 wds (12/yr). Responds in 6-8 wks. Seasonal 1 yr ahead. Accepts simultaneous submissions & reprints (tell when/where appeared). Prefers hard copy or e-mail submission (attached file). No sidebars. Prefers KJV. Guidelines/theme list; copy for #10 SAE/1 stamp.

> **Fillers:** Buys 10-12/yr. Cartoons, puzzles, quizzes, fun activities; 100-150 wds. Pays $7-25.
>
> **Columns/Departments:** Buys 12/yr. God's Wonders (science

themes); Around the World (missions story from child's perspective); 800-850 wds.

Tips: "A writer can best break into our publication by submitting manuscripts that are well-written and proofread, and conform to our word count. Should have a feel for the age level. Know your readers and what is appropriate in terms of concepts and vocabulary. Submit only best quality manuscripts. All must have a Christian emphasis." Uses ethnic short stories. Include Social Security number.

** This periodical was #65 on the 1998 Top 50 Christian Publishers List. (#61 in 1996, #67 in 1994). 1995 EPA Award of Merit & 1984 EPA Award of Excellence—Sunday School Take-Home.

*COURAGE, 1300 N. Meacham Rd., Schaumburg IL 60173-4888. (847)843-1600. Fax (847)843-3757. Regular Baptist Press. Joan Alexander, ed. For children, 9-12, in Sunday school. Weekly take-home paper. Note: This periodical is being redesigned as we go to press. Send for new guidelines before submitting.

CRUSADER, 1333 Alger SE, Grand Rapids MI 49507. (616)241-5616. Fax (616)241-5558. Website: http://www.gospelcom.net/Cadets. Calvinist Cadet Corp. G. Richard Broene, ed. To show cadets and their friends, boys 9-14, how God is at work in their lives and in the world around them. Mag published 7X/yr; 24 pgs; circ 14,000. Subscription $9.50. 35% freelance. Complete ms/cover letter. Pays .02-.05/wd on acceptance for 1st, one-time, or reprint rts. Articles 500-1,000 wds (7/yr); fiction 900-1,500 wds (14/yr). Responds in 4 wks. Seasonal 9 mos ahead. Accepts simultaneous submissions & reprints (tell when/where appeared). No disk. Regular sidebars. Prefers NIV. Guidelines/theme list; copy for 9x12 SAE/4 stamps. (Ads)

Fillers: Buys 12-18/yr. Cartoons, quizzes, word puzzles; 20-200 wds; $5 & up.

Tips: "Fiction tied to themes or fillers; request new theme list in February of each year. Also looking for simple projects/crafts, and puzzles (word, logic)."

** 1995 EPA Award of Merit—Youth.

DISCOVERIES, 6401 The Paseo, Kansas City MO 64131. (816)333-7000. Fax (816)333-4439. Website: http://www.nazarene.org. Nazarene/Word Action Publishing. Kathleen Johnson, asst ed. For 8-10 yr olds, emphasizing Christian values and holy living; follows theme of Sunday school curriculum. Weekly take-home paper; 4 pgs; circ 30,000. 75% freelance. Complete ms/cover letter; fax query OK. Pays .05/wd on publication for multi-use rts. Articles (10/yr) & fiction (30/yr), to 500 wds. Responds in 6 wks. Seasonal 1 yr ahead. Accepts simultaneous submissions & reprints (tell when/where appeared). No disk; accepts e-mail submission. Regular sidebars. Prefers NIV. Guidelines/theme list/copy for #10 SAE/2 stamps. (No ads)

Fillers: Buys 60/yr. Cartoons, facts, word puzzles, 75-200 wds. Pays $10-15.

Columns/Departments: Buys 30/yr. Complete ms. Pays $10-15.

Tips: "Follow guidelines and theme list. Most open to nonfiction and fiction."

DISCOVERY (NY), 475 Riverside Dr., Rm. 455, New York NY 10115. (212)870-3335. Fax (212)870-3229. E-mail: order@jmsblind.org. Website: http://www.jmsblind.org. The John Milton Society for the Blind. Ingrid Peck, asst ed. For blind children ages 8-18, in Braille; reprints articles from Christian and other magazines for youth. Quarterly mag; 44 pgs; circ 2,040. Free subscription. 5% freelance. Complete ms/cover letter; phone query OK. **NO PAYMENT** for reprint rts. Not copyrighted. Articles 500-1,500 wds (1/yr); fiction 500-1,500 wds (1/yr). Responds in 6 wks. Seasonal 9-12 mos ahead. Accepts simultaneous submissions & reprints (tell when/where appeared). Accepts disk. No sidebars. Guidelines (also on Website); free copy.

> **Poetry:** Accepts 1/yr. Any type; 5-30 lines.
>
> **Fillers:** Anecdotes, games, ideas, jokes, quizzes, prayers, quotes, short humor, word puzzles; 10-150 wds.
>
> **Tips:** "Most open to poems, prayers and personal inspirational pieces about more timeless themes: Christian holidays, overcoming challenges like visual impairment, prejudice, love, forgiveness, etc. If writing about blindness, don't be patronizing. Send complete manuscripts requiring little or no editing. Look at the magazines we typically reprint from (see guidelines)."

DISCOVERY TRAILS, (formerly Junior Trails) 1445 Boonville Ave., Springfield MO 65802-1894. (417)862-2781. Fax (417)862-6059. E-mail: discoverytrails@ag.org. Assemblies of God. Sinda S. Zinn, ed. Teaching of Christian principles through fiction stories about children (10-12 yrs). Weekly take-home paper; 4 pgs; circ 35,000. Subscription $9.60. 98% freelance. Complete ms/no cover letter. Pays .07-.10/wd on acceptance for one-time rts. Articles 200-300 wds (50/yr); fiction 700-1,000 wds (50/yr). Responds in 2-4 wks. Seasonal 18-24 mos ahead. Accepts simultaneous submissions & reprints. No disk; accepts e-mail submission (copied into message). No sidebars. Prefers NIV. Guidelines/theme list (also by e-mail); copy for #10 SAE/1 stamp.

> **Poetry:** Buys 6-8/yr. Free verse, haiku, light verse, traditional; $5 & up. Submit max 3 poems.
>
> **Fillers:** Buys 8-10/yr. Facts, short humor; 200-300 wds; .07-.10/wd.
>
> **Tips:** "Most open to fiction stories, especially mystery with a spiritual emphasis. We are featuring short, punchy items of interest to 9-12 year olds. Including a spiritual emphasis in them is a plus."
>
> ** This periodical was #33 on the 1998 Top 50 Christian Publishers list. (#36 in 1997, #17 in 1996, #23 in 1995)

+THE FLICKER MAGAZINE, PO Box 660554, Birmingham AL 35266-0544. Ann Dorer, assoc ed. Based on Christian values and principles; encourages balanced growth in all areas of life: physical, mental, spiritual, social and emotional; for 10-12 year olds. Bimonthly mag. Complete ms. Pays .10/wd on acceptance. Articles to 500 wds; fiction 800-850 wds. Guidelines/theme list.

> **Poetry:** Short, $25.
>
> **Fillers:** Jokes, $10, word puzzles, $50.
>
> **Note:** Not reviewing manuscripts until April 1999.

FOCUS ON THE FAMILY CLUBHOUSE, 8605 Explorer Dr., Colorado Springs CO 80920. (719)531-3400. Fax (719)531-3499. Website: http://www.family.org. Focus on the Family. Jesse Florea, ed. For children 8-12 yrs in Christian homes. Monthly mag; 24 pgs; circ 100,000. Subscription $15. 40% freelance. Complete ms/cover letter; fax query OK. Pays $25-250 (.10-.25/wd) for articles, $200 & up for fiction on acceptance for 1st rts. Articles 600-800 wds (5/yr); fiction 1,200-1,600 wds (30/yr). Responds in 4-6 wks. Seasonal 6 mos ahead. No disk. Kill fee. Regular sidebars. Prefers NIV. Guidelines; copy for $1/9x12 SAE. (Ads)

> **Fillers:** Buys 10/yr. Games, party ideas, quizzes, word puzzles; 150-500 wds; $35-150.
>
> **Tips:** "Biggest need is for historical fiction. Send mss with list of credentials. Read past issues."
>
> ** This periodical was #21 on the 1998 Top 50 Christian Publishers list. (#2 in 1997, #62 in 1996, #38 in 1995, #15 in 1994) Also 1997 & 1995 EPA Award of Merit—Youth.

#FOCUS ON THE FAMILY CLUBHOUSE JR., 8605 Explorer Dr., Colorado Springs CO 80920. (719)548-4595. Fax (719)531-3499. Website: http://www.family.org. Focus on the Family. Jesse Florea, ed. For ages 4-8 yrs. Monthly mag; 16 pgs; circ 75,000. Subscription $12. 25% freelance. Complete ms/cover letter; fax query OK. Pays $100 ($100-200 for fiction) on acceptance for 1st rts. Articles 300-750 wds (1-2/yr); fiction 300-1,000 wds (10/yr). Responds in 4 wks. Seasonal 5-6 mos ahead. Kill fee. No sidebars. Guidelines; copy for 9x12 SAE/2 stamps. (Ads)

> **Poetry:** Buys 3/yr. Free verse, light verse, traditional; 10-25 lines; $25-100.
>
> **Fillers:** Buys 1-2/yr. Cartoons, games, word puzzles; $15-30.
>
> **Special Needs:** Bible stories.
>
> **Tips:** "Most open to short, non-preachy fiction, beginning reader stories, and read-to-me."
>
> ** This periodical was #60 on the 1998 Top 50 Christian Publishers list. (#52 in 1997, #53 in 1996 & 1995, #15 in 1994) 1996 EPA Award of Excellence—Youth.

GOD'S WORLD NEWS (formerly God's World Today/It's God's World), PO Box 2330, Asheville NC 28802. (828)253-8063. Fax (828)253-1556. E-mail: nbomer@gwpub.com. God's World Publications. Norman W. Bomer, sr ed. Current events, published in 5 editions, for kindergarten through jr. high students, mostly in Christian and home schools. Weekly mag (during school yr); 8 pgs; circ 301,000. Subscription $19.95. 16% freelance. Complete ms/cover letter. Pays $100 on acceptance for one-time rts. Articles 700-900 wds. Responds in 9 wks. Accepts reprints (tell when/where appeared). Accepts disk or e-mail submission (attached file). Some sidebars. Guidelines; free copy. (Ads)

> **Tips:** "Keep vocabulary simple. Must present a distinctly Christian world view without being moralistic."

GOOD NEWS FOR CHILDREN, 330 Progress Rd., Dayton OH 45449. (937)847-5900. Fax (937)847-5910. E-mail: pliservice@aol.com. Website:

http://www.pflaum.com. Catholic. Joan Mitchell CSJ, ed. For 2nd & 3rd graders. Weekly (32X) take-home paper; 4 pgs. Not in topical listings.

GUIDE, 55 W. Oak Ridge Dr., Hagerstown MD 21740. (301)791-7000. Fax (301)790-9734. E-mail: Guide@chpa.org. Website: http://www.guide magazine.org. Seventh-day Adventist/Review and Herald Publishing. Tim Lale, ed.; Randy Fishell, assoc ed. A Christian journal for 10-14 yr olds, presenting true stories relevant to their needs. Weekly take-home paper; 32 pgs; circ 32,000. Subscription $39.97/yr. 100% freelance. Complete ms/cover letter; fax/e-query OK. Pays .08-.12/wd on acceptance for one-time, reprint, or electronic rts. True stories 500-1,000 wds (200/yr). Responds in 6-8 wks. Seasonal 6 mos ahead. Accepts reprints (tell when/where appeared; pays $50). Accepts disk or e-mail submission. Some sidebars. Prefers NIV. Guidelines/theme list (also by e-mail); copy for #10 SAE/2 stamps. (Ads)

> **Fillers:** Buys 100/yr. Games & word puzzles on a spiritual theme; 20-50 wds; $20-50.
>
> **Special Needs:** "Most open to true action/adventure and Christian humor. Kids want that—put it together with dialogue and a spiritual slant, and you're on the 'write' track for our readers. School life."
>
> **Tips:** "We use true or based-on-truth short stories, including school situations, humorous circumstances, adventure, short historical and biographical stories, and almost any situation relevant to 10-14 year olds. Best start for new writer: First-person story of a significant incident in your life between ages 10-14. Must have spiritual point or implications."
>
> ** This periodical was #27 on the 1998 Top 50 Christian Publishers list. (#22 in 1995, #38 in 1994)

GUIDEPOSTS FOR KIDS, PO Box 638, Chesterton IN 46304. (219)929-4429. Fax (219)926-3839. E-mail: WALLYT5232@aol.com. Website: http://www. guideposts.org. (Spring 1999: www.gp4k.org). Guideposts, Inc. Mary Lou Carney, ed; Betsy Kohn, articles ed; Tracey Dils, fiction ed. For kids 7-12 yrs (emphasis at upper level). Bimonthly mag; 32 pgs; circ 200,000. Subscription $15.95. 75% freelance. Query/clips (complete ms for fiction); no phone/fax/e-query. Pays $100-400 ($250-400 for fiction) on acceptance for all & electronic rts. Articles 300-1,200 wds (24/yr); fiction 500-1,200 wds (6/yr). Responds in 4-6 wks. Seasonal 6 mos ahead. No disk or e-mail submission. Kill fee. Regular sidebars. Prefers NIV. Guidelines; copy $3.25/ 10x13 SAE. (No ads)

> **Poetry:** Betsy Kohn. Buys 4-6/yr. Free verse, haiku, light verse, traditional; 3-20 lines; $15-50. Submit max 5 poems.
>
> **Fillers:** Buys 15-20/yr. Facts, games, jokes, quizzes, short humor, word puzzles; to 300 wds; $20-75.
>
> **Columns/Departments:** Buys 20/yr. Featuring Kids (true, interesting kid profiles), 300-600 wds; Tips from the Top (Christian celebrities/ sport figures), 500-700 wds; $150-350.
>
> **Tips:** "Looking for historical fiction; holiday fiction; folk/fairy tales; true action stories suitable comic book format."

** This periodical was #28 on the 1998 Top 50 Christian Publishers list. (#30 in 1997, #54 in 1996, #55 in 1995)

*HIGH ADVENTURE, 1445 Boonville Ave., Springfield MO 65802-1894. (417)862-2781x4178. Fax (417)831-8230. Assemblies of God. Marshall Bruner, ed-in-chief. For the Royal Rangers (boys), 5-17 yrs; slanted toward teens. Quarterly mag; 16 pgs; circ 86,000. 90% freelance. Complete ms/ cover letter. Pays .03-.04/wd on acceptance for 1st, one-time, simultaneous or reprint rts. Articles 500-900 wds (30/yr); fiction 500-900 wds (15/yr). Responds in 4-5 wks. Seasonal 7 mos ahead. Accepts simultaneous submissions & reprints (tell when/where appeared). Regular sidebars. Prefers NIV. Guidelines/theme list; copy for 9x12 SAE/3 stamps.

Fillers: Buys 30/yr. Cartoons, jokes, short humor; 50 wds; $2-20.

** This periodical was #14 on the 1997 Top 50 Christian Publishers list.

*JUNIOR COMPANION, PO Box 4060, Overland Park KS 66204. (913)432-0331. Fax (913)722-0351. Church of God (holiness)/Herald and Banner Press. Arlene McGehee, Sunday school ed. Denominational; for 4th-6th graders. Weekly take-home paper; 4 pgs; circ 3,500. Subscription $1.30. Complete ms/cover letter; phone/fax query OK. Pays .005/wd on publication for 1st rts. Fiction 500-1,200 wds. Seasonal 6-8 mos ahead. Accepts simultaneous submissions & reprints (tell when/where appeared). Prefers KJV. Guidelines/theme list; copy. Not in topical listings.

KEYS FOR KIDS, Box 1, Grand Rapids MI 49501. (616)451-2009. Fax (616)451-0032. E-mail: cbh@cbhonline.com. Website: http://www.cbhon line.com/kfk. Hazel Marett, ed. A daily devotional booklet for children (8-14) or for family devotions. Bimonthly booklet; 96 pgs; circ 40,000. No subscriptions. 100% freelance. Complete ms. Pays $12-16 on acceptance for 1st or simultaneous rts. Not copyrighted. Devotionals (includes short fiction story) 375-425 wds (60-70/yr). Responds in 2-4 wks. Seasonal 4-5 mos ahead. Accepts simultaneous submissions & reprints. Prefers KJV or NIV. Guidelines; copy for 6x9 SAE/$1.24 postage.

Tips: "If you are rejected, go back to the sample and study it some more."

+KIDZ CHAT, (formerly R-A-D-A-R) 8121 Hamilton Ave., Cincinnati OH 45231. (513)931-4050. Fax (513)931-0904. Standard Publishing. Gary Thacker, ed. For third and fourth graders; correlates with Sunday school lesson themes. Weekly take-home paper; 8 pgs; circ 56,000. Subscription $13. First issue fall 1999. 80-90% freelance. Complete ms/cover letter; no phone/fax query. Pays .03-.07/wd on acceptance for all, 1st, and reprint rts. Articles 225 wds (50/yr) & fiction 475 wds (50/yr). Responds in 3-4 wks. Seasonal 1 yr ahead. Accepts simultaneous submissions & reprints (tell when/where appeared). No disk or e-mail submission. Some sidebars. Prefers NIV. Guidelines/theme list/copy for #10 SAE/2 stamps.

Poetry: Buys 20-25/yr. Traditional, any length; pays .50/line. Submit any number.

Fillers: Buys 50/yr. Games, quizzes, prayers, word puzzles; .03-.07/ wd or $15-17.50.

Tips: "We mail theme list automatically if you request to be put on list. Follow our theme list (published quarterly). Articles should deal with issues relevant to third and fourth graders and use age-appropriate language."

** This periodical was #20 on the 1998 Top 50 Christian Publishers list. (#41 in 1997, #24 in 1996 & 1995, #13 in 1994)

*LAD, 4200 n. Point Pkwy, Alpharetta GA 30022-4174. Southern Baptist. Charlotte Teas, ed. For boys, grades 1-3; missions education. Monthly mag; 20 pgs; circ. 60,000. Subscription $12.36. Complete ms/cover letter; fax query OK. Pays variable rate on acceptance for all rts. Responds in 4 wks. Seasonal 1 yr ahead. Prefers NAS. Guidelines/theme list; copy $1.25/9x12 SAE/4 stamps.

Tips: "Be Southern Baptist—involved in Royal Ambassadors or children's missions education group."

LISTEN, 6401 The Paseo, Kansas City MO 64131. (816)333-7000 x2358. Fax (816)333-4439. E-mail: psmits@nazarene.org. Website: http://www.nazarene.org. Nazarene/Wesleyan/WordAction. Pamela Smits, ed. Weekly activity/story paper for 4-6 yr olds; 6 pgs; circ 20,000+. Subscription $9.50. 50% freelance. Complete ms/cover letter. Pays $25/story, $5-15/activity, on publication for first/multiple-use rts. Not copyrighted. Articles 100-200 wds (0/yr); contemporary fiction & true stories 400-500 wds (45/yr). Responds in 6-8 wks. Seasonal 10-12 mos ahead. No disk or e-mail submission. No sidebars. Prefers NIV. Guidelines/theme list/copy for #10 SAE/1 stamp.

Poetry: Buys 35/yr. Light verse, traditional; 8-10 lines; $2 or .25/line. Submit max 10 poems.

Fillers: Buys 15/yr. Games, ideas/activities (age-appropriate), prayers; $5-15.

Special Needs: Exciting, age-appropriate activities for back page; adventure stories and children's life situation stories; poetry. Parent-oriented helps with lessons.

LIVE WIRE, 8121 Hamilton Ave., Cincinnati OH 45231. (513)931-4050. Fax (513)931-0950. E-mail: standardpub@attmail.com. Carla J. Crane, ed. Geared to 10-12 year olds who want to connect to Christ. Weekly newspaper; 4 pgs; circ 40,000. Subscription $12. 50-65% freelance. Complete ms. Pays .05-.07/wd on acceptance for all, 1st, & reprint rts. Articles 250-350 wds. Responds in 9-13 wks. Seasonal 1 yr ahead. Accepts simultaneous submissions & reprints (tell when/where appeared). Accepts disk. Regular sidebars. Prefers NIV. Guidelines/theme list; copy for #10 SAE/2 stamps.

Fillers: Facts, games, ideas, jokes, party ideas, quotes.

** This periodical was #29 on the 1998 Top 50 Christian Publishers list.

MY FRIEND, The Catholic Magazine for Kids, 50 St. Paul's Ave., Boston MA 02130-3491. (617)522-8911. Fax (617)541-9805. E-mail: chaire@interramp.com. Website: http://www.pauline.org (click on Kidstuff). Pauline Books & Media. Sr. Kathryn James, mng ed. Christian values and basic Catholic doctrines for children, ages 6-12. Monthly (10X) mag; 32 pgs; circ 12,000. Subscription $18. 20-60+% freelance. Complete ms/cover letter; fax/e-query OK. Pays $35-100 after acceptance for all or 1st rts. Articles 150-800 wds (20/yr) & fiction 500-900 wds (8/yr). Responds in 9 wks. Seasonal 6 mos ahead. Accepts e-mail submission (attached file). Kill fee. Regular sidebars. Guidelines; copy $2.95.

Fillers: New area. Cartoons, jokes; $7-15.

Tips: "In fiction, include physically challenged, and universality or ethnic inclusion. Send fun fiction with values; polished fiction with original slant."

** This periodical was #66 on the 1997 Top 50 Christian Publishers list. (#32 in 1996, #34 in 1995, #39 in 1994)

NATURE FRIEND MAGAZINE, 2727 Pressrun Rd., Sugarcreek OH 44681. (330)852-1900. Fax (330)852-3285 or (800)852-4482. Carlisle Press. Marvin Wengerd, ed. For children (ages 4-14); about God's wonderful world of nature and wildlife. Monthly mag; 36 pgs; circ 8,000. Subscription $22. 50% freelance. Complete ms/cover letter; no phone/fax query. Pays .05/wd on publication for one-time rts. Articles 500-1,200 wds; or fiction 500-1200 wds (40/yr). Responds in 4-12 wks. Seasonal 3 mos ahead. Accepts simultaneous submissions & reprints (tell when/where appeared). No disk. Some sidebars. Prefers KJV. Guidelines; copy for 7x10 SAE/3 stamps. (No ads)

Poetry: Buys 10-20/yr. Traditional; $8-20. Submit max 5 poems.

Fillers: Buys 12/yr. Quizzes, word puzzles; 100-500 wds. Pays $10-25.

Tips: "Don't bother submitting to us unless you have seen our guidelines and a sample copy. We are very conservative in our approach. Everything must be nature-related. Write on a children's level, stories, facts, puzzles about animals and nature subjects. No evolution."

ON THE LINE, 616 Walnut Ave., Scottdale PA 15683-1999. (724)887-8500. Fax (724)887-3111. E-mail: otl@mph.org. Website: http://www.mph.org. Mennonite/Herald Press. Mary Clemens Meyer, ed. Reinforces Christian values in 10-14 yr olds. Monthly mag; 28 pgs; circ 6,000. Subscription $19.85. 90% freelance. Complete ms; fax/e-query OK. Pays .03-.05/wd on acceptance for one-time or reprint rts. Articles 300-500 wds (25-30/yr); fiction 1,000-1,800 wds (45-50/yr). Responds in 4 wks. Seasonal 6 mos ahead. Accepts simultaneous submissions & reprints (tell when/where appeared). No e-mail submission. Regular sidebars. Prefers NIV or NRSV. Guidelines; copy for 7x10 SAE/2 stamps.

Poetry: Buys 10-15/yr. Free verse, haiku, light verse, traditional; 3-24 lines; $10-25.

Fillers: Buys 25-30/yr. Cartoons, facts, games, jokes, party ideas, quizzes, word puzzles; to 350 wds; $10-25.

Tips: "Watch kids 10-14. Listen to them talk. Write stories that sound natural—not moralizing, preachy, with adults quoting Scripture. Our readers like puzzles, especially theme crosswords. Most sections of our magazine rely on freelancers for material."

** This periodical was #50 on the 1998 Top 50 Christian Publishers list. (#59 in 1997, #38 in 1996, #44 in 1995, #52 in 1994)

OUR LITTLE FRIEND, Box 5353, Nampa ID 83653-5353. (208)465-2580. Fax (208)465-2531. E-mail: ailsox@pacificpress.com. Website: http://www. pacificpress.com. Seventh-day Adventist. Aileen Andres Sox, ed. For theme and comments, see **Primary Treasure**. Weekly take-home paper for 1-6 yr olds (through 1st grade); 8 pgs; circ 45,000-50,000. 40% freelance (assigned), 10% unsolicited. Complete ms; fax/e-query OK (not preferred). Pays $25-50 on acceptance for one-time or reprint rts. True stories to 650 wds (52/yr). Responds in 13 wks. Seasonal 7 mos ahead. Accepts simultaneous submissions & reprints. No disk, e-mail submission OK. Guidelines (also on Website)/theme list; copy for 9x12 SAE/2 stamps.

> **Poetry:** 12 lines; $1/line. Rarely accepts.

> **Tips:** "Stories need to be crafted for this age reader in plot and vocabulary."

PARTNERS, Christian Light Publications, Inc., Box 1212, Harrisonburg VA 22801-1212. (540)434-0768. Fax (540)433-8896. Email: crystal@clp.org. Mennonite. Crystal Shank, ed. For 9-14 yr olds. Weekly take-home paper; 4 pgs; circ 6,000. Subscription $9.20. Almost 100% freelance. Complete ms. Pays up to .03/wd on acceptance for all, 1st, or reprint rts. Articles 200-1,000 wds (50/yr); fiction & true stories 1,000-1,600 wds (50-75/yr); serial stories up to 1,600/installment; short-short stories to 400 wds. Responds in 6 wks. Seasonal 6 mos ahead. Accepts simultaneous submissions (treated as reprints) & reprints (tell when/where appeared); serials 2-13 parts (2-4 parts preferred). Requires KJV. Guidelines/theme list/copy for 9x12 SAE/3 stamps. (No ads)

> **Poetry:** Buys 25/yr. Traditional, story poems; 4-24 lines; .50/line. Submit max 6 poems.

> **Fillers:** Buys 50-75/yr. Quizzes, word puzzles (Bible related). Payment varies, about $5.

> **Columns/Departments:** Character Corner; Cultures & Customs; Historical Highlights; Maker's Masterpiece; Missionary Mail; Torches of Truth; or Nature Nooks; all 200-800 or 1,000 wds.

> **Tips:** "Personal familiarity with conservative Mennonite applications of biblical truth is very helpful. Follow themes. We do not require that you be Mennonite, but we do send a questionnaire for you to fill out."
> ** This periodical was #43 on the 1998 Top 50 Christian Publishers list. (#44 in 1997, #63 in 1996, #66 in 1995)

POCKETS, PO Box 189, Nashville TN 37202-0189. (615)340-7333. Fax (615)340-7006. E-mail: pockets@upperroom.org. Website: http://www. upperroom.org/pockets. United Methodist. Janet Knight, ed; submit to Lynn W. Gilliam, assoc ed. Devotional magazine for children (6-11 yrs). Monthly (11X) mag; 48 pgs; circ 93,000. Subscription $16.95. 75% freelance. Complete ms/brief cover letter. Pays .14/wd on acceptance for 1st rts. (Will start buying software application rts if commissioned.) Articles 400-800 wds (20/yr) & fiction 500-1,600 wds (55/yr). Responds in 4 wks. Seasonal 1 yr ahead. Accepts reprints (tell when/where appeared). Kill fee 33%. No e-mail submission. Some sidebars. Prefers NRSV. Guidelines/ theme list (also by e-mail /Website); copy for 7x9 SAE/3 stamps.

> **Poetry:** Buys 30/yr. Free verse, haiku, light verse, traditional; 4-20 lines; $25-50 or $2/line. Submit max 7 poems.

> **Fillers:** Buys 44 games/puzzles/yr. Games, ideas, jokes, prayers, riddles, word puzzles; $25.

Columns/Departments: Buys 40/yr. Kids Cook; Pocketsful of Love (ways to show love), 200-300 wds; Peacemakers at Work, 500-800 wds; Pocketsful of Prayer, 400-600 wds.

Special Needs: "New feature is a 2-pg story for ages 5-8, 650 words max Need role model stories and retold Bible stories. Stories about someone you'd like to know. Interesting articles about children doing unusual things, 250-600 wds."

Contest: Fiction-writing contest; submit between 4/1 & 8/15 every yr. Prize $1,000. Length 1,000-1,600 wds. Must be unpublished and not historical fiction. Previous winners not eligible. Send to Pockets Fiction Contest at above address.

Tips: "Get our theme list first. Nonfiction probably easiest to sell and Peacemakers at Work."

** This periodical was #38 on the 1998 Top 50 Christian Publishers list. (#22 in 1997, #10 in 1996, #8 in 1995, #18 in 1994)

POWER AND LIGHT, 6401 The Paseo, Kansas City MO 64131. (816)333-7000x2243. Fax (816)333-4439. E-mail: bpostlewait@nazarene.org. Website: http://www.nazarene.org. Nazarene/WordAction Publishing Co. Beula Postlewait, ed. For pre-teens, 11-12 year olds. Weekly take-home paper; 8 pgs; circ 40,000. Subscription $28. 25% freelance. Query or complete ms/cover letter; fax/e-query OK. Pays .05/wd on publication for multiple use rts (writer retains right to reuse). Articles 600 wds (5/yr); fiction 700 wds (5/yr). Responds in 2 wks. Accepts simultaneous submissions & reprints (.035/wd—tell when/where appeared). Kill fee $15. Accepts disk or e-mail submission. No sidebars. NIV only. Guidelines/theme list; copy for #10 SAE/2 stamps.

Fillers: Buys 104/yr. Cartoons, games, jokes, short humor, word puzzles; $15.

Tips: "Most open to nonfiction based on real-life application of biblical principles/topics that effect daily living for preteens. Also needs a variety of puzzles. Request a theme list. Write about preteens from a preteen perspective. Especially needs holiday/seasonal material."

+POWER STATION, 4040 Lee Vance View, Colorado Springs CO 80918. (719)536-0100. Fax (719)533-3044. Cook Communication Ministries, Scripture Press Division. Janice K. Burton, ed. For 5th & 6th graders. Weekly take-home paper; 4 pgs. Subscription $12.45. Estab 1999. 90% freelance. Complete ms/cover letter; no phone/fax/e-query. Pays .08-.10/wd on acceptance for all, 1st, one-time & reprint rts. Articles 300-350 wds (68-70/yr); fiction 800-850 wds (36/yr). Responds in 3-4 wks. Seasonal 1 yr ahead. Accepts simultaneous submissions & reprints (tell when/where appeared). Requires disk or e-mail submission. Some sidebars. Prefers KJV. Guidelines/theme list; copy for #10 SAE/1 stamp (after 9/99). (No ads)

Fillers: Buys 20-25/yr. Cartoons, facts, games, quizzes, word puzzles 100-200 wds. Pays .08-.10/wd.

Columns/Departments: Buys 60/yr. Spark (activities) 150 wds; Live Wires (good role models for kids) 300-800 wds; By Design (nature, science) 300-350 wds; Contact (missions) 300-800 wds; crafts (seasonal or really fun) 150-300 wds. Pays .08-.10/wd.

Special Needs: True stories for 10-12 year olds that show God at work in a child's life. Also missions or true stories of kids involved in Christian service.

Tips: "We want lively stories, both true and fictional, and cameos of kids this age or older involved in service for the Lord. Clear, concise, grammatically correct manuscripts that enhance our evangelical Christian focus and conform to word counts."

*PRIMARY PAL (IL), 1300 N. Meacham Rd., Schaumburg IL 60173-4888. (847)843-1600. Fax (847)843-3757. Regular Baptist Press. Joan Alexander, ed. For ages 6-8; fundamental, conservative. Weekly take-home paper. Note: This periodical is being redesigned as we go to press. Send for new guidelines before submitting.

*PRIMARY PAL (KS), PO Box 4060, Overland Park KS 66204. (913)432-0331. Fax (913)722-0351. Church of God (holiness)/Herald and Banner Press. Arlene McGehee, Sunday school ed. Denominational; for 1st-3rd graders. Weekly take-home paper; 4 pgs; circ 2,900. Subscription $1.30. Complete ms/cover letter; phone/fax query OK. Pays .005/wd on publication for 1st rts. Fiction 500-1,000 wds. Seasonal 6-8 mos ahead. Accepts simultaneous submissions & reprints (tell when/where appeared). Prefers KJV. Guidelines/theme list; copy. Not in topical listings.

PRIMARY TREASURE, Box 5353, Nampa ID 83653-5353. (208)465-2500. Fax (208)465-2531. E-mail: ailsox@pacificpress.com. Website: http://www.pacificpress.com. Seventh-day Adventist. Aileen Andres Sox, ed. To teach children Christian belief, values, and practice. God's loving us and our loving Him makes a difference in every facet of life, from how we think and act to how we feel. Weekly take-home paper for 7-9 yr olds (2nd-4th grades); 16 pgs; circ 35,000. 25% freelance (assigned), 75% reprints or unsolicited. Complete ms; fax/e-query OK (not preferred). Pays $25-50 on acceptance for one-time or reprint rts. True stories 900-1,000 wds (52/yr); articles used rarely (query). Responds in 13 wks. Seasonal 7 mos ahead. Accepts simultaneous submissions; serials to 10 parts (query). No disk. Guidelines (also on Website); copy for 9x12 SAE/2 stamps.

Poetry: 12 lines; $1/line. Rarely uses.

Tips: "We need positive, lively stories about children facing modern problems and making good choices. We always need strong stories about boys. We need a spiritual element that frequently is missing from submissions. We're changing; refer to guidelines."

PROMISE, 330 Progress Rd., Dayton OH 45449. (937)847-5900. Fax (937)847-5910. E-mail: pliservice@aol.com. Website: http://www.pflaum.com. Catholic. Joan Mitchell CSJ, ed. For Kindergarten & Grade 1; encourages them to participate in parish worship. Weekly (32X) take-home paper. Not in topical listings.

*SEEDS, 330 Progress Rd., Dayton OH 45449. (937)847-5900. Fax (937)847-5910. E-mail: pliservice@aol.com. Website: http://www.pflaum.com. Catholic. Joan Mitchell CSJ, ed. For preschoolers. Weekly (32X) take-home paper; 4 pgs. Not in topical listings.

SKIPPING STONES, A Multicultural Children's Quarterly, PO Box 3939, Eugene OR 97403. Phone/fax (541)342-4956. E-mail: skipping@efn.org. Website: http://www.nonviolence.org/skipping. Not specifically Christian. Arun N. Toke', ed. A multi-cultural awareness and nature appreciation magazine for young people 7-17, world-wide. Bimonthly mag; 36 pgs; circ 2,500. Subscription $25. 80% freelance. Query or complete ms/cover letter; no phone query. **PAYS IN COPIES** for 1st, electronic or reprint rts. Articles (15-25/yr) 500-750 wds; fiction for teens, 750-1,000 wds; book reviews 100 wds; video reviews 50 wds. Responds in 3-6 wks. Seasonal 2-4 months ahead. Accepts simultaneous submissions. Accepts disk. Regular sidebars. Guidelines/theme list; copy $5/9x12 SAE/5 stamps. (No ads)

Poetry: Only from kids under 18. Accepts 100/yr. Any type; 3-30 lines. Submit max 4-5 poems.

Fillers: Accepts 10-20/yr. Anecdotes, cartoons, games, quizzes, short humor, word puzzles; to 250 wds.

Columns/Departments: Accepts 10/yr. Noteworthy News (multicultural/nature/international/social, appropriate for youth), 200 wds.

Special Needs: Challenging disability; living in other cultures/countries; cross-cultural communications; rewards and punishments.

Contest: Annual Youth Honor Awards. June 20, 1999 deadline for students 7-17. Send SASE for guidelines.

Tips: "We're seeking submissions by minority, multicultural, international, and/or youth writers. Do not be judgmental or preachy; be open or receptive to diverse opinions."

STORY FRIENDS, 616 Walnut St., Scottdale PA 15683. (724)887-8500. Fax (724)887-3111. E-mail: rstutz@mph.org. Website: http://www.mph.org. Herald Press/Mennonite. Rose Mary Stutzman, ed. For children 4-9 yrs; reinforces Christian values in a non-moralistic manner. Monthly mag; 20 pgs; circ 7,000. Subscription $18. 75% freelance. Complete ms/cover letter. Pays .03-.05/wd on acceptance for one-time rts. Articles (5-10/yr) & fiction (30/yr), 300-800 wds. Responds in 8 wks. Seasonal 6 mos ahead. Accepts simultaneous submissions & reprints (tell when/where appeared). Prefers NIV. Guidelines; copy for 9x12 SAE/2 stamps.

Poetry: Buys 12/yr. Traditional; 4-12 lines; $10. Submit max 3 poems.

Fillers: Buys 2-3/yr. Cartoons, word puzzles.

Ethnic: Targets all ethnic groups involved in the Mennonite church.

Tips: "Send stories that show rather than tell. Realistic fiction (no fantasy). Send good literary quality with a touch of humor that will appeal to children. Cover letter should give your experience with children."

STORY MATES, Christian Light Publications, Inc., Box 1212, Harrisonburg VA 22801-1212. (540)434-0768. Fax (540)433-8896. E--mail: crystal@clp.org. Mennonite. Crystal Shank, ed. For 4-8 yr olds. Weekly take-home paper; 4 pgs; circ 5,900. Subscription $9.20. 90% freelance. Complete ms/cover letter. Pays up to .03/wd on acceptance for all, 1st, & reprint rts. Realistic or true stories to 800-900 wds (50-75/yr); picture stories 120-150 wds. Responds in 6 wks. Seasonal 6 mos ahead. Accepts simultaneous submissions & reprints (tell when/where appeared). No disk. Requires

KJV. Guidelines/theme list/copy for 9x12 SAE/3 stamps. Will send questionnaire to fill out. (No ads)

Poetry: Buys 25/yr. Traditional, any length. Likes story poems. Pays up to .50/line.

Fillers: Quizzes, word puzzles, craft ideas. "Need fillers that correlate with theme list; Bible related." Pays about $5.

Tips: "We would welcome more puzzles for this age group. Carefully read our guidelines and understand our conservative Mennonite applications of Bible principles." Very conservative.

** This periodical was #64 on the 1998 Top 50 Christian Publishers list.

TOGETHER TIME, 6401 The Paseo, Kansas City MO 64131. (816)333-7000x2359. Fax (816)333-4439. E-mail: kjohnson@nazarene.org. Website: http://www.nazarene.org. WordAction Publishing Co./Church of the Nazarene. Kathleen Johnson, asst ed. For 3-4 yr olds and parents. Weekly take-home paper; 4 pgs; circ 19,000. Subscription $9.95. 75% freelance. Query; fax/e-query OK. Pays .05/wd on publication for all rts. Articles 150-200 wds, fiction 150-200 wds (30/yr). Responds in 8-10 wks. Seasonal 12 mos ahead. Accepts simultaneous submissions. Kill fee 5%. Prefers disk. Prefers NIV. Guidelines/theme list; copy for #10 SAE/1 stamp.

Poetry: Buys 52/yr. Free verse, traditional; 4-8 lines; .25/line. Submit max 5 poems.

Fillers: Games, ideas, activities; 150-200 wds. Pays $15 for crafts & ideas, finger plays.

Tips: "Know the age level of 3-4 year olds. Integrate Christian education throughout; don't tack it on the end."

#TOUCH, Box 7259, Grand Rapids MI 49510. (616)241-5616. Fax (616)241-5558. GEMS Girls Clubs (Christian Reformed, Reformed, and Presbyterian). Carol Smith, mng ed. To show girls, ages 9-14, that God is at work in their lives and the world around them. Monthly (10X) mag; 24 pgs; circ 14,000. Subscription $12.50. 70% freelance. Complete ms. Pays $5-20 ($15-50 for fiction) or .03/wd on publication for 1st, reprint or simultaneous rts. Articles 200-400 wds (10/yr); fiction 400-1,000 wds (30/yr). Responds in 3 wks. Seasonal 10 mos ahead. Accepts simultaneous submissions & reprints. Accepts disk. Regular sidebars. Prefers NIV. Guidelines/theme list; copy $1/9x12 SAE/3 stamps.

Poetry: Buys 3/yr. Haiku, light verse, traditional; 4-12 lines; $5-10. Poetry fits themes.

Fillers: Buys 10/yr. Games, party ideas, prayers, quizzes, short humor; 50-200 wds; $5-15.

Special Needs: Annual theme is "Come, Celebrate the King!" so all articles and stories should be of a celebrative nature. See Update for ideas.

Tips: "Fiction most open to freelancers. Know what girls face today and how they cope in their daily lives. We need angles from home life and friendships, peer pressure and the normal growing-up challenges girls deal with."

** This periodical was #42 on the 1996 Top 50 Christian Publishers list. (#45 in 1995)

TRAILS 'N' TREASURES, 119 S. Lakewood Dr., Ridgeley WV 26753. (304)738-2136. Fax (304)738-0555. Fountain Publishing. Patricia Timbrook, pub/ed-in-chief; Susan Titus Osborn, ed. Focus is on great literature and great art from a Christian perspective; for children 6-12 yrs. Estab 1998. Bimonthly mag; 32 pgs. Subscription $19.95. Complete ms/cover letter; e-query OK. Pays $50-150 ($75 for reprints) on publication for 1st or reprint rts. Articles & fiction. Accepts simultaneous submissions & reprints (tell when/where appeared). Accepts disk or e-mail submission. Some sidebars. Guidelines; copy $3.95/9x12 SAE/4 stamps. (No ads)

> **Tips:** "We select 1-2 freelance stories per issue. Think seasonally and write for kids today."

VENTURE, 330 Progress Rd., Dayton OH 45449. (937)847-5900. Fax (937)847-5910. E-mail: pliservice@aol.com or rscorpi9@mail.idt.net. Website: http://www.pflaum.com. Joan Mitchell, ed. Connects young people's real life experiences—successes and conflicts in family, neighborhoods, classrooms, playgrounds—with the Sunday gospels; for intermediate-age children, grades 4-6. Weekly (32X) take-home paper; 8 pgs; circ 140,000. 40% freelance. Query. Pays $125 on publication for all rts. Articles (6-8/yr) & fiction (8-10/yr), 850 wds. Responds in 2-8 wks. Seasonal 4-6 mos ahead. Accepts simultaneous query. Guidelines (also on Website); copy $1.85.

> **Tips:** "We want realistic fiction and nonfiction that raises current ethical religious questions and conflicts in multi-racial settings, believable and detailed, to which intermediate-age children can relate."

+WINNER, 55 W. Oak Ridge Dr., Hagerstown MD 21740. Seventh-day Adventist. Lincoln Steed, ed. For elementary school children. Guidelines; copy for 9x12 SAE/3 stamps.

WONDER TIME, 6401 The Paseo, Kansas City MO 64131. (816)333-7000. Fax (816)333-4439. Website: http://www.nazarene.org. Church of the Nazarene. Patty Craft, assoc ed. For 6-8 yr olds (1st & 2nd graders); emphasis on principles, character-building, and brotherhood. Weekly take-home paper; 4 pgs; circ 40,000. 75-85% freelance. Complete ms/with cover letter; no phone/fax query. Pays $25 on publication for all rts. Fiction 250-350 wds (52/yr). Responds in 4-6 wks. Seasonal 1 yr ahead. Accepts disk or e-mail submission (copied into message). Kill fee $15. No sidebars. Prefers NIV. Guidelines/theme list; copy for #10 SAE/2 stamps. (No ads)

> **Tips:** "We accept freelance stories that follow our theme list. Stories should be contemporary, life-related, at a 1st-2nd grade readability, and directly correlate with our Sunday school curriculum. Avoid trite situations."

WRITERS' INTERNATIONAL FORUM FOR YOUNG AUTHORS - See Writers' International Forum (now part of that online publication).

CHRISTIAN EDUCATION/LIBRARY MARKETS

BAPTIST LEADER, Box 851, Valley Forge PA 19482-0851. (610)768-2143. Fax (610)768-2056. E-mail: baptist.leader@abc-usa.org. Website: http://www.abc-em.org/ceboard.html. American Baptist. Ingrid Dvirnak, mng ed. Practical "how-to" or thought-provoking articles for local church Christian education lay leaders and teachers. Quarterly mag; 32 pgs; circ 5,000. Subscription $8. 5% freelance. Complete ms/cover letter; e-query OK. Pays $10-75 ($25-75 for fiction) on acceptance for one-time or reprint rts. Articles 1,300-2,000 wds (10/yr); fiction (2-3/yr); book & video reviews 200 wds (assigned). Responds in 12 wks. Seasonal 1 yr ahead. Accepts simultaneous submissions & reprints (tell when/where appeared). Prefers disk or e-mail submission (copied into message). Regular sidebars. Prefers NRSV. Guidelines (also by e-mail); copy $1.50. (Ads)

> **Poetry:** Accepts 2-3/yr. Haiku, light verse, traditional; $10-20.
>
> **Fillers:** Buys 4-8/yr. Cartoons, jokes, prayers; 25-100 wds; $10-20.
>
> **Special Needs:** Plays & skits related to holidays that churches celebrate: Christmas, Easter, Mother's Day, Children's Day, Reformation Sunday, Black History Month, etc.; 1,300-2,000 wds; pays $25-50. Plays & skits are the only fiction used.
>
> **Tips:** "Most open to feature articles, new program ideas for holidays, and holiday-related dramas or plays. Send us CE ideas that have worked well in your church."

BRIGADE LEADER, Box 150, Wheaton IL 60187. (630)665-0630. Fax (630)665-0372. E-mail: BrigadeCSB@aol.com. Christian Service Brigade. Deborah Christensen, mng ed. For men leading boy's clubs; emphasis on Brigade leadership. Quarterly mag; 16 pgs; circ 5,000. Subscription $10. 50% freelance. Query (most articles assigned); no e-query. Pays .05-.10/wd on publication for 1st or reprint rts. Articles 500-1,000 wds (4-8/yr). Responds in 2 wks. Accepts reprints (tell when/where appeared). Prefers disk. Kill fee $35. Regular sidebars. Prefers NIV. Guidelines; copy $1.50/9x12 SAE/4 stamps.

> **Tips:** "We're especially looking for men who are familiar with Christian Service Brigade and how to disciple boys."

*CARAVAN: A Resource for Adult Religious Educators, 90 Parent Ave., Ottawa ON K1N 7B1 Canada. (613)241-9461. Fax (613)241-8117. Canadian conference of Catholic Bishops. Joanne Chafe, ed. A resources for adult educators who work in church settings. Quarterly mag; 16 pgs; circ 1,500. Subscription $17.12. 100% freelance. Complete ms/cover letter. Pays variable rate on acceptance or publication. Copyrighted; rights released on request. Articles (30-40/yr). Responds in 4-6 wks. Seasonal 3 mos ahead. Accepts simultaneous submissions. Regular sidebars. Guidelines/copy.

> **Columns/Departments:** Adult religious education: New Initiatives, New Releases, Creative program ideas.
>
> **Special Needs:** Workshop models.

CATECHIST, 330 Progress Rd., Dayton OH 45449. (937)847-5900. Fax (937)847-5910. E-mail: raffio@aol.com. Website: http://www.catechist.com. Catholic. Patricia Fischer, ed. For Catholic school teachers and parish volunteer catechists. Mag. published 7X/yr; 52 pgs; circ 50,000. Query (preferred) or complete ms. Pays $25-150 on publication for all rts. Articles 1,200-1,500 wds. Responds in 9-18 wks. Guidelines (also on Website); copy $2.50.

+**CATHOLIC LIBRARY WORLD**, 291 Springfield St., Chicopee MA 01013-2839. (413)594-2761. Fax (413)594-7418. E-mail: gallagherm@dms.edu. Website: http://www.cathla.org. Catholic Library Assn. Mary E. Gallagher , editorial chairman. For libraries at al levels—pre-school to post-secondary to academic, parish, public and private. Quarterly journal; 80 pgs; circ 1,000. Subscription $60/$70 foreign. Query; phone/fax/e-query OK. **PAYS 1 COPY.** Articles; book/video reviews, 300-500 wds. Accepts disk. Some sidebars. No guidelines; copy for 9x12 SAE. Not in topical listings. (Ads)

> **Tips:** "Open to articles related to librarianship, archives, Parish ministry, theology and religious education; literature, children to adult."

C.E. CONNECTION, Box 12609, Oklahoma City OK 73157. (405)787-7110. Fax (405)789-3957. E-mail: kristy@iphc.com. Website: http://www. iphc.org. General Christian Education Dept./IPHC. Kristy Cofer, coordinating ed. Targets pastors and local Christian education workers/leaders for training/how-to. Quarterly newsletter; 12 pgs; circ 6,600. Free. 100% freelance. Complete ms/cover letter. **NO PAYMENT.** Not copyrighted. Articles (10/yr) & fiction to 450 wds. Responds in 2 wks. Seasonal 6 mos ahead. Accepts simultaneous submissions & reprints (tell when/where appeared). Accepts disks or e-mail submission (attached file).   Regular sidebars. Free copy.

> **Fillers:** Cartoons, ideas.

CE CONNECTION COMMUNIQUE, PO Box 12624, Roanoke VA 24027. Phone/fax (540)342-7511. E-mail: ccmbbr@juno.com. Betty Robertson, ed. Virginia Christian Education Assn. Bimonthly newsletter; 8 pgs; circ 1,350. Subscription $19.95. 25% freelance. Query; no phone/fax/e-query. Pays $5-10 on acceptance for 1st, one-time, simultaneous rts. Not copyrighted. Articles 100-600 wds. Responds in 6 wks. Seasonal 6 mos ahead. Accepts simultaneous submissions & reprints. Guidelines; copy $3.

CHILDREN'S MINISTRY, PO Box 481, Loveland CO 80539. (970)669-3836. Fax (970)679-4372. E-mail: info@grouppublishing.com. Website: http://www.grouppublishing.com. Group Publishing. Christine Yount, ed; Laurie Copley, asst ed. For Christians who work with kids from birth to 6th grade. Bimonthly mag; 85 pgs; circ 65,000. Subscription $24.95. 73% freelance. Query/clips or complete ms/cover letter; fax/e-query OK. Pays $35-175 on acceptance for all rts. Articles 500-1,700 wds (40/yr). Responds in 4-8 wks. Seasonal 5 mos ahead. Accepts disk. Regular sidebars. Prefers New Century. Guidelines; copy $2/9x12 SASE. (Ads)

> **Fillers:** Buys 5-10/yr. Cartoons, games, ideas; $15-35.
>
> **Columns/Departments:** Buys 50/yr. For Parents Only (practical parenting tips); Preschool Page (hints, songs, Bible activities); Nursery Notes; Group Games; Seasonal Specials (parties, service projects, worship celebrations—4-5 mos ahead); 5-Minute Messages; 50-125 wds; $15-35. Complete mss.

Special Needs: Crafts, hobbies, children's tends; tried and true ideas that work.

Tips: "Potential authors should be familiar with *Children's Ministry* and its style. Most successful authors are ones who have experience working with children in the church. We like new ideas with 'ahas.'"

+THE CHRISTIAN CLASSROOM, 2026 Exeter Rd. Ste. 2, Germantown TN 38138. (901)624-5911. Fax (901)624-5910. E-mail: tcc@grtriver.com. Great River Publishing. Sherry Campbell, ed. Ideas and information for teachers in Christian schools. Quarterly mag; 32-56 pgs; circ 22,000. Subscription $19.95. Estab 1997. 33% freelance. Complete ms/cover letter; phone/fax/e-query OK. Pays negotiable rates on publication for 1st rts. Articles 1,000-1,500 wds (8/yr); fiction 1,000-1,500 wds (6/yr). Responds in 6 wks. Seasonal 6 mos ahead. Accepts disk or e-mail submission (copied into message). Regular sidebars. Any version. Guidelines/theme list; copy for 9x12 SAE/5 stamps. (Ads)

Fillers: Buys 12/yr. Anecdotes, cartoons, facts, games, ideas, jokes, prayers, short humor, word puzzles; to 500 wds. No payment.

Columns/Departments: Accepts 10/yr. From the Teacher's Desk (ideas), 100-250 wds, no payment.

Tips: "Provide information to help Christian school teachers do their jobs better and easier."

CHRISTIAN EDUCATION COUNSELOR, 1445 Boonville Ave., Springfield MO 65802-1894. (417)862-2781. Fax (417)862-0503. E-mail: salee@ag.org. Website: http://www.we-build-people.org/cec. Assemblies of God. Sylvia Lee, ed. Presents teaching and administrative helps to lay leaders in local churches. Bimonthly mag; 32 pgs; circ 15,000. Subscription $12. 5% freelance. Complete ms/cover letter. Pays .08-.12/wd on acceptance for 1st, simultaneous & reprint rts. Articles 300-800 wds (50/yr); book reviews, 400-500 wds, $35. Responds in 4 wks. Seasonal 6 mos ahead. Accepts simultaneous submissions & reprints. Accepts disk. Regular sidebars. Guidelines; copy for 9x12 SAE/2 stamps. (No ads)

Fillers: Buys cartoons, games, ideas, quizzes; $35-85.

Tips: "We need short articles, 300 words or less, on an idea that works. We want practical helps for our readers and first-hand experience is best."

** This periodical was #52 on the 1996 Top 50 Christian Publishers list. (#62 in 1995, #64 in 1994)

CHRISTIAN EDUCATION JOURNAL, 2065 Half Day Rd., Deerfield IL 60015. Trinity Evangelical Divinity School. Dr. Perry G. Downs, ed. Complete ms (disk & hard copy)/cover letter. Articles 10-25 pgs, on Christian education topics. Guidelines. Not in topical listings.

Special Needs: All areas related to Christian education, including church ministry and leadership. Educational articles related to organizational development and leadership.

CHRISTIAN EDUCATION LEADERSHIP, 1080 Montgomery Ave., Cleveland TN 37311. (423)476-4512. Fax (423)478-7521. E-mail: lancewc@aol.com. Pentecostal Church of God/Pathway Press. Lance Colkmire, ed. For Christian education teachers and leaders. Quarterly mag; 32 pgs; circ 9,800.

Subscription $7. 40% freelance. Complete ms/cover letter. Pays $25-55 on acceptance for one-time, simultaneous or reprint rts. Articles 500-1,200 wds (12/yr). Responds in 4 wks. Seasonal 4 mos ahead. Accepts simultaneous submissions & reprints (tell when/where appeared). Accepts disk. Regular sidebars. Prefers NKJV or NIV. Guidelines; copy for 9x12 SAE/4 stamps. (Ads)

Columns/Departments: Sunday School; Teen Ministry; Outreach; The Pastor and C.E.; Kids Church; 400-800 wds; $25-50.

Special Needs: Articles on children's ministry and Sunday school.

CHRISTIAN EDUCATORS JOURNAL, Dordt College, 498 4th Ave. NE, Sioux Center IA 51250-1697. (712)722-6252. Fax (712)722-1185. E-mail: lgilst @dordt.edu. Website: http://www.dordt.edu. Christian Educators Journal Assn. Lorna Van Gilst, mng ed. For educators in Christian day schools at the elementary, secondary, and college levels. Quarterly journal; 36 pgs; circ 4,200. Subscription $7.50. 50% freelance. Query; phone query OK. Pays $30 on publication for one-time rts. Articles 600-1,200 wds (20/yr); fiction 600-1,200 wds. Responds in 5 wks. Seasonal 4 mos ahead. Accepts simultaneous submissions & reprints. Guidelines/theme list; copy $1 or 9x12 SAE/4 stamps. (Ads)

Poetry: Buys 6/yr. On teaching day school; 4-30 lines; $10. Submit max 5 poems.

Tips: "No articles on Sunday school, only Christian day school. Most open to theme topics and features."

THE CHRISTIAN LIBRARIAN, 4298 McKee Rd., Charlotte NC 28270. (704)847-5600. Fax (704)845-1747. E-mail: ses@perigee.net. Assn. of Christian Librarians. Ron Jordahl, ed. Christian librarianship. Quarterly (3X) journal; 40 pgs; circ 500. Subscription $25. 25% freelance. Query; phone/fax query OK. **NO PAYMENT** for one-time rts. Not copyrighted. Articles 1,000-3,500 words; research articles to 5,000 wds (6/yr); reviews 150-300 wds. Responds in 5 wks. Accepts simultaneous query & reprints. Prefers disk. Regular sidebars. Guidelines; copy $5.

Fillers: Anecdotes, cartoons, newsbreaks, short humor; 25-300 wds.

Special Needs: Articles on libraries, books, and reading.

CHRISTIAN LIBRARY JOURNAL, 801 S. Osage Ave., Bartlesville OK 74003-4946. (918)336-0813. Fax (918)336-0877. E-mail: nancyhclj@aol.com. Christian Library Services. Nancy Hesch, ed/pub.; Andrew Seddon, articles ed. Provides reviews of library materials and articles about books, authors, and libraries for the Christian librarian. Bimonthly (5X) mag; 88 pgs; circ. 1,000. Subscription $45. 10% freelance. Complete ms/cover letter. Pays to $20 on publication for 1st or reprint rts. Articles (10/yr) 1,500 wds; book /video reviews, 200-400 wds (ask Nancy Hesch to be a reviewer), no payment. Responds in 10-12 wks. Accepts reprints (tell when/ where appeared). Requires disk. Regular sidebars. Guidelines/theme list; copy for 9x12 SAE/5 stamps. (Ads)

Fillers: Quotes; 10-100 wds. No payment.

Columns/Departments: Accepts 4-6/yr. Book Nook (using books with students), 500-800 wds; no payment. Complete ms.

Tips: "Most open to articles, book reviews, especially written by librarians and teachers; library related articles and author profiles."

*CHRISTIAN SCHOOL, 1308 Santa Rosa, Wheaton IL 60187. (630)653-4588. Phil Landrum, pub. A publication for Christian-school educators and parents. Quarterly mag; 48 pgs; circ 3,000 schools. 2% freelance. Query; phone query OK. **NO PAYMENT.** Articles 500-1,500 wds (1/yr); fiction 1,000-1,500 (1/yr). Responds in 2-4 wks. Free guidelines/copy.

Poetry: Accepts 1/yr. Traditional. Submit max 5 poems.

Fillers: Accepts 1/yr. Anecdotes.

Special Needs: Education how-to; youth trends; training techniques; children's books.

+THE CHRISTIAN SCHOOL ADMINISTRATOR, 2026 Exeter Rd. Ste. 2, Germantown TN 38138. (901)624-5911. Fax (901)624-5910. E-mail: csa@grtriver.com. Great River Publishing. Sherry Campbell, ed. The information source for Christian school operations. Bimonthly mag; 40-56 pgs; circ 15,000. Subscription $15. 25% freelance. Complete ms/cover letter; phone/fax/e-query OK. Pays negotiable rates on publication for 1st rts. Articles 1,000-1,500 wds (6/yr); fiction 1,000-1,500 wds (4/yr). Responds in 6 wks. Seasonal 6 mos ahead. Accepts disk or e-mail submission (copied into message). Regular sidebars. Any version. Guidelines/theme list; copy for 9x12 SAE/5 stamps. (Ads)

Fillers: Buys 6-10/yr. Anecdotes, cartoons, facts, games, ideas, jokes, short humor; 50-250 wds. Pays $25-75.

Tips: "Provide how-to information on some aspect of operating a private Christian school."

CHURCH & SYNAGOGUE LIBRARIES, PO Box 19357, Portland OR 97280-0357. (503)244-6919. Fax (503)977-3734. E-mail: csla@worldaccessnet.com. Website: http://www.worldaccessnet.com/~csla. Church and Synagogue Library Assn. Judith Janzen, exec dir. To help librarians run congregational libraries. Bimonthly; 20 pgs.; circ. 3,000. Subscription $25, $35 CAN, $45 foreign. Query. **NO PAYMENT.** Requires disk. Articles. Book & video reviews 1-2 paragraphs. (Ads)

Fillers: Ideas.

*CHURCH EDUCATOR, 165 Plaza Dr., Prescott AZ 86303. (520)771-8601. Fax (520)771-8621. E-mail: edmin2@aol.com. Linda Davidson, ed. For mainline Protestant Christian educators. Monthly journal; 36 pgs; circ 4,500. Subscription $35, CAN $45, foreign $55. 90% freelance. Complete ms/cover letter; phone/fax/e-query OK. Pays .03/wd on publication for 1st rts. Articles 700-1,500 wds (100/yr). Responds in 4-6 wks. Seasonal 4 mos ahead. Accepts simultaneous submissions & reprints (tell when/where appeared). Regular sidebars. Guidelines/theme list; copy for 9x12 SAE/4 stamps.

Fillers: Bible games and Bible puzzles.

Columns/Departments: Buys 20/yr. Noah's Ark (crafts for children); Youth Notebook (tips for working with teens); 200-500 wds.

Tips: "Talk to the educator at your church. What would they find useful? Most open to seasonal articles dealing with the liturgical year.

Write up church programs with specific how-tos of putting the program together."

CHURCH LIBRARIES, 9731 Fox Glen Dr. #6F, Niles IL 60714-5861. (847)296-3964. Fax (847)296-0754. E-mail: linjohnson@compuserve.com. Website: http://members.aol.com/ECLAssoc/index.html. Evangelical Church Library Assn. Lin Johnson, ed. To assist church librarians in setting up, maintaining, and promoting church libraries and media centers. Quarterly mag; 40 pgs; circ 600. Subscription $25. 99% freelance. Complete ms; fax/e-query OK. Pays .04/wd on acceptance for 1st, one-time, or reprint rts. Articles 500-1,000 wds (20/yr); book/music/video/cassette reviews by assignment, 75-150 wds, free product. Responds in 4-6 wks. Seasonal 6 mos ahead. Accepts reprints (tell when/where appeared). Requires disk or e-mail submission (copied into message). Regular sidebars. Prefers NIV. Guidelines (also by e-mail/Website); copy for 9x12 SAE/6 stamps. (Ads)

> **Columns/Departments:** Buys 16/yr. Idea Exchange (brief hints on any aspect of running a library), 100-200 wds; pays a free book.
>
> **Tips:** "Talk to church librarians or get involved in library or reading programs. Most open to articles, Idea Exchange, and promotional ideas; profiles of church libraries; round-ups on best books in a category (query on topic first). Need for reviewers fluctuates; if interested send SASE for questionnaire."

*CHURCH MEDIA LIBRARY MAGAZINE, 127 9th Ave. N., Nashville TN 37234-0140. (615)251-2752. Fax (615)251-5607. Southern Baptist. Floyd B. Simpson, ed. Supports the establishment and development of church media libraries; provides how-to articles and articles of inspiration and encouragement to media library workers. Quarterly mag; 52 pgs; circ 30,000. Query. Pays .055/wd on publication for all, 1st, or reprint rts. Articles 600-1,500 wds (10-15/yr). Responds in 5 wks. Seasonal 14 mos ahead. Free guidelines/copy.

EVANGELIZING TODAY'S CHILD, Box 348, Warrenton MO 63383-0348. (314)456-4321. Fax (314)456-2078. E-mail: ETCLIP@aol.com. Child Evangelism Fellowship. Elsie C. Lippy, ed. To equip Christians to win the world's children (4-11) to Christ and disciple them. Bimonthly mag; 64 pgs; circ 18,000. Subscription $20. 50% freelance. Complete ms; no phone/fax/e-query. Pays .10-.12/wd (.07/wd for fiction) within 60 days of acceptance for one-time rts. Articles 1,200 wds (24/yr); fiction 700-900 (12/yr). Responds in 4-6 wks. Seasonal 1 yr ahead. Accepts reprints (tell when/where appeared). No disk or e-mail submission. Kill fee 30%. Regular sidebars. Prefers NIV. Guidelines; copy $2/9x12 SAE/6 stamps. (Ads)

> **Resource Center:** Buys 40-60/yr. Complete ms, 200-250 wds. Pays $25 for teaching hints, bulletin board ideas, object lessons, missions incentives, etc.
>
> **Special Needs:** Salvation testimonies of adults saved before age 12, 700-900 wds; 6/yr. Creative ideas for involving children in ministry.
>
> **Tips:** "Most open to Resource Center. Study the publication. Know children and/or children's workers."

** This periodical was #62 on the 1997 Top 50 Christian Publishers list. (#64 in 1995, #49 in 1994)

GROUP MAGAZINE, Box 481, Loveland CO 80538. (970)669-3836. Fax (970)669-3269. E-mail: kdieterich@grouppublishing.com. Kathleen Dieterich, asst ed. Aimed at leaders of junior and senior high Christian youth groups. Bimonthly mag; 85 pgs; circ 55,000. Subscription $25.95. 70% freelance. Query or complete ms/cover letter; fax/e-query OK. Pays $35-225 on acceptance for all rts. Articles 500-1,700 wds (30-40/yr). Responds in 4-8 wks. Seasonal 5 mos ahead. Accepts disk. Regular sidebars. Guidelines; copy $2/9x12 SASE. (Ads)

> **Fillers:** Buys 5-10/yr. Cartoons, games, ideas; $15-35.
>
> **Columns/Departments:** Buys 30-40/yr. Try This One (youth group activities), 300 wds; Strange But True (strange youth-ministry stories), 500 wds; Hands-on Help (tips for leaders), 300 wds; Good News About Kids (positive news about teens), 350 wds; $35. Complete ms.
>
> **Special Needs:** Articles geared toward working with teens; programming ideas; youth ministry issues.
>
> **Tips:** "Looking for articles that demonstrate cutting-edge activity in the area of youth ministry."

*INSIGHT INTO CHRISTIAN EDUCATION, Box 23152, Charlotte NC 28227-0272. (704)545-6161. Fax (704)573-0712. Advent Christian. Millie Griswold, ed. For local church Christian education volunteers. Quarterly mag; 8 pgs; circ 2,200. Subscription $6. 20% freelance. Query or complete ms. Pays $25 on publication. Articles 600-1,000 wds. Accepts reprints. Seasonal 6 mos ahead. Free copy.

THE JOURNAL OF ADVENTIST EDUCATION, 12501 Old Columbia Pike, Silver Springs MD 20904-6600. (301)622-9627. E-mail: 74617.1231@ compuserve.com. Seventh-day Adventist. Beverly J. Rumble, ed. For Seventh-day teachers teaching in the church's school system, K-University. Bimonthly (5X) journal; 48 pgs; circ 7,400. Subscription $17.25 (add $1 outside US). 10% freelance. Query or complete ms; phone/fax/e-query OK. Pays $25-150 on publication for 1st & translation rts. Articles to 1,000-1,500 wds (2-20/yr). Responds in 6 wks. Seasonal 6 mos ahead. Accepts reprints (tell when/where appeared). Accepts disk. Kill fee to 25%. Regular sidebars. Guidelines; copy for 9x12 SAE/$2 postage.

> **Fillers:** Cartoons only, no pay.
>
> **Special Needs:** "All articles in the context of parochial schools (*not* Sunday school tips); professional enrichment and teaching tips for Christian teachers. Need feature articles."

KIDS' MINISTRY IDEAS, 55 W. Oak Ridge Dr., Hagerstown MD 21740. (301)791-7000. Fax (301)790-9734. E-mail: KidsMin@rhpa.org. Seventh-day Adventist. Patricia Fritz, ed; Tamara Michalenko Terry, mng ed. For adults leading children (birth-eighth grade) to Christ. Quarterly mag; 32-40 pgs; circ. 7,500. Subscription $16.97. 10% freelance. Query; fax/e-query OK. Pays $25-125 on acceptance for one-time or reprint rts. Articles 500-1,300 wds (10/yr). Responds in 6-8 wks. Seasonal 9 mos ahead. Accepts simultaneous submissions & reprints (tell when/where appeared). Accepts e-mail submission. Regular sidebars. Prefers NIV. Guidelines (also by e-mail); copy for 9x12 SAE/4 stamps. (Ads- call [410]799-1955)

Columns/Departments: Try This (short ideas that have worked in teaching kids), 2-3 paragraphs. Pays free book.

Tips: "Looking for program ideas, outreach ideas, something that has worked to draw kids closer to Jesus. This is a how-to oriented magazine. I'd be interested in active teaching ideas on general themes, such as faith, trust, prayer and grace."

LEADER IN THE CHURCH SCHOOL TODAY, 201 Eighth Ave. N, Nashville TN 37203. (615)749-6488. Fax (615)749-6512. E-mail: smcgee@ umpublishing.org. United Methodist. Jill S. Reddig, ed. For pastors and Christian education leaders in the church. Quarterly mag; 64 pgs; circ 9,000. Subscription $16. 70% freelance. Complete ms/cover letter; phone/fax/e-query OK. Pays $25-125 (.05/wd) on publication for all, 1st, one-time or reprint rts. Articles 650-1,300 wds (98/yr); book reviews 150 wds. Responds in 6-8 wks. Seasonal 6-12 mos ahead. Accepts reprints (tell when/where appeared). Prefers disk or e-mail submission. Some sidebars. Prefers NRSV (never Living). Guidelines/theme list; copy $4.50/9x12 SAE. (No ads)

Fillers: Buys 25-30/yr. Games, ideas, word puzzles; 50-250 wds. Pays $15-50.

Columns/Departments: Buys 30/yr. Idea Exchange (what worked for us; for children/youth/adult classes), 50-150 wds; Teacher/leader Development (teacher training), 700-2,500 wds; Days & Seasons (seasonal Christian ed.), 700-2,500 wds.

Tips: "Most open to columns. Send a sample of your writing. "

** This periodical was #46 on the 1998 Top 50 Christian Publishers List. (#45 in 1997, #66 in 1996)

*LOLLIPOPS**, The Magazine for Early Childhood Educators, Good Apple, Inc., Box 2649, Columbus OH 43216-2649. Donna Borst, ed. Easy-to-use,hands-on, practical teaching ideas and suggestions for early childhood educators. Magazine published 5X/yr; circ 20,000. 20% freelance. Query or complete ms. Pays $10-100 on publication for all rts. Articles 200-1,000 wds; fiction (for young children) 500-1,200 wds. Seasonal 6 mos ahead. Guidelines (2 stamps); copy for 9x12 SAE/3 stamps.

Poetry: Light verse.

Tips: "Looking for something new and different for teachers of young children; seasonal material."

PARISH TEACHER, Box 1209, Minneapolis MN 55440-1209. (612)330-3423. E-mail: grinerr@augsburg-fortress.org. ELCA/Augsburg Fortress Publishers. Randi Sundet Griner, ed. Articles and ideas for Lutheran and mainline Christian volunteers who are leaders in Christian education programs. Monthly (9X, Sept-May) mag; 16 pgs; circ 50,000. Subscription $9.95. 12.5% freelance. Complete ms/cover letter. Pays $50 on publication for all rts (preferred). Articles 550-650 wds (15/yr); plays 400-800 wds (1-2/yr). Responds in 12-16 wks. Seasonal 4-6 mos ahead. Requires disk. No sidebars. Prefers NRSV. Guidelines; copy for 9x12 SAE/4 stamps.

Fillers: Buys 70+ ideas/yr.; 100-200 wds; $20.

Tips: "Most open to ideas or feature articles that are practical and inspirational in Christian education settings."

PERSPECTIVE, Box 788, Wheaton IL 60189-0788. (630)876-5735. Fax (630)293-3053. E-mail: bparat@yahoo.com. Website: http://www. pioneerclubs.org. Pioneer Clubs. Rebecca Powell Parat, ed. To help and encourage Pioneer Clubs leaders (for children ages 2-18). Triennial mag; 32 pgs; circ 24,000. Subscription $6. 15% freelance. Query/clips (preferred); fax query OK. Pays .06-.10/wd on acceptance. Articles 1,000-1,500 wds (0-3/yr). Responds in 9 wks. Seasonal 9 mos ahead. Accepts simultaneous query & reprints (tell when/where appeared). Prefers disk or accepts e-mail submission if under 300 wds (copied into message). Regular sidebars. Prefers NIV. Guidelines; copy $1.75/9x12 SAE/6 stamps. (No ads)

> **Columns/Departments:** Buys 0-3/yr. Storehouse (ideas for crafts, games, service projects, tips for leaders, etc.); 150-250 wds; $9-15. Complete ms.

> **Tips:** "Most articles done on assignment. We'd like to hear from freelancers who have experience with, or access to, a Pioneer Clubs program or Camp Cherith. They should send samples of their work along with a letter introducing themselves."

RELIGION TEACHER'S JOURNAL, Box 180, Mystic CT 06355. (860)536-2611. Fax (860)572-0788. E-mail: ttpubsedit@aol.com. Twenty-Third Publications/ Catholic. Gwen Costello, ed. dir. For volunteer religion teachers who need practical, hands-on information as well as theological background for teaching religion to K through high school. 7X yearly mag; 40 pgs; circ 40,000. Subscription $19.95. 40% freelance. Query; fax/e-query OK. Pays to $100 on acceptance for 1st rts. Not copyrighted. Articles to 6 pgs (50/yr). Responds in 2-4 wks. Seasonal 2 mos ahead. Prefers disk. Regular sidebars. Guidelines/theme list; copy for 9x12 SAE/4 stamps. (Ads)

> **Fillers:** Buys 20-30/yr. Anecdotes (about teaching), games, ideas, prayers, successful class activities; to 1 pg; $5-25.

> **Tips:** "Know our audience and address their needs. Most open to feature articles about teaching skills, spirituality, successful class activities or projects."

RESOURCE, 6401 The Paseo, Kansas City MO 64131. (816)333-7000x2224. Fax (816)363-7092. E-mail: dfelter@nazarene.org. Website: http://www.naza rene.org. Church of the Nazarene. David Felter, ed. To provide information, training, and inspiration to those who are involved in ministering within the Christian Life and Sunday school departments of the local church. Quarterly journal; 34 pgs; circ 9,000. Subscription $6.25. 50-65% freelance. Query; fax/e-query OK. Query for electronic submissions. Pays .04/wd on acceptance for all, 1st, one-time, or reprint rts. Articles 1,000-4,000 wds (150/yr); book reviews 300 wds. Responds in 2 wks. Seasonal 6 mos ahead. Accepts reprints. Accepts disk. Regular sidebars. Prefers NIV or NRSV. Guidelines/ theme list; copy for 9x12 SAE/2 stamps. (Ads)

> **Poetry:** Buys 4/yr. Seasonal or on outreach/Sunday school; to 30 lines; .25/line, $5 minimum. Submit max 1 poem.

Fillers: Buys 4 cartoons/yr; $10-25.

Tips: "Looking for succinct pieces that instruct, train, motivate, etc." ** This periodical was #58 on the 1998 Top 50 Christian Publishers list. (#50 in 1997, #18 in 1996, #10 in 1995)

SHINING STAR MAGAZINE, 308 N. Pine St., New London IA 52645. (217)357-2280. Frank Schaeffer Publications. Mary Tucker, ed. Reproducible Bible activities for Sunday school, VBS & Christian schools; pre-K-6th grades. Quarterly mag; 80 pgs; circ 11,000. Subscription $16.95. 90% freelance. Query; phone query OK. Pays $15-40 on publication for all rts. Articles 1-2 pages (uses mostly activities-200/yr); little fiction (6-10/yr). Responds in 4-6 wks. Seasonal 9 mos ahead. Accepts simultaneous submissions. Hard copy only. No sidebars. Prefers NIV. Guidelines/theme list; copy $4.95/9x12 SAE. (No ads)

Poetry: Buys 10-12/yr. Light verse, traditional; 8-30 lines; $10-30. Submit max 5 poems.

Fillers: Buys 30/yr. Anecdotes, facts, games, ideas, quizzes, quotes, word puzzles; 100-300 wds; $10-40.

Special Needs: Puzzles, games, crafts for kids. Always needs more activities/ideas for preschoolers.

Tips: "Be familiar with what our mission/purpose is. Find a new, different, fun way to teach God's Word to children. Try out material on children before you consider it ready to submit."

TEACHERS IN FOCUS, 8605 Explorer Dr., Colorado Springs CO 80920. (719)531-3372. Fax (719)548-5860. E-mail: koernehd@fotf.org. Website: http://www.family.org. Focus on the Family. Mark Hartwig, ed; submit to Heather Koerner, assoc ed. To encourage, inform and support Christian teachers in public and private education (K-12). Monthly (9X) mag; 24 pgs; circ 30,000. Subscription $20. 80% freelance. Query; fax/e-query OK. Pays $200 & up on acceptance for 1st rts. Articles 1,500 wds (4/yr); book reviews (educational resources), $25-50. Responds in 4 wks. Accepts reprints (tell when/where appeared). Accepts disk or e-mail submission (copied into message). Kill fee 50%. Regular sidebars. Prefers NIV. Guidelines/theme list (also on Website); copy for 9x12 SAE/4 stamps.

Fillers: Buys 50/yr. Humorous classroom anecdotes; 50-150 wds; $25.

Columns/Departments: Teammates (profiles on support staff), 500 wds; Guest Speaker (misc. education and religious topics), 500 wds. Pays $75.

Tips: "Uses articles of interest to teachers trying to cope in the classroom situation. Education issues. Avoid educational and religious jargon." ** This periodical was #40 on the 1998 Top 50 Christian Publishers list (#23 in 1997, #12 in 1996, #29 in 1995, #55 in 1994). 1997 EPA Award of Merit—Christian Ministry (1995 EPA Award of Excellence—Christian Ministry).

TEACHERS INTERACTION, 3558 S. Jefferson Ave., St. Louis MO 63118-3968. (314)268-1083. Fax (314)268-1329. E-mail: nummelata@cphnet.org. Concordia Publishing House/Lutheran Church-Missouri Synod. Tom

Nummela, ed. A magazine church-school workers grow by. Quarterly mag; 32 pgs; circ. 20,400. Subscription $10.25. 25% freelance. Complete ms/cover letter; fax/e-query OK. Pays $20-100 on acceptance or publication for all rts. How-tos to 100 wds, articles 700 wds (10/yr). Responds in 4 wks. Seasonal 1 yr ahead. Prefers disk. Some sidebars. Prefers NIV. Guidelines/theme list; copy for 9x12 SAE/3 stamps.

Songs: Buys 4/yr. First rts. $50.

Fillers: Buys 48/yr. Teacher tips/ideas, 50 wds.

Special Needs: Practical, how-to articles that will help the volunteer church worker.

Tips: "We need feature articles in four areas—inspiration, theology, practical and informational—in the area of volunteer Christian education. Theology must be compatible with Lutheranism."

*TEAM, Box 7259, Grand Rapids MI 49510. (616)241-5616. Fax (616)241-5558. Young Calvinist Federation. Submit to The Editor. Geared to leaders of youth programs, not Sunday school. Quarterly mag; circ 2,000. 10% freelance. Complete ms. Pays $30 on publication for 1st, simultaneous or reprint rts. Articles 700-2,000 wds (6/yr). Responds in 5 wks. Seasonal 6 mos ahead. Kill fee 50%. Accepts simultaneous submissions & reprints. Guidelines; copy $1/9x12 SAE/2 stamps.

Fillers: Cartoons, ideas, party ideas, short humor.

Columns/Departments: Street Beat (issues in urban youth ministry).

TODAY'S CATHOLIC TEACHER, 330 Progress Rd., Dayton OH 45449-2386. (937)847-5900. Fax (937)847-5910. E-mail: tcteditor1@aol.com. Website: http://www.catholicteacher.com. Catholic/Peter Li Education Group. Mary C. Noschang, ed. Directed to personal and professional concerns of teachers and administrators in K-12 Catholic schools. Monthly mag (6X during school yr); 60 pgs; circ 50,000. Subscription $14.95. 40% freelance. Query; phone/fax query OK. Pays $65-250 after publication for all rts. Articles 600-800, 1,000-1,200 or 1,200-1,500 wds (40-50/yr). Responds in 18 wks. Seasonal 3 mos ahead. Accepts simultaneous submissions & reprints (tell when/where appeared). Prefers disk or e-mail submission (copied into message). Regular sidebars. Guidelines/theme list (also on Website); copy $3. (Ads)

Special Needs: Activity pages teachers can copy and pass out to students to work on. Try to provide classroom-ready material teachers can use to supplement curriculum.

Tips: "Looking for material teachers in grades 3-9 can use to supplement curriculum material. Most open to articles or lesson plans."

VISION MAGAZINE, Box 41300, Pasadena CA 91114. (626)798-1124. Fax (626)798-2346. E-mail: ceaieduca@aol.com. Christian Educators Assn., Intl. Denise Jones, ed. To encourage, equip and empower Christian educators and parents in serving in public and private schools. inserted in Teachers in Focus. Monthly (9X) insert; 4 pgs; circ 6,000. VISION Magazine is 16 pgs (3X/yr). Subscription $35 (free to donors). 50% freelance. Query; fax query OK. Pays $30-40 on publication for 1st & reprint rts. Articles 50-1,200 wds (2/yr); book reviews 40-50 wds, pays copies. Responds in 4-6 wks. Seasonal 4 mos ahead. Accepts simultaneous submissions &

reprints. Regular sidebars. Guidelines/theme list; copy for 9x12 SAE/6 stamps. (Ads)

Poetry: Accepts 3-4/yr. Free verse, haiku, light verse, traditional; 4-16 lines; no payment. Submit max 3 poems.

Fillers: Accepts 2-6/yr. Anecdotes, cartoons, facts, ideas, newsbreaks, prose, prayers, quotes; 100 wds; no payment. Educational only.

Special Needs: Legal and other issues in public education.

Tips: "Know public education, write from a positive perspective as our readers are involved in public education by calling and choice. Most open to tips for teachers for living out their faith in the classroom in legally appropriate ways."

DAILY DEVOTIONAL MARKETS

Due to the nature of the daily devotional market, the following market listings may include only the name, address, phone number (if available) and editor's name. Because most of these markets assign all material, they do not wish to be listed in the usual way, if at all.

If you are interested in writing daily devotionals, send to the following markets for guidelines and sample copies, write up sample devotionals to fit each one's particular format, and send to the editor with a request for an assignment. **DO NOT** submit any other type of material to these markets unless indicated.

*COME YE APART, Box 419527, Kansas City MO 64131. Paul Martin, ed.

DAILY DEVOTIONS FOR THE DEAF, 21199 Greenview Rd., Council Bluffs IA 51503-4190. (712)322-5493. Fax (712)322-7792. E-mail: DeafMissions @deafmissions.com. Website: http://www.deafmissions.com. Duane King, ed. Prefers to see completed devotionals; 225 wds. **NO PAYMENT.**

*DEVOTIONS, 8121 Hamilton Ave., Cincinnati OH 45231. (513)931-4050. Eileen Wilmoth, ed. No devotions or poetry. Buys photos only.

FORWARD DAY BY DAY, 412 Sycamore St., Cincinnati OH 45202-4195. (513)721-6659. Fax (513)721-0729. E-mail: forwardmovement@msn. com. Website: http://www.forwardmovement.org. Edward S. Gleason, ed. Send a couple of sample devotions to fit our format and request an assignment. Preferred length: 1150 characters. Pays honorarium, about $200 for a month's devotions. Uses almost no freelance.

+FRUIT OF THE VINE, Barclay Press, 110 S. Elliott St., Newberg OR 97132-2144. (503)538-7345. Fax (503)538-7033. E-mail: info@barclaypress. com. Website: http://www.barclaypress.com. Editorial team: Harlow Ankeny, Susan Fawver, Sherry Macy, Dan McCracken. Send samples and request assignment. Prefers 250-290 wds. **PAYS FREE SUBSCRIPTION.** Guidelines.

+GOD'S COURTROOM, 745 Hickory St., Akron OH 44303-2213. (330)434-1544. Fax (330)535-6452. E-mail: Wtai@mindspring.com. Website: http:// www.fovgc.org. Wanda J. Sprinkle, sr ed. Written specifically for inmates in jail, prisons, and residents of halfway house facilities. Pays $5 on acceptance. Guidelines/copy for #10 SAE/1stamp.

THE HOME ALTAR, Box 1209, Minneapolis MN 55440-1209. (612)330-3211. E-mail: grinerr@augsburg-fortress.org. Randi Sundet Griner, ed. Devotional material for families with elementary-school-aged children. Devotional booklet; 64 pgs. Pays $20/printed pg.

THE QUIET HOUR, 4050 Lee Vance View, Colorado Springs CO 80919. (719)536-0100. Cook Communications Ministries. Gary Wilde, ed. Pays $15 -25 on acceptance. Send resume and list of credits, rather than a sample.

REJOICE! 1218 Franklin St. NW, Salem OR 97304-3902. (503)585-4458. Mennonite. Philip Wiebe, ed. Quarterly. Pays $110 for 7-day assigned meditations, 300 wds. Doesn't send samples or guidelines to unsolicited writers. Prefers that you send a couple of sample devotions and inquire about assignment procedures. Don't apply for assignment unless you are familiar with the publication and Anabaptist theology.

THE SECRET PLACE, Box 851, Valley Forge PA 19482-0851. (610)768-2240. (800)ABC-3USA. Kathleen Hayes, sr ed. Prefers to see completed devotionals, 100-200 wds (use unfamiliar Scripture passages). Uses poetry and photos. 64 pgs. Pays $15 for 1st rts. Guidelines.

+THESE DAYS, 100 Witherspoon St., Louisville KY 40202-1396. Fax (502)569-5453. Presbyterian Publishing Corp. Kay Snodgrass, ed. Send for issue themes and scripture references; then query. Pays $10 for all rts (makes work-for-hire assignments); 200-250 wds. Uses poetry (2-6/yr).

THE UPPER ROOM, PO Box 189, Nashville TN 37202-0189. (615)340-7252 (no "cold" calls; get guidelines first). Fax (615)340-7006. E-mail: The UpperRoomMagazine@upperroom.org. Website: http://www.upper room.org. Mary Lou Redding, mng ed. 95% freelance. Pays $25/devotional. 72 pgs. Note: This publication wants freelance submissions and does not make assignments. Phone/fax/e-query OK. Send devotionals of 250-300 wds. Buys one-time use of art work (transparencies/slides requested). No disk. Guidelines; copy for 5x7 SAE/2 stamps.

> **Tips:** "We do not return submissions. Accepted submissions will be notified in 6-9 wks. Follow guidelines."

*THE WORD IN SEASON, PO Box 1209, Minneapolis MN 55440-1209. (800)426-0115x216. Fax (612)330-3455. Andrea Lee Schieber, ed. 96 pgs. Devotions 250 wds. Pays $15/devotion. Guidelines for #10 SAE/2 stamps.

> **Tips:** "We prefer that you write for guidelines. We will send instructions for preparing sample devotions. We accept new writers based on the sample devotions we request and make assignments after acceptance."

WORDS OF LIFE, St. Paul University, 223 Main St., Ottawa ON K1S 1C4 Canada. (613)782-3036. Fax (613)752-3004. E-mail: cgreen@spu.stpaul. uottawa.ca. Caryl Green, ed. Send samples and request an assignment. Prefers 125 wds. Pays $40 CAN. Buys photos.

MISSIONS MARKETS

AMERICAN BAPTISTS IN MISSION, PO Box 851, Valley Forge PA 19482-0851. (610)768-2077. Fax (610)768-2320. E-mail: richard.schramm@abc-usa.org. Website: http://www.abc-usa.org. Richard W. Schramm, ed. Denominational. Bimonthly mag; 24-32 pgs; circ 39,000. Subscription free. 10% freelance. Query; fax/e-query OK. Pays negotiable rates on publication. Articles 750-1,000 wds (few/yr). Prefers e-mail submission (attached file). Some sidebars. Prefers NRSV. Guidelines (also by e-mail); copy. Not in topical listings but will accept any article of substantial interest to American Baptists. (Ads)

#AMERICAN HORIZON, 1445 Boonville Ave., Springfield MO 65802-1894. (417)862-2781x3264. Fax (417)863-7276. Assemblies of God. Dan Van Veen, ed. Denominational magazine of home missions, mostly on assignment. Bimonthly mag; 20 pgs; circ 40,200. Free to contributors. 75% freelance. Query or complete ms/cover letter; phone query OK. Pay .03/wd on publication for 1st rts. Articles 750-1,200 wds (17/yr). Responds in 6 wks. Seasonal 5 mos ahead. Accepts simultaneous submissions & reprints. Free guidelines/copy. (Ads)

***AREOPAGUS MAGAZINE**, PO Box 33, Shatin, New Territories, Hong Kong. (852)691-1904. Fax (852)265-9885. Website: http://www.areopagus.com. Tao Fong Shan Christian Centre. John G. LeMond, ed. Provides a forum for dialogue between the good news of Jesus Christ and people of faith both in major world religions and new religious movements. Quarterly mag; 50 pgs; circ 1,000. Subscription $24. 75% freelance. Complete ms; e-mail submission OK. Pays $100-300 on publication for 1st rts. Articles 1,000-5,000 wds (40/yr); book reviews, 500-750 wds, $100. Responds in 6-13 wks. Seasonal 6 mos ahead. Accepts simultaneous submissions & reprints. Prefers disk. Kill fee 50%. Guidelines; copy $4.

> **Columns/Departments:** Buys 10/yr. Complete ms. Pays $50-100.
> **Special Needs:** Interfaith dialogue.
> **Tips:** "We look for compassionate, direct, and unself-conscious prose that reflects a writer who is firmly rooted in his/her own tradition but is unafraid to encounter other religions."

CATHOLIC NEAR EAST, 1011 First Ave., New York NY 10022-4195. (212)826-1480. Fax (212)826-8979. Catholic Near East Welfare Assn. Michael La Civita, ed. Interest in cultural, religious, human rights development in Middle East, NE Africa, India and Eastern Europe. Bimonthly mag; 32 pgs; circ 100,000. Subscription $12. 50% freelance. Query/clips; fax query OK. Pays .20/edited wd ($200) on publication for 1st rts. Articles 1,500-2,000 wds (15/yr). Responds in 8 wks. Accepts disk. Kill fee $200. Regular sidebars. Prefers NAS. Guidelines; copy for 7x10 SAE/3 stamps.

> **Tips:** "We strive to educate our readers about the culture, faith, history, issues and people who form the Eastern Christian churches. Material should not be academic."

EAST-WEST CHURCH AND MINISTRY REPORT, Dept. IEWCS, Wheaton College, Wheaton IL 60187-5593. (630)752-5917. Fax (630)752-5916. E-mail: lewcw@wheaton.edu. Website: http://www.wheaton.edu/bgc/iewcs. Institute for East-West Christian Studies. Dr. Mark Elliot, ed. Encourages Western Christian ministry in East Central Europe and the former Soviet Union that is effective, culturally sensitive and cooperative. Quarterly newsletter; 16 pgs; circ 430. Subscription $44.95. 75% freelance. Query; query for electronic submissions; e-query OK. **NO PAYMENT** for all rts.

Articles 1,500 wds (3/yr); book reviews, 100 wds. Responds in 4 wks. Prefers disk or e-mail submission. Regular sidebars. Any version. Guidelines (also by e-mail/Website); copy $10. (No ads)

Tips: "All submissions must relate to East-Central Europe, the former Soviet Union or evangelical missions."

EVANGELICAL MISSIONS QUARTERLY, PO Box 794, Wheaton IL 60189. (630)752-7158. Fax (630)752-7155. E-mail: emqjournal@aol.com. Evangelism & Missions Information Service. Gary Corwin, ed. For missionaries and others interested in missions trends, strategies, issues, problems, and resources. Quarterly journal; 128 pgs; circ 7,000. Subscription $21.95. 65% freelance. Query; fax e-query OK. Pays $100 on publication for all rts. Articles 2,500 wds (70/yr); book reviews 400 wds (query), $25. Responds in 4 wks. Accepts few reprints (tell when/where appeared). Prefers disk or e-mail submission (copied into message). Some sidebars. Prefers NIV. Free guidelines (also by e-mail)/copy. (Ads)

Columns/Departments: Buys 4/yr. In the Workshop (tips to increase missionary effectiveness), 1,500-2,000 wds. Pays $100.

Tips: "Present an article idea and why you are qualified to write it. All articles must target evangelical, cross-cultural missionaries."

HEARTBEAT, PO Box 5002, Antioch TN 37011-5002. (615)731-6812. Fax (615)731-5345. E-mail: heartbeat@nafwb.org. Website: http://www. nafwb.org. Free Will Baptist. Don Robirds, ed. To inform and challenge church members with mission needs. Bimonthly mag; 12 pgs; circ 20,000. Subscription free. 1% freelance. Complete ms/cover letter; fax/e-query OK. Pays .04/wd on publication for one-time rts. Articles 800 wds (2/yr). Responds in 6 wks. Seasonal 4 mos ahead. Accepts reprints (tell when/where appeared). Prefers disk or e-mail submission (copied into message). No sidebars. Prefers KJV. Guidelines; copy for #10 SAE. (No ads)

INTERNATIONAL JOURNAL OF FRONTIER MISSIONS, 7665 Wenda Way, El Paso TX 79915. (915)775-2464. Fax (915)775-8588. E-mail: 103121. 2610@compuserve.com. Hans Weerstra, ed. Dedicated to frontier missions in people groups that have no viable Christian church. Quarterly journal; 55 pgs; circ 600. Subscription $15. 100% freelance. Complete ms/cover letter; phone/fax/e-query OK. **NO PAYMENT** for one-time rts. Articles 6-7 pgs. Seasonal 3 mos ahead. Accepts simultaneous submissions & reprints. Accepts e-mail submission. No sidebars. Prefers NKJV or NIV. Guidelines/theme list (also by e-mail); copy $2/10x13 SAE. (Ads)

Special Needs: Contextualization, church in missions, comparative religions, training for missions, trends for missions, biblical basis for missions.

Tips: "Although the circulation is small, the print run is 3,000 and used for motivational purposes."

LATIN AMERICA EVANGELIST, Box 52-7900, Miami FL 33152-7900. (305)884-8400. Fax (305)885-8649. E-mail: evangelist@lam.org. Website: http://www.lam.org. Latin America Mission. Susan G. Loobie, ed (sgloobie@lam.org). To present God's work through the churches and missionaries in Latin America. Quarterly & online mag; 24 pgs; circ 22,000. Subscription $10. 10% freelance. Query/clips first; phone/fax/e-query OK. Pays $125 on publication for 1st rts. Articles 1,000 wds. Reporting time varies. Accepts simultaneous submissions. Accepts e-mail submission. Regular sidebars. Prefers NIV. Guidelines (also by e-mail); free copy. (No ads)

Tips: "Looking for news and analysis of the religious climate and social conditions in Latin America."

#LEADERS FOR TODAY, Box 13, Atlanta GA 30370. (770)449-8869. Fax (770)449-8457. Haggai Institute. Billy Grimes, ed. Primarily for donors to ministry; focus is alumni success stories. Quarterly mag; 24 pgs; circ 7,500. Free subscription. 75% freelance. Query; fax query OK. Pays .10-.25/wd on acceptance for all rts. Articles 1,000-2,000 wds. Responds in 2-3 wks. Requires disk. Kill fee 100%. Regular sidebars. Prefers NIV. Guidelines/theme list; copy for 9x12 SAE/4 stamps. (No ads)

Tips: "All articles are pre-assigned. Query first."

*MESSAGE OF THE CROSS, 6820 Auto Club Rd., Ste D, Minneapolis MN 55438. (612)829-2492. Fax (612)829-2753. Bethany Fellowship, Inc. George Foster, ed. Deeper life and Christian missions for a general Christian public. Quarterly mag; 32 pgs; circ 10,000. Subscription free. 20% freelance. Query or complete ms/cover letter; fax query OK. Pays $20-35 on publication for 1st or reprint rts. Articles (8/yr). Responds in 4 wks. Seasonal 6 mos ahead. Accepts reprints. No sidebars. Copy for 6x9 SAE. (Ads)

MISSIOLOGY: An International Review, Asbury Theological Seminary, 204 N. Lexington Ave., Wilmore KY 40390. (606)858-2216. Fax (606)858-2375. E-mail: Darrell_Whiteman@ats.wilmoreky.us. Website: http://www.asmweb.org. American Society of Missiology. Darrell L. Whiteman, ed. A professional organization for mission studies. Quarterly journal; 128 pgs; circ 2,000. Subscription $28. 70% freelance. Complete ms/cover letter; phone/fax/e-query OK. **PAYS 20 COPIES** for all rts. Articles 5,000 wds (20/yr); book reviews, 200-300 wds. Responds in 6 wks. Requires disk, no e-mail submission. No sidebars. Any version. Guidelines; free copy. (Ads)

Tips: "Whole journal is open to freelancers as long as they write from a missiological perspective and have adequate documentation."

NEW WORLD OUTLOOK, 475 Riverside Dr., Room 1467, New York NY 10115-0122. (212)870-3765. Fax (212)870-3940. E-mail: nwo@gbgm-umc.org. Website: http://www.gbgm-ums.org/nwo. United Methodist. Alma Graham, ed.; submit to Christie R. House. Denominational missions. Bimonthly mag; 48 pgs; circ 25,000. Subscription $15. 20% freelance. Query; phone/fax query OK. Pays $50-200 on publication for all rts. Articles 500-2,000 wds (24/yr); book reviews 200-500 wds (assigned). No guaranteed response time. Seasonal 4 mos ahead. Kill fee 50%. Prefers e-mail submission (WordPerfect 6.1 in attached file). Regular sidebars. Prefers NRSV. Guidelines; copy $3. (Ads)

Tips: "Ask for a list of United Methodist mission workers and projects in your area. Investigate them, propose a story, and consult with the editors before writing. Most open to articles and/or color photos of US or foreign mission sites visited as a stringer, after consultation with the editor."

PFI WORLD REPORT, Box 17434, Washington DC 20041. (703)481-0000. Fax (703)481-0003. E-mail: cnicholson@pfi.org. Prison Fellowship, Intl. Christopher P. Nicholson, mng ed. Targets issues and needs of prisoners, ex-prisoners, justice officials, victims, families and PFI staff, and volunteers in 75 countries. Bimonthly newsletter; 4-8 pgs; circ 4,750. Free subscription. 10% freelance. Query; phone/fax/e-query OK. Pays $100-300 on acceptance for all rts. Articles 500-750 wds (4/yr). Responds in 2 wks. Seasonal 4 mos ahead. Accepts simultaneous submissions & reprints (tell when/where appeared). Accepts disk. Kill fee. Regular sidebars. Copy for #10 SAE/ 1 stamp.

> **Special Needs:** Prison issues, justice issues, anything that relates to international prison ministry.
> **Tips:** "Looking for personal profiles of people active in prison ministry (preferably PFI officials); ex-prisoner success stories; how-to articles about various aspects of prison ministry. Avoid American slant."

P.I.M.E. WORLD, 17330 Quincy St., Detroit MI 48221-2765. (313)342-4066. Fax (313)342-6816.Website: http://www.rc.net/pime. Pontifical Inst. for Foreign Missions/Catholic. Paul W. Witte, mng ed. For those interested in and supportive of foreign missions. Monthly (10X) mag; 16 pgs; circ 26,000. Subscription $5. 15% freelance. Complete ms/cover letter; query for electronic submissions. Pays .06/wd on publication for all rts. Photos $10. Not copyrighted. Articles 800-1,200 wds. Responds in 4 wks. Seasonal 2 mos ahead. Accepts simultaneous submissions & reprints (tell when/where appeared). Prefers disk; no e-mail submission. Regular sidebars. Prefers NAB. Guidelines; copy for 2 stamps. (No ads)

> **Tips:** "Issues like hunger, human rights, women's rights, peace and justice as they are dealt with in developing countries by missionaries and locals alike; stories of missionary service."

THE QUIET HOUR ECHOES, 630 Brookside Ave., Box 3000, Redlands CA 92373. (909)793-2588. Fax (909)793-4754. E-mail: cwest@thequiethour. com. Website: http://www.thequiethour.com. The Quiet Hour (radio broadcast). Bill Tucker, ed. Provides radio listeners with challenges from the mission field and heart-to-heart messages from God. Monthly mag; 36 pgs; circ. 80,000. Subscription $5. 50% freelance. Query only. **NO PAYMENT**. Not copyrighted. Some sidebars. Prefers KJV.

> **Poetry:** Accepts 12-36/yr. Traditional.
> **Tips:** Only accepting poetry with a strict meter (rhyme).

THE RAILROAD EVANGELIST, PO Box 5026, Vancouver WA 98668-5026. (360)699-7208. Fax (360)750-5618. E-mail: rejoe@integrityonline.com. Joe Spooner, ed. For railroad and transportation employees and their families. Quarterly mag; 16 pgs; circ 2,500. Subscription $6. 100% freelance. Complete ms/no cover letter; phone query OK. **NO PAYMENT**. Articles 100-700 wds (10-15/yr). Seasonal 4 months ahead. Accepts simultaneous submissions & reprints. Accepts e-mail submission. No sidebars. Guidelines; copy for 9x12 SAE/2 stamps. (No ads)

> **Poetry:** Accepts 4-8/yr. Traditional, any length. Send any number.
> **Fillers:** Accepts many. Anecdotes, cartoons, quotes; to 100 wds.

Tips: "We need 400-700 word railroad-related salvation testimonies; or railroad-related human-interest stories."

#SO ALL MAY HEAR (formerly Save Our World), 2490 Keith St. NW, PO Box 8016, Cleveland TN 37320-8016. (423)478-7190. Fax (423)478-7155. E-mail: tlr@cogwm.org. Website: http://www.cogwm.org. Church of God (Cleveland TN). Robert D. McCall, ed. Denominational publication for missions awareness. Quarterly tabloid; 16 pgs; circ. 97,000. Free. 10% freelance. Query/clips; phone/fax/e-query OK. **NO PAYMENT** (pays $50 for some) for one-time rts. Articles 400-650 wds. Responds in 4 wks. Accepts reprints. Prefers disk. Regular sidebars. Prefers KJV. Copy $3/9x12 SAE.

Fillers: Accepts 4/yr. Facts, newsbreaks; 50-100 wds.

Tips: "Most open to missions trips made to foreign fields, missions experiences, material promoting missions giving and its rewards, missions-related stories, etc."

*URBAN MISSION, Box 27009, Philadelphia PA 19118. (215)887-5511. Fax (215)887-5404. Westminster Theological Seminary. H. M. Conn, ed. Dedicated to advancement of Christ in cities throughout the world. Quarterly journal; circ 1,300. Subscription $16. 100% freelance. Complete ms/cover letter. **PAYS 3 COPIES.** Articles 2,100-6,000 wds (40/yr). Responds in 1-2 wks. Accepts reprints.

+VOICES IN THE WILDERNESS, PO Box 5303, Charlottesville VA 22905. (804)293-8829. Fax (804)293-7586. E-mail: anm@adnamis.org. Advancing Native Missions. Virginia Tobias, ed. To communicate the story/message/needs of indigenous missionaries to North American Christians. Quarterly mag; circ 7,000. Subscription free. Query. Not in topical listings. (No ads)

+WOMEN OF THE HARVEST, PO Box 151297, Lakewood CO 80215-1297. (303)914-0191. Fax (303)986-4062. E-mail: gln@uswest.net. Website: Http://www.womenoftheharvest.com. Women of the Harvest Ministries Intl., Inc. Stephanie Nelson, ed; Kimberly Staub, submissions ed. To support and encourage women serving in cross-cultural missions. Quarterly mag; 16 pgs. Complete ms. **NO PAYMENT** for one-time rts. Articles 350-650 wds. Seasonal 3 mos ahead. Prefers e-mail submission or disk. Guidelines; copy for SASE.

Poetry: Free verse, traditional, haiku; variable length. Submit max 5 poems.

Fillers: Accepts; 100 wds. Anecdotes, short humor.

Tips: "This is a magazine designed especially for women serving cross-culturally. We need articles, humor, and anecdotes related to this topic."

+WORLD CHRISTIAN MAGAZINE, PO Box 1525, Oak Park, IL 60304. (708)524-5070. Fax: (708) 524-5174. E-mail:winpress@juno.com. WIN Press, a division of World In Need, USA. Tonya Eichelberger, ed. To inform, encourage, provoke and mobilize this generation in obedience to the Great Commission. Quarterly mag; circ 30,000+ (March, September and December), 150,000+ (June). Subscription $14.95. 85% freelance. Prefers 1-page query; fax/e-query OK. Payment varies for all rts (usually).

Articles 800-2,000 words. Some sidebars. Guidelines/theme list; sample copy $3. (Ads)

WORLD MISSION PEOPLE, PO Box 535002, Indianapolis IN 46253-5002. (317)244-3660. Fax (317)244-1247. E-mail: FMCpeople@aol.com. Website: http://ourworld.compuserve.com/homepages/world_mission_people. Free Methodist World Missions. Daniel V. Runyon, ed. People features and worldwide news for supporters of Free Methodist missions. Bimonthly mag; 32 pgs; circ 7,000. Subscription $10. 90% freelance. Complete ms/ cover letter; no phone/fax query OK. **NO PAYMENT** for one-time rts. Articles 100-2,000 wds. Responds in 4 wks. Considers simultaneous submissions & reprints (tell when/where appeared). Prefers e-mail submission (copied into message). Regular sidebars. Prefers NIV. No guidelines/copy. (No ads)

   Tips: "Visit a Free Methodist overseas ministry and tell us about your experience."

WORLD PULSE, PO Box 794, Wheaton IL 60189. (630)752-7158. Fax (630)752-7155. E-mail: pulsenews@aol.com. Evangelism & Missions Information Service (EMIS). Stan Guthrie, mng ed. Articles and news items from around the world, related to missions and Christians. Bimonthly newsletter; 8 pgs; circ 5,000. Subscription $29.95. Query; fax/e-query OK. Pays $100 on publication for all rts. Articles 800-900 wds. Responds in 2 wks. Accepts reprints (tell when/where appeared). Prefers disk or e-mail submission (copied into message). Kill fee 60%. No sidebars. Prefers NIV. Free guidelines (also by e-mail)/copy for #10 SAE. (No ads)

   Tips: "Send specific ideas on what missions and national churches are actually doing and tell why you are qualified to write it."

WORLDWIDE CHALLENGE, 100 Sunport Ln., Dept. 1600, Orlando FL 32809. (407)826-2390. Fax (407)826-2374. E-mail: WChallenge@ccci.org. Website: http://www.ccci.org/WWC. Campus Crusade for Christ. Bill Sundstrom, ed. For financial supporters of Campus Crusade. Bimonthly mag; 48 pgs; circ 90,000. Subscription $12.95. 5% freelance. Query only/ clips. Pays .10/wd + a flat fee of $100-200 (depending on research) on acceptance for 1st rts (all rts for assigned articles). Articles 800-1,600 wds (6/yr). Responds in 6-8 wks. Seasonal 6-8 mos ahead. Accepts simultaneous submissions. Prefers disk. Kill fee 50%. Regular sidebars. Prefers NAS. Guidelines; copy for 9x12 SAE/5 stamps. (Ads)

   Columns/Departments: Buys 6/yr. Upfront (personal experience/ commentary); 400-800 wds; query or complete ms; Susie Hilsman, ed. History's Heroes (positive examples), 1,250 wds, query, Lisa Master, ed.

   Tips: "Give the human face behind a topic or story. Show how the topic relates to evangelism and/or discipleship."

   ** This periodical was #43 on the 1996 Top 50 Christian Publishers List. (#35 in 1994) Also 1996 EPA Award of Merit—Organizational.

MUSIC MARKETS

CCM MAGAZINE, 107 Kenner Ave., Nashville TN 37205. (615)386-3011. Fax

(615)385-4112. E-mail: feedback@ccmcom.com. Website: http://www. ccmcom.com. April Hefner, mng ed. Encourages spiritual growth through contemporary music; provides news and information about the Christian music market. Monthly & online mag; 80 pgs; circ 100,000+. Subscription $21.95. 75% freelance. Query/clips; phone/fax query OK. Pays .20/wd for short pieces, or $100/published page for features, on publication for all rts. Articles 500-2,500 wds; music reviews 250-350 wds. Responds slowly. Seasonal 3 mos ahead. Kill fee 50%. Prefers disk or e-mail submission (copied into message). Regular sidebars. Guidelines; copy for 9x12 SAE/$4. (Ads)

   ** 1996 EPA Award of Merit—Youth.

*CHRISTIAN COMPOSER, Box 448, Jacksonville OR 97530. (541)899-8888. James Lloyd, ed/pub. The only songwriter and artists Top Sheet in the business; includes a relevant essay on music-related subjects. Bimonthly newsletter, supplement to Christian Media; circ 2,000-6,000. Query; prefers phone query. **PAYS IN COPIES OR PRODUCT** for all rts. Articles; book & music reviews, 3 paragraphs. Responds in 3 wks. Accepts simultaneous submissions & reprints. Prefers disk. KJV only. Copy for 9x12 SAE/2 stamps. Not in topical listings.

   Special Needs: Material should focus on the craft of song writing, musical performance, or marketing of the same.

   Tips: "We like 'street-smarts' when it comes to articles. Tell it like it is in the music industry; we want our readers forewarned about the various pitfalls in Christian music."

CHRISTIAN COUNTRY RESEARCH BULLETIN (CCRB), 7057 Bluffwood Ct., Brownsburg IN 46112. (317)892-5031. Fax (317)892-5034. Website: http://www.christiancountry.com/ccrb. Joyful Sounds. Les Roberts, ed. Trade journal for Christian country radio industry. Biweekly trade journal; 8-12 pgs; circ. 300-1,200. Subscription $36. 75% freelance. Query or complete ms/cover letter; phone/fax/e-query OK. Negotiable payment & rights. Articles 600-2,000 wds; music reviews, 100-300 wds. Responds in 2 wks. Seasonal 2 mos ahead. Accepts reprints. Requires disk (DOS-ASCII). Copy for 9x12 SAE/2 stamps. (Ads)

   Fillers: Cartoons, short humor.

   Columns/Departments: Insider (artist interview); Programming 101 (radio technique); retail, inspirational, especially for musicians and radio people; 600-2,000 wds.

   Tips: "Most open to artist interviews. Must be familiar with Christian country music."

CHURCH MUSICIAN TODAY, 127 9th Ave. N., Nashville TN 37234-0140. (615)251-2913. Fax (615)251-2869. E-mail: churchmusician@lifeway.com. Southern Baptist. Jere Adams, design ed. A ministry resource for music and worship leaders. Monthly mag; 34 pgs; circ 10,000. Subscription $3. 10% freelance. Complete ms/cover letter; e-query OK. Pays .055/wd (.06/wd on disk or by e-mail submission) on publication for all rts. Articles (12-15/yr) 1,200 wds; book reviews 300 wds. Responds in 12 wks. Seasonal 1 yr ahead. Accepts few reprints (pays 50%—tell when/where appeared). Accepts disk or e-mail submission. Some sidebars. Guidelines; copy for 10x13 SAE/3 stamps. (Ads)

Fillers: Short humor (with a musical slant); 15-25 wds; $5-15.

Special Needs: Only uses articles that deal with church music ministry and worship planning for the church.

Tips: "Material must be relevant and practical to trained, practicing ministers of music, pastors, and other worship leaders."

THE CHURCH MUSIC REPORT, Box 1179, Grapevine TX 76099-1179. (817)488-0141. Fax (817)481-4191. E-mail: tcmrtalk@airmail.net. Website: http://www.tcmr.com. Bill Rayborn, ed. For church music leaders. Monthly newsletter; 12-36 pgs; circ 6,200. Ideas, tips, Special Offers, New Products, Articles. (Space ads, advertising inserts)

*CHURCH PIANIST/SAB CHOIR/THE CHOIR HERALD, Box 268, Alcoa TN 37701. Now a division of The Lorenz Corp. Hugh S. Livingston Jr., ed. Each of these music magazines has one page devoted to articles that deal with problems/solutions of choirs and accompanists. Bimonthly mag; 36-52 pgs; circ 25,000. 45% freelance. Complete ms/cover letter. Pay $15-150 on publication for all rts. Articles 250-1,250 wds (10-20/yr). Seasonal 1 yr ahead. Responds in 3-6 wks. Guidelines; copy for 9x12 SAE/3 stamps.

Poetry: Accepts 25/yr. Free verse, light verse, traditional, or poetry suitable for song lyrics; $10. Submit max 5 poems.

Fillers: Accepts 5-10/yr. Anecdotes, cartoons.

Special Needs: Choir experiences; pianist/organist articles.

Tips: "Best approach is from direct experience in music with the small church."

CREATOR MAGAZINE, 735 Industrial Rd., San Carlos CA 94070-3310. E-mail: creatormag@aol.com. Website: http://www.creatormagazine.com. Marshall Sanders, pub. For interdenominational music ministry; promoting quality, diverse music programs in the church. Bimonthly mag; 48-56 pgs; circ 6,000. Subscription $32.95. 35% freelance. Query or complete ms/ cover letter; fax/e-query OK. Pays $35-75 on publication for 1st or one-time rts. Articles 1,000-10,000 wds (20/yr); book reviews $20. Responds in 4-12 wks. Seasonal 4 mos ahead. Accepts simultaneous submissions & reprints (tell when/where appeared). Prefers disk. Regular sidebars. Prefers NRSV. Guidelines/theme list; copy for 9x12 SAE/5 stamps. (Ads)

Fillers: Buys 20/yr. Anecdotes, cartoons, ideas, jokes, party ideas, short humor; 10-75 wds; $5-25.

Special Needs: Articles on worship; staff relationships.

*GLORY SONGS, 127 9th Ave. N. Nashville TN 37234-0140. (615)251-2913. Fax (615)251-2614. Southern Baptist. Jere V. Adams, ed. Easy choral music for church choirs; practical how-to articles for small church music programs. Quarterly mag; 26 pgs; circ 85,000. 100% freelance. Complete ms. Pays .055/wd on acceptance for 1st rts. Articles 550-1,000 wds (6-7/yr). Responds in 2-4 wks. Seasonal 1 yr ahead. Accepts simultaneous submissions & reprints. Guidelines; free copy.

Poetry: Buys 2-3/yr. Free verse, traditional.

Fillers: Cartoons, ideas, party ideas, musical quizzes, short humor.

Special Needs: Vocal techniques, choir etiquette, mission/outreach ideas, music training, etc.

GOSPEL INDUSTRY TODAY, 761 Old Hickory Blvd., Ste. 205, Brentwood TN 37027-4513. E-mail: gospel@usit.net. Website: http://www.gospeltoday. com/gospel_industry.htm. Horizon Concepts, Inc. Teresa Harris, pub. About the Christian and Gospel music industry. Monthly (10X) mag; 20 pgs; circ 3,500. Subscription $24. 50% freelance. Query; fax/e-query OK. Pays $75-250 on publication for 1st rts. Articles 1,500-3,000 wds. Responds in 5-9 wks. Seasonal 3 mos ahead. Prefers disk. Kill fee 10%. Regular sidebars. Prefers KJV. Guidelines/theme list; copy for 10x13 SAE/8 stamps. (Ads)

THE HYMN, School of Theology, Boston University, 745 Commonwealth Ave., Boston MA 02215-1401. (800)THEHYMN. E-mail: hymneditor@worldnet. att.net, Hymn Society in the US & Canada. Carol A. Pemberton, ed, Box 46485, Eden Prairie MN 55344. For church musicians, hymnologists, scholars; articles related to the congregational song. Quarterly journal; 60 pgs; circ 3,000. Subscription $45. 100% freelance. Query; phone query OK. **NO PAYMENT** for all rts. Articles any length (12/yr); book & music reviews any length. Responds in 4 wks. Seasonal 4 mos ahead. Prefers disk, no e-mail submission. Regular sidebars. Any version. Guidelines; free copy. (Ads)

Poetry: Hymn poetry.

Special Needs: Hymns (text or music) and articles on history of hymns. Contact editor.

+THE LIGHTHOUSE ELECTRONIC MAGAZINE, 983 Clopper Rd. #B2, Gaithersburg MD 20878. (301)519-9155. Fax (301)519-9114. E-mail: lighthouse@tlem.org. Website: Http://tlem.org. Soditus, Inc./NetCentral, Inc. J. Warner Soditus, mng ed. A free online only Christian music magazine. Online mag 75% freelance. Complete ms by e-mail submission; e-query OK. **NO PAYMENT** for electronic rts. Articles (100/yr). Response time varies. Seasonal 2 mos ahead. Accepts reprints (tell when/where appeared). Requires disk or e-mail submission. Any version. Guidelines (by e-mail submission/Website); copy (see Website). (Ads)

Tips: "Most open to music reviews. Ask to join our staff mailing list. We are the first Christian music site rated in top 5% of the WWW."

*MUSIC MAKERS, 127 9th Ave. N., Nashville TN 37234-0140. (615)251-2000. Southern Baptist. Darrell Billingsley, ed. For children ages 6-11. Quarterly mag; circ 105,000. Pays .06/wd on acceptance for all rts. Articles & fiction 250-500 wds. Responds in 4 wks. Guidelines/copy. Not in topical listings.

*MUSIC TIME, 127 9th Ave. N., Nashville TN 37234-0140. (615)251-2000. Southern Baptist. Darrell Billingsley, literary design ed. For 4 & 5 yr olds; directly related to unit material found in The Music Leader. Quarterly mag; circ 60,000. Complete ms. Pays .05/wd for stories. Pays $9-12 on acceptance for all rts. Stories for 4 & 5 yr olds. Responds in 2-5 wks. Not in topical listings. Guidelines; free copy.

Poetry: 1-7 lines; $5-9.

+PROFILE MAGAZINE, 2525-C Lebanon Pike, Box 6, Nashville TN 37214.

(615)872-8080. Fax (615)872-9786. E-mail: profile@profilemagazine. com. Website: http://www.profilemagazine.com. VoxCorp, Inc. Chris Well, ed-in-chief; submit to Suzie Waltner, ed coordinator. Covers music, books and media for the retail shopper. Bimonthly mag; 100 pgs; circ 80,000. Subscription $15.95. 80% freelance. Query for electronic submissions. E-query OK. Pays .08-.10/wd, 45 days after publication. Prefers e-mail submission (copied into message). No guidelines. Not in topical listings. (Ads)

> **Tips:** "Send us clips and demonstrate that you have knowledge of the products and personalities we cover."

*QUEST, PO Box 14804, Columbus OH 43214. Rick Welke, ed. Geared to 16-30 year olds and radio personnel. Monthly newsletter. Query; fax query OK. **PAYS A SUBSCRIPTION.** Articles 100-500 wds (4/yr); fiction, 150-750 wds (4/yr); book/music reviews, 30-75 wds. Seasonal 3 mos ahead. Accepts simultaneous submissions & reprints. Theme list; copy for #10 SAE/2 stamps.

> **Poetry:** Accepts 12/yr. Any type, 4-24 lines. Submit max 4 poems.
>
> **Fillers:** Accepts 36/yr. Cartoons, facts, jokes, quizzes, quotes, short humor, word puzzles.
>
> **Columns/Departments:** Artist Action (any specific artist information).
>
> **Special Needs:** Organizational pieces; new music releases/photos; artist's concert schedules; radio station playlists.
>
> **Tips:** "Submit between the 10th and 20th of each month for best review."

+RELEASE, 2525-C Lebanon Pike, Box 6, Nashville TN 37214. (615)872-8080. Fax (615)872-9786. E-mail: release@releasemagazine.com. Website: Http://www.releasemagazine.com. Vox Corp Inc. Suzie Waltner, ed coordinator. Bimonthly mag; circ 100,000. Subscription $19.95. 60% freelance. Query/clips; e-query OK. Pays .08-.12/wd, 45 days after publication, for 1st & electronic rts. Articles. Accepts e-mail submission (copied into message). Kill fee. Some sidebars. No guidelines. Not in topical listings. (Ads)

> **Tips:** "Show us you know the music and give us an idea of the styles you're most comfortable with."

*RENAISSANCE, The Resource Publication for the Christian Musician, Box 2134, Lynnwood WA 98036. Renaissance Artists Group/Christian Artists International. Nathan L. Csakany, ed. Issues of interest to Christian musicians. Not in topical listings. Copy.

*RING! PO Box 1179, Grapevine TX 76099-1179. (817)488-0141. Fax (817)481-4191. TCMR Communications Inc. Lynann Rayborn, ed. For handbell choir members. Monthly (10X) newsletter.

*THE SENIOR MUSICIAN, 127 9th Ave. N, Nashville TN 37234-0140. (615)251-2913. Fax (615)251-2614. Southern Baptist. Jere V. Adams, ed. For music directors and choir members of senior adult choirs. Quarterly mag; 26 pgs; circ 32,000. 100% freelance. Complete ms. Pays .055/wd on acceptance for 1st rts. Articles 500-900 wds (6-7/yr). Responds in 2-4 wks.

Seasonal 1 yr ahead. Some simultaneous submissions; reprints. Guidelines; free copy.

Poetry: Buys 2-3/yr. Traditional.

Fillers: Buys 3-4/yr. Cartoons, ideas, party ideas, musical quizzes, short humor.

Special Needs: Senior adults' testimonials, inspirational stories, personal growth and development, music training, and choir projects.

Tips: "All topics must relate to senior adult musicians and senior choirs—anything else will be returned."

7BALL, 2525-C Lebanon Pike, Box 6, Nashville TN 37214. (615)872-8080. Fax (615)872-9786. E-mail: 7ball@7ball.com. Website: http://www.7ball.com. VoxCorp, Inc. Chris Well, ed-in-chief; submit to Suzie Waltner, ed coordinator. Covers modern and alternative Christian rock. Bimonthly mag; circ 60,000. Subscription $19.95. 60% freelance. Query for electronic submissions. E-query OK. Pays .08-.10/wd, 45 days after publication. Prefers e-mail submission (copied into message). No guidelines. Not in topical listings. (Ads)

*SING! JR., PO Box 1179, Grapevine TX 76099-1179. (817)488-0141. Fax (817)481-4191. TCMR Communications Inc. Lynann Rayborn, ed. For children's choir members & their parents. Monthly (9X) newsletter.

+SONGWRITER MAGAZINE, PO Box 25879, Colorado Springs CO 80936-5879. (719)591-5866. Roberta Redford, ed. For songwriters, from beginning to professional. Monthly mag; 36 pgs; circ 3,000. Estab 1998. 100% freelance. Query/clips or complete ms/cover letter; no phone query. Pays $50-300 on acceptance for one-time rts. Articles 1,000-3,000 wds (150/yr); book reviews, 250-1,000 wds, $50. Responds in 2-3 wks. Seasonal 4 mos ahead. Accepts reprints (tell when/where appeared). Prefers disk. Kill fee. Regular sidebars. Guidelines; copy $3. (Ads)

Poetry: Free verse, light verse, traditional; lines.

Fillers: Buys 50/yr. Anecdotes, cartoons, facts, games, ideas, newsbreaks, quotes, short humor, 50-250 wds. Pays $5-20.

Columns/Departments: Buys 100-120/yr. Grace Notes (songwriters making a difference), 1,500 wds; Ad Lib (song writer's personal experiences), 1,200-1,500 wds; Open Mike (advice), 1,000-1,500 wds; Ledger Lines (short items on songwriting), 50-250 wds. Pays $30-75.

Contest: Monthly lyric contest, plus a major songwriting contest each year.

Tips: "Any area open to writers who are willing to do their homework. Songwriters can write about their own experiences for Ad Lib and Open Mike (columns). Always looking for good interviews with songwriters. The Story Behind the Song section tells how a hit song came to be. Just remember that the focus is on songwriters, not musicians or performers."

PASTOR/LEADERSHIP MARKETS

+AFRICAN AMERICAN PULPIT, PO Box 851, Valley Forge PA 19482-0851. (610)768-2128. Fax (610)768-2441. Website: Http://www.judsonpress.

com. Judson Press/American Baptist Churches. Submit to: African American Pulpit, Judson Press Ed Dept. The only journal focused exclusively on the art of black preaching. Quarterly journal; 96 pgs; circ 1,600. Subscription $29.95. 60% freelance. Complete ms/cover letter; phone query OK. Pays on publication for 1st rts. Articles/sermons to 2,500 wds, or audio tapes of sermons. Responds in 13-26 wks. Seasonal 6-9 mos ahead. Requires disk. No sidebars. Any version. Guidelines; no copy. (Ads)

Special Needs: Any type of sermon by African American preachers, and related articles or essays.

ART+PLUS, Reproducible Resources, Box 3588, Sarasota FL 34230-3588. (941)955-2950. Fax (941)955-5723. E-mail: Mail@MMI-art.com. Website: http://www.mmi-art.com. Mission Media Inc. Wayne Hepburn, pub. Reproducible illustrations and verse for church bulletins and newsletters. Quarterly mag; 26 pgs; circ 3,000. Subscription $39.97. 100% freelance. Complete ms; phone/fax/e-query OK. Pays $5-25 on acceptance for all rts only. Anecdotes 100 wds max. Responds in 12 wks. Seasonal 6 mos ahead. Accepts simultaneous submissions. Accepts disk. Guidelines/ theme list; copy $2/9x12 SAE.

Poetry: Buys 12-20/yr. Traditional only; 4-24 lines; $15. Submit max 20 poems.

Fillers: Buys 40-100/yr. Anecdotes, cartoons; to 50 wds; $8.

Tips: "We are seasonally oriented; more open to art/images than writing. We need 3-5 poems per quarter and 3-10 anecdotes or fillers."

*CATECHUMENATE, A Journal of Christian Initiation, 1800 N. Hermitage Ave., Chicago IL 60622-1101. (773)486-8970. Fax (800)933-7094. E-mail: editors@ltp.org. Catholic. Victoria M. Tufano, ed. For clergy and laity who work with those who are planning to become Catholic. Bimonthly journal; 48 pgs; circ 5,600. Subscription $20. Complete ms/cover letter; phone/fax/e-query OK. Pays $100-250 on publication for all rts (poetry, one-time rts). Articles 1,500-3,000 wds (10/yr). Responds in 2-6 wks. Accepts simultaneous submissions. Prefers disk. Kill fee. No sidebars. Guidelines; copy for 6x9 SAE/4 stamps.

Poetry: Buys 6/yr. Free verse, traditional; 5-20 lines; $75. Submit max 5 poems.

Columns/Departments: Buys 12/yr. Sunday Word (Scripture reflection on Sunday readings, aimed at catechumers); 450 wds; $200-250. Query for assignment.

Special Needs: Christian initiation; reconciliation.

Tips: "It helps if the writer has experience working with Christian initiation. Approach is that this is something we are all learning together through experience and scholarship."

*THE CATHOLIC SERVANT, PO Box 24142, Minneapolis MN 55410. (612)929-8110. Fax (612)929-8146. Catholic. John Sondag, pub. For Catholic evangelization, catechesis, and apologetics. Monthly newspaper; 12 pgs; circ 24,000. Query/clips; fax query OK. Pays $50-60 on publication. Articles 1,000 wds (12/yr). Responds in 4 wks. Seasonal 3 mos ahead. Prefers disk. Some sidebars. (Ads)

Fillers: Cartoons & short humor.

Tips: "We buy features only."

*CELEBRATION, 207 Hillsboro Dr., Silver Spring MD 20902-3125. William J. Freburger, ed. National Catholic Reporter Publishing House. Monthly mag; 48 pgs; circ 9,000. Subscription $64.95. 15% freelance. Complete ms/cover letter. Pays $100-200 on acceptance for one-time rts. Articles 1,000-2,500 wds (15-20/yr). Responds in 2 wks. Seasonal 7 mos ahead. Prefers disk. No sidebars. Copy for 10x13 SAE/4 stamps. (Ads)

> **Contest:** Monthly contest on different themes, usually worship ideas for specific occasions (New Year, Easter, etc.).

> **Tips:** "I am always looking for descriptions of worship services (texts), ideas for worship occasions (seasonal., special), unsentimental and non-obvious stories as teaching/preaching aids, etc."

CELL CHURCH MAGAZINE, PO Box 19888, Houston TX 77224. (281)497-7901. Fax (281)497-0904. E-mail: eliz@touchusa.org. Website: http://www.touchusa.org. Touch Outreach Ministries. Randall Neighbour, ed dir; Elizabeth A. Bruns, mng ed. For Cell Church pastors, leaders and consultants working to impact the world for Christ through the church. Quarterly mag; 32 pgs; circ 12,000. Subscription $14. 70-80% freelance. Query/clips; fax/e-query OK. **PAYS 10 COPIES.** Articles 1,000-1,500 wds (20-30/yr). Responds in 2 wks. Seasonal 3 mos ahead. Accepts simultaneous submissions & reprints (tell when/where appeared). Prefers disk. Some sidebars. Prefers NIV. Guidelines/theme list; copy $3.50/9x12 SAE/3 stamps. (Ads)

> **Columns/Departments:** Accepts 20-25/yr. Youth, Children's Ministry, Transitioning (to Cell Church), Global Input, Pastor's Pilgrimage (pastor's testimonial about Cell Church), ToolKit (500-wd testimonies about cell life, tips from cell leaders/interns, icebreakers), and Heart to Heart (heartfelt testimony about cell life); all 1,000-1,500 wds.

> **Special Needs:** Global issues; practical tips and ideas relevant to Cell Church concept. Needs youth Cell Church writers.

CELL LIFE FORUM, 131 Tilman Cir., Markham ON L3P 6A4 Canada. (905)471-5015. Fax (905)471-6912. E-mail: 75273,3241@compuserve.com. World Team Canada. Nancy J. Lindquist, ed. A resource to connect cell-based churches across Canada. Quarterly mag; 16 pgs; circ. 300+. Subscription $12 CAN. 75% freelance. Query; phone/e-query OK. Pays .05/wd on publication for 1st or one-time rts. Not copyrighted. Articles 500-2,000 wds (8-12/yr); book/music reviews, 100-500 wds, $5-25. Responds in 3-4 wks. Accepts simultaneous submissions & reprints. Accepts disk (prefers e-mail submission). Regular sidebars. Prefers NIV. Guidelines/theme list; copy for 9x12 SAE. (Ads)

> **Poetry:** Buys 4/yr. Any type as long as on theme; 5-30 lines; $5-10. Submit max 4 poems.

> **Fillers:** Buys 8+/yr. Anecdotes, cartoons, tips; to 100 wds; $5-10.

> **Tips:** "All material must relate to Canadian cell churches or Canadians involved in cell churches. Most open to profiles, My Story, or fillers."

CHRISTIAN CAMP & CONFERENCE JOURNAL, 405 W. Rockrimmon Blvd. Colorado Springs CO 80919. (719)260-9400. Fax (719)260-6398. E-mail:

editor@cciusa.org. Website: http://www.cciusa.org. Christian Camping Intl./USA. Dean Ridings, ed. To inform, inspire, and motivate all who serve in Christian camping. Bimonthly mag; 32-40 pgs; circ 7,500. Subscription $24.95. 80% freelance. Query; fax/e-query OK. Pays .12/wd on publication for 1st & electronic rts. Articles 1,000-2,500 wds (12/yr). Responds in 4-6 wks. Seasonal 4 mos ahead. Accepts simultaneous submissions & reprints (tell when/where appeared). Prefers e-mail submission (attached file) with fax back-up. Kill fee. Regular sidebars. Prefers NIV. Guidelines (also by e-mail); copy $2.25/9x12 SAE/5 stamps. (Ads)

Special Needs: Outdoor setting; purpose and objectives; administration and organization; personnel development; camper/guest needs; programming; health and safety; food service; site/facilities maintenance; business/operations; marketing and PR; and fund raising.

Tips: "Get guidelines first. Don't send general camping-related articles. We print stories specifically related to Christian camp and conference facilities; changed lives or innovative programs; how a Christian camp or conference experience affected a present-day leader."

#CHRISTIAN CENTURY, 407 S. Dearborn St., Ste. 1405, Chicago IL 60605-1150. (312)427-5380. Fax (312)427-1302. Website: http://www.christian century.org. Christian Century Foundation. Submit to Manuscripts. For ministers, educators and church leaders interested in events and theological issues of concern to the ecumenical church. Weekly magazine; 32 pgs; circ 30,000. Subscription $40. 90% freelance. Query (complete ms for fiction); phone/fax query OK. Pays $75-200 ($75-150 for unsolicited) on publication for all rts. Articles 1,000-3,000 wds (150/yr); fiction 1,000-3,000 wds (3/yr); book reviews, 800-1,500 wds; music or video reviews 1,000 wds; pays $0-75. Responds in 1-9 wks. Seasonal 4 mos ahead. Accepts simultaneous submissions. No disk. Kill fee. Regular sidebars. Prefers NRSV. Guidelines/theme list; copy $3. (Ads)

Poetry: Buys 50/yr. Any type (religious but not sentimental); to 20 lines; $50. Submit max 10 poems.

Tips: "Looking for more fiction. Keep in mind our audience of sophisticated readers, eager for analysis and critical perspective that goes beyond the obvious."

CHRISTIAN MANAGEMENT REPORT, 2310 S. McClintock Ste.3, Tempe AZ 85282. (602)967-9122. Fax (602)967-8298. E-mail: Herbrandson @com puserve.com. Church Management Association. DeWayne Herbrandson, exec ed. Management resources and leadership training for Christian organizations. Bimonthly journal; 32 pgs; circ 4,000. Subscription $29.95. 75% freelance. Query or complete ms/cover letter; fax query OK. **NO PAYMENT** for all rts. Articles 700 wds/bio; book reviews 100-200 wds. Responds in 6 wks. Seasonal 6 mos ahead. Accepts simultaneous submissions & reprints. CMA members first choice. Guidelines; free copy. (Ads)

Fillers: Anecdotes, cartoons, quotes, short humor; 20-50 wds.

Columns/Departments: Board Governance, CEO/Leadership, Human Resources, Communications/Public Relations, Fund Development/Marketing, Financial Management, Church Management, Tax & Legal Trends; 650 wds. Query.

Special Needs: Evangelical Calendar of Events, Ministry Profiles/Case Studies.

THE CHRISTIAN MINISTRY, 407 S. Dearborn St., Ste. 1405, Chicago IL 60605-1150. (312)427-5380. Fax (312)472-1302. E-mail: cmin@christian century.org. Website: http://www.christianmin.org. The Christian Century Foundation. Victoria Rebeck, mng ed; submit to Manuscripts. For clergy seeking practical advice for ministry and on up-to-date theological developments (mainline to liberal). Bimonthly mag; 40 pgs; circ 6,500. Subscription $17. 60% freelance. Complete ms/cover letter; fax query OK. Pays $50-100 on publication for all rts. Articles 1,200-1,800 wds (30/yr); book reviews, 500 wds (keep book). Responds in 6 wks. Seasonal 8 mos ahead. Kill fee 50%. Regular sidebars. Prefers disk or e-mail submission (copied into message).   Kill fee 50%. Regular sidebars. Prefers NRSV. Guidelines/theme list; copy for 9x12 SAE/8 stamps. (Ads)

> **Columns/Departments:** Buys 20/yr. Tricks of the Trade (brief practical tips), 500 wds; Women by the Word (about women pastors), 1,800 wds; Congregational Computing (software for congregational ministry), 1,800 wds. Complete ms. Pays $20-100.
>
> **Special Needs:** Communicating theology to laypeople; laywomen's changing ministries; local church public relations; educating new members.
>
> **Contest:** Sponsors a sermon contest. Send #10 SASE for qualifications and requirements; send $5 for back issue with sermon winners.
>
> **Tips:** "Most open to Reflections on Ministry; pastors offering personal thoughts on a real-life experience they have had. Writer should understand the life and intellectual abilities of the mainline pastor. Should have a sophisticated theology. Articles should not be preachy."

*CHURCH ADMINISTRATION, MSN 157, 127 9th Ave. N., Nashville TN 37234-0140. (615)251-2062. Fax (615)251-3866. Southern Baptist. Submit to The Editor. Practical pastoral ministry/church administration ideas for pastors and staff. Monthly mag; 50 pgs; circ 12,000. 15% freelance. Query. Pays .065/wd on acceptance for all rts. Articles 1,600-2,000 wds (60/yr). Responds in 8 wks. Guidelines/copy for #10 SAE/2 stamps.

> **Columns/Departments:** Buys 60/yr. Weekday Dialogue; Minister's Mate; Secretary's File; all 2,000 wds.

CHURCH GROWTH NETWORK, PO Box 892589, Temecula CA 92589-2589. Phone/fax (909)506-3086. E-mail: gary_mcintosh@peter.biola.edu. Website: http://www.mcintoshcgn.com. Dr. Gary L. McIntosh, ed. For pastors and church leaders interested in church growth. Monthly newsletter; 2 pgs; circ 8,000. Subscription $16. 10% freelance. Query; fax query OK. **PAYS IN COPIES** for one-time rts. Not copyrighted. Articles 1,000-2,000 wds (2/yr). Responds in 4 wks. Accepts simultaneous submissions & reprints. Accepts disk. No sidebars. Copy for #10 SAE/1 stamp. (No ads)

> **Tips:** "All articles must have a church-growth slant. Should be very practical, how-to material; very tightly written with bullets, etc."

*CHURCH WORSHIP, 165 Plaza Dr., Prescott AZ 86303. (520)771-8601. Fax (520)771-8621. E-mail: edmin2@aol.com. Robert Davidson, ed. Supplementary resources for church worship leaders. Monthly journal; 24 pgs; circ 1,200. Subscription $24. 75% freelance. Complete ms/cover letter; phone/fax/e-query OK. Pays .03/wd on publication for 1st rts. Articles to 100-1,500 wds; fiction 100-1,500 wds. Responds in 2-6 wks. Seasonal 4 mos ahead. Guidelines/theme list; copy for 9x12 SAE/3 stamps.

> **Special Needs:** Complete worship services; seasonal sermons.
>
> **Tips:** "Most open to creative worship services using music, drama or art."

THE CLERGY JOURNAL, 6160 Carmen Ave. E., Inver Grove Heights MN 55076-4422. (612)451-9945. Fax (612)457-4617. Logos Productions, Inc. Sharilyn Figueroa, mng ed. "How-to" articles on church administration, ministry/personal issues for Protestant ministers, Christian educators and church personnel. Monthly mag; 96 pgs; circ 10,000. Subscription $27. 60% freelance. Query/clips or complete ms/cover letter. Pays $50-150 on publication for 1st rts. Articles 1,000-3,000 wds (50/yr); fiction 1,000 wds (10/yr). Responds in 2 wks. Seasonal 1 yr ahead. Accepts reprints (tell when/where appeared). Prefers disk. Regular sidebars. Prefers NRSV. Guidelines/theme list; copy for 9x12 SAE/4 stamps. (Ads)

> **Fillers:** Cartoons, prayers; 50-150 wds; $10-25.
>
> **Special Needs:** Humorous fiction for pastors and children's sermons.
>
> **Tips:** "On the religious spectrum from very conservative to very liberal, our audience is in the middle to left. We are interested in meeting the personal and professional needs of clergy in areas like worship planning, church and personal finances, and self-care—spiritual, physical and emotional. "

CROSS CURRENTS, College of New Rochelle, 29 Castle Pl., New Rochelle NY 10805-2339. (914)235-1439. Fax (914)235-1584. E-mail: aril@ecunet.org. Website: http://www.aril.org. Association for Religion and Intellectual Life. Shelley Schiff, mng ed. For thoughtful activists for social justice and church reform. Quarterly journal; 144 pgs; circ 5,000. Subscription $30. 99% freelance. Mostly written by academics. Complete ms/cover letter; phone/fax query OK. **PAYS IN COPIES** for all rts. Articles 3,000-5,000 wds; book reviews 1,000 wds (James Giles). Responds in 6-8 wks. Seasonal 6 mos ahead. Accepts simultaneous submissions & reprints. Requires disk. No sidebars. Guidelines; copy for 6x9 SAE/4 stamps. (Ads)

> **Poetry:** Tom O'Brien. Accepts 12/yr. Any type or length; no payment. Submit max 5 poems.
>
> **Tips:** "Send 3 double-spaced copies; SASE; use Chicago Manual of Style; non-sexist language."

CURRENT THOUGHTS & TRENDS, PO Box 35004, Colorado Springs CO 80935-3504. (719)531-3584. Fax (719)598-7128. E-mail: ctt@navpress. com. Website: http://www.navpress.com/ctt. The Navigators. Dennis Cone, ed. To enhance the ministry of Christian leaders by providing concise, timely summaries of contemporary trends in Christian and secular thought. Monthly newsletter; 32 pgs; circ 17,000. Subscription $36. Open to freelance. Query; e-query OK. Buys 1st & electronic rts. Responds in 4 wks. Seasonal 3 mos ahead. Prefers disk or e-mail submission (copied into message). Prefers NIV. Guidelines (also by e-mail); copy. (Ads)

Columns/Departments: Buys 6/yr. Trend Scope (latest trends affecting church, families or individuals), 500-575 wds, $150. Query.

DIOCESAN DIALOGUE, 16565 S. State St., South Holland IL 60473. (708)331-5485. Fax (708)331-5484. Catholic. Fr. Michael Gilligan, editorial dir. Targets Latin-Rite dioceses in the US that sponsor a mass broadcast on TV or radio. Annual newsletter; 8 pgs; circ. 750. Free. 20% freelance. Complete ms/cover letter; no phone/fax query. Pays on publication for all rts. Responds in 10 wks. Accepts simultaneous submissions & reprints. Some sidebars. Prefers NAB (Confraternity). No guidelines; copy $3/9x12 SAE/2 stamps.

    Fillers: Cartoons, 2/yr.

    Tips: "Writers should be familiar with TV production of the Mass and/or the needs of senior citizens, especially shut-ins."

*EMMANUEL, 5384 Wilson Mills Rd., Cleveland OH 44143-3092. (440)449-2103. Fax (440)449-3862. Catholic. Rev. Anthony Schueller, ed; book reviews to Dr. Patrick Riley. Eucharistic spirituality for priests and others in church ministry. Monthly (10X) mag; 60 pgs; circ 4,000+. Subscription $19.95. 75% freelance. Query or complete ms/cover letter; fax query OK. Pays $75-150 for articles, $50 for meditations, on publication for all rts. Articles 2,000-2,750 wds; meditations 1,000-1,250 wds; book reviews 500-750 wds. Responds in 2 wks. Seasonal 4 mos ahead. Accepts disk. Prefers RNAB. Guidelines/theme list. (Ads)

    Poetry: Buys 15/yr. Free verse; 25-100 lines. Pays $35-50. Submit max 2-3 poems.

ENRICHMENT, A Journal for Pentecostal Ministry, 1445 Boonville Ave., Springfield MO 65802. (417)862-2781. Fax (417)862-0416. E-mail: enrichment@ag.org. Website: http://www.enrichmentjournal.ag.org. Assemblies of God. Rick Knoth, mng ed. Directed to part- or full-time denominational ministers and church leaders. Quarterly journal; 144 pgs; circ 32,000. Subscription $20. 5-10% freelance. Complete ms/cover letter. Pays .03-.10/wd ($75-175) on publication for one-time rts. Articles 1,200-2,500 wds (25/yr); book reviews, 250 wds, $25. Responds in 8-12 wks. Seasonal 6 mos ahead. Accepts simultaneous submissions & reprints (tell when/where appeared). Requires disk or e-mail submission (copied into message). Kill fee 50%. Regular sidebars. Prefers NIV. Guidelines/theme list; copy for $3/10x13 SAE. (Ads)

    Fillers: Cartoons. Pays $50-75.

    Columns/Departments: Buys many/yr. For Women in Ministry (leadership ideas), Associate Ministers (related issues), Managing Your Ministry (how-to), Financial Concepts (church stewardship issues), Family Matters (ministers family), View from the Pew (layperson's perspective on ministry); all 1,200-1,500 wds. Pays $125-150.

    Tips: "Most open to sermon outlines, how-to articles (fillers), sermon illustrations, practical ideas on ministry-related topics."

** 1997 EPA Award of Merit—Denominational & Most Improved Publication 1997.

*ENVIRONMENT & ART LETTER, 1800 N. Hermitage Ave., Chicago IL 60622-1101. (773)486-8970x64. Fax (773)486-7094. Catholic. David Philippart, ed. For artists, architects, building professionals, pastors, parish committees interested in church architecture, art and decoration. Monthly newsletter; 12 pgs; circ 2,500. Subscription $20. 80% freelance. Query/clips; phone/fax query OK. Pays $25/ms page on publication for all rts. Responds in 18 wks. Seasonal 2 mos ahead. Accepts simultaneous submissions. Theme list; copy for 9x12 SAE/3 stamps.

> **Tips:** "Need a thorough knowledge of the liturgical documents pertaining to architecture and art, especially environment and art for Catholic worship."

*EUCHARISTIC MINISTER, 115 E. Armour Blvd., Box 419493, Kansas City MO 64111. (816)531-0538. Fax (816)968-2280. E-mail: newsward@aol.com. Website: http://www.natcath.com. Catholic. Beatrice Fleo, ed. For Eucharistic ministers. Monthly newsletter; 4-8 pgs; circ 50,000. 90% freelance. Complete ms. Pays $20-200 on acceptance for one-time rts. Articles 200-2,000 wds (30+/yr). Responds in 1-2 wks. Seasonal 4-6 mos ahead. Accepts simultaneous submissions & reprints. Guidelines; free copy.

> **Fillers:** Buys 10-12/yr. Anecdotes, cartoons, short humor.

> **Tips:** "We want articles to be practical, inspirational, or motivational. They need to be simple and direct enough for the average person to read easily—no heavy theology, pious inspiration, or excess verbiage."

THE EVANGELICAL BAPTIST, 679 Southgate Dr., Guelph ON N1G 4S2 Canada. (519)821-4830. Fax (519)821-9829. E-mail: president@fellowship.ca. Website: http://www.fellowship.org. Fellowship of Evangelical Baptist Churches in Canada. Ginette Cotnor, mng ed, 18 Louvigny, Lorraine QC J6Z 1T7 Canada. To enhance the life and ministry of denominational leaders in local churches. Bimonthly (5X) mag (soon to be online); 28-32 pgs; circ 5,000. Subscription $10. 10% freelance. Query or complete ms/cover letter; fax/e-query OK. Pays $25-50 on publication for one-time rts. Articles 700-1,500 wds. Responds in 6 wks. Accepts simultaneous submissions & reprints (tell when/where appeared). Accepts disk; prefers e-mail submission. Some sidebars. Guidelines (also by e-mail/Website); copy for 9x12 SAE/.90 Canadian postage. (Ads)

> **Columns/Departments:** Buys 5/yr. Joy in the Journey (inspiration in everyday life), 600-900 wds; View From the Pew (humorous, first-person essay with a twist), 600-900 wds. Pays $25-50. Complete ms.

> **Tips:** "This magazine has been redesigned and refocused for church leaders. Need are much more specific and most articles are assigned. Most open to columns."

THE FIVE STONES, 135 Pine St., Norton MA 02766-2812. Phone/fax (508)285-7145. E-mail: pappas@ma.ultranet.com. Website: http://www.tabcom.org. American Baptist. Anthony G. Pappas, ed. Primarily to small church pastors and laity, denominational staff, and seminaries; to equip for service. Quarterly journal; 24 pgs; circ 1,200. Subscription $8-12.

100% freelance. Complete ms/cover letter. Pays $5 on publication for one-time rights. Not copyrighted. Articles (20/yr) & fiction (4/yr), 500-2,000 wds; book reviews 500 wds, $5. Responds in 10-12 wks. Seasonal 10 mos ahead. Accepts simultaneous submissions & reprints. Accepts disk or e-mail submission. Some sidebars. Any version. Guidelines/theme list; copy for 9x12 SAE/4 stamps. (No ads)

> **Fillers:** Buys 12/yr. Anecdotes, cartoons, ideas, jokes, short humor; 20-200 wds; $5.
>
> **Tips:** "Always looking for everything related to small church life (nature and dynamics of small churches); fresh programming. Good place for unpublished to break in. Use first-person. Best to call and talk."

+GROWING CHURCHES, 127 Ninth Ave. N, Nashville TN 37234-0157. (615)251-3837. Fax (615)251-3609. E-mail: erowell@bssb.com. Southern Baptist. Ed Rowell, ed.

*ISSACHARFILE, PO Box 12609, Oklahoma City OK 73157. (405)787-7110. Fax (405)789-3957. Intl. Pentecostal Holiness Church. Shirley G. Spencer, ed. Denominational; keeping church leaders in touch with the times. Monthly mag; circ 3,000. Subscription $9.75. Open to freelance. Query. Not in topical listings. (Ads)

THE IVY JUNGLE REPORT, 1025 Austin St., Bellingham WA 98226-2643. (360)733-6212. Fax (360)738-8057. E-mail: ivyjungle@aol.com. Website: http://www.ivyjungle.org. Woodruff Resources. Mike Woodruff, pub. For people who minister to collegians. Quarterly mag; 16 pgs; circ 800. Subscription $20. 75% freelance. Query; fax/e-query OK. **NO PAYMENT** for one-time rts. Not copyrighted. Articles 500-1,500 wds (16/yr); book/music reviews, 500 wds. Responds in 2 wks. Accepts simultaneous submissions & reprints. Prefers e-mail submission (attached file). Regular sidebars. Copy for 2 stamps. (Ads)

> **Fillers:** Accepts 10+/yr. Anecdotes, cartoons, facts, jokes, newsbreaks, quizzes, quotes, short humor; 15-100 wds.
>
> **Columns/Departments:** Out of the Classroom (student missions), 750-1,000 wds (4/yr). Query.
>
> **Tips:** "We are looking for writers who understand the unique demands and challenges of college ministry, both church and parachurch."

*JOURNAL OF CHRISTIAN HEALING, 6728 Old McLean Village Dr., McLean VA 22101. (703)556-9222. Fax (703)556-8729. Assoc. of Christian Therapists. Father Louis Lussier, OSCAS, ed. Focuses on the healing power and presence of Jesus Christ, for health and mental health professionals and healing ministries. Quarterly journal; 40 pgs; circ 1,200. 100% freelance. Complete ms/cover letter; phone query OK. **PAYS IN COPIES** for all rts. Articles 10-20 pgs (12/yr); fiction 2-5 pgs; book reviews, 2-5 pgs. Accepts reprints. Responds in 8 wks. Guidelines; copy $8.

> **Poetry:** Charles Zeiders. Accepts 12/yr. Free verse, haiku, light verse or traditional; to 40 lines. Submit max 10 poems.
>
> **Fillers:** Accepts 10/yr. Various; to 250 wds.
>
> **Columns/Departments:** Accepts 12/yr. Resources, Medical Practices,

Nursing, Pastoral Ministry, Psychiatry, Prayer Ministry, Sexuality, Dreams; 2-5 pgs.

Tips: "All articles or short stories must relate to healing."

THE JOURNAL OF PASTORAL CARE, 1068 Harbor Dr. SW, Calabash NC 28467. Phone/fax (910)579-5084. E-mail: OrloS@aol.com. Website: http:// www.jpcp.org. Orlo Strunk, Jr., mng ed. For chaplains/pastors/professionals involved with pastoral care and counseling in other than a church setting. Quarterly journal; 116 pgs; circ. 10,000. Subscription $22.50. 80% freelance. Query; phone/fax/e-query OK. **PAYS IN COPIES** for 1st rts. Articles 5,000 wds or 20 pgs (30/yr); book reviews 5 pgs. Responds in 8 wks. Accepts disk. No sidebars. Guidelines (on Website);no copy. (Ads)

   Poetry: Accepts 16/yr. Free verse; 5-16 lines. Submit max 3 poems.

   Tips: "Readers are highly trained clinically, as well as holding professional degrees in religion/theology. Writers need to be professionals on topics covered."

JOURNAL OF THE AMERICAN SOCIETY FOR CHURCH GROWTH, c/o Dr. Gary L. McIntosh, ed, Talbot School of Theology, 13800 Biola Ave., LaMirada CA 90639. (562)944-0351. Fax (562)906-4502. E-mail: gary-mcintosh@peter.biola.edu. American Society for Church Growth. Dr. Gary L. McIntosh, ed. Targets professors, pastors, denominational executives and seminary students interested in church growth and evangelism. Quarterly journal (3X—fall, winter, spring); 100 pgs; circ 400. Subscription $24. 100% freelance. Complete ms/cover letter; phone/fax query OK. **PAYS IN COPIES** for one-time rts. Not copyrighted. Articles 15 pgs or 4,000-5,000 wds (10/yr); book reviews 750-2,000 wds. Responds in 8-12 wks. Accepts simultaneous submissions & reprints (tell when/where appeared). Prefers disk or e-mail submission (copied into message). No sidebars. Any version. Guidelines/theme list; copy $10. (Ads)

   Tips: "All articles must have a church-growth slant. We're open to new writers at this time."

THE JOYFUL NOISELETTER, PO Box 895, Portage MI 49081-0895. (616)324-0990. Fax (616)324-3984. E-mail: JoyfulNZ@aol.com. Cal Samra, ed. To provide pastors and local church bulletin editors of all denominations with clean jokes, uplifting anecdotes, and cartoons to use and reprint. Monthly newsletter; circ 10,000. Subscription $22. Open to freelance. Query. **NO PAYMENT.** Partial topical listings. (No ads)

LEADERSHIP JOURNAL, 465 Gundersen Dr., Carol Stream IL 60188. (630)260-6200. Fax (630)260-0114. E-mail: LeaderJ@aol.com. Website: http://www.christianity.net/leadership. Christianity Today, Inc. Marshall Shelley, ed. Practical help for pastors/church leaders. Quarterly journal; 130 pgs; circ 70,000. Also online edition. Subscription $22. 75% freelance. Query or complete ms; fax/e-query OK. Pays $75-375 (.10/wd) on acceptance for 1st rts, rt. to reprint & electronic rts. Articles 500-3,000 wds (50/yr). Responds in 6-9 wks. Seasonal 6 mos ahead. Accepts reprints (tell when/where appeared). Accepts disk or e-mail submission (copied into message). Kill fee 50%. Regular sidebars. Prefers NIV or NLT. Guidelines/theme list (also on Website); copy $3. (Ads)

Fillers: Buys 80/yr. Anecdotes, cartoons, ideas, short humor; to 150 wds. Pays $25-50.

Columns/Departments: Buys 80/yr. Ideas That Work, 150 wds; To Illustrate (sermon illustrations), 150 wds; To Quip (humorous sermon illustrations). Complete ms. Pays $25-50.

Special Needs: Material on pastoral care, church health, contemporary preaching, and the pastor's soul.

Tips: "Writers should be involved in the ministry/leadership of the church; write a personal experience piece; offer to write book/software reviews."

** This periodical was #14 on the 1998 Top 50 Christian Publishers list. (#14 in 1996, #27 in 1995, #16 in 1994)

LET'S WORSHIP, MSN 157, 127 9th Ave. N., Nashville TN 37234. (615)251-2496. Fax (615)251-3609. E-mail: Ed_Rowell@lifeway.com. Southern Baptist/LifeWay Christian Resources. Ed Rowell, design ed. Resources for worship leaders: music, drama, litanies, prayers, children's sermons, orders of worship and family worship. Quarterly mag; 100 pgs; circ 7,000. Subscription $62.25. Estab 1996. 40% freelance. Complete ms/cover letter; e-query OK. Pays $200 (.055/wd) on acceptance for all or 1st rts. Articles 1,500 wds (50/yr). Responds in 6 wks. Seasonal 1 yr ahead. Accepts reprints rarely (tell when/where appeared). Prefers disk or e-mail submission (attached file). Some sidebars. Prefers NIV. No guidelines; theme list & copy for 9x12 SAE.

Poetry: Buys 16/yr. Free verse, traditional; 4-48 lines. Pays $20-120.

Tips: "Most open to short dramas, dramatic readings, dramatic monologues/dialogues."

LUTHERAN FORUM, PO Box 327, Delhi NY 13753-0327. (607)746-7511. Fax (607)829-2158. E-mail: dkralpb@juno.com. American Lutheran Publicity Bureau. Ronald Bagnall, ed. For church leadership—clerical and laity. Quarterly journal; 64 pgs; circ 3,200. 100% freelance. Complete ms/cover letter. **NO PAYMENT.** Articles 1,000-3,000 wds. Responds in 26-32 wks. Accepts simultaneous submissions & reprints. Requires disk. Guidelines; copy for 9x12 SAE/6 stamps. (Ads)

LUTHERAN PARTNERS, 8765 W. Higgins Rd., Chicago IL 60631-4195. (800)638-3522x2875 or 2884. (773)380-2875. Fax (773)380-2829. E-mail: 1partmag@elca.org or LUTHERAN_PARTNERS.parti@ecunet.org. Website: http://www.elca.org/dm/lp. Evangelical Lutheran Church in America. Carl E. Linder, ed. To encourage and challenge rostered leaders in the ELCA, including pastors and lay ministers. Bimonthly mag; 40-48 pgs; circ 20,000. Subscription $10 (free to leaders), $15 outside North America. 10-15% freelance. Query or complete ms/cover letter; phone/fax/e-query OK. Query for electronic submissions. Pays $100-150 on publication for one-time rts. Articles 500-2,500 wds (12-15/yr). Responds in 16 wks. Seasonal 9 mos ahead. Accepts simultaneous submissions & reprints (tell when/where appeared). Kill fee (rare). Prefers disk or e-mail submission (copied into message). Regular sidebars. Prefers NRSV. Guidelines/theme list (also by e-mail/Website); copy $2/9x12 SAE/5 stamps. (Ads)

Poetry: Buys 6-10/yr. Free verse, traditional: $50-75. Keep concise. Submit max 6-10 poems.

Fillers: Buys 4-5/yr. Cartoons; ideas for parish ministry (called Jottings); to 500 wds; $25.

Special Needs: Book reviews. Query Thelma Megill-Cobbler, Trinity Lutheran Seminary, 2199 E. Main St., Columbus OH 43209, (614)235-4136. Uses books predominately from mainline denominational publishers. Payment is copy of book.

Tips: "Query us with solid idea. Understand Lutheran Christian theology and congregational life. Be able to see life from a pastor/lay leader's point of view. With limited freelance, most sections hard to get into, but you might try the Jottings section first (see Fillers)."

*THE MINISTER'S FAMILY, MSN 157, 127 9th Ave. N., Nashville TN 37234. (615)251-3837. Fax (615)251-3609. Southern Baptist. Dean Richardson, ms asst. A leisure-reading magazine designed to encourage, inspire, inform, and enrich the lives of ministers and their families. Quarterly mag; 52 pgs. Subscription $17.95. 20% freelance. Complete ms/cover letter; no phone/fax query. Pays $200 (.065/wd) on acceptance for all rts. Articles 1,600-2,000 wds. Responds in 6-8 wks. Seasonal 6-12 mos ahead. Accepts simultaneous submissions. Prefers disk. Kill fee. Regular sidebars. Prefers NIV. Guidelines; copy for 9x12 SAE.

Poetry: Buys 5/yr. Light verse; 4-20 lines. Pays $20-100. Submit max 4 poems.

Fillers: Games & ideas.

Tips: "Most open to experience-based humor."

MINISTRIES TODAY, 600 Rinehart Rd., Lake Mary FL 32746. (407)333-0600. Fax (407)333-7133. E-mail: grady@strang.com. Website: http://www. ministriestoday.com. Strang Communications. Lee Grady, exec ed; Lary Keefauver, mng ed (keefauv@strang.com); Jimmy Stewart, book & music review ed. Helps for pastors and church leaders primarily in Pentecostal/charismatic churches. Bimonthly mag; 90 pgs; circ 30,000. Subscription $24.95. 60-80% freelance. Query; fax/e-query OK. Pays $50 or $500-800 on publication for all rts. Articles 2,000-2,500 wds (25/yr); book/music/video reviews, 300 wds, $25. Responds in 4 wks. Prefers disk. Kill fee. Regular sidebars. Prefers NIV. Guidelines; copy $4/9x12 SAE. (Ads)

Columns/Departments: Buys 36/yr.

Tips: "Most open to columns. Write for guidelines and study the magazine."

MINISTRY & LITURGY (formerly Modern Liturgy), 160 E. Virginia St. #290, San Jose CA 95112. (408)286-8505. Fax (408)287-8748. E-mail: mdrnlitrgy@aol.com. Resource Publications, Inc. Nick Wagner, ed dir. To help liturgists and ministers make the imaginative connection between liturgy and life. Monthly (10X) mag; 50 pgs; circ 20,000. Subscription $45. Query only; fax/e-query OK. Query for electronic submissions. **PAYS IN COPIES & SUBSCRIPTION** on publication for 1st rts. Articles 1,000 wds (30/yr). Responds in 4 wks. Seasonal 6 mos ahead. Accepts reprints (tell when/where appeared). Requires disk. Regular sidebars. Guidelines/theme list; copy $4/11x14 SAE/2stamps. (Ads)

Contest: Visual Arts Awards.

*MINISTRY MAGAZINE: International Journal for Pastors, 12501 Old Columbia Pike, Silver Spring MD 20904. (301)680-6510. Fax (301)680-6502. E-mail: 74532.2425@compuserve.com. Seventh-day Adventist. Julia W. Norcott, asst ed. For Pastors. Monthly journal; 32 pgs.; circ 20,000. Subscription $26.95. 90% freelance. Query; fax/e-query OK. Pays $50-150 on acceptance for all rts. Articles 1,000-1,500 wds; book reviews 100-150 wds ($25). Responds in 2-3 wks. Prefers disk. No sidebars. Guidelines/theme list; copy for 9x12 SAE/5 stamps. (Ads)

MINISTRY NOW, (formerly Sermon Notes), 1420 Osborne St., Ste. 10, Humboldt TN 38343. (901)784-9239. Fax (901)784-8154. E-mail: stevemay@ministrynow.com. Website: http://www.ministrynow.com. Alderson Press. Stephen May, ed. Sermon helps for ministers. Quarterly & online mag; 96 pgs; circ 5,000. Subscription $39. 25% freelance. Complete ms/cover letter; fax/e-query OK. Pays $35-50 for articles & sermons ($5 for illustrations on publication for one-time rts. Sermons & articles (8/yr) 1,500 wds; illustrations 80-100 wds; book reviews 500 wds ($20). Responds in 5 wks. Seasonal 4 mos ahead. Accepts reprints (tell when/where appeared). Prefers disk. Regular sidebars. Prefers NIV. Guidelines/theme list; copy $2/6x9 SAE. (Ads)

   Fillers: Buys 12/yr. Cartoons, short humor or church newsletter ideas. Pays $15.

   Columns/Departments: Buys 6/yr. Q & A (interview with Christian leader), 1,000-1,500 wds; Pastor's Library (book or product review), 500 wds. Pays $35-50.

   Tips: "We are always interested in sermons. Right now we have an even greater interest in articles about church growth, preaching, or about a particular minister who is pastoring a growing church of any size." Also publishes on diskette.

MINISTRY NOW PROFILES, PO Box 2430, Cleveland TN 37320-2430. (423)478-7055. Fax (423)478-7966. E-mail: MNprofiles@aol.com. Church of God (Cleveland TN). Tom George, ed. To provide denominational ministers with church news and inspirational, informational, and practical how-to articles. Monthly mag; circ 13,500. Subscription free. Open to freelance. Query. Not in topical listings.

NATIONAL DRAMA SERVICE, MSN 170, 127 Ninth Ave. N, MSN 158, Nashville TN 37234. (615)251-5045. Fax (615)251-2614. Email: Christy_M_Haines@compuserve.com. Southern Baptist. Christy Haines, ed. Conservative, evangelical dramas for stage, street and sanctuary. Drama, puppets, clowns, mime, movement, comedy, seeker-oriented, dramatic worship service plans. Quarterly script collections; 48 pages; 5,000 subscription base. 100% freelance. Complete ms/cover letter. Pays about $25/published page. Scripts 5-7 minutes in length. No one-acts, full length or musicals. Responds in 10 wks. Seasonal 9 mos ahead. Accepts simultaneous submissions. Guidelines.

*NETWORKS, Box 685, Cocoa FL 32923. (407)632-0130. Fax (407)631-8207. Christian Council on Persons with Disabilities. Linda G. Howard, ed. For those with specialized ministry to the mentally retarded. Bimonthly newsletter; 8 pgs; circ 1,700. 80% freelance. Query or complete ms. **NO PAY-MENT** for 1st rts. Articles 250-450 wds (12/yr); book reviews 350 wds. Responds in 6 wks. Seasonal 4 mos ahead. Accepts simultaneous submissions & reprints. Guidelines; copy for 9x12 SAE/6 stamps.

Poetry: Accepts 4/yr. Any type; to 66 lines. Submit max 10 poems.

Columns/Departments: Accepts 8/yr. Program Highlights, 1,000 wds; Teachers' Tips, 750 wds.

Special Needs: Advocacy, normalization/integration, church/state issues. June 15 deadline for annual issue on the Christian Council on Persons with Disabilities.

THE NEWSLETTER NEWSLETTER, 4150 Belden Village St. 4th Floor, Canton OH 44718. (330)493-7880. Fax (330)493-7897. E-mail: spurdum@ comresources.com. Communication Resources. Stan Purdum, ed. To help church secretaries and church newsletter editors prepare their newsletter. Monthly newsletter; 12 pgs. Subscription $39.95. 30% freelance. Complete ms. Pays $150 on acceptance for all rts. Articles 800-1,000 wds (8/yr). Responds in 4 wks. Seasonal 8 mos ahead. Accepts simultaneous submissions. Requires disk; accepts e-mail submission. Kill fee. Regular sidebars. Copy for 9x12 SAE/3 stamps.

PARISH LITURGY, 16565 S. State St., South Holland IL 60473. (708)331-5485. Fax (708)331-5484. Catholic. Father Michael Gilligan, ed dir. A planning tool for Sunday and Holyday liturgy. Quarterly mag; 32 pgs; circ 22,000. Subscription $18/2 yrs. 10% freelance. Query; no phone query. All rts. Articles 400 wds. Responds in 4 wks. Seasonal 4 mos ahead. Accepts simultaneous submissions & reprints (tell when/where appeared). Some sidebars. Prefers NAB.

PASTORAL LIFE, 9531 Akron-Canfield Rd., Canfield OH 44406-0595. (330)533-5503. Fax (330)533-1076. Catholic. Rev. Anthony Chenevey, ed. Focuses on the current problems, needs, issues and all important activities related to all phases of pastoral work and life. Monthly (11X) mag; 64 pgs; circ 1,800. Subscription $17. 50% freelance. Query; phone/fax query OK. Pays .04/wd on publication for one-time rts. Not copyrighted. Articles (50/yr) to 3,000 wds; book reviews 300-500 wds (no pay). Responds in 3 wks. Seasonal 4 mos ahead. No disk. Some kill fees. Prefers NAB. Guidelines/theme list; copy for 6x9 SAE/4 stamps. (Ads)

Tips: "We feature pastoral homilies for Sundays and Holydays. Articles should be eminently pastoral in approach and content."

*****PASTOR'S TAX & MONEY**, PO Box 50188, Indianapolis IN 46250. (800)877-3158. Daniel D. Busby, ed. Guidance for pastors in management of church and personal finances. Quarterly newsletter; 8 pgs; circ 6,000. Subscription $59.95. 50% freelance. Complete ms/cover letter. Pays $50 on publication for 1st rts. Articles 600-800 wds (8/yr). Responds in 13 wks. No sidebars. Copy $1/6x9 SAE/2 stamps.

Special Needs: Minister's taxes; computers; personal finances and church finances.

PLUGGED IN, 8605 Explorer Dr., Colorado Springs CO 80920. (719)531-3360. Fax (719)531-3347. Website: http://www.family.org. Focus on the Family. Bob Smithouser, ed; Steven Isaac, assoc ed. Helping parents and youth leaders guide teens through the world of popular youth culture. Monthly newsletter; 12 pgs; circ 50,000. Subscription $20. Freelance OK. Query. **NO PAYMENT.** No guidelines. Not in topical listings. (No ads)

Columns/Departments: Youth Leader's Perspective (message to youth leader), 600 wds.

+POLICY REVIEW: The Journal of American Citizenship, 214 Massachusetts Ave. NE, Washington DC 20002. (202)546-4440. The Heritage Foundation. D.W. Miller, mng ed. Highlights communities or organizations, including churches and other religious organizations, that are effectively solving problems more effectively than the bureaucratic government. Bimonthly mag; circ 30,000. Complete ms. Pays $500 on publication. Articles 2,000-6,000 wds (4/yr)

Tips: "Most open to articles on private and local institutions that are putting the family back together, cutting crime, improving education, and repairing bankruptcy in government."

PRAY! PO Box 35008, Colorado Springs CO 80935-3504. (719)531-3555. Fax (719)598-7128. E-mail: pray.mag@navpress.com. Website: http://www.nav press.com/pray.html. Jonathan L. Graf, ed. A magazine entirely about prayer, geared toward intercessors and prayer mobilizers (pastors and leaders who encourage prayer). Bimonthly mag; 32-40 pgs; circ 35,000. Subscription $14.97. 75% freelance. Complete ms/cover letter; fax/e-query OK. Pays .10/ wd (.05/wd for reprints) on acceptance for 1st, reprint & electronic rts. Articles 600-1,500 wds (30/yr). Responds in 8-12 wks. Accepts simultaneous submissions & reprints (tell when/where appeared). Accepts disk or e-mail submission (copied into message). Kill fee 50%. Regular sidebars. Prefers NIV. Guidelines/theme list (also by e-mail/Website); copy for 9x12 SAE/6 stamps. (Ads)

Fillers: Ideas on prayer; 75-500 wds. Pays $20.

Special Needs: Non-theme feature articles on various aspects of prayer.

Tips: "We most frequently purchase short material for our Ideas section. If you submit a general article it better be unique. Most of our theme articles are assigned."

** This periodical was #31 on the 1998 Top 50 Christian Publishers list.

THE PREACHER, PO Box 757800, Memphis TN 38175-7800. (901)757-7977. Fax (901)757-1372. E-mail: olford@memphisonline.com. Encounter Ministries, Inc. Mark N. Boorman, assoc ed. Triennial & online mag; 20-24 pgs; circ 4,500. Subscription $10 (voluntary). 10% freelance. Query; phone query OK. **NO PAYMENT** for one-time rts. Articles (1-3/yr) 500 wds; book/video reviews 250 wds. Responds in 2-3 wks. Seasonal 3-4 mos ahead. Might accept reprints (tell when/where appeared). Prefers disk or e-mail submission (attached file). Regular sidebars. Prefers NKJV. Copy for 9x12 SAE/4 stamps. (No ads)

Poetry: Accepts 1-2 /yr. Traditional; 4-20 lines. Submit max 2 poems.

Fillers: Accepts 4-6/yr. Prayers, 100-200 wds.

Tips: "Call and ask if we need article complementary to theme of upcoming issue."

PREACHER'S ILLUSTRATION SERVICE, Box 3102, Margate NJ 08402. (609)822-9401. Fax (609)822-1638. Website: http://www.voicings.com. James Colaianni, pub. Sermon illustration resource for professional clergy. Bimonthly loose-leaf booklet, 16 pgs. 15% freelance. Complete ms. Pays .15/wd on publication for any rts. Illustrations/anecdotes 50-250 wds. Responds in 6 wks. Seasonal 4 mos ahead. Accepts reprints. Prefers disk. Guidelines/topical index; copy for 9x12 SAE.

> **Poetry:** Light verse, traditional; 50-250 lines; .15/wd. Submit max 3 poems.

> **Fillers:** Various; sermon illustrations; 50-250 wds; .15/wd.

#THE PREACHER'S MAGAZINE, 10814 E. Broadway, Spokane WA 99206. (509)226-1545. Fax (509)926-8740. Nazarene. Rev. Randal E. Denny, ed. A professional journal for holiness pastors and other preachers. Quarterly mag; 80 pgs; circ 18,000. Subscription $12. 30% freelance. Complete ms/ cover letter; phone query OK. Pays .035/wd on publication for one-time rts. Articles 700-2,500 wds (40/yr); book reviews 300-400 wds. Responds in 4-6 wks. Seasonal 6 mos ahead. Accepts simultaneous submissions & reprints (tell when/where appeared). No disk. Some sidebars. Prefers NIV. Guidelines.

> **Fillers:** Buys 10/yr. Anecdotes, cartoons, ideas; 300-700 wds.

> **Tips:** "Material must be relevant to pastor's ministry or personal life."

#PREACHING, PO Box 369, Jackson TN 38302-0369. (901)668-9948. Fax (901)668-9633. E-mail: preaching@compuserve.com or 74114.275@ compuserve.com. Website: http://www.preaching.com. Preaching Resources, Inc. Dr. Michael Duduit, ed; submit to Mark Johnson, mng ed. Professional magazine for evangelical preachers; focus is on preaching and worship leadership. Bimonthly mag; 64 pgs; circ 10,000. Subscription $24.95. 75% freelance. Query or complete ms/cover letter; phone/ fax/e-query OK. Pays $35-50 on publication for 1st rts. Articles 1,000-2,000 wds (8-24/yr). Responds in 18 wks. Seasonal 1 yr ahead. Prefers disk. Regular sidebars. Prefers NIV. Some sidebars. Guidelines; copy $3.50. (Ads)

> **Fillers:** Buys 10-15/yr. Cartoons only; $25.

> **Tips:** "Need how-to articles about specific areas of preaching and worship leadership. We only accept articles from pastors or seminary/ college faculty."

THE PRIEST, 200 Noll Plaza, Huntington IN 46750-4304. (219)356-8400. Fax (219)359-0029. E-mail: tpriest@osv.com. Website: http://www.osc.com. Catholic/Our Sunday Visitor, Inc. Msgr. Owen F. Campion, ed. For Catholic priests, deacons and seminarians; to help in all aspects of ministry. Monthly mag; 48 pgs; circ 8,000. Subscription $35.95. 80% freelance. Query or complete ms/cover letter; phone/fax/e-query OK. Pays $175-250 on acceptance for 1st rts. Articles to 1,500-5,000 wds (96/yr); some 2-parts. Responds in 10-12 wks. Seasonal 6 mos ahead. Some sidebars. Prefers NAB. Free guidelines/copy. (Ads)

> **Fillers:** George Foster. Cartoons; $35.

> **Columns/Departments:** Buys 36/yr. Viewpoint (about priests or the church), under 1,000 wds, $50. Complete ms.

Tips: "Write to the point, with interest. Most open to features. Keep the audience in mind. Include Social Security number."
** This periodical was #57 on the 1998 Top 50 Christian Publishers list (#62 in 1994).

PROCLAIM, 127 Ninth Ave. N, Nashville TN 37234-0140. (615)251-3837. Fax (615)251-3609. E-mail: erowell@lifeway.com Southern Baptist. Ed Rowell, ed. Strives to provide quality sermons and preaching resources for biblical preachers. Quarterly journal; 50 pgs; circ 15,000. Subscription $13.30. 75% freelance. Query first; fax/e-query OK. Pays .065/wd ($8 min) on acceptance for all or 1st rts. Articles 600-4,000 wds (50-60/yr); book reviews, 400 wds, $26. Responds in 2-16 wks. Seasonal 6 mos ahead. Accepts reprints. Prefers e-mail submission (attached file). Some sidebars. Guidelines/theme list; copy for 9x12 SAE/6 stamps. (No ads)

> **Special Needs:** Sermons, sermon outlines, and sermon series ideas.
> ** #68 on the 1994 Top 50.

PULPIT HELPS, 6815 Shallowford Rd., Chattanooga TN 37421. (800)251-7206. Fax (423)894-6863. E-mail: AMGpublish@aol.com. Website: http://www.pulpithelps.com. Bob Dasal, ed. To help preachers and serious students of the Bible. Monthly & online tabloid; 32 pgs; circ 106,000. Subscription $15. 20% freelance. Complete ms; fax/e-query OK. **NO PAYMENT.** Articles to 100-1,200 wds, prefers 1,000 (60-80/yr). Responds in 3 wks. Seasonal 4 mos ahead. Accepts simultaneous submissions & reprints (tell when/where appeared). Accepts disk or e-mail submission (attached file). Some sidebars. Prefers KJV or NIV. Guidelines/theme list (also by e-mail); copy for 9x12 SAE/2 stamps. (Ads)

> **Poetry:** Accepts 10-12/yr. Traditional; short. Submit max 3 poems.
> **Fillers:** Anecdotes, prose; quotes; 50-250 wds.
> **Columns/Departments**: Family Helps, 100-1,000 wds; Illustrations (for sermons), 50-100 wds; Sermon Starters (brief).
> **Tips:** "Most open to Illustrations & Sermon Starters—short, pointed anecdotes/articles preachers can use as illustrations. "

QUARTERLY REVIEW, A Journal of Theological Resources for Ministry, 1001 19th Ave. S., Nashville TN 37202-0871. (615)340-7334. Fax (615)340-7048. E-mail: shels@gbhem.org. United Methodist. Dr. Sharon J. Hels, ed. A theological approach to subjects of interest to clergy—Scripture study, ethics, and practice of ministry in Wesleyan tradition. Quarterly journal; 112 pgs; circ 1,500. Subscription $24. 75% freelance. Complete ms/cover letter; phone/fax query OK. **PAYS IN COPIES** for 1st rts. Articles to 5,000 wds (20/yr); book reviews to 1,000 wds. Responds in 6-8 wks. Seasonal 8 mos ahead. Prefers disk, no e-mail submission. No sidebars. Prefers NRSV. Guidelines/theme list; copy for 9x12 SAE/$2 postage. (No ads)

> **Tips:** "We look for writers who have strong academic/theological training and whose work addresses concerns and interests of those in ministry. Awareness of current scholarly literature, a well-developed argument, and clear expository prose are essential."

+REACHING CHILDREN AT RISK, PO Box 633, Oxford OX2 ONX, England

UK. Phone + 44 1865 450 800. Fax + 44 1865 203 567. E-mail: rrobinson@viva.org. Website: http://www.viva.org. The Viva Network. B. Ripley Robinson, ed. To meet the needs of project leaders and workers ministering to children at high risk (street children of the world). Quarterly journal; 36 pgs; circ 2,000. Subscription $3.75/copy. Estab 1996. 95% freelance. Query; phone/e-query OK. Query for electronic submissions. **PAYS IN COPIES.** Articles 1,500-3,000 wds. Accepts disk or e-mail submission. Regular sidebars. Prefers NIV. Guidelines/theme list (by e-mail submission); copy $3.75. (Ads)

> **Special Needs:** Identifying issues/problem areas common to many children's ministries worldwide, analyzing, and providing practical solutions. Such issues might include worker/worker or worker/child relationships; administration; psychological, emotional, spiritual, practical or legal obstacles to third-world children's ministries.
>
> **Tips:** "All articles must relate directly to ministry to children at risk and the issue's theme. We are forming a pool of writers who would contribute material on an ongoing basis. A contributing writer may be asked to write one or two articles a year. Topics will pertain to theme of issue."

REFORMED WORSHIP, 2850 Kalamazoo SE, Grand Rapids MI 49560-0001. (616)224-0785. Fax (616)224-0834. E-mail: rw@crcpublications.org. Website: http://www.reformedworship.org. Christian Reformed Church in North America. Dr. Emily R. Brink, ed. To provide liturgical and musical resources for pastors, church musicians, and other worship leaders. Quarterly mag; 48 pgs; circ 4,000. Subscription $23.95. 5% freelance. Complete ms/cover letter; e-query OK. Query for electronic submissions. Pays .05/wd on publication for all rts (negotiable). Articles 2,000 wds; book reviews 250 wds, $25. Responds in 4 wks. Seasonal 6 mos ahead. Rarely accepts reprints (tell when/where appeared). Kill fee 50%. Prefers e-mail submission (copied into message). Regular sidebars. Prefers NIV or NRSV. Guidelines/theme list (also by e-mail); copy for 9x12 SAE/$2 postage. (No ads)

> **Fillers:** Buys 4-5/yr. Cartoons, prayers; $20-50.
>
> **Columns/Departments:** View From the Pew (humorous or reflective vignettes on worship experiences), 1,000-1,500 wds.
>
> **Tips:** "You need to understand the Reformed tradition of worship. Need articles on prayer this year."

RESOURCE, The National Leadership Magazine, 6745 Century Ave., Mississauga ON L5N 6P7 Canada. (905)542-7400. Fax (905)542-7313. E-mail: resource@paoc.org. Website: http://www.paoc.org. Pentecostal Assemblies of Canada. Michael Horban, ed. For church leadership and practical how-tos on leadership issues. Bimonthly mag; 48 pgs; circ 10,000. Subscription $20. 20% freelance. Query; fax/e-query OK. Pays $30-100 on publication for all rts. Articles 500-1,500 wds (8-10/yr); book reviews 250 wds, $20. Responds in 4-6 wks. Seasonal 3 mos ahead. Accepts reprints. Prefers disk or e-mail submission (copied into message). Regular sidebars. Prefers NIV. Guidelines/theme list; copy $2/9x12 SAE. (Ads)

> **Fillers:** Buys 4-8/yr. Anecdotes, cartoons, short humor; 200-300 wds; $20-30.

Special Needs: Good missions promotional features.

Tips: "Say something positive to leaders that stretches and enriches them."

#REVIEW FOR RELIGIOUS, 3601 Lindell Blvd., Rm. 428, St. Louis MO 63108-3393. (314)977-7363. Fax (314)977-7362. E-mail: foppema@slu. edu. Catholic/Jesuits of Missouri Province. Rev. David L. Fleming, S.J., ed. For Catholic Women and Men Religious, clergy and laity involved in church ministry; to reflect on the church's rich heritage of spirituality. Bimonthly mag; 112 pgs; circ 9,000. Subscription $20. 100% freelance. Complete ms/cover letter; no phone/fax/e-query. Pays $6/pg on publication for 1st rts. Articles 1,500-5,000 wds (50/yr). Responds in 9 wks. Seasonal 8 mos ahead. Accepts disk. No sidebars. Prefers RSV or NAB. Guidelines; copy for 10x13 SAE/5 stamps.

Poetry: Buys 10/yr. Light verse, traditional; 3-12 lines; $6. Submit max 4 poems.

Tips: "Be familiar with at least three past issues."

SABBATH SCHOOL LEADERSHIP, 55 W. Oak Ridge Dr., Hagerstown MD 21740. (301)393-4095. Fax (301)393-4055. E-mail: fcrumbly@rhpa.org. Website: http://www.rhpa.org. Faith Johnson Crumbly, ed. Denominational; nurtures, educates and supports adult Sabbath school leaders by providing program helps, resources, instructional material, and networking opportunities. Open to freelance. Complete ms. Pays on publication (on acceptance for solicited material) for 1st rts. Articles 70-800 wds. Responds in 6-8 wks. Seasonal 4-6 mos ahead. Requires disk. Guidelines/theme list; copy.

SCROLL, (formerly Church Bytes), 8992 Preston Rd., Ste. 110-120, Frisco TX 75034-3964. (972)335-3201. Fax (972)377-9705. E-mail: mnsurratt@aol. com. Deerhaven Press. Marshall N. Surratt, ed. Reviews of faith-based software, as well as stories about how churches, ministries, individuals and families are using computer technology. Bimonthly mag; 48 pgs; circ 10,000. Subscription $24. 50% freelance. Query; e-query OK. Pays $50 on publication for 1st, simultaneous, electronic rts. Articles 1,200-2,000 wds (15-20/yr); book reviews, 1,200-1,600 wds, $50. Responds in 1-3 wks. Seasonal 3 mos ahead. Accepts simultaneous submissions & reprints (tell when/where appeared). Requires disk. Regular sidebars. Guidelines; copy for 9x12 SAE/5 stamps. (Ads)

Special Needs: Computing; computer technology, multimedia, Internet, and software.

Tips: "We want articles that tell a story about people using computer technology to enhance ministry or to enhance their families' lives. We are also interested in how computer technology is being used and what difference that makes in our lives and for our faith."

+SHARING THE PRACTICE, 720 W. Church St., Hagerstown, MD. 21740-4560. (800) 456-8115. E-mail: darryl.zoller@erols.com Website: http://www.bright.net/danned/apc.html. Academy of Parish Clergy/Ecumenical/Interfaith. Darryl Zoller, ed-in-chief. Growth toward Excellence through Sharing the Practice of parish ministry. Quarterly international journal; 40 pages; circ 350 (includes 100 seminary libraries). Subscription $25/

yr.(send to: APC, PO Box 96, Wade, NC 28395-0096). 100% freelance. Complete ms/cover letter; phone/E-query OK. **PAYS IN COPIES FOR NOW** for 1st, reprint, or simultaneous rts. Articles 500-2500 words (25/yr.). Accepts simultaneous submissions & reprints (tell when/where appeared). Regular sidebars. Prefers NRSV or NIV. Guidelines/theme list; copy/9X12 SAE/4 stamps. (Ads)

Poetry: Free verse, traditional. Submit max 2 poems.

Fillers: Humorous, true anecdotes, 25-150 words.

Contest: Book of the Year award ($100+), Top Ten Books of the Year list, Parish Pastor of the Year award ($200+). Inquire by E-mail to Bob_Yoder.parti@pcusa.org

Tips: " We desire articles by clergy of all kinds who wish to share their practice of ministry. Also articles on spiritual direction or spiritual companionship."

SINGLE ADULT MINISTRIES JOURNAL, Box 36670, Colorado Springs CO 80936. (800)487-4726. Fax (719)536-3202. E-mail: KJHurst@aol.com. Cook Communications Ministries. Kim Hurst, ed. For pastors and lay leaders involved in ministry with single adults. Bimonthly journal; 32 pgs; circ 3,000. Subscription $24. 10% freelance. Query; fax/e-query OK. Query for electronic submissions. **USUALLY NO PAYMENT** for 1st rts. Articles 200-2,500 wds (2/yr); book reviews 50-300 wds/$15-75. Responds in 4 wks. Seasonal 1 yr ahead. Accepts simultaneous submissions & reprints (tell when/where appeared). Prefers e-mail submission (copied into message). Regular sidebars. Prefers NIV. Theme list; copy for 9x12 SAE/4 stamps. (Ads)

Fillers: Buys 0-5/yr. Facts, newsbreaks, quotes; 25-200 wds; $10-50.

Tips: "Write to the pastor or leader, not to singles themselves. Interview singles or the leaders who work with them. Want very practical, how-to or 600-word essay on a controversial topic of interest to single adult leaders."

+SMALL GROUP DYNAMICS, 5513 Emmerson Way, Anderson IN 46017. E-mail: micmac@smallgroups.com. How-to for small groups. Query; e-query OK. Pays $20-50 for one-time rts. Articles 500-1,000 wds. Seasonal 2-3 mos ahead. Prefers disk or e-mail submission (attached file). Accepts reprints. Prefers NIV. Guidelines/theme list. Incomplete topical listings.

Fillers: Cartoons.

Special Needs: Brief testimonies of how God has worked in your group; humor in groups; ice-breaker ideas, etc.

Tips: "Follow our themes. We use mostly practical, how-to oriented articles."

SUNDAY SERMONS, PO Box 3102, Margate NJ 08402. (609)822-9401. Fax (609)822-1638. Website: http://www.voicings.com. Ecumenical. J. Colaianni, ed-in-chief. Full-text sermon resource for clergy. Bimonthly bound workbook; 54-60 pgs. 5% freelance. Pays on publication for all rts. Responds in 6 wks. Seasonal 6 mos ahead. Accepts reprints. Prefers disk. Guidelines/theme list; copy for 9x12 SAE. Not in topical listings.

Tips: "Sermons must include several relevant illustrations."

TECHNOLOGIES FOR WORSHIP, PO Box 35, Aurora ON L4G 3H1 Canada. (905)830-4300. Fax (905)853-5096. E-mail: amip@inforamp.net. Website:

http://www.TFWM.com. TWM Media. Neil Sutton, ed. Bimonthly mag; 32-40 pgs; circ 10,000. Subscription $29.95. 90% freelance. Query; phone/fax/e-query OK. **NO PAYMENT** for one-time rts. Articles 700-1,200 wds. Responds in 2 wks. Seasonal 2 mos ahead. Accepts simultaneous submissions & reprints (tell when/where appeared). Accepts disk. Some sidebars. Free guidelines/theme list/copy. (Ads)

> **Special Needs:** Technologies: audio, video, music, computers, broadcast, lighting, and drama; 750-2,500 wds.

> **Tips:** Call the editor to discuss idea for article or column. Should know a lot about today's technologies.

*__THEOLOGY TODAY,__ PO Box 29, Princeton NJ 08542. (609)497-7714. Fax (609)497-7870. Submit to The Editor. Explores key issues, current thoughts and trends in the fields of religion and theology. Quarterly journal; 144-160 pgs; circ 13,000+. Subscription $24. Little unsolicited accepted. Complete ms/cover letter; phone query OK. Pays to $200 on publication for all rts. Articles 13-17 manuscript pgs; book reviews 500-750 pgs. Responds in several wks. Seasonal 1 yr ahead. No disk. Regular sidebars. Guidelines; free copy. (Display ads)

> **Poetry:** Buys 12/yr. Free verse, traditional; $50. Submit max 5 poems.

> **Tips:** "We rarely accept unsolicited material, but do look for new talent. The best route to acceptance is strong familiarity with the journal and types of articles we publish. We expect exclusive language."

*__TODAY'S CHRISTIAN PREACHER__, 162 E Main St., Elverson PA 19520-9700. Marketing Partners. Jerry Thacker, ed. To provide material on current topics to help preachers in their personal lives. Quarterly mag; 24 pgs; circ 25,000. Free subscription. 20% freelance. Complete ms/cover letter; fax query OK. Pays $150 on publication for one-time or simultaneous rts. Not copyrighted. Articles 800-1,000 wds (10-15/yr). Responds in 3-4 wks. Seasonal 1 yr ahead. Accepts simultaneous submissions & reprints (tell when/where appeared). Prefers disk. Regular sidebars. Prefers KJV. Guidelines; copy for 9x12SAE/3stamps. (Ads)

TODAY'S PARISH, Box 180, Mystic CT 06355. (860)536-2611. Fax (860)572-0788. E-mail: ttpubsedit@aol.com. Catholic. Daniel Connors, ed. Practical ideas and issues relating to parish life, management and ministry. Mag published 7X/yr; 40 pgs; circ 14,800. Subscription $22.95. 25% freelance. Query or complete ms. Pays $75-100 on publication for 1st rts. Articles 800-1,800 wds (15/yr). Responds 13 wks. Seasonal 6 mos ahead. Guidelines; copy for 9x12 SASE.

VITAL MINISTRY, PO Box 481, 1515 Cascade Ave., Loveland CO 80538. (970)669-3836. Fax (970)679-4372. E-mail: krector@grouppublishing.com. Website: http://www.grouppublishing.com. Group Publishing, Inc. Paul Allen, ed. For senior pastors and church leaders who provide vision and cultivate the spiritual life of the church; practical. Bimonthly mag; 45 pgs; circ 25,000. 70% freelance. Query or complete ms/cover letter; fax/e-query OK. Pays $300-400 on acceptance for all rts. Articles 1,000-3,000 wds. Responds in 4-8 wks. Seasonal 5 mos ahead. Prefers disk or e-mail submission (attached file). Regular sidebars. Guidelines; copy $2/9x12 SAE/ 5 stamps. (Ads)

Fillers: Buys 5-10/yr. Cartoons, games, ideas. Pays $15-35.

Columns/Departments: Family Ministry, Effective Outreach, Meaningful Worship, Preaching & Teaching, Staff & Layleaders, Practical Discipleship, Generational Trends, all 250-350 wds. Pays $35-50.

Tips: "We are most open to short (300 word) practical articles for our departments."

VOICE OF THE VINEYARD, PO Box 18329, Anaheim CA 92817. (714)777-1433. Fax (714)777-8841. E-mail: editor@vov.org. Assn. of Vineyard Churches. Jon Bogart, ed. Quarterly mag; 24 pgs; circ 25,000. Subscription $14. Little freelance. Query; fax/e-query OK. Pays negotiable rates on publication for 1st rts. Articles 750-1,200 wds; book reviews 300 wds. Responds in 2 wks. Accepts simultaneous submissions & reprints (tell when/where appeared). Requires disk. Kill fee, Prefers NIV. Regular sidebars. Copy for 9x12 SAE/2 stamps. (Ads)

Fillers: Anecdotes, cartoons, facts, games, ideas, jokes, newsbreaks, quizzes, quotes, short humor, word puzzles; 50 wds.

WCA NEWS (formerly WCA Monthly), PO Box 3188, Barrington IL 60011-5046. (847)765-0070. Fax (847)765-5046. E-mail: BraoudaP@willow creek.org. Website: http://www.willowcreek.org. Willow Creek Assn. Paul Braoudakis, mng ed. For church leaders who are willing to take risks for the sake of the gospel. Bimonthly & online newsletter; 16-20 pgs; circ 6,000. Subscription $29. 10% freelance. Query/clips; phone/fax/e-query OK. Pays $25 on publication for all rts. Articles 500-1,000 wds; book/music reviews 500 wds, video reviews 300 wds. Responds in 2 wks. Seasonal 2 mos ahead. Accepts simultaneous submissions & reprints (tell when/where appeared). Requires disk or e-mail submission (attached file). Some sidebars. Prefers NIV. Guidelines (e-mail submission or Website); free copy. (No ads)

Fillers: Accepts many. Cartoons, ideas, short humor; 50-75 wds. Pays $10.

Columns/Departments: On the Lighter Side (humor), 100 wds; News From the Frontlines (creative ministries within the church), 50-100 wds; Strategic Trends (trends from growing churches), 200-250 wds. Pays $10-25. Complete ms.

Tips: "Any articles that pertain to doing a seeker-sensitive type of ministry will be considered. Also leadership issues in the church, outreach ideas, and effective evangelism."

*WORD & WORLD: Theology for Christian Ministry, 2481 Como Ave., St. Paul MN 55108. (612)641-3482. Fax (612)641-3354. E.L.C.A./Luther Northwestern Theological Seminary. Frederick J. Gaiser, ed. Addresses ecclesiastical and secular issues from a theological perspective and addresses pastors and church leaders with the best fruits of theological research. Quarterly journal; 104 pgs; circ 3,100. Subscription $18. 10% freelance. Complete ms/cover letter; phone query OK. Pays $50 on publication for all rts. Articles 5,000-6,000 wds. Responds in 2-8 wks. Guidelines/theme list; copy $5.

Tips: "Most open to general articles. We look for serious theology addressed clearly and interestingly to people in the practice of ministry. Creativity and usefulness in ministry are highly valued."

WORSHIP LEADER, 107 Kenner Ave., Nashville TN 37205-2207. (615)386-3011. Fax (615)385-4112 or (615)386-3380. E-mail: mriddle@ccmcom.com. CCM Communications. Melissa L. Riddle, mng ed. Intellectual tone with practical advice on leading worship. Bimonthly mag; 64 pgs; circ 48,000. Subscription $19.95. 20-40% freelance. Query/clips or complete ms. Pays .20/wd on publication for 1st rts. Articles 800-2,000 wds (15/yr). Responds in 6-8 wks. Seasonal 6-8 mos ahead. Kill fee 50%. Prefers disk. Regular sidebars. Prefers NIV. Guidelines. (Ads)

Fillers: Buys 6-12/yr. Anecdotes, quotes; 150-300 wds.

Columns/Departments: Buys 6-12/yr. Viewpoint (op/ed), 600-800 wds; Putting it All Together (experience with church), 1,200 wds. Several others, see guidelines.

Tips: "We need writers from all parts of the country to do profiles of churches, worship leaders/ministers of music in their home cities. Also, suggest articles on worship applications outside the church."

YOUR CHURCH, 465 Gundersen Dr., Carol Stream IL 60188. (630)260-6200. Fax (630)260-0114. E-mail: YCEditor@aol.com. Website: http://www.christianity.net/yc. Christianity Today Inc. Phyllis Ten Elshof, ed. Focuses on church business/administration, purchasing and facilities management. Bimonthly mag; 80+ pgs; circ 150,000. Subscription free to church administrators. 20% freelance. Query or complete ms/cover letter; fax/e-query OK. Query for electronic submissions. Pays $100 & up on acceptance for 1st rts. Articles 1,000-1,500 wds (60/yr). Responds in 2-4 wks. Seasonal 6 mos ahead. Accepts reprints (tell when/where appeared). Prefers e-mail submission (copied into message). Kill fee 50%. Regular sidebars. Prefers NIV. Guidelines/theme list; copy for $1 postage. (Ads)

Fillers: Cartoons, $125.

Columns/Departments: Query. Pays $100.

Special Needs: Church management articles; audio/visual equipment; books/ curriculum resources; music equipment; church products; furnishings; office equipment; computers/software.

Tips: "Almost all articles are assigned to writers with expertise in a certain area. Write and ask for an assignment; tell your strengths, interests and background."

** This periodical was #25 on the 1998 Top 50 Christian Publishers list (#42 in 1997).

YOUTHWORKER, The Contemporary Journal for Youth Ministry, PO Box 2638, El Cajon CA 92021. (619)440-2333. Fax (619)440-4939. E-mail: urb@youthspecialties.com, or YS@YouthSpecialties.com. Website: http://www.youthspecialties.com. Youth Specialties Inc. Dave Urbanski, ed. For youth workers/church and parachurch. Bimonthly & online journal; 72 pgs; circ 13,200. Subscription $25.95. 90% freelance. Query or complete ms; phone query OK. Pays $100-150 on acceptance for 1st & reprint rts. Articles 2,000-3,500 wds (30/yr). Responds in 5 wks. Seasonal 10 mos ahead. Accepts reprints. Kill fee $50. Guidelines/theme list (also by e-mail: Leslie@ YouthSpecialties.com); copy $3/10x13 SAE.

Columns/Departments: Buys 10/yr. High School Minister; Middle School Minister; 2,000-3,000 wds; $100-150.

Special Needs: Upcoming themes include Music in Ministry, Growing Up: pitfalls, conflict, conflict, expectations.

Tips: "Read Youthworker; imbibe its tone (professional, though not academic; conversational, though not chatty). Query me with specific, focused ideas that conform to our needs. Writer needs to be a youth minister."

** This periodical was #59 on the 1998 Top 50 Christian Publishers list. (#60 in 1997, #46 in 1995, #53 in 1994) Also 1995 EPA Award of Merit—Christian Ministry.

TEEN/YOUNG ADULT MARKETS

ALIVE! PO Box 779, Minneapolis MN 55440-0779. (612)338-0500. Fax (612)335-1299. E-mail: alive@graham-assn.org. Website: http://www.alive.org. Billy Graham Evangelistic Assn. Ann McCaffrey Elder, ed. Evangelistic publication for teens. Accepting no freelance submissions.

***BEAUTIFUL CHRISTIAN TEEN,** #7 Bergoo Rd., Webster Springs WV 26288. (304)847-7537. Fax (304)847-7552. Baptist. Kimberly Short Wolfe, ed. Conservative publication for Christian teen girls. Bimonthly mag; 24-28 pgs; circ under 5,000. 75% freelance. Complete ms/cover letter. **NO PAYMENT.** Columns & fiction. Guidelines; copy $3. (Ads)

#BREAKAWAY, 8605 Explorer Dr., Colorado Springs CO 80920. (719)548-4576. Fax (719)531-3499. Website: http://www.family.org. Focus on the Family. Michael Ross, ed. The 14-year-old, unchurched teen (boy) in the public school is our target; boys 11-18 yrs. Monthly mag; 24-32 pgs; circ 84,000. Subscription $15. 60-70% freelance. Complete ms/cover letter; phone query OK. Pays .12-.15/wd on acceptance for all, 1st, one-time & reprint rts. Articles 400-1,800 wds (40/yr); fiction 1,200-2,200 wds (15/yr); music reviews, 300 wds, $30-40. Responds in 5 wks. Seasonal 8 mos ahead. Accepts simultaneous submissions & reprints. Kill fee 33-50%. Guidelines/theme list; copy for 9x12 SAE/3 stamps. (Ads)

　　Fillers: Buys 50/yr. Cartoons ($75), facts, quizzes; 200-600 wds; .20-.25/wd.

　　Columns/Departments: Buys 12/yr. Plugged In (devotional); 700-900 wds.

　　Tips: "Need strong lead. Brevity and levity a must. Have a teen guy or two read it. Make sure the language is up-to-date, but not overly hip."

　　** This periodical was #3 on the 1998 Top 50 Christian Publishers list. (#9 in 1997, #3 in 1996, #6 in 1995, #5 in 1994)

#BRIO, 8605 Explorer Dr., Colorado Springs CO 80920. (719)548-4577. Fax (719)531-3499. Website: http://www.family.org. Focus on the Family. Susie Shellenberger, ed; submit to Susan Stevens. For teen girls, 12-16 yrs. Monthly mag; 32 pgs; circ 170,000. Subscription $15. 60% freelance. Complete ms/cover letter; phone query OK. Pays .08-.15/wd on acceptance for 1st rts. Articles 800-1,000 wds (10/yr); fiction 1,200-2,000 wds

(10/yr). Responds in 4-9 wks. Seasonal 5 mos ahead. Kill fee $100. Guidelines; copy $1.50. (No ads)

Fillers: Buys 15/yr. Cartoons, facts, ideas, quizzes, short humor; 50-200 wds. Pays $75-100.

Special Needs: All topics of interest to female teens are welcome: boys, make-up, dating, weight, ordinary girls who have the extraordinary, female adjustments to puberty, etc. Also teen-related female fiction.

Tips: "Study at least 3 issues of *Brio* before submitting. We're looking for a certain, fresh, hip-hop conversational style. Most open to fiction, articles and quizzes."

** This periodical was #63 on the 1998 Top 50 Christian Publishers list (#58 in 1997, #60 in 1996, #61 in 1995, #37 in 1994). Also 1995 EPA Award of Merit—Youth.

CAMPUS LIFE, 465 Gundersen Dr., Carol Stream IL 60188. (708)260-6200. Fax (708)260-0114. E-mail: cledit@aol.com. Website: http://www. campus life.net. Christianity Today, Inc. Christopher Lutes, ed. Seeks to help teenagers navigate adolescence with their Christian faith intact. Bimonthly (plus 3 special Christian College issues) mag; 68-94 pgs; circ 100,000. Subscription $19.95. 35% freelance. Query/clips; fax query OK. Pays .15-.25/wd on acceptance for 1st or one-time rts. Articles 750-1,200 (5-10/yr); fiction 1,000-2,000 wds (1-5/yr); photo essays. Responds in 5-9 wks. Seasonal 5 mos ahead. Accepts simultaneous submissions & reprints (tell when/where appeared). Accepts disk. Kill fee 50%. Regular sidebars. Guidelines; copy $3/9x12 SAE/3 stamps. (Ads)

Poetry: Buys 1-5/yr. Free verse; 5-20 lines; $25-50. Submit max 2 poems. Rarely purchase.

Fillers: Buys 30 cartoons/yr; $50; anecdotes, facts, short humor, 25-250 wds, $10-50.

Columns/Departments: Buys 20/yr. Making the Grade (study tips), 100-250 wds, $25-50.

Tips: "Most open to as-told-to stories. Interview students and get their stories."

** This periodical was #35 on the 1998 Top 50 Christian Publishers list. (#37 in 1996, #49 in 1995, #63 in 1994)

*****CERTAINTY**, 1300 N. Meacham Rd., Schaumburg IL 60173-4888. (847)843-1600. Fax (847)843-3757. Regular Baptist Press. Joan E. Alexander, ed. For senior high youth (15-18); conservative/fundamental. Weekly take-home paper. Note: This periodical is being redesigned as we go to press. Send for new guidelines before submitting.

CHALLENGE (GA), 4200 N. Point Pkwy, Alpharetta GA 30022-4176. (770)410-6000. Fax (770)410-6018. E-mail: shsmith@namb.net. Website: http:// www.namb.net, or http://www.student2.com. North American Mission Board/Southern Baptist. Shelley Smith, ed. Missions interest articles for young men, ages 12-18. Monthly mag; 24 pgs; circ 24,500. Subscription $13.08. 5% freelance. Query/clips. Pays $20-100 on publication for 1st or simultaneous rts. Articles 500-800 wds (36/yr); fiction 700-1,000 wds (12/

yr); book/music/video reviews 250 wds, $20. Responds in 4-5 wks. Seasonal 8 mos ahead. Accepts simultaneous submissions & reprints. Accepts disk. Regular sidebars. Prefers NAS. Guidelines/theme list; copy for 9x12 SAE/3 stamps.

Special Needs: Internet computer innovation for youth.

Tips: "Looking for articles of male youth interest and articles with a Christian testimony, especially sports. Mission stories involving youth are also very good. Present relevant youth issues in an entertaining way."

*CHALLENGE (IL), 1300 N. Meacham Rd., Schaumburg IL 60173-4888. (847)843-1600. Fax (847)843-3757. Regular Baptist Press. Joan E. Alexander, ed. For junior high youth (12-14); conservative/fundamental. Weekly take-home paper. Note: This periodical is being redesigned as we go to press. Send for new guidelines before submitting.

+THE CHRISTIAN COLLEGE HANDBOOK, PO Box 1357, Oak Park, IL 60304. (708)524-5070. Fax: (708) 524-5174. E-mail: kipland@juno.com. Website: http://www.collegefocus.com. Kipland Publishing House. Tonya Eichelberger, ed. College planning guide for high school juniors and seniors. Annual mag; circ 265,000+. Free to college-bound high schoolers. 85% freelance. Prefers 1-page query; fax/e-query OK. Payment varies for all rts (usually). purchased. Articles 800-1,200 wds. Some sidebars. Guidelines/theme list; copy $3. Not in topical listings. (Ads)

Special Needs: First-person and how-to features that express the value of a Christian college or university education and focus on all topics of interest to high schoolers planning for college including: the college application process, paying for college, choosing a major, selecting a school, financial aid and scholarships, spending time with God, campus life, time management, short-term missions.

Tips: "We are open to working with new/unpublished authors, especially college graduates, current college students, college professors, admissions personnel, career counselors and financial aid officers. Visit our Website to view articles previously published."

*THE CONQUEROR, 8855 Dunn Rd., Hazelwood MO 63042. (314)837-7300. United Pentecostal Church, Intl. Nathan C. Reever, ed. For teenagers in the denomination. Bimonthly mag; 16 pgs; circ 6,000. Subscription $7.50. 90% freelance. Complete ms. Pays $20-30 on publication for various rts. Articles & fiction (many/yr) 600-800. Responds in 10 wks. Seasonal 4 mos ahead. Accepts simultaneous submissions & reprints. Prefers KJV. Guidelines; copy for 11x14 SAE/2 stamps.

Fillers: Various.

Tips: "Articles should be written with the idea of strict morals, standards and ethics in mind."

CROSS WALK, 6401 The Paseo, Kansas City MO 64131. (816)333-7000x2211. Fax (816)333-4315. E-mail: crosswalk@nazarene.org. Website: http://www.nazarene.org. Holiness denominations. James K. Hampton, ed. Written by teens (and youth leaders) for teens. Weekly take-home paper; circ 35,000. Subscription $7.60. By assignment only. Query only. Pays on acceptance for all rts. Responds in 2 wks. Kill fee 50%. No sidebars. Guidelines; copy for 9x12 SAE/2 stamps.

Tips: "Open only to a youth worker (professional or volunteer) and five teens from his/her youth group. The youth leader will write devotionals for Saturday and Sunday, and the five teens will write devotionals for Monday-Friday." Writers must be subscribers.

DEVO'ZINE, 1908 Grand Ave., Nashville TN 37202-9890. (615)340-7247. Fax (615)340-7267. E-mail: devozine@upperroom.com. Website: http://www.upperroom.org/devozine/default.html. The Upper Room. Robin Pippin, ed. Devotional; to help teens (12-18) develop and maintain their connection with God and other Christians. Bimonthly mag; 64 pgs; circ 75,000. Subscription $16.95. Estab 1996. 100% freelance. Query; phone/fax/e-query OK. Pays $20 for meditations, $75 for feature articles (assigned) on acceptance for one-time, electronic rts (newspaper, software-driven format). Meditations 150-250 wds (350/yr), articles 350-500 wds; book/music/video reviews, 350-500 wds, $75. Responds in 16 wks. Seasonal 6-8 mos ahead. Accepts reprints (tell when/where appeared). Accepts disk or e-mail submission. Regular sidebars. Prefers NRSV, NIV, CEV. Guidelines/theme list; copy/7x10 SAE.

Poetry: Buys 25-30/yr. Free verse, light verse, haiku, traditional; to 150 wds or 10-20 lines. Pays $20. Submit max 1 poem/theme, 9 themes/issue.

Tips: "Call with ideas for week-end features related to specific themes."

** This periodical was #10 on the 1998 Top 50 Christian Publishers list (#6 in 1997).

ESSENTIAL CONNECTIONS, 127 Ninth Ave. N., Nashville TN 37234-0140. (615)251-5679. Fax (615)251-2795. E-mail: DwayneUlmer@bssb.com. Website: http://www.youthscape.com. Southern Baptist. Dwayne Ulmer, ed. Christian leisure reading and devotional guide for 7th-12th graders. Monthly mag; 60 pgs; circ 130,000. Subscription $3.84 (per quarter - 3 issues). 15% freelance. Complete ms/cover letter; e-query OK. Pays $40-80 on publication for all (preferred), 1st, one-time or reprint rts. Articles 750-800 wds (20/yr); fiction 1,100-1,200 wds. Responds in 10 wks. Seasonal 8 mos ahead. Accepts simultaneous submissions & reprints. Accepts disk or e-mail submission (attached file). Kill fee. Some sidebars. Prefers NIV. No guidelines; free copy. (No ads)

Poetry: Accepts 30/yr. All types. From teens only.

Special Needs: Always in search of Christian humor.

+GUIDEPOSTS FOR TEENS, PO Box 638, Chesterton IN 46304. (219)929-4429. Fax (219)926-3839. E-mail: gp4t@aol.com. Website: Http://www.guideposts.org. Guideposts, Inc. Tanya Dean, mng ed. For teens, 13-21; features teens who show courage, strength, and positive attitudes through faith in God. Bimonthly mag; 48 pgs. Subscription $19.95. 95% freelance. Query/clips; query for electronic submissions. Pays $300-500 for true stories, $100-300 for shorter pieces on acceptance for all, 1st, one-time or reprint rts. Articles 750-1,000 wds. Responds in 4-6 wks. Seasonal 6+ mos ahead. Accepts reprints (tell when/where appeared). Accepts disk or e-mail submission. Kill fee 25%. Some sidebars OK. Prefers NIV. Guidelines; copy $4.50. (No ads)

Poetry: Buys 3-6/yr. Avant-garde, free verse, traditional; 8-16 lines. Pays $25-100. Submit max 3 poems.

Fillers: Buys 25-100/yr. Anecdotes, cartoons, facts, jokes, prose, quizzes, short humor, 50-250 wds. Pays $25-100.

Columns/Departments: Buys 30-40/yr. Send complete ms. My Most Embarrassing Moment, 200-300 wds; Are You Laughing at Me? (humor, true or fictional), 500-1,000 wds; Seen and Heard (fun clips of weird news items), 100 wds; Who's in Charge? (teens initiating volunteer activities), 200-300 wds. Pays $25-300.

Special Needs: Need 1st-person true stories of teens with a spiritual point (7-8/issue); see guidelines.

Contest: Laws of Life essay contest for teens, 13-18. Prizes of $5,000, $3,000 and $2,000. Send SASE for guidelines.

Tips: "Most open to how-to features, Humor/embarrassing moment; Who's in Charge? (column). Want true stories of teens in the Guideposts' tradition; teens in dangerous, inspiring, miraculous situations. Study guidelines."

+HYPE, Hyper Young People Evangelizing, 16 Barclay Rd., North Rocks, Sydney NSW 2151. E-mail: ranita@cheerful.com. Ranita Row, sr ed. Estab 1997. Open to freelance. **NO PAYMENT.** Not in topical listings.

*I.D., 4050 Lee Vance View, Colorado Springs CO 80918. (719)536-0100. Fax (719)536-3296. Cook Communications Ministries.

** 1997 EPA Award of Excellence, Sunday School Take-home paper.

INSIGHT, 55 W. Oak Ridge Dr., Hagerstown MD 21740-7301. (301)393-4037. Fax (301)393-4055. E-mail: insight@rhpa.org. Website: http://www.insight magazine.org. Review and Herald/Seventh-day Adventist. Lori Peckham, ed. A magazine of positive Christian living for Seventh-day Adventist teenagers, 14-18 years. Weekly mag; 16 pgs; circ 18,000. Subscription $37.97. 60% freelance. Complete ms/cover letter; e-query OK. Pays $25-125 on acceptance for one-time rts. Articles 500-1,500 wds (100/yr). Responds in 4 wks. Seasonal 6 mos ahead. Accepts reprints (tell when/where appeared). Prefers disk or e-mail submission. Kill fee. Regular sidebars. Prefers NIV. Guidelines (also by e-mail/Website); copy $2/9x12 SAE. (Ads)

Poetry: Buys to 36/yr. All types; to 1 pg. By teens only. Pays $10.

Columns/Departments: Buys 50/yr. On the Edge (drama in real life), 800-1,500 wds, $50-100; It Happened To Me (personal experience in first-person), 600-900 wds, $50-75; Big Deal (big topics, such as prayer, premarital sex, knowing God's will, etc.) with sidebar, 1,200-1,700 wds, $75 + $25 for sidebar; So I Said (first-person opinion), 300-500 wds, $25-50.

Contest: Sponsors a fiction & poetry contest; includes a category for students under 21. Prizes to $250. May or June deadline (may vary). Send SASE for rules.

Tips: "We are desperately in need of true, dramatic stories involving Christian teens. Also need stories by male authors, particularly some humor. Also profiles of Seventh-day Adventist teenagers who are making a notable difference."

** This periodical was #6 on the 1998 Top 50 Christian Publishers list. (#5 in 1997, #8 in 1996, #18 in 1995, #6 in 1994)

+INTEEN, 1551 Regency Ct., Calumet City IL 60409. (708)868-7100x239. Fax (708)868-6759. E-mail: umi1551@aol.com. Website: http://www.urban ministries.com. Urban Ministries, Inc. Katara Washington, ed. Teen curriculum for ages 14-17 (student and teacher manuals). Quarterly booklet; 32 pgs; circ 20,000. Subscription $11.25. 80% freelance. Query/clips; phone query OK. Pays $75-150 on acceptance for all rts. Articles & fiction 1,200 wds. Responds in 4 wks. Seasonal 9 mos ahead. Accepts some reprints (tell when/where appeared). Accepts disk or e-mail submission (copied into message). Prefers NIV. Free guidelines/theme list/copy for 10x13 SAE. (No ads)

Poetry: Buys 4/yr. Free verse; variable length. Pays $25-60.

Tips: "Most open to Bible study guides."

LISTEN, 55 W. Oak Ridge Dr., Hagerstown MD 21740. (301)745-3888. Fax (301)393-4055. E-mail: lsteed@RHPH.org. Review and Herald/Seventh-day Adventist. Lincoln Steed, ed. To educate teens against alcohol/drugs in a uniquely positive way; emphasizes moral values in a secular tone. Monthly mag; 32 pgs; circ 30,000. Subscription $24.97. 50% freelance. Complete ms. Pays .05-.10/wd ($40-250) on acceptance for 1st or reprint rts. Articles 1,200 wds (45/yr); fiction 1,200 wds (15/yr). Responds in 12 wks. Seasonal 1 yr ahead. Accepts simultaneous submissions & reprints (tell when/where appeared). Accepts disk. Regular sidebars. Guidelines; copy $1/9x12 SAE/2 stamps. (No ads)

Fillers: Buys 12/yr. Quizzes, word puzzles, 150-300 wds. Pays $15.

Tips: "Most open to stories, self-help, well-known personalities who are positive role-models for teens."

** This periodical was #36 on the 1998 Top 50 Christian Publishers List. (#21 in 1997, #15 in 1996)

REAL TIME   (formerly Teen Power), PO Box 36640, Colorado Springs CO 80936. (719)533-3044. Fax (719)533-3045. Cook Communications/Scripture Press. Chris Lyon, ed. To help young teens (11-15 yrs) explore ways Jesus relates to them in everyday life. Weekly take-home paper; 8 pgs, circ 30,000. Subscription $11.50. 90% freelance. Complete ms/no cover letter; no phone/fax query. Pays $50-125 on acceptance for one-time or pick-up (reprint) rts. Articles 800-1,200 wds (10/yr); fiction & true stories 800-1,200 wds (20/yr). Responds in 6-8 wks. Seasonal 1 yr ahead. Accepts simultaneous submissions & reprints. Prefers disk or e-mail, but will request. Regular sidebars. Any version. Guidelines/theme list/copy for #10 SAE/1 stamp. (No ads)

Poetry: From teens only. Free verse, light verse, traditional.

Fillers: Buys 10/yr. Cartoons, jokes, prose, quizzes, word puzzles; $15.

Tips: "Looking for remarkable Christian teens doing remarkable things, and how their Christianity affects that. Also looking for humor that teaches biblical truth." Send Social Security number.

** This periodical was #34 on the 1997 Top 50 Christian Publishers list. (#21 in 1996 & 1995, #41 in 1994)

*RIGHTSIDE UP MAGAZINE, PO Box 2041, Grand Rapids MI 49501-2041. Website: http://www.gospelcom.net/uplook/home.html. Uplook Ministries. Estab 1997. Quarterly; circ. 1,500. Not in topical listings.

THE ROCK, 4050 Lee Vance View, Colorado Springs CO 80918-7100. "We are not currently accepting freelance material; perhaps in a year or two."

SHARING THE VICTORY, 8701 Leeds Rd., Kansas City MO 64129-1680. (816)921-0909. Fax (816)921-8755. E-mail: stv@fca.org. Website: http://www.fca/org. Fellowship of Christian Athletes (Protestant and Catholic). John Dodderidge, ed. Equipping and encouraging athletes and coaches to take their faith seriously, in and out of competition. Monthly (Sept-May, 9X) mag; 32 pgs; circ 60,000. Subscription $18. 50% freelance. Query only/clips. Pays $50-200 on publication for 1st rts. Articles 500-1,500 wds (5-20/yr). Responds in 9 wks. Seasonal 3 mos ahead. Accepts reprints (pays 50%). Accepts disk or e-mail submission (copied into message). Kill fee. Regular sidebars. Prefers NIV. Guidelines; copy $1/9x12 SAE/3 stamps. (Ads)

Poetry: Buys 9/yr. Free verse; 8-24 lines; $25. Submit max 3 poems.

Special Needs: Articles on FCA camp experiences (40th anniversary of camps). All articles must have an athletic angle.

Tips: "FCA angle important; pro & college athletes and coaches giving solid Christian testimony; we run stories according to athletic season; need articles/poetry on female athletes."

** 1997 EPA Award of Merit—Organizational.

SPIRIT, Lectionary-based Weekly for Catholic Teens, 1884 Randolph Ave., St. Paul MN 55105-1700. (612)690-7005. Fax: (612)690-7039. E-mail: jmcsj9@mail.idt.net. Catholic/Good Ground Press. Joan Mitchell, CSJ, ed; Therese Sherlock, CSJ, mng ed. For the religious education of high schoolers (14-18 yrs). Weekly newsletter; 4 pgs; circ 26,000. 50% freelance. Query. Pays $200 on publication for all rts. Articles (4/yr) & fiction (10/yr) 1,000-1,200 wds. Responds in 5-26 wks. Seasonal 6 mos ahead. Accepts simultaneous submissions. Free guidelines/copy.

STRAIGHT, 8121 Hamilton Ave., Cincinnati OH 45231. (513)931-4050. Fax (513)931-0950. Standard Publishing. Heather Wallace, ed. For Christian teens (12-19 yrs). Weekly take-home paper; 12 pgs; circ 30,000. Subscription $11.99. 90% freelance. Complete ms/cover letter; no phone/fax query. Pays .05-.07/wd on acceptance for 1st, one-time, or reprint rts. Articles to 900-1,100 wds (40/yr); fiction 900-1,500 wds (100/yr). Responds in 6-8 wks. Seasonal 9-12 mos ahead. Accepts simultaneous submissions & reprints. No disk. Some sidebars. Prefers NIV. Guidelines/theme list; copy for #10 SAE/2 stamps. (No ads)

Poetry: Buys 20/yr. Free verse, light verse, traditional; from teens only; $10. Submit max 5 poems.

Fillers: Buys 10-15/yr. Prayers, short humor, 300-700 wds.

Columns/Departments: Buys 12/yr. Straight Spotlight (teens making a difference), 900-1,100 wds. Pays .05-.06/wd.

Tips: "Request to be put on our theme list. Writers should have a

good grasp of what today's teens are like. How do they act? What do they like/dislike? What are their concerns?"
** This periodical was #8 on the 1998 Top 50 Christian Publishers list. (#17 in 1997, #13 in 1996, #5 in 1995, #17 in 1994)

STUDENT LEADERSHIP JOURNAL, Box 7895, Madison WI 53707-7895. (608)274-9001x425. Fax (608)274-7882. E-mail: slj@ivcf.org. Website: http://www.ivcf.org/slj. InterVarsity Christian Fellowship. Jeff Yourison, ed. Undergraduate college student Christian leaders, single, ages 18-26. Triannual & online journal; 32 pgs; circ 8,500. Subscription $12. 20% freelance. Query/clips. Pays $35-125 on acceptance for 1st or one-time rts. Articles to 2,000 wds (1/yr); book reviews 150-400 wds, $25-50. Responds in 16 wks. Seasonal 8 mos ahead. Accepts reprints. No e-mail submission. Regular sidebars. Guidelines/theme list; copy $4/9x12 SAE/4 stamps. (Ads)
   Poetry: Buys 4-6/yr. Avant-garde, free verse; to 15 lines; $25-50. Submit max 5 poems.
   Fillers: Buys 0-5/yr. Facts, games, party ideas, quizzes; to 200 wds; $10-50.
   Columns/Departments: Buys 6-10/yr. Collegiate Trends, 20-100 wds; Student Leadership Network, 500-800 wds; Chapter Strategy (how-to planning strategy for campus groups), 500-800; $10-75. Query.
   Special Needs: Campus issues/trends/ministry/spiritual growth/leadership; Kingdom values; multi-ethnic reconciliation.
   Tips: "Most open to main features targeted to college-age students. Be upbeat, interesting and fresh. Writers who were involved in campus fellowship as students have the 'write' perspective and experience."
   ** 1997 & 1996 EPA Award of Merit—Christian Ministry.

TAKE FIVE, 1445 Boonville Ave., Springfield MO 65802. (417)862-2781x4359. Fax (417)862-8558. E-mail: takefive@ag.org. Assemblies of God. Tammy Bicket, youth ed. A daily devotional for teens, grades 7-12. Quarterly booklet; 128 pgs; circ 34,000. Subscription $9.60. 80% freelance. Write for assignment. Pays $30/devotion on acceptance for all rts (one-time rts for poetry). Responds in 13 wks. Seasonal 15 mos ahead. Accepts simultaneous submissions & reprints on poetry only. Prefers disk. Guidelines; copy for 6x9 SAE/3 stamps.
   Poetry: Buys 36/yr. Any type; 8-20 lines; $15. Submit max 5 poems. "Poetry is held on file unless writer requests its return."
   Special Needs: Photos; photos of ethnic groups are a plus. Poetry from teens (SASE required for return).
   Tips: "All devotional writing is done on assignment to Assemblies of God writers only. Sample devotional or similar writing can be submitted for editors evaluation and for future consideration when writing assignments are made."

*TEENAGE CHRISTIAN**, PO Box 549, Murray KY 42071-0549. (800)637-2613. Church of Christ/Christian Publishing Inc. Jim Pounders, ed. Spiritual answers to tough questions for Christian teens (13-19 yrs). Bimonthly mag; 32 pgs; circ 10,500. Subscription $14.95. 50% freelance.

Complete ms/cover letter. Pays $35 on publication for one-time & reprint rts. Articles 600-1,200 wds (20/yr); fiction 600-1,500 wds (9/yr). Responds in 3-4 wks. Accepts disk. Seasonal 6 mos ahead. Accepts simultaneous submissions & reprints (tell when/where appeared). Rarely uses sidebars. Prefers NIV. Copy for 9x12 SAE/$2.50. (Ads)

Poetry: Buys 3-4/yr. Free verse; 10-25 lines; $15-25. Submit max 5 poems.

Fillers: Buys 5-10/yr. Cartoons, quizzes, prayers, word puzzles; 150-350 wds; $15-25.

Tips: "Most open to practical nonfiction. Fiction should be excellent, realistic, and up to date."

TEEN LIFE, 1445 Boonville Ave., Springfield MO 65802-1894. (417)862-2781. Fax (417)862-6059. E-mail: teenlife@ag.org. Assemblies of God. Tammy L. Bicket, ed. To emphasize Christian living through biblical principles for Spirit-filled young people ages 12-19. Quarterly mag; 64 pgs; circ 44,000. Subscription $10.40. 10% freelance. Complete ms/cover letter; no phone/fax query. Pays $25-200 ($25-100 for fiction) or .05-.08/wd on acceptance for 1st, one-time, reprint or simultaneous rts. Articles 500-1,000 wds (5/yr); fiction 500-800 wds (5/yr). Responds in 8-10 wks. Seasonal 18 mos ahead. Accepts simultaneous submissions & reprints (tell when/where appeared). Prefers disk or e-mail submission. Some sidebars. Prefers NIV. Guidelines; copy for 9x12 SAE/2 stamps. (No ads)

Fillers: Buys 5/yr. Anecdotes, cartoons, facts, jokes, newsbreaks, short humor, Top 10 lists; to 25 wds; payment negotiable.

Special Needs: We like to highlight actual events/testimonies of teens: what they're doing in their church or community. Need filler material: weird news, facts and filler stuff. (Sources of information must be included.)

Tips: "The best opening is in the area of short story, true or fiction. It should be relevant to what teens are facing, but not provide pat, clichd answers. Be willing to address the tough issues. Good humor pieces always needed." Current teen issues, trends and testimonies are needed. Accepts freelance on a very limited basis.

** This periodical was #62 on the 1998 Top 50 Christian Publishers list. (#37 in 1996, #37 in 1995, #11 in 1994)

TEENS ON TARGET, 8855 Dunn Rd., Hazelwood MO 63042. (314)837-7300. Fax (314)837-4503. E-mail: wapeditor@aol.com. Website: http://www.upci.org. Word Aflame Publications. P. Daniel Buford, assoc ed. For teens 12-14 years. Weekly take-home paper; circ 7,000. Subscription $4.40. 75% freelance. Complete ms/cover letter. Pays .01-.02/wd on publication for 1st or simultaneous rts. Articles 1,200-1,400 wds; fiction 1,200-1,400 wds (40/yr). Seasonal 1 yr ahead. Accepts simultaneous submissions & reprints. Some sidebars. Prefers KJV. Guidelines; copy for 6x9 SAE/2 stamps.

Fillers: Buys 2-3/yr. Quizzes, word puzzles; $5-12.

Tips: "Articles should be human interest with practical application of Christian principles for 12-14 year olds."

#TODAY'S CHRISTIAN TEEN, PO Box 329, Elverson PA 19529. (610)286-8800. Fax (610)286-8881. Marketing Partners. Jerry Thacker, ed. To help today's Christian teens by presenting material which applies the Bible to contemporary issues; conservative. Quarterly mag; 24 pgs; circ 39,800. Free subscription. 20% freelance. Complete ms/cover letter; fax/e-query OK. Pays $150 on publication for first, one-time or reprint rts. Not copyrighted. Articles 800-1,000 wds (4/yr). Responds in 6 wks. Seasonal 6 mos ahead. Accepts reprints (tell when/where appeared). Prefers disk. Regular sidebars. Prefers KJV. Guidelines; copy for 9x12 SAE/4 stamps.

Contest: Essay contest. Prize is full scholarship to a youth conference for high school students. Send SASE for information.

VISIONS, Lectionary-based Weekly for Catholic Junior Highs, 330 Progress Rd., Dayton OH 45449. (937)847-5900. Fax (937)847-5910. E-mail: pliservice@aol.com, or rscorpi9@mail.idt.net. Website: http://www. pflaum.com. Peter Li, Inc./Catholic. Joan Mitchell, CSJ, mng ed. Connects young people's real-life experiences—successes and conflicts in family, neighborhood, classroom—with the Sunday gospels; for grades 7-9. Weekly (32X during school yr) take-home paper; circ 140,000. 40% freelance. Query; e-query OK. Pays $150 on publication for all rts. Articles (6-8/yr) & fiction (8-10/yr), 950 wds. Responds in 2-8 wks. Seasonal 4-6 mos ahead. Accepts simultaneous query. Guidelines; copy $1.85.

WITH, The Magazine for Radical Christian Youth, Box 347, Newton KS 67114-0347. (316)283-5100. Fax (316)283-0454. Faith & Life Press/Mennonite, Brethren & Mennonite Brethren. Carol Duerksen, ed. For high-school teens (15-18 yrs), Christian and non-Christian. 8X/yr mag; 32 pgs; circ 6,000. Subscription $18.95. 80% freelance. Query (on first-person and how-to articles); complete ms on others/cover letter; no phone/fax query. Pays .05/wd (.03/wd for reprints) on acceptance for 1st, one-time, simultaneous or reprint rts. Articles 500-1,800 wds (15/yr); fiction 1,000-2,000 wds (15/yr); music reviews, 500 wds, .05/wd (query for assignment). Responds in 4 wks. Seasonal 6 mos ahead. Accepts simultaneous submissions & reprints (tell when/where appeared). No disk. Kill fee 25-50%. Regular sidebars. Prefers NRSV. Guidelines/theme list; copy for 9x12 SAE/4 stamps. Separate guidelines for 1st-person and how-to articles sent only when requested. (Ads)

Fillers: Buys 20 cartoons/yr; $35-40.

Contest: Sponsors contests for teen writers only.

Tips: "Most open to true life stories about an experience a teen has gone through."

** This periodical was #41 on the 1998 Top 50 Christian Publishers list (#35 in 1997, #23 in 1996, #17 in 1995, #12 in 1994). Also 1997 EPA Award of Merit—Youth.

#YOU! MAGAZINE, Youth for the Next Millennium, 29963 Mulholland Hwy., Agoura Hills CA 91301-3009. E-mail: youmag@earthlink.net. Catholic. Submissions Editor. An alternative teen magazine (13-23 yrs) aimed at bridging the gap between religion and pop culture. Monthly (10X) mag; 35 pgs; circ 35,000. (Youthbeat, a newspaper insert, also available.) Subscription $19.95. 40% freelance. Query; fax/e-query OK. **PAYS IN COPIES** for all rts. Articles 200-1,000 wds (130/yr); fiction 900 wds (15/yr); book reviews 200 wds; music reviews 150 wds; video reviews 100 wds. Responds in 2 wks. Seasonal 3 mos ahead. Accepts simultaneous query & reprints (tell when/where appeared). Accepts disk. Regular sidebars. Prefers NAB. Guidelines/theme list; copy $2/9x12 SAE/4 stamps. (Ads)

Poetry: Accepts 24/yr. Free verse, light verse, traditional, 5-30 lines. Submit max 3 poems.

Fillers: Cartoons, games, jokes, prayers, quizzes, quotes, and word puzzles; to 300 wds.

Columns/Departments: Patrick Lorenz. Watch It/Hear It (positive movie & music reviews), 50-150 wds.

Special Needs: Teen issues, sports, back to school, pro-life issues, religious vocations, and alternative Christian music.

Tips: "Write in the language of teens. Must be 'hip.' Most open to sports, school, friends & family, sexuality, and Your Stuff. Be brief, positive and powerful."

YOUNG ADULT TODAY, 1551 Regency Ct., Calumet City IL 60409. (708)868-7100x239. Fax (708)868-6759. E-mail: umi1551@aol.com. Website: http://www.urbanministries.com. Urban Ministries, Inc. Katara Washington, ed. Young adult curriculum for ages 18-24 (student and teacher manuals). Quarterly booklet; 80 pgs; circ 10,000. Subscription $14.75. 90% freelance. Query/clips; phone query OK. Pays $75-150 on acceptance for all rts. Articles (24/yr) to & fiction (12/yr); under 1,000 wds. Responds in 4 wks. Seasonal 9 mos ahead. Accepts some reprints (tell when/where appeared). Accepts disk or e-mail submission (copied into message). Prefers KJV. Free guidelines/theme list/copy for 10x13 SAE. (No ads)

Poetry: Buys 4/yr. Free verse; variable length. Pays $25-60.

Tips: "Most open to fiction/nonfiction stories related to Bible study guides."

YOUNG AND ALIVE, Box 6097, Lincoln NE 68506. (402)488-0981. Christian Record Services. Richard Kaiser, mng ed., Gaylena Gibson, ed. For sight-impaired young adults, 16-20 yrs; for interdenominational Christian audience. Quarterly mag; 65-70 pgs; circ 26,000. 90% freelance. Complete ms; no phone query. Pays .03-.05/wd on acceptance for one-time rts. Articles & true stories 800-1,400 wds (30/yr). Responds in 9-13 wks. Seasonal 1 yr ahead. Accepts simultaneous submissions & reprints. Accepts disk. No sidebars. Guidelines; copy for 9x12 SAE/5 stamps. (No ads)

Special Needs: Adventure and careers for the handicapped.

Tips: "Although many blind and visually impaired young adults have the same interests as their sighted counterparts, the material should meet their needs specifically." Follow guidelines.

YOUNG CHRISTIAN, PO Box 1264, Huntington WV 25714. (304)523-2162. Tellstar Productions/Interdenominational. Shannon Bridget Murphy, ed. A take-home paper for Christian children and teens; also produces a quarterly newsletter with writing/publishing guidance for Christian writers and artists; Bimonthly mag; 80100 pgs; circ 50,000. Subscription $18. 90% freelance. Complete ms/cover letter. Pays variable rates on publication for 1st or one-time rts. Articles 500+ wds (100/yr); fiction 500+ wds (100/yr); book review (exchange for the book or product). Responds in 4-8 wks. Seasonal 3-6 mos ahead. Accepts simultaneous submissions & reprints (tell when/where appeared). No disk. Regular sidebars. Any version. Guidelines; copy $8. (Ads)

Poetry: Buys many/yr. Any type or length. Pays variable rates. Submit any number.

Fillers: Buys many/yr. Anecdotes, cartoons, facts, games, ideas, newsbreaks, party ideas, prayers, prose, quizzes, word puzzles. Pays variable rates.

Columns/Departments: Market Place (reviews of products/news). Send product, flyers, etc.

Special Needs: How to write and make sales; articles for or by teens/young adults; food/recipes; party ideas for children and young adults.

Contest: Sponsors contests throughout the year. Send SASE for details.

Tips: "Submissions always welcome from children, teens or young adults. Need more material on writing how-to; writers, artists, or photographers should send a resume or letter with information on experiences and background." Supplies material to writer's groups on request.

YOUNG SALVATIONIST, PO Box 269, Alexandria VA 22313. (703)684-5500. Fax (703)684-5539. E-mail: ys@usn.salvationarmy.org. Website: http://publications.salvationarmyusa.org. The Salvation Army. Tim Clark, mng ed. For teens & young adults in the Salvation Army. Monthly (10X) & online mag; 20 pgs; circ 48,000. Subscription $4. 90% freelance. Complete ms; e-query OK. Pays .15/wd (.10 for reprints) on acceptance for 1st, one-time or reprint rts. Articles (40/yr) & fiction (10/yr); 1,000-1,500 wds. Responds in 4-6 wks. Seasonal 6 mos ahead. Accepts reprints (tell when/where appeared). Accepts disk or e-mail submission. Some sidebars. Prefers NIV. Guidelines/theme list (also on Website); copy for 9x12 SAE/3 stamps. (No ads)

Contest: Sponsors a contest for fiction, nonfiction, poetry, original art and photography. Send SASE for details.

Tips: "Well-written, brief evangelistic or devotional pieces are the best way to break in. We also need, but don't often find, relevant topical pieces on contemporary issues that affect a teen's daily life. We want pieces that not only tell how the Christian life is lived but also show faith in action. Write in contemporary style, but no slang unless you know it's current and properly used."

** This periodical was #16 on the 1998 Top 50 Christian Publishers list. (#24 in 1997, #36 in 1996, #43 in 1995, #14 in 1994)

YOUTH CHALLENGE, 8855 Dunn Rd., Hazelwood MO 63042. (314)837-7300. Fax (314)837-4503. E-mail: wapeditor@aol.com. Website: http://www.upci.org. Word Aflame Publications. P. Daniel Buford, assoc ed. For teens in 10th-12th grades. Weekly take-home paper; circ 5,500. Subscription $4.40. 75% freelance. Complete ms/cover letter. Pays .01-.02/wd on publication for 1st or simultaneous rts. Articles 1,200-1,400 wds; fiction 1,200-1,400 wds (40/yr). Seasonal 1 yr ahead. Accepts simultaneous submissions & reprints. Some sidebars. Prefers KJV. Guidelines; copy for 6x9 SAE/2 stamps.

Fillers: Buys 2-3/yr. Quizzes, word puzzles; $5-12.

Tips: "Articles should be human interest with practical application of Christian principles for 15-17 year olds."

*YOUTH COMPASS (KS), PO Box 4060, Overland Park KS 66204. (913)432-0331. Fax (913)722-0351. Church of God (holiness)/Herald and Banner Press. Arlene McGehee, Sunday school ed. Denominational; for teens. Weekly take-home paper; 4 pgs; circ 4,800. Subscription $1.30. Complete ms/cover letter; phone/fax query OK. Pays .005/wd on publication for 1st rts. Fiction 800-1,500 wds. Seasonal 6-8 mos ahead. Accepts simultaneous submissions & reprints (tell when/where appeared). Prefers KJV. Guidelines/theme list; copy. Not in topical listings.

YOUTH UPDATE, 1615 Republic St., Cincinnati OH 45210-1298. (513)241-5615. Fax (513)241-0399. E-mail: CarolAnn@americancatholic.org. Website: http://www.AmericanCatholic.org. St. Anthony Messenger Press/Catholic. Carol Ann Morrow, ed. For high-school teens, to support their growth in a life of faith. Monthly newsletter; 4 pgs; circ 20,000. 90% freelance. Query. Pays .15/wd ($350-400) on acceptance for 1st & electronic rts. Articles 2,200-2,300 wds (12/yr). Responds in 13 wks. Seasonal 6 mos ahead. Prefers disk. Regular sidebars. Prefers NAB. Guidelines; copy for #10 SAE/1 stamp.

WOMEN'S MARKETS

*ADAM'S RIB, 5620 Hummer Lake Rd., Oxford MI 48371. Phone/fax (810)628-5953. Website: http://crossplaza.com/wotp. Women of the Promise (wives of Promise Keepers). Gina Lawton, ed-in-chief. For women who desire to walk with God. Bimonthly newsletter. Subscription $9. Open to freelance. Complete ms; fax/e-query/submission OK. **PAYS IN COPIES.** Articles to 1,000 wds; fiction to 1,000 wds. Seasonal 3 mos ahead. Accepts reprints (tell when/where appeared). Prefers disk. Prefers KJV or NIV. Guidelines/theme list; copy for 6x9 SAE/ 2 stamps. (Ads)

Poetry: Accepts.

Tips: "Follow themes and have mss in our hands no later than 8 weeks before an issue is printed (earlier is better)."

ANNA'S JOURNAL, PO Box 341, Ellijay GA 30540. Phone/fax (706)276-2309. E-mail: annas@ellijay.com. Catherine Ward-Long, ed. Spiritual support for childless couples who for the most part have decided to stay that way. Quarterly newsletter; 8 pgs; circ 40. Subscription $14. 90% freelance. Complete ms/cover letter; fax/e-query OK. **PAYS IN COPIES** for 1st, simultaneous or reprint rts. Not copyrighted. Articles 500-2,000 wds (8-12/yr); fiction 1,000-2,000 wds (1-3/yr). Responds in 4-8 wks. Seasonal 3 months ahead. Accepts simultaneous submissions & reprints (tell when/where appeared). No disk; E-mail OK (copied into message). No sidebars. Prefers KJV. No guidelines; copy $3/9x12 SAE/3 stamps. (No ads)

Poetry: Accepts 4-10/yr. Any type. Submit max 3 poems.

Fillers: Accepts 3-4/yr. Anecdotes, facts, newsbreaks, prose, prayers, quizzes, quotes, letters; 50-250 wds.

Special Needs: Articles from married, childless men; articles discussing the meaning of childless, childfree and childless by choice.

Tips: "Looking for innovative ways to improve the child-free lifestyle and self-esteem. It helps if writer is childless."

#ASPIRE, 107 Kenner Ave., Nashville TN 37205. (615)386-3011. Fax (615)385-4112. E-mail: aspire@ccmcom.com. CCM Communications. Wendy Lee Nentwig, mng ed. For women who feel they don't always fit the stereotype prescribed by the world, and sometimes the church, but who want to understand what it means to be fully of God and fully human. Bimonthly mag; circ 50,000. Subscription $19.95. 80% freelance. Query/clips; fax/e-query OK. Pays .30/wd on acceptance (for assigned) and publication (for unsolicited) for 1st rts. Articles 500-2,000 wds (6/yr). Responds in 8-15 wks. Seasonal 6 mos ahead. Accepts simultaneous submissions & some reprints (tell when/where appeared). Regular sidebars. Prefers NKJV. Guidelines; copy $2.50/9x12 SAE/$1.50 postage. (Ads)

Columns/Departments: Family Matters, Food for Thought, BodyWise, Your Image, Money Sense, The Great Outdoors, and On the Job; 1,000 wds; $200-300.

Special Needs: Stories about the latest news and trends on weddings for an annual wedding section.

Tips: "Read us and other women's magazines. Be in touch with latest journalism techniques. Have a savvy sense on what's news, and what's revealing, insightful, and unique for Christian women. Look for fresh twists to put on every story. Back up the relevance of a story with anecdotes, statistics, expert opinion, and real women's candid thoughts and insights."

** This periodical was #34 on the 1998 Top 50 Christian Publishers list. (#26 in 1997, #19 in 1996, #59 in 1995)

THE CHURCH WOMAN, 475 Riverside Dr., Ste. 500, New York NY 10115. (212)870-2347. Fax (212)870-2338. E-mail: cwu@churchwomen.org. Website: http://www.churchwomen.org. Church Women United. Elizabeth Young, mng ed; Martha M. Cruz, ed. Highlights women's, peace and justice issues. Quarterly mag; 24 pgs; circ 10,000. Little freelance. Query. **PAYS IN COPIES.** Articles to 3 pgs. Guidelines; copy $1.

+CLARITY, 104 Kenner Ave. Ste 202, Nashville TN 37205 or 16 E. 34th St., New York NY 10016. Guideposts, Inc. Mary Bailey, ed-in-chief; Susan Trotman, asst ed. Addresses contemporary issues for women from a Christian perspective. Bimonthly mag; 48 pgs; circ 140,000. Estab 1998. Query only.

Tips: "We concentrate on the inner woman, rather than outer appearance. Material should focus on a woman's personal and spiritual growth and well-being to provide spiritual encouragement for today's woman."

#COLABORER, Box 5002, Antioch TN 37011-5002. (615)731-6812. Fax (615)731-0071. E-mail: colaborer@nafwb.com. Free Will Baptist/Women Nationally Active for Christ. Suzanne Franks, ed. To help Free Will Baptist women fulfill the great commission. Bimonthly mag; 32 pgs; circ 11,000.

Subscription $6. 5% freelance. Query; e-query OK. **PAYS IN COPIES** for one-time rts. Articles (1/yr) 1,500-2,000 wds; fiction (1/yr) 1,000-2,000. Responds in 4 wks. Seasonal 6 mos ahead. Accepts reprints (tell when/where appeared). Accepts disk. Some sidebars. Guidelines; copy $1.25. (No ads)

Fillers: Accepts 1-2/yr. Anecdotes, party ideas; 200-500 wds.

Tips: "Most open to missions nonfiction stories."

Contest: Creative Arts Contest open to women in the Free Will Baptist Church. March 1 deadline each year. $25 first prize, plus others. Categories include art, feature articles, plays, poetry, and programs. Send SASE for details.

#CONSCIENCE, A Newsjournal of Prochoice Catholic Opinion, 1436 U St. NW, Ste. 301, Washington DC 20009-3997. (202)986-6093. E-mail: cffc@ige.apc.org. Catholic. Submit to The Editor. For lay people, theologians, policy makers, and clergy. Quarterly newsjournal; 48 pgs; circ 12,000. Subscription $10. 80% freelance. Query/clips or complete ms/cover letter. Pays $25-150 on publication for 1st rts. Articles 1,000-3,500 wds (8-12/yr); book reviews 500-800 wds, $25-150. Responds in 18 wks. Seasonal 6 mos ahead. Accepts simultaneous submissions & reprints (tell when/where appeared). Kill fee. Guidelines; copy for 9x12 SAE/4 stamps.

Poetry: Buys 16/yr. Any type, on subject, to 50 lines; $10 + copies. Submit max 5 poems.

Fillers: Buys 6/yr. Newsbreaks; 100-300 wds; $25-35.

Tips: "Focus on issues of reproductive choice. Raise serious ethical questions within a generally prochoice framework. Most open to feature articles and book reviews."

ESPRIT, Evangelical Lutheran Women, 302-393 Portage Ave., Winnipeg MB R3B 3H6 Canada. (204)984-9160. Fax (204)984-9162. E-mail: esprit@elcic.ca. Evangelical Lutheran Church in Canada. Gayle Johonnesson, ed. For denominational women. Quarterly mag; 56 pgs; circ 7,000. Subscription $15.50 CAN, $25 US. 50% freelance. Complete ms/cover letter; phone/fax/e-query OK. Pays $12.50-15/pg CAN on publication for 1st, one-time or reprint rts. Articles (34/yr) and fiction (4/yr) 325-1,400 wds; book reviews 150 wds ($6.25 CAN). Responds in 2-4 wks. Seasonal 4 mos ahead. Accepts simultaneous submissions & reprints (tell when/where appeared). Accepts disk (Macintosh) or e-mail submission (copied into message). Regular sidebars. Prefers NRSV. Guidelines/theme list (also by e-mail submission); copy for 6x9 SAE/.90 CAN postage or $1 US. (No ads)

Poetry: Buys 4-8/yr. Free verse, light verse, traditional; 8-100 lines; $10-20. Submit max 2 poems.

Columns/Departments: Buys 4/yr, 325 wds. Pays $12.50-15/pg.

Tips: "Be a Lutheran woman living in Canada. Use inclusive language (no male pronoun references to God), focus on women and spiritual/faith issues. Check our theme calendar; almost all articles and poems are theme related."

+HEARTH, 320 Spring Ridge Dr., Roswell GA 30076-2614. Phone/fax (770)458-4236. E-mail: canticle@mindspring.com. Website: http://www.

catholicity.com/market/hearth/magmissn.htm. Catholic. Genevieve S. Kineke, ed. Covers basic societal issues for Catholic women. Quarterly mag; Complete ms; e-query OK. **PAYS IN COPIES.** for one-time rts. Articles to 3,500 wds. Prefers disk. Guidelines (also by e-mail); copy $3. Incomplete topical listings.

THE HELPING HAND, Box 12609, Oklahoma City OK 73142-2609. (405)787-7110. Fax (405)789-3957. E-mail: MBJohnson@RDC. Pentecostal Holiness Church/Women's Ministries. Mary Belle Johnson, ed. Denominational; for women. Bimonthly mag; 16 pgs; circ 3,000. Subscription $9.95. 50% freelance. Complete ms/cover letter. Pays $20 on publication for one-time or simultaneous rts. Articles 500-1,300 wds (30/yr); fiction 500-1,300 wds (20/yr). Responds in 3 wks. Seasonal 3-4 mos ahead. Accepts simultaneous submissions & reprints (tell when/where appeared). Accepts disk. Some sidebars. Prefers NIV. Guidelines; copy for 9x12 SAE/2 stamps.

> **Poetry:** Buys 5/yr. Traditional; $10-20. Submit max 4 poems.

HORIZONS, 100 Witherspoon St., Louisville KY 40202-1396. (502)569-5379. Fax (502)569-8085. E-mail: MarieC@ctr.pcusa.org. Website: www.pcusa. org/pcusa/horizons. Presbyterian Church (USA). Submit to The Editor. Justice issues and spiritual life for Presbyterian women. Bimonthly (7X) mag & annual Bible study; 40 pgs; circ 25,000. Subscription $14. 40% freelance. Complete ms/cover letter; fax query OK. Pays $50/printed page on publication for all rts. Articles 500-1,200 wds (10/yr) & fiction 500-1,200 wds (5/yr); book/music/video reviews 100-150 wds. Responds in 4 wks. Seasonal 5 mos ahead. Accepts reprints (tell when/where appeared). Prefers disk or e-mail submission (attached file). Regular sidebars. Prefers NRSV. Guidelines (also by e-mail); copy for 9x12 SAE/2 stamps. (No ads)

> **Poetry:** Buys 5/yr. All types; $50-100. Submit max 5 poems.
> **Fillers:** Cartoons, church-related graphics; $50.
> **Tips:** "Poetry, features, fiction are open to freelancers. Should be relevant to Presbyterian women and church leadership. Devotionals for the inside front cover are also accepted. Seasonal fiction or nonfiction are most likely to be used."

JOURNAL OF WOMEN'S MINISTRIES, 919 Pleasant St. #F-2, Oak Park IL 60302-3105. (800)334-7626. Fax (708)763-9454. E-mail: wimm@dfms. org. Website: http://www.dfms.org/women. Episcopal/Women in missions and ministries. Marcy Darin, ed. Deals with issues of interest to women from a liberal perspective. Biannual mag; 36 pgs; circ 10,000. Query. Pays $50 on publication for 1st rts. Articles 1,200-1,500 wds. Responds in 5 wks. Seasonal 3 mos ahead. Guidelines; copy for 9x12 SAE/3 stamps.

> **Poetry:** Free verse, traditional. Submit max 2 poems.

*JOURNEY, 127 Ninth Ave. N., Nashville TN 37234. (615)251-5659. Fax (615)251-5008. Southern Baptist. Pamela Nixon, mng ed. Devotional magazine for women of the 90s (30-45 years old). Monthly mag; 44 pgs; circ 150,000. 20% freelance. Subscription $18.95. Query/clips or complete ms/cover letter; no phone/fax/e-query. Pays $25-150 on acceptance for all, 1st, one-time or reprint rts. Articles 350-1,000 wds (10-12/yr). Responds in 8 wks. Seasonal 6-7 mos ahead. Accepts simultaneous submissions & reprints (tell when/where appeared). Regular sidebars. Prefers NIV. Accepts disk. Guidelines; copy for 6x9 SAE/2 stamps.

Fillers: Prayers, short humor; 200-350 wds.

Special Needs: Strong feature articles 90-1,000 words; profiles of Christian women in leadership positions.

Tips: "Would like to see articles for our week-end pages and an occasional 3-page feature article on topics of interest to women 30-45 years old."

** This periodical was #54 on the 1997 Top 50 Christian Publishers List. (#55 in 1996)

THE JOYFUL WOMAN, PO Box 90028, Chattanooga TN 37412-6028. (706)866-5522. (706)866-2432. E-mail: JoyfulCMI@aol.com. Joyful Christian Ministries. Joy Rice Martin, ed. For and about Bible-believing women who want God's best. Bimonthly mag; 32 pgs; circ 6,000. Subscription $19. 50% freelance. Query with first page of article; fax/e-query OK. Pays $20-30 (.03-.04/wd) on publication for 1st rts. Articles & fiction 500-1,000 wds (45/yr). Responds in 6 wks. Seasonal 3 mos ahead. Accepts simultaneous submissions & reprints (tell when/where appeared). Accepts disk or e-mail submission (attached file). Kill fee. Some sidebars. KJV only. Guidelines; copy for 9x12 SAE/6 stamps. (Ads)

Poetry: Buys 6/yr. Free verse, light verse, traditional; 15-40 lines; $15-40. Submit max 2 poems.

Fillers: Buys few. Cartoons, jokes, newsbreaks, prayers, quotes, short humor; 25-300 wds; $15-25.

Columns/Departments: Buys 6/yr. Positively Single, 300 wds. Complete ms. Pays $25.

Tips: "Our biggest need is true-life stories and inspirational articles. We prefer 1,000 word or less manuscripts, and would like color pictures of author and/or manuscript subject. Please allow 16 weeks before you call about your manuscript."

#JUST BETWEEN US, 777 S. Barker Rd., Brookfield WI 53045. (414)786-6478 or (800)260-3342. Fax (414)796-5752. Elmbrook Church, Inc. Shelly Esser, ed. Ideas, encouragement and resources for wives of evangelical ministers. Quarterly mag; 32 pgs; circ 5,000. Subscription $14.95. 90% freelance. Query; phone/fax query OK. **NO PAYMENT** for one-time rts. Articles 250-500 wds or 800-1,500 wds (50/yr). Responds in 6 wks. Accepts simultaneous submissions & reprints. Regular sidebars. Prefers NIV. Guidelines/theme list; copy $2/9x12 SAE. (Ads)

Fillers: Buys 15/yr. Anecdotes, cartoons, ideas, prayers, quotes, short humor; 50-250 wds.

Columns/Departments: Buys 12/yr. Money Savers; Keeping Your Kids Christian; Women's Ministry (program ideas); all 500-700 wds.

Tips: "Articles need to relate to unique ministry issues. Most open to columns or feature articles. Follow themes."

*KANSAS CITY WOMAN, One Heart, Many Faces, PO Box 1860, Blue Springs MO 64013-1860. Phone/fax (816)228-9838. E-mail: kcwoman@

discoverynet.com. Secular. Submit to The Editor. Publishes the best profiles, business and family news, how-tos, features and spiritual encouragement to keep the woman's heartbeat going strong. Monthly mag. Estab 1998. Query or query/clips (for cover stories & features). Pays .10/wd on publication for 1st (preferred), one-time, or reprint rts. Cover stories 1,500-2,500 wds, profiles 400-800 wds, features 750-1,000 wds, personal experience 750-850 wds, how-to 375-750 wds; fiction 3,000-5,000 wds (to be serialized in 3 issues); book/music reviews 50-100 wds. Seasonal 9-12 mos ahead. Accepts reprints (tell when/where appeared). Guidelines.

Poetry: Assigned only.

Tips: "We want to see light, inspirational material."

+**KEEPERS AT HOME**, 2727 Township Rd. 421, Sugarcreek OH 44681. (30)852-1900. Fax (330)852-3285. Elaine Troger, ed. Homemaking advice and encouragement for mothers. Quarterly mag; 40 pgs. 80% freelance. Complete ms. Pays .02-.06/wd on publication. Articles 500-1,500 wds. Accepts reprints (tell when/where appeared). Prefers KJV. Copy for 9x12 SAE/6 stamps. (No ads)

Poetry: Buys 12/yr. Traditional. Pays .02-.06/wd..

Fillers: Buys 10/yr. Ideas, prose.

+**LEAH'S SISTERS, A Newsletter for Woman Conquering Rejection and Loss**, PO Box 17-1234, Irving TX 75017. Mary Dunham, ed. Bimonthly newsletter. Subscription $12.50.

THE LINK & VISITOR, 30 Arlington Ave., Toronto ON M6G 3K8 Canada. (416)651-7192. Fax (416)651-0438. Baptist Women's Missionary Society of Ontario and Quebec. Esther Barnes, ed. A positive, practical magazine for Canadian Baptist women who want to make a difference in our world. Monthly (9X) mag; 16 pgs; circ 4,500. Subscription $12 CAN, $15 US. 50% freelance. Complete ms/cover letter; phone query OK. Pays .05/wd CAN, on publication for one-time or simultaneous rts. Articles 700-2,000 wds (15/yr). Responds in 36 wks. Seasonal 3 mos ahead. Accepts simultaneous submissions & reprints (tell when/ where appeared). Accepts disk. Some sidebars. Prefers NIV (inclusive language), NRSV, or LB. Guidelines/theme list; copy for 9x12 SAE/.90 Canadian postage. (Ads - limited/Canadian)

Poetry: Buys 6/yr. Free verse; 12-32 lines; $10-25. Submit max 4 poems.

Special Needs: Mentoring, sharing our faith, and cross-cultural relationships.

Tips: "Looking for articles on joy. Canadian writers preferred. If US writers send US postage for returns, they will be rejected. Too many writers seem too focused on themselves and their own experiences. Canadian perspective, please."

*****LUTHERAN WOMAN'S QUARTERLY**, 1860 Greenfield Dr., El Cajon CA 92021. Phone/fax (619)444-6089. Lutheran Women's Missionary League. Donna Streufert, ed-in-chief. For women of the Lutheran Church—Missouri Synod. Quarterly mag; 48 pgs; circ 200,000. Subscription $2.50. 100% freelance. Complete ms/cover letter. **NO PAYMENT.** Not copyrighted. Articles 750-1,200 wds (4/yr); fiction 750-1,200 wds (4/yr). Responds in 2 wks. Seasonal 5 mos ahead. Regular sidebars. Prefers NIV. Guidelines/theme list.

Tips: "Most open to articles. Must reflect the Missouri Synod teachings. Most of our writers are from the denomination."

#LUTHERAN WOMAN TODAY, 8765 W. Higgins Ave., Chicago IL 60631-4189. (800)638-3522x2743 or (773)380-2743. E-mail: kelliott@elca.org. Website: http://www.elca.org/wo/lwthome.html. Evangelical Lutheran Church in America. Kate Elliott, assoc ed. For women in the denomination. Monthly (11X) mag: 48 pgs; circ 230,000. 25% freelance. Complete ms/ cover letter or query; e-query or submissions OK. Pays $60-280 on acceptance for 1st or one-time rts. Articles (24/yr) & fiction (5/yr), to 1,250 wds. Responds in 16 wks. Seasonal 7 mos ahead. Guidelines/theme list (also on Website at: http://www.elca.org/wo/lwtguid.html); copy $1.

Poetry: Buys 5/yr. Free verse, haiku, light verse, traditional; to 60 lines; $15-60. Submit max 3 poems. Poetry must have a spiritual and women's focus.

Columns/Departments: Buys 5/yr. Devotion, 350 wds; Season's Best (reflection on the church year), 350-700 wds; About Women; Forum (essay); $50-250.

Tips: "Submit a short, well-written article using inclusive language and offering a women's and spiritual focus."

*THE PROVERBS 31 HOMEMAKER, PO Box 17155, Charlotte NC 28227. (704)849-2270. Fax (704)849-2270. E-mail: P31home@aol.com. Mary Ellen Bianco, ed. Encouragement and information for stay-at-home mothers. Monthly newsletter; 10 pgs; circ 2,000. Subscription $15. 90% freelance. Query. **NO PAYMENT** for one-time rts. Articles 200-400 wds (24/yr); book reviews 200-250 wds. Responds in 4 wks. Seasonal 4 mos ahead. Accepts simultaneous submissions & reprints (tell when/where appeared). No disk. Regular sidebars. Prefers NIV. Guidelines/theme list; copy for 9x12 SAE/2 stamps.

Poetry: Accepts up to 12/yr.

Fillers: Accepts 12/yr. Anecdotes, cartoons, ideas, party ideas, prose, prayers, quotes, short humor; to 100 wds.

Tips: "Looking for articles on relationship with God; how homemakers organize time; marital relationships; how to keep kids busy."

+SHARE, 10 W. 71st St., New York NY 10023-4201. (212)877-3041. Fax (212)724-5923. Catholic Daughters of the Americas. Peggy Eastman, ed. For Catholic women. Quarterly mag; circ 118,000. Free with membership. Most articles come from membership, but is open. **NO PAYMENT.** Buys color photos and covers. Guidelines/copy. Not in topical listings. (Ads)

+THE SILENT WOMAN IN THE PEW, 5351 NW 11th St., Lauderhill FL 33313. Ellen Waldron, pub. Open to freelance.

SISTERS TODAY, The Liturgical Press, St. John's Abbey, PO Box 7500, Collegeville MN 56321-7500. (320)363-7065. Fax (320)363-7130. E-mail: mwagner@csbsju.edu. Website: http://www.csbsju.osb.sisters/public. html. Catholic. Sr. Mary Anthony Wagner, ed. Exploration of the role of women and the church. Bimonthly mag; 80 pgs; circ 3,000-4,000. Subscription $22. 25% freelance. Complete ms; phone/e-query OK. Pays $5 or by the page on publication for 1st rts. Articles to 10 pgs. Responds in several wks. Accepts reprints (tell when/where appeared). No disk or e-mail submission. Free guidelines; copy $4.50. (Ads)

Poetry: Sr. Mary Virginia Micka, C.S.J. Buys 6-8/yr; 3-20 lines. Pays $10/poem.

+SPIRIT-LED WOMAN, 600 Rinehart Rd., Lake Mary FL 32746. E-mail:spiritledwoman@strang.com. Website: http://www.spiritledwoman.com. Strang Communications. Brenda J. Davis, ed. To help women, ages 20-60, develop intimacy with God. Monthly mag. Estab 1998.

Columns/Departments: Testimonies; Final Fun (funny stories or embarrassing moments).

Tips: "Articles need to deal with the heart issues that hold a woman back."

TODAY'S CHRISTIAN WOMAN, 465 Gundersen Dr., Carol Stream IL 60188-2498. (630)260-6200. Fax (630)260-0114. E-mail: TCWedit@aol.com. Website: http://www.TodaysChristianWoman.net. Christianity Today, Inc. Submit to Camerin Courtney, assoc ed. To help Christian women grow in their relationship to God by providing practical, biblical perspectives on marriage, sex, parenting, work, health, friendship, and self. Bimonthly mag; 80-150 pgs; circ 351,000. Subscription $17.95. 25% freelance. Query only; fax/e-query OK. Query for electronic submissions. Pays .15/wd on publication (on acceptance for assignments) for 1st or reprint rts. Articles 1,500-1,800 wds (6-12/yr); no fiction. Responds in 4-6 wks. Seasonal 6 mos ahead. Accepts reprints (tell when/where appeared). Accepts e-mail submission (copied into message). Some sidebars. Prefers NIV. Guidelines (also by e-mail); copy $5. (Ads)

Columns/Departments: Buys 6/yr. One Woman's Story (dramatic story of overcoming a difficult situation), 1,000-1,500 wds, $150, query; Faith on Job (sharing faith at work), 100-200 wds, $50; Small Talk (humorous, inspirational anecdotes), 50-100 wds, $50. Send complete ms for last two/not acknowledged or returned.

Tips: "Most open to practical, fresh, relational articles; including work-related friendships."

** This periodical was #57 on the 1996 Top 50 Christian Publishers List. (#34 in 1994) Also 1997 EPA Award of Merit—General.

+TRUE WOMAN, E-mail: agape114@juno.com. Panya Yarber, ed-in-chief. For Christian women. Online mag. Complete ms by e-mail submission. **NO PAYMENT.** Guidelines on Website.

Fillers: Beauty, health and household tips..

Special Needs: Arts and crafts, mentoring, mothering, any articles of interest to women.

Tips: "If you are the writer, please send information about yourself as well (a short bio and contact e-mail submission address for readers). If you are not the writer, please include proper credits."

VIRTUE, Helping Women Build Christ-Like Character, 465 Gundersen Dr., Carol Stream IL 60188. (630)260-6200. Fax (630)260-0114. E-mail: VirtueMag@aol.com. Website: http://www.christianity.net. Christianity Today, Inc. Linda Piepenbrink, ed. For Christian women who want to grow spiritually and apply biblical truths to their daily life. Bimonthly mag. Subscription $17.95. 75% freelance. Query/clips; fax query OK. Pays .15-.20/ wd on acceptance for 1st rts. Articles 500-1,800 wds (30/yr). Responds in 6-8 wks. Seasonal 6 mos ahead. Accepts reprints only from non-competing markets (tell when/where appeared). Encourages sidebars. Prefers NASB. Guidelines; copy for 9x12 SAE/9 stamps or $5. (Ads)

Departments: Buys 50/yr. On the Home Front (enriching your relationship with family and friends) to 600 wds; Virtue in Action (serving God, serving others), to 600 wds. (Query not needed for previous two departments.) "The Virtue of . . . (topic)" (first-person story about the impact a certain virtue has had on your life). Pays $200.

Tips: "Writers who clearly know our target audience, demonstrate an understanding of the issues our readers care about, and write a strong, specific query have the best chance of attracting our interest." ** This periodical was #42 on the 1994 Top 50 Christian Publishers list.

*VIRTUOUS WOMAN, 241 Old Mobile Rd., McCaysville GA 30555. (706)492-3332. E-mail: virtuouswoman@wingnet.net. Website: http://www.virtuous woman.com. Sonja S. Key, ed. Interdenominational. Quarterly mag; 40-60 pgs; circ 350. And online mag (see Website above). Subscription $16. 60% freelance. Complete ms/cover letter; e-query OK. **PAYS 3 COPIES** for 1st & electronic rts. Articles 1,200 wds (25/yr); book reviews 200 wds, music reviews 100 wds. Responds in 8 wks. Accepts simultaneous submissions. No disk. Regular sidebars. Prefers Amplified Bible. Guidelines; copy for 9x12 SAE/$2 postage. (Ads)

Poetry: Accepts 50/yr. Free verse, light verse, traditional; 8-25 lines. Submit max5 poems.

Fillers: Accepts 8/yr. Anecdotes, cartoons, prayers, prose, quizzes, quotes; 50-100 wds.

Columns/Departments: Accepts 25/yr. Rivers of Living Waters (work of the Holy Spirit); Earthen Vessels (body, diet, grooming, etc.); Broken & Poured Out (soul, mind, will, emotions); all 1,000 wds.

Tips: "Most open to articles which offer advice to women already established in ministry, such as better or innovative ways to reach women with the gospel, how to train women for ministry, or how to build a thriving women's ministry."

WELCOME HOME, 8310A Old Courthouse Rd., Vienna VA 22182. (703)827-5903 or (800)783-4MOM. Fax(703)790-8587. E-mail: mah@mah.org. Website: http://www.mah.org. Mothers at Home, Inc. Submit to Manuscript Coordinator. For women who have chosen to stay at home with their children. Monthly journal; 30 pgs; circ. 15,000. Subscription $18. 100% freelance. Complete ms/cover letter. **NO (OR LIMITED) PAYMENT** for one-time rts. Articles to 2,400 wds, most 500-1,500 wds (20/yr). Responds in 6-12 wks. Seasonal 1 yr ahead. No e-mail submission. Some sidebars. Guidelines (request specific guidelines for departments interested in; also available on Website); copy $2/7x10 SAE. (No ads)

Poetry: Winnie Peterson Cross. Accepts 48/yr. Free verse, haiku, light verse, traditional.

Columns/Departments: Accepts 36/yr. From a Mother (surprising/ sudden insights); Resource Roundup (books/resources); New Dimensions (personal growth/development); Heartwarming (cooking/recipes); Health & Safety (mother's/child's health, family safety); Time to Care (volunteer work; all 700-1,000 wds.

Tips: "This is a publication for all mothers at home, and not for those with any particular religious background. Articles which focus on a religious theme will not be accepted."

THE WESLEYAN WOMAN, PO Box 50434, Indianapolis IN 46250-0434. (317)570-5164. Fax (317)570-5254. E-mail: wwi@wesleyan.org. Website: http://www.wesleyan.org. Wesleyan Church. Martha Blackburn, mng ed. Inspiration, education and sharing to meet the needs of Wesleyan women. Quarterly mag; 24 pgs; circ 3,500. Subscription $12.95. 75% freelance. Complete ms/cover letter; phone/fax query OK. Pays .04/wd (.02-.03/wd for reprints) on publication for one-time or reprint rts. Articles 500-700 wds (1-10/yr). Responds in 10-12 wks. Seasonal 6 mos ahead. Accepts simultaneous submissions & reprints (tell when/where appeared). Accepts disk. Regular sidebars. Guidelines/theme list; free copy.

Poetry: Accepts 4/yr. Free verse, light verse, traditional. Pays .04/wd, up to $10. Submit max 2 poems.

Fillers: Accepts few. Anecdotes, cartoons, ideas, party ideas, quotes, short humor; 150-350 wds.

Tips: "Most open to personal stories of 'guts' and grace to follow the Lord. Ways you see God at work in your life—personal, not preachy."

WOMAN'S TOUCH, 1445 Boonville Ave., Springfield MO 65802-1894. (417)862-2781. Fax (417)862-0503. E-mail: womanstouch@ag.org. Assemblies of God. Lillian Sparks, ed. A general readership magazine committed to providing help and inspiration for Christian women, strengthening family life, and reaching out in witness to others; also leadership edition. Bimonthly mag; 36 pgs; circ 16,000+. Subscription $7/ leader $8.50. 90% freelance. Complete ms/cover letter. Pays $10-40 (.03/ wd) on publication for 1st, one-time, or reprint rts. Articles to 1,000 wds (50-60/yr). Responds in 10 wks. Seasonal 10-12 mos ahead. Accepts simultaneous submissions & reprints (tell when/where appeared). Accepts disk. Kill fee. Regular sidebars. Prefers KJV or NIV. Guidelines/theme list; copy for 9x12 SAE/3 stamps.

Fillers: Buys 10/yr. Anecdotes, ideas; 50-200 wds; $5-15.

Columns/Departments: Buys 30/yr. A Better You (health/fitness), 500 wds; A Final Touch (human interest on home/family/career), 350 wds; A Lighter Touch (true humorous anecdotes); 100 wds; History's Women (great women of faith), 500 wds. Pays $10-40.

** This periodical was #35 on the 1996 Top 50 Christian Publishers List.

WOMEN ALIVE! Box 4683, Overland Park KS 66204. Phone/fax (913)649-8583. Website: http://www.womenalivemagazine.org. Aletha Hinthorn, ed. To encourage women to live holy lives by applying Scripture to their daily lives. Bimonthly mag; 20 pgs; circ 3,500-4,000. Subscription $13.95. 50% freelance. Complete ms/no cover letter; no phone/fax query. Pays

$25-50 on publication for 1st or reprint rts. Articles 900-1,800 wds (7/yr). Responds in 4-6 wks. Seasonal 4 mos ahead. Accepts reprints. Some sidebars. No disk. Prefers KJV or NIV. Guidelines/theme list; copy for 9x12 SAE/4 stamps. (No ads)

Fillers: Buys 0-1/yr. Cartoons, jokes, short humor.

Tips: "We look for articles that draw women into a deeper spiritual life—articles on surrender, prayer, Bible study—yet written with personal illustrations."

WOMEN OF SPIRIT, 55 W. Oak Ridge Dr., Hagerstown MD 21740-7390. (301)393-4125. Fax (301)393-4055. E-mail: WomenofSpirit@rhpa.org. Website: http://www.rhpa.org/main/wos/docs/wos.htm. Review and Herald/Seventh-day Adventist. Heide Ford, assoc ed. To inspire, nurture and challenge Christian women. Bimonthly mag; 32 pgs; circ 18,000. Subscription $16.95. Complete ms/cover letter; fax/e-query OK. Pays on acceptance. Articles 500-1,000 wds. Responds in 12 wks. Seasonal 6 mos ahead. Accepts reprints (tell when/where appeared). Accepts disk, prefers e-mail submission (attached file). Regular sidebars. Prefers NIV. Guidelines (also by e-mail); copy for 9x12 SAE. (Ads)

+WOMEN TODAY, Box 300, Vancouver BC V6C 2X3, Canada. (604) 514-2000. Fax (604)514-2002. E-mail: katherine@mkehler.com. Website: Http://www.crusade.org/wto. Campus Crusade for Christ, Canada. Katherine Kehler, exec ed. For the professional, non-Christian woman, 20-40 years. Monthly mag; 20 pgs. Estab 1995. 30 % freelance. Query for electronic submissions; e-query OK. Pays $25-100 on publication. Articles 100-1,200 wds. Seasonal 4 mos ahead. Accepts reprints (tell when/where appeared). Prefers e-mail submission. Regular sidebars. Guidelines.

Fillers: Will consider newsbreaks, quizzes.

Columns/Departments: Life Stories (testimony of adult conversion), 250 wds; Feature (Christ-centered, but not religious), 1,200 wds; Potpourri (women's interests), 100 wds.

Tips: "The writer needs to have global perspective, and have a heart to reach women with the gospel, build them in their faith, and help develop them to win others."

+WOMEN TODAY ONLINE, Box 300, Vancouver BC V6C 2X3, Canada. (604) 514-2000. Fax (604)514-2002. E-mail: katherine@mkehler.com. Website: http://www.womantodaymagazine.com. Campus Crusade for Christ, Canada. Katherine Kehler, exec ed. For the professional, Christian woman, 20-40 years. Monthly mag; 20 pgs. Estab 1996. 30% freelance. Query for electronic submissions; e-query OK. Pays $25-100 on publication. Articles 100-1,200 wds. Seasonal 4 mos ahead. Accepts reprints (tell when/where appeared). Prefers e-mail submission. Regular sidebars. Guidelines.

Fillers: Will consider newsbreaks, quizzes.

Columns/Departments: Life Stories (testimony of adult conversion), 250 wds; Feature (Christ-centered, but not religious), 1,200 wds; Potpourri (women's interests), 100 wds.

Tips: "The writer needs to have global perspective, and have a heart to reach women with the gospel, build them in their faith, and help develop them to win others."

WRITER'S MARKETS

ADVANCED CHRISTIAN WRITER, 9731 N. Fox Glen Dr., #6F, Niles IL 60714-5861. (847)296-3964. Fax (847)296-0754. E-mail: linjohnson@compuserve.com. American Christian Writers. Lin Johnson, ed. A professional newsletter for published writers. Bimonthly newsletter; 8 pgs; circ 500. Subscription $19. 75% freelance. Query by e-mail submission or complete ms. Pays $20 on publication for 1st or reprint rts. Articles 500-1,000 wds (18/yr); book reviews 200-400 wds, $10. Responds in 6-8 wks. Seasonal 6 mos ahead. Accepts reprints (tell when/where appeared). Regular sidebars. Requires e-mail submission. Prefers NIV. Guidelines; copy for #10 SAE/1 stamp (order from ACW, PO Box 110390, Nashville TN 37222). (Ads)

> **Special Needs:** Behind the Scenes look at a publishing house (how it started, how editorial operates, current needs, submission procedures).

> **Tips:** "We accept articles only from professional, well-published writers. We need manuscripts about all aspects of being a published freelance writer and how to increase sales and professionalism; on the advanced level; looking for depth beyond the basics."

BYLINE, Box 130596, Edmond OK 73013-0001. Phone/fax (405)348-5591. E-mail: ByLineMP@aol.com. Website: http://www.BylineMag.com. Secular. Kathryn Fanning, mng ed. Offers practical tips, motivation and encouragement to freelance writers and poets. Monthly (11X) mag; 32 pgs; circ 3,000+. Subscription $22. 80% freelance. Query or complete ms; no phone/fax/e-query; no electronic submissions. Pays $50 for features; $100 for fiction; less for shorts, on acceptance for 1st rts. Articles 1,500-1,800 wds (100/yr); personal experiences 800 wds; fiction 2,000-4,000 wds (10/yr). Responds in 6 wks. Seasonal 6 mos ahead. Accepts simultaneous submissions. Encourages sidebars. Guidelines (also on Website); copy $4. (Ads)

> **Poetry:** Sandra Soli. Buys 50-100/yr. Any type; to 30 lines; $5-10. Writing themes. Submit max 3 poems.

> **Fillers:** Anecdotes, prose, short humor for humor page, 200-400 wds, pays $15-20.

> **Columns/Departments:** Buys 50-60/yr. End Piece (personal essay on writing theme), 700 wds, $35; First Sale accounts, 200-400 wds, $20; Only When I Laugh (writing humor), short, $15-25. Complete ms.

> **Contests:** Sponsors many year round; details included in magazine.

> **Tips:** "Most open to First Sale account; be upbeat about writing. Need articles, essays and poetry on writing topics; general interest short stories (no religious)."

*CANADIAN WRITER'S JOURNAL, White Mountain Publications, Box 5180, New Liskeard ON P0J 1P0 Canada. (705)647-5424. Fax (705)647-8366. E-mail: cwj@ntl.sympatico.ca. Deborah Ramchuk, ed. How-to articles for writers. Quarterly digest; 64 pgs; circ 385. Subscription $15. 95% freelance. Complete ms/cover letter; e-query OK. Pays $5 CAN/published pg on publication for 1st or one-time rts. Articles to 2,000 wds (45-50/yr); book reviews to 1,000 wds/$5. Responds in 12 wks. Seasonal 6 mos ahead. Accepts simultaneous submissions & reprints (tell when/where appeared). Prefers e-mail submission. Regular sidebars. Guidelines; copy $5. (Ads)

Poetry: Elizabeth St. Jacques (406 Elizabeth St., Saulte St. Marie ON P6B 3H4 Canada). Buys 16-20/yr. Free verse, haiku: on writing; to 8 lines. Pays $1. Send 5 poems max

Fillers: Anecdotes, cartoons, quotes; 20-50 wds. Pays $3-5.

Contest: Sponsors annual poetry contest (June 30 deadline). Also a fall fiction contest.

THE CHRISTIAN COMMUNICATOR, 4701 Aspen Dr., Des Moines IA 50265-2924. (410)995-0831. E-mail: JeanetteDL@aol.com. American Christian Writers/Reg Forder, Box 110390, Nashville TN 37222, (800)21-WRITE (for advertising or subscriptions), fax (615)834-0450; regaforder@aol.com. Jeanette Gardner Littleton, ed. For Christian writers/speakers who want to polish writing skills, develop public-speaking techniques, and sell their mss. Monthly (11X) mag; 24 pgs; circ 4,000. Subscription $25. 50% freelance. Complete ms/cover letter; phone/fax/e-query OK. Pays $5-10 on publication for 1st, one-time or reprint rts. Articles 600-1,200 wds (62/yr). Responds in 6-8 wks. Seasonal 6 mos ahead. Accepts reprints. Free guidelines/copy. (Ads)

Poetry: Accepts 12/yr. Poems on writing; $5. Submit max 4 poems.

Columns/Departments: Buys 20/yr. Interviews (published authors or editors), 800-1,200 wds; Speaker's Corner (techniques for speakers), 600-1,000 wds; Book Reviews (writing/speaking books), 300-400 wds; $5-10.

THE CHRISTIAN RESPONSE, PO Box 125, Staples MN 56479-0125. (218)894-1165. E-mail: hapco@brainerd.net. Website: http://www.brainerd.net/hapco. Hap Corbett, ed. Exposes anti-Christian bias in America & encourages readers to write letters in defense of such bias. Bimonthly newsletter; 6 pgs; circ 400. Subscription $15. 10% freelance. Complete ms/cover letter; phone/e-query OK. Pays $2.50-20 on acceptance for 1st or simultaneous rts. Articles 50-500 wds (6/yr). Responds in 2 wks. Seasonal 6 mos ahead. Accepts simultaneous submissions & reprints. No sidebars. Guidelines; copy for $1 or 3 stamps.

Fillers: Anecdotes, facts, quotes; 25-100 wds; $2.50-10.

Special Needs: Articles on anti-Christian bias; tips on writing effective letters to the editor; pieces on outstanding accomplishments of Christians in the secular media.

Tips: "We are looking for news/articles about anti-Christian bias in the media, and how you, as a writer, responded to such incidents."

CROSS & QUILL, Rt. 3 Box 1635, Jefferson Davis Rd., Clinton SC 29325-9542. (864)697-6035. Fax (864)697-4326. E-mail: cwfi@aol.com, or cwfi@juno.com. Website: http://members.aol.com/cwfi/writers.htm. Christian Writers Fellowship Intl. Sandy Brooks, ed/pub. For Christian writers, editors, agents, conference directors. Bimonthly newsletter; 12 pgs; circ 1,000+. Subscription $20; CWFI membership $40. 75% freelance. Complete ms; query for electronic submissions. Pays small honorarium for feature articles on publication for 1st or reprint rts. Articles 800-1,000 wds (24/yr); book reviews 100 wds (pays copies). Responds in

2 wks. Seasonal 6 mos ahead. Accepts reprints (tell when/where appeared). Regular sidebars. Accepts disk, no e-mail submission. Guidelines; copy $2/9x12 SAE/2 stamps. (Ads)

Poetry: Accepts 12/yr. Any type; to 12 lines. Submit max 3 poems. Must pertain to writing/publishing. Currently overstocked.

Fillers: Accepts 12/yr. Anecdotes, cartoons, prayers; to 100 wds. Pays in copies.

Columns/Departments: Accepts 36/yr. Writing Rainbows! (devotional), 600 wds; Writer to Writer (how-to), 900 wds; Editor's Roundtable (interview with editor), 200-800 wds; Tots, Teens & In-Betweens (juvenile market), 200-800 wds; BusinessWise (business side of writing), 200-800 wds; Connecting Points (how-to on critique group), 200-800 wds.

Special Needs: Articles on screenwriting, poetry writing, news writing, greeting cards, and gift books.

Tips: "Most open to feature articles, devotions for writers, good informational articles. Personal experiences and personal journey articles have little chance."

+**DREAM WEAVER, The Write Readers' Source**, 2440 Indian Mound Ave., Cincinnati OH 45212. (513)631-5995. Fax (513)631-5978. E-mail: pen drago@goodnews.net. Website: http://www.pendragon-ent.com. Epsilon Computing. Robin J. Mace, ed-in-chief & poetry ed; Robert Mace, articles/columns/fillers ed; Wes Gilbert or L.J. Shook, fiction ed. Covers all forms of writing and publishes local/regional writers of all ages. Monthly mag; 48-64 pgs; circ 5000. Subscription $18. 50% freelance. Complete ms/cover letter. **PAYS IN COPIES** for 1st rts. Articles 1,000-3,000 wds (25/yr); fiction 2,000 wds (60/yr); book reviews 250 wds. Responds in 8 wks. Seasonal 2 mos ahead. Accepts simultaneous submissions & reprints (tell when/where appeared); but prefers new writers. Accepts disk. Some sidebars. Prefers KJV. Guidelines (also on Website); copy for 10x13 SAE/5 stamps. Limited topical listings, considers most topics. (Ads)

Poetry: Accepts 250/yr. Any type; to 40 lines. Submit max 4 poems.

Fillers: Accepts 10-25/yr. Cartoons, facts, prose, short humor; to 25 wds.

Columns/Departments: Accepts 10-20/yr. How-to on all aspects of writing.

Special Needs: Does a Halloween and a Valentines anthology each year.

Contest: Has several fiction contests each year; no fees.

Tips: "Our magazine is divided into two parts, the how-to articles on all aspects of writing, and the published pieces of the local amateur/semi professional writers."

EXCHANGE, 15 Torrance Rd. #104, Toronto ON M1J 3K2 Canada. (416)439-4320. Fax (416)439-5089. E-mail: exchange@ica.net. Audrey Dorsch, ed. A forum for Christian writers to share information and ideas. Quarterly newsletter; 8 pgs; circ 185. Subscription $11.50 US/$16 CAN. 75% freelance. Complete ms/cover letter; fax/e-query OK. Pays .08/wd (CAN) on publication for one-time rts. Not copyrighted. Articles 400-600 wds (20/

yr). Responds in 4-6 wks. Accepts reprints (tell when/where appeared). Accepts disk, prefers e-mail submission (attached file). No sidebars. Prefers NIV. Guidelines (also by e-mail)/copy for #10 SAE/2 Canadian stamps (.52). (Ads—classified)

Special Needs: Material geared to experienced, professional writers.

Tips: "Take a very deliberate approach to the 'how' of good writing. Send me a strong article that an experienced writer will learn from and I'll love you forever."

FELLOWSCRIPT, 121 Morin Maze, Edmonton AB T6K 1V1 Canada. Fax (403)461-1809. E-mail: nathan_harms@enabel.ab.ca. Alberta Christian Writers' Fellowship-CanadaWide. Nathan Harms, ed. To provide encouragement, instruction and news to Christians who write. Quarterly (+1) newsletter; 24 pgs; circ 250. Subscription $30 (includes membership). 100% freelance. Complete ms/cover letter; fax/e-query OK. Pays $10-30 (.02-.05/wd) on publication for 1st, one-time, reprint or simultaneous rts. Not copyrighted. Articles 350-1,000 wds (6/yr); book reviews, 300-350 wds, $5. Responds in 12 wks. Seasonal 4 mos ahead. Accepts simultaneous submissions & reprints (tell when/where appeared). Accepts disk. Regular sidebars. Prefers KJV. Guidelines; copy $1. (Ads)

Fillers: Anecdotes, cartoons, facts, ideas, quotes, market updates; to 140 wds. Buys 8-25/yr. Pays $2-7.

Columns/Departments: Open to ideas for columns.

Special Needs: Articles of practical help to writers; how to put together a promotional package for the writer.

Contest: Sponsors two a year, one in March for members, one in August that is open. Send #10 SAE/$1 to "Contest Info."

Tips: "Most open to writer's tips and market information, personal experiences with writing, first sales, submitting via the Internet, etc. Appreciate submissions by e-mail submission, marked 'Attention Fellowscript.'"

GOTTA WRITE NETWORK LITMAG, 515 E. Thacker St., Hoffman Estates IL 60194-1957. E-mail: netera@aol.com. Secular/Maren Publications. Denise Fleischer, ed. A support system for writers, beginner to well established. Semiannual mag; circ 300. Subscription $12.75. 80% freelance. Query or complete ms/cover letter; e-query OK. Pays $5 ($10 for fiction) after publication for 1st rts. Articles 3-5 pgs (25/yr); fiction to 5-10 pgs (10+/yr) on writing techniques; book reviews 2.5 pgs. Responds in 18 wks. Seasonal 6 mos ahead. Guidelines; copy $5.

Poetry: Accepts 75+/yr. Avant-garde, free verse, haiku, experimental; 4 lines to 1 pg. Submit max 5 poems.

Tips: "Most open to articles on writing techniques. Give me something different and in-depth. No I-love-writing, how-I-did-it." No religious material. Seeking GWN state representatives.

*HEAVEN, HCR-13 Box 21AA, Artemas PA 17211. (814)458-3102. Kay Weems, ed. Published for Easter. New publication. $5/copy. Annual booklet. 100% freelance. **NO PAYMENT.** Short stories to 2,500 wds. Responds in 4-12 wks. Accepts simultaneous submissions & reprints.

Poetry: All types of poetry on heaven, to 36 lines. Submit max 10 poems.

Tips: "Does different themes throughout the year."

INKLINGS, Threads of Truth from Art and Story, 1650 Washington St., Denver CO 80203-1407. (303)861-8191. Fax (303)861-0659. E-mail: inkhick@aol.com, or inklings@paradoxpub.com. Website: http://www. paradoxpub.com. Paradox Publishing. Brad Hicks, pub; Laura Robinson, fiction ed. For thinking Christians and seekers interested in the arts and literature. Quarterly mag; 32-48 pgs; circ 10,000. Subscription $15. 50-75% freelance. Query or complete ms/cover letter; phone/fax/e-query OK. Pays $100 for fiction (nothing for others) on publication for 1st rts. Articles 250-3,000 wds (8/yr); fiction 250-3,000 wds (4/yr); book/music/film reviews, 300 wds (pays in copies). Responds in 3 wks. Seasonal 6 mos ahead. Prefers disk or e-mail submission (copied into message). Some sidebars. Guidelines/theme list; copy $4. (Ads)

Poetry: Susan Kauffman. Accepts 16-24/yr. All types, 2-100 lines. Submit max 10 poems. No payment.

Tips: "We will never publish a submission which refuses to acknowledge the legitimate human needs of all individuals and cultures."

*MERLYN'S PEN, The National Magazine of Student Writing, Box 1058, East Greenwich RI 02818. Secular. R. James Stahl, ed. Written by students in grades 7-12 only. Mag printed in 2 editions: Intermediate, 6th-9th grades; Senior, 9th-12th grades. Fiction to 3,500 wds; reviews and travel pieces to 1,000 wds. Pays $5-25, plus copies. Not in topical listings. Students send for guidelines.

Poetry: To 200 lines.

*MY LEGACY, HCR-13 Box 21AA, Artemas PA 17211. (814)458-3102. Kay Weems, ed. For young adults and up. Quarterly booklet; 70-80 pgs; circ 200+. 100% freelance. **NO PAYMENT.** No articles; fiction to 2,500 wds (100/yr). Responds in 14-16 wks. Accepts simultaneous submissions & reprints. Guidelines; copy for 6x9 SAE/4 stamps & $3.50.

Poetry: Accepts 200+/yr. Any type; to 36 lines.

NORTHWEST CHRISTIAN AUTHOR, 10663 NE 133rd Pl., Kirkland WA 98034-2030. (425)821-6647. Fax (206)823-8590. E-mail: newton@integ rityol.com. Website: http://www.integrityol.com/newton/ncwa/ncwahome. htm. Northwest Christian Writers' Assn. Lorinda Newton, ed. To encourage Christian authors to share the gospel through the written word and to promote excellence in writing. Bimonthly newsletter; 8 pgs; circ 80. Subscription $10. 70% freelance. Complete ms/cover letter; e-query OK. Query for electronic submissions. **PAYS 3 COPIES** for 1st, one-time, reprint or simultaneous rts. Not copyrighted. Articles 500-1,000 wds (18/yr). Responds in 8 wks. Accepts simultaneous submissions & reprints (tell when/where appeared). Prefers disk or e-mail submission (attached file). Regular sidebars. Guidelines/theme list (also by e-mail/Website); copy for 6x9 SAE/2 stamps. (No ads)

Fillers: Accepts 1-2 cartoons/yr.

Contest: For members only; see Website.

Tips: "Most open to articles on writing techniques, particularly for specific genres. We've had too many how-to-submit articles. Stay within word count. E-queries should have 'NW Christian Author' in subject line. Include 1-2 sentence author bio with article."

*OMNIFIC, HCR-13 Box 21AA, Artemas PA 17211. (814)458-3102. Kay Weems, ed. Family-type publication for writers/adults. Quarterly booklet; 100+ pgs; circ 300+. Subscription $16. 100% freelance. **SMALL AWARDS GIVEN.** Accepts simultaneous submissions & reprints. No articles; poetry only. Guidelines; copy for 6x9 SAE/4 stamps & $4.

Poetry: Any type; to 36 lines. Submit max 4-8 poems.

ONCE UPON A TIME . . . , 553 Winston Ct., St. Paul MN 55118. (651)457-6223. Fax (651)457-9565. E-mail: AUDREYOUAT@aol.com. Website: http://members.aol.com/ouatmag. Audrey B. Baird, ed/pub. A support publication for children's writers and illustrators. Quarterly mag; 32 pgs; circ 1,000. Subscription $23. 50% freelance. Complete ms/cover letter; phone/fax/e-query OK. Query for electronic submissions. **PAYS IN COPIES** for one-time rts. Articles to 800 wds (80-100/yr). Responds in 4-5 wks. Seasonal 6 mos ahead. Accepts simultaneous submissions & reprints (tell when/where appeared). Prefers disk or e-mail submission (copied into message). Some sidebars. Guidelines; copy $4.50. (Ads)

Poetry: Buys 25/yr. Free verse, haiku, light verse, traditional; any length. Writing/illustrating related. Submit max 6 poems.

Fillers: Buys 50/yr. Anecdotes, cartoons, prose, quizzes, short humor (all writing/illustrating related); to 100 wds.

Special Needs: How-to articles on writing & illustrating up to 800 wds; short pieces on writing & illustrating, 100-400 wds.

Tips: "Emphasis is on children's writing, but we take general writing pieces too. I don't get enough humor. Half our magazine is open to freelancers. I like how-to pieces. No rejection pieces. Looking for articles on viewpoint, collaboration, avoiding clichés and how-tos. Short shorts to 150 words, writing related."

THE POETRY CONNECTION, 13455 SW 16th Ct. #F-405/CWM, Pembroke Pines FL 33027. (954)431-3016. Sylvia Shichman, ed/pub. Information for poets, writers and song writers; also greeting card markets. Monthly newsletter; flyer format; circ 200. Subscription $20. Phone query OK. Not copyrighted. Responds immediately. Accepts simultaneous submissions. Guidelines; copy $7/10x13 SAE. (Ads)

Poetry: All forms, any length. Magic Circle membership required.

Contests: Lists contests in newsletter.

Note: Also offers membership in the Magic Circle, a poetry reading network service for poetry. Membership $30 (50 copies) or $60 (100 copies). Your bio and one poem sent directly to publishers. In addition, rents a mailing list that includes poets.

+SONGWRITER MAGAZINE, Box 25044, Colorado Springs CO 80936-5044. (719)591-5866. Secular. Roberta C. Redford, pub/ed. Helps readers learn about the craft and business of songwriting. Estab 6/98. Open to freelance. Query with/without clips. Pays negotiable rates on publication for 1st rts. Articles 200-2,500 wds. Responds in 2-4 wks. Guidelines.

Columns/Departments: Looking for columnists.

Special Needs: Interviews with songwriters, how-to pieces on writing lyrics and melodies, how-to pieces on promotion and marketing of songs.

Tips: "Write in a way that is both informational and personal." Very open to unpublished writers.

SOUTHWESTERN WRITERS NEWSLETTER, 7144 Misty Meadow Dr. S., Ft. Worth TX 76133-7131. (817)346-2447. Fax (817)292-1025. E-mail: tillietx@flash.net. Protestant. Tillie Read, pub. Informative articles, market news, writer's resources, tools of the trade, and book reviews. Triannual newsletter; 8-15 pgs. Subscription $10. 75% freelance. Query; fax query OK. **PAYS IN COPIES** for one-time rts. Not copyrighted. Articles 1-2 pgs; short book reviews. Responds in 2 wks. Accepts reprints (tell when/where appeared). No disk; accepts e-mail submission. Regular sidebars. Prefers NIV. Guidelines; copy $2.50. (No ads)

Poetry: Free verse, haiku, light verse, traditional. Submit max 4 poems.

Fillers: Anecdotes, prayers, quotes, word puzzles.

Columns/Departments: Writing tips.

Tips: "Most open to tips, how-tos, and short 1-2-3 items."

TEACHERS & WRITERS, 5 Union Square W, New York NY 10003. (212)691-6590. Fax (212)675-0171. Website: http://www.twc.org. Ron Padgett & Chris Edgar, eds. On teaching creative and imaginative writing for children. Mag published 5X/yr & online mag; circ 1,500-2,000. Query. **PAYS IN COPIES.** Articles 3,000-6,000 wds. Copy $2.50.

TICKLED BY THUNDER, 7385 129 St., Surrey BC V3W 7B8 Canada. Phone/fax (604)591-6095. E-mail: thunder@ista.ca. Website: http://home.istar.ca/thunder. Larry Lindner, ed. For writers wanting to better themselves. Quarterly chapbook (3-4X); 24 pgs; circ 1,000. Subscription $12 (or $10 US). 95% freelance. Complete ms/cover letter; e-query OK. Pays $2-5 (in Canadian or US stamps) on publication for one-time rts. Articles 2,000 wds (5/yr); fiction 2,000 wds (20/yr); book/music/video reviews 1,000 wds. Responds in 16 wks. Seasonal 6 mos ahead. Accepts simultaneous submissions. Prefers disk, no e-mail submission. Some sidebars. Guidelines (also by e-mail/ Website); copy $2.50/9x12 SAE. (Ads)

Poetry: Accepts 20-40/yr. Any type; to 40 lines. Submit max 7 poems.

Contest: For fiction, articles and poetry. For subscribers only. Send SASE for guidelines.

Tips: "Be original, creative, and have something to say-some reason to read your piece. And simple is often best."

WIN-INFORMER, Box 11337, Bainbridge Island WA 98110. (206)842-9103. Fax (206)842-0536. E-mail: writersinfonetwork@juno.com, or writersinfo network@mci2000.com (if sending attachments). Website: http://www.bluejaypub.com/win or http://www.ecpa.org/win. Writers Information Network. Elaine Wright Colvin, ed. Professional Christian writers marketing news. Bimonthly (5X) mag; 40-44 pgs; circ 1,000+. Subscription $33 ($38 Canada/foreign). 30% freelance. Complete ms/cover letter; phone/fax/e-query OK. Query for electronic submissions. Pays $10-50 (copies or subscription) on publication for 1st rts. Articles 100-800 wds (30/yr); book reviews, 300 wds. Accepts e-mail submission. Some sidebars. Guidelines (also by e-mail/Website); copy $5/9x12 SAE/$1.70 postage. (Ads—members and writing-related)

Poetry: Any type.

Fillers: Anecdotes, facts, ideas, newsbreaks, quizzes, quotes, prayers, short humor; 50-300 wds; $10-50.

Columns/Departments: Buys 42/yr. News, Bulletin Board, Computer Corner, Speakers' Microphone, Prayer Requests Poetry News, Agency News, Changes in the Industry, Watch on the World, Look Over My Shoulder, and Readers Q & A; $10-25.

Tips: "Give us cutting-edge, out-of-the-box tips on how to not only survive, but grow your freelance writing career in the face of tightening and shrinking markets. Tell us what your editors or agent are telling you. Give us breaking news stories. No beginner material."

+WRITER ON LINE, 190 Mount Vernon Ave., Rochester NY 14620. (716)271-2250. Fax (716)271-5602. E-mail: email@novalearn.com. Website: http://www.novalearn.com/wol. Novation Learning Systems, Inc. Mr. Terry Boothman, mng ed. For writers seeking timely, professional advice on the art, craft, and marketing of writing. Biweekly online newsletter; circ 13,000. Free subscription. Estab 1998. 30-70% freelance. Prefers hardcopy queries, but do accept e-mail submission. Query by e-mail submission with "Writer" in the body of e-mail submission. Pays $20-50 on publication for one-time or reprint rts. Articles 800-1,800 wds (30-50/yr); book reviews, 800-1,800 wds, $50 ($20 for reprint). Responds in 2-4 wks. Accepts reprints (tell when/where appeared). Requires e-mail submission (attached file). Some sidebars. Guidelines (also by e-mail/Website); copy on Website. (Ads)

Columns/Departments: Buys 110/yr. Creative Nonfiction; International Writer; Children's Writer; Writer's Advocate (legal); Technical Writer; Public Relations Writer; Interview; Book Reviews; M.O.: Mystery and Mayhem; Guest (various topics), 800-1,200 wds, $20-50. Query.

Tips: "Most open to Guest columns on writing how-tos: markets, craft, technique. Also interviews with famous or well-published writers."

THE WRITER, 120 Boylston St., Boston MA 02116-4615. (617)423-3157. Fax (617)423-2168. E-mail: writer@user1.channel1.com. Website: http://www.channel1.com/the writer. Secular. Sylvia Burack, ed/pub. How-to for writers; lists religious markets in December. Monthly mag; 52 pgs; circ 50,000. Subscription $28. 75% freelance. Query; no phone/fax/e-query. Pays $100 (varies) on acceptance for 1st rts. Articles to 2,000 wds (60/yr). Responds in 3 wks. No sidebars. Guidelines (also by e-mail); copy $3.50. (Ads)

Poetry: Accepts poetry for critiques in "Poet to Poet" column; to 30 lines; no payment. No religious poetry. Submit max 3 poems.

Fillers: Prose.

Columns/Departments: Buys 24+/yr. Rostrum (shorter pieces on the craft of writing), 1,000 wds; Off the Cuff (somewhat more personal tone), 1,000-1,200 wds; $75.

Special Needs: How-to on the craft of writing only.

WRITER'S DIGEST, 1507 Dana Ave., Cincinnati OH 45207. (513)531-2222. Fax (513)531-1843. E-mail: writersdig@fwpubs.com. Website: http://www.writersdigest.com. Secular/F & W Publications. Dawn Simonds Ramirez, assoc ed. To inform, instruct or inspire the freelancer. Monthly mag; 76 pgs; circ 225,000. Subscription $27. 90% freelance. Query/clips; e-query OK. Pays .15-.40/wd on acceptance for 1st and reprint rts. Articles 500-3,000 wds (100/yr). Responds in 9 wks. Seasonal 8 mos ahead. Accepts reprints (tell when/where appeared). Prefers disk or e-mail submission (copied into message). Kill fee 20%. Regular sidebars. Guidelines (also by e-mail/Website); copy $3.50 ($3.70 in OH). (Ads—Call Joan Wright, 800-234-0963)

Poetry: Buys 10-15/yr. Light verse on writing; 2-20 lines; $10-50. Submit max 8 poems.

Fillers: Buys to 50/yr. Anecdotes & short humor on writing; 50-250 wds; .10-.15/wd.

Columns/Departments: Buys 100-150/yr. The Writing Life (anecdotes about writing life & short profiles), 50-800 wds; Tip Sheet (short solutions to writer/business-related problems), 50-600 wds; Chronicle (1st-person narrative about writing life), 1,200-1,500 wds. Pays .10-.15/wd.

Contests: Sponsors annual contest for articles, short stories, poetry and scripts. Also The National Self-Publishing Book Awards. Send SASE for rules.

Tips: "Always in the market for technique pieces. Writing Life and Tip sheet items are great ways to break in."

WRITER'S EXCHANGE, 100 Upper Glen Dr., Blythewood SC 29016. E-mail: Eboone@aol.com.Website: http://members.aol.com/WriterNet. R.S.V.P. Press. Eugene Boone, ed. Features writings and small press markets for writers and poets at all levels. Quarterly mag; 36-40 pgs; circ 350. Subscription $12. 100% freelance. Complete ms/cover letter; query for electronic submissions. **PAYS IN COPIES** for one-time rts. Articles 350-5,000 wds (20-30/yr); book reviews 500 wds. Responds in 2-4 wks. Seasonal 6-12 mos ahead. Accepts reprints (tell when/where appeared). Accepts disk. Regular sidebars. Guidelines; copy for 6x9 SAE/3 stamps. (Ads)

Poetry: Accepts 100-150/yr. Any type; 3-35 lines. Submit max 8 poems.

Fillers: Accepts 300/yr. Various; 10-750 wds.

Special Needs: Poetry how-to; writing techniques; personal experiences with writing groups, conferences, writing courses, using computers, etc. What worked and what didn't.

Contest: Quarterly poetry contest; send SASE for rules.

WRITER'S FORUM, Writer's Digest School, 1507 Dana Ave., Cincinnati OH 45207. (513)531-2222. Fax (513)531-1843. Secular F&W Publications. Amanda Boyd, ed. Writing techniques, marketing and inspiration for Writer's Digest correspondence school students. Quarterly newsletter; 16 pgs; circ 13,000. Subscription $10. 100% freelance. Complete ms/cover letter. Pays $10-25 on acceptance for reprint rts. Articles 500-1,000 wds (20/yr). Responds in 6 wks. Seasonal 4 mos ahead. Accepts reprints (tell when/where appeared). Free guidelines/copy for #10 SAE/3 stamps.

Tips: "A great market for reprints. How-to pieces geared toward beginning writers always stand a good chance. Articles must have a how-to slant; focus on writing technique."

+WRITER'S GUIDELINES & NEWS, PO Box 18566, Sarasota FL 34276. (941)924-3201. Fax (941)925-4468. E-mail: WritersGN@aol.com. Independent Publishing Co. Ned Burke, ed-in-chief. For new writers in particular. Quarterly mag; 48 pgs; circ 2,500. Subscription $20. 60% freelance. Complete ms/cover letter; no phone/fax/e-query. Pays $5-30 ($15 for fiction) on publication for one-time rts. Articles 500-1,500 wds (50+/yr); fiction to 2,000 wds; book review 500 wds, $5-10. Responds in 6-8 wks. Seasonal 3 mos ahead. No disk or e-mail submission. Some sidebars. Guidelines; copy $4/9x12 SAE/7 stamps. (Ads)

Poetry: Accepts 10/yr. Light verse, traditional; to 24 lines. No payment. Submit max 4 poems.

Fillers: Accepts 5-10/yr. Anecdotes, cartoons, jokes, quotes, short humor; to 150 wds. No payment.

Special Needs: Up-close and personal interview with published writer or publisher.

Contest: Planning a short-short fiction contest.

Tips: "A First Sale article is the best way to break in."

*WRITER'S INK, PO Box 93156, Henderson NV 89009-3156. (800)974-8465. Panabaker Publications. Darla R. Panabaker, ed. Supplies writers with information on writing and selling. Monthly newsletter; 12 pgs; circ. 100. Subscription $24. 90-95% freelance. Query or complete ms. **PAYS IN COPIES** for 1st, one-time or simultaneous rts. Articles 50-1,000 wds (200/yr); book reviews, 500 wds. Responds in 4 wks. Seasonal 3-6 mos ahead. Accepts simultaneous submissions & reprints. Regular sidebars. Guidelines; copy for 9x12 SAE/2 stamps.

Poetry: All types; on writing topics; to 50 lines. Send any number.

Fillers: Ideas, newsbreaks, quizzes, quotes; to 50 wds.

Columns/Departments: Looking for freelancers to write columns. Topics and subject matter open. Please inquire.

Contest: 1999 Poetry Competition. $100 grand prize. Deadline November 15. Send SASE for rules.

Tips: "Send article with letter describing your previous experience. All areas open. We use a different writer for each cover article. "

WRITERS' INTERNATIONAL FORUM, PO Box 516, Tracyton WA 98393. Website: http://www.bristolservicesintl.com. Bristol Services Intl. Sandra E. Haven, ed. For writers of all ages (young writers through adults). On-line publication, updated frequently. Offshoot of in-print publication by the same name established in 1990. Includes pages for "Featured Manuscripts," including one page just for Christian fiction, essays and articles-which includes author bio and editor's comments. Also a page of winning manuscripts from past competitions. Mail complete ms/cover letter & competition entry form; no phone/fax/e-query. Merchandise awards, competition fees, and prizes vary. Fiction and essays for adult and young readers. 1st & electronic rts. Length varies per competition. Prefers NIV or any version. Guidelines/entry form (also on Website). (No ads)

Contest: Sponsors three or more contests a year for adult or young writers. Send SASE or see Website for details. Some winners published online. You don't have to be online to enter.

Tips: "We prefer fiction and essays that are heartfelt, provide humor, and/or have surprising twists. Although we will consider fresh ideas. and methods, we prefer and appreciate well-crafted traditional approaches. We feature both stories written for adults and stories written for children."

WRITER'S JOURNAL, PO Box 394, Perham MN 56573-0394. (218)346-7921. Fax (218)346-7924. E-mail: writersjournal@wadena.net. Website: http://www.sowashco.com/writersjournal.   Val-Tech   Media/Secular.   Leon Ogroske, ed. For current, aspiring, amateur, and professional writers. Bimonthly mag; 64 pgs; circ 33,000. 40% freelance. Complete ms/cover letter; fax/e-query OK. Pays subscription up to $25 on publication for one-time rts. Articles to 2,000 wds (30-40/yr); book reviews 200 wds, $5. Responds in 12 wks. Seasonal 6 mos ahead. Accepts simultaneous submissions & reprints (tell when/where appeared). Accepts disk or e-mail submission (copied into message). Some sidebars. Guidelines; copy $4/9x12 SAE. (Ads)

Poetry: Esther M. Leiper. Buys 70/yr. All types; to 25 lines; .25/line. Submit as contest entries only.

Fillers: Anecdotes, cartoons, facts, ideas, jokes, short humor, 50 wds. Pay varies.

Contest: Runs 2 poetry contests each year, spring and fall. Prizes $15-50. Reading fee $5/entry (4 max). Also fiction contests.

WRITER'S LIFELINE, Box 1641, Cornwall ON K6H 5V6 Canada. (613)932-2135. Fax (613)932-7735. E-mail: sgill@ican.net. Stephen Gill, mng ed. For professional freelancers and beginning writers. Bimonthly mag; 16-35 pgs; circ 1,500. Needs articles of interest to writers, news items of national and international interest, letters to the editor, poetry, interviews. Needs book reviewers; **PAYS IN BOOK REVIEWED & COPIES.** Not in topical listings.

+WRITER'S POTPOURRI, 55 Binks Hill Rd., Plymouth NH 03264. (603)536-2641. Fax (603)536-4851. E-mail: me.allen@juno.com. MEA Productions. Mary Emma Allen, ed. Tips and information of interest to writers. Quarterly newsletter; 4-6 pgs; circ 100. Subscription $6. Estab 1996. 25% freelance. Pays $5, plus 2 copies, on acceptance for one-time, reprint or simultaneous rts. Articles 250-500 wds (4-6/yr); book reviews 250 wds, $5. Responds in 4 wks. Accepts simultaneous submissions & reprints (tell when/where appeared). Accepts disk or e-mail submission (copied into message). Some sidebars. Guidelines (also by e-mail); copy $1/#10 SAE/1 stamp. (No ads)

Special Needs: Market trends for writers and self-publishing information.

Tips: "Most open to helpful tips for writers."

*THE WRITE TOUCH, PO Box 695, Selah WA 98942. (509)966-3524. Tim Anderson, ed. For writers trying to get published. Monthly newsletter; 12 pgs; circ 40. Subscription $15/yr. 100% freelance. Complete ms/cover letter. **PAYS 3 COPIES**, for one-time rts. Essays on various subjects (120/yr) & fiction for all ages (120/yr), 100-500 wds. Responds in 2-4 wks. Seasonal 2 mos ahead. Discourages simultaneous submissions & reprints. Accepts disk. Guidelines; copy $1.

> **Poetry:** Any type; 4-30 lines. Submit maximum 3 poems.

> **Fillers:** Anecdotes, facts, ideas, prose, short humor; 15-50 wds.

*WRITING WORLD, 44 Tarleton Rd., Newton MA 02159. Submit to The Editor. Bimonthly newsletter; 8 pgs. Subscription $39. Little freelance. Copy for $5/#10 SAE. Not in topical listings.

> **Contest:** Occasionally; see sample issues.

> **Tips:** "Look at back issues and send a fantastic query that shows you've read us."

MARKET ANALYSIS

PERIODICALS IN ORDER BY CIRCULATION

ADULT/GENERAL
Guideposts 3,800,000
Focus on the Family 2,500,000
Decision 1,800,000
Columbia 1,500,000
Angels on Earth 800,000
Plus 600,000
Catholic Digest 501,024
Marion Helpers 500,000
Oblates 500,000
Mature Living 350,000
St. Anthony Messenger
345,000
Miraculous Medal 340,000
Lutheran Witness 325,000
War Cry 300,000
Anglican Journal 272,000
Pentecostal Evangel 265,000
Liberty 250,000
Liguorian 250,000
Power for Living 250,000
Signs of the Times 245,000
Upscale Magazine 242,000
Charisma & Christian Life
220,000
Christian Reader 210,000
Episcopal Life 180,000
Ideals 180,000
Christianity Today 178,000
Real FamilyLife 165,000
Lutheran Digest 155,000
The Family Digest 150,000
The Lutheran 150,000
Standard 150,000
Smart Families 140,000
The Plain Truth 135,000
Live 130,000
Lutheran Journal 130,000
On Mission 130,000
Message 125,000
Company 124,000
Our Sunday Visitor 120,000
ParentLife 115,000
Moody 112,000
Discipleship Journal 110,000
United Church Observer
110,000
The Lookout 105,000

Presbyterian Survey 105,000
Catholic Forester 100,000+
CGA World 100,000
Christian Entertainment
100,000
Christian Parenting Today
100,000
Computing Today 100,000
Kaleidoscope 100,000
Foursquare World Advance
98,000
Christian Computing 90,000
Living (tabloid) 90,000
Total Health 90,000
Celebrate Life 80,000
Physician 74,000
Christian History 70,000
Gospel Tract 70,000
Mature Years 70,000
alive now! 65,000
Good News (KY)65,000
Christian Home & School
64,000
Catholic Answer 60,000
Good News Journal 60,000
Stand Firm 60,000
Christian Standard 58,000
Conquest 55,000
Marriage Partnership 55,000
Northwestern Lutheran
55,000
Presbyterian Record 55,000
Church of God Evangel 51,000
Bridal Guides 50,000
Creation Ex Nihilo 50,000
Gospel Today 50,000
Pursuit 50,000
Sports Spectrum 50,000
Today's Christian Senior
50,000
Trumpeter, The 50,000
Who Cares 50,000
Annals of St. Anne 45,000
Seek 45,000
Living with Teenagers 42,000
America 40,000
Christian Motorsports 40,000
A Positive Approach 40,000

U.S. Catholic 40,000
Vibrant Life 40,000
Weavings 40,000
Cornerstone 38,000
Single-Parent Family 36,000
Good News Journal 35,000-
50,000
Christian Research Journal
35,000
Highway News 35,000
Pray! 35,000
Church & State 33,000
Catholic Parent 32,000
First Things 31,500
The Banner 30,000
Catholic Twin Circle 30,000
Lifeglow 30,000
Progress 30,000
ProLife News Canada 30,000
Cathedral Age 29,000
Common Boundary 26,000
African-American Heritage
25,000
Catholic Heritage 25,000
Homeschooling Today 25,000
Interim 25,000
Sojourners 24,000
Messenger of St. Anthony
23,000
Pentecostal Testimony 21,700
The Mennonite 21,600
Canada Lutheran 20,000
Canadian Mennonite 20,000
Covenant Companion 20,000
The Evangel 20,000
God's Revivalist 20,000
Light and Life 20,000
New Covenant 20,000
Visitation 20,000
Evangel 19,000-20,000
Commonweal 19,000
Accent on Living 18,000
Faith Today 18,000
SCP Journal 18,000
Experiencing God 17,000
The Door 16,000
Visitation 16,000
AXIOS 15,670

St. Joseph's Messenger 15,500
Christian Edge 15,000
Mennonite Brethren Herald
 15,000
Messenger/Sacred Heart
 15,000
Over the Back Fence/NW
 15,000
Over the Back Fence/SW
 15,000
Wesleyan Advocate 15,000
Gems of Truth 14,000
Purpose 13,800
Bible Advocate 13,500
Emphasis on Faith & Living
 13,000
Island Christian Info 13,000
Presbyterian Outlook 12,734
Books & Culture 12,000
Marketplace 12,000
Peoples Magazine 12,000
E Street 11,000
Spiritual Life 11,000
Review for Religious 10,200
A.M.E. Christian Recorder
 10,000
Breakthrough Intercessor
 10,000
CBA Frontline 10,000
Disciple's Journal 10,000
Immaculate Heart Messenger
 10,000
Romantic 10,000
Sacred Journey 10,000
The Vision 10,000
The Christian Leader 9,800
Montana Catholic 9,300
the standard 9,300
Celebration (Catholic) 9,000
Companions 9,000
Journal of Christian Nursing
 9,000
Living Church 9,000
Prism 9,000
Religious Broadcasting 9,000
Sharing 9,000
Brethren Evangelist 8,150
CBA Marketplace 8,000
Our Family 8,000
The Family 8,000
Atlantic Baptist 7,500
Lutheran Parent 7,300
Prairie Messenger 7,300
The Gem 7,000
Master's Community 7,000
MN Christian Chronicle 7,000
MovieGuide 7,000
2 Soar 7,000

Christian Courier (CAN) 6,000
Heartlight Internet 6,000
Impact 6,000
Bread of Life 5,200
Contact 5,200
AGAIN 5,000
Companion 5,000
The Evangelical Advocate
 5,000
Evangelical Baptist 5,000
Green Cross 5,000
Hallelujah! 5,000
Healing Inn 5,000
A New Heart 5,000
The Plowman 5,000
Way of St. Francis 5,000
Christian Living 4,900
Social Justice Review 4,750
Cresset 4,700
Christian Civic League/ME
 4,600
Message/Open Bible 4,300
ADVOCATE 4,000
Christianity & the Arts 4,000
Christian Renewal 4,000
Preserving Christian Homes
 4,000
The Witness 4,000
Cross Currents 3,500
Culture Wars 3,500
Life@Work 3,500
Servant Life 3,500
Perspectives on Science 3,300
Advent Christian Witness
 3,200
Catholic Insight 3,100
Alive! 3,000
Chrysalis Reader 3,000
New Moon 3,000
North American Voice 3,000
Perspectives 3,000
Poets' Paper 3,000
Quiet Revolution 3,000
Rural Landscapes 3,000
Queen of All Hearts 2,800
The Kansas Christian 2,700
Mennonite Historian 2,600
The Inspirer 2,500
The Messenger (NC) 2,500
Railroad Evangelist 2,500
Gospel Tidings 2,300
Apocalypse Chronicles 2-3,000
Answers in Action 2,000
Baptist History & Heritage
 2,000
Christian Chronicle 2,000
Christian Social Action 2,000
Fellowship Link 2,000

Forefront 2,000
Legions of Light 2,000
No-Debt Living 2,000
Re:Generation 2,000
Religious Education 2,000
Touchstone 1,800
Church Herald/Holiness
 Banner 1,700
Journal/Church & State 1,700
Christian Arts Review 1,500
Dovetail 1,500
Jewel Among Jewels 1,500
Grail 1,300
Comments From the Friends
 1,200
Bible Reflections 1,100
Canadian Catholic Review
 1,000
Connecting Point 1,000
Head to Head 1,000
Methodist History 1,000
Pourastan 1,000
Right Road 1,000
Broken Streets 500
Hearing Hearts 500
Hidden Manna 500
St. Willibrord Journal 500
Heavenly Thoughts 430
Burning Light 400
Poetry Forum 400
Christian Poet 350
Explorer 300+
Lighthouse Fiction 300
Smile 300
Time of Singing 250
Dreams & Visions 200
Silver Wings 200
TEAK Roundup 200
Family Network 150
Keys to Living 125
Pegasus Review 115
Time for Rhyme 100
Upsouth 75
New Creation 64
Times of Refreshing 60

CHILDREN

God's World Today 301,000
Guideposts for Kids 200,000+
Venture 140,000
FOF Clubhouse 100,000
Pockets 93,000
High Adventure 86,000
FOF Clubhouse Jr. 75,000
Our Little Friend 45-50,000
Courage 40,000
Live Wire 40,000
Power & Light 40,000

Wonder Time 40,000
Discovery Trails 35,000
Primary Treasure 35,000
GUIDE 32,000
Listen 20,000
Together Time 19,000
Club Connection 18,000-
20,000
Venture 18,000
Touch 14,000
My Friend 12,000
Crusader (MI) 12,300
BREAD for God's Children
10,000
CLUBHOUSE 8,000
Nature Friend 8,000
Story Friends 7,000
On the Line 6,000
Partners 5,800
Story Mates 5,500
Junior Companion 3,500
Primary Pal 2,900
Beginner's Friend 2,700
Skipping Stones 2,500

CHRISTIAN EDUCATION/ LIBRARY

Children's Ministry 65,000
GROUP 55,000
Catechist 50,000
Parish Teacher 50,000
Today's Catholic Teacher
50,000
Religion Teacher's Journal
40,000
Church Media Library 30,000
Teachers in Focus 30,000
Group's Jr. High Ministry
25,000
Perspective 24,000
Christian Classroom 22,000
Lollipops 20,000
Evangelizing Today's Child
18,000
CE Counselor 15,000
Christian School
Administrator 15,000
Teachers Interaction 14,000
Shining Star 11,000
CE Leadership 9,800
Leader/Church School Today
9,000
Resource 9,000
Journal/Adventist Ed 7,400
Kids' Ministry Ideas 7,500
CE Connection 6,600
Vision (CA) 6,000
Church Educator 4,500

Christian Educator's Journal
4,200
Leader 3,500
Church & Synagogue Libraries
3,000
The Youth Leader 2,800
Insight into CE 2,200
Team 2,000
Changing Lives 1,800
Caravan 1,500
CE Connection Communique
1,350
Catholic Library World 1,000
Christian Library Journal
1,000
Church Libraries 600
Christian Librarian 500

MISSIONS

Catholic Near East 100,000
Worldwide Challenge 90,000
Quiet Hour Echoes 80,000
Faith in Action 50,000
American Horizon 40,000
World Christian 40,000
American Baptist in Mission
39,000
P.I.M.E. World 26,000
New World Outlook 25,000
Latin America Evangelist
22,000
Heartbeat 20,000
Wherever 17,000
Message of the Cross 10,000
Leaders for Today 7,500
Evangelical Missions 7,000
Voices in the Wilderness 7,000
World Mission People 7,000
World Pulse 5,000
PFI World Report 4,750
Missiology 2,000
Urban Mission 1,300
Areopagus 1,000
Intl. Journal/Frontier 600
East-West Church 430

MUSIC

Music Makers 105,000
CCM Magazine 100,000+
Release 100,000
Glory Songs 85,000
Profile 80,000
Music Time 60,000
7ball 60,000
Church Pianist 35,000
Senior Musician 32,000
Church Musician 10,000

Church Music Report 6,200
Creator 6,000
Gospel Industry Today 3,500
The Hymn 3,000
Songwriter 3,000
Tradition 2,500
Christian Composer 2,000-
6,000
Christian Country 300-1,200

NEWSPAPERS

Presbyterian Layman 575,000
Christian American 400,000
Inside Journal 400,000
Anglican Journal 272,000
Living 250,000
Episcopal Life 170,000
Together 150,000
Catholic New York 130,000
Our Sunday Visitor 125,000
Alabama Baptist 110,000
Pulpit Helps 106,000
So All May Hear 97,000
Something Better News
75,000
Arlington Catholic Herald
53,000
Good News Journal
(MO)50,000
Catholic Courier 48,000
National Catholic Reporter
48,000
Dallas/Ft Worth Heritage
45,000
Good News Etc. 40,000
Live Wire 40,000
Metro Voice 35,000
You! 35,000
Indian Life 32,000
Catholic Faith & Family 30,000
Interim, The 30,000
Single Connection 30,000
Christian Ranchman 28,000
Catholic Telegraph 27,000
NW Christian Journal 27,000
Christian Crusade 25,000
Christian News NW 25,000
Discovery 25,000
Catholic Servant 24,000
Life Gate 23,000
Family Journal 22,000
B.C. Catholic 20,000
Catholic Peace Voice 20,000
Good News (AL) 20,000
Harvest Press 20,000
Living Light News 20,000
Shantyman 17,000
Catholic Sentinel 15,000

Expression Christian 15,000
Messenger 15,000
Network 15,000
Church Advocate 13,000
Interchange 12,600
Michigan Christian 12,000
Mennonite Weekly 11,000
Awareness TN Christian
 10,000
Baptist Informer 10,000
Christian Courier (WI) 10,000
Disciple's Journal 10,000
Montana Catholic 8,300
Star of Zion 8,000
Arkansas Catholic 7,000
Minnesota Chr. Chronicle
 7,000
John Milton 5,188
Christian Courier (Canada)
 5,000
The Parent Paper 5,000
Christian Renewal 4,500
Home Times 4,000
Day Star Tribune 3,000
Inland NW Christian 2,500
Christian Media 2-6,000
Christian Observer 2,000
Christian Edge 1,500
Prayerworks 600

PASTORS/LEADERS

Your Church 150,000
Pulpit Helps 105,000
Leadership Journal 70,000
Eucharistic Minister 50,000
Plugged In 50,000
Worship Leader 48,000
Enrichment 32,000
Christian Century 30,000
Policy Review 30,000
Today's Christian Preacher
 25,000
Vital Ministry 25,000
Voice of the Vineyard 25,000
Parish Liturgy 22,000
Lutheran Partners 20,000
Ministry 20,000
Ministry & Liturgy 20,000
Preacher's Magazine 18,000
Current Thoughts & Trends
 17,000
Proclaim 15,000
Today's Parish 14,800
Ministry Now Profiles 13,500
Youthworker 13,200
Theology Today 13,000+
Cell Church 12,000
Church Administration 12,000

Church Bytes 10,000
Clergy Journal 10,000
Jour/Pastoral Care 10,000
Joyful Noiseletter 10,000
Preaching 10,000
Resource 10,000
Technologies/Worship 10,000
Celebration 9,000
Review for Religious 9,000
Student Leadership Journal
 8,500
Church Growth Network
 8,000
Faith & Renewal 8,000
The Priest 8,000
Christian Camp & Conference
 7,500
Let's Worship 7,000
Christian Ministry 6,500
Journal/Christian Camping
 6,000
Pastor's Tax & Money 6,000
WCA Monthly 6,000
Catechumenate 5,600
Baptist Leader 5,000
Brigade Leader 5,000
Cross Currents 5,000
National Drama Service 5,000
The Preacher 4,500
Emmanuel 4,000+
Christian Management Report
 4,000
Reformed Worship 4,000
Lutheran Forum 3,200
Word & World 3,100
Art+Plus 3,000
Issachar File 3,000
Ministry Now 3,000
Single Adult Min Jour 3,000
Environment & Art 2,500
Reaching Children at Risk
 2,000
Pastoral Life 1,800
Networks 1,700
African American Pulpit 1,600
Quarterly Review 1,500
Church Worship 1,200
Five Stones 1,200
Jour/Christian Healing 1,200
Ivy Jungle Report 800
Jour/Amer Soc/Chur Growth
 400
Cell Life 300+

TEEN/YOUNG ADULT

Brio 170,000
Visions 140,000
essential connection 130,000

The Rock 125,000
Campus Life 100,000
Breakaway 84,000
Devo'Zine 75,000
Sharing the Victory 60,000
Teen Life 50,000
Young Christian 50,000
Young Salvationist 48,000
Youth 98 40,000
Today's Christian Teen 39,800
Cross Walk 35,000
You! 35,000
Take Five 34,000
Listen 30,000
Spirit 30,000
Straight 30,000
Young & Alive 26,000
Challenge (GA) 24,500
Inteen 20,000
Youth Update 20,000
Certainty 18,000
Insight 18,000
Challenge (IL) 16,000
Teenage Christian 10,500
Young Adult Today 10,000
Student Leadership 8,500
Teens on Target 7,000
The Conqueror 6,000
With 6,000
Youth Challenge 5,500
Beautiful Christian Teen 5,000
Youth Compass 4,800

WOMEN

Today's Christian Woman
 351,000
Lutheran Woman Today
 230,000
Lutheran Woman's Quarterly
 200,000
Journey 150,000
Share 118,000
Virtue 110,000
Aspire 50,000
Horizons 25,000
Women of Spirit 18,000
Woman's Touch 16,000+
Welcome Home 15,000
CoLaborer 11,000
Church Woman 10,000
Conscience 10,000
Journal/Women's Ministries
 10,000
Esprit 7,000
Joyful Woman 6,000
Just Between Us 5,000
Link & Visitor 4,500
Women Alive 3,500-4,000

Sisters Today 3,500
Wesleyan Woman 3,500
Helping Hand 3,000
Probe 3,000
Proverbs 31 Homemaker 2,000
Virtuous Woman 350
Salt & Light 300
Anna's Journal 40

WRITERS

Writer's Digest 225,000
The Writer 50,000
Writers' Journal 33,000
Writer On Line 13,000
Writer's Forum (OH) 13,000
Inklings 10,000

Dream Weaver 5,000
Christian Communicator
   4,000
Byline 3,000+
Writer's Guidelines & News
   2,500
Housewife-Writers Forum
   2,000
Teachers & Writers 1,500-
   2,000
Writers Connection 1,500
Writer's Lifeline 1,500
Cross & Quill 1,000+
Writers Information Network
   1,000+
New Writing 1,000

Once Upon a Time 1,000
Tickled By Thunder 1,000
Advanced Christian Writer 500
Christian Response 400
Canadian Writer's Journal 385
Writer's Exchange 350
Omnific 300+
Gotta Write Network 300
FellowScript 250
My Legacy 200+
The Poetry Connection 200
Exchange 185
Writer's Ink 100
Writer's Potpourri 100
Northwest Christian Author 80
Southwestern Writers 42
The Write Touch 40

PERIODICAL TOPICS IN ORDER OF POPULARITY

NOTE: Following is a list of topics in order by popularity. To find the list of publishers interested in each of these topics, go to the Topical Listings for periodicals and find the topic you are interested in. The numbers indicate how many periodical editors said they were interested in seeing something of that type or topic. There are 296 photography markets this year. (*—new topic this year)

Non-topics:
   -Photographs 290
   -Newspapers 73
   -Contests 70
   -Canadian/Foreign 61
   -Online Magazines 56
   -Take-home Papers 46
1. Christian Living 270
2. Inspirational 257
3. Family Life 256
4. Personal Experience 256
5. Prayer 254
6. Current/Social Issues 246
7. Interviews/Profiles 245
8. Holiday/Seasonal 240
9. Poetry 230
10. Spirituality 222
11. Evangelism/Witnessing 221
12. Humor 203
13. Marriage 200
14. Devotions/Mediations 186
15. Discipleship 186
16. Relationships 185
17. Worship 184
18. Christian Education 182
19. Book Reviews 181
20. Women's Issues 176
21. Parenting 175
22. Fillers: Cartoons 171
23. True Stories 171
24. Missions 170
25. How-to 164

26. Youth Issues 160
27. Leadership 158
28. Church Outreach 155
29. Controversial Issues 153
30. Ethics 152
31. Theological 142
32. World Issues 139
33. Bible Studies 130
34. Health 130
35. Short Story: Adult 130
36. Historical 128
37. Fillers: Anecdotes 125
38. Ethnic/Cultural 122
39. Men's Issues 120
40. Fillers: Short Humor 118
41. Think Pieces 117
42. Church Life 116
43. Essays 116
44. Money Management 115
45. Opinion Pieces 113
46. Celebrity Pieces 109
47. Environmental Issues 108
48. Short Story: Humorous
   108
49. Divorce 107
50. Singles Issues 107
51. Religious Freedom 106
52. Senior Adult Issues 106
53. Church Growth 100
54. Death/Dying 99
55. Healing 97
56. Salvation Testimonies 97

57. Doctrinal 96
58. Stewardship 96
59. Short Story:
   Contemporary 95
60. Social Justice 95
61. Short Story: Biblical 93
62. Fillers: Ideas 92
63. Christian Business 91
64. Sports/Recreation 91
65. Book Excerpts 87
66. Fillers: Newsbreaks 87
67. Fillers: Facts 85
68. Liturgical 84
69. Church Management 83
70. Miracles 82
71. Short Story: Parables 82
72. Music Reviews 77
73. Spiritual Warfare 76
74. Cults/Occult 75
75. Fillers: Word Puzzles 74
76. Fillers: Quizzes 72
77. Short Story: Historical 72
78. Economics 71
79. Short Story: Adventure 71
80. Political 70
81. Fillers: Games 69
82. Fillers: Quotes 69
83. Home Schooling 69
84. How-to Activities 68
85. Nature 68
86. *Personal Growth 60
87. Short Story: Juvenile 60

88. Short Story: Teen/YA 59
89. Self-Help 58
90. Fillers: Jokes 57
91. Fillers: Prayers 57
92. Fillers: Prose 57
94. Food/Recipes 55
94. Travel 53
95. Psychology 50
96. Science 50
97. Prophecy 49
98. Writing How-to 49
99. Creation Science 48

100. Short Story: Mystery 48
101. Short Story: Allegory 47
102. Short Story: Literary 47
103. *Church Traditions 44
104. Sermons 41
105. Sociology 41
106. Short Story: Fantasy 39
107. Video Reviews 37
108. Short Story: Romance 36
109. Short Story: Frontier 32
110. *Time Management 29
111. Short Story: Ethnic 28

112. Short Story: Plays 27
113. Short Story: Science Fiction 25
114. *Exegesis 22
115. *Homiletics 18
116. Puppet Plays 18
117. Short Story: Frontier/ Romance 18
118. Short Story: Skits 18
119. Short Story: Historical/ Romance 17
120. Short Story: Mystery/ Romance 17

Comments:

If you are a short story writer, the biggest market is for adult fiction (130 markets—up 1 from last year). Children's has moved back into second place with 59 (5 more than last year), followed by teen with 59 (3 more than last year). The most popular genres (in order) are Humorous, Contemporary, Biblical, Parables, Historical, Adventure, Mystery, and Allegory. Compared to last year, they are in the same order, except for Historical which moved ahead of Adventure again, and Mystery which moved ahead of Allegory. The least popular are still the genre romances.

This year poetry dropped to 230 markets, from 246 last year and 260 the year before. It also dropped from the seventh most popular topic last year to the ninth most popular this year. Nevertheless the poetry market remains strong with a total number of poems expected to be bought or accepted by those markets at about 4,310—over 3,000 less than last year (we've lost some of the big poetry buyers). The book market for poetry gained two markets this year, from 30 to 32, but I still recommend that the serious poet pursue the periodical markets and establish a good reputation as a poet before every attempting to sell a book of poetry.

This year the same topics are in the top 11, although all but two are in a different position than last year. Personal Experience moved from first to fourth, Christian Living moved from second to first, and Inspirational moved up three places to second. Except for current social issues and poetry which dropped two places, and Interviews/ profiles that went up two, the others only moved up or down one position. In fiction, most genres increased in the number of markets, with Literary, Mystery, and Romance gaining the most, and Allegory and Skits the only ones to drop.

Because of the difference in the way the information for topics was collected this year, there were few significant changes in the interest in specific topics. The only ones to increase significantly in interest were Death/Dying, Church Life, Church Growth, Health, and Spiritual Warfare, in that order. Those showing a decease are Home Schooling, Cult/Occult, True Stories, Sociology, Think Pieces, and Salvation Testimonies.

SUMMARY OF INFORMATION ON CHRISTIAN PERIODICAL PUBLISHERS FOUND IN THE ALPHABETICAL LISTINGS

NOTE: The following numbers are based on the maximum total estimate for each periodical. For example, if they gave a range of 4-6, the average was based on the higher number, 6. These figures were all calculated from those periodicals that reported information in each category.

WANTS QUERY OR COMPLETE MANUSCRIPT:
Of those periodicals that indicated a preference, 72% will accept a complete manuscript (up 23% from last year), and 26% require or will accept a query (up 11% from last year). Only 2% require a query. Only a little over 2% of all reporting will accept either (down 12% from last year). The tendency seems to be moving toward complete manuscripts again.

ACCEPTS PHONE QUERY:
This year, 154 periodical publishers are accepting phone queries—just one more than last year. Many seem to now prefer fax or e-mail to phone queries. It is suggested that you reserve phone queries for timely material that won't wait for the regular mailed query. If you phone in a query, be sure you have your idea well thought out and can present it succinctly and articulately.

ACCEPTS FAX QUERY:
More and more publishers have fax numbers and a good many are willing (and even prefer) to accept fax queries, but some are also beginning to say no to them. Last year, over 40% of all the periodical publishers accepted fax queries. This year, 220 publishers (39%) will accept them. Since a fax query will not have an SASE, it is suggested that you make fax queries only if you have your own fax machine to accept their response.

ACCEPTS E-MAIL QUERY:
This is the fourth year we have asked about e-mail queries, and as expected, the number of publishers with e-mail addresses continues to grow. Last year only 183 publishers were open to receiving messages or submissions by e-mail. This year 454 publications have e-mail, and 223 publishers (almost 50%) are open to e-mail queries. In addition, 317 publishers have Websites (up from 145 last year).

SUBMISSIONS ON DISK:
Of the 372 periodicals that responded to the question about whether or not they accepted, preferred, or required submissions on disk, 133 (36%) said they accepted disks, 133 (36%) preferred disks, only 46 (12%) required disk, and 60 (16%) do not want disks.

SUBMISSIONS BY E-MAIL:
This is a new category this year. When asked if they would accept submissions by e-mail, the 214 that answered were split with 186 saying yes, and 28 saying no. Of those who would accept them, 37% wanted them copied into the message, 26% wanted them sent an as attached file, and the last 37% would accept them either way.

PAYS ON ACCEPTANCE OR PUBLICATION:
Of the 433 publishers that indicated, 39 percent of the publishers pay on acceptance, while 61% pay on publication. These figures are the same as last year's.

PERCENTAGE OF FREELANCE:
Most of the publishers responded to the question about how much freelance material they use. The average indicates that 55% of material used is from freelancers (up .5% from last year).

CIRCULATION:
In dividing the list of periodicals into three groups, according to size of circulation, the list comes out as follows: Publications with a circulation of 100,000 or more (up to 3,800,000), 14% (12% last year); publications with circulations between 50,000 and

100,000, only 9% (10% last year); the remaining 77% have circulations of 50,000 or less (78% last year). If we break that last group into three more groups by circulation, we come out with 8% of those from 33,000-50,000 (up 1% from last year); 19% from 17,000-32,000 (same as last year); and the remaining 72% with less than 17,000. That means that nearly 56% of all the periodicals that reported their circulation are at a circulation of 17,000 or less.

RESPONSE TIME:

According to the 516 publishers who indicated response time, the average response time is back up to just over 7 weeks (was below 7 weeks last year). Those who are writing and submitting regularly will have no problem believing that most publishers are taking longer than they used to to respond to submissions.

REPRINTS:

Just under 55% of the periodicals reporting accept reprints, that's about the same as the last two years. Although in the past it has not been necessary to tell a publisher where a piece has been published previously, that seems to be changing. Most Christian publishers are now wanting a tear sheet of the original publication and a cover letter telling when and where it appeared originally. Be sure to check the listings to see if a publisher wants to know when and where a piece has appeared previously. Many are also paying less for reprints than for original material.

PREFERRED BIBLE VERSION:

Again this year, the most preferred Bible version is the NIV, the preference of 51% of the publishers (down 2% from last year). Other preferred versions are the KJV with 18%; the New Revised Standard Version at 14% the New American Bible with 6%; New American Standard, Revised Standard Version, and New King James with 3% each. The NIV seems a good choice for those that didn't indicate a preference, although the more conservative groups seem to favor the KJV.

PERIODICALS THAT HAVE CHANGED NAMES OR CEASED PUBLICATION

This information is now included in the General Index. See introduction to that section.

PERIODICALS NOT INTERESTED IN FREELANCE SUBMISSIONS, OR WHO ASKED NOT TO BE LISTED

This information is now included in the General Index. See introduction to that section.

GREETING CARD/GIFT/SPECIALTY MARKETS

PLEASE NOTE: This listing contains both Christian/religious card publishers and secular publishers who have religious lines or produce some religious or inspirational cards. Keep in mind that the secular companies may produce other lines of cards that are not consistent with your beliefs, and that for a secular company, inspirational cards usually do not include religious imagery.

(*) Indicates that publisher did not return questionnaire.
(#) Indicates that listing was updated from guidelines or other sources.
(+) Indicates new listing.

NOTE: See the end of this listing for specialty product lists.

CARD PUBLISHERS

BLUE MOUNTAIN ARTS, PO Box 1007, Boulder CO 80306. (303)449-0536. Fax (303)447-0939. E-mail: mail@bluemountainarts.com. Web site: http://www.bluemountainarts.com. Submit to Editorial Department. General card publisher. Open to freelance. Prefers outright submissions. Pays $200 for all rts, or $25 for one-time use in a book, on publication. No royalties. Responds in 8-12 wks. Uses unrhymed or traditional poetry; usually longer than 15 lines. Produces inspirational and sensitivity. Needs anniversary, birthday, Christmas, congratulations, Easter, friendship, get well, graduation, keep in touch, love, miss you, new baby, please write, relatives, sympathy, thank you, Valentines, wedding. Holiday/seasonal 5 mos ahead. Open to ideas for new card lines. Send any number of ideas. Open to ideas for calendars, gift books. Guidelines; no catalog.
> **Contest:** Periodically sponsors a poetry card contest online. Details on their Website.
> **Tips:** "We are interested in reviewing poetry and writings for greeting cards, and expanding our field of freelance poetry writers." They sponsor a tri-annual poetry contest (last one was September 1997).

BOB SIEMON DESIGNS INC., 3501 W. Segerstrom Ave., Santa Ana CA 92704-6497. (714)549-0678. Fax (714)979-2627. Web site: http://www.bobsiemon.com. No freelance.

CATHEDRAL ART METAL CO., 25 Manton Ave., Providence RI 02909-3349. (401)273-7200x227. E-mail: camco@cathedralart.com. Website: http://www.cathedralart.com. Fritzi Frey, art dir. General card publisher that does a few inspirational/religious card and specialty products. 10% freelance; buys 6-12 ideas/yr. Outright submissions. Pays $50-150 on acceptance for all rights. Royalties 5%. Responds in 1-4 wks. Open to ideas for figurines, pins, bookmarks, gift/novelty items, magnets and plaques. No guidelines; catalog for 9x12 SAE/$3.

CELEBRATION GREETINGS (A div. of Leanin' Tree), Box 9500, Boulder CO 80301. (303)530-1442. Fax (303)530-2152. Nancy Trumble Fox, V.P. Product. Christian/religious card publisher and specialty products. 50% free-lance. Buys 30 ideas/yr. Query. Pays $100 on publication for all rts. No royalties. Responds in 12 wks. Any type of verse, including humorous; to 8 lines. Produces conventional, humorous, informal, inspirational, religious. Needs anniversary, birthday, Christmas, Easter, friendship, get well, graduation, keep in touch, love, miss you, Mother's Day, new baby, sympathy, thank you, Valentines, wedding, and encouragement. Christmas ideas 12 mos ahead. Not open to new card lines. Prefers 12-20 ideas. Open to ideas for magnets, mugs, and posters. Guidelines; no catalog.

CREATIVE CHRISTIAN MINISTRIES, PO Box 12624, Roanoke VA 24027. (540)342-7511. Fax (540)342-7929. E-mail: ccmbbr@juno.com. Christian/religious card publisher. 50% freelance. Outright submissions. Pays $5-10 on acceptance for reproduction rts. No royalties. Responds in 6 wks. Rhymed, unrhymed and traditional. Produces inspirational, religious and sensitivity. Seasonal 6 mos ahead. Open to ideas for new card lines. Submit any number. Also open to ideas for magnets, plaques, and post cards. Guidelines; catalog for 9x12 SAE/4 stamps.

> **Tips:** "We are expanding our personalized Heart Impressions line and desperately need inspirational submissions which 'touch the heart' for our plaques and cards. We need poetry about real emotions and feelings, written from personal experience to: husband, mother, father, brother, sister, grandparents, aunt, uncle, friend, daughter, son, cousin, nephew, like-a-mother, like-a-daughter, pastor, Sunday school teacher, etc."

*CREATIVE GRAPHICS, 785 Grant, Eugene OR 97402. (541)484-2726. Fax (541)345-2550. Terry Dusseault, corp sec. General card publisher/religious lines and specialty products. 10% freelance. Query. Usage rights on designs. Pays on acceptance. No royalties. Responds in 4 wks. Uses rhymed and light verse; short. Produces inspirational, religious, and soft line. Needs Christmas, friendship, Valentines, and Mother's Day. Seasonal 10 mos ahead. Open to ideas for new card lines. Send 5 ideas. Open to ideas for magnets and post cards. No guidelines/catalog.

*CURRENT, INC., PO Box 2559, Colorado Springs CO 80901. (719)594-4100. Fax (719)534-6259. Mar Porter, freelance coordinator. General card publisher with a few inspirational and religious cards, and specialty products. 30-40% freelance (100+ ideas/yr). Follow guidelines for submissions. Pays $100 on acceptance for all rts. Royalties only on licensed property. Responds in 2-4 wks. Uses rhymed, unrhymed, traditional, light verse; open length (but uses a lot of short copy). Produces announcements, conventional, humorous, informal, inspirational, invitations, juvenile, novelty, religious, sensitivity, and soft line. Needs all types except relative and St. Patrick's Day. Needs "additional copy" ideas—plaque copy, "What is Easter?" format or "What is a Friend?" Holiday/seasonal 4-6 mos ahead. Open to ideas for new card lines. Send 4 ideas. Open to ideas for banners, calendars, coloring books, gift books, gift/novelty items, greeting books, magnets, mugs, plaques, post cards, posters, puzzles, T-shirts. Guidelines/needs list; catalog for 9x12 SAE/2 stamps.

DAYSPRING GREETING CARDS, Box 1010, 20984 Oak Ridge Rd., Siloam Springs AR 72761. (501)549-6303. Fax (501)524-8959. E-mail: info@dayspring.com (type "write" in message or subject line). Ann Woodruff, ed. Christian/religious card publisher. Currently only accepting submissions from previously published greeting card authors. Please read guidelines before submitting. Prefer outright submission. Pays from $50/idea on acceptance for all rts. No royalty. Responds in 4-8 wks. Uses unrhymed, traditional, light verse, conversational, contemporary; various lengths. Looking for inspirational cards for all occasions including: anniversary, birthday, relative birthday, congratulations, encouragement, friendship, get well, new baby, sympathy, thank you, wedding. Also needs seasonal cards for friends and family members for Christmas, Valentines, Easter, Mother's Day, Father's Day, Thanksgiving, graduation, and Clergy Appreciation Day. Seasonal 13 mos ahead. Send 10 ideas or less. Guidelines (also by e-mail); no catalog.

> **Tips:** This company now accepts submissions from published card writers only, or by request of an editor. Published writers send up to 5 copies of published cards. Also write "Previously Published" on lower, left corner of envelope.

*DIVINE INSPIRATION, 2110 Hobson Rd., #C101, Fort Wayne IN 46805-4873. Lori George, pres. Christian/religious card publisher. Does inspirational and religious cards. All need to contain scriptures. Open to ideas for new card lines. Open to ideas for calendars, post cards, posters, bookmarks, wallet cards, note cards and spiral-bound booklets. No guidelines or catalog.

FREEDOM GREETING CARD COMPANY, 774 American Dr., Bensalem PA 19020-7342. (215)604-0300. Fax (215)604-0436. J. Levitt, pres. General card publisher/religious and inspirational lines. 100% freelance; buys 100s of ideas/yr. Outright submission. Buys greeting card rights. Pays negotiable rates on acceptance. No royalties. Responds in 2 wks. Prefers rhymed, unrhymed, traditional or light verse; 4-24 lines. Produces announcements, conventional, humorous, informal, inspirational, invitations, juvenile, novelty, religious, sensitivity, softline. Needs all types/holidays. Holiday/seasonal 10 mos ahead. Open to new card lines. Prefers 10 ideas/submission. Open to ideas for specialty products. No guidelines; free catalog.

GALLANT GREETINGS CORP., PO Box 308, Franklin Park IL 60131. (847)671-6500. Fax (847)671-7500. E-mail: sales@gallantgreetings.com. Website: http://gallantgreetings.com. General card publisher with a religious line and several inspirational lines. Chris Allen, VP/Sales & Marketing. 25% freelance. Query. Responds in 12 wks. Pays on publication for world-wide rts. No royalties. Uses rhymed, unrhymed, traditional and light verse. Produces announcements, conventional, humorous, informal, inspirational, invitations, juvenile, religious, sensitivity, softline. Needs all types of greetings, except Halloween. Holiday/seasonal 6 months ahead. Open to new card lines. Prefers 20 ideas/submission. No guidelines/catalog.

*GENESIS MARKETING GROUP, 16 Wellington Ave., Greenville SC 29609. (803)233-2651. Fax (803)232-0059. Peter Sullivan, pres. Christian/religious card publisher. 100% freelance. Buys 10 ideas/yr. Outright submission. Royalty 5%. Traditional and light verse. Produces inspirational, religious, sensitivity. Needs anniversary, birthday, Christmas, congratulations, Easter, friendship, get well, graduation, keep in touch, love, miss you, new baby, please write, relatives, sympathy, thank you, valentines, wedding. Also produces calendars, gift books, magnets, mugs, plaques, posters, T-shirts.

+GIBSON GREETINGS, PO Box 371804, Cincinnati OH 45222-1804. Submit to Editorial Dept. General card publisher with inspirational and religious lines. 30% freelance, buys 300-400 ideas/yr. Pays $150 for humor and $100 for non-humor. Responds in 2-12 wks. Uses all types of poetry, 15-35 wds. Produces all kinds of cards. Needs anniversary, birthday, Christmas, congratulations, Easter, friendship. Get well, graduation, Halloween, love, new baby, relative, St. Patrick's Day, Sympathy, Thanksgiving, thank you, Valentines, wedding, woman-to-woman, encouragement. Holiday/seasonal 3-6 mos ahead. Not open to ideas for new card lines or specialty products. Send 10-12 ideas. See Tips for special submission guidelines.

> **Tips:** "Unsolicited writing will not be reviewed, and we will solicit writing only from a pre-selected list of contributors. Inclusion on list will be based on previous performance with Gibson, evidence of proficiency in the social expression industry, or performance on a writing test. Any writer may request a humor test, a non-humor test, or both. Selected writers will become eligible to receive assignments or needs lists at the discretion of the editors. To receive one or both tests, send a 9½ x12½ SAE/$1.10 postage for one or $1.70 postage for two (available by mail only). Allow 2-4 wks to receive test and 2 months for response."

*THE HERITAGE COLLECTION, 79 5th Ave., 4th Floor, New York NY 10003. (212)647-1000. Fax (212)647-0188. Allison Powe, creative dir. General card publisher with a religious line. 20% freelance; buys 50-60 ideas/yr. Outright submission. Pays $35 on publication for domestic rights. No royalties. Responds in 4 wks. Prefers unrhymed; to 3 paragraphs. Produces announcements, inspirational, religious, and sensitivity. Needs anniversary, birthday, congratulations, friendship, get well, keep in touch, love, miss you, new baby, sympathy, thank you, and wedding. Also open to ideas for mugs. Guidelines/needs list; free catalog.

*IMAGE CRAFT, INC. and **LAWSON FALLE LTD.,** 1245 Franklin Blvd., Box 814, Cambridge ON N1R 5X9 Canada. (519)622-4310. Fax (519)621-6774. Jeanette W. Gilmour or Manny Dutra, Product Dev. Dept. Christian/religious card publisher and general card publisher with a religious line. Open to freelance. Query. Pays on acceptance. No royalties. Responds in 4-6 wks. Prefers unrhymed, traditional and humorous, 6-12 lines. Produces announcements, conventional, humorous, informal, inspirational, invitations, juvenile, religious, sensitivity and studio cards. Needs anniversary, birthday, Christmas, congratulations, Easter, friendship, get well, graduation, Halloween, keep in touch, love, miss you, new baby, Mother's Day/Father's Day, new baby, relatives/St. Patrick's Day, all occasion, sympathy, Thanksgiving, thank you, Valentines, wedding, confirmation, and First Communion. Seasonal 8 mos ahead. Not open to new card lines. Send 6-8 ideas.

Tips: "We need good, but clean humor."

J-MAR, PO Box 23149, Waco TX 76702-3149. (254)751-0100. Fax (254)751-0054. E-mail: amyb@calpha.com. Amy Brown, product marketing mgr. Christian/religious publisher that does 2x3 cards, posters and pocket-size cards. 25% freelance; buys 50 ideas/yr. Outright submission. Pays variable rates on acceptance for all rts; no royalties. Responds in 6 wks. Prefers unrhymed (short, focused submissions receive the most attention). Produces humorous, informal, inspirational, novelty, softline. Needs friendship, love, and thank you cards. Seasonal 9 mos ahead. Open to new card lines. Send 5-10 ideas. Open to ideas for bookmarks, 2x3 inspirational cards, gift/novelty items, posters, pocket-size verse cards, stationery. Guidelines; no catalog.

Tips: "We appreciate writing submissions that are focused on inspirational Christian themes. These themes can include biblical references or verses, poems and/or text."

*LIFE GREETINGS, Box 468, Little Compton RI 02837. (401)635-8535. Kathy Brennan, ed. Christian/religious card publisher. Open to freelance. Outright purchases. Pays $10 on acceptance for all rts. No royalties. Responds in 6 wks. Uses rhymed, unrhymed, traditional; 6-8 lines. Produces announcements, conventional, humorous, inspirational, and religious. Needs congratulations, friendship, get well, new baby, sympathy, thank you and wedding. Also clergy reassignment, ordination, anniversary of ordination, and pro-life Christmas. Seasonal 6 mos ahead. Open to new card lines. Prefers 6 ideas/submission. Guidelines; no catalog.

*MANHATTAN GREETING CARD CO., 150 E 52 St. c/o Platzer/Fineberg, New York NY 10022. (718)894-7600. Paula Haley, ed. General card publisher/inspirational line. 100% freelance. Pays $5-250. Responds in 3 wks. Produces announcements, conventional, humorous, informal, inspirational, invitations, juvenile, sensitivity, soft line, studio, Christmas (85% of the line). Holiday/seasonal 18 months ahead. Also open to ideas for bumper stickers, calendars, gift books, greeting books, post cards, and promotions. Free guidelines.

NOVO CARD PUBLISHERS, INC., 3630 W. Pratt Ave., Lincolnwood IL 60645. (847)763-0077. Fax (847)763-0020. Thomas Benjamin/Molly Morawski, art dirs. General card publisher that does a few inspirational and religious cards. 95% freelance; buys 200-500 ideas/yr. Prefers query for writers and outright submissions for art samples. Pays $2/line on publication for greeting card rts. No royalties. Responds in 9 wks. Uses any type verse, variable lengths. Produces all types of cards. Needs birthday, congratulations, friendship, graduation, keep in touch, relatives (all occasions), sympathy, thank you. Seasonal 8 mos ahead. Open to ideas for new card lines. Submit enough ideas to show style. Guidelines/needs list; samples for 9x12 SAE/5 stamps.

Tips: "Sympathy cards need to be a bit more inspirational than just 'my deepest sympathy.'"

*PACIFIC PAPER GREETINGS, INC., Box 2249, Sidney BC V8L 3S8 Canada. (604)656-0504. Louise Rytter, ed. Inspirational cards. 50% freelance; buys 20 ideas/yr. Pays on acceptance for all rts. Responds in 3 wks. Produces conventional, inspirational, romantic, sensitivity, soft line. Holiday/seasonal 12 months ahead. Guidelines for SAE/1 IRC.

*PAINTED HEARTS & FRIENDS, 1222 N. Fair Oaks Ave., Pasadena CA 91103-3614. (818)798-3633, Fax (818)798-7385. E-mail: teri@paintedhearts. com. Teri Willis, ed. General card publisher that does a few inspirational and religious cards. 20% freelance. Query or outright submission (copies only, no original artwork). Pays $25/message on acceptance. 5% royalty on artwork only. Responds in 1-2 wks. Uses unrhymed, traditional, light verse; 2-3 liners. Produces announcements, inspirational, invitations. Needs most types of greetings (no Please Write), plus graduation and Jewish holidays. Holiday/seasonal 3 mos ahead. See guidelines for submission schedule. Open to ideas for new card lines. Submit 12 art designs max, or 24 messages. Open to ideas for banners, gift books, invitations, postcards, posters and stationery. Guidelines/market list for #10 SASE.

*RED FARM STUDIO, 1135 Roosevelt Ave., Pawtucket RI 02862-0347. (401)728-9300. Fax (401)728-0350. Submit to Production Coordinator. General card publisher with a religious line. 100% freelance; buys 100 ideas/yr. Outright submission. Pays variable rates (about $4/line) within 1 mo. of acceptance for exclusive rts. No royalties. Responds in 2 mos. Use traditional and light verse; 1-4 lines. Produces announcements, invitations, religious. Needs anniversary, birthday, Christmas, friendship, get well, new baby, sympathy, wedding. Holiday 6 months ahead. Not open to ideas for new card lines. Submit any number of ideas. Guidelines/needs list for SASE.

*SUNRISE PUBLICATIONS, INC., 1145 Sunrise Greeting Ct., Box 4699, Bloomington IN 47402-4699. (812)336-9900. Fax (812)336-8712. Website: http://www.interart.com. Angeline R. Larimer, creative writer. General card publisher that does inspirational cards. 5% freelance; buys 15 ideas/yr. Outright submission. Pays $50 on acceptance for worldwide exclusive rts. No royalties. Responds in 3 mos. Prefers unrhymed, traditional; 2 stanzas max. Produces conventional, humorous, inspirational. Needs anniversary, birthday, belated birthday, Christmas, congratulations, Easter, friendship, get well, graduation, Halloween, keep in touch, love, miss you, new baby, please write, relatives, St. Patrick's Day, sympathy, Thanksgiving, thank you, Valentines, wedding; also baptism, confirmation, bar and bat mitzvah. Holiday/seasonal 6 mos ahead. Open to ideas for new card lines. Up to 15 ideas/submission. Also open to ideas for gift/novelty items, greeting books, magnets and posters. Guidelines/market list.

    Tips: "We use very little religious imagery or verse. However, it is sometimes used in sympathy, Easter and Christmas captions."

ADDITIONAL CARD PUBLISHERS

The following greeting card publishers did not complete a questionnaire, but are included for reference or to contact on your own. Do not submit to them before you send for guidelines or ascertain their needs. Card publishers who do not accept freelance submissions are now listed in the General Index.

ABUNDANT TREASURES, PO Box 605, Calimesa CA 92320-0605.

APPALACHIAN BIBLE CO. INC., 506 Princeton Rd, Johnson City TN 37601.

ART BEATS, 33 River Rd., Cos Cob CT 06807-2717.

BERG CHRISTIAN ENTERPRISES, 4525 SE 63rd Ave., Portland OR 97206.

BLACK FAMILY GREETING CARDS, 20 Cortlandt Ave., New Rochelle NY 10801. Bill Harte, pres.

CAROLE JOY CREATIONS, INC., 107 Mill Plain Rd., Danbury CT 06811. (203)798-2060. African-American greetings cards.

CAROLYN BEAN PUBLISHING, 1700 Corporate Cir., Petaluma CA 94954-6924.

CD GREETING CARDS, PO Box 5084, Brentwood TN 37024-5084.

EARTH CARE PAPER, INC., PO Box 8507, Ukiah CA 95482.

FREDERICK SINGER AND SONS, INC., 2-15 Borden Ave., Long Island City NJ 11101.

FRIENDLY SALES, PO Box 755, Quakertown PA 18951.

FRIENDS OF ISREAL GOSPEL MINISTRIES, PO Box 908, Bellmawr NJ 08099-9900.

GREENLEAF, INC., 200 Wending Way, Spartanburg SC 29306.

THE HERMITAGE ART COMPANY INC., 5151 N. Ravenswood Ave., Chicago IL 60640.

HIGHER HORIZONS, Box 78399, Los Angeles CA 90016.

IDESIGN, 12020 W. Ripley, Milwaukee WI 53226. (414)475-7176.

JONATHAN & DAVID INC., Box 1194, Grand Rapids MI 49501.

KIMBERLY ENTERPRISES INC., 15029 S. Figueroa St., Gardena CA 90248. Inspirational cards.

KRISTEN ELLIOTT, INC., 6 Opportunity Way, Newburyport MA 01950.

+LAURA LEIDEN CALLIGRAPHY, INC., PO Box 141, Watkinsville GA 30677. (706)769-6989. Inspirational cards.

LAWSON FALLE LTD., Eden Hall, 3330 Griswold Rd., Port Huron MI 48060.

THE LORENZ COMPANY, 1208 Cimmaron Dr., Waco TX 76712-8174.

+MAGIC IMAGE, PO Box 231217, Sacramento CA 95823. (800)684-1555. African-American Greetings

MCBETH CORP., PO Box 400, Chambersburg PA 17201.

MERI MERI, 11 Vista Ave., San Mateo CA 94403-4612.

MORE THAN A CARD, 5010 Baltimore Ave., Bethesda MD 20816.

OAKSPRINGS IMPRESSIONS, Box 572, Woodacre CA 94973.

PS GREETINGS/FANTUS PAPER PRODUCTS, 5060 N. Kimberly Ave., Chicago IL 60630-1744.

RANDALL WILCOX PUBLISHING, 826 Orange Ave. #544, Coronado CA 92118. (619)437-1321.

SENDJOY GREETING CARDS, Laurel Park, Wappingers Falls NY 12590.

+SOUL-SEARCHER GREETING CARDS, 1336 N 6th St., Mankato MN 56001-4216. Inspirational cards.

THESE THREE, INC., 2105 N. Scott St. #79, Arlington VA 22209-1023. Jean Bridgers, ed.

THINGS GRAPHIC & FINE ARTS, 1522 14th St. NW, Washington DC 20005.

T.S. DENISON GREETING CARDS, PO Box 1650, Grand Rapids MI 49501.

WEST GRAPHICS, 1117 California Dr., Burlingame CA 94010-3505. Carol West, ed.

NOTE: Most of the markets listed below for games, gift items and videos have not indicated their interest in receiving freelance submissions. Contact these markets on your own for information on submission procedures before sending them anything.

GAME MARKETS

#BIBLE GAMES CO., 14389 Cassell Rd., PO Box 237, Fredericktown OH 43019. (740)694-8042. Website: http://www.vozar.com. Kelly Vozar, asst. Produces Bible games. 10% freelance. Buys 1-2 ideas/yr. Query. Pays on publication for all rts (negotiable). Royalties 8%. Responds in 6-8 wks. Open to new ideas. One game per submission. Guidelines; catalog for 9x12 SAE/6 stamps.

> **Tips:** "Send developed and tested game play; target market and audience. Must be totally non-sectarian and fully biblical—no fictionalized scenarios." Board games, CD-roms, computer games and video games.

*CACTUS GAME DESIGN, INC., 8845 Stevens Chase Ct., Las Vegas NV 89129. Games.

+DIVINITY RELIGIOUS PRODUCTS, 5115 Avenida Encinas, Ste. B, Carlsbad CA 92008. (800)669-9200. Board games and games for PC or Mac.

+GOODE GAMES INTERNATIONAL, PO Box 21231, Columbia SC 29221. (800)257-7767.

*GOOD STEWARD GAME CO., 6412 Sunnyfield Way, Sacramento CA 95823-5781. (916)393-4263. William Parker, ed. Board games.

#LATE FOR THE SKY PRODUCTION COMPANY, 3000 Robertson Ave., Cincinnati OH 45209-1216. Fax (513)721-5757. Board games.

*MARTIN LEVY INC., 1405 Brewester Dr., El Cerrito CA 94530. (510)234-8888. Board games.

*M.J.N. ENTERPRISES, 1624 McMillan, Memphis TN 38106. (901)946-8185. Board games.

TALICOR, 4741 Murietta St., Chino CA 91710-5156. (909)517-0076. Fax (909)517-1962. E-mail: webmaster@Talicor.com. Website: http://www.Talicor.com. Lew Herndon, pres. Produces board games and puzzles. 100% freelance; buys 6-10 ideas/yr. Outright submissions. Pays variable rates on publication for all rts. Royalty 4-6%. Responds in 4 wks. Seasonal 4 mos ahead. Open to new ideas. Submit 1-4 ideas. No guidelines; free catalog.

WISDOM TREE, PO Box 8682, Tucson AZ 85738-8682. (520)825-5702. Fax (520)825-5710. E-mail: wisdom@elijah.christianlink.com. Web site: http://www.christianlink.com/media/wisdom. Brenda Huff, owner. Produces Bible-based computer games. 30% freelance (Beta versions). Query. Negotiable rights. Pays variable rates on acceptance or publication. Variable royalties. Responds in 1-6 wks. Seasonal 8 mos ahead. Open to ideas for computer games, computer software or video games. No guidelines; catalog on request.

GIFT/SPECIALTY ITEM MARKETS

*ARGUS COMMUNICATIONS**, 400 W. Bethany, Allen TX 75013. (972)396-6500. Fax (972)396-6789. Amy Craft, ed; submit to Beth Davis. Primarily interested in Christian posters. 90% freelance. Query. Outright purchase. Pays $75 on acceptance for all rts. Royalty 5-8%. Responds in 6-8 wks. Uses unrhymed, traditional, light verse; 1-2 lines. Produces humorous and inspirational (one line of sweet, light bear cards). Needs birthday, congratulations, friendship, get well, keep in touch, love, miss you, sympathy, thank you, and wedding. Submit maximum 20 ideas. Also open to calendars and postcards appropriate for Christian schools and Sunday school classrooms. Guidelines; no catalog .

   Special Needs: "We need Christian posters for teens and adults that are positive, inspirational and motivational."

+**B & H GIFTS**, a division of Broadman & Holman. See book listing.

*THE CALLIGRAPHY COLLECTION**, 2604 NW 74th Pl., Gainesville FL 32653. (352)375-8530. Fax (352)374-9957. Katy Fischer, ed. General publisher/inspirational line of framed prints. 40% freelance; 20 ideas/yr. Outright submission. Pays $75-150 for framed print idea on publication for all rts; no royalties. Responds in 6 months. Uses rhymed, unrhymed (preferred), traditional, light verse; under 50 words. Produces inspirational (not too specific or overly religious), framed prints for friends, family, teachers, etc. Holiday/seasonal 6 months ahead. Send 3 ideas/batch. Also open to ideas for gift books, plaques, and musical framed pieces. Guidelines; no catalog.

DICKSONS, INC., 709 B Ave. E., PO Box 368, Seymour IN 47274. (812)522-1308. Fax (812)522-1319. E-mail: productdev@dicksonsgifts.com. David McNabb, VP of Product Development. Produces gift items. 1% freelance; open. Submit cover letter/sample (no originals). Variable rights and payment on acceptance. Variable royalties. Responds ASAP. Uses religious/inspirational verses for bookmarks, Quik Notes, plaques, etc. Seasonal 1 yr ahead. Open to ideas for specialty items. Send any number. Produces board games, calendars/journals, coloring books, gift books, gift/novelty items, mugs, plaques, stationery and T-shirts. No guidelines or catalog.

*FIRST HOUSE PUBLISHING**, 2209 Hand Blvd., Orlando FL 32806. (407)895-3547. Posters.

GARBORG'S, INC., 2060 W. 98th St., Bloomington MN 55431. (612)888-5727. Fax (612)888-4775. E-mail: garborgbf@aol.com. Barbara Farmer, ed. Producer of specialty products. 2% freelance, buys 2-3 ideas/yr. Query or outright submission. Pays negotiable rates on publication. Negotiable royalties. Responds in 4-6 wks. Seasonal 9 mos ahead. Open to ideas for new card lines or calendars, bookmarks, gift books, journals, or stationery. Submit 1 idea. Guidelines; catalog for 9x12 SAE/4 stamps.

   Tips: "Our main product is a page-a-day perpetual calendar with inspirational thoughts, quotes and scripture. Looking for material with a relationship emphasis that will inspire a diverse audience, secular as well as Christian. No 'Christianese,' no clichés, just fresh language and gentle inspiration."

*INSPIRATIONS, Thomas Nelson Gifts, 506 Nelson Pl., Nashville TN 37214. (800)251-4000. Fax (800)448-8403. Stationery, journals, monthly planners, note pads, and gift collection.

*MARYCANA, 23 Great Oaks Blvd., Ste. S, San Jose CA 95119. (800)869-3733. Gift items, including: gift dolls, note paper, bookmarks, etc.

+NEW LEAF GIFTS, a division of New Leaf Press. See book listing.

*NEW VENTURES, RR 1 Box 2091, Moretown VT 05660-9511. (802)229-1020. Fax (802)229-1020. Action figures.

*PEELE ENTERPRISES SHIRT PRINTS, LTD., 3401 Hwy 25N, Hodges SC 29653. (803)374-7339. Christian T-shirts and sweatshirts.

RAYS OF SONSHINE, 910 Ave. E/Box 736, Wisner NE 68791. (402)529-6531. Marlene Colligan, owner. No submissions in 1999.

*SCANDECOR, 430 Pike Rd., Southampton PA 18966. (215)355-2410. Fax (215)364-8737. Lauren Harris Karp, product mngr. A general poster publisher that does a few inspirational posters for children, teens and adults. 40% freelance; buys 50 ideas/yr. Makes outright purchase, for world-wide, exclusive rts. Pays $100 on publication, depends on size of poster. No royalties. Responds in 9 wks. Uses rhymed, unrhymed and light verse; one line up to 20 lines. Produces humorous, inspirational, juvenile, novelty and soft line. No holiday posters. Submit several ideas. Open to ideas for calendars, posters and novelty products/copy. Guidelines; no catalog.

SWANSON INC., 1200 Park Ave., Murfreesboro TN 37133-1257. (615)896-4114. Fax (615)898-1313. E-mail: swanson@hotcom.net. Website: http://www.hotcom.net/swanson. Jason Crisler, marketing. Produces specialty products. Just opening up to freelancers. Query. Pays on publication. No royalties. Responds in 8-10 wks. Uses rhymed, unrhymed, traditional and light verse; short. Inspirational/Christian. Open to new ideas. Send any number. Open to ideas for coloring books, gift/novelty items, magnets, mugs, post cards, puzzles, T-shirts. No guidelines or catalog.

WARNER PRESS INC., 1200 E 5th St., PO Box 2499, Anderson IN 46018-9988. (765)644-7721. Fax (765)640-8005. E-mail: jennieb@warnerpress. org. Jennie Bishop, sr ed. Producer of specialty products. 30% freelance; buys 30-50 ideas/yr. Query for guidelines. Pays $30-35 on acceptance (for bulletins); material for bulletins cannot be sold elsewhere for bulletin use, but may be sold in any other medium. No royalties. Responds in 4-6 wks. Uses rhymed, unrhymed, traditional verse for bulletins; 16-32 lines. Holiday/seasonal 6 months ahead. Accepts 10 ideas/submission. Also open to ideas for coloring books, novelty items. Guidelines (must send for before submitting); no catalog.

Tips: "Most of our present purchases are for church bulletins. Verses may be general inspirational as well as specifically for holiday seasons. Verses should try to inspire worshippers before the church service begins."

*YOUTH LIFE CREATIONS, 2004 Carrolton, Muncie IN 47304. (800)784-0078. Action cards.

SOFTWARE DEVELOPERS

AGES SOFTWARE, PO Box 1926, Albany OR 97321-0509. (541)926-1370. Fax (541)917-0839. Steve Radda, president. Contact: Mario Aranda.

BAKER BOOK HOUSE. See book section.

BIBLESOFT, 22014 7th Ave. S., Seattle WA 98198-6235. (206)824-0547. Fax (206)824-1828. Website: http://www.biblesoft.com.

+BROADMAN & HOLMAN. See book listing.

*EPIPHANY SOFTWARE, 15897 Alta Bista Way, San Jose CA 95127. (408)251-9788.

EXEGESES BIBLES CD ROM—The Only Literal Translations and Transliterations—Ever. PO Box 1776, Orange CA 92856. Phone/fax (800)9BIBLE9. (714)835-1705. Website: http://www.exegesesbibles.org.

KIRKBRIDE TECHNOLOGIES, PO Box 606, Indianapolis IN 46206. (317)633-1900.

LOGOS RESEARCH SYSTEMS, 715 SE Fidalgo Ave., Oak Harbor WA 98277-4049. (360)679-6575. Fax (360)675-8169. E-mail: info@logos.com. Website: http://www.logos.com.

*LOIZEAUX BROTHERS. See book listing.

*NAVPRESS SOFTWARE, 16002 Pool Canyon Rd., Austin TX 78734. (512)266-1700.

PARSONS TECHNOLOGY, 1 Martha's Way, Hiawatha IA 52233-0100. (319)395-9626.

+TOMMY NELSON. See book listing.

ZONDERVAN CORP. See book listing.

VIDEO/CD MARKETS

*CHRISTIAN DUPLICATIONS INTL., INC., 1710 Lee Reed Rd., Orlando FL 32810. (800)327-9332. Videos.

*CITY ALIVE, PO Box 4952, Chicago IL 60680-4952. (312)433-3838. Fax (312)433-3839. Music and teaching videos.

*DALLAS CHRISTIAN VIDEO, 1878 Firman, Richardson TX 75081. (800)231-0095.

+EVERLAND ENTERTAINMENT, 3319 West End Ave., Ste. 200, Nashville TN 37203. (800)876-9673.

*HEARTSONG, PO Box 2455, Glenview IL 60025. (800)648-0755. Videos.

*PROPHECY PARTNERS, PO Box 2204, Niagara Falls NY 14302. (905)684-5561. Videos.

*PROPHECY PUBLICATIONS, PO Box 7000, Oklahoma City OK 73153. (800)475-1111. Religious education videos.

RANDOLF PRODUCTIONS, 18005 Sky Park Cir. Ste. K, Irvine CA 92614-6514. (800)266-7741. Videos.

RUSS DOUGHTEN FILMS, INC., 5907 Meredith Dr., Des Moines IA 50322. (515)278-4737. Fax (515)278-4738. E-mail: doughten@mustardseed-rdfilms.com. Submit to Production Dept. Produces feature-length Christian movies. Open to ideas. Guidelines; free catalog.

+ST. ANTHONY MESSENGER PRESS. See book listing.

*SOLDIERS OF LIGHT PRODUCTIONS, PO Box 16354, Encino CA 91416-6354. (813)345-3866. Fax (818)345-1162. Videos.

*THIS WEEK IN BIBLE PROPHECY, PO Box 1440, Niagara Falls NY 14302. (905)684-7700. Videos.

+THOMAS MORE. See book listing.

+TOMMY NELSON. See book listing.

*VISUAL PROGRESSIONS, PO Box 1327, Melbourne FL 32902. (800)922-1985. Videos.

+ZONDERVAN. See book listing.

PUBLISHERS PRODUCING SPECIALTY PRODUCTS

NOTE: Most of the following publishers are greeting card publishers, but some will be found in the book publisher listings.

ACTIVITY/COLORING BOOKS

Current
In Celebration
Rainbow Books
Chariot (Rainfall)
Regina Press
Shining Star
Standard
Swanson
Warner Press

AUDIO TAPES

Eldridge Publishing
In Celebration
Liguori Publications
Success Publishers
Tyndale House
Word
World Publishing
Zondervan

BANNERS

Argus Communications
Current
In Celebration
Painted Hearts & Friends

BOARD GAMES

Bethel Publishing
Bible Games Co.
Chariot (Rainfall Inc.)
Dicksons

Good Steward Game Co.
Late for the Sky
Lightwave Publishing
Master Books
Joshua Morris Publishing
M.J.N.Enterprises
Shining Star
Standard Publishing
Talicor
Tyndale House

BOOKMARKS

Cathedral Art
Dicksons
Divine Inspiration
Garborg's
J-Mar
Marycana

CALENDARS/DAILY JOURNALS

Abingdon
American Tract Society
Argus Communications
Barbour & Co.
Blue Mountain Arts
Current
Dicksons
Divine Inspiration
Garborg's
Genesis
Group Publishing

Manhattan Greeting Card
Neibauer Press
Pilgrim Press
Read 'N Run Books
Scandecor
Tyndale House
Women of the Promise

CD-ROMS

Bible Games Co.
Chariot
GROUP Publishing
Image Books/Doubleday
Lydia Press
NavPress
Our Sunday Visitor
World Publishing

CHARTS

Rose Publishing

COMIC BOOKS

Dicksons
Kaleidoscope Press
Thomas Nelson

COMPUTER GAMES

Bible Games Co.
Brown-ROA
Chariot Victor
NavPress Software
Wisdom Tree

Wood Lake Books

COMPUTER SOFTWARE

Baker (BakerBytes)
Biblesoft
Concordia
Epiphany Software
Gospel Light
In Celebration
Kirkbride Technology
Logos Research Systems
Loizeaux Brothers
NavPress Software
Parsons Technology
Resource Publications
Sage Software
Wisdom Tree
Zondervan

GIFT BOOKS

(See listing under Book Topics)
Blue Mountain Arts
Current
Dicksons
Garborg's
Genesis
Image Craft
Painted Hearts & Friends
Review and Herald

GIFT/NOVELTY ITEMS

Abingdon
Cathedral Art
Chariot Victor
Current
Dicksons
Garborg's
In Celebration
J-Mar
Manhattan Greeting Card
New Boundary Designs
Scandecor
Swanson
Sunrise Publications
Zondervan

GREETING BOOKS

Calligraphy Collection
Current
Joshua Morris (novelty books)
Manhattan Greeting Card
New Boundary Designs
Sunrise Publications

MAGNETS

Celebration Greetings

Creative Christian
Creative Graphics
Current
Genesis
New Boundary Designs
Sunrise Publications
Swanson

MUGS

Celebration Greetings
Current
Dicksons
Genesis
Heritage Collection
Swanson

PLAQUES

Dicksons
Calligraphy Collection
Cathedral Art
Creative Christian
Current
Dicksons
Genesis
New Boundary Designs

POST CARDS

Abingdon
Argus Communications
Creative Christian
Creative Graphics
Current
Divine Inspiration
In Celebration
J-Mar (pocket verse cards)
Manhattan Greeting Card
New Boundary Designs
Read 'N Run Books
Swanson
Warner Press
Zondervan

POSTERS

Argus Communications
Celebration Greetings
Current
Divine Inspiration
Eldridge Publishing
First House
Genesis
In Celebration
J-Mar
Read 'N Run Books
Scandecor
Standard Publishing
Sunrise Publications

PUZZLES

Current
Swanson
Talicor

STATIONERY

Dicksons
In Celebration
J-Mar
Painted Hearts & Friends

SUNDAY BULLETINS

Warner Press

T-SHIRTS

Current
Dicksons
Eldridge Publishing
Genesis
Peele Enterprises
Swanson
Women of the Promise

VIDEOS/VIDEO GAMES

Abingdon
Augsburg
Bible Games Co.
Brentwood Music
Broadman & Holman
Brown-ROA
Chariot (Rainfall)
Church Street Press
City Alive
Destiny Image
Diamante
Russ Doughten Films
Editorial Unilit
Focus on the Family
Gospel Light/Regal
Group Publishing
Howard Publishing
Integrity Music
InterVarsity
Liguori Publications
Master Books
Moody Press
Paraclete Press
Pauline Video
Prophecy Publications
Star Song
Tyndale Family Video
Vermont Story Works
Victor Books
Vision Video
Wisdom Tree
Word
Zondervan

CHRISTIAN WRITERS' CONFERENCES AND WORKSHOPS

(*) Indicates information was not verified or updated by the group leader.
(+) Indicates a new listing.

ALABAMA
*SOUTHERN CHRISTIAN WRITERS CONFERENCE. Birmingham/Samford University, June 1999. Contact: Joanne Sloan, SCWC, PO Box 1106, Northport AL 35476. (205)333-8603. Fax (205)339-4528. E-mail: Visionslo@ aol.com. Attendance: 150-200.

ARIZONA
AMERICAN CHRISTIAN WRITERS PHOENIX CONFERENCE. October 22-23, 1999. Contact: Reg A. Forder, Box 110390, Nashville TN 37222. 1-800-21-WRITE. Attendance: 35-50.
MINI WRITING WORKSHOPS. Held in various U.S. locations, throughout the year. Contact and speaker: Donna Goodrich, 648 S. Pima St., Mesa AZ 85210. (602)962-6694. One- to three-day-long workshops on various topics. Attendance: 20-30.
*SOUTH-EASTERN ARIZONA CHRISTIAN WRITERS SEMINAR. Tucson; September 1999. Contact: Bea Carlton, HCR 1 Box 153C, Willcox AZ 85643. (520)384-9232.
+TEMPE WRITERS WORKSHOP. September 18, 1999 & September 16, 2000. Sponsored by Creative Copy Ink. Contact: Kitty Bucholtz, PO Box 68114, Phoenix AZ 85082-8114. (602)267-8529. Fax (602)273-1314. E-mail: jkbuch@primenet.com. Website: http://www.primenet.com/jkbuch.

ARKANSAS
55TH ANNUAL ARKANSAS WRITERS' CONFERENCE. Little Rock; June 5, 1999 (held annually on 1st week-end of June). Contact: Barbara L. Mulkey, 17 Red Maple Ct., Little Rock AR 72211-3117. Attendance: 200+.

CALIFORNIA
AMERICAN CHRISTIAN WRITERS ANAHEIM CONFERENCE. Anaheim Ramada Inn, March 12-13, 1999. Contact: Reg Forder, Box 110390, Nashville TN 37222. 1-800-21-WRITE. Attendance: 20-50.
AMERICAN CHRISTIAN WRITERS RIVERSIDE CONFERENCE. October 15-16, 1999. Contact: Reg A. Forder, Box 110390, Nashville TN 37222. 1-800-21-WRITE. Attendance: 35-50.
AMERICAN CHRISTIAN WRITERS SACRAMENTO CONFERENCE. October 8-9, 1999. Contact: Reg A. Forder, Box 110390, Nashville TN 37222. 1-800-21-WRITE. Attendance: 35-50.

CASTRO VALLEY CHRISTIAN WRITERS SEMINAR. Castro Valley, February 26-27, 1999. Speakers: Francine Rivers, Ethel Herr, Lissa Halls Johnson. Contact: Pastor Jon Drury, 19300 Redwood Rd., Castro Valley CA 94546-3465. (510)886-6300. Fax (510)581-5022. E-mail: jond@redwoodchapel.org. Attendance: 120.

*CEHUC SPANISH CHRISTIAN WRITERS SEMINAR. Los Angeles, San Diego or Tijuana; April 1999. Contact: Magdalena Latorre, 9802 Quail Canyon Rd., El Cajon CA 92021-6000. Phone/fax (619)390-3747. New.

CHRISTIAN WRITERS CONFERENCE OF SANTA BARBARA. Westmont College; October 9, 1999. Contact: Rev. Opal Mae Dailey, PO Box 42429, Santa Barbara CA 93140. Phone/fax (805)563-9230. Offers track for advanced writers.

*CHRISTIAN WRITERS FELLOWSHIP OF ORANGE COUNTY WRITER'S DAYS. Lake Forest, April and October 1999. Contact: Carol Hutchins, PO Box 538, Lake Forest CA 92630. (310)379-5646. Attendance: 100.

LODI ALL-DAY WRITERS SEMINAR. Stockton, date not set for 1999 (usually July). General writing conference; not just Christian writers. Contact: Dee Porter, PO Box 1863, Lodi CA 95241. Phone/fax (209)334-0603. E-mail: crcomm@lodinet.com. Write and ask to be put on mailing list.

MASTER CLASS. Pine Valley Bible Conference Center, Pine Valley, March 18-21, 1999. A creative writing workshop co-sponsored by San Diego Co. Christian Writers Guild and AD LIB Christian Arts. Speakers include: David & Heather Kopp, Jean Janzen and Jerry Jenkins. Contact: Judith Deem Dupree, PO Box 365, Pine Valley CA 91962. Phone/fax (619)473-8683. E-mail: ADLIB@ixpres.com.

MOUNT HERMON CHRISTIAN WRITERS CONFERENCE. Mount Hermon (near Santa Cruz), March 26-30, 1999; April 14-18, 2000. Keynote speaker: Dr. Dick Foth; speakers include Penelope Stokes. Advanced track with Sally Stuart and Lauraine Snelling. Contact: David R. Talbott, Box 413, Mount Hermon CA 95041-0413. (831)335-4466. Fax (831)335-9218. E-mail: rachelw@mhcamps.org. Website: http://www.mounthermon.org. Attendance: 300-350.

+ORTHODOX AUTHOR'S ASSN. SEMINAR. Forestville, October 1999. Contact: Mrs. Michael Hoffman, 7777 Martinelli Rd., Forestville CA 95436.

SAN DIEGO CHRISTIAN WRITERS GUILD FALL CONFERENCE. San Diego, September 17-18, 1999. Contact: Robert Gillespie, 17041 Palacio Pl., San Diego CA 92127. Phone/fax (619)673-3921. E-mail: riters@adnc.com. Attendance: 150.

SAN DIEGO STATE UNIVERSITY WRITERS CONFERENCE. San Diego, January 17-18, 1999. To advanced writers offers a read and critique by editors and agents. Contact: Diane Dunaway, 5250 Campanile Dr., San Diego CA 92182-1920. (619)484-8575. Fax (619)594-8577. E-mail: ddunaway@aol.com. Website: http://www.ces.sdsu.edu. Attendance: 400.

+WRITERS SYMPOSIUM BY THE SEA. San Diego/Point Loma Nazarene University, February 18-20, 1999. Speakers: Michael Medved, Richard Lederer, Jannell Cannon, Chitra Divakaruni, John Ullmann. Contact: Dean Nelson, Professor, Journalism Dept. PLNU, 3900 Lomaland Dr., San

Diego CA 92106. (619)849-2592. Fax (619)849-2566. E-mail: dean nelson@ptloma.edu.

+THE WRITE TOUCH. A six-week School of Christian Writing class, teaching the basics of fiction, newspaper pieces, children's books, poetry, personal experience articles and marketing. Taught as requested in your area. For information or to book the school, contact: Glenda Palmer, 1687 Via Elisa Dr., El Cajon CA 92021-3559. (619)440-3020 or Peggy Leslie at (619)447-6258.

COLORADO

AD LIB CHRISTIAN ARTS RETREAT. Black Forest/Colorado Springs, September 29- October 3, 1999. Contact: Judith Deem Dupree, PO Box 365, Pine Valley CA 91962-0365. Phone/fax (619)473-8683. E-mail: ADLIB@ ixpres.com. Designed as a forum and format for renewal. Solitude, issues and ideas, critiquing. Attendance: 40+.

COLORADO CHRISTIAN WRITERS CONFERENCE. Estes Park; May 20-22, 1999. Speakers: Jack Cavanaugh, Ethel Herr, Barbara Nicolosi, Gayle Roper, Jim Watkins. Director: Marlene Bagnull, 316 Blanchard Rd., Drexel Hill PA 19026-3507. Phone/fax (610)626-6833. E-mail: mbagnull@aol. com. Website: http://nancepub.com/cwf/co/. Offers track for advanced writers. Attendance: 250.

SPAN '99 CONFERENCE. Denver; October 22-24, 1999. Sponsored by the Small Publishers Assn. of North America. Speakers: Tom & Marilyn Ross. For pro-active authors who seek creative & proven ways to promote & sell their books, self-publishers and small presses. Contact: Marilyn Ross, PO Box 1306, Buena Vista CO 81211-1306. (719)395-4790. Fax (719)395-8374. E-mail: SPAN@SPANnet.org. Website: http://www.SPANnet.org. Attendance: 150.

CONNECTICUT

WESLEYAN WRITERS CONFERENCE. Wesleyan University/Middletown, last week of June 1999. Contact: Anne Green, c/o Wesleyan University, Middletown CT 06459. (860)685-3604. Fax (860)685-2441. E-mail: agreene@wesleyan.edu. Website: http://www.wesleyan.edu/writing/con feren.html. Attendance: 100.

FLORIDA

AMERICAN CHRISTIAN WRITERS FORT LAUDERDALE CONFERENCE. November 12-13, 1999. Contact: Reg A. Forder, Box 110390, Nashville TN 37222. 1-800-21-WRITE. Attendance: 35-50.

AMERICAN CHRISTIAN WRITERS JACKSONVILLE CONFERENCE. July 16-17, 1999. Contact: Reg Forder, Box 110390, Nashville TN 37222. 1-800-21-WRITE. Attendance: 20-50.

AMERICAN CHRISTIAN WRITERS ORLANDO CONFERENCE. July 9-10, 1999. Contact: Reg Forder, Box 110390, Nashville TN 37222. 1-800-21-WRITE. Attendance: 20-50.

AMERICAN CHRISTIAN WRITERS TAMPA CONFERENCE. November 26-27, 1999. Contact: Reg A. Forder, Box 110390, Nashville TN 37222. 1-800-21-WRITE. Attendance: 35-50.

EVANGELICAL PRESS ASSOCIATION CONVENTION. Orlando; May 2-5,1999 (held in different location each year). Sheraton World Resort. Speakers: Dr. Bill Bright, Peggy Wehmeyer, Clifton Taulbert, Carol Childress. Contact: Ron Wilson, dir., 314 Dover Rd., Charlottesville VA 22901. (804)973-5941. Fax (804)973-2710. E-mail: 74473.272@compu serve.com. Website: http://www.epassoc.org. Attendance: 300-400. Annual convention; freelance communicators welcome.

FLORIDA CHRISTIAN WRITERS CONFERENCE. Park Avenue Retreat Center/Titusville; January 28-February 1, 1999; January 27-31, 2000. Offers advanced track by application only. Contact: Billie Wilson, 2600 Park Avenue, Titusville FL 32780. (407)269-6702x202. Fax (407)383-1741. E-mail: writer@digital.net. Website: http://www.kipertek.com/writer. Attendance: 200 + 50 staff.

WRITING STRATEGIES FOR THE CHRISTIAN MARKET. Classes for basics, intermediate marketing & business; Building the Novel, January 30 & October 30, 1999. Speakers: Rosemary Upton & Kistler London.   Also material available for an independent studies program by mail. Contact: Rosemary J. Upton, 2712 S. Peninsula Dr., Daytona Beach FL 32118. Phone/fax (904)322-1111. E-mail: romy14@juno.com. Write to be put on mailing list. Attendance: 10-20.

GEORGIA

*NORTHEAST GEORGIA WRITERS CONFERENCE. Gainesville, October 2000 (biennial/even-numbered years). Contact: Elouise Whitten, 660 Crestview Terrace, Gainesville GA 30501-3110. (770)532-3007. Attendance: 50-60.

SOUTHEASTERN WRITERS CONFERENCE. St. Simons Island; June 20-26, 1999. Contact: Patricia S. Laye, Rt. 1 Box 102, Cuthbert GA 31740. (912)679-5445. E-mail: psl@sowega.net. Attendance: 100 (limited). Awards cash prizes in every genre and free manuscript critiques.

IDAHO

*INTERNATIONAL NETWORK OF COMMUNICATORS & THE ARTS CONFERENCE. Coeur d'Alene; September/October 1999. Contact: Sheri Stone, Box 1754, Post Falls ID 83854-1754. Phone/fax (208)667-9730. Attendance: 300.

ILLINOIS

AMERICAN CHRISTIAN WRITERS DANVILLE   CONFERENCE. Baptist Church, August 20-21, 1999. Contact: Reg A. Forder, Box 110390, Nashville TN 37222. 1-800-21-WRITE. Attendance: 35-50.

+CATHOLIC PRESS ASSOCIATION ANNUAL CONVENTION. Chicago, June 1999. Contact: Owen McGovern, exec dir, 3555 Veterans Memorial Hwy Ste. O, Ronkonkoma NY 11779-7636. (516)471-4730. Fax (516)471-4804. E-mail: CathJourn@aol.com. For media professionals. Attendance: 400.

*INTERNATIONAL BLACK WRITERS CONFERENCE. Chicago, June 1999. Contact: Mable Terrell, PO Box 1030, Chicago IL 60690-1030. (312)409-2292.

MISSISSIPPI VALLEY WRITERS CONFERENCE. (24th) Augustana College/ Rock Island, June 6-12, 1999. Contact: David R. Collins, 3403 45th St., Moline IL 61265-6608. (309)762-8985. Offers advanced novel track. Attendance: 75.

*THE SALVATION ARMY CHRISTIAN WRITERS' CONFERENCE. Des Plaines IL, April 2000 (held every other year). Contact: Elizabeth Kinzie, 10 W. Algonquin Rd., Des Plaines IL 60016-6006. (847)294-2050. Attendance: 60. For S.A. officers, laymen, and employee staff.

WRITE-TO-PUBLISH CONFERENCE. Wheaton (Chicago area); June 2-5, 1999. Speakers: Dr. Dennis Hensley and Gayle G. Roper. Contact: Lin Johnson, 9731 Fox Glen Dr., #6F, Niles IL 60714-5861. (847)296-3964. Fax (847)296-0754. E-mail: linjohnson@compuserve.com. Website: http://www.ccu.edu/christiansandmedia. Offers advanced track. Attendance: 150.

INDIANA

AMERICAN CHRISTIAN WRITERS INDIANAPOLIS CONFERENECE. Holiday Inn, August 27-28, 1999. Contact: Reg Forder, Box 110390, Nashville TN 37222. 1-800-21-WRITE. Attendance: 35-50.

BETHEL COLLEGE CHRISTIAN WRITERS' WORKSHOP. Mishawaka; may not be held every year. Contact: Jeanne Haverstick, 1001 W. McKinley Ave., Mishawaka IN 46545-5509. (219)257-3352. Attendance: 120.

+EARLHAM SCHOOL OF RELIGION ANNUAL COLLOQUIUM/THE MINISTRY OF WRITING. Richmond; October 1999. Contact: '99 Writing Colloquium, J. Brent Bill, Earlham School of Religion, 228 College Ave., Richmond IN 47374. (765)983-1423. Fax (765)983-1688. E-mail: wetheph@earlham.edu. Website: http://www.earlham.edu/esr. Attendance: 200.

IMAGE FESTIVAL OF LITERATURE AND THE ARTS. Location undecided; early November 1999. Contact: Gregory Wolfe, IMAGE, PO Box 674, Kennett Square PA 19348. (302)652-8279. Fax (302)652-1344. E-mail: gwolfe@compuserve.com. Website: http://www.imagejournal.org.

MIDWEST WRITERS WORKSHOP. Muncie, July 28-31, 1999. Speaker: Jim Watkins.(nonfiction). Contact: Dr. Earl Conn, Dept. of Journalism, Ball State University, Muncie IN 47306-0675. (765)285-5587. Fax (765)285-7997. E-mail: 00ELCONN@bsu.edu. Attendance: 125.

IOWA

AMERICAN CHRISTIAN WRITERS DES MOINES CONFERENCE. Sheraton Hotel, August 6-7, 1999. Contact: Reg A. Forder, Box 110390, Nashville TN 37222. 1-800-21-WRITE. Attendance: 35-50.

KANSAS

BOONDOCKS RETREAT. Dodge City; possibly June, date not set. Contact: Linda Fergerson, 2500 Memory Ln., Dodge City KS 67801. (316)225-1126. Attendance: 25-40. Offers a spiritual retreat for writers, rather than a nuts & bolts conference.

KANSAS CITY CHRISTIAN WRITERS' NETWORK FALL CONFERENCE. Kansas City area; October 1999. Contact: Cheryl Gochnauer, conference

Registrar, PO Box 6883, Lee's Summit MO 64064-6883. Phone/fax (816) 524-4716. E-mail: KCCWN@aol.com. Attendance: 100.

PITTSBURG CHRISTIAN WRITERS' WORKSHOP. Pittsburg; April 10, 1999. Speaker: Debi Stack. Contact: LeAnn Campbell, 267 SW 1st Ln., Lamar MO 64759. (417)682-2713. E-mail: campbell@talleytech.com. Attendance: 25.

KENTUCKY

AMERICAN CHRISTIAN WRITERS LOUISVILLE CONFERENCE. Executive Inn, January 29-30, 1999. Contact: Reg A. Forder, Box 110390, Nashville TN 37222. 1-800-21-WRITE. Attendance: 35-50.

*WRITERS WORKSHOP AT LOUISVILLE PRESBYTERIAN SEMINARY. Louisville; March 1999. Co-directors/keynote speakers: Cec Murphy & Perry Biddle. Contact: Dr. James Andrews, Louisville Presbyterian Seminary, 1044 Alta Vista Rd., Louisville KY 40205. (800)264-1839. Fax (502)895-1096. Attendance: 40.

LOUISIANA

AMERICAN CHRISTIAN WRITERS NEW ORLEANS CONFERENCE. April 16-17, 1999. Contact: Reg A. Forder, Box 110390, Nashville TN 37222. 1-800-21-WRITE. Attendance: 35-50.

MAINE

SIXTH ANNUAL (99) CHRISTIAN WRITERS' CONFERENCE. China Lake Conference Center, August 12-14, 1999. Contact: Dr. Ken Parker, Minister of Conferencing & Camping, China Lake Conference Center, PO Box 149, China ME 04926. (207)968-2101. Fax (207)968-2434. E-mail: jvschad @larck.net. Website: http://www.chinalake.net. Sponsors Dorothy Templeton Writer's Contest. Attendance: 35-50.

*STATE OF MAINE WRITERS' CONFERENCE. Ocean Park; August 1999. Contact: Richard F. Burns, PO Box 7146, Ocean Park ME 04063-7146. (207)934-9806. Attendance: 25-40. Contest announcement available March 1; brochure available June 1. Half-price tuition for teens.

MARYLAND

SANDY COVE CHRISTIAN WRITERS CONFERENCE. Sandy Cove/North East, October 3-7, 1999. Offers Advanced Track. Contact: Jim Watkins, Writers' Conference Director, Sandy Cove Ministries, Box B, North East MD 21901. (800)234-2683. E-mail: info@sandycove.com. Website: http://www.noblecan.org/watkins/sandycov.htm. Attendance: 150.

MASSACHUSETTS

*CAPE COD WRITERS' CONFERENCE. Craigville Conference Center, August 1999. Contact: Joseph Ryan, c/o Cape Cod Conservatory, Rt. 132, West Barnstable MA 02668. (508)375-0516. Attendance: 125. Also offers **CAPE LITERARY ARTS WORKSHOPS**: 6 simultaneous week-long workshops (poetry, romance novels, juvenile writing, children's book illustrating, and play writing), August 1999. Limited to 10 in each workshop.

MICHIGAN

AMERICAN CHRISTIAN WRITERS ANN ARBOR CONFERENCE. June 4-5, 1999. Contact: Reg Forder, Box 110390, Nashville TN 37222. 1-800-21-WRITE. Attendance: 20-50.

AMERICAN CHRISTIAN WRITERS GRAND RAPIDS CONFERENCE. Holiday Inn, May 28-29, 1999. Contact: Reg Forder, Box 110390, Nashville TN 37222. 1-800-21-WRITE. Attendance: 35-50.

+CHRISTIAN WRITERS CONFERENCE. Almont, April 25-27, 1999. Speakers: Dr. Thomas Long and Jonellen Heckler. Contact: Dr. Richard Henderson and Dr. Kate Thoreson, PO Box 1, Novi MI 48376-0001. (248)349-5666. Fax (248)349-2345. Attendance: 40.

*JOURNEY WRITING WORKSHOPS/LIFELINE: A SPIRITUAL JOURNEY FOR WRITERS. Leelanau Center for Education. Glen Arbor MI. Held every 6 weeks. Contact: Elizabeth Hawkins, 1049 Floral Dr. SE, East Grand Rapids MI 49506. (616)245-9245. Classes limited to 20.

MARANATHA CHRISTIAN WRITERS SEMINAR. Maranatha Bible & Missionary Conference/Muskegon, August 23-27, 1999. Speakers: Jack Metzler, Verna Kokmeyer, Leona Hertel. Contact: Leona Hertel, 4759 Lake Harbor Rd., Muskegon MI 49441-5299. (616)798-2161. Attendance: limited to 50.

"SPEAK UP WITH CONFIDENCE" SEMINARS. Hillsdale/Michindoh Ministries Conference Center, July 29-31, 1999. Contact: Carol Kent, 1614 Edison Shores Pl., Port Huron MI 48060. (810)982-0898. Fax (810)987-4163. E-mail: speakupinc@aol.com. Speaker: Carol Kent. Speaking seminar. Offers advanced training. Also offers a seminar on writing for publication. Attendance: 100.

*WRITERS CONFERENCE AT SKYLINE. Skyline Conference Center/Calumet; November 1999. Contact: Nancy A. Regensburger, 615 Wightman St., Vassar MI 48768. Attendance: 50.

MINNESOTA

AMERICAN CHRISTIAN WRITERS MINNEAPOLIS CONFERENCE. Hilton Hotel, August 13-14, 1999. Contact: Reg Forder, Box 110390, Nashville TN 37222. 1-800-21-WRITE. Attendance: 35-50

MINNESOTA CHRISTIAN WRITERS GUILD SPRING SEMINAR. Minneapolis/St. Paul, March 1999. Contact: Joyce Ellis, 9266 Dunbar Knoll Circle N., Brooklyn Park MN 55444. Attendance: 80-100.

+WRITING CLASSES AT NORTH HENNEPIN COMMUNITY COLLEGE. Minneapolis; 2 fall, 2 winter, 2 spring. Instructor: Louise B. Wyly. Topics include fiction, children's writing, personal experiences, memoirs and nonfiction. Contact: Louise Wyly, 6916 65th Ave. N, Minneapolis MN 55428-2515. (612)533-6207. E-mail: lsnowbunny@aol.com.

MISSOURI

AMERICAN CHRISTIAN WRITERS SPRINGFIELD CONFERENCE. Holiday Inn, July 30-31, 1999. Contact: Reg A. Forder, Box 110390, Nashville TN 37222. 1-800-21-WRITE. Attendance: 35-50.

*MARK TWAIN WRITERS CONFERENCE. Hannibal, Heartland Lodge, four separate weeks in June, July, August & September, 1999. Contact: Cyndi

Allison, 921 Center St., Hannibal MO 63401. (800)747-0738. (573)221-2462. Fax (573)221-6409. Attendance: 25 per conference. Note: This is a general conference under the direction of evangelical Christians.

THE WRITING ACADEMY SEMINAR. Sponsors year-round correspondence writing program and annual seminar in various locations. 1999 seminar is in St. Louis MO, August 5-9. Contact: Nancy Remmert, (314)524-3718. E-mail: nremm10335@aol.com. Call after 4/01/99. Website: http://www.wams.org.

NEBRASKA

+MY THOUGHTS EXACTLY WRITERS RETREAT. St. Benedict Retreat Center/Schuyler. April and October 1999 & April 2000. Contact: My Thoughts Exactly Writers Group, PO Box 1073, Fremont NE 68026-1073. (402)727-6508. Geared toward the beginning writer. Attendance: Limited to 50.

NEW HAMPSHIRE

+WRITING WORKSHOPS. Plymouth State College/Plymouth. Classes held in May and October at the college (others as requested). Contact: Mary Emma Allen (teacher), 55 Binks Hill Rd., Plymouth NH 03264. (603)536-2641. Fax (603)536-4851. E-mail: me.allen@juno.com. Attendance: 5-15.

NEW MEXICO

*GHOST RANCH WRITING WORKSHOPS. Abiquiu; October 1999. Contact: Ghost Ranch, HC 77 Box 11, Abiquiu NM 87510-9601.

THE GLEN WORKSHOP. Ghost Ranch/Abiquiu NM; August 9-16, 1999. Includes fiction, poetry, nonfiction, memoir, on-site landscape painting, figure drawing, book arts, songwriting, master class on journal writing. Contact: Image, PO Box 674, Kennett Square PA 19348. (302)652-8279. Fax (302)652-1344. gwolfe@compuserve.com. Website: http://www.imagejournal.org. Attendance: 100.

GLORIETA CHRISTIAN WRITERS' CONFERENCE. Glorieta (18 mile N. of Santa Fe); November 9-13, 1999. Speakers: Bill Myers, Luci Shaw. Offers 6 continuing classes (including writing for children), 42 workshops, editorial appointments, evening critique groups, a writing contest, and paid critiques. Contact: Glorieta Conference Center at (800)797-4222 or Mona Hodgson, PO Box 999, Cottonwood AZ 86326-0999. Fax (520)634-3145. E-mail: mona@sedona.net. Attendance: 225.

SOUTHWEST CHRISTIAN WRITERS ASSN. SEMINAR. Hesperus, September 18, 1999. Contact: Kathy Cordell, PO Box 1008, Flora Vista NM 87415. (505)334-0617. E-mail: acampbell@cyberport.com (Anne Campbell, vice pres). Attendance: 30.

SOUTHWEST WRITERS WORKSHOP. Albuquerque, late summer 1999 (tentative). Contact: Carol Bruce-Fritz, 1338 Wyoming Blvd. NE, Ste. B, Albuquerque NM 87112-5067. (505)293-0303. Fax (505)237-2665. E-mail: SWriters@aol.com. Attendance: 500.

WRITERS' CONFERENCE AT SANTA FE. Santa Fe, February 12-14, 1999. Speaker: John Nichols. Contact: Program Coordinator, Dept. of Continuing Education, Santa Fe Community College, Box 4187, Santa Fe NM

87502-4187. (505)428-1251or (505)428-1675. Fax (505)428-1302. E-mail: rsimpson@santa-fe.cc.nrn.us. Website: http://www.santa-fe.cc.nrn.us. Attendance: 100-120.

NEW YORK
AMERICAN CHRISTIAN WRITERS BUFFALO CONFERENCE. June 25-26, 1999. Contact: Reg A. Forder, Box 110390, Nashville TN 37222. 1-800-21-WRITE. Attendance: 35-50.

NORTH CAROLINA
AMERICAN CHRISTIAN WRITERS CHARLOTTE CONFERENCE. Wyndam Garden Hotel, February 12-13, 1999. Contact: Reg Forder, Box 110390, Nashville TN 37222. 1-800-21-WRITE. Attendance: 35-50.
*ASSOCIATED CHURCH PRESS 1999 ANNUAL CONVENTION. Hendersonville; April 1999. Contact: John Stapert, The Associated Church Press, PO Box 30215, Phoenix AZ 85046-0215. E-mail: John_Stapert@Ecunet.org. Workshops, individual critique, meet editors, discuss potential assignments, etc.

OHIO
AMERICAN CHRISTIAN WRITERS AKRON CONFERENCE. Holiday Inn, June 11-12, 1999. Contact: Reg Forder, Box 110390, Nashville TN 37222. 1-800-21-WRITE. Attendance: 35-50.
AMERICAN CHRISTIAN WRITERS COLUMBUS CONFERENCE. Radisson Hotel, May 21-22, 1999. Hosted by Columbus Christian Writers Assn./Pat Zell, (937)593-9207. Contact: Reg Forder, Box 110390, Nashville TN 37222. 1-800-21-WRITE. Attendance: 35-50.
#CINCINNATI BIBLE COLLEGE CHRISTIAN WRITERS WORKSHOP. Cincinnati, September 1999. Contact: Dr. Ward Patterson, 2700 Glenway Ave., Cincinnati OH 45211. (513)244-8445. Fax (513)244-8140. E-mail: ward.patterson@cincybible.edu. Website: http://www.cincybible.edu/cw/main.htm. Attendance: 80-100.
*COLUMBUS CHRISTIAN WRITERS CONFERENCE. Columbus, fall 1999 (tentative). Contact: Brenda Custodio, 3069 Bocastle Ct., Reynoldsburg OH 43068. (614)861-1011. Attendance: 60.
*HEIGHTS WRITERS CONFERENCE. Beechwood, May 1,1999 (always 1st Saturday of May). Contact: Lavern Hall, Writer's World Press, PO Box 24684, Cleveland OH 44124-0684. (216)481-1974.
NORTHWEST OHIO CHRISTIAN WRITERS SEMINAR. Toledo; September 18, 1999. Contact: Linda Tippett, 4221 Woodmont Rd., Toledo OH 43613. (419)475-9169. E-mail: ANDAMIJA@juno.com. Attendance: 75-100.
SET FORTH CHRISTIAN WRITERS GUILD SEMINAR. North Central OH/Mansfield area; Spring 1999. Contact: Donna Caudill, 836 Delph Ave., Mansfield OH 44906. (419)747-1755.
*STATELINE CHRISTIAN WRITER'S CLUB PEOPLE IN PRINT SEMINAR. Celina, October 1999. Contact: Shirley Knox, 54106 Club Island Rd., Celina OH 45822. (419)268-2040.

WEST-DAYTON CHRISTIAN WRITERS CONFERENCE. Englewood; July 1999. Speaker: Donna Goodrich. Contact: Tina V. Toles, PO Box 251, Englewood OH 45322-2049. Phone/fax (937)832-0541. E-mail: Poet11 @ix.netcom.com. Website: http://activedayton.com/DaytonChristian Writers.

OKLAHOMA

AMERICAN CHRISTIAN WRITERS OKLAHOMA CITY CONFERENCE. Fifth Season Hotel, April 23-24, 1999. Contact: Reg Forder, Box 110390, Nashville TN 37222. 1-800-21-WRITE. Attendance: 35-50.

*WRITING WORKSHOPS. Various locations and dates. Contact: Kathryn Fanning, PO Box 18472, Oklahoma City OK 73154-0472.

OREGON

+HEART TALK. A workshop for women beginning to write for publication. Portland/Western Seminary, March 6, 1999; beginners March 11, 1999. Speakers: Jane Kirkpatrick, Marilyn McAuley, Melody Carlson, Deborah Hedstrom. Contact: Beverly Hislop, Women's Center for Ministry, Western Seminary, 5511 SE Hawthorne Blvd., Portland OR 97215. (503)233-8561. Fax (503)239-416. E-mail: bwhislop@westernseminary.edu. Website: http://www.westernseminary.edu. Attendance: 150+.

OREGON CHRISTIAN WRITERS COACHING CONFERENCE. Salem, June 28-July 1, 1999. Contact: Duane Young, 3619 NE 91st Ave., Portland OR 97220. (503)252-4433. Website: http://cs.georgefox.edu/rzempel/ocw. Attendance: 125-150.

PENNSYLVANIA

GREATER PHILADELPHIA CHRISTIAN WRITERS' CONFERENCE. Dresher (N. of Philadelphia), April 15-17, 1999. Especially encourages African-American writers. Contact: Marlene Bagnull, 316 Blanchard Rd., Drexel Hill PA 19026-3507. Phone/fax (610)626-6833. E-mail: mbagnull@aol. com. Website: http://nancepub.com/cwf/cwf/. Attendance: 270.

MONTROSE CHRISTIAN WRITERS CONFERENCE. Montrose, July 25-30, 1999. Speakers: Ethel Herr, Roger Palms. Barbara Hibschman, Pat Timbrook. Contact: Patti Souder, c/o Montrose Bible Conference, 5 Locust St., Montrose PA 18801-1112. (800)598-5030. (717)278-1001. Fax (717)278-3061. E-mail: mbc@epix.net. Includes advanced track. Attendance: 75.

ST. DAVIDS CHRISTIAN WRITERS' CONFERENCE. Geneva College/Beaver Falls, near Pittsburgh, June 20-25, 1999. Offers advanced track. Susan Swan, director. Contact: Audrey Stallsmith, registrar, 87 Pines Rd. E., Hadley PA 16130-1019. (724)253-2738. Fax (724)946-3689. E-mail: audstall@nauticom.net. Attendance: 100.

WEST BRANCH CHRISTIAN WRITERS SEMINAR. Williamsport, no date set for 1999. Contact: Barbara Sutryn, RR 3 Box 399, Montoursville PA 17754-9546. (717)322-1984. E-mail: bars@csrlink.net.

TEXAS

AMERICAN CHRISTIAN WRITERS AUSTIN CONFERENCE. Chariot Inn, February 26-27, 1999. Contact: Reg Forder, Box 110390, Nashville TN 37222. 1-800-21-WRITE. Attendance: 35-50.

AMERICAN CHRISTIAN WRITERS DALLAS CONFERENCE. Holiday Inn, September 10-11, 1999. Contact: Reg Forder, Box 110390, Nashville TN 37222. 1-800-21-WRITE. Attendance: 35-50.

AMERICAN CHRISTIAN WRITERS HOUSTON CONFERENCE. September 17-18, 1999. Contact: Reg A. Forder, Box 110390, Nashville TN 37222. 1-800-21-WRITE. Attendance: 35-50.

+AUSTIN CHRISTIAN WRITERS' SEMINAR. February 26-27, 1999. Contact: Lin Harris, 8409 Farm Road 1625, Austin TX 78747-9624. (512)243-2305. Fax (512)243-2317. E-mail: linjer@ix.netcom.com. Website: http://www2.netcom.com/linjer/acwg.html.

GREENVILLE CHRISTIAN WRITERS' CONFERENCE. Greenville; October 2, 1999. Contact: Jim Pence, 1551 Hunt Co. Rd. 4109, Campbell TX 75422-1201. (903)450-4944. E-mail: jhpence@yahoo.com. Attendance: 35.

INSPIRATIONAL WRITERS ALIVE!/AMARILLO SEMINAR. April 10, 1999. Speaker: Holly G. Miller. Contact: Helen Luecke, 2921 S. Dallas, Amarillo TX 79103-6713. (806)376-9671.

TEXAS CHRISTIAN WRITERS FORUM. Houston; August 5, 2000 (first Saturday in August in even numbered years). Contact: Maxine E. Holder, Rt. 4 Box 81-H, Rusk TX 75785-9410. (903)795-3986. Attendance: 70.

*YWAM HANDS-ON WRITERS TRAINING WORKSHOPS. Lindale; various dates. Contact: Pamela Warren, PO Box 1380, Lindale TX 75771-1380. (903)882-5591x288. Fax (903)882-5710. E-mail: 104564.2036@compuserve.com. Send SASE for list of workshops.

VIRGINIA

HELP! I'M A CHRISTIAN WRITER OR I'D LIKE TO BE ONE. Held in various locations by invitation. Contact: Betty B. Robertson, PO Box 12624, Roanoke VA 24027-2624. Phone/fax:(540)342-7511. E-mail: ccmbbR@juno.com.

NORTHERN VIRGINIA CHRISTIAN WRITERS CONFERENCE. Burke; March 13, 1999; March 11, 2000. Speakers for 1999: Dan Wooding, Judith Couchman, Roger Palms, Holly Miller, James Scott Bell. Contact: Jennifer Ferranti, dir., PO Box 12390, Burke VA 22009. Phone/fax (703)503-5366. E-mail: JenniferF@compuserve.com. Attendance: 150.

PRESBYTERIAN WRITER'S GUILD WORKSHOP. No information on 1999 at this time. Contact: Jack Purdy, director, 209 Rendon Rd., Santa Fe NM 87501. (505)988-9254.

WASHINGTON

AMERICAN CHRISTIAN WRITERS SEATTLE CONFERENCE. March 19-20, 1999. Contact: Reg Forder, Box 110390, Nashville TN 37222. 1-800-21-WRITE. Attendance: 35-50.

*SDA CAMP MEETING WRITING CLASS. Auburn, June 1999. Open to non-Adventists; free. Contact: Marian Forschler, PO Box 58785, Renton WA 98058-1785. (425)235-1435. Fax (425)204-2070. Attendance: 50.

YAKIMA WRITERS WORKSHOP. Yakima, may not be held in 1999. Contact: Helen Heavirland, PO Box 146, College Place WA 99324. Phone/fax (541)938-3838. E-mail: hlh@bmi.net. Attendance: 35.

SEATTLE PACIFIC CHRISTIAN WRITERS CONFERENCE. Seattle. Nothing scheduled at this time. Contact: Linda Wagner, Humanities Dept., Seattle Pacific University, Seattle WA 98119. (206)281-2000.

WENATCHEE CHRISTIAN WRITERS MINI-SEMINAR. Wenatchee, September 18 or 25, 1999. Contact: Shirley Pease, 1818 Skyline Dr. #31, Wenatchee WA 98801-2302. (509)662-8392. E-mail: mocrane@aol.com. Attendance: 35-40.

#WRITERS HELPING WRITERS. Spokane; March 18-20, 1999. This is not a conference, but a booth offering manuscript evaluation and help to writers during the annual Christian Workers Conference. Contact: Pat Pfeiffer, PO Box 104, Otis Orchards WA 97027-0140. (509)927-9460. Fax (509)922-7030. Attendance: 20-35.

WRITER'S WEEKEND AT THE BEACH. Ocean Park, February/March 1999. Contact: Pat Rushford, 3600 Edgewood Dr., Vancouver WA 98661. (206)695-2263 or Birdie Etchison, PO Box 877, Ocean Park WA 98640. (360)665-6576. E-mail: BLEtchison@aol.com. Attendance: Limited to 45-50.

WISCONSIN

GREEN LAKE CHRISTIAN WRITER'S CONFERENCE. Green Lake, July 3-10, 1999. Contact: Program Dept., American Baptist Assembly, W2511 State Hwy 23, Green Lake WI 54941-9300. (800)558-8898 or (920)294-7364. Fax (920)294-3848. E-mail for information: glcc@worldnet.att.net. Website: http://www.abc-usa.org. Attendance: 80. Also provides Christian Writer's Weeks when you can stay at the conference center for writing time; January 10-15, March 7-12, November 7-12.

*TIMBER-LEE CHRISTIAN WRITER'S CONFERENCE. Timber-Lee Christian Center/East Troy, February or April 1999. Contact: Mary Kay Meeker, N8705 Scout Rd., East Troy WI 53120. (414)642-7345. Attendance: 30-40.

WORD & PEN CHRISTIAN WRITERS CONFERENCE. Oshkosh, next conference 2000. Contact: Beth A. Ziarnik, 1963 Indian Point Rd., Oshkosh WI 54901. (920)235-0664. Attendance: 75.

CANADA

*ALBERTA CHRISTIAN WRITERS' SEMINARS. Sponsored by Alberta Christian Writers Fellowship—CanadaWide. Last week-end of April (Rocky Mountain College, Calgary AB) & last Friday/Saturday of September 1999 (King's University College in Edmonton AB). Contact: Elsie Montgomery, pres., 34 - 1130 Falconer Rd., Edmonton AB T6R 2J6, Canada. (403)988-5622. Fax (403)430-0139.

GOD USES INK WRITERS CONFERENCE/ON. Guelph, Ontario; June 17-19, 1999. Contact: Marianne Meed Ward, c/o Faith Today, M.I.P. Box 3745, Markham ON L3R 0Y4 Canada. (905)479-6071x245. Fax (905)479-4742. E-mail: ft@efc-canada.com. Website: http://www.efc-canada.com. Attendance: 100.

WORDPOWER. Clearbrook, schedule for 1999 unknown. Contact: Susan Brandt, MB Herald, 3-169 Riverton Ave., Winnipeg MB R2L 2E5 Canada. (204)669-6575. Fax (204)654-1865. E-mail: mbherald@cdnmbconf.ca. Offers workshops for advanced and young writers. Attendance: 100-150.

FOREIGN COUNTRIES

ASSOCIATION OF CHRISTIAN WRITERS SEMINARS. London, England; February 10 & June 3, 1999. Speakers: Fay Sampson, Geoffrey Daniel, Stewart Henderson. Contact: Warren Crawford, 73 Lodge Hill Rd., Farnham, Surrey, UK GU10 3RB. Phone/fax: +44 (0)1252 715746. Fax +44 (0)1252 715746. E-mail: christian-writers@dial.pipex.com. Website: http://dspace.pipex.com/christian-writers. Attendance 60+.

ASSOCIATION OF CHRISTIAN WRITERS WEEKEND. Hothorpe Hall, Leicestershire, England. Contact: Warren Crawford, 73 Lodge Hill Rd., Farnham, Surrey, UK GU10 3RB. Phone/fax: +44 (0)1252 715746. Fax +44 (0)1252 715746. E-mail: christian-writers@dial.pipex.com. Website: http://dspace.pipex.com/christian-writers. Next weekend is July 13-15, 2000. Attendance 90.

CHRISTIAN COMICS TRAINING COURSES. For information on these conferences held around the world, visit the ROX35Media, Inc. Website at: http://www.ROX35Media.org. E-mail: ROX35Media@xc.org. Hong Kong, March 11-14, 1999; Manila, March 19-20, 1999.

LITT-WORLD 2000. Hoddesdon, Hertfordshire, England; October 2000. Contact: John D. Maust, 120 N. Bloomingdale Rd., Bloomingdale IL 60108. (630)893-1977. Fax (630)893-1141. E-mail: MAI_LittWorld@compuserve.com. Attendance 140.

WRITERS' SUMMER SCHOOL. Swanwick, Derbyshire, England; August 14-20,1999. Contact: Brenda Courtie, The New Vicarage, Parsons St., Woodford Halse, Daventry, Northants, NN11 3RE, England, United Kingdom. Phone/fax: +44-7050-630949. E-mail: bcourtie@aol.com. Website: http://dspace.dial.pipex.com/royder. A secular conference attended by many Christians. Attendance: 300-350.

+WRITERS' TOUR OF ENGLAND AND IRELAND. England, Ireland and you decide where else; April 2002. For details, send an SASE to: Rowena Hughes, PO Box 514, Troutdale OR 97060-0514. (503)491-8067. E-mail: 101461,2252@compuserve.com. If very interested, send three .32 stamps (no envelope) for a full planning packet.

CONFERENCES THAT CHANGE LOCATIONS

AMERICAN CHRISTIAN WRITERS CONFERENCES. Various dates and locations (see individual states where held). Also sponsors an annual Caribbean cruise, November 14-21, 1999. Contact: Reg A. Forder, Box 110390, Nashville TN 37222. 1-800-21-WRITE.

*ASSOCIATED CHURCH PRESS 1999 ANNUAL CONVENTION. Hendersonville, North Carolina, April 1999. Contact: Director, The Associated Church Press, PO Box 30215, Phoenix AZ 85046-0215. Workshops, individual critique, meet editors, discuss potential assignments, etc.

CATHOLIC PRESS ASSOCIATION ANNUAL CONVENTION. Chicago, June 1999. Contact: Owen McGovern, exec. dir., 3555 Veterans Memorial Hwy Ste. O, Ronkonkoma NY 11779-7636. (516)471-4730. Fax (516)471-4804. E-mail: CathJourn@aol.com. For media professionals. Attendance: 400.

CHRISTIAN BOOKSELLERS ASSN. CONVENTION. (held in a different location each year), July 10-15, 1999, Orlando FL; July 8-13, 2000, New Orleans LA. Contact: CBA, Box 200, Colorado Springs CO 80901. (719)576-7880. Entrance badges available through book publishers.

CHRISTIAN LEADERS AND SPEAKERS SEMINARS (The CLASSeminar). Various dates & locations across the country. For anyone who wants to improve their communication skills for either the spoken or written word, for professional or personal reasons. Speakers: Florence Littauer and Marita Littauer. Contact: Marita Littauer, PO Box 66810, Albuquerque NM 87193. (800)433-6633. (505)899-4283. Fax (505)899-9282. E-mail: classrvcs@aol.com. Website: http://www.classervices.com. Attendance: 100.

EVANGELICAL PRESS ASSOCIATION CONVENTION. Orlando, Florida; May 2-5,1999 (held in different location each year); Nashville TN in May 2000. Sheraton World Resort. Contact: Ron Wilson, dir., 314 Dover Rd., Charlottesville VA 22901. (804)973-5941. Fax (804)973-2710. E-mail: 74473.272@compuserve.com. Attendance: 300-400. Annual convention; freelance communicators welcome.

"WRITE HIS ANSWER" SEMINARS. Various locations around U.S.; dates throughout the year; choice of article writing or books (includes self-publishing). Contact: Marlene Bagnull, 316 Blanchard Rd., Drexel Hill PA 19026-3507. Phone/fax (610)626-6833. E-mail: mbagnull@aol.com. Website: http://nancepub.com/cwf/wha/. Attendance: 30-100. One and two-day seminars by the author of *Write His Answer—Encouragement for Christian Writers.*

THE WRITING ACADEMY SEMINAR. Sponsors year-round correspondence writing program and annual seminar in various locations. 1999 seminar is in St. Louis MO, August 5-9. Contact: Nancy Remmert, (314)524-3718. E-mail: nremm10335@aol.com. Website: http://www.wams.org. Membership (75) open.

AREA CHRISTIAN WRITERS' CLUBS, FELLOWSHIP GROUPS, AND CRITIQUE GROUPS

(*) An asterisk before a listing means the information was not verified or updated by the group leader.

(+) A plus sign before a listing indicates a new listing.

ALABAMA

*CHRISTIAN FREELANCERS. Tuscaloosa. Contact: Joanne Sloan, 3230 Mystic Lake Way, Northport AL 35476. (205)333-8603. Fax (205)339-4528. Membership (25) open.

ARIZONA

FOUNTAIN HILLS CHRISTIAN WRITERS. Contact: Nelia Greer, 15929 E. Cholla Dr., Fountain Hills AZ 85268. (602)837-2913. Membership (25) open.

MESA CHRISTIAN WRITERS CLUB. Contact: Donna Goodrich, 648 S. Pima St., Mesa AZ 85210. (602)962-6694. Membership (15-20) open.

*PHOENIX CHRISTIAN WRITERS' FELLOWSHIP. Contact: Victor J. Kelly Sr., 2135 W. Cactus Wren Dr., Phoenix AZ 85021. (602)864-1390. Membership (20) open.

*SOUTH-EASTERN ARIZONA CHRISTIAN WRITERS GROUP. Benson. Contact: Bea Carlton, HCR 1 Box 153C, Willcox AZ 85643. (520)384-9232. Membership (18) open. Sponsoring a September 1999 seminar.

TEMPE CHRISTIAN WRITERS CLUB. Contact: Kitty Bucholtz, PO Box 68114, Phoenix AZ 85082-8114. (602)267-8529. Fax (602)273-1314. E-mail: jkbuch@primenet.com. Website: http://www.primenet.com/jkbuch. Membership (30) open.

ARKANSAS

+ROGERS AREA CHRISTIAN WRITERS GUILD. Contact: Brian Stiles, PO Box 1115, Rogers AR 72757-1115. (501)631-9431. Monthly interactive workshops. Rogers Public Library. Membership (6) open.

CALIFORNIA

CASTRO VALLEY CHRISTIAN WRITERS GROUP. Contact: Pastor Jon Drury, 19300 Redwood Rd., Castro Valley CA 94546-3465. (510)886-6300. Fax (510)581-5022. E-mail: jond@redwoodchapel.org. Membership (10-20) open. Sponsoring a Christian Writers Seminar, February 26-27, 1999.

*CEHUC SPANISH CHRISTIAN WRITERS GROUP. El Cajon. Contact: Magdalena Latorre, 9802 Quail Canyon Rd., El Cajon CA 92021-6000. Phone/fax (619)390-3747. Fax (619)561-6172. Membership (34) open.

Sponsors a contest open to non-members. Planning a Spanish conference for February 1999 in Tijuana, Mexico.

*CHILDREN'S WRITERS GROUP. Lake Forest. Contact: Eileen Reinoehl, 24902 Winterwood Dr., Lake Forest CA 92630. (949)859-6294. For serious children's writers.

*CHRISTIAN WRITERS FELLOWSHIP OF ORANGE COUNTY. Santa Ana. Contact: Carol Fitzpatrick, PO Box 538, Lake Forest CA 92630. (949)768-3891. Membership (100) open. Monthly newsletter. Sponsors critique groups throughout southern California (contact critique group coordinator, Jessica Shaver, 186 E. Cameron Pl., Long Beach CA 90807-3851, (562)595-4162). Sponsors two annual Writers' Days: April and October 1999.

DIABLO VALLEY CHRISTIAN WRITERS GROUP. Danville. Contact: Marcy Weydemuller, 3623 Corte Segundo, Concord CA 94519. (925)676-6555. Fax (925)681-1771. E-mail: mcyweyde@hotcoco.infi.net. Membership (6-8) open.

HAYWARD AREA WRITERS GROUP. Castro Valley. Contact: Launa Herrmann, 21555 Eden Canyon Rd., Castro Valley CA 94552-9721. (510)889-7564. Fax (510)583-1841. E-mail: wordroom@aol.com. Membership (10) open.

HIGH DESERT CHRISTIAN WRITERS GUILD. Throughout Antelope Valley. Contact: Ellen Bergh, 3600 Brabham Ave., Rosamond CA 93560-6891. (805)256-1266. E-mail: mastermedia@hughes.net. Membership (15) open.

LODI WRITERS ASSOCIATION. (General membership, not just Christian). Contact: Dee Porter, PO Box 1863, Lodi CA 95241. Phone/fax (209)334-0603. E-mail: crcomm@lodinet.com. Membership (70) open. Sponsors one-day workshop, usually in July.

*NATIONAL WRITER'S ASSN./SOUTHERN CALIFORNIA CHAPTER. Fountain Valley. Liaison: Shirl Thomas, 9379 Tanager Ave., Fountain Valley CA 92708-6557. (714)968-5726. Membership (142) open. Secular group/ many Christians.

SACRAMENTO CHRISTIAN WRITERS. Contact: Patricia Sedgwick, 3031 Tilden Dr., Roseville CA 95661. (916)773-0693. E-mail: PininiFarm@aol.com. Website: http://home.att/Rossbach3. Membership (25) open.

SAN DIEGO COUNTY CHRISTIAN WRITERS' GUILD. Contact: Robert Gillespie, 17041 Palacio Pl., San Diego CA 92027. (619)487-7929. Fax (619)673-3921. E-mail: riters@adnc.com. Membership (250+) open. Sponsors fall seminar and March awards banquet. Contest for members.

COLORADO
*CHRISTIAN WRITERS OF SOUTHERN COLORADO. Colorado Springs. Contact: Sue Sutherland or Sharon McAllister, 4605 Splendid Cir. S., Colorado Springs CO 80917. (719)591-0370. Membership (8) open.

CHRISTIAN WRITERS IN TOUCH. Denver. Contact: Chris Adams, PO Box 40971, Denver CO 80204-0971. (303)595-5857. Membership (6) open.

DELAWARE

DELMARVA CHRISTIAN WRITERS' FELLOWSHIP. Georgetown. Contact: Candy Abbott, PO Box 777, Georgetown DE 19947-0777. (302)856-6649. Fax (302)856-7742. E-mail: dabbott@dmv.com. Membership (12) open.

FLORIDA

ADVENTURES IN CHRISTIAN WRITING. Orlando. Contact: Mary F. Shaw, 350 E. Jackson St. #811, Orlando FL 32801. (407)841-4866. Membership (20) open.

CHRISTIAN WRITERS CRITIQUE GROUP. Miami Area. Contact: Eva Sartorio at (305)234-7378 or Karen Whiting at (305)388-8656. E-mail: whiting@icanect.net or eva@cs.miami.edu. Membership (7-12) open.

FAMU CHRISTIAN WRITERS GUILD. Tallahassee. Contact: Rev. Larry Hunt, BSM Director, Baptist Student Ministries Center, Florida A&M University, Tallahassee FL 32307. (850)224-7151. E-mail: ebonyink@hotmail.com. Ebony Thomas, 1999 Chairperson. Membership (15+) open.

SUNCOAST CHRISTIAN WRITERS GROUP. Largo. Contact: Elaine Creasman, 13014 - 106th Ave. N., Largo FL 34644-5602. (727)595-8963. Fax (727)398-5730. E-mail: emcreasman@aol.com. Membership (20) open.

TITUSVILLE CHRISTIAN WRITERS' FELLOWSHIP. Contact: Nancy Otto Boffo, 2625 Riviera Dr., Titusville FL 32780-5144. (407)267-7604. Membership (10) open.

WRITING STRATEGIES CRITIQUESHOP. Daytona Beach. Meets monthly (10X). Sponsors seminars the 2nd Tuesday of each month (except July & August) for working authors who have completed one course of Writing Strategies (see conference listing). Speakers: Rosemary Upton & Kistler London. Send SASE for brochure. Contact: Rosemary J. Upton, 2712 S. Peninsula Dr., Daytona Beach FL 32118. Phone/fax (904)322-1111. E-mail: romy14@juno.com. Membership (20) open.

GEORGIA

LAMBLIGHTER'S CRITIQUE GROUP. Lilburn/Snellville. Contact: Cisi Morrow-Smith, 1056 Sawgrass Ct., Lilburn GA 30047-1864. (770)978-9129. Membership (4-6) open.

IDAHO

*INTERNATIONAL NETWORK OF COMMUNICATORS & THE ARTS. Couer d Alene. Contact: Sheri Stone, Box 1754, Post Falls ID 83854-1754. Phone/fax (208)667-9730. Membership (25) open. Sponsors a contest and an annual fall seminar.

ILLINOIS

*INTERNATIONAL BLACK WRITERS. Chicago & New York. Contact: Mable Terrell, PO Box 1030, Chicago IL 60690-1030. (312)409-2292. Membership (2,000) open. Sponsors a contest open to nonmembers. Conference in Chicago, June 1999.

JUVENILE FORUM. Moline. Contact: David R. Collins, 3403 45th St., Moline IL 61265-6608. (309)762-8985. Membership (12) open to those writing for children or youth.

INDIANA

BLOOMINGTON AREA CHRISTIAN WRITERS. Bloomington & Ellettsville. Contact: Kathi Adams, 9576 W. St. Rd. 48, Bloomington IN 47404-9737. (812)876-8265. E-mail: tkjadams@bluemarble.net. Membership (12) open.

EVANSVILLE-AREA CHRISTIAN WRITERS' FELLOWSHIP. Contact: Jay Beuoy, 450 Albert St., Evansville IN 47720. (812)426-1539. E-mail: jbevoy@evansville.net. Membership (21) open.

FORT WAYNE CHRISTIAN WRITERS CLUB. Fort Wayne. Contact: Linda R. Wade, 739 W. Fourth St., Fort Wayne IN 46808-2613. (219)422-2772. E-mail: linda_wade@juno.com. Membership (32) open. Also publishes a bimonthly newsletter called Fort and Field (editor: Phyllis Posey, PO Box 127, Hicksville OH 43526).

OPEN DOOR CHRISTIAN WRITERS. Westport. Contact: Janet Teitsort, PO Box 129, Westport IN 47283-0129. Phone/fax (812)591-2210. E-mail: teitsort@hsonline.net. Membership (20) open.

IOWA

*CEDAR RAPIDS CHRISTIAN WRITER'S CRITIQUE GROUP. Contact: Billie Parr, 2222 - 1st Ave. NE, Cedar Rapids IA 52402. (319)363-0039. Membership (12) open. A day and a night group.

RIVER CITY WRITERS. Council Bluffs. Contact: Dee Barrett, 16 Susan Lane, Council Bluffs IA 51503. (712)322-7692. Fax (712)329-9615. E-mail: barrett@mitec.net. Membership (30) open.

SIOUXLAND CHRISTIAN WRITERS. Sioux City. Contact: William B. Tucker, 4881 Bradford Ln., Sioux City IA 51106-9519. (712)943-1412. E-mail: wbt@willinet.net. Membership (8) open.

KANSAS

KANSAS CITY CHRISTIAN WRITERS' NETWORK. Kansas City Metro area. Contact: Teresa Vining, 1438 N Lucy Montgomery Way, Olathe KS 66061-6706. Phone/fax: (913)764-4610. E-mail: KCCWN@aol.com. Membership (200) open. Sponsors monthly meetings, retreats, conferences and workshops. Fall conference, October 1999.

PITTSBURG CHRISTIAN WRITERS FELLOWSHIP. Pittsburg. Contact: LeAnn Campbell, 267 SW 1st Ln., Lamar MO 6475-92339. (417)682-2713. E-mail: campbell@talleytech.com. Membership (15) open. Sponsors an occasional seminar; next one April 10, 1999.

KENTUCKY

JACKSON CHRISTIAN WRITERS' CLUB. Vancleve/Kentucky Mt. Bible College. Contact: Donna J. Woodring, Box 10, Vancleve KY 41385-0010. (606)666-5000. E-mail: donnaw@kmbc.edu. Membership (8) open.

LOUISIANA

SCRIBES OF NEW ORLEANS. Contact: Jack Cunningham, PO Box 55601, Metairie LA 70055-5601. (504)837-4397. E-mail: 72440.1623@compuserve. com. Membership (10) not open.

MAINE

MAINE FELLOWSHIP OF CHRISTIAN WRITERS. China. Contact: Vicki Schad, RR 1 Box 540, N. Vassalboro ME 04962-9709. (207)923-3956. E-mail: jvschad@larck.net. Website: http://www.chinalake.net. Membership (15) open. Sponsors contest open to non-members. Conference, August 12-14, 1999.

MARYLAND

*ANNAPOLIS FELLOWSHIP OF CHRISTIAN WRITERS. Annapolis. Contact: Mark Littleton, 5350 Eliot's Oak Rd., Columbia MD 21044. Phone/Fax (410)995-0831 or Jeri Sweany (410)267-0924. E-mail: MarkLitt@aol.com. Membership (15-20) open. Sponsors occasional seminars.

MASSACHUSETTS

WESTERN MASSACHUSETTS CHRISTIAN WRITERS FELLOWSHIP. Springfield. Contact: Barbara A. Robidoux, 127 Gelinas Dr., Chicopee MA 01020-4813. (413)592-4386. Fax 594-8375. Membership (50) open. Monthly newsletter.

MINNESOTA

MINNESOTA CHRISTIAN WRITERS GUILD. Minneapolis. Contact: Jane Kise, 5504 Grove St., Edina MN 55436. (612)926-4343. E-mail: jagkise@aol.com. Membership (125) open. Sponsors a contest (open to non-members) and an annual spring seminar in March.

MISSOURI

CHRISTIAN WRITERS WORKSHOP. St. Louis. Contact: Ruth McDaniel, 15233 Country Ridge Dr., Chesterfield MO 63017-7432. (314)532-7584. Membership (25) open.

GREATER ST. LOUIS CHRISTIAN WRITERS. This group is no longer meeting, but contact person for writers in the area is: Lila Shelburne, 707 Gran Lin Dr., St. Charles MO 63303-6025. (314)441-2131. Fax (314)441-2452. E-mail: lila@anet-stl.com.

KANSAS CITY CHRISTIAN WRITERS' NETWORK. Kansas City Metro area. Contact: Teresa Vining, 1438 N Lucy Montgomery Way, Olathe KS 66061-6706. Phone/fax: (913)764-4610. E-mail: KCCWN@aol.com. Membership (200) open. Sponsors monthly meetings, retreats, conferences and workshops. Fall conference, October 1999.

NORTHLAND CHRISTIAN WRITERS. Kansas City. Contact: Margaret Owen, 207 NW 67th St., Gladstone MO 64118. (816)436-5240. E-mail: MadgeO@aol.com. Membership (10) open.

*SPRINGFIELD CHRISTIAN WRITERS CLUB. Contact: Owen Wilkie, 4909 Old Wire Rd., Brookline MO 65619-9655. (417)882-5185. Fax (417)862-4382. Membership (7) open.

MONTANA
MONTANA CHRISTIAN WRITERS. Helena. Contact: Lori Soloman, 659 N. Warren, Helena MT 59601. (406)443-8528. E-mail: Lsolomon_mt@ hotmail.com.

NEBRASKA
*MY THOUGHTS EXACTLY WRITERS GROUP. Fremont. Contact: Cheryl Paden, 1959 E. 10th St., Fremont NE 68025. (402)727-6508. Membership (4) open. Periodically sponsors a writers' retreat, April 1999.
WRITERS IN THE BIG SKY. Helena. Contact: Lenore Puhek, 1215 Hudson, Helena MT 59601. (406)443-2552. Membership (10) open as space allows.

NEW HAMPSHIRE
LIVING WORD WRITERS FELLOWSHIP. West Lebanon. Contact: James A. Blaine, 80 1/2 Mascoma St., Lebanon NH 03766-2646. (603)448-4609. Membership (20) open.
WORDSMITHS' CHRISTIAN WRITERS' FELLOWSHIP. Nashua. Contact: Cynthia Vlatas, 5 Jeremy Ln., Hudson NH 03051. (603)882-2851. E-mail: sasacindy@aol.com. Website: http://members.aol.com/nh4jesus/ wrd smith.htm. Membership (32) open. Sponsors occasional workshop.

NEW JERSEY
*CENTRAL JERSEY CHRISTIAN WRITERS' FELLOWSHIP. Somerset. Contact: Catherine J. Barrier, 13 Oliver St., Somerset NJ 08873-2142. (732)545-5168. Membership open. New group. Morning and evening meetings.
NEW JERSEY SOCIETY OF CHRISTIAN WRITERS. Millville. Contact: Dr. Mary Ann Diorio, PO Box 405, Millville, NJ 08332-0405. (609)327-1231. Fax (609)327-0291. madiorio@aol.com. Website: http://daystarministries. com/njscw.html. Meets monthly at the Millville Public Library. Membership open.

NEW MEXICO
SOUTHWEST CHRISTIAN WRITERS ASSOCIATION. Farmington. Contact: Patti Cordell, #74 RD 3535, Flora Vista NM 87415. (505)334-2258. Membership (14) open. Sponsors annual one-day seminar the third Saturday in September in Hesperus CO.
SOUTHWEST WRITERS WORKSHOP. Albuquerque. Contact: Carol Bruce-Fritz, 1338 Wyoming Blvd. NE, Ste. B, Albuquerque NM 87112-5067. (505)293-0303. Fax (505)237-2665. swriters@aol.com. Membership (1,200) open. Sponsors a contest (open to non-members)and a conference in Albuquerque, late summer 1999.

NEW YORK

BROOKLYN WRITER'S CLUB. Contact: Ann Dellarocco, PO Box 184, Bath Beach Station, Brooklyn NY 11214-0184. (718)837-3484. Membership (500+) open.

*INTERNATIONAL BLACK WRITERS. New York & Chicago. Contact: Mable Terrell, PO Box 1030, Chicago IL 60690-1030. (312)409-2292. Membership (2,000) open. Sponsors a contest open to nonmembers. Conference in Chicago, June 1999.

NEW YORK CHRISTIAN WRITERS GROUP. New York City. Contact: Zoe Blake, 361 Clinton Ave., #7H, Brooklyn 11238, (718)636-5547; or Marilyn Driscoll, 350 First Ave., New York NY 10010, (212)529-6087. Membership (10-20) open.

SOUTHERN TIER CHRISTIAN WRITERS' FELLOWSHIP. Binghamton/Johnson City area. Contact: Kenneth Cetton, 20 Pine St., Port Crane NY 13833-1512. (607)648-7249. E-mail: KC1933@juno.com. Membership (6) open.

NORTH CAROLINA

COVENANT WRITERS. Lincolnton. Contact: Janice Stroup, 403 S. Cedar St., Lincolnton NC 28092-3342. (704)735-8851. Membership (6) open.

OHIO

*CHRISTIAN WRITERS GUILD. Youngstown area. Contact: Susan K. Virgalitte, 240 Sawmill Run Dr., Canfield OH 44406. Phone/fax (330)533-5833. E-mail: TOVIR@aol.com. Membership (30) open.

COLUMBUS CHRISTIAN WRITERS ASSN. Contact: Pat Zell, 545 S. Madriver St., Bellefontaine OH 43311-1833. (937)593-9207. Membership (15-25) open. Co-sponsoring a writers workshop with the American Christian Writers, May 21-11, 1999.

COLUMBUS CHRISTIAN WRITERS/PATASKALA. Reynoldsburg & Pataskala. Contact: Melissa Morgan, PO Box 667, Pataskala OH 43062. (740)964-5575. E-mail: wisestewards@sprynet.com. Website: http://wise.home.ml.org/writers.htm. Membership (6-20) open.

DAYTON CHRISTIAN SCRIBES. Kettering. Contact: Lois Pecce (secretary), Box 41613, Dayton OH 45441-0613. (937)433-6470. Fax (937)435-2175. Membership (35) open.

GREATER CINCINNATI CHRISTIAN WRITERS' FELLOWSHIP. Contact: Teresa Cleary, 895 Garnoa St., Cincinnati OH 45231-2618. Phone/fax (513)521-1913. E-mail: tcwriter@aol.com. Membership (25) open. Dues $15.

NORTHWESTERN OHIO CHRISTIAN WRITERS. Bowling Green. Contact: Linda R. Tippett, 4221 Woodmont Rd., Toledo OH 43613. (419)475-9169. E-mail: ANDAMIJA@juno.com. Membership (30) open. Sponsors a Saturday seminar, September 18, 1999.

*SET FORTH WRITERS GUILD. North Central OH/Mansfield area. Contact: Donna Caudill, 836 Delph Ave., Mansfield OH 44906. (419)747-1755. Membership (35) open. Planning seminar for July 1999.

STATELINE CHRISTIAN WRITER'S CLUB. Celina. Contact: Peg Dorsten, 600 Bruns Ave., Apt. 27, Celina OH 45822. (419)586-2662. Membership (24) open.

WEST-DAYTON CHRISTIAN WRITERS GUILD. Contact: Tina V. Toles, PO Box 251, Englewood OH 45322-2049. Phone/fax (937)832-0541. E-mail: Poet11@ix.netcom.com. Website: Http://activedayton.com/DaytonChristianWriters. Membership (50) open. Sponsoring a July 1999 seminar, and a contest open to non-members.

OKLAHOMA

TULSA CHRISTIAN WRITERS. Contact: Donna M. Cowan, PO Box 35625, Tulsa OK 74135. (918)665-8844. E-mail: 104676.1742@compuserve.com. Membership (50) open.

WORDWRIGHTS. Oklahoma City. Contact: Mary Murphy, 428 Brookside Dr., Guthrie OK 73044. (405)282-6170. Fax (405)282-6318. E-mail: faithpub @theshop.net. Membership (30) open. Sponsors an annual writing seminar, April 1999, in Oklahoma City; send SASE for information.

OREGON

***CHRISTIAN WRITERS SUPPORT GROUP.** Portland area. Contact: Karen Taylor, 5530 NW Osprey Pl., Portland OR 97229-1089. (503)645-4906. Membership (6) open.

WRITERS DOZEN CRITIQUE GROUP. Eugene/Springfield. Contact: Denise Carlson, 1509 D St., Springfield OR 97477-4974. (541)741-8678 E-mail: dcarlson@efn.org. Membership (11) may be open.

MILWAUKIE CHRISTIAN WRITERS GROUP. Contact: Geneva Iijima, (503)656-3632. Serious group; must write regularly. Waiting list available.

+OREGON CITY CHRISTIAN WRITERS GROUP. Contact: Geneva Iijima, (503)656-3632. Meets third Thursday of each month. Openings from time to time. Membership: 5.

OREGON CHRISTIAN SCRIBES. Portland. Contact: Ed Schwisow, (503)255-7300. Membership (12+) open. Annual conference in Yakima WA, May 1999.

OREGON CHRISTIAN WRITERS. Contact: Debbie Hedstrom, pres., 5490 - 8th Ave. SE, Salem OR 97306. (503)370-9153. Fax (503)365-1801. E-mail: dhdstrom@wbc.edu. Website: http://cs.georgefox.edu/rzempel/ocw. Attendance: Meets three times annually: February in Salem, May in Eugene, and October in Portland. All-day Saturday conferences. Membership (400) open. Sponsors annual conference, July 21-24 (Salem). Newsletter & critique groups.

OREGON CITY CHRISTIAN WRITERS GROUP. Contact: Geneva Iijima, (503)656-3632. Serious group; must write regularly. Waiting list available.

ORTHODOX AUTHOR'S ASSN. Eugene, Ashland, Forestville CA. Contact: Sarah Cowie, 25372 Eldale Dr., Eugene OR 97402. Phone/fax (541)935-6763. E-mail: eugeneoaa@aol.com. Membership (30) open. October writer's retreat in Forestville, CA.

PORTLAND CHRISTIAN WRITERS GROUP. Contact: Stan Baldwin, (503)659-2974. Serious group; must write regularly. Waiting list available.

SALEM I CHRISTIAN WRITERS GROUP. Contact: Marcia Mitchell, 4427 Rodeo Dr. NE, Salem OR 97305. (503)588-0372. Fax (03)375-8406. E-mail: 74747.1161@compuserve.com. Membership (7) open.

*SALEM II CHRISTIAN WRITERS GROUP. Contact: Diane Hopper, (503)378-7974. Membership (6) open.

SMITH ROCK CHRISTIAN WRITERS. Redmond. Contact: Toni Mackenroth, 4321 NE O'Neal Way, Redmond OR 97756. (541)548-6617. Membership (5) open.

WORDSMITHS. Gresham/Vancouver/Battle Ground/E. Portland. Contact: Susan Thogerson Maas, 27526 SE Carl St., Gresham OR 97080-8215. (503)663-7834. E-mail: STM663@aol.com. Membership (6-8) open. Christian and secular writers. Looking for writers in Gresham to start new group.

PENNSYLVANIA

*BETHEL WORDSPINNERS. Bethlehem. Contact: Wanda Dean, 4100 Birch Dr., Bethlehem PA 18017-4512. Membership (7) open. Monthly meetings and critique by mail.

*THE FIRST WORD. Sewickley. Contact: Shirley Stevens, 326 B Glaser Ave., Pittsburgh PA 15202-2910. (412)761-2618. Membership (12) open.

GREATER JOHNSTOWN CHRISTIAN WRITERS' GUILD. Contact: Betty Rosian, 108 Deerfield Ln., Johnstown PA 15905-5703. (814)255-4351. E-mail: BLRosian@aol.com. Membership (20) open.

GREATER PHILADELPHIA CHRISTIAN WRITERS' FELLOWSHIP. Broomall. Contact: Marlene Bagnull, 316 Blanchard Rd., Drexel Hill PA 19026. Phone/fax (610)626-6833. E-mail: mbagnull@aol.com. Website: http://nancepub. com/cwf/cwf/. Membership (40) open. Sponsors contest (open to non-members) and annual writers' conference (April 15-17, 1999).

INDIANA CHRISTIAN WRITERS FELLOWSHIP. Contact: Jan Woodard, 270 Sunset Dr., Indiana PA 15701. (724)465-5886. E-mail: jwoodard@wpia. net. Membership (12) open.

LANCASTER AREA CHRISTIAN WRITERS FELLOWSHIP. Contact: John Brenneman, 258 Brenneman Rd., Lancaster PA 17603-9623. (717)872-5183. Membership (8-13) open.

MONTROSE CHRISTIAN WRITERS FELLOWSHIP. Contact: Patti Souder, PO Box 159, Montrose PA 18801-1059. (717)278-4815. Membership (12) open. Holding a conference July 25-30,1999.

PUNXSUTAWNEY AREA CHRISTIAN WRITERS FELLOWSHIP. Contact: Michele T. Huey, RD 1 Box 112, Glen Campbell PA 15742-9604. (814)845-7683. Membership (12) open.

WEST BRANCH CHRISTIAN WRITERS. Williamsport. Contact: Barbara Sutryn, RR 3 Box 399, Montoursville PA 17754-9546. (717)322-1984. E-mail: bars@csrlink.net. Membership (14) open. Sponsors occasional workshop.

SOUTH CAROLINA

CHRISTIAN WRITERS GROUP. Greenville. Contact: Nancy Parker, 3 Ben St., Greenville SC 29601. (864)467-9653. Fax (864)467-9690. E-mail: NKPediting@aol.com. Membership (6-8) open. Meets monthly.

SOUTH DAKOTA

BLACK HILLS CHRISTIAN WRITERS. Rapid City. Contact: Loma Davies Silcott, 1777 Zinnia St., Rapid City SD 57703-6280. Phone/fax (605)393-2246. E-mail: 73500.3633@compuserve.com. Membership (6) open. Instruction at each meeting. This group will continue to meet only if enough interest.

TEXAS

AUSTIN CHRISTIAN WRITERS' GUILD. Contact: Lin Harris, 8409 Farm Road 1625, Austin TX 78747-9624. (512)243-2305. Fax (512)243-2317. E-mail: linjer@ix.netcom.com. Website: http://www2.netcom.com/linjer/acwg.html. Membership (80) open. Monthly newsletter, print and electronic. Seminar February 26-27, 1999.

GREENVILLE CHRISTIAN WRITERS' GROUP. Greenville. Contact: Jim Pence, 1551 Hunt Co. Rd. 4109, Campbell TX 75422-1201. (903)450-4944. E-mail: jhpence@yahoo.com. Membership (10) open. Sponsoring an October 2, 1999 seminar.

*INSPIRATIONAL WRITERS ALIVE! Pasadena. Contact: Pat Vance (713)477-4968. Membership (90-100) open. Sponsors summer seminar on even years, monthly newsletter, and annual contest (November 1-April 1).

INSPIRATIONAL WRITERS ALIVE!/AMARILLO CHAPTER. Contact: Helen Luecke, 2921 S. Dallas, Amarillo TX 79103-6713. (806)376-9671. Membership (25) open. Seminar April 10, 1999 in Amarillo.

*INSPIRATIONAL WRITERS ALIVE!/CENTRAL TX CHAPTER. Buffalo. Contact: Juanice Teer (903)322-4701.

*INSPIRATIONAL WRITERS ALIVE!/HOUSTON CHAPTER. Houston. Contact: Martha Rogers (713)686-7209 or Wanda Shadle (713)862-1115. Membership (30) open.

*INSPIRATIONAL WRITERS ALIVE!/NORTHWEST HOUSTON CHAPTER. Spring. Contact: Lynn Grice (713)370-7111. Membership open.

*INSPIRATIONAL WRITERS ALIVE!/JACKSONVILLE CHAPTER. Contact: Maxine Holder, Rt. 4 Box 81H, Rusk TX 75785. (903)795-3986. Or, Debra Smith (903)586-6423. Membership open.

*INSPIRATIONAL WRITERS ALIVE!/TRINITY CHAPTER. Anahuac. Contact: Mary Ann Evans, PO Box 1027, Anahuac TX 77514. (409)267-3284. Membership (13) open.

UTAH

UTAH CHRISTIAN WRITERS FELLOWSHIP. Salt Lake City & suburbs. Contact: Kimberly Malkogainnis, 117 W Park St., Bingham Canyon UT 84006-1134. (801)568-7761. Fax (801)568-3142. E-mail: akmalkos@aol.com. Membership (12) open.

VERMONT

*PROFESSIONAL WRITERS GROUP. Central Vermont and Eastern New York. Contact: Celeste Perrino Walker, RR #3 Box 4913, Rutland VT 05701. (802)773-0535. Membership open. Instruction given at monthly meetings. Secular group with Christian members.

VIRGINIA

+GREATER ROANOKE VALLEY CHRISTIAN WRITER'S GROUP. Roanoke. President: Amanda Davis, PO Box 497, Boones Mill VA 24065. Contact: Lisa Vest, (540)265-9183. E-mail: LNSV@hotmail.com. Membership (5) open.

NEW COVENANT WRITER'S GROUP. Hampton. Contact: Mary Tatem, 451 Summer Dr., Newport News VA 23606-2515. Phone/fax (757)930-1700. E-mail: rwtatem@juno.com. Membership (10) open.

NORTHERN VIRGINIA CHRISTIAN WRITERS FELLOWSHIP. Burke. Contact: Jennifer Ferranti, dir. PO Box 12390, Burke VA 22009. Phone/fax (703)503-5366. E-mail: JenniferF@compuserve.com. Membership (200+) open. Sponsors a spring seminar (March 13, 1999).

S.O.N. WRITERS. Alexandria. Contact: Susan Lyttek, 2434 Temple Ct., Alexandria VA 23307-1524. Phone/fax (703)768-5582. E-mail: SusanAJL@aol.com. Membership (5) open.

WASHINGTON

***ADVENTIST WRITERS ASSOCIATION OF WESTERN WASHINGTON.** Auburn. Contact: Marian Forschler, PO Box 58785, Renton WA 98058-1785. (425)235-1435. Fax (425)204-2070. Membership (40) open. Newsletter $10/yr. Sponsors annual writers' conference in late June.

***CAPITOL CHRISTIAN WRITERS ASSN.** Olympia. Contact: Teresa Graham, 1815 E. End St. NW, Olympia WA 98502-4135. Membership (19) open.

NORTHWEST CHRISTIAN WRITERS ASSN. Bellevue. Contact: John Blanchard or Lorinda Newton, 10663 NE 133rd Pl., Kirkland WA 98034-030. (425)821-6647.Fax (425)823-8590. E-mail: newton@integrityol.com. Website: http://www.integrityol.com/newton/ncwa/ncwahome.htm. Membership (63) open.

SPOKANE CHRISTIAN WRITERS. Contact: Niki Anderson, 1405 E 54th Ave., Spokane WA 99223-6374. (509)448-6622. Fax (509)448-2277. E-mail: Nander1405@aol.com. Or Christine Tangvald, 6016 E. Willow Springs Rd., Spokane WA 99223-9235. (509)448-0593. Membership (10) open.

***SPOKANE NOVELISTS.** Contact: Joan Mochel, 12229 N. Ruby Rd., Spokane WA 99218-1924.(509)466-2938. E-mail: MOCHEL@aol.com. Membership (18) open. Secular group with mostly Christian members.

+WALLA WALLA VALLEY CHRISTIAN SCRIBES. College Place. Contact: Helen Heavirland, PO Box 146, College Place WA 99324-0146. Phone/fax (541)938-3838. E-mail: hlh@bmi.net. Newsletter $6/yr. September-May. Membership (20) open.

WALLA WALLA CHRISTIAN WRITERS. Contact: Dolores Walker, 904 Ankeny, Walla Walla WA 99362-3705. (509)529-2974. Membership (7) open.

WENATCHEE CHRISTIAN WRITERS' FELLOWSHIP. Contact: Shirley R. Pease, 1818 Skyline Dr. #31, Wenatchee WA 98801. (509)662-8392. E-MAIL: mocrane@aol.com. Membership (30-35) open. Holds one-day seminar in September.

WISCONSIN
WORD & PEN CHRISTIAN WRITERS CLUB. Menasha. Contact: Linda DeVries, W4897 Escarpment Terrace, Sherwood WI 54169-9760. (920)989-2844. E-mail: devries4@mail.tds.net. Membership (17) open.

CANADA
ALBERTA CHRISTIAN WRITERS' FELLOWSHIP—CANADAWIDE. Calgary & Edmonton. Contact: Elsie Montgomery, pres, 1130 Falconer Rd., Edmonton AB T6R 2J6, Canada. (403)988-5622. Fax (403)430-0139. Membership (150) open. Newsletter. Membership fee $30. Sponsors seminars the last week-end of April & September. See conference listing. Sponsors 2 contests, spring & fall (fall open to non-members).

*ARTISTIC LICENSE. Langley, BC. Contact: Christy Bowler, Box 56040, Valley Center PO, Langley BC V3A 8B3 Canada. (604)532-0401. Membership (20) open.

*CHRISTIAN WRITERS CLUB. Montreal, Quebec. Contact: Mary Ann Lipscombe , 7428 Stuart (Park Extension District), Montreal QB H3N 2R4 Canada. (514)273-5356. Annual membership fee, $15. Membership (18) open. Holds occasional writers' seminar.

FRASER VALLEY CHRISTIAN WRITERS GROUP. Abbotsford. Contact: Ingrid Shelton, 2082 Geneva Ct., Clearbrook BC V2T 3Z2 Canada (Box 783, Sumas WA 98295). (604)859-7530. Membership (30) open.

+LAMBTON CHRISTIAN WRITERS GROUP. Sarnia. Contact: Teresa Arseneau, pres, 486 Wellington St., Sarnia ON N7T 1H9 Canada. Tnt@rcv.org. Membership (16) open.

MANITOBA CHRISTIAN WRITERS ASSN. Winnipeg. Contact: Edward D. Hughes, 39 Valleyview Dr., Winnipeg MB R2Y 0R5 Canada. (204)889-0460. E-mail: hughes@aecc.escape.ca. Membership (15) open.

*SOUTHERN MANITOBA FELLOWSHIP OF CHRISTIAN WRITERS. Winkler, Roland or Carman. Contact: Ellie Reimer, 173 10th St., Winkler MB R6W 1W8 Canada. (204)325-7701. Membership (4) open.

*SPIRITWOOD SCRIBES. Meets 19X/yr. Contact: Elmer Bowes, Spiritwood SK, S0J 2M0. (306)883-2003. Annual dues $5. Membership open.

*SWAN VALLEY WRITERS GUILD. Swan River, Manitoba. Contact: Julie Bell, Box 2115, Swan River MB R0L 1Z0 Canada. (204)734-7890. Membership (7-8) open. Sponsors a seminar.

FOREIGN
ASSOCIATION OF CHRISTIAN WRITERS. London + network of area group in England. Contact: Warren Crawford, 73 Lodge Hill Rd., Farnham, Surrey, UK GU10 3RB. Phone/fax: +44 (0) 1252 715746. Fax +44 (0)1252 715746. E-mail: christian-writers@dial.pipex.com. Website: http://dspace.pipex.com/christian-writers. Membership (750) open. Sponsors a biennial writers weekend. Next one July 13-15, 2000 (Leicestershire, England).

NATIONAL/INTERNATIONAL GROUPS (no state location)

AMERICAN CHRISTIAN WRITERS SEMINARS. Sponsors conferences in various locations around the country (see individual states for dates and places). Call for dates and locations. Contact: Reg Forder, Box 110390, Nashville TN 37222. 1-800-21-WRITE.

CHRISTIAN WRITERS FELLOWSHIP INTL. Contact: Sandy Brooks, Rt. 3 Box 1635, Jefferson Davis Rd., Clinton SC 29325-9542. (864)697-6035. E-mail: cwfi@aol.com. Website: http://members.aol.com/cwfi/writers.htm. No meetings, but offers market consultations, critique service, writers books and conference workshop tapes. Connects writers living in the same area, and helps start writer's groups.

*THE PRESBYTERIAN WRITERS GUILD. No regular meetings. National writers' organization with a quarterly newsletter. Dues $15 per year (send to Alice Bostrom, 33255 N Valley View Dr., Wildwood IL 60030). Contact: Vic Jameson, PO Box 6551, Hendersonville NC 28793. (314)725-6290. Membership (220) open. Sponsors contests for members each year. Sponsors annual conference.

WRITERS INFORMATION NETWORK. The Professional Association for Christian Writers, PO Box 11337, Bainbridge Island WA 98110. (206)842-9103. Newsletter, seminars, editorial services.

THE WRITING ACADEMY. Contact: Nancy Remmert, (314)524-3718. E-mail: nremm10335@aol.com. Call after 4/01/98. Website: http://www.wams.org. Membership (75) open. Sponsors year-round correspondence writing program and annual seminar in August (held in various locations). 1999 seminar in St. Louis MO, August 5-9.

ON-LINE WRITER'S GROUPS. (See resources section in front of book.)

Note: If your group is not listed here, please send information to Sally Stuart, 1647 SW Pheasant Dr., Aloha OR 97006. November 1 is deadline for the next year's edition.

EDITORIAL SERVICES

The following listing is included because so many writers contact me looking for experienced/qualified editors who can critique or evaluate their manuscripts. These people from all over the country offer this kind of service. I cannot personally guarantee the work of any of those listed, so you may want to ask for references or samples of their work.

The following abbreviations indicate what kinds of work they are qualified to do: GE indicates general editing/manuscript evaluation; LC—line editing or copy editing; GH—ghostwriting; CA—co-authoring; B—brochures; NL—newsletters; SP—special projects; and BC—book contract evaluation. The following abbreviations indicate the types of material they evaluate: A—articles, SS—short stories, P—poetry, F—fillers, N—novels, NB—nonfiction books, BP—book proposals, JN—juvenile novels, PB—picture books, BS—Bible studies, TM—technical material, E—essays, D—devotionals, S—scripts. Note: If you need a co-author or ghostwriter, for your convenience, you will find a list of those at the end of this section.

Always send a copy they can write on and an SASE for return of your material.

(*) Indicates that editorial service did not return questionnaire.
(+) Indicates new listing.

ARIZONA

CARLA'S MANUSCRIPT SERVICE/CARLA BRUCE, 4326 N. 50th Ave., Phoenix AZ 85031-2031. Phone/fax (602)247-0174. E-mail: CarlaBruce@juno. com. Call/e-mail/write. GE/LC/GH/typesetting. Does A/SS/P/F/N/NB/BP/QL/ BS/TM/E/D. Charges by the page or gives project estimate after evaluation. Does ghostwriting for pastors & teachers; professional typesetting. Eighteen years ghostwriting/editing; 5 years typesetting.

JOY P. GAGE, 2370 S. Rio Verde Dr., Cottonwood AZ 86326-5923. (520)646-6534. E-mail: joypg@juno.com. Send material with $25 deposit. GE. Does A/N/NB/BS/D. Charges $25/hr for articles or devotionals; $2/page for books. Author of 13 books and many articles.

DONNA GOODRICH, 648 S. Pima St., Mesa AZ 85210. (602)962-6694. Call/ write. GE/LC. Does A/SS/P/F/N/NB/BP/D. Also types ($1/pg) and proofreads ($15/hr) manuscripts. Editing $1.50/pg.

'LEEN POLLINGER, 14805 W. Ravenswood Dr., Sun City West AZ 85375-5705. (602)546-4757. E-mail: FRALEEN@worldnet.att.net. Write. GE/LC. Does SS/F/ N/NB/BP/JN/BS/D. Charges $12-35/hr depending on work done. Fee schedule available for SASE.

CALIFORNIA

+PATRICIA M. BELCHER TRANSCRIPTION SERVICE, 1197 Bacon Way, Lafayette CA 94549-6238. (510)284-5905. Transcribes tapes and the spoken word into the computer.

CHRISTIAN COMMUNICATOR MANUSCRIPT CRITIQUE SERVICE/SUSAN TITUS OSBORN, 3133 Puente St., Fullerton CA 92835-1952. (714) 990-1532. Fax (714) 990-0310. E-mail: Susanosb@aol.com. Website: http://www.christiancommunicator.com. Call/write. For book, send material with $90 deposit. Staff of 14 editors. GE/LC/SP book contract evaluation. Edits all types of material. Articles/stories/picture books $65. Three chapter-book proposal $90. Additional editing $25/hr.

+COMMUNICORP/EDWARD CARY HAYES, PhD, 4125A Mt. Alifan Pl., San Diego CA 92111. Phone/fax (619)278-6265. Call. GH/CA. Specialties: biographies and historical novels. Does A/SS/P (rhymed)/TM. Initial consultation $25. Published 1,450 pages.

+CORNERSTONE INDEXING/SHIRLEY WARKENTIN, 1862 Tenaya Ave., Clovis CA 93611-0630. (559)322-2145. Call for fax. E-mail: indexer@juno.com. Website: http://home.earthlink.net/warkentin4. Writes subject and scripture indexes for nonfiction books from a Christian perspective. Call or e-mail. Charges $20-25/hr, or on a per page rate. Member, American Society of Indexers; 3 years experience.

DIANE FILLMORE PUBLISHING SERVICES, PO Box 489, La Habra CA 90633-0489. (562)697-1541. E-mail: dibofi@aol.com. E-mail/write. GE/LC/GH/CA/B/NL/SP. Does A/F/QL/BS/TM/E/D/small group or SS curriculum. Charges $20/hr. Member of Assn. of Professional Writing Consultants; book editor, former magazine editor.

VICKI HESTERMAN, Ph.D/WRITING, EDITING, PHOTOGRAPHY, PO Box 6788, San Diego CA 92166. (619)849-2260. E-mail: vhesterm@ptloma.edu. E-mail preferred. Phone consultation/print evaluation: $60/hr. Estimates given for longer projects. Edits/develops nonfiction material, including editorials; works with book and article writers and publishers as co-author, line editor, or in editorial development.

DARLENE HOFFA, 512 Juniper St., Brea CA 92821. (714)990-5980. E-mail: Jackho@genesisnetwork.net. Write. GE. Does A/F/NB/BP/BS/D. Charges $35/article or short piece; $65 for book ms up to 52 pgs, plus $1.25/pg; or $15/hr.

+HELEN HOSIER ENTERPRISES, 117 Broadview Ln., Winters CA 95694. (530)795-4008. Call/write. GE/LC. Author of 58 books.

MAIN ENTRY EDITIONS/REBECCA JONES, 1057 Chestnut Dr., Escondido CA 92025. (619)741-3750. Fax (619)480-0252. E-mail: Perejone@mailhost2.csusm.edu. E-mail. GE/LC/GH/B/NL/basic formatting. Does A/SS/P/F/N/ NB/BP/JN/PB/BS/E/D. Send payment and SASE. Content $20-25/hr; copy-editing $15-20/hr; rewriting $25-30/hr, formatting/indexing $25/hr. Graduate writing instructor, Westminster Theological Seminary in California.

KIMURA CREATIONS/DENELLA KIMURA, PO Box 785, Benicia CA 94510-0785. (707)746-8421. E-mail: dkimura@juno.com. E-mail or write/$30 deposit. GE/LC. Does P/poetry book proposals & chapbooks. Send no more than 5 pages, double-spaced with $30 (for poetry editing and critique). For poetry books, send $150.

LIGHTHOUSE EDITING/DR. LON ACKELSON, 13326 Community Rd., #11, Poway CA 92064-4734. (619)748-9258. Fax (619)748-7134. E-mail:

Isaiah68LA@aol.com. E-mail/write. GE/LC/GH/CA. Does A/SS/NB/BP/QL/ BS/D. Charges $30 for article/short story critique; $40 for book proposal. Editor since 1981; senior editor since 1984; edited over 300 books.

MARY CARPENTER REID, 925 Larchwood Dr., Brea CA 92821. (714)529-3755. E-mail: MARYCREID@aol.com. Call/write. GE. Does A/SS/N/BP/JN/ PB/E. Charges $25/hr., $75 minimum.

SHIRL'S EDITING SERVICE/SHIRL THOMAS, 9379 Tanager Ave., Fountain Valley CA 92708-6557. (714)968-5726. E-mail: ShirlTH@aol.com. Call or write, or send material with $50 deposit. GE/LC/GH/CA/Rewriting. Does A/SS/P/F/ N/NB/BP/TM/greeting cards. Consultation/evaluation, $30/hr; copy editing $40/hr; content editing/rewriting, $50/hr. Teaches two, 6-week classes, three times a year, "Stepping Stones to Getting Published," and "Writing for the Greeting Card Market."

LAURAINE SNELLING, 19872 Highline Rd., Tehachapi CA 93561-7796. (805)823-0669. E-mail: TLSnelling@aol.com. Call/write. GE. Does N/BP/ JN. Charges $50/hr ($50 minimum), or by the project after discussion with client.

COLORADO

ARIEL COMMUNICATIONS/DEBBIE BARKER, 2868 CR 46, Berthoud CO 80513. (970)532-0950. E-mail: dkbarker@cris.com. Call or e-mail. GE/LC. Does A/SS/N/NB/BP/JN/PB/E/TM. Negotiable rates on a project basis.

ECLIPSE EDITORIAL SERVICES/TRACI MULLINS, 5110 Golden Hills Ct., Colorado Springs CO 80919. (719)265-5741. Fax (719)265-5752. E-mail: tlmullins@earthlink.net. E-mail/write. GE/LC/CA/SP/book proposal preparation and some agenting.. Does NB/BP/QL/BS/D. Charges $45/hr or flat fee by project. B.A. Journalism; 12 years in-house editing; 2 years freelance editing.

+STANFORD CREATIVE SERVICES/ERIC STANFORD, 7645 N. Union Blvd. #235, Colorado Springs CO 80920. (719)599-7808. Fax (719)590-7555. E-mail: stanford@pcisys.net. Call. GE/LC/GH/CA. Does A/NB/BS/D. Charges $25/hr and up. An editor for 10 years at David C. Cook.

CONNECTICUT

KAREN ORFITELLI, 105 Shepard Dr., Manchester CT 06040. (860)645-1100. E-mail: KarenOrf@aol.com. Write. GE/LC/GH. Does A/F/BS/E/D. Charges $25/hr. Estimates given.

FLORIDA

*JULIA LEE DULFER, 705 Hibiscus Trail, Melbourne Beach FL 32951. (407)727-8192. Call. GE/LC. Does A/SS/F/N/NB/BP/JN/PB/BS/TM/E/D. Charges $20/hr for all functions.

KNUTH EDITORIAL SERVICES/DEBORAH L. KNUTH, 3965 Magnolia Lake Ln., Orlando FL 32810. (407)293-2029. E-mail: knuth101@aol.com. E-mail/write. GE/LC/B/NL/SP/BCE. Does SS/F/N/NB/BP/QL/JN/PB. Send SASE for price sheet. Specializes in historical fiction. Has a B.A. in creative writing and 1 year's experience editing.

LESLIE SANTAMARIA, PO Box 780066, Orlando FL 32878-0066. E-mail: santamar@magicnet.net. E-mail inquiry or send material (3-chapter book proposal, article up to 2,500 words, or poems to 5 pages) with $30 for an initial review. Will give a brief critique and description of editing services available for your material, including cost estimate. GE/LC/GH/CA/SP. Does A/SS/N/NB/BP/JN/BS/TM/E/D/S/query letters. Charges $30 for initial review; by the page or project for additional editing.

+WILDE CREATIVE SERVICES/GARY A. WILDE, 382 Raleigh Pl., Oviedo FL 32765. (407)977-3869. Fax (407)359-2850. E-mail: wilde@ao.net. GE/GH/CA/SP. Negotiated flat fee based on $40/hr. Former staff editor.

GEORGIA

+BONNIE C. HARVEY, Ph.D., 309 Carriage Place Ct., Decatur GA 30033-5939. (404)299-6149. E-mail: BoncaH@aol.com. Call or send with $100 deposit. GE/LC/CA/SP. Does A/SS/NB/BP/QL/BS/E/D. Charges $20/hr for reading/critiquing or proofreading; $25/hr for editing, $35/hr for rewriting.

LAMBLIGHTER'S WRITING SERVICE/CISI MORROW-SMITH, 1056 Sawgrass Ct., Lilburn GA 30047. (770)978-9129. Call/Write; send non-book material with $35 deposit. GE/LC/GH/CA/SP/tutoring writing (child or adult). Does A/SS/F/ N/NB/BP/QL/JN/PB/BS/TM/E/D/other letters. Phone consultation $20-40 (initial 1/2 hour free). Charges $15-35/hr, $35 minimum; long-term projects negotiable. Degree in Jounralism.

POSITIVE DIFFERENCE COMMUNICATIONS/ROSS WEST, 100 Martha Dr., Rome GA 30165-4138. (706)232-9325. Fax (706)235-2716. E-mail: drrwest@aol.com. Write, call or e-mail. GE/LC/GH/ CA/SP. Does A/NF/BP/BS/E/D. Charges by the page or provides a project cost estimate. Published professional; author of two books and several articles.

SANDRA A. HUTCHESON, 210 Montrose Dr., McDonough GA 30253-4239. (770)507-6665. Fax (770)474-8880. Call. GE/LC/CA/B/NL/SP. Does A/SS/F/ N/NB/BP/ JN/PB/BS/TM/E/D. Charges $25/hr ($25 min.), plus expenses (telephone, research, postage).

ILLINOIS

DEBORAH CHRISTENSEN, PO Box 354, Addison IL 60101. (630)665-3044. E-mail: christen@stametinc.net. Send with $20 deposit. GE/LC/B/NL. Does A/SS/F/N/NB/JN/D. Charges $20/hour.

*EDITECH/DOUGLAS C. SCHMIDT, 872 S. Milwaukee Ave., Ste. 272, Libertyville IL 60048. Write. GE/LC/SP. Does A/SS/F/BS/D; Sunday school curriculum. Charges $25/hr or negotiated flat fee.

JOY LITERARY AGENCY, 3 Golf Center, Ste. 141, Hoffman Estates IL 60195-3710. (847)310-0003. Fax (847)310-0893. E-mail: joyco2@juno.com. Write. GE/LC. Does A/SS/N/NB/JN. Charges $1.50/pg for line editing; $15/hr for reading & critique.

VIRGINIA J. MUIR EDITORIAL SERVICES, 130 Windsor Park Dr. #C205, Carol Stream IL 60188. (708)665-2994. Write or e-mail. GE/LC/CA. Does A/SS/N/NB/JN/ BS/TM/E/D. Charges $40/hr; $40 minimum, plus telephone, research expenses and postage.

THE WRITER'S EDGE, PO Box 1266, Wheaton IL 60189. E-mail: writersedge @usa.net. Website: http://members.tripod.com/!WRITERSEDGE. No phone calls. A manuscript screening service for 50 cooperating Christian publishers. Charges $45 to evaluate a book proposal and if publishable, they will send a synopsis of it to 50 publishers who might be interested. If not publishable they will tell how to improve it. If interested, send an SASE for guidelines and a Book Information Form, request a form via e-mail or copy from Website. The Writer's Edge now handles previously published books that are out of print and available for reprint. Requires a different form, but cost is the same.

INDIANA

DENEHEN, INC./DR. DENNIS E. HENSLEY, 6824 Kanata Ct., Fort Wayne IN 46815-6388. Phone/Fax (219)485-9891 (Fax 10 a.m-6 p.m., M-F). E-mail: DENEHEN@juno.com. Write. GE/LC/GH. Does A/SS/N/NB/BS/D/academic articles/editorials/op-ed pieces. Rate sheet for SASE. Author of 29 books; Ph.D in English.

*PMN PUBLISHING/GEORGE ALLEN, Box 47024, Indianapolis IN 46247. (317) 888-7156. Fax (317)791-8113. Write. Various editorial services and newsletters. Call or write for services available and charges.

JAMES N. WATKINS, PO Box 117, LaOtto IN 46763-0117. (219)897-4121. (219)897-3700. E-mail: watkins@noblecan.org. Website: http://www. noblecan.org/watkins. Write/e-mail. GE. Does A/NB/BP/E/D. Charges $25 to critique up to 2,000 wds; book proposals with one sample chapter. Awarded four Evangelical Press Assn. awards for editing, former editorial director, recipient of Amy Award.

+WRITING AND CREATIVE SERVICES/STEPHEN R. CLARK, 5287 Crestview Ave., Indianapolis IN 46220-3216. (317)726-0621. Fax (317)726-0623. Website: http://www.indy.net/srclark.

KANSAS

*ESTHER L. VOGT, 113 S. Ash, Hillsboro KS 67063. (316)947-3796. Write. GE/LC/CO/GH. Does SS/N/JN. $15 for first chapter (to 20 pgs); $12 for each chapter thereafter.

LOUISIANA

+INSPIRATION COVE COMMUNICATIONS/NINA HARRIS, 605 Bass Haven Resort Dr, Anacoco LA 71403. (318)286-5307. Write/ send material/$20 deposit. GE/LC/GH. Does A/SS/P/F/N/NB/BP/QL/JN/PB/BS/E/D. Complete literary services. Overall evaluation of manuscripts up to 200 pages for $50; line edit $2/pg; rewrite $5/pg; query/proposal $25; market consultation $25. Ghostwriting (200 pgs, nonfiction) $10,000. Ghostwriting (200 pgs fiction) $10,000.

MARYLAND

+OWEN-SMITH & ASSOCIATES, INC./RHONDA OWEN-SMITH, 34 Market Place, Ste. 317, Baltimore MD 21202. (410)659-2247. Fax (410)659-9758. E-mail: mapreos@aol.com. Does GH/CA/B/NL/SP/BP/Biographies/Market

Analysis/Marketing & PR Plans/Potential Publisher Identification/Press Kits/Interview Scheduling/Book Signings. Will consider other requests. Charges a flat fee or hourly rate based upon the project.

MASSACHUSETTS

CRAIGVILLE PRESS & VIDEO/MARION VUILLEUMIER, 579 Buck Island Rd. #147, West Yarmouth MA 02673-3225. (508)775-4811. Write. GE/LC (readies mss for presentation to publishers). Does NB. Initial reading $75, plus $30/hour; consultations $75; ten-session writing classes $100. Author of 20 books; editor of 5 books.

WORD PRO/BARBARA ROBIDOUX, 127 Gelinas Dr., Chicopee MA 01020-4813. (413)592-4386. Fax (413)594-8375. Call/write. GE/LC/GH/CA/B/NL/SP. Does A/F/ NB/TM/E/D. Fee negotiable; estimate given.

MICHIGAN

THE LITTFIN PRATT AGENCY/VALINDA LITTFIN/LONNI COLLINS PRATT, 518 W. Nepessing, Ste. 201, Lapeer MI 48446. (810)664-4610. Fax (810)664-1267. E-mail: lcollpr@tir.com. Write/e-mail/send with $25 deposit.. GE/SP/BCE/publicist. Does A/N/NB/BP/QL/D. Charges $50 for 500-1,500 wds, $100 for 1,500-3,000 words; call for longer manuscripts. Send for complete list of services and fees. Also offers mentoring programs for serious new or intermediate writers (must have access to e-mail). Send for application information. National Press Assn. Awards, author of 9 books and over 1,500 articles, writers' conference instructor.

LONNIE HULL DUPONT & ASSOCIATES, PO Box 2618, Ann Arbor MI 48106-2618.(734)213-5255. Fax (734)747-8986. E-mail: Lonniehd@aol.com. Call/write/e-mail; don't send material without OK. GE/GH/SP/condensing. Does N/NB/BP/QL. Charges by the hour. Sixteen years full-time experience in publishing, mostly editorial.

MINNESOTA

PTL TRANSCRIPTION/SECRETARIAL SERVICES/CONNIE PETTERSEN, R 4 Box 289, Aitkin MN 56431. (218)927-6176. E-mail: Pett289@mlecmn.net. Call/write. Manuscript typing; edit punctuation/spelling/grammar, etc. Published freelance writer; 25 years secretarial/Dictaphone experience. IBM compatible computer, WordPerfect 5 & 6, Corel 7 and Microsoft Word 97 software; microcassette transcriber. Fees: Negotiable, plus postage. By the line (.10) or by the page: $1.25 + postage, for legible writing or $1.15/pg for microcassette. Internet/e-mail/fax access. Confidentiality guaranteed.

MISSOURI

*TIM PATRICK MILLER, 4131 Manchester Blvd., St. Louis MO 63110. Line edit, $1/pg; copy edit, $2/pg; structural edit, $7/hr; proofing, .95/pg. literary consultations/new writers, $10/hr; literary consultations/published writers, $25-150/hr.

PRO WORD WRITING & EDITORIAL SERVICES/MARY R. RUTH, PO Box 155, Labadie MO 63055-0155. (314)742-3663. Call/write. GE/LC/SP/manuscript or script typing, scan hard copy to disk, proofreading, indexing.

Does A/SS/N/ NB/BP/JN/BS/TM/E/D/S/biographies/textbooks. Call to discuss your project. Reasonable rates/professional results. MC/Visa available.

NEW HAMPSHIRE
SALLY WILKINS, Box 273, Amherst NH 03031-0393. (603)673-9331. Write. GE/LC. Does A/F/JN/PB/ BS/TM. Rate sheet for SASE.

NEW JERSEY
DAYSTAR COMMUNICATIONS/DR. MARY ANN DIORIO, Box 405, Millville NJ 08332-0405. (609)327-1231. Fax (609)327-0291. E-mail: daystar405 @aol.com or madiorio@aol.com. Website: http://www.daystarministries. com. E-mail/write. GE. Does A/SS/P/QL/D/copy for ads and PR material/resumes/business letters; also translations in French, Italian, and Spanish. Rate sheet for SASE. Freelance writer, 20 yrs; editor, 11yrs; former college instructor; Ph.D.

NEW MEXICO
*K.C. MASON, 1882 Conejo Dr., Santa Fe NM 87501. Write for information, fees, and availability.

NEW YORK
+ELIZABETH CRISPIN, Box 134 Schulyer Rd., Oswegatchie NY 13670-3126. (315)848-7401. Fax (315)848-9860. E-mail: Ecrispin@juno.com. E-mail, write, or send with $25 deposit and SASE. GE/LC/CA/NL. Does A/P/F/D. Charges $5-15/pg for copy editing, $10/hr for articles or newsletters (nontechnical), $5/pg for poetry or devotionals; $5-15/pg for fillers.
+LAST WORD OFFICE WORKS/MARY A. LACLAIR, PO Box 435, Vernon NY 13476-0435. (315)829-3356. Fax (315)829-3356 (auto switch). E-mail: mlaclair1@juno.com. Write; send material with $25 deposit. GE/LC. Does A/SS/N/JN/BS/D. Estimates for projects, about $2-5/pg or $10-20/hr (depending on amount of editing needed). Published writer; op-ed guest column in NY and FL newspapers.
*STERLING DIMMICK, 86 Route 34, Waverly NY 14892-9793. (607)565-4470. Write. GE/GH/CA. Does A/SS/P/F/N/NB/BP/JN/PB/BS/TM/E/D/S. Charges $15-20/hour or by the project.

NORTH CAROLINA
*ANNA FISHEL, 3416 Hunting Creek Dr., Pfafftown NC 27040. (336)924-5880. Call. GE/CA/SP. Does A/SS/N/JN. Charges variable rates depending on job.

OHIO
BOB HOSTETLER, 2336 Gardner Rd., Hamilton OH 45013-9317. Phone/fax (513)737-1102. E-mail: BobHoss@compuserve.com. Call/write. GE/LC/ GH/ CA/B/N. Does A/SS/P/N/NB/BP/JN/PB. Rate sheet available for SASE.
+PREP PUBLISHING/ANNE MCKINNEY, 1110 1/2 Hay St., Fayetteville NC 28305. (910)483-6611. Fax (910)483-2439. E-mail: PREPPub@aol.

com.Website: http://www.prep-pub.com. Write for guidelines/SASE. GE/
LC/GH/CA/B/SP/BCE. Does A/N/BP/or others. Writes resumes and cover
letters. Author of 10 books, MBA and BA in English.

OKLAHOMA

+EPISTLE WORKS/JOANN R. WRAY, 812 W Glenwood Ave., Broken Arrow
OK 74011-6419. (918)451-4017. Artwork, ads, brochures, business cards,
critiques, editing, ghost writing and letters.

*KATHRYN FANNING, Critique Service, PO Box 18472, Oklahoma City OK
73154-0472. N/NB; no poetry. Charges $3.50/page.

THE WRITE WORD/IRENE MARTIN, PO Box 300332, Midwest City OK
73140-5641. Write. GE/LC/GH. Does A/SS/N/JN/PB. For fee schedule send
SASE/query letter detailing project. Charges $3/pg or $15/hr. Has M.A. in
English-Creative Writing; published novelist; writing teacher.

OREGON

*NASIRA ALMA, 8851-A SE 11th Ave. #2, Portland OR 97202-7050. Call. GE/
GH. Does A/SS/P/N/NB/BP/BS/E/D. For an initial overview, which includes
a single-spaced report of not less than 10 pgs, charges $400 (for book of
average size). Sometimes negotiates a flat fee for the project.

*BESTSELLER CONSULTANTS/URSULA BACON, PO Box 922, Wilsonville
OR 97070. (503)682-3235. Fax (503)682-8684. Write. GE/LC/GH. Does A/
SS/N/NB/ BP. Fees are quoted on a per project basis. Ms evaluation for
250-325 pgs starts at $550. Full report and chapter-by-chapter recommen-
dations included. Secular, but handles Christian books.

+BOOKHOUSE/TRICIA A. TONEY, PO Box 277, Brownsville OR 97327-
0277. E-mail: bookhouse@ivillage.com. E-mail/write. GE/LC. Does SS/N.
Charges $95 for 3-chapter/proposal evaluation; $55 for shorter fiction;
Starts at $195 for complete manuscript evaluation. Specializes in plotting,
theme work, characterization, and dramatic content for fiction.

MARION DUCKWORTH, 2495 Maple NE, Salem OR 97303. (503)364-9570.
E-mail: marion.duckworth@bbs.chemek.cc.or.us. Call/e-mail/write. GE.
Does A/SS/N/NB/BP/QL/BS/D. Charges $25/hr. for critique or consultation.
Author of 20 books and many articles.

LIT.DOC/KRISTEN JOHNSON INGRAM, 955 S. 59TH St., Springfield OR
97478. (541)726-8320. Fax (541)988-9126. Pager: (541)710-3764. E-mail:
kris64@worldnet.att.net. Call. GE/LC/CA/B. Does A/SS/P/F/N/NB/BP/E/D.
Charges $25/hr, or negotiates on longer manuscripts.

*LYON'S LITERARY SERVICES/ELIZABETH LYON, 2123 Marlow Ln., Eugene OR 97401-6431. (541)344-9118. Fax (541)485-2216. Call/write. GE/
LC/ SP. Does A/SS/N/NB/BP/JN/PB/TM/E/D. Charges $45/hr or $75, plus $3/
pg. for longer projects.

*PRIMA FACIE PUBLISHERS/BEN RIGALL, 13002 SE Alder St., Portland OR
97233-1629. (503)735-1924. Write or call. GE/LC. Contact for information
and fees.

+SKIP SELLERS, 12700 SW Sara Dr, Gaston OR 97119. (503)985-7281.
Skipdave@teleport.com. E-mail, call or write. GE/LC/B/NL/SP. Does A/SS/

P/F/N/NB/JN/PB/BS/TM/E/D. Charges about $30/hr, plus .01/wd. Bachelor's degree in Journalism & English; creative writer and editor.

CONNIE'S EASY WRITER SERVICE/CONNIE SOTH, 4890 SW Menlo Dr., Beaverton OR 97005-2612. (503)644-4972. Call/Write. GE/LC/SP/book doctoring & guidance. Does A/N/NB/BP/JN/PB/E/D. Charges $10/hour.

*ANNA LLOYD STONE, PO Box 2251, Lake Oswego OR 97035. (503)638-3705. Fax (503)638-3811. Call. LC/special projects/word processing. Does A/SS/P/ F/N/NB/BP/JN/PB/BS/TM/E/D/S. Charges $20/hr for copyediting or word processing; $30/hr for both.

SALLY STUART, 1647 SW Pheasant Dr., Aloha OR 97006. (503)642-9844. Fax (503)848-3658. E-mail: stuartcwmg@aol.com. Website: http://www.stuart market.com. Call/write. GE. Does A/SS/N/NB/ BP/JN/PB/E. Charges $30/hr. for critique; $40/hr. for consultations. Comprehensive publishing contract evaluation $50-80. Author of 25 books, and over 30 years experience as a writer, teacher, marketing expert.

+THE WRITE CONNECTION/MARY HAMPTON, 1535 NE 86TH Ave., Portland OR 97220. (503)251-8678. Offers help in promoting your published book. Will help you develop a marketing plan to help get the best exposure for you and your book. Send an SASE for details.

+WRITING CONSULTS/DARLENE STAFFELBACH, 6950 SW Hampton, Ste. 107, Tigard OR 97223. (503)684-5228. E-mail: writingconsults@ juno.com. Write/e-mail. GE/LC/SP. Assists writers with idea clarification and development; literature synthesis; integration of critical thinking. Specializes in scholarly writing such as theses and dissertations; letters and correspondence; formulation and review of reports and manuscripts; development of teaching syllabi and other presentation materials.

PENNSYLVANIA

*VAL CINDRIC EDITING & PUBLISHING SERVICES, 536 Monticello Dr., Delmont PA 15626. Phone/Fax (412)468-6185. Call/write. GE/GH/CA. Does NB. Charges $20/hr.

IMPACT COMMUNICATIONS/DEBRA PETROSKY, 11331 Tioga Rd., N. Huntingdon PA 15642-2445. Phone/fax (724)863-5906. E-mail: Editing 4U@aol.com. Call/e-mail. GE/LC. Does NB/BP. Charges $20/hr. Satisfied self-publishers endorse our typesetting services. Very reasonable rates.

SPREAD THE WORD/MAURCIA DELEAN HOUCK, 1618 Rockwell Rd., Abington PA 19001. Phone/fax (215)659-2912. E-mail: mhouck@voicenet. com. E-mail/write. GE/LC/B/SP. Does A/SS/F/N/NB/BP/QL/BS. Charges $1.75/pg., or as quoted. Discount for over 200 pgs. Author of over 200 articles and former newspaper editor.

WRITE HIS ANSWER MINISTRIES/MARLENE BAGNULL, 316 Blanchard Rd, Drexel Hill PA 19026-3507. Phone/fax: (610)626-6833. E-mail: mbagnull @aol.com. Website: http://nancepub.com/cwf/wha/. Call/write. GE/LC/ typesetting. Does A/SS/N/NB/BP/JN/BS/D. Charges $25/hr; estimates given. Call or write for information on At-Home Writing Workshops, a correspondence study program.

SOUTH CAROLINA
NANCY KOESY PARKER WRITING & EDITING SERVICES, 3 Ben St., Greenville SC 29601. (864)467-9653. Fax (864)467-9690. E-mail: NKPediting@aol.com. Send SASE for resume, services and references.
+JULIE SALE, 208 B Croft St., Greenville SC 29609. (864)242-2824.

TENNESSEE
CHRISTIAN WRITERS INSTITUTE MANUSCRIPT CRITIQUE SERVICE, PO Box 110390, Nashville TN 37222. (800)21-WRITE. Call/write. GE/LC/GH/CA/SP/BCE. Does A/SS/P/F/N/NB/BP/JN/PB/BS/TM/E/D/S. Send SASE for rate sheet and submission slip.
JOHNSON LITERARY AND TALENT SERVICES/JOSEPH S. JOHNSON JR., 2915 Walnut Crest Dr., Antioch TN 37013-1337. Phone/fax (615)361-8627. Call. GE/LC/GH/CA/B/N/SP/BCE/consultations. Does A/SS/P/F/N/NB/BP/QL/JN/PB/BS/TM/E/D/S/advice on song writing. Reasonable rates; negotiable. Fifty years experience as a professional writer.
*WILLIAM PENS/WILLIAM D. WATKINS, 500 - 5th Ave. N, Apt 402, Nashville TN 37219-1229. Write. GE/CA/B/NL/SP/BC/consulting, contract negotiations, book proposal evaluations & creations, market analysis of book ideas. Does A/SS/N/NB/BP/BS/ TM/E/D. Send SASE for rate sheet.
+WRITEWAY COMMUNICATIONS/BEN JOBE, PO Box 1293 Gallatin TN 37066-1293. (615)230-7165. Call/write. LC/B. Does A/SS/N/NB/BP/QL/JN/BS/D. Charges $10/hr for proofreading, or $1/pg; charges $12/hr for copyediting, $1.50/hr. Volume discounts available. Nine years experience as copyeditor for Broadman.

TEXAS
SYLVIA BRISKEY, PO Box 9053, Dallas TX 75209-9053. (214)521-7507. Call. GE/LC. Does SS/P/N/JN/PB/children's stories/secular articles. Poetry, charges $5.60 plus $1/line; fiction $30 to 2,000 wds, $2.50/page thereafter. Writing teacher; writes children's books and poetry.
JAN E. KILBY, Ph.D., PO Box 171390, San Antonio TX 78217-8390. (210)657-0171. Fax (210)657-0173. E-mail: jkilby@stic.net. Call. GE/LC. Does A/SS/P/F/N/NB/BP/JN/PB/TM/E/ D/S/speeches. Charges by the hour; call for prices/information.

VIRGINIA
CREATIVE CHRISTIAN MINISTRIES/BETTY ROBERTSON, PO Box 12624, Roanoke VA 24027-2624. Phone/fax (540)342-7511. E-mail: ccmbbr@juno.com. Send with full payment. GE/LC. Does A/SS/F/NB/BP/BS/D/S. Charges $1/page for everything.
*IRENE BOYER, 8836 Burbank Rd., Annandale VA 22003-3859. (703)425-1080. Fax (703)425-1090. E-mail: caboyer@mnsinc.com. Write. LC/GH/CA/B/NL/SP. Does A/F/NB/BS/E/D. Word processing, typesetting, hard copy, electronic. Charge depends on type/scope. Brochure for SASE.
*HCI EDITORIAL SERVICES/DAVID HAZARD, PO Box 568, Round Hill VA 20142-0568. Write. GE. Does N/NB/BP. Works with agents and self-publishers. Fees on request.

*PUBLICATIONS MANAGEMENT, INC./JANETTE G. BLACKWELL, 1507 N. Amelia St., Sterling VA 20164-3612. Write. GE/LC/GH/CA/B/ NL/SP. Does A/ SS/N/NB/TM/E/D/biographies; design and production of brochures, newsletters, books. Charges $25/hr. for writing/editing, or as negotiated.

SCRIVEN COMMUNICATIONS/KATHIE NEE SCRIVEN, 1462 California St., Woodridge VA 22191. (703)494-4866. Fax (703)583-1505. E-mail: danzndave@aol.com. Call/write. GE/LC. Does A/SS/P/F/NB/BP/QL/JN/BS/ E/D/S/tracts/pamphlets/ resumes/job application letters/biographical sketches. Charges $10-12/hr; 1/3 deposit. Brochure available for SASE. Has a BS in Mass Communication/Journalism; 13 years experience in print media.

WASHINGTON

+BRISTOL SERVICES INTL./SANDRA E. HAVEN, PO Box 516, Tracyton WA 98393. E-mail: services@bristolservicesintl.com. GE/LC/NL/SP. Does A/SS/ N/NB/BP/JN/PB/BS/TM/E/D. Charges $2/pg for most services or gives project estimate for special projects. Fees and services fully explained at Website: http://www.bristolservicesintl.com, or send SASE for rate sheet. Offers project overview for $20 for up to 20 manuscript pages for those unsure of services needed; $20 credit them applied to further services desired on the same manuscript.

*DUE NORTH PUBLISHING/SCOTT R. ANDERSON, 7372 Guide Meridian, Lynden WA 98264. Phone/fax (360)354-0234 (call first for fax). Write. GE/ LC/ GH/CA/B/NL/SP. Does A/NB/BP/E. Charges $25/hr for copy and content editing or by the project (estimate given). Offers wide range of editorial & pre-press (design/layout) services, including layout and design for brochures.

MARY ARMSTRONG LITERARY SERVICES, 8018 38th Dr. NE, Marysville WA 98270. (360)653-6548. E-mail: bobnmarya@aol.com. Call, e-mail, write. GE/LC. Does A/SS/F/N/NB/BP/BS/E/D. No picture books. Line-editing $1.50/pg.; evaluations $25/hr.

+ENGLISHWORKS/LORINDA NEWTON, 10663 NE 133RD Pl., Kirkland WA 98034-2030. Phone/fax (425)823-8590. E-mail: newton@integrityol.com. Website: http://ww2.integrityol.com/newton/englishworks.htm. Call/e-mail/write. LC/B/NL. Does A/N/NB/TM/E. Charges $10-30/hour, depending on client and service provided. Has certificate of manuscript editing from Univ. of Wisconsin.

BIRDIE ETCHISON, Box 877, Ocean Park WA 98640. (360)665-6576. Write. GE/LC. Does A/SS/F/N/BP/PB. Charges according to length, $15 minimum.

*KALEIDOSCOPE PRESS/PENNY LENT, 2507 94th Ave. E., Puyallup WA 98371-2203. Phone/Fax (253)848-1116. Call/write. GE/LC/GH/CA/B/NL/ SP/BC. Does A/SS/F/N/NB/BP/JN/PB/E/D. Also market analysis. Line item editing $3/pg; other projects negotiated individually.

GLORIA KEMPTON, 2139 52nd Ave. SW #B, Seattle WA 98116-1803. Phone/ fax: (206)935-3075. Call/write. GE. Does A/SS/F/N/NB/BP/JN/E. Free estimates; generally $25-50 for article/short story, $100-250 for book proposal.

AGNES C. LAWLESS, 17462 NE 11th St., Bellevue WA 98008-3814. (425)644-5012. E-mail: AGNESLAW@aol.com. Write. GE/LC/CA. Does A/SS/P/F/NB/

BP/BS/E/D. Articles/stories $65; book proposal (3 chapters) $90; additional $25/hr.

MOODY LITERARY AGENCY/VIRGINIA A. MOODY, 17402 114th Pl. NE, Granite Falls WA 98252-9667. (360)691-5402. Call/write. GE/LC/GH/CA/BC. Does A/SS/F/N/NB/BP/JN/BS/D/S. Charges $2/pg or as agreed.

PATRICIA H. RUSHFORD, 3600 Edgewood Dr., Vancouver WA 98661. (360)695-2263. E-mail: PRushford@aol.com. Call. GE/personal consultation and conference; Weekend With a Writer. Does A/SS/N/NB/BP. Fee $15-35/hr (negotiable). Offers private week-end workshop for $300, plus expenses.

NANCY SWANSON, 10234 38th Ave. SW, Seattle WA 98146-1118. (206)932-2161. Any contact. GE/LC/GH/CA/NL/SP. Does A/SS/N/NB/BP/QL/BS/TM/E/D/S. Charges $1/pg or as agreed by project. Twenty-five years experience editing.

WRITERS INFORMATION NETWORK/ELAINE WRIGHT COLVIN, Box 11337, Bainbridge Island WA 98110. (206)842-9103. Fax (206)842-0536. E-mail: writersinfonetwork@juno.com. Website: http://www.bluejaypub.com/win. Send material/ $150 deposit. GE/LC/GH/CA. Does N/NB/BP/QL/JN/PB/BS. Send SASE for rate sheet & list of all services. Christian writers consultant for 22 years.

WISCONSIN

BETHESDA LITERARY SERVICE/MARGARET L. BEEN, South 63 West 35530 Piper Rd., Eagle WI 53119-9726. (414)392-9761. Write/send with $15 deposit/SASE. GE/LC. Does A/SS/P/F/E/D. Charges $15/hr. Also does devotional & inspirational readings. Teaches writers' classes/poetry seminars for all ages, with emphasis on classical literature. Many years experience editing and teaching literary arts. Note: When submitting, be specific about what editorial services you want, what your goals are, etc.

MARCIA HOEHNE, 609 Walter St., Kaukauna WI 54130. (920)766-5028. Fax (920)766-9667. E-mail: donmar@execpc.com. Call/write/e-mail. GE/LC/proofreading. Does A/SS/N/NB/JN/E/D. Charges $20/hr or $2.50/page for GE/LC ($20 min.); $10/hr or $1.25/page for proofreading ($10 min.).

MARGARET HOUK, West 2355 Valleywood Ln., Appleton WI 54915-8712. (920)687-0559. Fax (920)687-0259. E-mail: marghouk@juno.com. Call/write. GE/LC. Does A/NB/BP/BS. Charges *Writer's Market* rates, or will negotiate. Author of 3 books and 700 articles; has taught writing for years.

CANADA

*****A. BIENERT**, Box 1358, Three Hills AB T0M 2A0 Canada. 443-2491. GE/LC. Does N/NB. Charges negotiable.

BERYL HENNE, 541 56th Street, Delta BC V4L 1Z5 Canada (U.S. address: Box 40, Pt. Roberts WA 98281-0040). (604)943-9676. Fax (604)943-9651. Write. GE/LC/ B/NL/SP. Does A/SS/NB/E/D. Charges $20/hr.

*****DANIEL YORDY,** Box 6855, Fort St. John BC V1J 4J3 Canada. (250)774-1020. GE/LC. Does A/SS/P/N/NB/BS/E/D. Charges $25/hr. Call/write for fee/services list. Estimates given.

*WINDFLOWER COMMUNICATIONS/THE WRITER'S EDGE, 844-K McLeod Ave., Winnipeg MB R2G 2T7, Canada. (204)668-7475. Fax (204)661-8530. Write first. Charges $100.

WRITING SERVICES INSTITUTE (WSI)/MARSHA L. DRAKE, 6341 Beatrice St., Vancouver BC V5P 3R5, Canada. Phone/fax (604)321-3555. E-mail: 103270.1722@compuserve.com. Website: http://www.vsb-adult-ed.com. Call/e-mail/write. GE/LC/GH/CA/B; also biographies, resumes, or company history. Does A/SS/N/NB/BP/D. Offers correspondence course: Write for Fun and Profit. Charges $20/hr. for critique; $30/hr for consultation. Write for details and information on correspondence course.

CHRISTIAN LITERARY AGENTS

Note: Visit these Websites to find information on agents—or agents other writers have found less than desirable: http://members.aol.com/writeconol/agents.html or http://www.agentresearch.com, or contact: Professor Jim Fisher, Criminal Justice Dept., Edinboro University of Pennsylvania, Edinboro PA 16444, (814)732-2409, e-mail: Jfisher@edinboro.edu. Another such site, http://www.sfwa.org.beware/agents.html, is sponsored by the Association of Author's Representatives, http://www.bookwire.com/AAR (on this site you will find a list of agents who don't charge fees, except for office expenses). You may also send for their list of approved agents (send $7 with a #10 SAE/1 stamp) to: 10 Astor Pl., 3rd Floor, New York NY 10003. I also suggest that you check out any potential agent at their local Better Business Bureau or local Attorney General's office.

(*) Indicates that agent did not return questionnaire.
(#) Indicates that listing was updated from guidelines or other sources.
(+) Indicates new listing.

+AGENT RESEARCH & EVALUATION, INC., 332 E. 30th St., New York, New York 10016. Phone/fax (212)481-5721. E-mail: bmii@ziplink.net. This is not an agency, but a service that tracks the public record of literary agents, and helps authors use the data to obtain effective literary representation. Charges fees for this service.

*ALIVE COMMUNICATIONS, 1465 Kelly Johnson Blvd. #320, Colorado Springs CO 80920-3955. (719)260-7080. Fax (719)260-8223. Agents: Rick Christian/Greg Johnson/Jeff Tikson/Kathryn Yanni. Well known in the industry. Est. 1989. Represents over 50 clients. Open to unpublished authors occasionally. Occasionally open to new clients. Handles any material except poetry, for all ages. Deals in both Christian (80%) and general market (20%). Also runs a speaker's bureau.

> **Contact:** Query with letter, previous history and future ideas (no calls)/ SASE.
> **Commission:** 15%
> **Fees:** Only extraordinary costs with client's pre-approval; no review/reading fee.

*ALLEGRA LITERARY AGENCY, 2806 Pine Hill Dr., Kennesaw GA 30144-2834. Phone/fax (770)795-8318. Agent: Cynthia Lambert. Est. 1994. Establishing reputation. Represents 4 clients. Open to unpublished authors. Handles adult & teen (rarely) novels, adult nonfiction, scripts (rarely). Interested in Christian science fiction, romance and mainstream novels. Books only.

> **Contact:** By mail, phone, or fax.
> **Commission:** 12%.

Fees: Requires a $150 retainer for postage and copying: 100% refundable when manuscript sells.

Tips: "We're interested in fictional manuscripts that are spiritually uplifting as well as educational."

*AUTHOR AID ASSOCIATES, 7542 Bear Canyon Rd. NE, Albuquerque NM 87109-3847. Agent: Arthur Orrmont. Not known in industry but expanding Christian/religious client list. Est. 1967. Represents 10 Christian clients. Open to unpublished authors. Handles novels for all ages, nonfiction for all ages, and scripts.

    Contact: By mail or phone.

    Commission: 15%.

    Fees: Evaluation fees for new/unpublished authors.

+AUTHORS ADVENTURE ASSISTANCE LITERARY AGENCY, PO Box 17070, San Diego CA 92177. (619)276-0308. E-mail: mmaine@axnet.net. Agent: Mark Maine. Founded by a Christian fiction adventure writer. Open to unpublished authors & new clients. Handles adult, teens and children's novels, adult, teens, and children's nonfiction, picture books, gift books, scripts. Books only.

    Contact: Submit by e-mail a one-page synopsis of your project.

    Commission: 15%.

    Tips: "We offer every service imaginable from copyrighting to ghost writing, combined with expert negotiating."

+LORETTA BARRETT BOOKS, INC., 101 5th Ave., New York NY 10003. (212)242-3120. Fax (212)691-9418. E-mail: lbarbooks@aol.com. Agent: Loretta Barrett. Estab 1991. Represents 10-15 clients. Open to unpublished authors & new clients. Handles adult novels and nonfiction; scholarly, sophisticated; religious philosophy.

    Contact: Letter.

    Commission: 15%.

    Fees: For office expenses only.

+BIG SCORE PRODUCTIONS, INC., PO Box 4575, Lancaster PA 17604. (717)293-0247. Fax (717)293-1945. E-mail: bigscore@starburstpublishers.com. Website: http://www.starburstpublishers.com/bigscore. Agent: David A. Robie. Estab 1995. Represents 5-10 clients. Open to unpublished or new clients. Handles adult fiction and nonfiction, self-help.

    Contact: Query or proposal. See Website for guidelines.

    Commission: 15%, foreign 20%.

    Tips: Very open to taking on new clients. Submit a well-prepared proposal that will take minimal fine tuning for presentation to publishers. Nonfiction writers must be highly marketable and media savvy-the more established in speaking or your profession, the better.

+BOOKS & SUCH/JANET KOBOBEL GRANT, 3093 Maiden Ln., Altadena CA 91001. (626)797-1716. Fax (626)398-0246. E-mail: jkgbooks@aol.com. Agent: Janet Kobobel Grant. Recognized in industry. Estab 1997. Represents 17 clients. Open to new or unpublished authors. Handles fiction and nonfiction for all ages, picture books, gift books. Focus is on fiction.

    Contact: Letter.

    Commission: 15%.

Fees: Photocopying and phone calls.

Tips: "While I'm open to representing additional authors, I can only take on a few more. I need to be very impressed with someone's writing to represent him or her. "

BRANDENBURGH & ASSOCIATES LITERARY AGENCY, 24555 Corte Jaramillo, Murrieta CA 92562. (909)698-5200. E-mail: donbrand@vmicro. m. Agent: Don Brandenburgh. Recognized in industry. Est. 1986. Represents 8 clients. No unpublished authors. No new fiction clients at this time. Handles adult novels (limited) and nonfiction. Specializes in nonfiction for the religious market only. Books only.

Contact: Query/SASE (or no response).

Commission: 15%; 20% for foreign or dramatic rights.

Fees: $35 for mailing/materials when contract is signed.

+ELIZABETH BROOME AGENCY, Box 507, Nye MT 59061. E-mail: agent@writeme.com. Website: http://members.tripod.com/beattitude/indx.html. Agent: Elizabeth Broome-Hardy. Estab 1981. Recognized in the industry. Open to unpublished authors & new clients. Handles novels and nonfiction for all ages, scripts. Articles & short stories only for establish clients.

Contact: Submit entire manuscript on disk or hard copy. Send nothing attached to e-mail (it will not be read).

Commission: 15%.

Fees: Charges for editorial services. (see Website for rates).

Tips: "Christian material receives high priority, but I do handle other material. No poetry books. No previously published or self-published books.."

PEMA BROWNE LTD., Pine Rd., HCR Box 104B, Neversink NY 12765. (914)985-2936. Fax (914)985-7635. Website: http://www.geocities.com/pemabrowneltd. Agents: Perry & Pema Browne. Recognized in industry. Est. 1966. Represents 6 clients. Open to unpublished authors and to new clients. Handles novels and nonfiction (preferred) for all ages; picture books, screenplays, TV/movie scripts. Prefers nonfiction. Only wishes mss not sent previously to publishers.

Contact: Letter query with credentials & SASE.

Commission: 15%; 20% foreign

Fees: None.

Tips: Check at the library in reference section, in Books in Print, for books similar to yours.

+THE CAEDMON AGENCY, 2418 19th St. NW, Suite 28, Washington DC 20009. (202)462-7097. E-mail: cameronpowell@bigplanet.com. Website: http://dwp.bigplanet.com/powelc20. Agent: Cameron Powell.   Estab 1998. Not yet recognized in the industry. Represents 2 clients. Open to unpublished authors & new clients. Handles adult novels and nonfiction, short stories.

+CASTIGLIA LITERARY AGENCY, 1155 Camino del Mar CA 92014. (619)755-8761. Fax (619)755-7063. Agent: Julie Castiglia. Estab 1993. Recognized in the industry. Represents 4 clients. Open to unpublished authors (with restrictions) & new clients. Handles adult novels and non-fiction.

Contact: Letter.

Commission: 15%.

Fees: None.

Tips: "I do not look at unsolicited complete manuscripts. For fiction send synopsis and two chapters; for nonfiction, an outline and two chapters or full proposal."

#CISKE & DIETZ LITERARY AGENCY, 6693 State Hwy 57 Lot 23, Greenleaf WI 54126-9734. (920)722-5944. Agents: Patricia Dietz & Fran Ciske. Recognized in industry. Open to unpublished authors and new clients at this time. Handles romance novels only, contemporary and historical.

Contact: One-two page query letter, with an SASE.

Commission: 15%.

Fees: None.

Tips: We prefer query letters that sum up the book in one paragraph, giving word length and whether contemporary or historical. If historical, give date. Additional information on the author is important if it pertains to their writing or the manuscript.

CREATIVE LITERARY AGENCY, PO Box 506, Birmingham MI 48012-0506. Agent: Michele Rooney. Recognized in the industry. Est. 1987. Represents 12 clients. Open to unpublished authors and new clients. Handles fiction and nonfiction for all ages, gift books.

Contact: Send brief description of book in letter, plus sample chapters.

Commission: Negotiable.

Fees: Charges $95 to critique a full manuscript.

Tips: Write from the heart, that's how the best books always start. Persist in your efforts to be published. Having the right attitude is 95% of the key to success.

*CVK INTERNATIONAL, 277 Smith St., New York NY 11231. (718)237-4570. Fax (718)237-4571. Agent: Cynthia Neeseman. Handles adult fiction and nonfiction; screenplays; and seeks foreign sales for translations of books published in the US.

Contact: Query.

DANAN LITERARY SERVICES, 10605 W. Wabash Ave., Milwaukee WI 53224-2315. Phone/fax (414)355-8930. E-mail: danan@milwpc.com. Agent: Andrea Boeshaar. Recognized in the industry. Est. 1997. Represents only Christian authors. Open to unpublished authors and new clients. Handles adult novels, gift books, novellas.

Contact: Query letter, brief bio, synopsis and first three chapters (up to 50 pages). Send SASE for submission guidelines first.

Commission: 15%.

Fees: Charges $45 reading fee; $25 marketing fee (upon a signed, non-binding terms agreement).

Comments: "Read books already published and be analytical. Figure out how and why they work (plot, characterization, etc.)."

+ECLIPSE EDITORIAL SERVICES/TRACI MULLINS, 5110 Golden Hills Ct., Colorado Springs CO 80919. (719)265-5741. Fax (719)265-5752. E-mail: tlmullins@earthlink.net. Does some agenting.

+THE ETHAN ELLENBERG LITERARY AGENCY, 548 Broadway, Ste. 5E, New York NY 10012. (212)431-4554. Fax (212)941-4652. E-mail: eellenberg@aol.com. Agent: Ethan Ellenberg. Estab. 1984. Building reputation in the industry. Represents 10 clients. Open to unpublished authors & new clients. Handles novels and nonfiction for all ages, picture books.

> **Contact:** Letter only.
> **Commission:** 15%.
> **Fees:** Copying and postage expense only.
> **Tips:** "Submit synopsis and first three chapters with SASE in initial query."

*JOYCE FARRELL AND ASSOCIATES, 669 Grove St., Upper Montclair NJ 07043. (973)746-6248. Fax (973)746-7348. Agent: Joyce Farrell. Recognized in the industry. Est. 1985. Represents 20-25 clients. Open to unpublished authors; selectively open to new clients. Handles fiction and nonfiction for children and adults. No fantasy novels. In nonfiction, prefers issue books, or books with historical, scientific, psychological or theological orientation.

> **Contact:** Prefers phone or fax. If by mail, send query letter, author bio, synopsis and SASE.
> **Commission:** 15%.
> **Fees:** Reading fee: up to 50 pgs, $35; complete manuscript $65 additional. Author provides copies for multiple submissions.
> **Tips:** "Check the marketplace to see what is currently available, and whether your treatment of a subject presents a fresh, somewhat different angle than books already published. If not, choose another subject."

SARA A. FORTENBERRY LITERARY AGENCY, PO Box 8177, Hermitage TN 37076-8177. (615)902-9471. Fax (615)902-9479. E-mail: safberry@aol. com. Recognized in the industry. Est. 1995. Represents 50 clients. Open to unpublished authors or new clients only by referral. Handles nonfiction and novels for all ages, picture books, and gift books.

> **Contact:** Query (by letter or e-mail) with overview of work in progress and brief bio, including publishing and writing history. Include SASE.
> **Commission:** 15%.
> **Fees:** Standard expenses (printing, mailing, phone, supplies, etc.) are charged back to the client.
> **Tips:** "I don't represent science fiction or fantasy. Rarely do I accept unpublished authors who write children's books or young adult."

+FOUR EMERALDS LITERARY SERVICES/AGENCY, PO Box 438, Vernon NY 13476-0438. (315)829-3356. Fax (315)829-3356 (auto switch). E-mail: MLaClair1@juno.com. Agent: Mary Adele LaClair. Estab 1995. Establishing reputation. Represents 4 clients. Open to unpublished authors; no new clients at this time. Handles adult novels and nonfiction, teen/young adult novels; children's novels and nonfiction; poetry books, gift books; articles, short stories and poetry. Christian books only; no New Age.

    Contact: Letter or e-mail.

    Commission: 10%.

    Fees: Office expenses.

    Tips: "Don't send original or only copy. If on computer, send disk with hard copy indicating software program and version used."

THE FRANKLIN LITERARY AGENCY, 310 Pine Burr St., Vidor TX 77662-6527. (409)769-7938. Fax (409)276-1527. Agent: Larry V. Franklin. Recognized in industry. Est. 1996. Represents 28 clients/15 religious. Open to new and unpublished clients. Handles adult fiction and nonfiction; teen/young adult fiction and nonfiction; juvenile novels; stage plays; short story collections.

    Contact: Query with synopsis and 1-3 chapters or e-mail.

    Commission: 10-15%.

    Fees: Representation fees charged to represent contracts. No reading fees.

    Tips: "Send cover/query letters with SASE for replies. Avoid justified right margins."

+GENESIS LITERARY GROUP, 28126 Peacock Ridge, Ste. 104, Rancho Palos Verdes CA 90275. (310)541-9232. Fax (310)541-9532. E-mail: KenRUnger @aol.com. Agents: Ken Unger or Austin Bosarge. Est. 1998; not yet recognized in industry. Represents few clients. Open to unpublished authors and new clients. Handles fiction for all ages, nonfiction for adults, screenplays, TV/Movie scripts, Television documentary, treatments and multimedia.

    Contact: Send one-page query with personal information, project description and target market, by e-mail or fax.

    Commission: 15%; may vary by type of project.

    Fees: No regular fees; only if special development of film or TV requires it.

    Tips: "We formed this company to represent material to film and television community, but we will also handle select books, especially if they have film or TV possibilities. We want material that presents values based on Judeo-Christian tradition. In nonfiction we have no interest in rehashed dogma."

GOOD NEWS LITERARY SERVICE, Box 587, Visalia CA 93279. Phone/fax (209)627-6241 (call first for fax). Agent: Cynthia A. Wachner. Recognized in industry. Est. 1986. Represents 6 clients. Not open to unpublished authors (must have one published title). Open to new clients. Handles fiction and nonfiction for all ages, picture books, screenplays, TV/Movie scripts, photos and games.

    Contact: Mail; query first. Short phone queries OK.

    Commission: Varies according to project.

    Fees: Requires $250 retainer fee. Charges for editorial services, when needed. Query for rates.

    Tips: "Believe your message. Work hard. Write eloquently. Package professionally to sell. "

*STEPHEN GRIFFITH, PO Box 939, Leicester NC 28748. Unlisted phone. Fax (704)683-2851. Recognized in industry. Est. 1990. Not open to unpublished authors. Open only to referrals from existing clients. Handles novels for all ages and adult nonfiction.

    Contact: By mail or fax.

    Commission: 15% (10% on reprinted books).

    Fees: None.

HARTLINE LITERARY AGENCY, 123 Queenston Dr., Pittsburgh PA 15235. (412)829-2483. Fax (412)829-2450. Agent: Joyce Hart. Recognized in industry. Est. 1992. Represents 14 clients. Published authors preferred. Open to new clients. Handles adult or teen novels (no science fiction) and adult or teen nonfiction. Handles books only.

    Contact: Phone or query.

    Commission: 15%.

    Fees: Fee schedule available on request.

    Tips: "Send your manuscript as professionally done as possible by e-mail and the hard copy printed on a laser or inkjet printer is best."

+JEFF HERMAN AGENCY, 332 Bleecker St., New York NY 10014. (212)941-0540. Fax (212)941-0614. E-mail: JHerman7@ix.netcom.com. Website: http://www.writersguide.com. Agent: Deborah Levine. Estab 1986. Recognized in the industry.

*HOLUB & ASSOCIATES, 24 Old Colony Rd., North Stonington CT 06359. (203)535-0689. Agent: William Holub. Recognized by Catholic publishers. Est. 1966. Open to unpublished authors. Handles adult nonfiction; possibly picture books; Christian living in secular society.

    Contact: Query with outline, 2 sample chapters, intended audience, and bio.

    Commission: 15%.

    Fees: Postage and photocopying.

+HELEN HOSIER ENTERPRISES, 117 Broadway Ln., Winters CA 95694. (530)795-4008. E-mail: nextech@mindspring.com. Agent: Helen Hosier. Recognized in the industry. Open to unpublished authors & new clients. Handles novels and nonfiction for all ages, gift books. Especially issues, historical, Christian living and inspirational.

    Contact: Query by mail. Include bio, brief synopsis, $25 evaluation fee, and SASE.

    Commission: 15%.

    Fees: Office expenses and full reading fee, depending on length of manuscript.

    Tips: "I am a published author of over 50 books and have been an acquisitions editor for a major publisher. It's difficult to get published these days, but I have knowledge of the industry and can help you if you are committed and have something to offer. I have a heart for would-be authors."

JOY LITERARY AGENCY, 3 Golf Center, Ste. 141, Hoffman Estates IL 60195-3710. (847)310-0003. Fax (847)310-0893. E-mail: joyco2@juno.com. Agent: Carol S. Joy. Recognized in industry. Est. 1996. Represents 5 clients. Open to unpublished authors. No new clients at this time. Handles adult novels and nonfiction. Always include SASE. Proofread your work carefully.

Contact: Letter.

Commission: 15%.

Fees: Charges only for extra editorial services.

+THE KNIGHT AGENCY, PO Box 550648, Atlanta GA 30355. (404)816-9620. Fax (404)237-3439. E-mail: Deidremk@aol.com. Website: http://www .knightagency.net. Agent: Deidre Knight. Recognized in industry. Estab. 1996. Open to unpublished and new clients (very selective). Handles adult & teen fiction & nonfiction, picture books.

Contact: Letter or e-mail; no phone or fax.

Commission: 15%; 25% on foreign & film rights.

Fees: Charges only for office expenses.

Tips: "We're always looking for strong nonfiction, particularly with cross-over appeal to the ABA. In children's or young adult, we're only considering authors who have published previously. In fiction, we're no longer accepting mystery or action-adventure submissions."

THE LITTFIN PRATT AGENCY, 518 W. Nepessing, Ste. 201, Lapeer MI 48446. Phone/fax (810)664-1267. E-mail: lcollpr@tir.com. Agents: Lonni Collins Pratt and Valinda Littfin. Recognized in industry. Represents 4 clients. Open to unpublished authors; no new clients at this time. No overtly evangelical themes, no fiction with an evangelism agenda, must be written to include persons of different faiths; their market is religious books for secular publishers, mainline and Catholic. Considers adult fiction and limited nonfiction; teen/young adult fiction and nonfiction, gift books, articles, and art books/text.

Contact: E-mail or UPS. Do not fax. Will answer questions by phone.

Commission: 15%; more for subsidiary rights.

Fees: No fees. Author pays office expenses.

Tips: "We are a publicity agency that handles a very limited number of authors, but will consider fresh, creative projects."

+DONALD MAASS LITERARY AGENCY, 157 W. 57th St., Ste. 703, New York NY 10019. (212)757-7755. Website: http://www.javanet.com/~nephilim/ study.html. Agent: Donald Maass. Estab 1980. Represents 100 clients. Open to unpublished authors and new clients. Handles religious fiction.

Contact: One-page query letter/SASE, by mail only.

Commission: 15%; foreign 20%.

Fees: None.

+MULTIMEDIA PRODUCT DEVELOPMENT, INC., 40 S. Michigan Ave., Ste 724, Chicago IL 60605. (312)922-3063. Fax (312)922-1905. Agent: Jane Jordan Browne. Recognized in the industry. Estab 1971. Represents 10 clients. Not open to unpublished authors. Will consider new clients with a track record. Handles adult fiction and nonfiction for the Christian market.

Contact: Query letter/SASE only.

Commission: 15%, foreign 20%.

Fees: Office costs.

BK NELSON LITERARY AGENCY, 84 Woodland Rd., Pleasantville NY 10570 and 139 S. Beverly Dr., Beverly Hills CA 90212. (914)741-1322 (NY) and

(310)858-7006 (CA). Fax (914)741-1324 and (310)858-7967. E-mail: bknelson@compuserve.com. Website: http://www.cmonline.com/bknelson. Agents: Jennifer Ng and Leonard C. Recognized in the industry. Est. 1980. Represents 9 clients. Open to unpublished authors & new clients. Handles adult & teen fiction and nonfiction, TV/movie scripts, screenplays, gift books, business, self-help, how-to. Also CD-ROM, audio tapes and lecturers.

Contact: Query by letter, fax or e-mail.

Commission: 20%, foreign 25%.

Fees: $375 reading fee for complete mss or $3/pg for proposals with sample chapters.

Comments: "Our success with first-book authors is outstanding. We work with you if you work with us to get published. If we suggest an edit, we expect you will have it done. After all, we share a common interest which is getting your book published."

+A PICTURE OF YOU AGENCY, 1176 Elizabeth Dr., Hamilton OH 45013. Phone/fax (513)863-1108. E-mail: apoy1@aol.com. Agent: Lenny Minelli. Estab 1995. Branching out into Christian market. Represents 3 clients. Open to unpublished authors & new clients. Handles novels and nonfiction for all ages, screenplays, TV/movie scripts.

Contact: Query with proposal.

Commission: 10%; 15% foreign.

Fees: Postage and phone calls only.

Tips: "Make sure your material is the best it can be before seeking an agent. Always enclose an SASE."

+SCHIAVONE LITERARY AGENCY, INC., 236 Trails End, West Palm Beach FL 33413-2135. Phone/fax (561)966-9294. E-mail: profschia@aol.com. Recognized in the industry. Estab 1997. Represents 4 clients. Open to unpublished or new clients. Handles adult, teen and children's fiction and nonfiction; picture books; screenplays; TV/movie scripts.

Contact: Query letter/SASE only.

Commission: 15%, foreign 20%.

Fees: Office costs.

Tips: Works primarily with published authors; will consider first-time authors with excellent material. Actively seeking books on spirituality, major religions, and alternative health. Very selective on first novels.

+THE SEYMOUR AGENCY/MARY SUE SEYMOUR, 475 Miner St. Rd., Canton NY 13617. (315)379-0028. Fax (315)386-1037. E-mail: marysue@slic.com. Website: http://www.slic.com/marysue. Agent: Mary Sue Seymour. Estab. 1982. Not yet recognized in the industry. Represents 5 religious clients (out of 50). Open to unpublished authors & new clients. Handles novels and nonfiction for all ages, picture books.

Contact: Query letter with first 50 pages.

Commission: 15%; less for published authors.

Fees: None.

Tips: "I'm interested in Christian romance, nonfiction and any good Christian books."

+THE SEYMOUR AGENCY/MIKE SEYMOUR, 475 Miner St. Rd., Canton NY 13617. (315)379-0028. Fax (315)386-1037. E-mail: mseymour@slic.com. Agent: Mike Seymour. Estab. 1982. Not yet recognized in the industry. Represents 5 religious clients (out of 50). Open to unpublished authors & new clients. Handles novels and nonfiction for all ages, picture books.

    Contact: Query letter with first 50 pages.

    Commission: 15%; less for published authors.

    Fees: None.

    Tips: "Would like to see any good Christian book-length works."

*THE SHEPARD AGENCY, Pawling Savings Bank Bldg., Brewster (Rt. 22) NY 10509. (914)279-2900/3236. Fax (914)279-3239. Agents: Jean or Lance Shepard. Recognized in the industry. Est. 1986. Represents 8 clients. Open to unpublished authors. Handles fiction and nonfiction for all ages; no picture books; especially business, reference, professional, self-help, cooking and crafts. Books only.

    Contact: Query letter and sample material.

    Commission: 15%

    Fees: None except long-distance calls and copying.

+THE THORNTON LITERARY AGENCY, 1431 SE Knight, Portland OR 97202. (503)232-8729. Fax (503)233-8633. E-mail: roxy@thornlit.com. Website: http://www.thornlit.com. Agent: Roxann Caraway. Est. 1997. Not recognized in the industry. Represents 2 clients. Open to unpublished authors and actively seeking new clients. Handles fiction and nonfiction for all ages, picture books, poetry books, anthologies.

    Contact: Query by e-mail, if possible.

    Commission: 15%.

    Fees: None.

    Tips: "We are a very young agency, but are aggressively marketing manuscripts. Please pay close attention to the technical merit of manuscripts."

SCOTT WAXMAN AGENCY, INC., 1650 Broadway Ste. 1011, New York NY 10019. (212)262-2388. Fax (212)262-0119. E-mail: waxman@interport. net. Agent: Scott Waxman. Recognized in the industry. Estab. 1996 (5 years experience). Represents 11 clients. Open to unpublished authors and new clients. Handles adult fiction and nonfiction.

    Contact: Query letter or e-mail.

    Commission: 15%.

    Fees: Copy/shipping if unable to sell book.

+WILLIAMS' LITERARY AGENCY, Rt. 1 Box 157, Gordo AL 35466. (888)724-3108 (enter code 5460925). Fax (205)752-3906. E-mail: williamsagency@geocities.com. Website: http://www.geocities.com/Paris/ Parc/1954. Agent: Sheri Homan. Estab. 1997. Recognized in the industry. Represents 15+ clients. Open to unpublished authors & new clients (currently backlogged on requests, allow 3-8 weeks for response). Handles novels and nonfiction for all ages, picture books, poetry books, gift books, articles/short stories/poetry.

    Contact: Letter or e-mail.

Commission: 5-10%.

Fees: None.

Tips: "On articles and short stories, query first with samples and writing history."

WOLGEMUTH & ASSOCIATES, INC., 330 Franklin Rd. Ste. 135A-106, Brentwood TN 37027. (615)370-9937. Fax (615)370-9939. E-mail: rwolge@ usit.net. Agents: Robert D. Wolgemuth, David Dunham, and Drew Robinson. Well recognized in the industry. Est. 1992. Represents 30 clients. Open to new clients, but accept few unpublished authors. Handles adult nonfiction and fiction, children's nonfiction, and gift books. Handles mostly adult nonfiction, most other types of books handled only for current clients.

Contact: By letter or e-mail.

Commission: 15%.

Fees: Charges for photocopying.

Tips: "We work with authors who are either best-selling authors or potentially best-selling authors. Consequently, we want to represent clients with broad market appeal."

+DAVID WOMACK, 2931 E. Lark St., Springfield MO 65804-6670. (417)889-0967. E-mail: davewomack@aol.com. Website: http://www.dwomack. com.

Contact: Prefers e-mail.

THE WRITER'S EDGE—See listing under Editorial Services—Illinois.

+THE YEOMAN'S SERVICE, 6563 Hwy 100, Bon Aqua TN 37025. E-mail: yeomanservice@mindspring.com. Website: http://www.mindspring.com/ yeomanservice. Agent: Virginia S. Youmans.

ADDITIONAL AGENTS

NOTE: The following agents did not return a questionnaire, but most have been identified as secular agents who handle religious manuscripts. Be sure to send queries first if you wish to submit to them. Always check out an agent thoroughly before committing to work with him/her. Ask for references, a list of books represented, check with the Better Business Bureau, and ask your writing friends.

+ABBEY HOUSE LITERARY AGENCY, 6960 Magnolia Ave., Ste. 101, Riverside CA 92506. (909)683-7010. Website: http://www.concentric.net/ abbeyhse. Agent: L. Steven Hattendorf. Estab. 1995. Open to unpublished authors & new clients. Handles religious fiction.

Contact: Visit Website for query and submission information.

Tips: "This agency is headed by an attorney, and we're actively seeking writers."

+AGENCY ONE, 87 Hamilton St., S. Portland ME 04106. (207)779-5689. E-mail: mmccutc642@aol.com. Agent: Marc McCutcheon. Estab 1997. Open to unpublished authors & new clients. Handles religious nonfiction.

Contact: Query or outline/proposal.

Commission: 15%; foreign 20%.

Fees: Charges for photocopying.

+**THE CHRISTINA ARNESON AGENCY**, Box 1302, Cathedral Station, New York NY 10025. (212)932-3468. Fax (212)932-3468. E-mail: CAANYC@aol.com. Estab 1996. Agent: Christina Arneson. Open to unpublished authors & new clients. Handles religious fiction and nonfiction, picture books, gift books.

> **Contact:** Prefers e-mail.

+**BARBARA BAUER LITERARY AGENCY**, 179 Washington Ave., Matawan NJ 07747-2944. (732)566-1213. E-mail: cannoliq@msn.com. Agent: Barbara Bauer. Estab. 1984. Handles religious fiction and nonfiction; picture books; poetry books.

+**CAMBRIDGE LITERARY ASSOCIATES**, Riverfront Landing, 150 Merrimac St., Ste. 301, Newburyport MA 01950. (508)499-0374. Fax (508)499-0374. E-mail: MrMV@aol.com. Website: http://members.aol.com/MrMV/index.html. Agent: Michael Valentino. Open to unpublished authors & new clients. Handles religious fiction and nonfiction, scripts.

> **Tips:** "We have branches in New York and California. Come see our Website, or contact us directly."

+**CATHERINE CRONIN LITERARY AGENCY**, 180 Harry L. Dr., Ste. 3B, Johnson City NY 13790-1566. (607)770-1098. Fax (607)798-1074. E-mail: stuckart@spectra.net. Website: http://www.e-lit.com. Agent: Catherine Cronin. Open to new clients. Handles religious fiction, screenplays.

> **Contact:** See Website.

*B.R. CROWN INTL. LITERARY & ARTS AGENCY**, 50 E. 10th St., New York NY 10003. (212)475-1999. Agent: Bonnie Crown. Handles adult novels, adult nonfiction.

+**ANITA DIAMANT LITERARY AGENCY**, 310 Madison Ave., New York NY 10017-6009. (212)687-1122. Agent: Robin Rue. Estab. 1917. Represents clients. Open to new clients through recommendations. Handles religious fiction and nonfiction.

> **Commission:** 15%; foreign 20%.

+**JANE DYSTEL LITERARY MANAGEMENT**, 1 Union Square W, New York NY 10003. (212)627-9100. Fax (212)627-9313. Website: http://www.dystel.com. Agent: Miriam Goderich. Estab. 1994. Represents 200 clients. Open to unpublished authors & new clients through recommendations. Handles religious nonfiction.

> **Contact:** Query.
>
> **Commission:** 15%; foreign 19%.
>
> **Fees:** Charges for photocopying.

+**ERICA BOOKS LITERARY AGENCY**, PO Box 1109, Frederick MD 21702. (301)631-0747. Fax (301)631-1922. Agent: Erica Feberwee. Open to unpublished U.S. authors & new clients. Handles religious fiction and nonfiction.

> **Contact:** By mail or e-mail (no attached files).
>
> **Fees:** No fees for in-house editing.

+**FINESSE LITERARY AGENCY**, 655 N 1ST St., Wood River IL 62095. Phone/Fax (618)254-9737. E-mail: angel@mvp.net. Website: http://walden.mvp.

net/angel. Agent: Karen Carr. Open to unpublished authors & new clients. Handles religious fiction and nonfiction, picture books, poetry books, gift books.

+**FIRST LOOK TALENT AND LITERARY AGENCY**, 511 Avenue of the Americas, New York NY 10022. (212)216-9522. E-mail: Afirstlook@aol.com. Agent: Anthony West. Open to unpublished authors & new clients. Handles religious fiction and scripts.

+**LEW GRIMES LITERARY AGENCY**, 250 W 54th St. #800, New York NY 10019-5586. E-mail: bookagency@msn.com, or agent@inch.com. Agent: Lew Grimes. Open to unpublished authors & new clients. Handles religious fiction.

Fees: Enclose $25 US for handling in the US and Canada. Foreign submissions enclose $100 US for return handling.

+**HAMILTON HOUSE LITERARY AGENCY**, PO Box 382, Alliance NE 69301. E-mail: hhla@webquarry.com. Website: http://www.webquarry.com/hhla. Agent: M.G. Hamilton. Open to new clients. Handles religious fiction and nonfiction, scripts.

Contact: E-mail query only.

+**HEACOCK LITERARY AGENCY, INC.**, 1523 Sixth St. Ste. 14, Santa Monica CA 90401-2514. (310)393-6227. Agent: Rosalie Grace Heacock. Estab. 1978. Open to unpublished authors & new clients. Handles religious/inspirational nonfiction.

Contact: Mail query/sample chapters.

Commission: 15%; foreign 25%.

Fees: Office expenses.

+**SHERRY JACKSON, Agent**, 2448 E. 81st St., Ste. 154, Tulsa OK 74137. (918)488-9339, ext. 246.

+**MICHAEL LARSEN/ELIZABETH POMADA LITERARY AGENTS**, 1029 Jones St., San Francisco CA 94109-5023. (415)673-0939. Website: http://www.Larsen-Pomada.com. Agents: Michael Larsen or Elizabeth Pomada. Estab. 1972. Represents 100 clients. Open to unpublished authors & new clients. Handles religious/inspirational fiction and nonfiction.

Contact: Send title of book with promotion plan.

Commission: 15%; foreign 20%.

*****THE NED LEAVITT AGENCY**, 70 Wooster St. #4F, New York NY 10012. (212)334-0999. Agent: Ned Leavitt. Handles religious fiction and nonfiction.

+**THE LITERARY GROUP**, 270 Lafayette St., #1505, New York NY 10012. (212)274-1616. Fax (212)274-9876. Agent: Frank Weimann. Estab 1985. Open to new clients. Handles religious fiction, picture books, poetry books.

Contact: Query with outline and 3 sample chapters.

Commission: 15%; foreign 20%.

Tips: "We offer a written contract which may be canceled after 30 days."

+**MARGARET MCBRIDE LITERARY AGENCY**, 7744 Fay Ave. Ste 201, La Jolla CA 92037. (619)454-1550. Fax (619)454-2156. Agent: Lys Chard. Estab.

1980. Represents 50 clients. Open to unpublished authors & new clients. Handles religious/inspirational nonfiction.

Contact: Query with synopsis.

Commission: 15%; foreign 25%.

Fees: Office expenses.

+MCKENZIE, OPPENHEIMER AND JAMES CREATIVE MANAGEMENT GROUP, 13610 N Scottdale Rd. #10-257A, Scottsdale AZ 85254-4037. (602)992-3436. Fax (602)992-3436. E-mail: OwensAdWiz@aol.com. Agent: Jan McKenzie. Open to unpublished authors & new clients. Handles religious fiction and nonfiction.

Contact: Query letter/brief synopsis/SASE; by mail only.

+THE MIDWEST LITERARY AND ENTERTAINMENT MANAGEMENT GROUP, 2545 Hilliard-Rome Rd. Ste. 320, Hilliard OH 43026. (614)888-9670. Fax (614)885-2813. E-mail: Midwestlit@aol.com. Website: http://www.hwei.com. Agent: Vivian Hall. Open to new clients. Handles religious fiction.

Fees: None.

+NEW WRITING LITERARY AGENCY, Box 1812, Amherst NY 14226. (716)834-1067. E-mail: wordfellow@aol.com. Agent: Mason Deitz. Open to unpublished authors & new clients. Handles Religious fiction and non-fiction, picture books, poetry books, gift books.

Contact: Complete ms (if available), reading fee and SASE.

Commission: 12½%; foreign 18½%.

Fees: $40 reading fee and office expenses.

+P.S. BOOKS & CO., A LITERARY AGENCY, 5735 S. Pennsylvania Ave., Oklahoma City OK 73119-7016. (405)685-8735. Agent: Paula Sneed. Open to unpublished authors & new clients. Handles religious fiction and nonfiction, picture books, poetry books, gift books.

Contact: Query with synopsis and first 5 pages of your project.

Commission: 15%; foreign 10%.

Fees: Office expenses. No reading fees. Editing services available.

+REYNOLDS COMPANIES, 321 N 46th Ave. W, Duluth MN 55807-1450. (218)624-1669. E-mail: reygen@uslink.net. Agent: Thomas Reynolds. Open to new clients. Handles religious fiction. Specializes in marketing books to the movie and television industry.

+SEDGEBAND LITERARY ASSOCIATES, 1209 Vincent St. Ste 314, Fort Worth TX 76120. E-mail: Sedgeband@aol.com. Website: http://pwl.net com.com/agency. Agent: D. Duperre. Open to unpublished authors & new clients. Handles religious fiction.

Contact: E-mail queries encouraged.

+SUSAN TRAVIS LITERARY AGENCY, 1317 N San Fernando Blvd. #175, Burbank CA 91504-4236. (818)557-6538. Fax (818)557-6549. Agent: Susan Travis. Estab 1995. Represents 10 clients. Open to unpublished authors & new clients. Handles religious/inspirational nonfiction.

Contact: Query.

Commission: 15%; foreign 20%.

Fees: Photocopying.

+WESTCHESTER LITERARY AGENCY, 2533 Egret Lake Dr., West Palm Beach FL 33413. (561)642-2908. Fax (561)439-2228. E-mail: neilagency @msn.com. Agent: Neil McCluskey. Estab 1991. Open to unpublished authors & new clients. Handles religious fiction and nonfiction.

DENOMINATIONAL LISTING OF BOOK PUBLISHERS AND PERIODICALS

An attempt has been made to divide publishers into appropriate denominational groups. However, due to the extensive number of denominations included, and sometimes incomplete denominational information, some publishers may have inadvertently been included in the wrong list. Additions and corrections are welcome.

ASSEMBLIES OF GOD
Book Publishers:
Gospel Publishing House
Logion Press
Periodicals:
American Horizon
CE Counselor
Club Connection
Discovery Trails
Enrichment
High Adventure
Live
Paraclete
Pentecostal Evangel
Pentecostal Testimony
 (Canada)
Resource (Canada)
Teen Life
Take Five
Woman's Touch
Youth Leader

BAPTIST, SOUTHERN
Book Publishers:
Baylor Univ. Press
Broadman & Holman
New Hope Publishers
Southern Baptist Press
Periodicals:
Baptist History & Heritage
Challenge
Church Administration
Church Media Library
Church Musician
Crusader
Experiencing God
Glory Songs
Journey
Let's Worship
Living With Teenagers
Mature Living
Minister's Family

Music Makers
Music Time
National Drama Service
On Mission
ParentLife
Proclaim
Senior Musician
Stand Firm

BAPTIST, OTHER
Book Publishers:
Judson Press (American)
National Baptist (Missionary)
Sword of the Lord Publishers
 (Independent)
Periodicals:
African American Pulpit
 (American)
American Baptist in Missions
Atlantic Baptist
Baptist Informer (General)
Baptist Leader (American)
Beautiful Christian Teen
Certainty (Regular)
Challenge (Regular)
Co-Laborer (Free Will)
Conquest
Courage (Regular)
E Street (GA Baptist)
Fundamentalist Journal
God's Special People
 (Independent)
Heartbeat (Free Will)
LIGHT...For/Christian Walk
 (Independent)
The Link (Fellowship/Canada)
Link & Visitor
Messenger, The (Pentecostal
 Free Will)
Messenger, The (Regular)
Friends Journal

Moments with God (North
 American)
Primary Pal (Regular)
Secret Place (American)
Standard, The (General)
Writer's Forum

CATHOLIC
Book Publishers:
ACTA Publications
Alba House
American Catholic Press
Brown Publishing
Catholic Book Publishing
Catholic University of America
 Press
Cistercian Publications
Dimension Books
Franciscan University
 Press
HarperSF (Cath. bks)
ICS Publications
Libros Liguori
Liguori Publications
Liturgical Press
Loyola Press
Thomas More
Orbis Books
Our Sunday Visitor
Pauline Books
Paulist Press
Regina Press
Regnery Publishing
Resurrection Press
St. Anthony Messenger
St. Bede's Publications
Sheed & Ward
Periodicals:
America
Annals of St. Anne
Arkansas Catholic
Arlington Catholic Herald

Bread of Life
Canadian Catholic Review
Caravan
Catechist
Catechumenate
Catholic Answer
Catholic Courier
Catholic Digest
Catholic Forester
Catholic Heritage
Catholic Insight
Catholic Library World
Catholic Near East
Catholic New York
Catholic Parent
Catholic Peace Voice
Catholic Rural Life
Catholic Sentinel
Catholic Servant
Catholic Telegraph
Catholic Twin Circle
Celebration
CGA World
Columbia
Commonweal
Companion
Conscience
Culture Wars
Diocesan Dialogue
Environment & Art
Emmanuel
Eucharistic Minister
Family Digest, The
Forefront
Good News for Children
Immaculate Heart Messenger
Interim, The
Liguorian
Living Words
Marian Helpers Bulletin
Messenger/Sacred Heart
Messenger (KY)
Messenger/St. Anthony
Miraculous Medal
Montana Catholic
My Friend
National Catholic Reporter
New Covenant
N.A. Voice of Fatima
Oblates
Oblate World
Our Family
Our Sunday Visitor
Parish Liturgy
Pastoral Life
Prairie Messenger
Priest, The
Queen of All Hearts

Religion Teacher's Journal
Review for Religious
St. Anthony Messenger
St. Joseph's Messenger
St. Willibrord Journal
Seeds
Share
Sisters Today
Social Justice Review
Spirit
Spiritual Life
Sursum Corda!
This Rock
Today's Catholic Teacher
Today's Parish
U.S. Catholic
Visions
Way of St. Francis
YOU! Magazine
Youth Update

CHRISTIAN CHURCH/ CHURCH OF CHRIST

Book Publishers:
CBP Press (Disciples of Christ)
Chalice Press (Disciples of Christ)
College Press (Church of Christ)
Pilgrim Press, The (United Church of Christ)
Periodicals:
Christian Standard
Disciple, The (Disciples of Christ)
Four and Five
Lookout, The
R-A-D-A-R
Straight
Teenage Christian (Church of Christ)
Weekly Bible Reader

CHURCH OF GOD (Anderson, IN)

Book Publisher:
Warner Press

CHURCH OF GOD (Cleveland, TN)

Book Publisher:
Editorial Evangelica
Periodicals:
Church of God EVANGEL
So all May Hear

Youth and CE Leadership

CHURCH OF GOD (holiness)

Beginner's Friend
Church Herald and Holiness Banner
Gems of Truth
Junior Companion
Primary Pal (KS)
Youth Compass

CHURCH OF GOD, OTHER

Periodicals:
Bible Advocate (Seventh-day)
Bible Advocate Online (Seventh-day)
Church Advocate
Gem, The
2 Soar (Church of God in Christ)

CHURCH OF THE NAZARENE

Book Publishers:
Lillenas (music)
Beacon Hill Press
Periodicals:
Children's Church Exch.
Discoveries
Herald of Holiness
Listen
Power and Light
Preacher's Magazine
Resource
Standard
Teens Today
Together Time
Wonder Time

EPISCOPAL/ANGLICAN

Book Publishers:
Alban Institute
Forward Movement
Morehouse Publishing
Periodicals:
Cathedral Age
Episcopal Life
Interchange
Living Church

FREE METHODIST

Book Publishers:
Light and Life Communications
Periodicals:
Evangel
Light and Life

World Mission People

FREE WILL BAPTIST
Periodicals:
CoLaborer
Heartbeat

LUTHERAN
Book Publishers:
Concordia
Langmarc Publishing
Openbook Publishers
Periodicals:
Canada Lutheran (ELCC)
Cresset
Esprit (ELCC)
Evangelism (MO Synod)
Lutheran, The (ELCA)
Lutheran Digest
Lutheran Educ. (MO Synod)
Lutheran Forum
Lutheran Journal
Lutheran Parent
Lutheran Parent's Wellspring
Lutheran Partners (ELCA)
Lutheran Witness (MO Synod)
Lutheran Woman's Quarterly
   (MO Synod)
Lutheran Woman Today
   (ELCA)
Northwestern Lutheran
Parenting Treasures (MO
   Synod)
Parish Teacher (ELCA)
Word & World (ELCA)
Teachers Inter. (MO Synod)

MENNONITE
Book Publishers:
Kindred Press
Periodicals:
Canadian Mennonite
Christian Leader, The
Christian Living
Companions
Mennonite Brethren Herald
Mennonite Historian
Mennonite Weekly Review
On the Line
Partners
Purpose
Story Friends
Story Mates
With

MISSIONARY CHURCH
Periodicals:
Emphasis/Faith & Living

PENTECOSTAL HOLINESS CHURCH
Periodicals:
CE Connection
Helping Hand, The
Worldorama

PRESBYTERIAN
Book Publishers:
Presbyterian & Reformed
Westminster John Knox
Periodicals:
About Such Things
Covenanter Witness
Horizons (USA)
PCA Messenger
Presbyterian Layman (USA)
Presbyterian Outlook (USA)
Presbyterian Record
Presbyterian Today

QUAKER/FRIENDS
Book Publishers:
Barclay Press
Friends United Press
Periodicals:
Fruit of the Vine

REFORMED CHURCHES
Periodicals:
Perspectives
Reformed Worship
Vision (MI)

SEVENTH-DAY ADVENTIST
Book Publishers:
Pacific Press
Review and Herald
Periodicals:
GUIDE Magazine
Insight (MD)
Journal/Adventist Ed
Kids' Ministry Ideas
Liberty
Listen
Message
Ministry
Our Little Friend
Primary Treasure
Sabbath School Leadership
Signs of the Times

Vibrant Life
Young and Alive

UNITED METHODIST
Book Publishers:
United Methodist Publishing
   House
Abingdon Press
Cokesbury
Dimensions for Living
Upper Room Books
Periodicals:
alive now!
Christian Social Action
Good News
Kaleidoscope
Leader/Church School Today
Magazine/Christian Youth!
Mature Years
Methodist History
Michigan Christian Advocate
New World Outlook
Pockets
Quarterly Review
Upper Room

UNITED PENTECOSTAL
Periodicals:
Conqueror, The
Preserving Christian Homes
Vision

WESLEYAN CHURCH
Book Publishers:
Wesleyan Publishing House
Periodicals:
Changing Lives
Friend
In Touch
Wesleyan Advocate
Wesleyan World

MISCELLANEOUS DENOMINATIONS
African Methodist Episcopal
A.M.E. Christian Recorder
Armenian Holy Apostolic
Pourastan
Brethren Church
Brethren Evangelist
Christian Reformed
The Banner
**Christian & Missionary
   Alliance**
Christian Publications

**Evangelical Covenant
  Church**
Cornerstone
Covenant Companion
Evangelical Free Church
Evangelical Beacon
Pursuit
**Fellowship of Christian
  Assemblies**

**Fellowship of Evangelical
  Bible Churches**
Gospel Tidings
Foursquare Gospel Church
Foursquare World Advance
Greek Orthodox
Holy Cross Orthodox Press
**Open Bible Standard
  Churches**

MESSAGE of the Open Bible
United Church of Canada
United Church Publishing
  House
United Church Observer
United Church of Christ
United Church Press

LIST OF BOOK PUBLISHERS AND PERIODICALS BY CORPORATE GROUP

Following is a listing of book publishers and periodicals that belong to the same group or family of publications.

CCM COMMUNICATIONS

Aspire
CCM (Contemporary Christian Music)
Worship Leader
Youthworker
The CCM Update

CHRISTIAN BOOKSELLERS ASSN.

CBA Frontline
CBA Marketplace

CHRISTIANITY TODAY, INC.

Books & Culture
Campus Life
Christian Computing
Christian History
Christianity Today
Christian Parenting Today
Christian Reader
Computing Today
Leadership Journal
Marriage Partnership
Today's Christian Woman
Virtue
Your Church

CHRISTIAN MEDIA

Christian Media (books)
The Apocalypse Chronicles
Christian Composer
Christian Media

COOK COMMUNICATIONS MINISTRIES

Accent Publications (books)
Chariot Victor Books
Lion Publishing (books)
Counselor
I.D.
Power for Living
Primary Days
Quiet Hour, The
Real Time
The Rock
Single Adult Ministries Journal

FOCUS ON THE FAMILY

Focus on the Family (books)
Breakaway
Brio
Citizen
Clubhouse
Clubhouse Jr.
Focus on the Family
Physician
Plugged-In
Single-Parent Family
Teachers in Focus

GROUP PUBLICATIONS, INC.

Children's Ministry
Group Publishing, Inc. (books)
Group Magazine
Group's Bible Curriculum
Vital Ministry

GUIDEPOSTS

Guideposts Books
Angels on Earth
Clarity
Guideposts
Guideposts for Kids
Guideposts for Teens

THOMAS NELSON PUBLISHERS

J. Countryman
Thomas Nelson Publishers (books)
Tommy Nelson (books)
Word (books)

STANDARD PUBLISHING

Standard Publishing (books)
Christian Standard
Kidz Chat
The Lookout
Seek
Straight

STRANG COMMUNICATIONS

Creation House (books)
Charisma & Christian Life
Christian Retailing
Ministries Today
New Man
Vida Cristiana

THE UPPER ROOM

Upper Room Books
alive now!
Devo'Zine
The Upper Room
Weavings

GLOSSARY OF TERMS

NOTE: This is not intended to be an exhaustive glossary of terms. It includes primarily those terms you will find within the context of this market guide.

Advance. Amount of money a publisher pays to an author up front, against future royalties.

All rights. An outright sale of your material. Author has no further control over it.

Anecdote. A short, poignant, real-life story, usually used to illustrate a single thought.

Assignment. When an editor asks a writer to write a specific piece for an agreed-upon price.

Avant-garde. Experimental; ahead of the times.

Backlist. A publisher's previously published books that are still in print a year after publication.

Bar code. Identification code and price on the back of a book read by a scanner at checkout counters.

Bible Versions. KJV—King James Version; NAS—New American Standard; NJB—New Jerusalem Bible; NIV—New International Version; NKJV—New King James Version; NRSV—New Revised Standard Version; RSV—Revised Standard Version.

Bimonthly. Every two months.

Biweekly. Every two weeks.

Bluelines. Printer's proofs used to catch last-minute errors before a book is printed.

Book proposal. Submission of a book idea to an editor, usually includes a cover letter, thesis statement, chapter-by-chapter synopsis, market survey, and 1-3 sample chapters.

Byline. Author's name printed just below the title of a story, article, etc.

Camera-ready copy. The text and artwork for a book that are ready for the press.

Circulation. The number of copies sold or distributed of each issue of a publication.

Clips. See "Published Clips."

Column. A regularly appearing feature, section, or department in a periodical using the same heading; written by the same person or a different freelancer each time.

Contributor's copy. Copy of an issue of a periodical sent to the author whose work appears in it.

Copyright. Legal protection of an author's work.

Cover letter. A letter that accompanies some manuscript submissions. Usually needed only if you have to tell the editor something specific, or to give your credentials for writing a piece of a technical nature.

Critique. An evaluation of a piece of writing.

Devotional. A short piece which shares a personal spiritual discovery, inspires to worship, challenges to commitment or action, or encourages.

Editorial guidelines. See "Writer's guidelines."

Endorsements. Flattering comments about a book; usually carried on the back cover or in promotional material.

EPA/Evangelical Press Assn. A professional trade organization for periodical publishers and associate members.

E-Proposals. Proposals sent via e-mail.

E-Queries. Queries sent via e-mail.

Essay. A short composition usually expressing the author's opinion on a specific subject.

Evangelical. A person who believes that one receives God's forgiveness for sins through Jesus Christ, and believes the Bible is an authoritative guide for daily living.

Feature article. In-depth coverage of a subject, usually focusing on a person, event, process, organization, movement, trend or issue; written to explain, encourage, help, analyze, challenge, motivate, warn, or entertain—as well as to inform.

Filler. A short item used to "fill" out the page of a periodical. It could be a timeless news item, joke, anecdote, light verse or short humor, puzzle, game, etc.

First rights. Editor buys the right to publish your piece for the first time.

Foreign rights. Selling or giving permission to translate or reprint published material in a foreign country.

Foreword. Opening remarks in a book introducing the book and its author.

Freelance. As in 50% freelance: means that 50% of the material printed in the publication is supplied by freelance writers.

Freelancer or freelance writer. A writer who is not on salary, but sells his material to a number of different publishers.

Free verse. Poetry that flows without any set pattern.

Genre. Refers to type or classification, as in fiction or poetry. In fiction, such types as westerns, romances, mysteries, etc., are referred to as genre fiction.

Glossy. A black and white photo with a shiny, rather than matte finish.

Go-ahead. When a publisher tells you to go ahead and write up or send your article idea.

Haiku. A Japanese lyric poem of a fixed 17-syllable form.

Holiday/seasonal. A story, article, filler, etc. that has to do with a specific holiday or season. This material must reach the publisher the stated number of months prior to the holiday/season.

Humor. The amusing or comical aspects of life that add warmth and color to an article or story.

Interdenominational. Distributed to a number of different denominations.

International Postal Reply Coupon. See "IRC."

Interview article. An article based on an interview with a person of interest to a specific readership.

IRC or IPRC. International Postal Reply Coupon: can be purchased at your local post office and should be enclosed with a manuscript sent to a foreign publisher.

ISBN number. International Standard Book Number; an identification code needed for every book.

Journal. A periodical presenting news in a particular area.

Kill fee. A fee paid for a completed article done on assignment that is subsequently not published.

Light verse. Simple, light-hearted poetry.

Mainstream fiction. Other than genre fiction, such as romance, mystery or science fiction. Stories of people and their conflicts handled on a deeper level.

Ms. Abbreviation for manuscript.

Mss. Abbreviation for more than one manuscript.

NASR. Abbreviation for North American serial rights.

Newsbreak. A newsworthy event or item sent to a publisher who might be interested in publishing it because it would be of interest to his particular readership.

Nondenominational. Not associated with a particular denomination.

Not copyrighted. Publication of your piece in such a publication will put it into public domain and it is not then protected. Ask that the publisher carry your copyright notice on your piece when it is printed.

On acceptance. Periodical pays a writer at the time an article is accepted for publication.

On assignment. Writing something at the specific request of an editor.

On publication. Periodical pays a writer when his/her article is published.

On speculation. Writing something for an editor with the agreement that he will buy it only if he likes it.

One-time rights. Selling the right to publish a story one-time to any number of publications (usually refers to publishing for a non-overlapping readership).

Overrun. The number of extra copies of a book printed during the initial print run.

Payment on acceptance. See "On acceptance."

Payment on publication. See "On publication."

Pen name. Using a name other than your legal name on an article in order to protect your identity or the identity of people included in the article. Put the pen name in the byline under the title, and your real name in the upper, left-hand corner.

Permissions. Asking permission to use the text or art from a copyrighted source.

Personal experience story. A story based on a real-life experience.

Personality profile. A feature article that highlights a specific person's life or accomplishments.

Photocopied submission. Sending an editor a photocopy of your manuscript, rather than an original. Some editors prefer an original.

Press kit. A compilation of promotional materials on a particular book or author, usually organized in a folder, used to publicize a book.

Published clips. Copies of actual articles you have had published.

Quarterly. Every three months.

Query letter. A letter sent to an editor telling about an article you propose to write and asking if he or she is interested in seeing it.

Reporting time. The number of weeks or months it takes an editor to get back to you about a query or manuscript you have sent in.

Reprint rights. Selling the right to reprint an article that has already been published elsewhere. You must have sold only first or one-time rights originally, and wait until it has been published the first time.

Review copies. Books given to book reviewers or buyers for chains.

Royalty. The percentage an author is paid by a publisher on the sale of each copy of a book.

SAE. Self-addressed envelope (without stamps).

SAN. Standard Account Number, used to identify libraries, book dealers, or schools.

SASE. Self-addressed, stamped envelope. Should always be sent with a manuscript or query letter.

SASP. Self-addressed, stamped postcard. May be sent with a manuscript submission to be returned by publisher indicating it arrived safely.

Satire. Ridicule that aims at reform.

Second serial rights. See "Reprint rights."

Semiannual. Issued twice a year.

Serial. Refers to publication in a periodical (such as first serial rights).

Sidebar. A short feature that accompanies an article and either elaborates on the human interest side of the story or gives additional information on the topic. It is often set apart by appearing within a box or border.

Simultaneous rights. Selling the rights to the same piece to several publishers simultaneously. Be sure everyone is aware that you are doing so.

Simultaneous submissions. Sending the same manuscript to more than one publisher at the same time. Usually done with non-overlapping markets (such as denominational) or when you are writing on a timely subject. Be sure to state in a cover letter that it is a simultaneous submission and why.

Slanting. Writing an article in such a way that it meets the needs of a particular market.

Speculation. See "On speculation."

Staff-written material. Material written by the members of a magazine staff.

Subsidiary rights. All those rights, other than book rights, included in a book contract—such as paperback, book club, movie, etc.

Subsidy publisher. A book publisher who charges the author to publish his book, as opposed to a royalty publisher who pays the author.

Tabloid. A newspaper-format publication about half the size of a regular newspaper.

Take-home paper. A periodical sent home from Sunday School each week (usually) with Sunday School students, children through adults.

Think piece. A magazine article that has an intellectual, philosophical, or provocative approach to a subject.

Third World. Reference to underdeveloped countries of Asia and Africa.

Transparencies. Positive color slides, not color prints.

Trade magazine. A magazine whose audience is in a particular trade or business.

Traditional verse. One or more verses with an established pattern that is repeated throughout the poem.

Unsolicited manuscripts. A manuscript an editor did not specifically ask to see.

Vanity publisher. See "Subsidy publisher."

Vitae/Vita. An outline of one's personal history and experience.

Work-for-hire assignment. Signing a written contract with a publisher stating that a particular piece of writing you are doing for him is "work for hire." In the agreement you give the publisher full ownership and control of the material.

Writers' guidelines. An information sheet provided by a publisher which gives specific guidelines for writing for the publication. Always send an SASE with your request for guidelines.

GENERAL INDEX

This index includes only periodicals, books, and greeting cards. Conferences, groups, and editorial services are listed alphabetically by state; agents are listed alphabetically by the name of the agency. Check the Table of Contents for the location of these supplementary listings.

Note: Due to the many changes in the market, and to help you determine the current status of any publisher you might be looking for, again this year all markets will be listed in this index. If they are not viable markets, their current status will be indicated here, rather than in separate listings as they have been in prior years. The following codes will be used: (ABD) - asked to be deleted, (BA) - bad address or phone number, (ED) - editorial decision, (NF) - no freelance, (NR) - no recent response, (OB) - out of business. These changes will be noted in this listing for 5 years before being dropped altogether.